STUDENTS...

Want to get **better grades**? *(Who doesn't?)*

Prefer to do your **homework online**? *(After all, you are online anyway...)*

Need **a better way** to **study** before the big test?
(A little peace of mind is a good thing...)

 With **McGraw-Hill's *Connect*® *Plus* Economics,**

STUDENTS GET:

- **Easy online access** to homework, tests, and quizzes assigned by your instructor.

- **Immediate feedback** on how you're doing.
(No more wishing you could call your instructor at 1 a.m.)

- **Quick access** to lectures, practice materials, e-book, and more. (All the material you need to be successful is right at your fingertips.)

- **LearnSmart**--intelligent flash cards that adapt to your specific needs and provide you with customized learning content based on your strengths and weaknesses.

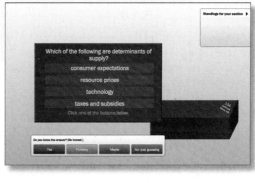

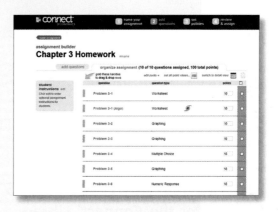

Want an online, **searchable version** of your textbook?

Wish your textbook could be **available online** while you're doing your assignments?

 ### Connect® Plus Economics e-book

If you choose to use *Connect® Plus Economics*, you have an affordable and searchable online version of your book integrated with your other online tools.

Connect® Plus Economics e-book offers features like:

- Topic search
- Direct links from assignments
- Adjustable text size
- Jump to page number
- Print by section

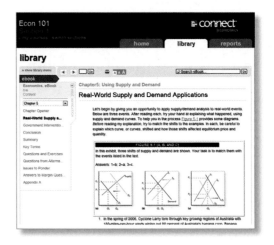

 Want to get more **value** from your textbook purchase?

Think learning economics should be a bit more **interesting**?

 ### Check out the STUDENT RESOURCES section under the *Connect®* Library tab.

Here you'll find a wealth of resources designed to help you achieve your goals in the course. Every student has different needs, so explore the STUDENT RESOURCES to find the materials best suited to you.

Microeconomics

The McGraw-Hill Series in Economics

Microeconomics

NINTH EDITION

David C. Colander

Middlebury College

McGraw-Hill
Irwin

Dedicated to the memory of
Helen Reiff (1928–2012),
my personal editor and long-time friend.

McGraw-Hill
Irwin

MICROECONOMICS, NINTH EDITION
Published by McGraw-Hill/Irwin, a business unit of The McGraw-Hill Companies, Inc., 1221 Avenue of the Americas, New York, NY, 10020.
Copyright © 2013 by The McGraw-Hill Companies, Inc. All rights reserved. Printed in the United States of America. Previous editions © 2010,
2008, and 2006. No part of this publication may be reproduced or distributed in any form or by any means, or stored in a database or retrieval system,
without the prior written consent of The McGraw-Hill Companies, Inc., including, but not limited to, in any network or other electronic storage or
transmission, or broadcast for distance learning.

Some ancillaries, including electronic and print components, may not be available to customers outside the United States.

This book is printed on acid-free paper.

2 3 4 5 6 7 8 9 0 RJE/RJE 1 0 9 8 7 6 5 4 3

ISBN   978-0-07-750180-8
MHID 0-07-750180-2

Senior Vice President, Products & Markets: *Kurt L. Strand*
Vice President, General Manager, Products & Markets: *Brent Gordon*
Vice President, Content Production & Technology Services: *Kimberly Meriwether David*
Managing Director: *Douglas Reiner*
Brand Manager: *Scott Smith*
Executive Director of Development: *Ann Torbert*
Managing Development Editor: *Christina Kouvelis*
Development Editor: *Alyssa Lincoln*
Director of Digital Content: *Doug Ruby*
Digital Development Editor: *Kevin Shanahan*

Marketing Manager: *Katie White*
Director, Content Production: *Sesha Bolisetty*
Content Project Manager: *Bruce Gin*
Senior Buyer: *Carol A. Bielski*
Cover/Interior Designer: *Pam Verros*
Cover Image: ©*Getty Images/Southern Stock*
Content Licensing Specialist: *Joanne Mennemeier*
Photo Researcher: *Michelle Buhr*
Typeface: *10.5/12 Times*
Compositor: *Aptara®, Inc.*
Printer: *R. R. Donnelley*

All credits appearing on page or at the end of the book are considered to be an extension of the copyright page.

Library of Congress Cataloging-in-Publication Data

Colander, David C.
    Microeconomics / David C. Colander. — 9th ed.
       p. cm.
    Includes index.
    ISBN-13: 978-0-07-750180-8 (alk. paper)
    ISBN-10: 0-07-750180-2 (alk. paper)
    1. Microeconomics. I. Title.
HB172.C558 2013
338.5—dc23

                                                                2012034264

The Internet addresses listed in the text were accurate at the time of publication. The inclusion of a website does not indicate an endorsement by the
authors or McGraw-Hill, and McGraw-Hill does not guarantee the accuracy of the information presented at these sites.

www.mhhe.com

David Colander is the Christian A. Johnson Distinguished Professor of Economics at Middlebury College. He has authored, coauthored, or edited over 40 books and over 150 articles on a wide range of economic topics.

He earned his B.A. at Columbia College and his M.Phil. and Ph.D. at Columbia University. He also studied at the University of Birmingham in England and at Wilhelmsburg Gymnasium in Germany. Professor Colander has taught at Columbia University, Vassar College, the University of Miami, and Princeton University as the Kelley Professor of Distinguished Teaching. He has also been a consultant to Time-Life Films, a consultant to Congress, a Brookings Policy Fellow, and Visiting Scholar at Nuffield College, Oxford.

He has been president of both the History of Economic Thought Society and the Eastern Economics Association. He has also served on the editorial boards of the *Journal of Economic Perspectives, The Journal of Economic Education, The Journal of Economic Methodology, The Journal of the History of Economic Thought, The Journal of Socio-Economics,* and *The Eastern Economic Journal.* He has been chair of the AEA Committee on Electronic Publishing, a member of the AEA Committee on Economic Education, and is currently the associate editor for content of the *Journal of Economic Education.*

He is married to a pediatrician, Patrice. In their spare time, the Colanders designed and built an oak post-and-beam house on a ridge overlooking the Green Mountains to the east and the Adirondacks to the west. The house is located on the site of a former drive-in movie theater. (They replaced the speaker poles with fruit trees and used the I-beams from the screen as support for the second story of the carriage house and the garage.) They now live in both Florida and Vermont.

"Imagine . . . a textbook that students enjoy!"
That comment, from an instructor who taught at Purdue, was e-mailed to me as I was struggling to write the preface to an earlier edition. That comment still captures what I believe to be the most distinctive feature of the core of this edition. It speaks to students.

An Entire Learning Platform

That comment continues to guide this edition. But because students today learn differently than they did twenty years ago, it does so in new ways. Students today grew up with the Internet and social media that provide them with access to a broad range of digital resources and instant feedback. That changes the way they learn, and if we are to reach them, we have to present material to them in ways that fit their learning style. They want to be able to bring their course with them—to access it anywhere, anytime—at a coffee shop in the afternoon, in their dorm room late at night, or at lunch hour at work. They still want material that speaks to them, but it has to speak to them in their language at the time they want to listen. Modern learning is blended learning in which online presentations, review and testing of material, and feedback are seamlessly blended with the narrative of the text.

The strengths of previous editions translate well in this new environment. Students don't want an automaton. They want a person who speaks to them, even if it is online. They don't differentiate a "virtual" world from a "real" world. Both are real and students seek the same thing in both—the presentation of material that engages them. And that's what I do. I tell stories. I use colloquial language, and I offer material that they read about in the newspaper—today's economic issues. The material speaks to them in ways that they can hear and enjoy.

A guiding principle of this edition has been to reach out to students in the digital language of online communication. To teach modern students effectively, we've got to get their attention and hold it, and digital tools give us that opportunity. That's why I've worked hard in this revision to provide the material that students can engage in a single, seamless, and fully digital product.

Embracing the digital environment has led to some significant pedagogical improvements. All of the content, including end-of-chapter questions, lines up directly with learning objectives. These learning objectives serve as the

organizational structure for the material. As a result, within McGraw Hill's online Connect Plus platform, students can learn the core building blocks online with instant feedback; instructors can assess student learning data and know what their students understand, and what they don't. With that information, they can devote class time to those issues with which students are having problems.

The end-of-chapter material has been revised for optimal online delivery: All of the standard questions and problems are auto-gradable and integrated with the eBook experience. Such integration allows students to move seamlessly between homework problems and portions of the narrative to get the information they need, when they need it. This is a significant advance in pedagogy. Now, even professors in large lecture classes can assign questions and exercises at the end of chapters and provide feedback to students at the point of need.

In addition to the standard questions and exercises at the end of every chapter I also provide a set of Issues of Ponder and Alternative Perspective Questions that have no "correct" answer, but instead are designed to get the students to think. In a blended learning environment, these are the questions that can form the basis for rich classroom discussions that engage the students with broad issues as much as the online material engages them with the building blocks. Classes become discussion and thinking time, not regurgitation and repetition time.

I am confident that the combination of the digital tools via Connect Plus, the modern material presented, and the colloquial style I have worked so hard to perfect will engage students in the ninth edition like never before. (Additional information about Connect is presented on p. xv.)

Modern, Not Outdated 1950s Economics

You can have the best online platform and presentation in the world, but if the content isn't relevant or engaging, it serves little purpose. My goal is to present students with the best economics I can. That means that I want to teach *modern economics,* not neoclassical economics (or whatever else the collection of models that developed in the 1950s is called). That doesn't mean that I don't teach the traditional models; it just means that I integrate modern interpretations and insights with them. That approach makes the tone and format somewhat different from the 1950s' tone and format of many competitors that make it seem as if economics hasn't changed in 60 years.

Why haven't competitors changed? Because it is really, really hard to deviate from the standard template developed in the 1950s. I fully recognize the difficulty. (After all I'm the one who coined the "15 percent rule" for revising textbooks.) I know and accept that if we are going to teach modern economics, it has to involve an evolutionary, not revolutionary, template. But recognizing the importance of the existing template is not a call for laziness and complacency in what we teach; it is a call for creativity. Economics has changed from what it was, and that means the content of the texts has to change as well. Texts that don't embrace that change are becoming more and more out-of-date.

If we are to consider ourselves serious teachers of economics, we can and should be doing whatever we can to teach students modern economics, not some vestige from the past. Over the past decade I have been working on ways to introduce modern economics into the principles course—trying different ideas on my students and colleagues and discovering what works and what doesn't. In the last edition I started to integrate modern economics into the standard principles template, and I continue that integration in this edition after getting useful comments from many of my users about the best way to do it.

One of the biggest problems that many people have pointed out with presenting students with the subtleties of modern economics is that many of their students are, shall we say, less-than-perfect students. I am not unaware of the nature of students—in fact I was one of those far-less-than-perfect students. I am no utopian; I am a realist who recognizes that many, perhaps most, students could care less about how economists think. They are taking the course because it is required, because their parents told them they had to, or because it was what fit in their schedule. That is the reality, and they are the students I'm writing for.

Why do I take this approach? Because I figure that if I can excite these marginal students about economics, I will likely also excite those more perfect, self-motivated students who professors dream of having in class. So my target student is a non-economics major who doesn't especially care about the content they are learning; he or she is much more likely to be concerned with what is going to be on the exam (and sometimes they don't even care about that). I regard this fact as liberating, not confining. It makes it even more important that we teach them modern economics, not a set of models from an outdated template. I want students to know TANSTAAFL, to know the strengths of markets, the weaknesses of markets, the importance of incentives, and why economic policy is so complicated and messy.

How does a teacher excite students who are less than excited about economics? My answer to that question is that you challenge them, you talk to them, you speak a language that they can understand, and you recognize their pain. That's what I try to do. I will fail with many of them, but if I don't try, then I don't deserve to be called a teacher, which in my view is the highest calling an economist can have.

A Student-Friendly Colloquial Style

To reach these less-than-perfect students, I convey ideas in a highly colloquial manner; I don't lecture students, or talk to them in textbookese; I talk to them in conversational English. I strongly believe that most students have the ability to understand economic concepts even though on exams it often appears as if they have serious problems. In my opinion, many of their problems in exams are not conceptual; rather, they are problems of motivation, reading, and math. The economics found in principles courses is not the student's highest priority; it certainly wasn't mine when I was 18. I'm continuously amazed at how many supposedly not-so-good students are conceptually bright. The reality is that most principles books bore this Internet generation. To teach them effectively, we've got to get their attention and hold it.

My colloquial style helps get their attention. It makes them feel that they are getting an additional tutor to back up the professor. This secondary tutor, while a bit of a pain in the ass at times, is at least human. That colloquial style helps with one of the biggest problems in the course—getting students involved with the material.

I get lots of e-mails from students—some ask me if I have sons who share my perverse sense of humor because they'd like to marry them; others tell me that I goofed somewhere in the book. Others complain about their professor—to which I answer the professor is always right. My point is not the content of the e-mails; my point is that students feel comfortable e-mailing and even phoning me. Students hear my voice in the book. It is the only economics textbook that establishes a connection with the student. To toot my own horn (what else are prefaces for?), let me share an e-mail that the publisher received from a friend of theirs (an insider to the publishing business) and that they forwarded to me. It said:

Dear X, My son is a freshman at The University of X. Like many kids he has grown to be less-and-less a reader until fairly recently. He is in the business school at college and he is wandering in search of an eventual major, like so many. He took the Principles Micro in the Fall and "hated" economics. On Monday he told me that his favorite course is Macro. His instructor is "not so helpful" but he is reading the book and making straight A's because the book is "so much fun to read" and he is "learning a ton of stuff." He has registered for the WSJ online and reads it every day. He is thinking of pursuing Econ as a major. It is actually the most positive review by an "end user" of a text-book that I've heard in a long time and, although it took me three days to find out the author and publisher (he didn't know; he just liked reading the book), the book is the latest edition of Colander. So: Thanks!

One of the reasons I keep working on this book is that I get a number of letters and e-mails like this one, and it boosts my admittedly already big ego, but what is life if not a big ego trip? (Yes, I recognize that that last statement is not standard textbookese, but I include it here to give you a sense of what I mean by my colloquial style, and to explain to you how I keep the students' attention as I am pounding into them the need to equate marginal cost and marginal benefits.)

Numerous students tell me that they actually break a smile when they read my book, and a few tell me they crack up. Just about everyone tells me that they recognize that the person writing this book is very human—all too human in some people's view. My colloquial style allows me greater flexibility in the material I present to students than most textbook authors have. Because I'm having a conversation with the students, I can explain to them what material is new and is to be read casually rather than to be memorized. Then, elsewhere where I am presenting material that will likely be on their exam, I can tell them that it is time to buckle down and memorize. So my colloquial style allows me to vary the presentation and I take full advantage of it in explaining to students what modern economics is.

Modern Critical Thinking Economics

Modern economics can mean different things to different people, and my interpretation of it centers around critical thinking. Modern economics is economics that is based on the traditional models, but that subjects them to critical thinking, and does not apply the models where they don't fit empirically. It focuses on the real world, rather than on abstract models.

To maintain that critical thinking approach, two principles stand out: (1) institutions and history are important in policy discussions and (2) good economics is open to dealing with all ideas. The mantra of modern critical thinking economics is, "Tell me something I don't already know, using whatever method works." Let me discuss each of these principles briefly.

Institutions and History Are Important to Understand Policy

If one opens up Adam Smith's *Wealth of Nations,* John Stuart Mill's *Principles of Political Economy,* or Alfred Marshall's *Principles of Economics,* one will see economic analysis placed in historical and institutional context. The modern textbook template moved away from that, and in previous editions, I tried to return the principles of economics toward that broader template, presenting models in a historical and institutional context. This edition continues that emphasis on institutions and history. Modern work in game theory and strategic decision making is making it clear that the implications of economic reasoning depend on the institutional setting. To understand economics requires an understanding of existing institutions and the historical development of those institutions. In a principles course we don't have time to present much about history and institutions, but that does not preclude us from letting students know that we know that these issues are important. And that's what I try to do.

When I say that institutions and history are important, I am talking about economic policy. As I stated above, this text and accompanying package is *not* designed for future economics majors. Most principles students aren't going to go on in economics. I write for students who will probably take only one or two economics courses in their lifetime. These students are interested in policy, and what I try to present to them are the basics of modern economic reasoning as they relate to policy questions.

Because I think policy is so important in explaining how to apply economic reasoning, I utilize a distinction made by J.N. Keynes (John Maynard Keynes' father) and Classical economists generally. That distinction is between *theorems*—the deductive conclusions of models— and *precepts*—the considered judgments of economists about the policy implications of the models. I make it clear to students that models do not tell us what to do about policy—they give us theorems. Only when we combine the model's results with our understanding of institutions, our understanding of the social context, and the normative goals one wants to achieve, can we arrive at policy conclusions, which are embodied in precepts.

Openness to Various Views

While I present modern economics, I present it in such a way that it is open to many different points of view. I don't present the material as "the truth" but simply as the conventional wisdom, the learning of which is a useful hurdle for all students to jump over. To encourage students to question conventional wisdom, the end of each chapter includes a set of questions—Questions from Alternative Perspectives—written by economists from a variety of different perspectives. These include Post-Keynesian, feminist, Austrian, Radical, Institutionalist, and religious questions. The Radical questions come from the Dollars and Sense Collective, a group with whom I've worked to coordinate their readers (www.dollarsandsense.org/bookstore.html) with this text. I also often integrate Austrian ideas into my class; I find that *The Free Market* (www.mises.org) is a provocative resource.

I often pair an article in *The Free Market* with one in *Dollars and Sense* in my assignments to students for supplementary reading. Having students read both radical and Austrian views, and then integrate those views into their own, generally middle-of-the-road, views is, for me, a perfect way of teaching the principles course. (If I have radicals and libertarians in the class, I argue in favor of middle-of-the-road views.) If you like to teach the course emphasizing alternative views, you might want to assign the brief survey of different approaches to economics in the "Preface for the Student" close to the beginning of the course, and then have the students discuss the alternative perspective questions at the end of each chapter.

There are many other ways to teach this open view approach, and for shorter classes, I have students read the various chapters on their own, and then do a presentation or have a discussion in class of how they really feel about various policies. The idea is to engage students about policy and policy debates as part of the course.

Teaching both Models and Critical Thinking

The goal in most principles courses is to teach students economic insights by presenting them a collection of models. Models are central to modern economics. Robert Solow nicely captured its importance when he said that, for better or worse, economics is a modeling science. This means that an important aspect of teaching students modern economics involves introducing them to the modeling approach to understanding the world. But teaching models, in my view, should be along the lines of Alfred Marshall, not Mas-Colell, Whinston, and Green. Marshall emphasized that economics was an approach to problems, not a body of confirmed truths.

In my view, *the modeling method, not the models,* is the most important to an economics class. In my presentation of models, I carefully try to guide students in the modeling method, rather than having them memorize truths from models. I carefully emphasize the limitations of the models and the assumptions that underlie them, and am constantly urging students to think beyond the models. This approach pushes the students a bit harder than the alternative, but it is, in my view, the best pedagogical approach; it is the critical thinking approach.

Changes in This Edition

I strongly believe that content has to be both up to date and relevant. Economic understanding and the economy in which we live are continually evolving. This means that course materials have to continually evolve as well so that they are teaching modern economics. For that reason, you will see many more changes in the text's organization and presentation than you will see in other long-standing principles texts. This is not a "change a few words here and there" revision. This is a substantial revision. They are changes that will keep your teaching fresh and engaging. The first change is obvious: All data, institutional detail and policy discussion had to be brought up to date. But that was only the beginning.

The biggest change in the micro section is how it is organized. The guiding principles were to simplify the presentations so that the text is more accessible, and to get policy discussion up front so that students see the relevance of economics early on. That meant moving the discussions of choice theory, game theory, and behavioral economics to later sections in the text, and moving the discussion of trade policy, market failure, and government failure up earlier in the text.

In revising, I use my students as sounding boards, and one of them reported back to me that "these chapters were a sudden jolt of reality; they were addictive; I couldn't put them down until I had finished them." He had multiple questions, as I suspect most readers will. So, if you want to teach students about the problems currently facing the economy—problems that students read on the Internet and in the newspapers—then this text is for you.

In-Depth Chapter-by-Chapter Discussion of Changes

Major changes include:

Chapter 1, Economics and Economic Reasoning

Deleted the discussion of induction, deduction, and abduction to simplify the presentation.

Chapter 2, The Production Possibility Model, Trade, and Globalization

The discussion of opportunity costs and its relationship to tradeoffs has been clarified. The "combined PPC with trade" diagram has been removed to simplify the discussion. The presentation now includes two simple graphs, each showing the production possibility curve for one country. The discussion allows the identification of a new level of possible consumption based on trade for each country separately.

I changed the discussion of outsourcing so it fits better with the broader term, "globalization." The issues go beyond U.S. companies moving production abroad and include the impact of global competition for U.S. firms, including shutting down U.S. production as well as retooling into more competitive sectors. This sets the stage for an expanded discussion of globalization throughout the text.

Chapter 3, Economic Institutions

I simplified the discussion of evolving economic systems by cutting the discussion of feudalism, mercantilism, and the Industrial Revolution. These topics are covered in the chapter's appendix. I added a discussion of for-benefit corporations, a rising form of business that includes social goods along with profit in their charters. I added a new box, "Who Are the 1 Percent" to include recent conversations in the Occupy Movement.

Chapter 4, Supply and Demand

I focused the discussion of the shift factors of supply on technology, while continuing to list the same four from the eighth edition.

Chapter 5, Using Supply and Demand

I replaced the example of the effect of Cyclone Larry with the more recent example of Hurricane Irene. I moved the discussion of the determination of exchange rates to Chapter 9, "Comparative Advantage, Exchange Rates, and Globalization."

Chapter 6, Describing Supply and Demand: Elasticities

This is Chapter 7 from the eighth edition. I deleted the box, "Calculating Elasticity at a Point," so that students can focus on the calculation using the average between two points. I cut the section "Substitution and Supply" and cut the detailed tables listing estimates of elasticities and provided a few examples. Finally, I eliminated the specific calculations illustrating the advanced topic: effect of shifting supply and demand based on relative elasticities of supply and demand.

Chapter 7, Taxation and Government Intervention

This is eighth edition Chapter 8. It has been updated, but otherwise is similar.

Chapter 8, Market Failure versus Government Failure

This is eighth edition Chapter 21. It has been moved up so policy can be discussed earlier. I added short discussions about the moral hazard problem and screening in the section about informational problems.

Chapter 9, Comparative Advantage, Exchange Rates, and Globalization

This chapter is based on the first part of Chapter 9 in the eighth edition and now incorporates material about exchange rates. Much of the institutional and data discussion about government policy is moved to Chapter 10. I added a number of new concepts to the chapter, including exchange rate determination and the distributional effects of international trade. It discusses how international adjustment are "supposed" to work in theory, but it also discusses how reality often does not quickly adjust, causing complications for economies when trade flows are unequal. It introduces the concept of import-led stagnation as the mirror image of export-led growth.

Chapter 10, International Trade Policy

This chapter looks more closely at trade and trade policy, and is based on portions of the eighth edition Chapter 9.

Chapter 11, Production and Cost Analysis I

This is eighth edition Chapter 12. It has been updated, but otherwise is similar. Some of the graphs have been simplified.

Chapter 12, Production and Cost Analysis II

This is eighth edition Chapter 13 updated. I added a short discussion of for-benefit corporations.

Chapter 13, Perfect Competition

This is eighth edition Chapter 14. I shortened the discussion of the condition for perfect competition, and streamlined the presentation so that the discussion of marginal revenue facing the perfect competitive firm follows immediately from the conditions for perfect competition.

Chapter 14, Monopoly and Monopolistic Competition

This chapter now presents both monopoly and monopolistic competition, drawing material from eighth edition Chapters 15 and 16. This allows for a significantly shortened presentation of antitrust policy that is integrated with the oligopoly chapter. I also added a graphical presentation of how price-discriminating monopolists eliminate welfare loss.

Chapter 15, Oligopoly and Antitrust Policy

This chapter combines the eighth edition Chapter 16 presentation of oligopoly and the Chapter 18 discussion of antitrust policy. I significantly simplified the antitrust portion of the chapter.

Chapter 16, Real-World Competition and Technology

This is eighth edition Chapter 17 updated, but otherwise largely unchanged.

Chapter 17, Work and the Labor Market

This is eighth edition Chapter 19 updated, but otherwise largely unchanged.

Chapter 18, Who Gets What? The Distribution of Income

This is eighth edition Chapter 20 updated, but otherwise largely unchanged. I added a discussion of the effect of globalization on the distribution of income across industries and classes of workers.

Chapter 19, The Logic of Individual Choice: The Foundation of Supply and Demand

This is eighth edition Chapter 10, which is updated.

Chapter 20, Game Theory, Strategic Decision Making, and Behavioral Economics

This is eighth edition Chapter 11 repositioned later in the text.

Chapter 21, Thinking Like a Modern Economist

This is eighth edition Chapter 6, which is updated, but other than being repositioned, it is largely unchanged.

Chapter 22, Behavioral Economics and Modern Economic Policy

This is the same chapter as the eighth edition. It is updated but is largely unchanged.

Chapter 23, Microeconomic Policy, Economic Reasoning, and Beyond

This is the same chapter as the eighth edition. It is updated, but largely unchanged.

Key Pedagogical Features

Learning Objectives

Four or five learning objectives are presented at the beginning of each chapter and are referenced again in the summary and end-of-chapter review questions and exercises to which they relate. The learning objectives (LO) serve as a quick introduction to the material and concepts to be mastered before moving to the next chapter. All of the assignable content within Connect is also organized around learning objectives to make it easier to plan, track, and analyze student performance across learning outcomes.

Margin Comments

Located throughout the text in the margin, these key takeaways underscore and summarize the importance of the material, at the same time helping students focus on the most relevant topics critical to their understanding.

Margin Questions

These self-test questions are presented in the margin of the chapter to enable students to determine whether the preceding material has been understood and to reinforce understanding before students read further. Answers to Margin Questions are found at the end of each chapter.

Web Notes

Jenifer Gamber has updated the Web Notes; this feature extends the text discussion onto the web. Web Notes are denoted in the margin and are housed on the Online Learning Center at **www.mhhe.com/colander9e** and within Connect Plus.

Podcasts

Written and recorded by Robert Guell of Indiana State University, more than 50 three- to five-minute audio clips delve deeper into the concepts. The audio clips (and summaries) occur throughout the text wherever you see the iPod icon in the margin. The podcasts are also housed on the Online Learning Center at **www. mhhe.com/colander9e** and within Connect Plus.

Supplements

McGraw-Hill has established a strong history of top-rate supplements to accompany this text, and this ninth edition strives to carry on the tradition of excellence.

For the Instructor

The following ancillaries are available for quick download and convenient access via the Online Learning Center at **www.mhhe.com/colander9e** and within Connect Plus. Both are password protected for security.

Instructor's Manual

This text boasts one of the strongest Instructor's Manuals on the market. Paul Fisher of Henry Ford Community College worked incredibly hard to maintain the high standard set in previous editions. Elements include:

- *Learning Objectives:* Lists the learning objectives for each chapter for a quick review.

- *Teaching Objectives:* Alerts new professors to common student difficulties with the material and provides help for addressing them.
- *For Professors New to Colander:* Notes some of the names, notations, definitions, and symbols that Colander uses as compared to other products to help professors transition into this product.
- *Problem Sets with Solutions:* Additional questions for each chapter are included here. They are designed to be photocopied and distributed for student use.

Solutions Manual

Prepared by Jenifer Gamber and me, this manual provides answers to all end-of-chapter questions—the Questions and Exercises, Questions from Alternative Perspectives, and Issues to Ponder.

Test Banks

The test bank contains thousands of unique quality questions for instructors to draw from in their classrooms. Brian Lynch of Lakeland Community College and Timothy Terrell of Wofford College worked diligently to make sure that this revised version is clear and useful. Each question is categorized by learning objective, level of difficulty, economic concept, AACSB learning categories, and Bloom's Taxonomy objectives. Questions were reviewed by professors and students alike to ensure that each one was effective for classroom use. All of the test bank content is available for assigning within Connect.

Computerized Test Banks

McGraw-Hill's EZ Test is a flexible and easy-to-use electronic testing program. The program allows you to create tests from text-specific items. It accommodates a wide range of question types and you can add your own questions. Multiple versions of the test can be created and any test can be exported for use with course management systems such as WebCT, BlackBoard, or Page Out. EZ Test Online is a service that gives you a place to easily administer your EZ Test-created exams and quizzes online. The program is available for Windows and Macintosh environmnents.

PowerPoint Presentations

Shannon Aucoin of the University of Louisiana at Lafayette and Edward Gullason of Dowling College worked tirelessly to revise the PowerPoint slide program, animating graphs and emphasizing important concepts. Each chapter has

been scrutinized to ensure an accurate, direct connection to the text.

For the Student

Online Learning Center

www.mhhe.com/colander9e

This Online Learning Center provides a number of useful study tools including practice quizzes, a set of study PowerPoints, Web Notes, and web chapters. Premium content is also available for purchase. The premium content contains podcasts and Paul Solman videos, which are downloadable to MP3 devices.

Study Guide

The study guide—written by Jenifer Gamber and me—provides a review of the concepts from each chapter. It gives students options to match a variety of learning styles: short-answer questions, matching terms with definitions, problems and applications, multiple-choice questions, and potential essay questions. To make the guide a true study tool, each answer includes an explanation of why it is correct.

Digital Solutions

McGraw-Hill Connect Economics

Less Managing. More Teaching. Greater Learning.

Connect Economics is an online assignment and assessment solution that offers a number of powerful tools and features that make managing assignments easier so faculty can spend more time teaching. With *Connect Economics,* students can engage with their coursework anytime and anywhere, making the learning process more accessible and efficient.

Simple Assignment Management

With *Connect Economics,* creating assignments is easier than ever, so you can spend more time teaching and less time managing. The assignment management function enables you to:

- Create and deliver assignments easily with selectable end-of-chapter questions and test bank items.
- Streamline lesson planning, student progress reporting, and assignment grading to make classroom management more efficient than ever.
- Go paperless with the eBook and online submission and grading of student assignments.

Smart Grading

Connect Economics helps students learn more efficiently by providing feedback and practice material when they need it, where they need it. The grading function in *Connect Economics* also enables instructors to:

- Score assignments automatically, giving students immediate feedback on their work and side-by-side comparisons with correct answers.
- Access and review each response; manually change grades or leave comments for students to review.
- Reinforce classroom concepts with practice tests and instant quizzes.

Instructor Library

The *Connect Economics* Instructor Library is your repository for additional resources to improve student engagement in and out of class. You can select and use any asset that enhances your lecture.

Student Study Center

The *Connect Economics* Student Study Center is the place for students to access additional resources. The Student Study Center:

- Offers students quick access to lectures, practice materials, eBooks, and more.
- Provides instant practice material and study questions, easily accessible on the go.

Diagnostic and Adaptive Learning of Concepts: LearnSmart

The LearnSmart adaptive self-study technology within *Connect Economics* provides students with a seamless combination of practice, assessment, and remediation for major concepts in the course. LearnSmart's intelligent software adapts to every student response and automatically delivers concepts that advance the student's understanding while reducing time devoted to the concepts already mastered. LearnSmart:

- Applies an intelligent concept engine to identify the relationships between concepts and to serve new concepts to each student only when he or she is ready.
- Adapts automatically to each student, so students spend less time on the topics they understand and more on those they have yet to master.
- Provides continual reinforcement and remediation, but gives only as much guidance as students need.

- Enables you to assess which concepts students have efficiently learned on their own, thus freeing class time for more applications and discussion.

Student Progress Tracking

Connect Economics keeps instructors informed about how each student, section, and class is performing, allowing for more productive use of lecture and office hours. The progress-tracking function enables you to:

- View scored work immediately and track individual or group performance with assignment and grade reports.
- Access an instant view of student or class performance relative to learning objectives.
- Collect data and generate reports required by many accreditation organizations like AACSB.

McGraw-Hill *Connect Plus Economics*

McGraw-Hill reinvents the textbook learning experience for the modern student with *Connect Plus Economics*. A seamless integration of an eBook and *Connect Economics*, *Connect Plus Economics* provides all of the *Connect Economics* features plus the following:

- An integrated eBook, allowing for anytime, anywhere access to the text.
- Dynamic links between the problems or questions you assign to your students and the location in the eBook where that problem or question is covered.
- A powerful search function to pinpoint and connect key concepts in a snap.

In short, *Connect Economics* offers you and your students powerful tools and features that optimize your time and energies, enabling you to focus on course content, teaching, and student learning. *Connect Economics* also offers a wealth of content resources for both instructors and students. This state-of-the-art, thoroughly tested system supports you in preparing students for the world that awaits.

For more information about Connect, go to **www.mcgrawhillconnect.com** or contact your local McGraw-Hill sales representative.

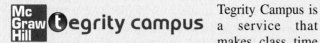

Tegrity Campus is a service that makes class time available 24/7 by automatically capturing every lecture in a searchable format for students to review when they study and complete assignments. With a simple one-click start-and-stop process, you capture all computer screens and corresponding audio. Students can replay any part of any class with easy-to-use browser-based viewing on a PC or Mac.

Educators know that the more students can see, hear, and experience class resources, the better they learn. In fact, studies prove it. With Tegrity Campus, students quickly recall key moments by using Tegrity Campus's unique search feature. This search helps students efficiently find what they need, when they need it, across an entire semester of class recordings. Help turn all your students' study time into learning moments immediately supported by your lecture.

To learn more about Tegrity watch a two-minute Flash demo at **http://tegritycampus.mhhe.com.**

Assurance of Learning Ready

Many educational institutions today are focused on the notion of *assurance of learning,* an important element of some accreditation standards. *Microeconomics, 9e* is designed specifically to support your assurance of learning initiatives with a simple yet powerful solution.

Each test bank question for *Microeconomics, 9e* maps to a specific chapter learning outcome/objective listed in the text. You can use our test bank software, EZ Test and EZ Test Online, or *Connect Economics* to easily query for learning outcomes/objectives that directly relate to the learning objectives for your course. You can then use the reporting features of EZ Test to aggregate student results in similar fashion, making the collection and presentation of assurance of learning data simple and easy.

AACSB Statement

The McGraw-Hill Companies is a proud corporate member of AACSB International. Understanding the importance and value of AACSB accreditation, the author of *Microeconomics, 9e* recognizes the curricula guidelines detailed in the AACSB standards for business accreditation by connecting questions in the test bank and end-of-chapter material to the general knowledge and skill guidelines found in the AACSB standards.

The statements contained in *Microeconomics, 9e* are provided only as a guide for the users of this textbook. The AACSB leaves content coverage and assessment within the purview of individual schools, the mission of the school, and the faculty. While *Microeconomics, 9e* and the teaching package make no claim of any specific AACSB qualification or evaluation, we have within *Microeconomics, 9e* labeled selected questions according to the general knowledge and skills areas.

McGraw-Hill Customer Care Contact Information

At McGraw-Hill, we understand that getting the most from new technology can be challenging. That's why our services don't stop after you purchase our products. You can e-mail our Product Specialists 24 hours a day to get product-training online. Or you can search our knowledge bank of Frequently Asked Questions on our support website. For Customer Support, call **800-331-5094** or visit **www.mhhe.com/support.** One of our Technical Support Analysts will be able to assist you in a timely fashion.

CourseSmart

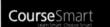

CourseSmart is a new way for faculty to find and review eTextbooks. It's also a great option for students who are interested in accessing their course materials digitally. CourseSmart offers thousands of the most commonly adopted textbooks across hundreds of courses from a wide variety of higher education publishers. It is the only place for faculty to review and compare the full text of a textbook online. At CourseSmart, students can save up to 50% off the cost of a print book, reduce their impact on the environment, and gain access to powerful web tools for learning including full text search, notes and highlighting, and e-mail tools for sharing notes between classmates. Complete tech support is also included with each title.

Finding your eBook is easy. Visit **www.CourseSmart.com** and search by title, author, or ISBN.

Dollars and Sense Readers

While not directly an ancillary to the book, the *Dollars and Sense* readers are annotated to fit with chapters of this book for professors who want to supplement the text with a radical perspective. Contact your McGraw-Hill representative for more information.

Package Pricing

To help lower costs of using ancillaries, McGraw-Hill has developed a variety of separate packages in which the book can be bought together with the ancillaries for a price that is close to the price of the book alone. Each of these packages has a separate ISBN number. For information on these packages, contact your McGraw-Hill sales representative.

People to Thank

Let me conclude this preface by thanking the hundreds of people who have offered suggestions, comments, kudos, and criticism on this project since its inception. This book would not be what it is without their input. So many people have contributed to this text in so many ways that I cannot thank everyone. So, to all the people who helped—many, many thanks. I specifically want to thank the ninth edition reviewers, whose insightful comments kept me on track. Reviewers include:

John Abell
Randolph College

Rose-Marie Avin
University of Wisconsin, Eau Claire

John Beck
Gonzaga University

Anthony Becker
St. Olaf College

Susan Bell
Seminole State College of Florida

Randall Bennett
Gonzaga University

Tami Bertelsen
Arapahoe Community College

Gerald Bialka
University of North Florida

John Blair
Wright State University

John Boschen
College of William & Mary

Taggert Brooks
University of Wisconsin–La Crosse

Keith Brouhle
Grinnell College

Neil Browne
Bowling Green State University

Joan Buccino
Florida Southern College

Douglas Bunn
Blackburn College

Eric Burns
Herbert W. Armstrong College

Colleen Callahan
American University

Kaycea Campbell
West Los Angeles Community College

Regina Cassady
Valencia County College

Suparna Chakraborty
Baruch College

Darian Chin
California State University–Los Angeles

Lisa Citron
Cascadia Community College

Jennifer Clark
Roosevelt University

George Darko
Tusculum College

Dennis Edwards
Coastal Carolina University

Gregory DeFreitas
Hofstra University

Diana Denison
Red Rocks Community College

Liang Ding
Macalester College

Justin Dubas
Texas Lutheran University

Sarah Estelle
Rhodes College

Doug Fain
Regis University

Christine Farrell
University of the Ozarks

Lucia Farriss
Saint Leo University Center for Online Learning

Fadi Fawaz
Texas Tech University

Shelby Frost
Georgia State University

Julie Gallaway
Missouri State University

Karen Gebhardt
Colorado State University

Scott Gilbert
Southern Illinois University–Carbondale

Robert Gitter
Ohio Wesleyan University

Nicholas Gomersall
Luther College

Michael Goode
Central Piedmont Community College

Mehdi Haririan
Bloomsburg University

Kevin Henrickson
Gonzaga University

Kermelle Hensley
Columbus Technical College

Elizabeth Hickman
Oakland City University–Bedford

Jannett Highfill
Bradley University

Reza Hossain
Mount Saint Mary College

Jack Hou
California State University–Long Beach

Chris Inama
Golden Gate University

Miren Ivankovic
Anderson University

Donna Rue Jenkins
National University

Paul Jones
National University

Lillian Kamal
University of Hartford

Jonathan Kaplan
California State Sacramento

Michele Kegley
Southern State Community College

Logan Kelly
Bryant University

Farida Khan
University of Wisconsin, Parkside

Chong-Uk Kim
Sonoma State University

Judy Klein
Mary Baldwin College

Rachel Kreier
Deanza College

Paul Kubik
DePaul University

Anil Lal
Pittsburgh State University

Simon Yuexing Lan
Auburn University–Montgomery

Gary Langer
Roosevelt University

Anthony Laramie
Merrimack College

Mark Lautzenheiser
Earlham College

Samuel Liu
West Valley College

Christine Lloyd
Western Illinois University

John Marcis
Coastal Carolina University

Ann Mari May
University of Nebraska–Lincoln

Warren Mazek
U.S. Merchant Marine Academy

Chris McNamara
Finger Lakes Community College

Lewis Metcalf
Parkland College

Peter Mikek
Wabash College

Garrett Milam
University of Puget Sound

William Milberg
The New School for Social Research

Frannie Miller
Texas A&M University–Commerce

Daniel Mizak
Frostburg State University

Karla Morgan
Whitworth College

Wayne Morra
Arcadia University

Muhammad Mustafa
South Carolina State University

Ronald Nate
Brigham Young University–Idaho

Nasrin Nazemzadeh
Lone Star College–Tomball

Brendan O'Flaherty
Columbia University

Ozgur Orhangazi
Roosevelt University

Peter Paluch
State University of New York–Delhi

Jodi Pelkowski
Wichita State University

Nathan Perry
University of Utah–Salt Lake

Liz Peterson
Eastern Washington University

Chiara Piovani
University of Utah

Brennan Platt
Brigham Young University–Provo

Roxanna Postolache
Capital University–Columbus

Ayman Reda
Grand Valley State University

Robert Rogers
Ashland University

Jonathan Sandy
University of San Diego

Richard Schatz
Whitworth University

Carol Schwartz
New York Institute of Technology

Robert Shoffner
Central Piedmont Community College

Jeffrey Silman
Paul Smith's College

Kevin Simmons
Austin College

John Somers
Portland Community College–Sylvania

Robert Sonora
Fort Lewis College

Robin Sturik
Cuyahoga Community College, Western Campus

Della Sue
Marist College

Thom Swanke
Morningside College

John Swinton
Georgia College & State

Richard Tarmey
Colorado Mountain College

Eric Taylor
Central Piedmont Community College

Zdravka Todorova
Wright State University

Dossee Toulaboe
Fort Hays State University

Stephen Tubene
University of Maryland–East Shore

Don-Joseph Uy-Barreta
Deanza College

Ramya Vijaya
Richard Stockton College of New Jersey

Randy Wade
Rogue Community College

Lynn Wallis
Clackamas Community College

Bruce Webb
Gordon College

Katherine Whitman
Mount St. Mary's College–Doheny

Van Wigginton
San Jacinto College–Pasadena

Andrew Williams
Delaware Tech Community College–Dover

Dmitry Yarushkin
Grand View University

In addition to the comments of the formal reviewers listed above, I have received helpful suggestions, encouragement, and assistance from innumerable individuals via e-mails, letters, symposia, and focus groups. Their help made this edition even stronger than its predecessor. They include James Wetzel, Virginia Commonwealth University; Dmitry Shishkin, Georgia State University; Amy Cramer, Pima Community College–West; Andrea Terzi, Franklin College; Shelby Frost, Georgia State University; Doris Geide-Stevenson, Weber State University; James Chasey, Advanced Placement Economics Teaching Consultant and Homewood-Flossmoor High School (ret.); David Tufte, Southern Utah University; Eric Sarpong, Georgia State University; Jim Ciecka, DePaul University; Fran Bradley, George School; Ron Olive, University of Massachusetts–Lowell; and Rachel Kreier, Hofstra University.

I want to give a special thank-you to the supplements authors including Shannon Aucoin, the University of Louisiana at Lafayette; Edward Gullason, Dowling College; Timothy Terrell, Wofford College; Brian Lynch, Lakeland Community College; and Paul Aaron Fisher,

Henry Ford Community College. They all did an outstanding job.

I'd also like to thank the economists who wrote the alternative perspective questions. These include Ann Mari May of the University of Nebraska–Lincoln, John Miller of Wheaton College, Dan Underwood of Peninsula College, Ric Holt of Southern Oregon University, and Bridget Butkevich of George Mason University. I enjoyed working with each of them, and while their views often differed substantially, they were all united in wanting questions that showed economics as a pluralist field that encourages students to question the text from all perspectives.

I have hired numerous students to check aspects of the book, to read over my questions and answers to questions, and to help proofread. These include Kelly Liss, Anne Sexton Powers, Taran Jondaro, Alexander Veerman, Andrew Vollmer, Elena Zhang, Emily Duh, Olivia Lau, William Gamber, and Samatha Gluck. I thank them all.

A special thank-you for this edition goes to two people. The first is Jenifer Gamber, whose role in the book cannot be overestimated. She helped me clarify its vision by providing research, critiquing expositions and often improving them, and being a good friend. She has an amazing set of skills, and I thank her for using them to improve the book. The second is Christina Kouvelis, who came into this project and with her hard work, dedication, and superb ability made it possible to get the book done on time, even during a period of turmoil. She and Jenifer are two amazing women.

Next, I want to thank the entire McGraw-Hill team, including Douglas Reiner, managing director; Scott Smith, the brand manager; Alyssa Lincoln, the development editor; Bruce Gin, the content project manager; Pam Verros, the designer; Carol Bielski, the senior buyer; and Katie White, the marketing manager. All of them have done a superb job, for which I thank them sincerely.

Finally, I want to thank Pat, my wife, and my sons, Kasey and Zach, for helping me keep my work in perspective, and for providing a loving environment in which to work.

Preface for the Student: Alternative Perspectives

This text is written for you, the student. It's meant to give you a sense of what economics is, how economists think, and how they approach policy problems. There's only so much that an introductory course can cover, which means that much is left out. That includes much of the subtlety of economic thinking. So if you have a problem swallowing some of the ideas, and you believe that there's more to the issue than is presented here, rest assured; generally you're right. Hard choices have to be made for pedagogical purposes—issues have to be simplified and presentations curtailed. Otherwise this would be a 1,600-page book and much too heavy to carry around in a backpack.

Economics as a Method of Reasoning, Not the Truth

The approach I use is what would be called mainstream (it presents the conventional wisdom of economists) both because I'm mainstream and because most economists are as well. But pedagogically, I also believe that students learn by questioning—to say, no, that's not right, that's not the way I see things, and then to compare their way of thinking with the conventional way. Despite my being mainstream, I'm by nature also a skeptic, and in terms of pedagogy often find myself in sympathy with Joan Robinson, a famous economist, who argued that "the purpose of studying economics is not to acquire a set of ready-made answers to economic questions, but to learn how to avoid being deceived by economists." So, to encourage questioning everything, I don't present models and insights of economists as the truth (the field of economics is far too complicated to have arrived at a single truth) but as a set of technical hurdles, reasoning processes, and arguments that students should know, and that will help prepare them to deal with economic issues. Economics primarily teaches you how to approach problems; it does not provide definitive answers about what is right and what is wrong. It is a method, not a set of truths.

Alternative Perspectives in Economics

One of the pedagogical choices I made was to concentrate almost exclusively on the mainstream view. I strongly believe that focusing on that view is the best way to teach the course. However, I also believe that students should be aware of the diversity in economics and know that the mainstream view is not the only view out there. In fact, there are probably as many views out there as there are economists. Still, for a majority of economists, the concepts presented are an acceptable pedagogical simplification of the myriad views held by economists.

Some economists, however, might see this presentation as misleading, or as diverting the discussion away from other, more relevant, issues. These economists are generally called nonmainstream or heterodox economists. A heterodox economist is *one who doesn't accept the basic underlying model used by a majority of economists as the most useful model for analyzing the economy.*

In this preface, I will briefly introduce six heterodox economic approaches to give you a sense of how their analyses differ from the mainstream analyses presented. The six heterodox approaches are Austrian, Post-Keynesian, Institutionalist, Radical, feminist, and religious. Below are brief descriptions of each group, written with the help of the team of alternative-perspective economists.

Austrian Economists

Austrian economists believe in methodological individualism, by which they mean that social goals are best met through voluntary, mutually beneficial interactions. Lack of information and unsolvable incentive problems undermine the ability of government to plan, making the market the best method for coordinating economic activity. Austrian economists oppose state intrusion into private property and private activities. They are not economists from Austria; rather, they are economists from anywhere who follow the ideas of Ludwig von Mises and Friedrich Hayek, two economists who were from Austria.

Austrian economists are sometimes classified as conservative, but they are more appropriately classified as libertarians, who believe in liberty of individuals first and in other social goals second. Consistent with their views, they are often willing to support what are sometimes considered radical ideas, such as legalizing addictive drugs or eliminating our current monetary system—ideas that most mainstream economists would oppose. Austrian economists emphasize the uncertainty in the economy and the inability of a government controlled by self-interested politicians to undertake socially beneficial policy.

One proposal of Austrian economists will give you a flavor of their approach. That proposal is to eliminate the Federal Reserve System and to establish a free market in money—a policy that would leave people free to use any money they want and that would significantly reduce banking regulation. In a sense, their proposal carries the Classical argument in favor of laissez-faire to its logical conclusions. Why should the government have a monopoly of the money supply? Why shouldn't people be free to use whatever money they desire, denominated in whatever unit they want? Why don't we rely upon competition to prevent inflation? Why don't we have a free market in money? Well-known Austrian economists include Peter Boettke, Veronique de Rugy, Mario Rizzo, David Gordon, Israel Kirzner, Peter Leeson, Chris Coyne, Steve Horwitz, Roger Garrison, and Roger Koppl.

Institutionalist Economists

Institutionalist economists argue that any economic analysis must involve specific considerations of institutions. The lineage of Institutionalist economics begins with the pioneering work of Thorstein Veblen, John R. Commons, and Wesley C. Mitchell. Veblen employed evolutionary analysis to explore the role of institutions in directing and retarding the economic process. He saw human behavior driven by cultural norms and conveyed the way in which they were with sardonic wit and penetrating insight, leaving us with enduring metaphors such as the leisure class and conspicuous consumption. Commons argued that institutions are social constructs that could improve general welfare. Accordingly, he established cooperative investigative programs to support pragmatic changes in the legal structure of government. Mitchell was a leader in developing economics as an empirical study; he was a keen observer of the business cycle and argued that theory must be informed by systematic attention to empirical data, or it was useless.

Contemporary Institutionalists employ the founders' "trilogy"—empirically informed evolutionary analysis directed toward pragmatic alteration of institutions shaping economic outcomes—in their policy approach. Examples include indicative planning—a macroeconomic policy in which the government sets up an overall plan for various industries and selectively directs credit to certain industries; and income support programs, including those assuring employment for all willing. Well-known

Institutionalists include Greg Hayden, Geoff Hodgson, Anne Mayhew, James Peach, and Ronnie Phillips.

Radical Economists

Radical economists believe substantial equality-preferring institutional changes should be implemented in our economic system. Radical economists evolved out of Marxian economics. In their analysis, they focus on the lack of equity in our current economic system and on institutional changes that might bring about a more equitable system. Specifically, they see the current economic system as one in which a few people—capitalists and high-level managers—benefit enormously at the expense of many people who struggle to make ends meet in jobs that are unfulfilling or who even go without work at times. They see the fundamental instability and irrationality of the capitalist system at the root of a wide array of social ills that range from pervasive inequality to alienation, racism, sexism, and imperialism. Radical economists often use a class-oriented analysis to address these issues and are much more willing to talk about social conflict and tensions in our society than are mainstream economists.

A policy favored by many Radicals is the establishment of worker cooperatives to replace the corporation. Radicals argue that such worker cooperatives would see that the income of the firm is more equitably allocated. Likewise, Radical theorists endorse policies such as universal health care insurance that conform to the ethic of "putting people before profits."

There are a number of centers of Radical thought, including The Political Economy Research Institute, The New School for Social Research, and some campuses of the University of Massachusetts. A good place to find Radical views is the *Dollars and Sense* magazine. Well-known Radical economists include Lourdes Beneria, Sam Bowles, Arthur MacEwan, Robert Pollin, Gerald Epstein, Anwar Shaikh, Michael Reich, Richard Wolff, and Stephen Resnick, as well as a number of feminist economists who would be considered both Radicals and feminists.

Feminist Economists

Feminist economics offers a substantive challenge to the content, scope, and methodology of mainstream economics. Feminist economists question the boundaries of what we consider economics to be and examine social arrangements surrounding provisioning. Feminist economists have many different views, but all believe that in some way traditional economic analysis misses many important issues pertaining to women.

Feminist economists study issues such as how the institutional structure tends to direct women into certain types of jobs (generally low-paying jobs) and away from other types of jobs (generally high-paying jobs). They draw our attention to the unpaid labor performed by women throughout the world and ask, "What would GDP look like if women's work were given a value and included?" They argue for an expansion in the content of economics to include women as practitioners and as worthy of study and for the elimination of the masculine bias in mainstream economics. Is there such a bias? To see it, simply compare the relative number of women in your economics class to the relative number of women at your school. It is highly likely that your class has relatively more men. Feminist economists want you to ask why that is, and whether anything should be done about it.

The historical roots of feminist economics can be found in the work of such authors as Mary Wollstonecraft, John Stuart Mill, Harriet Taylor Mill, and Charlotte Perkins Gilman. Feminist economics has expanded significantly in the past 25 years and has emerged as an influential body of thought. Well-known feminist economists include Myra Strober, Diana Strassmann, Barbara Bergmann, Julie Nelson, Jane Humphries, Marianne Ferber, Randy Albelda, Nancy Folbre, and Heidi Hartmann.

Religious Economists

Religion is the oldest and, arguably, the most influential institution in the world—be it Christianity, Islam, Judaism, Buddhism, Hinduism, or any of the many other religions in the world. Modern science, of which economics is a part, emphasizes the rational elements of thought. It attempts to separate faith and normative issues from rational analysis in ways that some religiously oriented economists find questionable. The line between a religious and non-religious economist is not hard and fast; all economists bring elements of their ethical considerations into their analysis. But those we call "religious economists" integrate the ethical and normative issues into economic analysis in more complex ways than the ways presented in the text.

Religiously oriented economists have a diversity of views; some believe that their views can be integrated reasonably well into standard economics, while others see the need for the development of a distinctive faith-based methodology that focuses on a particular group of normative concerns centered on issues such as human dignity and caring for the poor.

One religious perspective that is represented by a defined group in the U.S. economics profession is Christianity, and a number of Christian economists have joined together in the Association of Christian Economists (ACE). Its stated goal is "to encourage Christian scholars to explore and communicate the relationship between their faith and the discipline of economics, and to promote interaction and communication among Christian economists." Centers of ACE are Pepperdine University, Calvin College, and Gordon College. Leading Christian economists include Kurt Schaefer, Andrew Yuengert, and Stephen Smith.

Many of the religious alternative perspective questions that we provide in the text are from the Judeo-Christian perspective, the perspective most familiar to U.S. students. However, we intersperse some questions from other religious perspectives, both to show the similarity of views and to encourage students to think in a multicultural framework.

Post-Keynesian Economists

Post-Keynesian economists believe that uncertainty is a central issue in economics. They follow J. M. Keynes' approach more so than do mainstream economists in emphasizing institutional imperfections in the economy and the importance of fundamental uncertainty that rationality cannot deal with. They agree with Institutionalists that the study of economics must emphasize and incorporate the importance of social and political structure in determining market outcomes.

While their view about the importance of uncertainty is similar to the Austrian view, their policy response to that uncertainty is quite different. They do not see uncertainty as eliminating much of government's role in the economy; instead, they see it leading to policies in which government takes a larger role in guiding the economy.

One of their policy proposals that gives you a flavor of their approach is tax-based income policies—policies in which the government tries to directly affect the nominal wage- and price-setting institutions. Under a tax-based income policy, any firm raising its wage or price would be subject to a tax, and any firm lowering its wage or price would get a subsidy. Such a plan, they argue, would reduce the upward pressure on the nominal price level and reduce the rate of unemployment necessary to hold down inflation. Well-known Post-Keynesian economists include Paul Davidson, Jamie Galbraith, Barkley Rosser, John Cornwall, Shelia Dow, Malcolm Sawyer, Philip Arestis, Victoria Chick, Jan Kregel, and Geoff Harcourt.

Consistency of the Various Approaches

A characteristic of almost all heterodox economists of all types is that their analyses tend to be less formal than mainstream analysis. *Less formal* doesn't mean better or worse. There are advantages and disadvantages to formality, but *less formal* does mean that there's more potential for ambiguity in interpretation. It's easy to say whether the logic in a formal model is right or wrong. It's much harder to say whether the logic in an informal model is right or wrong because it's often hard to see precisely what the logic is. The advantage of an informal model is that it can include many more variables and can be made more realistic, so you can discuss real-world problems more easily with that model. Nonmainstream economists often want to talk about the real world, which is why they use informal models.

Often, after I discuss the mainstream and heterodox approaches, some student asks which is right. I respond with a story told by a former colleague of mine, Abba Lerner:

> "But look," the rabbi's wife remonstrated, "when one party to the dispute presented their case to you, you said, 'You are quite right,' and then when the other party presented their case you again said, 'You are quite right.' Surely they cannot both be right?" To which the Rabbi answered, "My dear, you are quite right!"

The moral of the story is that there's nothing necessarily inconsistent among mainstream and heterodox economists' approaches. Their approaches are simply different ways of looking at the same event. Which approach is most useful depends on what issues and events you are analyzing. The class analysis used by radicals is often more appropriate to developing countries than it is to the United States, and, in analyzing developing countries, many mainstream economists also include class fights in their approach. Similarly, Austrian analysis provides more insight into the role of the entrepreneur and individual in the economy than does mainstream analysis, while Post-Keynesian and Institutionalist analyses are useful when considering major institutional changes.

The distinctions between heterodox and mainstream economists can be overdone. One economist may well fall into two or three different groupings and use a combination of various analyses.

I follow the work of heterodox economists carefully. Their writing is often more interesting than mainstream writing, which can often get rather technical and boring.

But in this book, I present primarily mainstream views. I do that because that's what I see as the job of the principles of economics course. My goal, however, is to present those views to you, not to indoctrinate you with those views, and throughout the text I include some challenges to the standard views. At the end of each chapter, I also include some questions that challenge the view presented in the chapter. These questions are written by representatives of different heterodox groups. I also encourage you to look for these other views in your outside reading. The *Dollars and Sense* companion to the book has radical critiques and *Free Market,* an Austrian newsletter found at www.mises.org, has Austrian critiques. There are many other sources and websites for heterodox groups. Exploring these sites and learning about the many different views that are competing in the marketplace for ideas make your economics course more interesting.

A Concluding Thought

There are many ways to explore economics, and in your exploration, this text and accompanying package is only a map. You and your professor determine what you discuss and learn and what path you will take. Ultimately, that's the way it has to be. Most of you are in this course for the grade—college is a way of progressing up the ladder. That's how it was for me. But the process also can be transforming; it can change how you look at issues, how you think, and who you are. The economics courses I took were especially important in determining who I have become.

Much of the principles course is what I call hurdle jumping—calisthenics of the mind. It is a set of mind-strengthening exercises. Separately, each is not especially relevant, but combined, they help turn your weak cranial muscle into a strong muscle better able to handle the problems that life throws at you. So, do the work, even if it seems boring; follow your professor's reasoning, even if you don't agree with what he or she is arguing; and keep thinking. Take advantage of this product's digital tools, even if they aren't required. Read newspapers and try to apply the lessons, deciding when they apply and when they don't. But, in the process, be happy—enjoy the moment because that moment will never be again.

Brief Contents

Contents

PART **II**

MICROECONOMICS

SECTION I
THE POWER OF TRADITIONAL
ECONOMIC MODELS

Introduction:
Thinking Like an Economist

Part I is an introduction, and an introduction to an introduction seems a little funny. But other sections have introductions, so it seemed a little funny not to have an introduction to Part I; and besides, as you will see, I'm a little funny myself (which, in turn, has two interpretations; I'm sure you will decide which of the two is appropriate). It will, however, be a very brief introduction, consisting of questions you may have had and some answers to those questions.

Some Questions and Answers

Why study economics?
Because it's neat and interesting and helps provide insight into events that are constantly going on around you.

Why is this book so big?
Because there's a lot of important information in it and because the book is designed so your teacher can pick and choose. You'll likely not be required to read all of it, especially if you're on the quarter system. But once you start it, you'll probably read it all anyhow. (Would you believe?)

Why does this book cost so much?
To answer this question, you'll have to read the book.

Will this book make me rich?
No.

Will this book make me happy?
It depends.

This book doesn't seem to be written in a normal textbook style. Is this book really written by a professor?
Yes, but he is different. He misspent his youth working on cars; he married his high school sweetheart after they met again at their 20th high school reunion, they remain happily married today, still totally in love. Twenty-five years after graduating from high school, his wife went back to medical school and got her MD because she was tired of being treated poorly by doctors. Their five kids

make sure he doesn't get carried away in the professorial cloud.

Will the entire book be like this?
No, the introduction is just trying to rope you in. Much of the book will be hard going. Learning happens to be a difficult process: no pain, no gain. But the author isn't a sadist; he tries to make learning as pleasantly painful as possible.

What do the author's students think of him?
Weird, definitely weird—and hard. But fair, interesting, and sincerely interested in getting us to learn. (Answer written by his students.)

So there you have it. Answers to the questions that you might never have thought of if they hadn't been put in front of you. I hope they give you a sense of me and the approach I'll use in the book. There are some neat ideas in it. Let's now briefly consider what's in the first five chapters.

A Survey of the First Five Chapters

This first section is really an introduction to the rest of the book. It gives you the background necessary so that the later chapters make sense. Chapter 1 gives you an overview of the entire field of economics as well as an introduction to my style. Chapter 2 focuses on the production possibility curve, comparative advantage, and trade. It explains how trade increases production possibilities but also why, in the real world, free trade and no government regulation may not be the best policy. Chapter 3 gives you some history of economic systems and introduces you to the institutions of the U.S. economy. Chapters 4 and 5 introduce you to supply and demand, and show you not only the power of those two concepts but also the limitations.

Now let's get on with the show.

chapter 1

Economics and Economic Reasoning

> *In my vacations, I visited the poorest quarters of several cities and walked through one street after another, looking at the faces of the poorest people. Next I resolved to make as thorough a study as I could of Political Economy.*
>
> —Alfred Marshall

When an artist looks at the world, he sees color. When a musician looks at the world, she hears music. When an economist looks at the world, she sees a symphony of costs and benefits. The economist's world might not be as colorful or as melodic as the others' worlds, but it's more practical. If you want to understand what's going on in the world that's really out there, you need to know economics.

I hardly have to convince you of this fact if you keep up with the news. You will be bombarded with stories of unemployment, interest rates, how commodity prices are changing, and how businesses are doing. The list is endless. So let's say you grant me that economics is important. That still doesn't mean that it's worth studying. The real question then is: How much will you learn? Most of what you learn depends on you, but part depends on the teacher and another part depends on the textbook. On both these counts, you're in luck; since your teacher chose this book for your course, you must have a super teacher.[1]

What Economics Is

Economics is *the study of how human beings coordinate their wants and desires, given the decision-making mechanisms, social customs, and political realities of the society.* One of the key words in the definition of the term "economics" is *coordination.* Coordination can mean many things. In the study of economics,

[1]This book is written by a person, not a machine. That means that I have my quirks, my odd sense of humor, and my biases. All textbook writers do. Most textbooks have the quirks and eccentricities edited out so that all the books read and sound alike—professional but dull. I choose to sound like me—sometimes professional, sometimes playful, and sometimes stubborn. In my view, that makes the book more human and less dull. So forgive me my quirks—don't always take me too seriously—and I'll try to keep you awake when you're reading this book at 3 a.m. the day of the exam. If you think it's a killer to read a book this long, you ought to try writing one.

coordination refers to how the three central problems facing any economy are solved. These central problems are:

1. What, and how much, to produce.
2. How to produce it.
3. For whom to produce it.

How hard is it to make the three decisions? Imagine for a moment the problem of living in a family: the fights, arguments, and questions that come up. "Do I have to do the dishes?" "Why can't I have piano lessons?" "Bobby got a new sweater. How come I didn't?" "Mom likes you best." Now multiply the size of the family by millions. The same fights, the same arguments, the same questions—only for society the questions are millions of times more complicated. In answering these questions, economies find that inevitably individuals want more than is available, given how much they're willing to work. That means that in our economy there is a problem of **scarcity**—*the goods available are too few to satisfy individuals' desires.*

> Three central coordination problems any economy must solve are what to produce, how to produce it, and for whom to produce it.

> The coordination questions faced by society are complicated.

Scarcity

Scarcity has two elements: our wants and our means of fulfilling those wants. These can be interrelated since wants are changeable and partially determined by society. The way we fulfill wants can affect those wants. For example, if you work on Wall Street, you will probably want upscale and trendy clothes. In Vermont, I am quite happy wearing Levi's and flannel.

The degree of scarcity is constantly changing. The quantity of goods, services, and usable resources depends on technology and human action, which underlie production. Individuals' imagination, innovativeness, and willingness to do what needs to be done can greatly increase available goods and resources. Who knows what technologies are in our future—nannites or micromachines that change atoms into whatever we want could conceivably eliminate scarcity of goods we currently consume. But they would not eliminate scarcity entirely since new wants are constantly developing.

> The quantity of goods, services, and usable resources depends on technology and human action.

So, how does an economy deal with scarcity? The answer is coercion. In all known economies, coordination has involved some type of coercion—limiting people's wants and increasing the amount of work individuals are willing to do to fulfill those wants. The reality is that many people would rather play than help solve society's problems. So the basic economic problem involves inspiring people to do things that other people want them to do, and not to do things that other people don't want them to do. Thus, an alternative definition of economics is: the study of how to get people to do things they're not wild about doing (such as studying) and not to do things they are wild about doing (such as eating all the lobster they like), so that the things some people want to do are consistent with the things other people want to do.

Microeconomics and Macroeconomics

Economic theory is divided into two parts: microeconomic theory and macroeconomic theory. Microeconomic theory considers economic reasoning from the viewpoint of individuals and firms and builds up to an analysis of the whole economy. **Microeconomics** is *the study of individual choice, and how that choice is influenced by economic forces.* Microeconomics studies such things as the pricing policies of firms, households' decisions on what to buy, and how markets allocate resources among alternative ends.

> Microeconomics is the study of how individual choice is influenced by economic forces.

As we build up from microeconomic analysis to an analysis of the entire economy, everything gets rather complicated. Many economists try to uncomplicate matters by taking a different approach—a macroeconomic approach—first looking at the aggregate, or whole, and then breaking it down into components. **Macroeconomics** is *the study of the*

> Macroeconomics is the study of the economy as a whole. It considers the problems of inflation, unemployment, business cycles, and growth.

economy as a whole. It considers the problems of inflation, unemployment, business cycles, and growth. Macroeconomics focuses on aggregate relationships such as how household consumption is related to income and how government policies can affect growth.

Q-1 Classify the following topics as primarily macroeconomic or microeconomic:

1. The impact of a tax increase on aggregate output.
2. The relationship between two competing firms' pricing behavior.
3. A farmer's decision to plant soy or wheat.
4. The effect of trade on economic growth.

Consider an analogy to the human body. A micro approach analyzes a person by looking first at each individual cell and then builds up. A macro approach starts with the person and then goes on to his or her components—arms, legs, fingernails, feelings, and so on. Put simply, microeconomics analyzes from the parts to the whole; macroeconomics analyzes from the whole to the parts.

Microeconomics and macroeconomics are very much interrelated. What happens in the economy as a whole is based on individual decisions, but individual decisions are made within an economy and can be understood only within its macro context. For example, whether a firm decides to expand production capacity will depend on what the owners expect will happen to the demand for their products. Those expectations are determined by macroeconomic conditions. Because microeconomics focuses on individuals and macroeconomics focuses on the whole economy, traditionally microeconomics and macroeconomics are taught separately, even though they are interrelated.

A Guide to Economic Reasoning

People trained in economics think in a certain way. They analyze everything critically; they compare the costs and the benefits of every issue and make decisions based on those costs and benefits. For example, say you're trying to decide whether a policy to eliminate terrorist attacks on airlines is a good idea. Economists are trained to put their emotions aside and ask: What are the costs of the policy, and what are the benefits? Thus, they are open to the argument that security measures, such as conducting body searches of every passenger or scanning all baggage with bomb-detecting machinery, might not be the appropriate policy because the costs might exceed the benefits. To think like an economist involves addressing almost all issues using a cost/benefit approach. Economic reasoning also involves abstracting from the "unimportant" elements of a question and focusing on the "important" ones by creating a simple model that captures the essence of the issue or problem. How do you know whether the model has captured the important elements? By collecting empirical evidence and "testing" the model—matching the predictions of the model with the empirical evidence—to see if it fits. Economic reasoning—how to think like a modern economist, making decisions on the basis of costs and benefits—is the most important lesson you'll learn from this book.

Economic reasoning is making decisions on the basis of costs and benefits.

The book *Freakonomics* gives examples of the economist's approach. It describes a number of studies by University of Chicago economist Steve Levitt that unlock seemingly mysterious observations with basic economic reasoning. For example, Levitt asks the question: Why do drug dealers on the street tend to live with their mothers? The answer he arrives at is that it is because they can't afford to live on their own; most earn less than $5 an hour. Why, then, are they dealing drugs and not working a legal job that, even for a minimum-wage job, pays over $7.00 an hour? The answer to that is determined through cost/benefit analysis. While their current income is low, their potential income as a drug dealer is much higher since, given their background and current U.S. institutions, they are more likely to move up to a high position in the local drug business (and *Freakonomics* describes how it is a business) and earn a six-figure income than they are to move up from working as a Taco Bell technician to an executive earning a six-figure income in corporate America. Levitt's model is a very simple one—people do what is in their best interest financially—and it assumes that people rely on a cost/benefit analysis to make decisions. Finally, he supports his argument through careful empirical work, collecting and organizing the data to see if they fit the model. His work is a good example of "thinking like a modern economist" in action.

Economic Knowledge in One Sentence: TANSTAAFL

Once upon a time, Tanstaafl was made king of all the lands. His first act was to call his economic advisers and tell them to write up all the economic knowledge the society possessed. After years of work, they presented their monumental effort: 25 volumes, each about 400 pages long. But in the interim, King Tanstaafl had become a very busy man, what with running a kingdom of all the lands and all. Looking at the lengthy volumes, he told his advisers to summarize their findings in one volume.

Despondently, the economists returned to their desks, wondering how they could summarize what they'd been so careful to spell out. After many more years of rewriting, they were finally satisfied with their one-volume effort, and tried to make an appointment to see the king. Unfortunately, affairs of state had become even more pressing than before, and the king couldn't take the time to see them. Instead he sent word to them that he couldn't be bothered with a whole volume, and ordered them, under threat of death (for he had become a tyrant), to reduce the work to one sentence.

The economists returned to their desks, shivering in their sandals and pondering their impossible task. Thinking about their fate if they were not successful, they decided to send out for one last meal. Unfortunately, when they were collecting money to pay for the meal, they discovered they were broke. The disgusted delivery man took the last meal back to the restaurant, and the economists started down the path to the beheading station. On the way, the delivery man's parting words echoed in their ears. They looked at each other and suddenly they realized the truth. "We're saved!" they screamed. "That's it! That's economic knowledge in one sentence!" They wrote the sentence down and presented it to the king, who thereafter fully understood all economic problems. (He also gave them a good meal.) The sentence?

There **A**in't **N**o **S**uch **T**hing **A**s **A** **F**ree **L**unch— **TANSTAAFL**

Economic reasoning, once learned, is infectious. If you're susceptible, being exposed to it will change your life. It will influence your analysis of everything, including issues normally considered outside the scope of economics. For example, you will likely use economic reasoning to decide the possibility of getting a date for Saturday night, and who will pay for dinner. You will likely use it to decide whether to read this book, whether to attend class, whom to marry, and what kind of work to go into after you graduate. This is not to say that economic reasoning will provide all the answers. As you will see throughout this book, real-world questions are inevitably complicated, and economic reasoning simply provides a framework within which to approach a question. In the economic way of thinking, every choice has costs and benefits, and decisions are made by comparing them.

Marginal Costs and Marginal Benefits

The relevant costs and relevant benefits to economic reasoning are the expected *incremental,* or additional, costs incurred and the expected *incremental* benefits that result from a decision. Economists use the term *marginal* when referring to additional or incremental. Marginal costs and marginal benefits are key concepts.

A **marginal cost** is *the additional cost to you over and above the costs you have already incurred.* That means not counting **sunk costs**—*costs that have already been incurred and cannot be recovered*—in the relevant costs when making a decision. Consider, for example, attending class. You've already paid your tuition; it is a sunk cost. So the marginal (or additional) cost of going to class does not include tuition.

Similarly with marginal benefit. A **marginal benefit** is *the additional benefit above what you've already derived.* The marginal benefit of reading this chapter is the *additional* knowledge you get from reading it. If you already knew everything in this chapter before you picked up the book, the marginal benefit of reading it now is zero.

Web Note 1.1
Costs and Benefits

Marginal Cost and
Marginal Benefit

The Economic Decision Rule

Comparing marginal (additional) costs with marginal (additional) benefits will often tell you how you should adjust your activities to be as well off as possible. Just follow the **economic decision rule:**

If the marginal benefits of doing something exceed the marginal costs, do it. If the marginal costs of doing something exceed the marginal benefits, don't do it.

If the marginal benefits of doing something exceed the marginal costs, do it.

If the marginal costs of doing something exceed the marginal benefits, don't do it.

As an example, let's consider a discussion I might have with a student who tells me that she is too busy to attend my classes. I respond, "Think about the tuition you've spent for this class—it works out to about $60 a lecture." She answers that the book she reads for class is a book that I wrote, and that I wrote it so clearly she fully understands everything. She goes on:

> I've already paid the tuition and whether I go to class or not, I can't get any of the tuition back, so the tuition is a sunk cost and doesn't enter into my decision. The marginal cost to me is what I could be doing with the hour instead of spending it in class. I value my time at $75 an hour [people who understand everything value their time highly], and even though I've heard that your lectures are super, I estimate that the marginal benefit of attending your class is only $50. The marginal cost, $75, exceeds the marginal benefit, $50, so I don't attend class.

I congratulate her on her diplomacy and her economic reasoning, but tell her that I give a quiz every week, that students who miss a quiz fail the quiz, that those who fail all the quizzes fail the course, and that those who fail the course do not graduate. In short, she is underestimating the marginal benefits of attending my classes. Correctly estimated, the marginal benefits of attending my class exceed the marginal costs. So she should attend my class.

Q-2 Say you bought a share of Oracle for $100 and a share of Cisco for $10. The price of each is currently $15. Assuming taxes are not an issue, which would you sell if you need $15?

Economics and Passion

www   Web Note 1.2
Blogonomics

Recognizing that everything has a cost is reasonable, but it's a reasonableness that many people don't like. It takes some of the passion out of life. It leads you to consider possibilities like these:

- Saving some people's lives with liver transplants might not be worth the additional cost. The money might be better spent on nutritional programs that would save 20 lives for every 2 lives you might save with transplants.

- Maybe we shouldn't try to eliminate all pollution because the additional cost of doing so may be too high. To eliminate all pollution might be to forgo too much of some other worthwhile activity.

- Providing a guaranteed job for every person who wants one might not be a worthwhile policy goal if it means that doing so will reduce the ability of an economy to adapt to new technologies.

- It might make sense for the automobile industry to save $12 per car by not installing a safety device, even though without the safety device some people will be killed.

Economic reasoning is based on the premise that everything has a cost.

You get the idea. This kind of reasonableness is often criticized for being cold-hearted. But, not surprisingly, economists disagree; they argue that their reasoning leads to a better society for the majority of people.

Economists' reasonableness isn't universally appreciated. Businesses love the result; others aren't so sure, as I discovered some years back when my then-girlfriend

Q-3 Can you think of a reason why a cost/benefit approach to a problem might be inappropriate? Can you give an example?

told me she was leaving me. "Why?" I asked. "Because," she responded, "you're so, so . . . reasonable." It took me many years after she left to learn what she already knew: There are many types of reasonableness, and not everyone thinks an economist's reasonableness is a virtue. I'll discuss such issues later; for now, let me simply warn you that, for better or worse, studying economics will lead you to view questions in a cost/benefit framework.

Opportunity Cost

Putting economists' cost/benefit rules into practice isn't easy. To do so, you have to be able to choose and measure the costs and benefits correctly. Economists have devised the concept of opportunity cost to help you do that. **Opportunity cost** is *the benefit that you might have gained from choosing the next-best alternative*. To obtain the benefit of something, you must give up (forgo) something else—namely, the next-best alternative. The opportunity cost is the value of that next-best alternative; it is a cost because in choosing one thing, you are precluding an alternative choice. The TANSTAAFL story in the box on page 7 embodies the opportunity cost concept because it tells us that there is a cost to everything; that cost is the next-best forgone alternative.

Let's consider some examples. The opportunity cost of going out once with Natalie (or Nathaniel), the most beautiful woman (attractive man) in the world, is the benefit you'd get from going out with your solid steady, Margo (Mike). The opportunity cost of cleaning up the environment might be a reduction in the money available to assist low-income individuals. The opportunity cost of having a child might be two boats, three cars, and a two-week vacation each year for five years, which are what you could have had if you hadn't had the child. (Kids really are this expensive.)

Examples are endless, but let's consider two that are particularly relevant to you: what courses to take and how much to study. Let's say you're a full-time student and at the beginning of the term you had to choose five courses. Taking one precludes taking some other, and the opportunity cost of taking an economics course may well be not taking a course on theater. Similarly with studying: You have a limited amount of time to spend studying economics, studying some other subject, sleeping, or partying. The more time you spend on one activity, the less time you have for another. That's opportunity cost.

Notice how neatly the opportunity cost concept takes into account costs and benefits of all other options, and converts these alternative benefits into costs of the decision you're now making.

The relevance of opportunity cost isn't limited to your individual decisions. Opportunity costs are also relevant to government's decisions, which affect everyone in society. A common example is what is called the guns-versus-butter debate. The resources that a society has are limited; therefore, its decision to use those resources to have more guns (more weapons) means that it will have less butter (fewer consumer goods). Thus, when society decides to spend $50 billion more on an improved health care system, the opportunity cost of that decision is $50 billion not spent on helping the homeless, paying off some of the national debt, or providing for national defense.

Opportunity costs have always made choice difficult, as we see in the early-19th-century engraving *One or the Other*.

Opportunity cost is the basis of cost/benefit economic reasoning; it is the benefit that you might have gained from choosing the next-best alternative.

Opportunity Cost

www Web Note 1.3
Opportunity Cost

Economics in Perspective

All too often, students study economics out of context. They're presented with sterile analysis and boring facts to memorize, and are never shown how economics fits into the larger scheme of things. That's bad; it makes economics seem boring—but economics is not boring. Every so often throughout this book, sometimes in the appendixes and sometimes in these boxes, I'll step back and put the analysis in perspective, giving you an idea from whence the analysis sprang and its historical context. In educational jargon, this is called *enrichment*.

I begin here with economics itself.

First, its history: In the 1500s there were few universities. Those that existed taught religion, Latin, Greek, philosophy, history, and mathematics. No economics. Then came the *Enlightenment* (about 1700), in which reasoning replaced God as the explanation of why things were the way they were. Pre-Enlightenment thinkers would answer the question "Why am I poor?" with "Because God wills it." Enlightenment scholars looked for a different explanation. "Because of the nature of land ownership" is one answer they found.

Such reasoned explanations required more knowledge of the way things were, and the amount of information expanded so rapidly that it had to be divided or categorized for an individual to have hope of knowing a subject. Soon philosophy was subdivided into science and philosophy. In the 1700s, the sciences were split into natural sciences and social sciences. The amount of knowledge kept increasing, and in the late 1800s and early 1900s social science itself split into subdivisions: economics, political science, history, geography, sociology, anthropology, and psychology. Many of the insights about how the economic system worked were codified in Adam Smith's *The Wealth of Nations*, written in 1776. Notice that this is before economics as a subdiscipline developed, and Adam Smith could also be classified as an anthropologist, a sociologist, a political scientist, and a social philosopher.

Throughout the 18th and 19th centuries, economists such as Adam Smith, Thomas Malthus, John Stuart Mill, David Ricardo, and Karl Marx were more than economists; they were social philosophers who covered all aspects of social science. These writers were subsequently called *classical economists*. Alfred Marshall continued in that classical tradition, and his book, *Principles of Economics*, published in the late 1800s, was written with the other social sciences much in evidence. But Marshall also changed the questions economists ask; he focused on those questions that could be asked in a graphical supply/demand framework.

This book falls solidly in the Marshallian tradition. It presents economics as a way of thinking—as an engine of analysis used to understand real-world phenomena. But it goes beyond Marshall, and introduces you to a wider variety of models and thinking than the supply and demand models that Marshall used.

Marshallian economics is primarily about policy, not theory. It sees institutions as well as political and social dimensions of reality as important, and it shows you how economics ties in to those dimensions.

Q-4 John, your study partner, has just said that the opportunity cost of studying this chapter is about 1/38 the price you paid for this book, since the chapter is about 1/38 of the book. Is he right? Why or why not?

The opportunity cost concept has endless implications. It can even be turned upon itself. For instance, thinking about alternatives takes time; that means that there's a cost to being reasonable, so it's only reasonable to be somewhat unreasonable. If you followed that argument, you've caught the economic bug. If you didn't, don't worry. Just remember the opportunity cost concept for now; I'll infect you with economic thinking in the rest of the book.

Economic Forces, Social Forces, and Political Forces

Q-5 Ali, your study partner, states that rationing health care is immoral—that health care should be freely available to all individuals in society. How would you respond?

The opportunity cost concept applies to all aspects of life and is fundamental to understanding how society reacts to scarcity. When goods are scarce, those goods must be rationed. That is, a mechanism must be chosen to determine who gets what.

Let's consider some specific real-world rationing mechanisms. Dormitory rooms are often rationed by lottery, and permission to register in popular classes is often rationed by a first-come, first-registered rule. Food in the United States, however, is generally rationed by price. If price did not ration food, there wouldn't be enough food to go around. All scarce goods must be rationed in some fashion. These rationing mechanisms are examples of **economic forces,** *the necessary reactions to scarcity.*

One of the important choices that a society must make is whether to allow these economic forces to operate freely and openly or to try to rein them in. A **market force** is *an economic force that is given relatively free rein by society to work through the market.* Market forces ration by changing prices. When there's a shortage, the price goes up. When there's a surplus, the price goes down. Much of this book will be devoted to analyzing how the market works like an invisible hand, guiding economic forces to coordinate individual actions and allocate scarce resources. The **invisible hand** is *the price mechanism, the rise and fall of prices that guides our actions in a market.*

Societies can't choose whether or not to allow economic forces to operate—economic forces are always operating. However, societies can choose whether to allow market forces to predominate. Social, cultural, and political forces play a major role in deciding whether to let market forces operate. Economic reality is determined by a contest among these various forces.

Let's consider an example in which social forces prevent an economic force from becoming a market force: the problem of getting a date for Saturday night. If a school (or a society) has significantly more heterosexual people of one gender than the other (let's say more men than women), some men may well find themselves without a date—that is, men will be in excess supply—and will have to find something else to do, say study or go to a movie by themselves. An "excess supply" person could solve the problem by paying someone to go out with him or her, but that would probably change the nature of the date in unacceptable ways. It would be revolting to the person who offered payment and to the person who was offered payment. That unacceptability is an example of the complex social and cultural norms that guide and limit our activities. People don't try to buy dates because social forces prevent them from doing so.

Now let's consider another example in which political and legal influences stop economic forces from becoming market forces. Say you decide that you can make some money delivering mail in your neighborhood. You try to establish a small business, but suddenly you are confronted with the law. The U.S. Postal Service has a legal exclusive right to deliver regular mail, so you'll be prohibited from delivering regular mail in competition with the post office. Economic forces—the desire to make money—led you to want to enter the business, but in this case political forces squash the invisible hand.

Often political and social forces work together against the invisible hand. For example, in the United States there aren't enough babies to satisfy all the couples who desire them. Babies born to particular sets of parents are rationed—by luck. Consider a group of parents, all of whom want babies. Those who can, have a baby; those who can't have one, but want one, try to adopt. Adoption agencies ration the available babies. Who gets a baby depends on whom people know at the adoption agency and on the desires of the birth mother, who can often specify the socioeconomic background (and many other characteristics) of the family in which she wants her baby to grow up. That's the economic force in action; it gives more power to the supplier of something that's in short supply.

If our society allowed individuals to buy and sell babies, that economic force would be translated into a market force. The invisible hand would see to it that the

quantity of babies supplied would equal the quantity of babies demanded at some price. The market, not the adoption agencies, would do the rationing.[2]

Most people, including me, find the idea of selling babies repugnant. But why? It's the strength of social forces reinforced by political forces. One can think of hundreds of examples of such social and political forces overriding economic forces.

What is and isn't allowable differs from one society to another. For example, in Cuba and North Korea, many private businesses are against the law, so not many people start their own businesses. In the United States, until the 1970s, it was against the law to hold gold except in jewelry and for certain limited uses such as dental supplies, so most people refrained from holding gold. Ultimately a country's laws and social norms determine whether the invisible hand will be allowed to work.

Social and political forces are active in all parts of your life. You don't practice medicine without a license; you don't sell body parts or certain addictive drugs. These actions are against the law. But many people do sell alcohol; that's not against the law if you have a permit. You don't charge your friends interest to borrow money (you'd lose friends); you don't charge your children for their food (parents are supposed to feed their children); many sports and media stars don't sell their autographs (some do, but many consider the practice tacky); you don't lower the wage you'll accept in order to take a job from someone else (you're no scab). The list is long. You cannot understand economics without understanding the limitations that political and social forces place on economic actions.

In summary, what happens in a society can be seen as the reaction to, and interaction of three sets of forces: (1) economic forces, (2) political and legal forces, and (3) social and historical forces. Economics has a role to play in sociology, history, and politics, just as sociology, history, and politics have roles to play in economics.

Using Economic Insights

Economic insights are based on generalizations, called theories, about the workings of an abstract economy as well as on contextual knowledge about the institutional structure of the economy. In this book I will introduce you to economic theories and models. Theories and models tie together economists' terminology and knowledge about economic institutions. Theories are inevitably too abstract to apply in specific cases, and thus a theory is often embodied in an **economic model**—*a framework that places the generalized insights of the theory in a more specific contextual setting*—or in an **economic principle**—*a commonly held economic insight stated as a law or principle.* To see the importance of principles, think back to when you learned to add. You didn't memorize the sum of 147 and 138; instead, you learned a principle of addition. The principle says that when adding 147 and 138, you first add $7 + 8$, which you memorized was 15. You write down the 5 and carry the 1, which you add to $4 + 3$ to get 8. Then add $1 + 1 = 2$. So the answer is 285. When you know just one principle, you know how to add millions of combinations of numbers.

Theories, models, and principles are continually "brought to the data" to see if the predictions of the model match the data. Increases in computing power and new statistical

---

[2]Even though it's against the law, some babies are nonetheless "sold" on a semilegal market, also called a gray market. At the turn of the century, the "market price" for a healthy baby was about $30,000. If selling babies were legal (and if people didn't find it morally repugnant to have babies in order to sell them), the price would be much lower because there would be a larger supply of babies. (It was not against the law to sell human eggs in the early 2000s, and one human egg was sold for $50,000. The average price was much lower; it varied with donor characteristics such as SAT scores and athletic accomplishments.)

Web Note 1.4
Hip Hop Economics

What happens in society can be seen as a reaction to, and interaction of, economic forces with other forces.

techniques have given modern economists a far more rigorous set of procedures to determine how well the predictions fit the data than was the case for earlier economists. This has led to a stronger reliance on quantitative empirical methods in modern economics than in earlier economics.

Modern empirical work takes a variety of forms. In certain instances, economists study questions by running controlled laboratory experiments. That branch of economics is called **experimental economics**—*a branch of economics that studies the economy through controlled laboratory experiments.* Where laboratory experiments are not possible, economists carefully observe the economy and try to figure out what is affecting what. To do so they look for **natural experiments**—*naturally occurring events that approximate a controlled experiment where something has changed in one place but has not changed somewhere else.* Economists can then compare the results in the two cases. An example of a natural experiment was when New Jersey raised its minimum wage and neighboring state Pennsylvania did not. Economists Alan Kruger and David Card compared the effects on unemployment in both states and found that increases in the minimum wage in New Jersey did not significantly affect employment. This led to a debate about what the empirical evidence was telling us. The reason is that in such natural experiments, it is impossible to hold "other things constant," as is done in laboratory experiments, and thus the empirical results in economics are often subject to dispute.

While economic models are less general than theories, they are still usually too general to apply in specific cases. Models lead to **theorems** (*propositions that are logically true based on the assumptions in a model*). To arrive at policy **precepts** (*policy rules that conclude that a particular course of action is preferable*), theorems must be combined with knowledge of real-world economic institutions and value judgments determining the goals for which one is striving. In discussing policy implications of theories and models, it is important to distinguish precepts from theorems.

Theories, models, and principles must be combined with a knowledge of real-world economic institutions to arrive at specific policy recommendations.

The Invisible Hand Theorem

Knowing a theory gives you insight into a wide variety of economic phenomena even though you don't know the particulars of each phenomenon. For example, much of economic theory deals with the *pricing mechanism* and how the market operates to coordinate *individuals' decisions.* Economists have come to the following theorems:

> *When the quantity supplied is greater than the quantity demanded, price has a tendency to fall.*
>
> *When the quantity demanded is greater than the quantity supplied, price has a tendency to rise.*

Q-7 There has been a superb growing season and the quantity of tomatoes supplied exceeds the quantity demanded. What is likely to happen to the price of tomatoes?

Using these generalized theorems, economists have developed a theory of markets that leads to the further theorem that, under certain conditions, markets are efficient. That is, the market will coordinate individuals' decisions, allocating scarce resources efficiently. **Efficiency** means *achieving a goal as cheaply as possible.* Economists call this theorem the **invisible hand theorem**—*a market economy, through the price mechanism, will tend to allocate resources efficiently.*

Theories, and the models used to represent them, are enormously efficient methods of conveying information, but they're also necessarily abstract. They rely on simplifying assumptions, and *if you don't know the assumptions, you don't know the theory.* The result of forgetting assumptions could be similar to what happens if you forget

Winston Churchill and Lady Astor

There are many stories about Nancy Astor, the first woman elected to Britain's Parliament. A vivacious, fearless American woman, she married into the English aristocracy and, during the 1930s and 1940s, became a bright light on the English social and political scenes, which were already quite bright.

One story told about Lady Astor is that she and Winston Churchill, the unorthodox genius who had a long and distinguished political career and who was Britain's prime minister during World War II, were sitting in a pub having a theoretical discussion about morality. Churchill suggested that as a thought experiment Lady Astor ponder the following question: If a man were to promise her a huge amount of money—say a million pounds—for the privilege, would she sleep with him? Lady Astor did ponder the question

Lady Astor

for a while and finally answered, yes, she would, if the money were guaranteed. Churchill then asked her if she would sleep with him for five pounds. Her response was sharp: "Of course not. What do you think I am—a prostitute?" Churchill responded, "We have already established that fact; we are now simply negotiating about price."

One moral that economists might draw from this story is that economic incentives, if high enough, can have a powerful influence on behavior. But an equally important moral of the story is that noneconomic incentives also can be very strong. Why do most people feel it's wrong to sell sex for money, even if they might be willing to do so if the price were high enough? Keeping this second moral in mind will significantly increase your economic understanding of real-world events.

---

that you're supposed to add numbers in columns. Forgetting that, yet remembering all the steps, can lead to a wildly incorrect answer. For example,

$$147$$
$$+138$$

1,608 is wrong.

Knowing the assumptions of theories and models allows you to progress beyond gut reaction and better understand the strengths and weaknesses of various economic theories and models. Let's consider a central economic assumption: the assumption that individuals behave rationally—that what they choose reflects what makes them happiest, given the constraints. If that assumption doesn't hold, the invisible hand theorem doesn't hold.

I find it useful to distinguish two types of modern economists: modern traditional economists and modern behavioral economists. Modern traditional economists use models that focus on traditional assumptions of rationality and self-interest; modern behavioral economists modify these assumptions, and are working on models that incorporate some predictably irrational behavior. Yet another group of modern economists deemphasizes deductive models almost completely and develops empirical models that are primarily based on statistical patterns they discover in data.

Presenting the invisible hand theorem in its full beauty is an important part of any economics course. Presenting the assumptions on which it is based and the limitations of the invisible hand is likewise an important part of the course. I'll do both throughout the book.

Economic Theory and Stories

Theory is a shorthand way of telling a story.

Economic theory, and the models in which that theory is presented, often developed as a shorthand way of telling a story. These stories are important; they make the theory come alive and convey the insights that give economic theory its power. In this book I

14

present plenty of theories and models, but they're accompanied by stories that provide the context that makes them relevant.

At times, because there are many new terms, discussing theories takes up much of the presentation time and becomes a bit oppressive. That's the nature of the beast. As Albert Einstein said, "Theories should be as simple as possible, but not more so." When a theory becomes oppressive, pause and think about the underlying story that the theory is meant to convey. That story should make sense and be concrete. If you can't translate the theory into a story, you don't understand the theory.

Economic Institutions

To know whether you can apply economic theory to reality, you must know about economic institutions—laws, common practices, and organizations in a society that affect the economy. Corporations, governments, and cultural norms are all examples of economic institutions. Many economic institutions have social, political, and religious dimensions. For example, your job often influences your social standing. In addition, many social institutions, such as the family, have economic functions. I include any institution that significantly affects economic decisions as an economic institution because you must understand that institution if you are to understand how the economy functions.

To apply economic theory to reality, you've got to have a sense of economic institutions.

Economic institutions differ significantly among countries. For example, in Germany banks are allowed to own companies; in the United States they cannot. This helps explain why investment decisions are made differently in Germany as compared to the United States. Alternatively, in the Netherlands workers are highly unionized, while in the United States they are not. Unions in the Netherlands therefore have the power to agree to keep wages lower in exchange for more jobs. This means that government policies to control inflation might differ in these two countries.

Economic institutions sometimes seem to operate in ways quite different than economic theory predicts. For example, economic theory says that prices are determined by supply and demand. However, businesses say that they set prices by rules of thumb—often by what are called cost-plus-markup rules. That is, a firm determines what its costs are, multiplies by 1.4 or 1.5, and the result is the price it sets. Economic theory says that supply and demand determine who's hired; experience suggests that hiring is often done on the basis of whom you know, not by market forces.

These apparent contradictions have two complementary explanations. First, economic theory abstracts from many issues. These issues may account for the differences. Second, there's no contradiction; economic principles often affect decisions from behind the scenes. For instance, supply and demand pressures determine what the price markup over cost will be. In all cases, however, to apply economic theory to reality—to gain the full value of economic insights—you've got to have a sense of economic institutions.

Economic Policy Options

Economic policies are *actions (or inaction) taken by government to influence economic actions.* The final goal of the course is to present the economic policy options facing our society today. For example, should the government restrict mergers between firms? Should it run a budget deficit? Should it do something about the international trade deficit? Should it decrease taxes?

I saved this discussion for last because there's no sense talking about policy options unless you know some economic terminology, some economic theory, and something about economic institutions. Once you know something about them, you're in a position

Economists and Market Solutions

Economic reasoning is playing an increasing role in government policy. Consider the regulation of pollution. Pollution became a policy concern in the 1960s as books such as Rachel Carson's *Silent Spring* were published. In 1970, in response to concerns about the environment, the Clean Air Act was passed. It capped the amount of pollutants (such as sulfur dioxide, carbon monoxide, nitrogen dioxides, lead, and hydrocarbons) that firms could emit. This was a "command-and-control" approach to regulation, which brought about a reduction in pollution, but also brought about lots of complaints by firms that either found the limits costly to meet or couldn't afford to meet them and were forced to close.

Enter economists. They proposed an alternative approach, called cap-and-trade, that achieved the same overall reduction in pollution but at a lower overall cost. In the plan they proposed, government still set a pollution cap that firms had to meet, but it gave individual firms some flexibility. Firms that reduced emissions by less than the required limit could buy pollution permits from other firms that reduced their emissions by more than their limit. The price of the permits would be determined in an "emissions permit market." Thus, firms that had a low cost of reducing pollution would have a strong incentive to reduce pollution by more than their limit in order to sell these permits, or rights to pollute, to firms that had a high cost of reducing pollution and therefore could reduce their pollution by less than what was required. The net reduction was the same, but the reduction was achieved at a lower cost.

In 1990 Congress adopted economists' proposal and the Clean Air Act was amended to include tradable emissions permits. An active market in emissions permits developed and it is estimated that the tradable permit program has lowered the cost of reducing sulfur dioxide emissions by $1 billion a year while at the same time, reducing emissions by more than half, to levels significantly below the cap. Economists used this same argument to promote an incentive-based solution to world pollution in an agreement among some countries known as the Kyoto Protocol. In this plan countries would agree to caps with emissions permits traded on a global market. You can read more about the current state of tradable emissions at www.epa.gov/airmarkets.

To carry out economic policy effectively, one must understand how institutions might change as a result of the economic policy.

Q-8 True or false? Economists should focus their policy analysis on institutional changes because such policies offer the largest gains.

to consider the policy options available for dealing with the economic problems our society faces.

Policies operate within institutions, but policies also can influence the institutions within which they operate. Let's consider an example: welfare policy and the institution of the two-parent family. In the 1960s, the United States developed a variety of policy initiatives designed to eliminate poverty. These initiatives provided income to single parents with children, and assumed that family structure would be unchanged by these policies. But family structure changed substantially, and, very likely, these policies played a role in increasing the number of single-parent families. The result was the programs failed to eliminate poverty. Now this is not to say that we should not have programs to eliminate poverty, nor that two-parent families are always preferable to one-parent families; it is only to say that we must build into our policies their effect on institutions.

Objective Policy Analysis

Good economic policy analysis is objective; that is, it keeps the analyst's value judgments separate from the analysis. Objective analysis does not say, "This is the way things should be," reflecting a goal established by the analyst. That would be subjective analysis because it would reflect the analyst's view of how things should be. Instead, objective analysis says, "This is the way the economy works, and if society (or the individual or firm for whom you're doing the analysis) wants to achieve a particular goal, this is how it might go about doing so." Objective analysis keeps, or at least tries to keep, subjective views—value judgments—separate.

To make clear the distinction between objective and subjective analysis, economists have divided economics into three categories: *positive economics, normative economics,* and the *art of economics.* **Positive economics** is *the study of what is, and how the economy works.* It explores the pure theory of economics, and it discovers agreed-upon empirical regularities. These empirical regularities are often called empirical facts—for example, large price fluctuations in financial markets tend to be followed by additional large price fluctuations. Economic theorists then relate their theories to those facts. Positive economics asks such questions as: How does the market for hog bellies work? How do price restrictions affect market forces? These questions fall under the heading of economic theory.

As I stated above, economic theory does not provide definitive policy recommendations. It is too abstract and makes too many assumptions that don't match observed behavior. In positive economic theory, one looks for empirical facts and develops *theorems*—propositions that logically follow from the assumptions of one's model. Theorems and agreed-upon empirical facts are almost by definition beyond dispute and serve as the foundation for economic science. But these theorems don't tell us what policies should be followed.

Policies are built on two other branches of economics: normative economics and political economy, or the art of economics. **Normative economics** is *the study of what the goals of the economy should be.* Normative economics asks such questions as: What should the distribution of income be? What should tax policy be designed to achieve? In discussing such questions, economists must carefully delineate whose goals they are discussing. One cannot simply assume that one's own goals for society are society's goals. For example, let's consider a debate that is currently ongoing in economics. Some economists are worried about global warming; they believe that high consumption in rich societies is causing global warming and that the high consumption is a result of interdependent wants—people want something only because other people have it—but having it isn't necessarily making people happier. These economists argue that society's normative goal should include a much greater focus on the implications of economic activities for global warming, and the distribution of income, than is currently the case. Discussion of these goals falls under the category of normative economics.

The **art of economics,** also called political economy, is *the application of the knowledge learned in positive economics to achieve the goals one has determined in normative economics.* It looks at such questions as: To achieve the goals that society wants to achieve, how would you go about it, given the way the economy works?[3] Most policy discussions fall under the art of economics. The art of economics branch is specifically about policy; it is designed to arrive at *precepts,* or guides for policy. Precepts are based on theorems and empirical facts developed in positive economics and goals developed in normative economics. The art of economics requires economists to assess the appropriateness of theorems to achieving the normative goals in the real world. Whereas once the assumptions are agreed upon, theorems derived from models are not debatable, precepts are debatable, and economists that use the same theorems can hold

Positive economics is the study of what is, and how the economy works.

Q-9 John, your study partner, is a free market advocate. He argues that the invisible hand theorem tells us that the government should not interfere with the economy. Do you agree? Why or why not?

Normative economics is the study of what the goals of the economy should be.

The art of economics is the application of the knowledge learned in positive economics to achieve the goals determined in normative economics.

---

[3]This three-part distinction was made back in 1891 by a famous economist, John Neville Keynes, father of John Maynard Keynes, the economist who developed macroeconomics. This distinction was instilled into modern economics by Milton Friedman and Richard Lipsey in the 1950s. They, however, downplayed the art of economics, which J. N. Keynes had seen as central to understanding the economist's role in policy. In his discussion of the scope and method of economics, Lionel Robbins used the term "political economy" rather than Keynes' term "the art of economics."

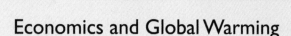

Economics and Global Warming

A good example of the central role that economics plays in policy debates is the debate about global warming. Almost all scientists are now convinced that global warming is occurring and that human activity such as the burning of fossil fuel is one of the causes. The policy question is what to do about it. To answer that question, most governments have turned to economists. The first part of the question that economists have considered is whether it is worth doing anything, and in a well-publicized report commissioned by the British government, economist Nicholas Stern argued that, based upon his cost/benefit analysis, yes it is worth doing something. The reason: Because the costs of not doing anything would likely reduce output by 20 percent in the future, and that those costs (appropriately weighted for when they occur) are less than the benefits of policies that can be implemented.

The second part of the question is: What policies to implement? The policies he recommended were policies that changed incentives—specifically, policies that raised the costs of emitting greenhouse gases and decreased the cost of other forms of production. Those recommended policies reflected the economist's opportunity cost framework in action: if you want to change the result, change the incentives that individuals face.

There is considerable debate about Stern's analysis—both with the way he conducted the cost/benefit analysis and with his policy recommendations. Such debates are inevitable when the data are incomplete and numerous judgments need to be made. I suspect that these debates will continue over the coming years with economists on various sides of the debate. Economists are generally not united in their views about complicated policy issues since they differ in their normative views and in their assessment of the problem and of what politically can be achieved; that's because policy is part of the art of economics, not part of positive economics. But the framework of the policy debate about global warming is the economic framework. Thus, even though political forces will ultimately choose what policy is followed, you must understand the economic framework to take part in the debate.

Q-10 Tell whether the following five statements belong in positive economics, normative economics, or the art of economics.

1. We should support the market because it is efficient.

2. Given certain conditions, the market achieves efficient results.

3. Based on past experience and our understanding of markets, if one wants a reasonably efficient result, markets should probably be relied on.

4. The distribution of income should be left to markets.

5. Markets allocate income according to contributions of factors of production.

Web Note 1.5
The Art of Economics

different precepts. For example, a model may tell us that rent controls will cause a shortage of housing. That does not mean that rent controls are necessarily bad policies since rent controls may also have some desirable effects. The precept that rent controls are bad policy is based upon a judgment about the importance of those other effects, and one's normative judgments about the benefits and costs of the policy. In this book, when I say that economists tend to favor a policy, I am talking about precepts, which means that alternative perspectives are possible even among economists.

In each of these three branches of economics, economists separate their own value judgments from their objective analysis as much as possible. The qualifier "as much as possible" is important, since some value judgments inevitably sneak in. We are products of our environment, and the questions we ask, the framework we use, and the way we interpret the evidence all involve value judgments and reflect our backgrounds.

Maintaining objectivity is easiest in positive economics, where you are working with abstract models to understand how the economy works. Maintaining objectivity is harder in normative economics. You must always be objective about whose normative values you are using. It's easy to assume that all of society shares your values, but that assumption is often wrong.

Maintaining objectivity is hardest in the art of economics because it can suffer from the problems of both positive and normative economics. Because noneconomic forces affect policy, to practice the art of economics we must make judgments about how these noneconomic forces work. These judgments are likely to reflect our own value judgments. So we must be exceedingly careful to be as objective as possible in practicing the art of economics.

Policy and Social and Political Forces

When you think about the policy options facing society, you'll quickly discover that the choice of policy options depends on much more than economic theory. Politicians, not economists, determine economic policy. To understand what policies are chosen, you must take into account historical precedent plus social, cultural, and political forces. In an economics course, I don't have time to analyze these forces in as much depth as I'd like. That's one reason there are separate history, political science, sociology, and anthropology courses.

While it is true that these other forces play significant roles in policy decisions, specialization is necessary. In economics, we focus the analysis on the invisible hand, and much of economic theory is devoted to considering how the economy would operate if the invisible hand were the only force operating. But as soon as we apply theory to reality and policy, we must take into account political and social forces as well.

An example will make my point more concrete. Most economists agree that holding down or eliminating tariffs (taxes on imports) and quotas (numerical limitations on imports) makes good economic sense. They strongly advise governments to follow a policy of free trade. Do governments follow free trade policies? Almost invariably they do not. Politics leads society in a different direction. If you're advising a policy maker, you need to point out that these other forces must be taken into account, and how other forces should (if they should) and can (if they can) be integrated with your recommendations.

Conclusion

Tons more could be said to introduce you to economics, but an introduction must remain an introduction. As it is, this chapter should have:

1. Introduced you to economic reasoning.

2. Surveyed what we're going to cover in this book.

3. Given you an idea of my writing style and approach.

We'll be spending long hours together over the coming term, and before entering into such a commitment it's best to know your partner. While I won't know you, by the end of this book you'll know me. Maybe you won't love me as my mother does, but you'll know me.

This introduction was my opening line. I hope it also conveyed the importance and relevance of economics. If it did, it has served its intended purpose. Economics is tough, but tough can be fun.

Summary

- The three coordination problems any economy must solve are what to produce, how to produce it, and for whom to produce it. In solving these problems, societies have found that there is a problem of scarcity.   *(LO1-1)*

- Economics can be divided into microeconomics and macroeconomics. Microeconomics is the study of individual choice and how that choice is influenced by economic forces. Macroeconomics is the study of the economy as a whole. It considers problems such as inflation, unemployment, business cycles, and growth.   *(LO1-1)*

- Economic reasoning structures all questions in a cost/benefit framework: If the marginal benefits of doing something exceed the marginal costs, do it. If the marginal costs exceed the marginal benefits, don't do it. *(LO1-2)*

- Sunk costs are not relevant in the economic decision rule. *(LO1-2)*

- The opportunity cost of undertaking an activity is the benefit you might have gained from choosing the next-best alternative. *(LO1-2)*

- "There ain't no such thing as a free lunch" (TANSTAAFL) embodies the opportunity cost concept. *(LO1-2)*

- Economic forces, the forces of scarcity, are always working. Market forces, which ration by changing prices, are not always allowed to work. *(LO1-3)*

- Economic reality is controlled and directed by three types of forces: economic forces, political forces, and social forces. *(LO1-3)*

- Under certain conditions, the market, through its price mechanism, will allocate scarce resources efficiently. *(LO1-4)*

- Theorems are propositions that follow from the assumptions of a model; precepts are the guides for policies based on theorems, normative judgments, and empirical observations about how the real world differs from the model. *(LO1-4)*

- Economics can be subdivided into positive economics, normative economics, and the art of economics. Positive economics is the study of what is, normative economics is the study of what should be, and the art of economics relates positive to normative economics. *(LO1-5)*

Key Terms

art of economics *(17)*	economics *(4)*	macroeconomics *(5)*	opportunity cost *(9)*
economic decision rule *(8)*	efficiency *(13)*	marginal benefit *(7)*	positive economics *(17)*
economic force *(11)*	experimental economics *(13)*	marginal cost *(7)*	precept *(13)*
economic model *(12)*	invisible hand *(11)*	market force *(11)*	scarcity *(5)*
economic policy *(15)*	invisible hand theorem *(13)*	microeconomics *(5)*	sunk cost *(7)*
economic principle *(12)*		natural experiment *(13)*	theorem *(13)*
		normative economics *(17)*	

Questions and Exercises

1. Why does the textbook author focus on coordination rather than on scarcity when defining economics? *(LO1-1)*

2. State whether the following are primarily microeconomic or macroeconomic policy issues: *(LO1-1)*
   a. Should U.S. interest rates be lowered to decrease the amount of unemployment?
   b. Will the fact that more and more doctors are selling their practices to managed care networks increase the efficiency of medical providers?
   c. Should the current federal income tax be lowered to reduce unemployment?
   d. Should the federal minimum wage be raised?
   e. Should Sprint and Verizon both be allowed to build local phone networks?
   f. Should commercial banks be required to provide loans in all areas of the territory from which they accept deposits?

3. List two microeconomic and two macroeconomic problems. *(LO1-1)*

4. Calculate, using the best estimates you can: *(LO1-2)*
   a. Your opportunity cost of attending college.
   b. Your opportunity cost of taking this course.
   c. Your opportunity cost of attending yesterday's lecture in this course.

5. List one recent choice you made and explain why you made the choice in terms of marginal benefits and marginal costs. *(LO1-2)*

6. You rent a car for $29.95. The first 150 miles are free, but each mile thereafter costs 15 cents. You plan to drive it 200 miles. What is the marginal cost of driving the car? *(LO1-2)*

7. Economists Henry Saffer of Kean University, Frank J. Chaloupka of the University of Illinois at Chicago, and Dhaval Dave of Bentley College estimated that the

government must spend $4,170 on drug control to deter one person from using drugs and the cost that one drug user imposes on society is $897. Based on this information alone, should the government spend the money on drug control? (*LO1-2*)

8. What is the opportunity cost of buying a $20,000 car? (*LO1-2*)

9. Suppose you currently earn $30,000 a year. You are considering a job that will increase your lifetime earnings by $300,000 but that requires an MBA. The job will mean also attending business school for two years at an annual cost of $25,000. You already have a bachelor's degree, for which you spent $80,000 in tuition and books. Which of the above information is relevant to your decision whether to take the job? (*LO1-2*)

10. Suppose your college has been given $5 million. You have been asked to decide how to spend it to improve your college. Explain how you would use the economic decision rule and the concept of opportunity costs to decide how to spend it. (*LO1-2*)

11. Give two examples of social forces and explain how they keep economic forces from becoming market forces. (*LO1-3*)

12. Give two examples of political or legal forces and explain how they might interact with economic forces. (*LO1-3*)

13. Individuals have two kidneys, but most of us need only one. People who have lost both kidneys through accident or disease must be hooked up to a dialysis machine, which cleanses waste from their bodies. Say a person who has two good kidneys offers to sell one of them to someone whose kidney function has been totally destroyed. The seller asks $30,000 for the kidney, and the person who has lost both kidneys accepts the offer. (*LO1-3*)
    a. Who benefits from the deal?
    b. Who is hurt?
    c. Should a society allow such market transactions? Why?

14. What is an economic model? What besides a model do economists need to make policy recommendations? (*LO1-4*)

15. Does economic theory prove that the free market system is best? Why? (Difficult) (*LO1-4*)

16. Distinguish between theorems and precepts. Is it possible for two economists to agree about theorems but disagree about precepts? Why or why not? (*LO1-4*)

17. What is the difference between normative and positive statements? (*LO1-5*)

18. State whether the following statements belong in positive economics, normative economics, or the art of economics. (*LO1-5*)
    a. In a market, when quantity supplied exceeds quantity demanded, price tends to fall.
    b. When determining tax rates, the government should take into account the income needs of individuals.
    c. When deciding which rationing mechanism is best (lottery, price, first-come/first-served), one must take into account the goals of society.
    d. California currently rations water to farmers at subsidized prices. Once California allows the trading of water rights, it will allow economic forces to be a market force.

Questions from Alternative Perspectives

1. Is it possible to use objective economic analysis as a basis for government planning? (Austrian)

2. In "Rational Choice with Passion: Virtue in a Model of Rational Addiction," Andrew M. Yuengert of Pepperdine University argues that there is a conflict between reason and passion.
   a. What might that conflict be?
   b. What implications does it have for applying the economic model? (Religious)

3. Economic institutions are "habits of thought" that organize society.
   a. In what way might patriarchy be an *institution* and how might it influence the labor market?
   b. Does the free market or patriarchy better explain why 98 percent of secretaries are women and 98 percent of automobile mechanics are men? (Feminist)

4. In October of 2004, the supply of flu vaccine fell by over 50 percent. The result was that the vaccine had to be rationed, with a priority schedule established: young children, people with weakened immunity, those over 65, etc., taking priority.
   a. Compare and contrast this allocation outcome with a free market outcome.
   b. Which alternative is more just? (Institutionalist)

5. The textbook model assumes that individuals have enough knowledge to follow the economic decision rule.
   a. How did you decide what college you would attend?
   b. Did you have enough knowledge to follow the economic decision rule?
   c. For what type of decisions do you not use the economic decision rule?
   d. What are the implications for economic analysis if most people don't follow the economic decision rule in many aspects of their decisions? (Post-Keynesian)

6. Radical economists believe that all of economics, like all theorizing or storytelling, is value-laden. Theories and stories reflect the values of those who compose them and tell them. For instance, radicals offer a different analysis than most economists of how capitalism works and what ought to be done about its most plaguing problems: inequality, periodic economic crises with large-scale unemployment, and the alienation of the workers.
   a. What does the radical position imply about the distinction between positive economics and normative economics that the text makes?
   b. Is economics value-laden or objective and is the distinction between positive and normative economics tenable or untenable? (Radical)

Issues to Ponder

1. At times we all regret decisions. Does this necessarily mean we did not use the economic decision rule when making the decision?

2. Economist Steven Landsburg argues that if one believes in the death penalty for murderers because of its deterrent effect, using cost/benefit analysis we should execute computer hackers—the creators of worms and viruses—because the deterrent effect in cost saving would be greater than the deterrent effect in saving lives. Estimates are that each execution deters eight murders, which, if one valued each life at about $7 million, saves about $56 million; he estimates that executing hackers would save more than that per execution, and thus would be the economic thing to do.
   a. Do you agree or disagree with Landsburg's argument? Why?
   b. Can you extend cost/benefit analysis to other areas?

3. Adam Smith, who wrote *The Wealth of Nations,* and who is seen as the father of modern economics, also wrote *The Theory of Moral Sentiments*. In it he argued that society would be better off if people weren't so selfish and were more considerate of others. How does this view fit with the discussion of economic reasoning presented in the chapter?

4. A *Wall Street Journal* article asked readers the following questions. What's your answer?
   a. An accident has caused deadly fumes to enter the school ventilation system where it will kill five children. You can stop it by throwing a switch, but doing so will kill one child in another room. Do you throw the switch?
   b. Say that a doctor can save five patients with an organ transplant that would end the life of a patient who is sick, but not yet dead. Does she do it?
   c. What is the difference between the two situations described in *a* and *b*?
   d. How important are opportunity costs in your decisions?

5. Economics is about strategic thinking, and the strategies can get very complicated. Suppose you kiss someone and ask whether the person liked it. You'd like the person to answer "yes" and you'd like that answer to be truthful. But they know that, and if they like you, they may well say that they liked the kiss even if they didn't. But you know that, and thus might not really believe that they liked the kiss; they're just saying "yes" because that's what you want to hear. But they know that you know that, so sometimes they have to convey a sense that they didn't like it, so that you will believe them when they say that they did like it. But you know that . . . You get the picture.
   a. Should you always be honest, even when it hurts someone?
   b. What strategies can you figure out to avoid the problem of not believing the other person?

6. Go to two stores: a supermarket and a convenience store.
   a. Write down the cost of a gallon of milk in each.
   b. The prices are most likely different. Using the terminology used in this chapter, explain why that is the case and why anyone would buy milk in the store with the higher price.
   c. Do the same exercise with shirts or dresses in Walmart (or its equivalent) and Saks (or its equivalent).

7. About 100,000 individuals in the United States are waiting for organ transplants, and at an appropriate price many individuals would be willing to supply organs. Given those facts, should human organs be allowed to be bought and sold?

8. Name an economic institution and explain how it affects economic decision making or how its actions reflect economic principles.

9. Tyler Cowen, an economist at George Mason University, presents an interesting case that pits the market against legal and social forces. The case involves payola—the payment of money to disk jockeys for playing a songwriter's songs. He reports that Chuck Berry was having a hard time getting his music played because of racism. To counter this, he offered a well-known disk jockey, Alan Freed, partial songwriting credits, along with partial royalties, on any Chuck Berry song of his choice. He chose *Maybellene,*

which he played and promoted. It went on to be a hit, Chuck Berry went on to be a star, and Freed's estate continues to receive royalties.

a. Should such payments be allowed? Why?

b. How did Freed's incentives from the royalty payment differ from Freed's incentives if Chuck Berry had just offered him a flat payment?

c. Name two other examples of similar activities—one that is legal and one that is not.

10. Name three ways a limited number of dormitory rooms could be rationed. How would economic forces determine individual behavior in each? How would social or legal forces determine whether those economic forces become market forces?

11. Prospect theory suggests that people are hurt more by losses than they are uplifted by gains of a corresponding size. If that is true, what implications would it have for economic policy?

12. Is a good economist always objective? Explain your answer.

Answers to Margin Questions

1. (1) Macroeconomics; (2) Microeconomics; (3) Microeconomics; (4) Macroeconomics. (*p. 6; LO1-1*)

2. Since the price of both stocks is now $15, it doesn't matter which one you sell (assuming no differential capital gains taxation). The price you bought them for doesn't matter; it's a sunk cost. Marginal analysis refers to the future gain, so what you expect to happen to future prices of the stocks—not past prices—should determine which stock you decide to sell. (*p. 8; LO1-2*)

3. A cost/benefit analysis requires that you put a value on a good, and placing a value on a good can be seen as demeaning it. Consider love. Try telling an acquaintance that you'd like to buy his or her spiritual love, and see what response you get. (*p. 8; LO1-2*)

4. John is wrong. The opportunity cost of reading the chapter is primarily the time you spend reading it. Reading the book prevents you from doing other things. Assuming that you already paid for the book, the original price is no longer part of the opportunity cost; it is a sunk cost. Bygones are bygones. (*p. 10; LO1-2*)

5. Whenever there is scarcity, the scarce good must be rationed by some means. Free health care has an opportunity cost in other resources. So if health care is not rationed, to get the resources to supply that care, other goods would have to be more tightly rationed than they currently are. It is likely that the opportunity cost of supplying free health care would be larger than most societies would be willing to pay. (*p. 10; LO1-3*)

6. Joan is wrong. Economic forces are always operative; market forces are not. (*p. 11; LO1-3*)

7. According to the invisible hand theorem, the price of tomatoes will likely fall. (*p. 13; LO1-4*)

8. False. While such changes have the largest gain, they also may have the largest cost. The policies economists should focus on are those that offer the largest net gain—benefits minus costs—to society. (*p. 16; LO1-5*)

9. He is wrong. The invisible hand theorem is a positive theorem and does not tell us anything about policy. To do so would be to violate Hume's dictum that a "should" cannot be derived from an "is." This is not to say that government should or should not interfere; whether government should interfere is a very difficult question. (*p. 17; LO1-5*)

10. (1) Normative; (2) Positive; (3) Art; (4) Normative; (5) Positive. (*p. 18; LO1-5*)

chapter 2

The Production Possibility Model, Trade, and Globalization

> *No one ever saw a dog make a fair and deliberate exchange of one bone for another with another dog.*
>
> —Adam Smith

Every economy must solve three main coordination problems:

1. What, and how much, to produce.
2. How to produce it.
3. For whom to produce it.

In Chapter 1, I suggested that you can boil down all economic knowledge into the single phrase "There ain't no such thing as a free lunch." There's obviously more to economics than that, but it's not a bad summary of the core of economic reasoning—it's relevant for an individual, for nonprofit organizations, for governments, and for nations. Oh, it's true that once in a while you can snitch a sandwich, but what economics tells you is that if you're offered something that approaches free-lunch status, you should also be on the lookout for some hidden cost.

Economists have a model, the production possibility model, that conveys the trade-offs society faces. This model is important for understanding not only the trade-offs society faces but also why people specialize in what they do and trade for the goods they need. Through specialization and trade, individuals, firms, and countries can achieve greater levels of output than they could otherwise achieve.

The Production Possibilities Model

The production possibilities model can be presented both in a table and in a graph. (Appendix A has a discussion of graphs in economics.) I'll start with the table and then move from that to the graph. A **production possibility table** is *a table that lists the trade-offs between two choices.*

A Production Possibility Curve for an Individual

Let's consider a study-time/grades example. Say you have exactly 20 hours a week to devote to two courses: economics and history. (So maybe I'm a bit optimistic.) Grades are given numerically and you know that the following relationships exist: If you study 20 hours in economics, you'll get a grade of 100; 18 hours, 94; and so forth.[1]

Let's say that the best you can do in history is a 98 with 20 hours of study a week; 19 hours of study guarantees a 96, and so on. The production possibility table in Figure 2-1(a) shows the highest combination of grades you can get with various allocations of the 20 hours available for studying the two subjects. One possibility is getting 70 in economics and 78 in history.

Notice that the opportunity cost of studying one subject rather than the other is embodied in the production possibility table. The information in the table comes from experience: We are assuming that you've discovered that if you transfer an hour of study from economics to history, you'll lose 3 points on your grade in economics and gain 2 points in history. Assuming studying economics is your next best alternative, the opportunity cost of a 2-point rise in your history grade is a 3-point decrease in your economics grade.

The information in the production possibility table also can be presented graphically in a diagram called a production possibility curve. A **production possibility curve (PPC)** is *a curve measuring the maximum combination of outputs that can be obtained from a given number of inputs.* It gives you a visual picture of the tradeoff embodied in a decision.

A production possibility curve is created from a production possibility table by mapping the table in a two-dimensional graph. I've taken the information from the table in Figure 2-1(a) and mapped it into Figure 2-1(b). The history grade is mapped, or plotted, on the horizontal axis; the economics grade is on the vertical axis.

As you can see from the bottom row of Figure 2-1(a), if you study economics for all 20 hours and study history for 0 hours, you'll get grades of 100 in economics and 58 in history. Point *A* in Figure 2-1(b) represents that choice. If you study history for all 20 hours and study economics for 0 hours, you'll get a 98 in history and a 40 in economics. Point *E* represents that choice. Points *B, C,* and *D* represent three possible choices between these two extremes.

Notice that the production possibility curve slopes downward from left to right. That means that there is an inverse relationship (a trade-off) between grades in economics and grades in history. The better the grade in economics, the worse the grade in history, and vice versa.

To summarize, the production possibility curve demonstrates that:

1. There is a limit to what you can achieve, given the existing institutions, resources, and technology.

2. Every choice you make has an opportunity cost. You can get more of something only by giving up something else.

Increasing Opportunity Costs of the Trade-off

In the study-time/grade example, the cost of one grade in terms of the other remained constant; you could always trade two points on your history grade for three points on your economics grade. This assumption of an unchanging trade-off made the production possibility curve a straight line. Although this made the example easier, is it realistic? Probably not, especially if we are using the PPC to describe the choices that a

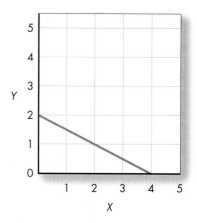

Q-1 In the graph below, what is the opportunity cost of producing an extra unit of good X in terms of good Y?

The production possibility curve is a curve measuring the maximum combination of outputs that can be obtained from a given number of inputs.

The slope of the production possibility curve tells you the trade-off between the cost of one good in terms of another.

Production Possibilities Curve

---

[1]Throughout the book I'll be presenting numerical examples to help you understand the concepts. The numbers I choose are often arbitrary. After all, you have to choose something. As an exercise, you might choose different numbers than I did, numbers that apply to your own life, and work out the argument using those numbers.

FIGURE 2-1 (A AND B)   A Production Possibility Table and Curve for Grades in Economics and History

The production possibility table (**a**) shows the highest combination of grades you can get with only 20 hours available for studying economics and history. The information in the production possibility table in (**a**) can be plotted on a graph, as is done in (**b**). The grade received in economics is on the vertical axis, and the grade received in history is on the horizontal axis.

Hours of Study in History	Grade in History	Hours of Study in Economics	Grade in Economics
20	98	0	40
19	96	1	43
18	94	2	46
17	92	3	49
16	90	4	52
15	88	5	55
14	86	6	58
13	84	7	61
12	82	8	64
11	80	9	67
10	78	10	70
9	76	11	73
8	74	12	76
7	72	13	79
6	70	14	82
5	68	15	85
4	66	16	88
3	64	17	91
2	62	18	94
1	60	19	97
0	58	20	100

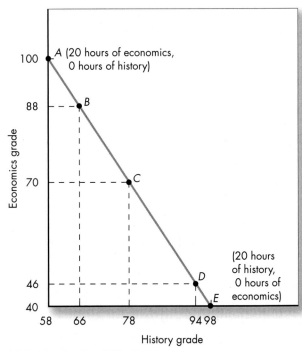

(a) Production Possibility Table

(b) Production Possibility Curve

society makes. For many of the choices society must make the perceived opportunity costs of society's next best alternative tend to increase as we choose more and more of an item. This principle can be summarized as follows:

> *In order to get more of something, generally one must give up ever-increasing quantities of something else.*

In other words, initially the opportunity costs of an activity are low, but they increase the more we concentrate on that activity. A production possibility curve that exhibits increasing opportunity costs of a trade-off is bowed outward, as in Figure 2-2(b).

Why are production possibility curves typically bowed outward? Because some resources are better suited for the production of certain kinds of goods than other kinds of goods. To understand what that means, let's talk about the graph in Figure 2-2(b), which is derived from the table in Figure 2-2(a). This curve represents society's choice between defense spending (guns) and spending on domestic needs (butter).

Suppose society is producing only butter (point *A*). Giving up a little butter (1 pound) initially gains us a lot of guns (4), moving us to point *B*. The next 2 pounds of butter we give up gain us slightly fewer guns (point *C*). If we continue to trade butter for guns, we find that at point *D* we gain very few guns from giving up a pound of butter. The opportunity cost of choosing guns in terms of butter increases as we increase the production of guns.

The principle of increasing marginal opportunity cost tells us that opportunity costs increase the more you concentrate on the activity.

FIGURE 2-2 (A AND B) **A Production Possibility Table and Curve**

The table in (**a**) contains information on the trade-off between the production of guns and butter. This information has been plotted on the graph in (**b**). Notice in (**b**) that as we move along the production possibility curve from *A* to *F*, trading butter for guns, we get fewer and fewer guns for each pound of butter given up. That is, the opportunity cost of choosing guns over butter increases as we increase the production of guns. The phenomenon occurs because some resources are better suited for the production of butter than for the production of guns, and we use the better ones first.

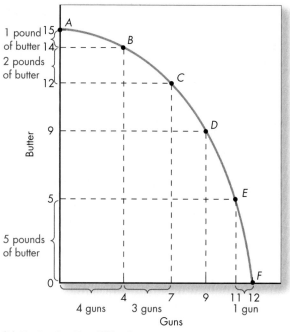

% of Resources Devoted to Production of Guns	Number of Guns	% of Resources Devoted to Production of Butter	Pounds of Butter	Row
0	0	100	15	A
20	4	80	14	B
40	7	60	12	C
60	9	40	9	D
80	11	20	5	E
100	12	0	0	F

(a) **Production Possibility Table**

(b) **Production Possibility Curve**

Comparative Advantage

The reason we must give up more and more butter as we produce more guns is that some resources are relatively better suited to producing guns, while others are relatively better suited to producing butter. Put in economists' terminology, some resources have a **comparative advantage**—*better suited to the production of one good than to the production of another good.* In this example, some resources have a comparative advantage over other resources in the production of butter, while other resources have a comparative advantage in the production of guns.

When making small amounts of guns and large amounts of butter, we primarily use those resources whose comparative advantage is in the production of guns to produce guns. All other resources are devoted to producing butter. Because the resources used in producing guns aren't good at producing butter, we're not giving up much butter to get those guns. As we produce more and more of a good, we must use resources whose comparative advantage is in the production of the other good—in this case, more suitable for producing butter than for producing guns. As we continue to remove resources from the production of butter to get the same additional amount of guns, we must give up increasing amounts of butter. Guns' costs in terms of butter increase because we're using resources to produce guns that have a comparative advantage in producing butter.

Let's consider two more examples. Say the United States suddenly decides it needs more wheat. To get additional wheat, we must devote additional land to growing it. This land is less fertile than the land we're already using, so our additional output of wheat per acre of land devoted to wheat will be less. Alternatively, consider the use of relief pitchers in a baseball game. If only one relief pitcher is needed, the manager sends in the best; if he must send in a second one, then a third, and even a fourth, the likelihood of winning the game decreases.

Q-2 If no resource had a comparative advantage in the production of any good, what would the shape of the production possibility curve be? Why?

Comparative Advantage

Production Possibility Curves

Definition	Shape	Shifts	Points In, Out, and On
The production possibility curve is a curve that measures the maximum combination of outputs that can be obtained with a given number of inputs.	The production possibility curve is downward sloping. Most are outward bowed because of the cost of producing a good increases as more is produced. If the opportunity cost doesn't change, the production possibility curve is a straight line.	Increases in inputs or increases in the productivity of inputs shift the production possibility curve out. Decreases have the opposite effect; the production possibility curve shifts along the axis whose input is changing.	Points inside the production possibility curve are points of inefficiency; points on the production possibility curve are points of efficiency; points outside the production possibility curve are not obtainable.

Efficiency

Efficiency

Q-3 Identify the point(s) of inefficiency and efficiency. What point(s) are unattainable?

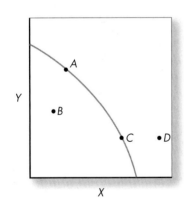

We would like, if possible, to get as much output as possible from a given amount of inputs or resources. That's **productive efficiency**—*achieving as much output as possible from a given amount of inputs or resources.* We would like to be efficient. The production possibility curve helps us see what is meant by productive efficiency. Consider point *A* in Figure 2-3(a), which is inside the production possibility curve. If we are producing at point *A,* we are using all our resources to produce 6 guns and 4 pounds of butter. Point *A* in Figure 2-3(a) represents **inefficiency**—*getting less output from inputs that, if devoted to some other activity, would produce more output.* That's because with the same inputs we could be getting either 8 guns and 4 pounds of butter (point *B*) or 6 pounds of butter and 6 guns (point *C*). As long as we prefer more to less, both points *B* and *C* represent **efficiency**—*achieving a goal using as few inputs as possible.* We always want to move our production out to a point on the production possibility curve.

Why not move out farther, to point *D?* If we could, we would, but by definition the production possibility curve represents the most output we can get from a certain combination of inputs. So point *D* is unattainable, given our resources and technology.

When technology improves, when more resources are discovered, or when the economic institutions get better at fulfilling our wants, we can get more output with the same inputs. What this means is that when technology or an economic institution improves, the entire production possibility curve shifts outward from *AB* to *CD* in Figure 2-3(b). How the production possibility curve shifts outward depends on how the technology improves. For example, say we become more efficient at producing butter, but not more efficient at producing guns. Then the production possibility curve shifts outward to *AC* in Figure 2-3(c).

Distribution and Productive Efficiency

In discussing the production possibility curve for a society, I avoided questions of distribution: Who gets what? But such questions cannot be ignored in real-world situations. Specifically, if the method of production is tied to a particular income

Choices in Context: Decision Trees

The production possibility curve presents choices without regard to time and therefore makes trade-offs clear-cut; there are two choices, one with a higher cost and one with a lower cost. The reality is that most choices are dependent on other choices; they are made sequentially. With sequential choices, you cannot simply reverse your decision. Once you have started on a path, to take another path you have to return to the beginning. Thus, following one path often lowers the costs of options along that path, but it raises the costs of options along another path.

Such sequential decisions can best be seen within the framework of a decision tree—a visual description of sequential choices. A decision tree is shown in the accompanying figure.

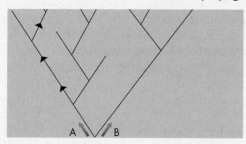

Once you make the initial decision to go on path A, the costs of path B options become higher; they include the costs

of retracing your path and starting over. The decision trees of life have thousands of branches; each decision you make rules out other paths, or at least increases their costs significantly. (Remember that day you decided to blow off your homework? That decision may have changed your future life.)

Another way of putting this same point is that *all decisions are made in context:* What makes sense in one context may not make sense in another. For example, say you're answering the question "Would society be better off if students were taught literature or if they were taught agriculture?" The answer depends on the institutional context. In a developing country whose goal is large increases in material output, teaching agriculture may make sense. In a developed country, where growth in material output is less important, teaching literature may make sense.

Recognizing the contextual nature of decisions is important when interpreting the production possibility curve. Because decisions are contextual, what the production possibility curve for a particular decision looks like depends on the existing institutions, and the analysis can be applied only in institutional and historical context. The production possibility curve is not a purely technical phenomenon. The curve is an engine of analysis to make contextual choices, not a definitive tool to decide what one should do in all cases.

FIGURE 2-3 (A, B, AND C)   **Efficiency, Inefficiency, and Technological Change**

The production possibility curve helps us see what is meant by efficiency. At point *A,* in (**a**), all inputs are used to make 4 pounds of butter and 6 guns. This is inefficient since there is a way to obtain more of one without giving up any of the other, that is, to obtain 6 pounds of butter and 6 guns (point *C*) or 8 guns and 4 pounds of butter (point *B*). All points inside the production possibility curve are inefficient. With existing inputs and technology, we cannot go beyond the production possibility curve. For example, point *D* is unattainable.

A technological change that improves production techniques will shift the production possibility curve outward, as shown in both (**b**) and (**c**). How the curve shifts outward depends on how technology improves. For example, if we become more efficient in the production of both guns and butter, the curve will shift out as in (**b**). If we become more efficient in producing butter, but not in producing guns, then the curve will shift as in (**c**).

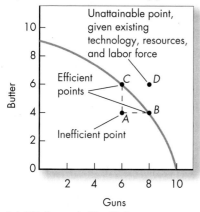

(a) Efficiency and Inefficiency

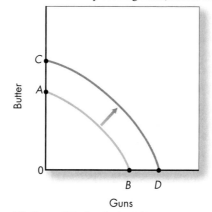

(b) Neutral Technological Change

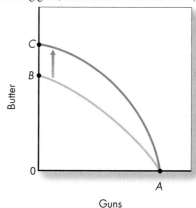

(c) Biased Technological Change

| FIGURE 2-4 (A, B, C, AND D) | **Examples of Shifts in Production Possibility Curves**

Each of these curves reflects a different type of shift. (The axes are left unlabeled on purpose. Manufactured and agricultural goods may be placed on either axis.) Your assignment is to match these shifts with the situations given in the text.

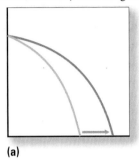
(a)

(b)

(c)

(d)

Q-4 Your firm is establishing a trucking business in Saudi Arabia. The managers have noticed that women are generally paid much less than men in Saudi Arabia, and they suggest that hiring women would be more efficient than hiring men. How should you respond?

distribution and choosing one method will help some people but hurt others, we can't say that one method of production is efficient and the other inefficient, even if one method produces more total output than the other. As I stated above, the term *efficiency* involves achieving a goal as cheaply as possible. The term has meaning only in regard to a specified goal. Say, for example, that we have a society of ascetics who believe that consumption above some minimum is immoral. For such a society, producing more for less (productive efficiency) would not be efficient since consumption is not its goal. Or say that we have a society that cares that what is produced is fairly distributed. An increase in output that goes to only one person and not to anyone else would not necessarily be efficient.

In our society, however, most people prefer more to less, and many policies have relatively small distributional consequences. On the basis of the assumption that more is better than less, economists use their own kind of shorthand for such policies and talk about efficiency as identical to productive efficiency—increasing total output. But it's important to remember the assumptions under which that shorthand is used: The distributional effects of the policy are deemed acceptable, and we, as a society, prefer more output.

Examples of Shifts in the PPC

To see whether you understand the production possibility curve, let us now consider some situations that can be shown with it. Below, I list four situations. To test your understanding of the curve, match each situation to one of the curves in Figure 2-4.

Q-5 When a natural disaster hits the midwestern United States, where most of the U.S. butter is produced, what happens to the U.S. production possibility curve for guns and butter?

1. A meteor hits the world and destroys half the earth's natural resources.
2. Nanotechnology is perfected that lowers the cost of manufactured goods.
3. A new technology is discovered that doubles the speed at which all goods can be produced.
4. Global warming increases the cost of producing agricultural goods.

The correct answers are: 1–d; 2–a; 3–b; 4–c.

If you got them all right, you are well on your way to understanding the production possibility curve.

Trade and Comparative Advantage

www   Web Note 2.1
Wine and Cloth

Now that we have gone through the basics of the production possibility curve, let's dig a little deeper. From the above discussion, you know that production possibility curves are generally bowed outward and that the reason for this is comparative advantage. To

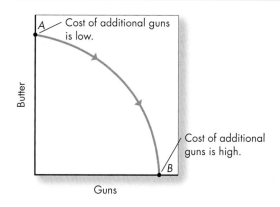

FIGURE 2-5 **Comparative Advantage and the Production Possibility Curve**

As we move down along the production possibility curve from point *A* to point *B,* the cost of producing guns is increasing since we are using resources less suited for gun production.

remind you of the argument, consider Figure 2-5, which is the guns and butter production possibility example I presented earlier.

At point *A,* all resources are being used to produce butter. As more guns are produced, we take resources away from producing butter that had a comparative advantage in producing guns, so we gain a lot of guns for little butter (the opportunity cost of additional guns is low). As we continue down the curve, the comparative advantage of the resources we use changes, and as we approach *B,* we use almost all resources to produce guns, so we are using resources that aren't very good at producing guns. Thus, around point *B* we gain few guns for a lot of butter (the opportunity cost of additional guns is high).

A society wants to be on the frontier of its production possibility curve. This requires that individuals produce those goods for which they have a comparative advantage. The question for society, then, is how to direct individuals toward those activities. For a firm, the answer is easy. A manager can allocate the firm's resources to their best use. For example, he or she can assign an employee with good people skills to the human resources department and another with good research skills to research and development. But our economy has millions of individuals, and no manager directing everyone what to do. How do we know that these individuals will be directed to do those things for which they have a comparative advantage? It was this question that was central to the British moral philosopher Adam Smith when he wrote his most famous book, *The Wealth of Nations* (1776). In it he argued that it was humankind's proclivity to trade that leads to individuals using their comparative advantage. He writes:

> This division of labour, from which so many advantages are derived, is not originally the effect of any human wisdom, which foresees and intends that general opulence to which it gives occasion. It is the necessary, though very slow and gradual consequence of a certain propensity in human nature which has in view no such extensive utility; the propensity to truck, barter, and exchange one thing for another . . . [This propensity] is common to all men, and to be found in no other race of animals, which seem to know neither this nor any other species of contracts . . . Nobody ever saw a dog make a fair and deliberate exchange of one bone for another with another dog. Nobody ever saw one animal by its gestures and natural cries signify to another, this is mine, that yours; I am willing to give this for that.

Adam Smith argued that it is humankind's proclivity to trade that leads to individuals using their comparative advantage.

As long as people trade, Smith argues, the market will guide people, like an invisible hand, to gravitate toward those activities for which they have a comparative advantage.

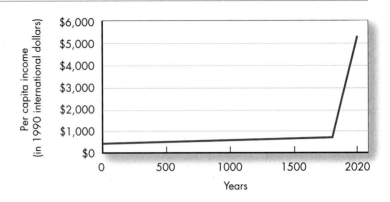

FIGURE 2-6   **Growth in the Past Two Millennia**

For 1,700 years the world economy grew very slowly. Then, since the end of the 18th century with the introduction of markets and the spread of democracy, the world economy has grown at increasing rates.

Source: Angus Maddison, *Monitoring the World Economy,* OECD, 1995; Angus Maddison, "Poor until 1820," *The Wall Street Journal,* January 11, 1999; and author extrapolations.

Markets, Specialization, and Growth

We can see the effect of trade on our well-being empirically by considering the growth of economies. As you can see from Figure 2-6, for 1,700 years the world economy grew very slowly. Then, at the end of the 18th century, the world economy started to grow, and it has grown at a high rate since then.

What changed? The introduction of markets that facilitate trade and the spread of democracy. There's something about markets that leads to economic growth. Markets allow specialization and encourage trade. The bowing out of the production possibilities from trade is part of the story, but a minor part. As individuals compete and specialize, they learn by doing, becoming even better at what they do. Markets also foster competition, which pushes individuals to find better ways of doing things. They devise new technologies that further the growth process.

The new millennium is offering new ways for individuals to specialize and compete. More and more businesses are trading on the Internet. For example, colleges such as the University of Phoenix are providing online competition for traditional colleges. Similarly, online stores are proliferating. As Internet technology becomes built into our economy, we can expect more specialization, more division of labor, and the economic growth that follows.

Markets can be very simple or very complicated.

The Benefits of Trade

The reasons why markets can direct people to use their comparative advantages follow from a very simple argument: When people freely enter into a trade, both parties can be expected to benefit from the trade; otherwise, why would they have traded in the first place? So when the butcher sells you meat, he's better off with the money you give him, and you're better off with the meat he gives you.

When there is competition in trading, such that individuals are able to pick the best trades available to them, each individual drives the best bargain he or she can. The end result is that both individuals in the trade benefit as much as they possibly can, given what others are willing to trade. This argument for the benefits from trade underlies the general policy of **laissez-faire**—*an economic policy of leaving coordination of individuals' actions to the market.* (*Laissez-faire,* a French term, means "Let events take their course; leave things alone.") Laissez-faire is not a theorem in economics; it is a precept because it extends the implications of a model to reality and draws conclusions about the real world. It is based on normative judgments, judgments about the relevance of the model, and assumptions upon which the model is based.

Web Note 2.2
Gains from Trade

Q-6 What argument underlies the general laissez-faire policy argument?

Let's consider a numerical example of the gains that accrue to two countries when they trade. I use an international trade example so that you can see that the argument

FIGURE 2-7 (A AND B)   The Gains from Trade

Trade makes those involved in the trade better off. If each country specializes and takes advantage of its comparative advantage, each can consume a combinations of goods beyond its production possibilities curve. In the example shown, Pakistan can consume at point *B* and Belgium at point *E*.

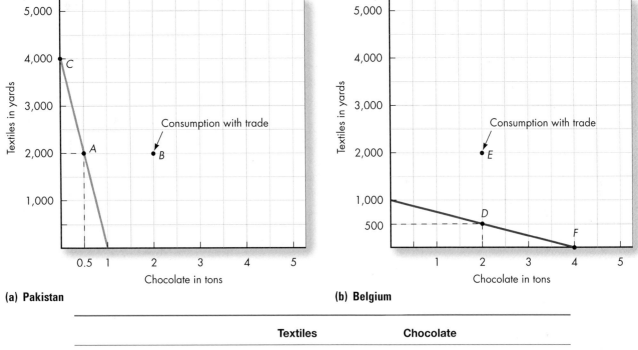

(a) **Pakistan**   (b) **Belgium**

	Textiles	Chocolate
Pakistan	2,000 yards	0.5 ton
Belgium	500 yards	2 tons

holds for international trade as well as domestic trade. Let's say that the two countries are Pakistan and Belgium, and that Pakistan has a comparative advantage in producing textiles, while Belgium has a comparative advantage in producing chocolate. Specifically, Pakistan can produce 4,000 yards of textiles a day or 1 ton of chocolate a day, or any proportional combination in between. Pakistan's production possibility curve is shown in Figure 2-7(a). Similarly, in a given day, Belgium can produce either 1,000 yards of textiles or 4 tons of chocolate, or any proportion in between. Its production possibility curve is shown in Figure 2-7(b).

In the absence of trade, the most each country can consume is some combination along its production possibility curve. Say Pakistan has chosen to produce and consume 2,000 yards of textiles and 0.5 ton of chocolate (point *A* in Figure 2-7(a)), while Belgium has chosen to produce and consume 500 yards of textiles and 2 tons of chocolate (point *D* in Figure 2-7(b)).

Let's now consider what would happen if each specialized, doing what it does best, and then traded with the other for the goods it wants. This separates the production and consumption decisions. Because Pakistan can produce textiles at a lower cost in terms of chocolate, it makes sense for Pakistan to specialize in textiles, producing 4,000 yards (point *C* in Figure 2-7(a)). Similarly, it makes sense for Belgium to specialize in chocolate, producing 4 tons (point *F* in Figure 2-7(b)). By specializing, the countries together produce 4 tons of chocolate and 4,000 yards of textiles. If the countries divide

Specialization and trade create gains that make all better off.

Q-7 Steve can bake either 4 loaves of bread or 8 dozen cookies a day. Sarah can bake either 4 loaves of bread or 4 dozen cookies a day. Show, using production possibility curves, that Steve and Sarah would be better off specializing in their baking activities and then trading, rather than baking only for themselves.

Q-8 True or false? Two countries can achieve the greatest gains from trade by each producing the goods for which it has a comparative advantage and then trading those goods.

production so that each country gets 2,000 yards of fabric and 2 tons of chocolate, Pakistan can consume at point *B* and Belgium at point *E*. Both are consuming beyond their production possibility curves without trade. This tells us an important principle about trade:

Trade lets countries consume beyond their "no-trade" production possibility curve.

It is primarily these gains that lead to economists' support of free trade and their opposition to barriers to trade.

The pressure to find comparative advantages is never ending, in part because comparative advantage can change. Two hundred years ago, the United States had a comparative advantage in producing textiles. It was rich in natural resources and labor, and it had a low-cost source of power (water). As the cost of U.S. labor went up, and as trade opportunities widened, that comparative advantage disappeared. As it did, the United States moved out of the textile industry. Countries with cheaper labor, such as Bangladesh, today have the comparative advantage in textiles. As firms have relocated textile production to Bangladesh, total costs have fallen. The gains from trade show up as higher pay for Bangladeshi workers and lower-priced cloth for U.S. consumers. Of course, trade is a two-way street. In return for Bangladesh's textiles, the United States sends computer software and airplanes, products that would be highly expensive, indeed almost impossible, for Bangladesh to produce on its own. So Bangladeshi consumers, on average, are also made better off by the trade.

Globalization and the Law of One Price

There is much more to be said about both trade and the gains from trade, and later chapters will explore trade in much more detail. But let me briefly discuss the relationship of the theory of comparative advantage to globalization.

Globalization

Globalization *is the increasing integration of economies, cultures, and institutions across the world.* In a globalized economy, firms think of production and sales at a global level. They produce where costs are lowest, and sell across the world at the highest price they can get. A globalized world is a world in which economies of the world are highly integrated. Globalization has two effects on firms. The first is positive; because the world economy is so much larger than the domestic economy, the rewards for winning globally are much larger than the rewards for winning domestically. The second effect is negative; it is much harder to win, or even to stay in business, competing in a global market. A company may be the low-cost producer in a particular country yet may face foreign competitors that can undersell it. The global economy increases the number of competitors for the firm. Consider the automobile industry. Three companies are headquartered in the United States, but more than 40 automobile companies operate worldwide. U.S. automakers face stiff competition from foreign automakers; unless they meet that competition, they will not survive.

The global economy increases the number of competitors for the firm.

These two effects are, of course, related. When you compete in a larger market, you have to be better to survive, but if you do survive the rewards are greater.

Globalization increases competition by allowing greater specialization and division of labor, which, as Adam Smith first observed in *The Wealth of Nations,* increases growth and improves the standard of living for everyone. Thus, in many ways globalization is simply another name for increased specialization. Globalization allows (indeed, forces) companies to move operations to countries with a comparative advantage.

Made in China?

Barbie and her companion Ken are as American as apple pie, and considering their origins gives us some insight into the modern U.S. economy and its interconnection with other countries. Barbie and Ken are not produced in the United States; they never were. When Barbie first came out in 1959, she was produced in Japan. Today, it is unclear where Barbie and Ken are produced. If you look at the box they come in, it says "Made in China," but looking deeper we find that Barbie and Ken are actually made in five different countries, each focusing on an aspect of production that reflects its comparative advantage. Japan produces the nylon hair. China provides much of what is normally considered manufacturing—factory spaces, labor, and energy for assembly—but it imports many of the components. The oil for the plastic comes from Saudi Arabia. That oil is refined into plastic pellets in Taiwan. The United States even provides some of the raw materials that go into the manufacturing process—it provides the cardboard, packing, paint pigments, and the mold.

The diversification of parts that go into the manufacturing of Barbie and Ken is typical of many goods today. As the world economy has become more integrated, the process of supplying components of manufacturing has become more and more spread out, as firms have divided up the manufacturing process in search of the least-cost location for each component.

But the global diversity in manufacturing and supply of components is only half the story of modern production. The other half is the shrinking of the relative importance of that manufacturing, and it is this other half that explains how the United States maintains its position in the world when so much of the manufacturing takes place elsewhere. It does so by maintaining its control over the distribution and marketing of the goods. In fact, of the $15 retail cost of a Barbie or Ken, $12 can be accounted for by activities not associated with manufacturing—design, transportation, merchandising, and advertising. And, luckily for the United States, many of these activities are still done in the United States, allowing the country to maintain its high living standard even as manufacturing spreads around the globe.

As they do so, they lower costs of production. Globalization leads to companies specializing in smaller portions of the production process because the potential market is not just one country but the world. Such specialization can lead to increased productivity as firms get better and better at producing through practice, what economists call *learning by doing*.

In a globalized economy production will shift to the lowest-cost producer. Globalization scares many people in the United States because, with wages so much lower in many developing countries than in the United States, they wonder whether all jobs will move offshore: Will the United States be left producing anything? Economists' answer is: Of course it will. Comparative advantage, by definition, means that if one country has a comparative advantage in producing one set of goods, the other country has to have a comparative advantage in the other set of goods. The real questions are: In what goods will the United States have comparative advantages? and: How will those comparative advantages come about?

One reason people have a hard time thinking of goods in which the United States has a comparative advantage is that they are thinking in terms of labor costs. They ask: Since wages are lower in China, isn't it cheaper to produce all goods in China? The answer is no; production requires many more inputs than just labor. Technology, institutional structure, specialized types of knowledge, and entrepreneurial know-how are also needed to produce goods, and the United States has significant advantages in these other factors. It is these advantages that result in higher U.S. wages compared to other countries.

Q-9 How does globalization reduce the costs of production?

Q-10 Is it likely that all U.S. jobs one day will have moved abroad? Why or Why not?

Web Note 2.3
Trade and Wages

The Developing Country's Perspective on Globalization

This book is written from a U.S. point of view. From that perspective, the relevant question is: Can the United States maintain its high wages relative to the low wages in China, India, and other developing countries? I suspect that most U.S. readers hope that it can. From a developing country's perspective, I suspect that the hope is that it cannot; their hope is that their wage rates catch up with U.S. wage rates. Judged from a developing country's perspective, the question is: Is it fair that U.S. workers don't work as hard as we do but earn much more?

The market does not directly take fairness into account. The market is interested only in who can produce a good or service at the lowest cost. This means that in a competitive economy, the United States can maintain its high wages only to the degree that it can produce sufficient goods and services cheaper than low-wage countries can at the market exchange rate. It must keep the trade balance roughly equal.

Developing countries recognize that, in the past, the United States has had a comparative advantage in creativity and innovation, and they are doing everything they can to compete on these levels as well as on basic production levels. They are actively trying to develop such skills in their population and to compete with the United States not only in manufacturing and low-tech jobs but also in research, development, finance, organizational activities, artistic activities, and high-tech jobs. Right now companies in China and India are working to challenge U.S. dominance in all high-tech and creativity fields. (For example, they too are working on nanotechnology.) To do this, they are trying to entice top scientists and engineers to stay in their country, or to return home if they have been studying or working in the United States. Since more than 50 percent of all PhD's given in science, engineering, and economics go to non-U.S. citizens (in economics, it is more than 70 percent), many observers believe that the United States cannot assume its past dominance in the innovative and high-tech fields will continue forever. The competitive front that will determine whether the United States can maintain much higher wages than developing countries is not the competition in current industries, but competition in industries of the future.

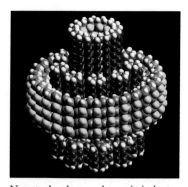

Nanotechnology—dynamic industry of the future?

The United States has excelled particularly in goods that require creativity and innovation. The United States has remained the leader of the world economy and has kept a comparative advantage in many goods even with its high relative wages, in part because of continual innovation. For example, the Internet started in the United States, which is why the United States is the location of so many information technology firms. The United States also has led the way in biotechnology innovation. Similarly, the creative industries, such as film, art, and advertising, have flourished in the United States. These industries are dynamic, high-profit, high-wage industries. (One of the reasons insourcing occurs is that the United States has such a great comparative advantage in these other aspects of production.) As long as U.S. production maintains a comparative advantage in innovation, the United States will be able to specialize in goods that allow firms to pay higher wages.

Exchange Rates and Comparative Advantage

There is, however, reason to be concerned. If innovation and creativity don't develop new industries in which the United States has a comparative advantage fast enough, as the current dynamic industries mature and move to low-wage areas, at current exchange rates (the value of a currency relative to the value of foreign currencies), the United States will not maintain comparative advantages in sufficient industries to warrant the relative wage differentials that exist today. In that case, U.S. demand for foreign goods and services will be higher than foreign demand for U.S. goods and services. For the last 20 years that has been the case. To bring them into equilibrium, the U.S. wage premium will have to decline to regain our comparative advantages. Since nominal wages (the wages that you see in your paycheck) in the United States are unlikely to fall, this will most likely occur through a decline in the U.S. exchange rate, large increases in foreign wages, or both. Either of these will make foreign products imported into the United States more expensive and U.S. products cheaper for foreigners, and eventually will balance the comparative advantages and trade flows.

The Law of One Price

Many Americans do not like the "exchange rate answer," but in terms of policy, it is probably the best the United States can hope for. If the United States tries to prevent production from moving to other countries with trade restrictions, U.S.-based companies will find that they can no longer compete internationally, and the United States will be in worse shape than if it had allowed outsourcing. The reality is that competition, combined with transferable technology and similar institutions, drives wages and prices of similar factors and goods toward equality. This reality often goes by the name of the **law of one price**—*the wages of workers in one country will not differ significantly from the wages of (equal) workers in another institutionally similar country.* As we will discuss in a later chapter, the debate is about what an "equal" worker is and what an equivalent institutional structure is.

Because of a variety of historical circumstances, the United States has been able to avoid the law of one price in wages since World War I. One factor has been the desire of foreigners to increase their holding of U.S. financial assets by trillions of dollars, which has let the United States consume more goods than it produces. Another is that the United States' institutional structure, technology, entrepreneurial labor force, and nonlabor inputs have given the United States sufficiently strong comparative advantages to offset the higher U.S. wage rates. The passage of time and modern technological changes have been eroding the United States' comparative advantages based on institutional structure and technology. To the degree that this continues to happen, to maintain a balance in the comparative advantages of various countries, the wages of workers in other countries such as India and China will have to move closer to the wages of U.S. workers.

The law of one price states that wages of workers in one country will not differ significantly from the wages of (equal) workers in another institutionally similar country.

Globalization and the Timing of Benefits of Trade

One final comment about globalization and the U.S. economy is in order. None of the above discussion contradicts the proposition that trade makes both countries better off. Thus, the discussion does not support the position taken by some opponents to trade and globalization that foreign competition is hurting the United States and that the United States can be made better off by imposing trade restrictions. Instead, the discussion is about the timing of the benefits of trade. Many of the benefits of trade already have been consumed by the United States during the years that the United States has been running trade deficits (importing more than it is exporting). The reality is that the United States has been living better than it could have otherwise precisely because of trade. It also has been living much better than it otherwise could because it is paying for some of its imports with IOUs promising payment in the future instead of with exports. But there is no free lunch, and when these IOUs are presented for payment, the United States will have to pay for some of the benefits that it already has consumed.

The reality is that the United States has been living better than it could have otherwise precisely because of trade and outsourcing.

Conclusion

While the production possibility curve model does not give unambiguous answers as to what government's role should be in regulating trade, it does serve a very important purpose. It is a geometric tool that summarizes a number of ideas in economics: trade-offs, opportunity costs, comparative advantage, efficiency, and how trade leads to

The production possibility curve represents the tough choices society must make.

efficiency. These ideas are all essential to economists' conversations. They provide the framework within which those conversations take place. Thinking of the production possibility curve (and picturing the economy as being on it) directs you to think of the trade-offs involved in every decision.

Look at questions such as: Should we save the spotted owl or should we allow logging in the western forests? Should we expand the government health care system or should we strengthen our national defense system? Should we emphasize policies that allow more consumption now or should we emphasize policies that allow more consumption in the future? Such choices involve difficult trade-offs that can be pictured by the production possibility curve.

Not everyone recognizes these trade-offs. For example, politicians often talk as if the production possibility curve were nonexistent. They promise voters the world, telling them, "If you elect me, you can have more of everything." When they say that, they obscure the hard choices and increase their probability of getting elected.

Economists continually point out that seemingly free lunches often involve significant hidden costs.

Economists do the opposite. They promise little except that life is tough, and they continually point out that seemingly free lunches often involve significant hidden costs. Alas, political candidates who exhibit such reasonableness seldom get elected. Economists' reasonableness has earned economics the nickname *the dismal science*.

Summary

- The production possibility curve measures the maximum combination of outputs that can be obtained from a given number of inputs. *(LO2-1)*

- In general, in order to get more and more of something, we must give up ever-increasing quantities of something else. *(LO2-1)*

- Trade allows people to use their comparative advantage and shift out society's production possibility curve. *(LO2-2)*

- The rise of markets coincided with significant increases in output. Specialization, trade, and competition have all contributed to the increase. *(LO2-2)*

- Points inside the production possibility curve are inefficient, points along the production possibility curve are efficient, and points outside are unattainable. *(LO2-2)*

- By specializing in producing those goods for which one has a comparative advantage (lowest opportunity cost), one can produce the greatest amount of goods

- with which to trade. Doing so, countries can increase consumption. *(LO2-3)*

- Globalization is the increasing integration of economies, cultures, and institutions across the world. *(LO2-4)*

- Because many goods are cheaper to produce in countries such as China and India, production that formerly took place in the United States is now taking place in foreign countries. *(LO2-4)*

- If the United States can maintain its strong comparative advantage in goods using new technologies and innovation, the jobs lost by production moving outside the United States can be replaced with other high-paying jobs. If it does not, then some adjustments in relative wage rates or exchange rates must occur. *(LO2-4)*

- Business's tendency to shift production to countries where it is cheapest to produce is guided by the law of one price. *(LO2-4)*

Key Terms

comparative advantage *(27)*	globalization *(34)*	law of one price *(37)*	production possibility table *(24)*
efficiency *(28)*	inefficiency *(28)*	production possibility	
	laissez-faire *(32)*	curve (PPC) *(25)*	productive efficiency *(28)*

Questions and Exercises

1. Show how a production possibility curve would shift if a society became more productive in its output of widgets but less productive in its output of wadgets. (*LO2-1*)

2. Show how a production possibility curve would shift if a society became more productive in the output of both widgets and wadgets. (*LO2-1*)

3. Design a grade production possibility table and curve that demonstrates a rising trade-off as the grade in each subject rises. (*LO2-1*)

4. In two hours JustBorn Candies can produce 30,000 Peeps or 90,000 Mike and Ikes or any combination in between. (*LO2-2*)
   a. What is the trade-off between Peeps and Mike and Ikes?
   b. Draw a production possibility curve that reflects this trade-off.
   c. Identify and label three points: efficient production, inefficient production, impossible.
   d. Illustrate what would happen if JustBorn candies developed a technology that increased productivity equally for both products.

5. How does the theory of comparative advantage relate to production possibility curves? (*LO2-2*)

6. A country has the following production possibility table: (*LO2-2*)

Resources Devoted to Clothing	Output of Clothing	Resources Devoted to Food	Output of Food
100%	20	0%	0
80	16	20	5
60	12	40	9
40	8	60	12
20	4	80	14
0	0	100	15

   a. Draw the country's production possibility curve.
   b. What's happening to the trade-off between food and clothing?

c. Say the country gets better at the production of food. What will happen to the production possibility curve?
d. Say the country gets equally better at producing both food and clothing. What will happen to the production possibility curve?

7. If neither of two countries has a comparative advantage in either of two goods, what are the gains from trade? (*LO2-3*)

8. Does the fact that the production possibilities model tells us that trade is good mean that in the real world free trade is necessarily the best policy? Explain. (*LO2-3*)

9. Suppose the United States and Japan have the following production possibility tables: (*LO2-3*)

Japan		United States	
Bolts of Cloth	Tons of Wheat	Bolts of Cloth	Tons of Wheat
1,000	0	500	0
800	100	400	200
600	200	300	400
400	300	200	600
200	400	100	800
0	500	0	1,000

   a. Draw each country's production possibility curve.
   b. In what good does the United States have a comparative advantage?
   c. Is there a possible trade that benefits both countries?
   d. Demonstrate your answer graphically.

10. What effect has globalization had on the ability of firms to specialize? How has this affected the competitive process? (*LO2-4*)

11. If workers in China and India become as productive as U.S. workers, what adjustments will allow the United States to regain its competitiveness? (*LO2-4*)

12. State the law of one price. How is it related to the movement of production out of the United States? (*LO2-4*)

Questions from Alternative Perspectives

1. Why might government be less capable than the market to do good? (Austrian)

2. The text makes it look as if maximizing output is the goal of society.
   a. Is maximizing output the goal of society?

   b. If the country is a Christian country, should it be?
   c. If not, what should it be? (Religious)

3. It has been said that "capitalism robs us of our sexuality and sells it back to us."
   a. Does sex sell?

b. Is sex used to sell goods from Land Rovers to tissue paper?

c. Who, if anyone, is exploited in the use of sex to sell commodities?

d. Are both men and women exploited in the same ways? (Feminist)

4. Thorstein Veblen wrote that *vested interests* are those seeking "something for nothing." In this chapter, you learned how technology shapes the economy's production possibilities over time so that a country becomes increasingly good at producing a subset of goods.

a. In what ways have vested interests used their influence to bias the U.S. economy toward the production of military goods at the expense of consumer goods?

b. What are the short-term and long-term consequences of that bias for human welfare, in the United States and abroad? (Institutionalist)

5. Writing in 1776, Adam Smith was concerned not only with the profound effects of the division of labor on productivity (as your textbook notes) but also its stultifying effect on the human capacity. In *The Wealth of Nations*, Smith warned that performing a few simple operations over and over again could render any worker, no matter his or her native intelligence, "stupid and ignorant."

a. Does the division of labor in today's economy continue to have both these effects?

b. What are the policy implications? (Radical)

Issues to Ponder

1. When all people use economic reasoning, inefficiency is impossible because if the benefit of reducing that inefficiency were greater than the cost, the inefficiency would be eliminated. Thus, if people use economic reasoning, it's impossible to be on the interior of a production possibility curve. Is this statement true or false? Why?

2. If income distribution is tied to a particular production technique, how might that change one's view of alternative production techniques?

3. Research shows that after-school jobs are highly correlated with decreases in grade point averages. Those who work 1 to 10 hours get a 3.0 GPA and those who work 21 hours or more have a 2.7 GPA. Higher GPAs are, however, highly correlated with higher lifetime earnings. Assume that a person earns $8,000 per year for working part-time in college, and that the return to a 0.1 increase in GPA gives one a 10 percent increase in one's lifetime earnings with a present value of $80,000.

a. What would be the argument for working rather than studying harder?

b. Is the assumption that there is a trade-off between working and grades reasonable?

4. Lawns produce no crops but occupy more land (25 million acres) in the United States than any single crop, such as corn. This means that the United States is operating inefficiently and hence is at a point inside the production possibility curve. Right? If not, what does it mean?

5. Groucho Marx is reported to have said "The secret of success is honesty and fair dealing. If you can fake those, you've got it made." What would likely happen to society's production possibility curve if everyone could fake honesty? Why? (Hint: Remember that society's production possibility curve reflects more than just technical relationships.)

6. Say that the hourly cost to employers per German industrial worker was $44. The hourly cost to employers per U.S. industrial worker was $34, while the average cost per Taiwanese industrial worker was $8.

a. Give three reasons why firms produce in Germany rather than in a lower-wage country.

b. Germany has an agreement with other EU countries that allows people in any EU country, including Greece and Italy, which have lower wage rates, to travel and work in any EU country, including high-wage countries. Would you expect a significant movement of workers from Greece and Italy to Germany right away? Why or why not?

c. Workers in Thailand are paid significantly less than workers in Taiwan. If you were a company CEO, what other information would you want before you decided where to establish a new production facility?

Answers to Margin Questions

1. You must give up 2 units of good *Y* to produce 4 units of good *X*, so the opportunity cost of *X* is ½ *Y*. (*p. 25; LO2-1*)

2. If no resource had a comparative advantage, the production possibility curve would be a straight line connecting the points of maximum production of each product as in the graph below.

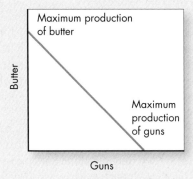

At all points along this curve, the trade-off between producing guns and butter is equal. (*p. 27; LO2-2*)

3. Points *A* and *C* are along the production possibility curve, so they are points of efficiency. Point *B* is inside the production possibility curve, so it is a point of inefficiency. Point *D* is to the right of the production possibility curve, so it is unattainable. (*p. 28; LO2-2*)

4. Remind them of the importance of cultural forces. In Saudi Arabia, women are not allowed to drive. (*p. 30; LO2-2*)

5. The production possibility curve shifts in along the butter axis as in the graph below. (*p. 30; LO2-2*)

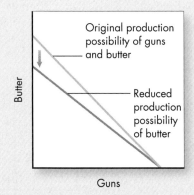

6. The argument that underlies the general laissez-faire policy argument is that when there is competition in trade, individuals are able to pick the best trades available to them and the end result is that both parties to the trade benefit as much as they possibly can. (*p. 32; LO2-3*)

7. Steve's and Sarah's production possibility curves are shown in the figure below. If they specialize, they can, combined, produce 4 loaves of bread and 8 dozen cookies, which they can split up. Say that Steve gets 2 loaves of bread and 5 dozen cookies (point *A*). This puts him beyond his original production possibility curve, and thus is an improvement for him. That leaves 2 loaves of bread and 3 dozen cookies for Sarah (point *B*), which is beyond her original production possibility curve, which is an improvement for her. Both are better off than they would have been without trade. (*p. 34; LO2-3*)

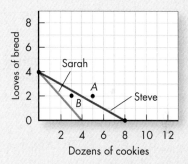

8. True. By producing the good for which it has a comparative advantage, a country will have the greatest amount of goods with which to trade and will reap the greatest gains from trade. (*p. 34; LO2-3*)

9. Globalization allows more trade and specialization. That specialization lowers costs of production since it allows the lowest-cost producer to produce each good. (*p. 35; LO2-4*)

10. No. By definition, if one country has a comparative advantage in producing one set of goods, the other country has a comparative advantage in the production in the other set. Jobs will be needed to support this production. Additionally, many jobs cannot be moved abroad effectively because they require physical proximity to the point of sale. (*p. 35; LO2-4*)

Graphish: The Language of Graphs

A picture is worth 1,000 words. Economists, being efficient, like to present ideas in **graphs,** *pictures of points in a coordinate system in which points denote relationships between numbers.* But a graph is worth 1,000 words only if the person looking at the graph knows the graphical language: *Graphish,* we'll call it. (It's a bit like English.) Graphish is usually written on graph paper. If the person doesn't know Graphish, the picture isn't worth any words and Graphish can be babble.

I have enormous sympathy for students who don't understand Graphish. A number of my students get thrown for a loop by graphs. They understand the idea, but Graphish confuses them. This appendix is for them, and for those of you like them. It's a primer in Graphish.

Two Ways to Use Graphs

In this book I use graphs in two ways:

1. To present an economic model or theory visually, showing how two variables interrelate.

2. To present real-world data visually. To do this, I use primarily bar charts, line charts, and pie charts.

Actually, these two ways of using graphs are related. They are both ways of presenting visually the *relationship* between two things.

Graphs are built around a number line, or axis, like the one in Figure A2-1(a). The numbers are generally placed in order, equal distances from one another. That number line allows us to represent a number at an appropriate point on the line. For example, point A represents the number 4.

The number line in Figure A2-1(a) is drawn horizontally, but it doesn't have to be; it also can be drawn vertically, as in Figure A2-1(b).

How we divide our axes, or number lines, into intervals is up to us. In Figure A2-1(a), I called each interval 1; in Figure A2-1(b), I called each interval 10. Point A appears after 4 intervals of 1 (starting at 0 and reading from left to right), so it represents 4. In Figure A2-1(b), where each interval represents 10, to represent 5, I place point B halfway in the interval between 0 and 10.

So far, so good. Graphish developed when a vertical and a horizontal number line were combined, as in Figure A2-1(c). When the horizontal and vertical number lines are put together, they're called *axes.* (Each line is an axis. *Axes* is the plural of *axis.*) I now have a **coordinate system**—*a two-dimensional space in which one point represents two numbers.* For example, point A in Figure A2-1(c) represents the numbers (4, 5)—4 on the horizontal number line and 5 on the vertical number line. Point B represents the numbers (1, 20). (By convention, the horizontal numbers are written first.)

Being able to represent two numbers with one point is neat because it allows the relationships between two numbers to be presented visually instead of having to be expressed verbally, which is often cumbersome. For example, say the cost of producing 6 units of something is $4 per unit and the cost of producing 10 units is $3 per

---

FIGURE A2-1 (A, B, AND C)   Horizontal and Vertical Number Lines and a Coordinate System

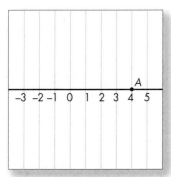

(a) Horizontal Number Line

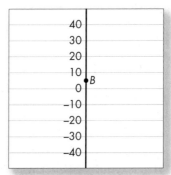

(b) Vertical Number Line

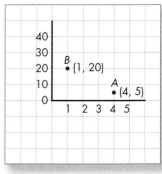

(c) Coordinate System

FIGURE A2-2 (A, B, C, AND D) A Table and Graphs Showing the Relationships between Price and Quantity

	Price per Pen	Quantity of Pens Bought per Day
A	$3.00	4
B	2.50	5
C	2.00	6
D	1.50	7
E	1.00	8

(a) Price Quantity Table

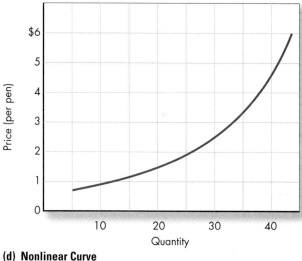

(b) From a Table to a Graph (1)

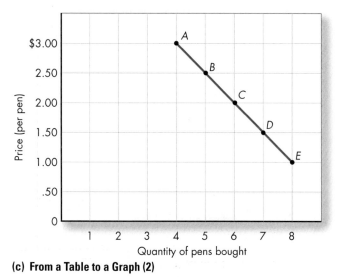

(c) From a Table to a Graph (2)

(d) Nonlinear Curve

unit. By putting both these points on a graph, we can visually see that producing 10 costs less per unit than does producing 6.

Another way to use graphs to present real-world data visually is to use the horizontal line to represent time. Say that we let each horizontal interval equal a year, and each vertical interval equal $100 in income. By graphing your income each year, you can obtain a visual representation of how your income has changed over time.

Using Graphs in Economic Modeling

I use graphs throughout the book as I present economic models, or simplifications of reality. A few terms are

often used in describing these graphs, and we'll now go over them. Consider Figure A2-2(a), which lists the number of pens bought per day (column 2) at various prices (column 1).

We can present the table's information in a graph by combining the pairs of numbers in the two columns of the table and representing, or plotting, them on two axes. I do that in Figure A2-2(b).

By convention, when graphing a relationship between price and quantity, economists place price on the vertical axis and quantity on the horizontal axis.

I can now connect the points, producing a line like the one in Figure A2-2(c). With this line, I interpolate the numbers between the points (which makes for a nice

Inverse and Direct Relationships

Inverse relationship:
When *X* goes up, *Y* goes down.
When *X* goes down, *Y* goes up.

Direct relationship:
When *X* goes up, *Y* goes up.
When *X* goes down, *Y* goes down.

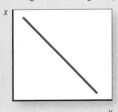

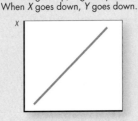

visual presentation). That is, I make the **interpolation assumption**—*the assumption that the relationship between variables is the same between points as it is at the points.* The interpolation assumption allows us to think of a line as a collection of points and therefore to connect the points into a line.

Even though the line in Figure A2-2(c) is straight, economists call any such line drawn on a graph a *curve.* Because it's straight, the curve in A2-2(c) is called a **linear curve**—*a curve that is drawn as a straight line.* Notice that this curve starts high on the left-hand side and goes down to the right. Economists say that any curve that looks like that is *downward-sloping.* They also say that a downward-sloping curve represents an **inverse relationship**—*a relationship between two variables in which when one goes up, the other goes down.* In this example, the line demonstrates an inverse relationship between price and quantity—that is, when the price of pens goes up, the quantity bought goes down.

Figure A2-2(d) presents a **nonlinear curve**—*a curve that is drawn as a curved line.* This curve, which really is curved, starts low on the left-hand side and goes up to the right. Economists say any curve that goes up to the right is *upward-sloping.* An upward-sloping curve represents a **direct relationship**—*a relationship in which when one variable goes up, the other goes up too.* The direct relationship I'm talking about here is the one between the two variables (what's measured on the horizontal and vertical lines). *Downward-sloping* and *upward-sloping* are terms you need to memorize if you want to read, write, and speak Graphish, keeping graphically in your mind the image of the relationships they represent.

Slope

One can, of course, be far more explicit about how much the curve is sloping upward or downward by defining it in terms of **slope**—*the change in the value on the vertical axis divided by the change in the value on the horizontal axis.* Sometimes the slope is presented as "rise over run":

$$\text{Slope} = \frac{\text{Rise}}{\text{Run}} = \frac{\text{Change in value on vertical axis}}{\text{Change in value on horizontal axis}}$$

Slopes of Linear Curves

In Figure A2-3, I present five linear curves and measures of their slopes. Let's go through an example to show how we can measure slope. To do so, we must pick two points. Let's use points *A* (6, 8) and *B* (7, 4) on curve *a.* Looking at these points, we see that as we move from 6 to 7 on the horizontal axis, we move from 8 to 4 on the vertical axis. So when the number on the vertical axis falls by 4, the number on the horizontal axis increases by 1. That means the slope is −4 divided by 1, or −4.

Notice that the inverse relationships represented by the two downward-sloping curves, *a* and *b,* have negative slopes, and that the direct relationships represented by the two upward-sloping curves, *c* and *d,* have positive slopes. Notice also that the flatter the curve, the smaller the numerical value of the slope; and the more vertical, or steeper, the curve, the larger the numerical value of the slope. There are two extreme cases:

1. When the curve is horizontal (flat), the slope is zero.

2. When the curve is vertical (straight up and down), the slope is infinite (larger than large).

Knowing the term *slope* and how it's measured lets us describe verbally the pictures we see visually. For example, if I say a curve has a slope of zero, you should picture in your mind a flat line; if I say "a curve with a slope of minus one," you should picture a falling line that makes a 45° angle with the horizontal and vertical axes. (It's the hypotenuse of an isosceles right triangle with the axes as the other two sides.)

Slopes of Nonlinear Curves

The preceding examples were of *linear* (straight) curves. With *nonlinear curves*—the ones that really do curve—the slope of the curve is constantly changing. As a result, we must talk about the slope of the curve at a particular point, rather than the slope of the whole curve. How can a point have a slope? Well, it can't really, but it can almost, and if that's good enough for mathematicians, it's good enough for us.

FIGURE A2-3 Slopes of Curves

The slope of a curve is determined by rise over run. The slope of curve *a* is shown in the graph. The rest are shown below:

	Rise	÷	Run	=	Slope
b	−1		+2		−.5
c	1		1		1
d	4		1		4
e	1		1		1

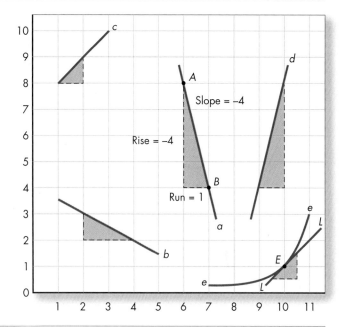

Defining the slope of a nonlinear curve is a bit more difficult. The slope at a given point on a nonlinear curve is determined by the slope of a linear (or straight) line that's tangent to that curve. (A line that's tangent to a curve is a line that just touches the curve, and touches it only at one point in the immediate vicinity of the given point.) In Figure A2-3, the line *LL* is tangent to the curve *ee* at point *E*. The slope of that line, and hence the slope of the curve at the one point where the line touches the curve, is +1.

Maximum and Minimum Points

Two points on a nonlinear curve deserve special mention. These points are the ones for which the slope of the curve is zero. I demonstrate those in Figure A2-4(a) and (b). At point *A* we're at the top of the curve, so it's at a maximum point; at point *B* we're at the bottom of the curve, so it's at a minimum point. These maximum and minimum points are often referred to by economists, and it's important to realize that the value of the slope of the curve at each of these points is zero.

There are, of course, many other types of curves, and much more can be said about the curves I've talked about. I won't do so because, for purposes of this course, we won't need to get into those refinements. I've presented as much Graphish as you need to know for this book.

FIGURE A2-4 (A AND B) A Maximum and a Minimum Point

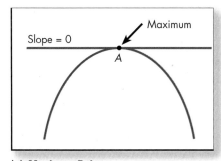

(a) Maximum Point

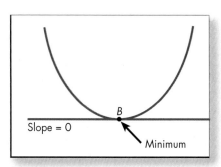

(b) Minimum Point

FIGURE A2-5 (A, B, AND C)   **A Shifting Curve versus a Movement along a Curve**

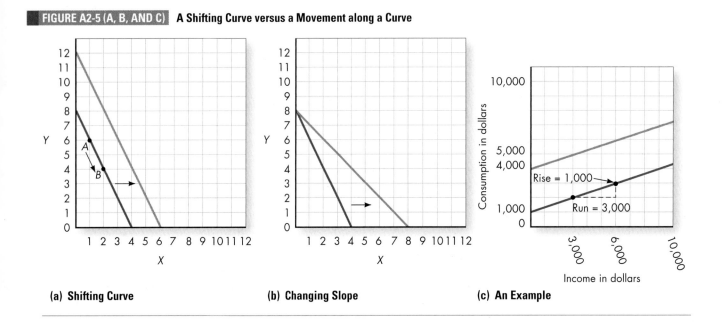

(a) **Shifting Curve**   (b) **Changing Slope**   (c) **An Example**

Equations and Graphs

Sometimes economists depict the relationships shown in graphs using equations. Since I present material algebraically in the appendixes to a few chapters, let me briefly discuss how to translate a linear curve into an equation. Linear curves are relatively easy to translate because all linear curves follow a particular mathematical form: $y = mx + b$, where y is the variable on the vertical axis, x is the variable on the horizontal axis, m is the slope of the line, and b is the vertical-axis intercept. To write the equation of a curve, look at that curve, plug in the values for the slope and vertical-axis intercept, and you've got the equation.

For example, consider the blue curve in Figure A2-5(a). The slope (rise over run) is -2 and the number where the curve intercepts the vertical axis is 8, so the equation that depicts this curve is $y = -2x + 8$. It's best to choose variables that correspond to what you're measuring on each axis, so if price is on the vertical axis and quantity is on the horizontal axis, the equation would be $p = -2q + 8$. This equation is true for any point along this line. Take point A (1, 6), for example. Substituting 1 for x and 6 for y into the equation, you see that $6 = -2(1) + 8$, or $6 = 6$. At point B, the equation is still true: $4 = -2(2) + 8$. A move from point A to point B is called a *movement along a curve*. A movement along a curve does not change the relationship of the variables; rather, it shows how a change in one variable affects the other.

Sometimes the relationship between variables will change. The curve will shift, change slope, or both shift

and change slope. These changes are reflected in changes to the m and b variables in the equation. Suppose the vertical-axis intercept rises from 8 to 12, while the slope remains the same. The equation becomes $y = -2x + 12$; for every value of y, x has increased by 4. Plotting the new equation, we can see that the curve has *shifted* to the right, as shown by the orange line in Figure A2-5(a). If instead the slope changes from -2 to -1, while the vertical-axis intercept remains at 8, the equation becomes $y = -x + 8$. Figure A2-5(b) shows this change graphically. The original blue line stays anchored at 8 and rotates out along the horizontal axis to the new orange line.

Here's an example for you to try. The lines in Figure A2-5(c) show two relationships between consumption and income. Write the equation for the blue line.

The answer is $C = \frac{1}{3}Y + \$1{,}000$. Remember, to write the equation you need to know two things: the vertical-axis intercept ($1,000) and the slope (⅓). If the intercept changes to $4,000, the curve will shift up to the orange line as shown.

Presenting Real-World Data in Graphs

The previous discussion treated the Graphish terms that economists use in presenting models that focus on hypothetical relationships. Economists also use graphs in presenting actual economic data. Say, for example, that you want to show how exports have changed over time. Then you would place years on the horizontal axis

FIGURE A2-6 (A, B, AND C) Presenting Information Visually

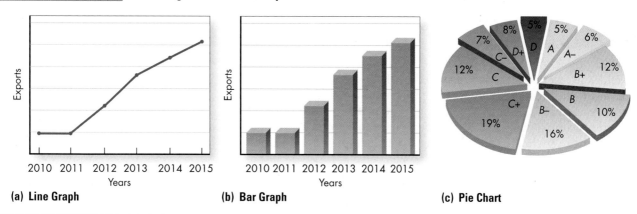

(a) Line Graph   (b) Bar Graph   (c) Pie Chart

(by convention) and exports on the vertical axis, as in Figure A2-6(a) and (b). Having done so, you have a couple of choices: you can draw a **line graph**—*a graph where the data are connected by a continuous line;* or you can make a **bar graph**—*a graph where the area under each point is filled in to look like a bar.* Figure A2-6(a) shows a line graph and Figure A2-6(b) shows a bar graph.

Another type of graph is a **pie chart**—*a circle divided into "pie pieces," where the undivided pie represents the total amount and the pie pieces reflect the percentage of the whole pie that the various components make up.* This type of graph is useful in visually presenting how a total amount is divided. Figure A2-6(c) shows a pie chart, which happens to represent the division of grades on a test I gave. Notice that 5 percent of the students got As.

There are other types of graphs, but they're all variations on line and bar graphs and pie charts. Once you understand these three basic types of graphs, you shouldn't have any trouble understanding the other types.

Interpreting Graphs about the Real World

Understanding Graphish is important because, if you don't, you can easily misinterpret the meaning of graphs. For example, consider the two graphs in Figure A2-7(a) and (b). Which graph demonstrates the larger rise in income? If you said (a), you're wrong. The intervals in the vertical axes differ, and if you look carefully you'll see that the curves in both graphs represent the same combination of points. So when considering graphs,

FIGURE A2-7 (A AND B) The Importance of Scales

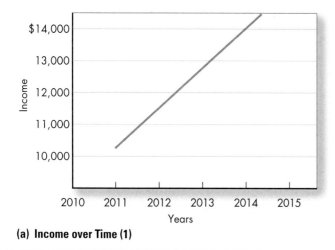

(a) Income over Time (1)

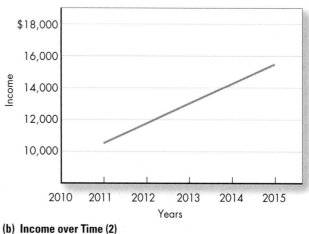

(b) Income over Time (2)

always make sure you understand the markings on the axes. Only then can you interpret the graph.

Quantitative Literacy: Avoiding Stupid Math Mistakes

The data of economics are often presented in graphs and tables. Numerical data are compared by the use of percentages, visual comparisons, and simple relationships based on quantitative differences. Economists who have studied the learning process of their students have found that some very bright students have some trouble with these presentations. Students sometimes mix up percentage changes with level changes, draw incorrect implications from visual comparisons, and calculate quantitative differences incorrectly. This is not necessarily a math problem—at least in the sense that most economists think of math. The mistakes are in relatively simple stuff—the kind of stuff learned in fifth, sixth, and seventh grades. Specifically, as reported in "Student Quantitative Literacy: Is the Glass Half-full or Half-empty?" (Robert Burns, Kim Marie McGoldrick, Jerry L. Petr, and Peter Schuhmann, 2002 University of North Carolina at Wilmington Working Paper), when the professors gave a test to students at a variety of schools, they found that a majority of students missed the following questions.

1. What is 25 percent of 400?
   a. 25   b. 50   c. 100
   d. 400   e. none of the above

2. Consider Figure A2-8, where U.S. oil consumption and U.S. oil imports are plotted for 1990–2000. Fill in the blanks to construct a true statement: U.S. domestic oil consumption has been steady while imports have been _____; therefore U.S. domestic oil production has been _____.
   a. rising; rising   b. falling; falling
   c. rising; falling   d. falling; rising

3. Refer to the following table to select the true statement.

Economic Growth in Poland Percent Increase in GDP, 1990–1994				
1990	1991	1992	1993	1994
−11.7	−7.8	−1.5	4.0	3.5

   a. GDP in Poland was larger in 1992 than in 1991.
   b. GDP in Poland was larger in 1994 than in 1993.
   c. GDP in Poland was larger in 1991 than in 1992.
   d. GDP in Poland was larger in 1993 than in 1994.
   e. Both b and c are true.

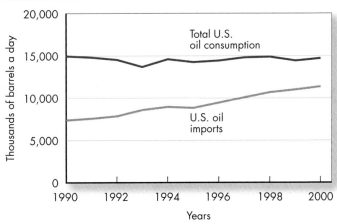

FIGURE A2-8

4. If U.S. production of corn was 60 million bushels in 2002 and 100 million bushels in 2003, what was the percentage change in corn production from 2002 to 2003?
   a. 40   b. 60   c. 66.67
   d. 100   e. 200

The reason students got these questions wrong is unknown. Many of them had had higher-level math courses, including calculus, so it is not that they weren't trained in math. I suspect that many students missed the questions because of carelessness: the students didn't think about the question carefully before they wrote down the answer.

Throughout this book we will be discussing issues assuming a quantitative literacy sufficient to answer these questions. Moreover, questions using similar reasoning will be on exams. So it is useful for you to see whether or not you fall in the majority. So please answer the four questions given above now if you haven't done so already.

Now that you've answered them, I give you the correct answers upside-down in the footnote at the bottom of the page.[1]

If you got all four questions right, great! You can stop reading this appendix now. If you missed one or more, read the explanations of the correct answers carefully.

1. The correct answer is c. To calculate a percentage, you multiply the percentage times the number. Thus, 25 percent of 400 is 100.

2. The correct answer is c. To answer it you had to recognize that U.S. consumption of oil comes from

---

1-c; 2-c; 3-e; 4-c.

U.S. imports and U.S. production. Thus, the distance between the two lines represents U.S. production, which is clearly getting smaller from 1990 to 2000.

3. The correct answer is e. The numbers given to you are percentage changes, and the question is about levels. If the percentage change is positive, as it is in 1993 and 1994, the level is increasing. Thus, 1994 is greater (by 3.5 percent) than 1993, even though the percentage change is smaller than in 1993. If the percentage change is negative, as it is in 1992, the level is falling. Because income fell in 1992, the level of income in 1991 is greater than the level of income in 1992.

4. The correct answer is c. To calculate percentage change, you first need to calculate the change, which in this case is $100 - 60$, or 40. So corn production started at a base of 60 and rose by 40. To calculate the percentage change that this represents, you divide the amount of the rise, 40, by the base, 60. Doing so gives us $40/60 = 2/3 = .6667$, which is 66.67 percent.

Now that I've given you the answers, I suspect that most of you will recognize that they are the right answers. If, after reading the explanations, you still don't follow the reasoning, you should look into getting some extra help in the course either from your teacher, from your TA, or from some program the college has. If, after reading the explanations, you follow them and believe that if you had really thought about them you would have gotten them right, then the next time you see a chart or a table of numbers being compared *really think about them*. Be a bit slower in drawing inferences since they are the building blocks of economic discussions. If you want to do well on exams, it probably makes sense to practice some similar questions to make sure that you have concepts down.

A Review

Let's now review what we've covered.

- A graph is a picture of points on a coordinate system in which the points denote relationships between numbers.
- A downward-sloping line represents an inverse relationship or a negative slope.
- An upward-sloping line represents a direct relationship or a positive slope.
- Slope is measured by rise over run, or a change of y (the number measured on the vertical axis) over a change in x (the number measured on the horizontal axis).
- The slope of a point on a nonlinear curve is measured by the rise over the run of a line tangent to that point.
- At the maximum and minimum points of a nonlinear curve, the value of the slope is zero.
- A linear curve has the form $y = mx + b$.
- A shift in a linear curve is reflected by a change in the b variable in the equation $y = mx + b$.
- A change in the slope of a linear curve is reflected by a change in the m variable in the equation $y = mx + b$.
- In reading graphs, one must be careful to understand what's being measured on the vertical and horizontal axes.

Key Terms

bar graph *(47)*	graph *(42)*	inverse relationship *(44)*	nonlinear curve *(44)*
coordinate system *(42)*	interpolation	line graph *(47)*	pie chart *(47)*
direct relationship *(44)*	assumption *(44)*	linear curve *(44)*	slope *(44)*

Questions and Exercises

1. Create a coordinate space on graph paper and label the following points:
   a. $(0, 5)$ b. $(-5, -5)$
   c. $(2, -3)$ d. $(-1, 1)$

2. Graph the following costs per unit, and answer the questions that follow.

Horizontal Axis: Output	Vertical Axis: Cost per Unit
1	$30
2	20
3	12
4	6
5	2
6	6
7	12
8	20
9	30

a. Is the relationship between cost per unit and output linear or nonlinear? Why?
b. In what range in output is the relationship inverse? In what range in output is the relationship direct?
c. In what range in output is the slope negative? In what range in output is the slope positive?
d. What is the slope between 1 and 2 units?

3. Within a coordinate space, draw a line with
   a. Zero slope.   b. Infinite slope.
   c. Positive slope.   d. Negative slope.

4. Calculate the slope of lines a through e in the following coordinate system.

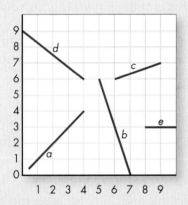

5. Given the following nonlinear curve, answer the following questions:

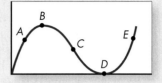

a. At what point(s) is the slope negative?
b. At what point(s) is the slope positive?
c. At what point(s) is the slope zero?
d. What point is the maximum? What point is the minimum?

6. Draw the graphs that correspond to the following equations:
   a. $y = 3x - 8$
   b. $y = 12 - x$
   c. $y = 4x + 2$

7. Using the equation $y = 3x + 1,000$, demonstrate the following:
   a. The slope of the curve changes to 5.
   b. The curve shifts up by 500.

8. State what type of graph or chart you might use to show the following real-world data:
   a. Interest rates from 1929 to 2013.
   b. Median income levels of various ethnic groups in the United States.
   c. Total federal expenditures by selected categories.
   d. Total costs of producing between 100 and 800 shoes.

chapter 3

Economic Institutions

> *Nobody can be a great economist who is only an economist—and I am even tempted to add that the economist who is only an economist is likely to become a nuisance if not a positive danger.*
>
> —Friedrich Hayek

The powerful U.S. economy generates a high standard of living and sense of economic well-being (compared to most other countries) for almost all those living in the United States. The reason why is often attributed to its use of markets, and to the wonders of a market economy. To some degree, that's true, but simply saying markets are the reason for the strength of the U.S. economy obscures as much information as it conveys. First, it misses the point that other countries have markets too, but many of those have much lower standards of living. Second, it conveys a sense that markets exist independently of social and cultural institutions, and that's just not correct. Markets are highly developed social constructs that are part of a country's social and economic institutions. Markets are based on **institutions,** which Nobel Prize–winning economist Douglass North defines as *"the formal and informal rules that constrain human economic behavior."* Institutions include laws that protect ownership of property and the legal system to enforce and interpret laws. They also include political institutions that develop those laws, the cultural traits of society that guide people's tastes and behaviors, and the many organizational structures such as corporations, banks, and nonprofit organizations that make up our economy. To understand markets, you need to understand institutions. In a principles course, we don't have time to develop a full analysis of institutions, but what we can do is to provide an overview of U.S. economic institutions and a brief discussion of why they are important. That's what we do in this chapter.

We begin by looking at the U.S. economic system in historical perspective, considering how it evolved and how it relates to other historical economic systems. Then we consider some of the central institutions of the modern U.S. economy and how they influence the way in which the economy works.

After reading this chapter, you should be able to:

LO3-1 Define *market economy* and compare and contrast socialism with capitalism.

LO3-2 Describe the role of businesses and households in a market economy.

LO3-3 List and discuss the various roles of government.

LO3-4 Explain why global policy issues differ from national policy issues.

Economic Systems

A market economy is an economic
system based on private property and
the market. It gives private property
rights to individuals and relies on
market forces to coordinate
economic activity.

The U.S. economy is a **market economy**—*an economic system based on private property and the market in which, in principle, individuals decide how, what, and for whom to produce.* In a market economy, individuals follow their own self-interest, while market forces of supply and demand are relied on to coordinate those individual pursuits. Businesses, guided by prices in the market, produce goods and services that they believe people want and that will earn a profit for the business. Prices in the market guide businesses in deciding what to produce. Distribution of goods is to each individual according to his or her ability, effort, inherited property, and luck.

Reliance on market forces doesn't mean that political, social, and historical forces play no role in coordinating economic decisions. These other forces do influence how the market works. For example, for a market to exist, government must allocate and defend **private property rights**—*the control a private individual or firm has over an asset.* The concept of private ownership must exist and must be accepted by individuals in society. When you say "This car is mine," you mean that it is unlawful for someone else to take it without your permission. If someone takes it without your permission, he or she is subject to punishment through the legal system.

Q-1 John, your study partner, is
telling you that the best way to
allocate property rights is through the
market. How do you respond?

How Markets Work

Markets work through a system of rewards and payments. If you do something, you get paid for doing that something; if you take something, you pay for that something. How much you get is determined by how much you give. This relationship seems fair to most people. But there are instances when it doesn't seem fair. Say someone is unable to work. Should that person get nothing? How about Joe down the street, who was given $10 million by his parents? Is it fair that he gets lots of toys, like Corvettes and skiing trips to Aspen, and doesn't have to work, while the rest of us have to work 40 hours a week and maybe go to school at night?

I'll put those questions about fairness off at this point—they are very difficult questions. For now, all I want to present is the concept of fairness that underlies a market economy: "Them that works, gets; them that don't, starve."[1] In a market economy, individuals are encouraged to follow their own self-interest.

In market economies, individuals are free to do whatever they want as long as it's legal. The market is relied on to see that what people want to get, and want to do, is consistent with what's available. Price is the mechanism through which people's desires are coordinated and goods are rationed. If there's not enough of something to go around, its price goes up; if more of something needs to get done, the price given to individuals willing to do it goes up. If something isn't wanted or doesn't need to be done, its price goes down. In a market economy, fluctuations in prices play a central role in coordinating individuals' wants.

Fluctuations in prices play a central
role in coordinating individuals' wants
in a market economy.

---

[1] How come the professor gets to use rotten grammar but screams when he sees rotten grammar in your papers? Well, that's fairness for you. Actually, I should say a bit more about writing style. All writers are expected to know correct grammar; if they don't, they don't deserve to be called writers. Once you know grammar, you can individualize your writing style, breaking the rules of grammar where the meter and flow of the writing require it. In college you're still proving that you know grammar, so in papers handed in to your teacher, you shouldn't break the rules of grammar until you've proved to the teacher that you know them. Me, I've done lots of books, so my editors give me a bit more leeway than your teachers will give you.

What's Good about the Market?

Is the market a good way to coordinate individuals' activities? Much of this book will be devoted to answering that question. The answer that I, and most U.S. economists, come to is: Yes, it is a reasonable way. True, it has problems; the market can be unfair, mean, and arbitrary, and sometimes it is downright awful. Why then do economists support it? For the same reason that Oliver Wendell Holmes supported democracy—it is a lousy system, but, based on experience with alternatives, it is better than all the others we've thought of.

The primary debate among economists is not about using markets; it is about how markets should be structured, and whether they should be modified and adjusted by government regulation. Those are much harder questions, and on these questions, opinions differ enormously.

Web Note 3.1
What Are Markets?

The primary debate among economists is not about using markets but about how markets are structured.

Capitalism and Socialism

The view that markets are a reasonable way to organize society has not always been shared by all economists. Throughout history strong philosophical and practical arguments have been made against markets. The philosophical argument against the market is that it brings out the worst in people—it glorifies greed. It encourages people to beat out others rather than to be cooperative. As an alternative some economists have supported socialism. In theory, **socialism** is *an economic system based on individuals' goodwill toward others, not on their own self-interest, and in which, in principle, society decides what, how, and for whom to produce.* The concept of socialism developed in the 1800s as a description of a hypothetical economic system to be contrasted with the predominant market-based economic system of the time, which was called capitalism. **Capitalism** is defined as *an economic system based on the market in which the ownership of the means of production resides with a small group of individuals called capitalists.*

You can best understand the idea behind theoretical socialism by thinking about how decisions are made in a family. In most families, benevolent parents decide who gets what, based on the needs of each member of the family. When Sabin gets a new coat and his sister Sally doesn't, it's because Sabin needs a coat while Sally already has two coats that fit her and are in good condition. Victor may be slow as molasses, but from his family he still gets as much as his superefficient brother Jerry gets. In fact, Victor may get more than Jerry because he needs extra help.

Markets have little role in most families. In my family, when food is placed on the table, we don't bid on what we want, with the highest bidder getting the food. In my family, every person can eat all he or she wants, although if one child eats more than a fair share, that child gets a lecture from me on the importance of sharing. "Be thoughtful; be considerate. Think of others first" are lessons that many families try to teach.

In theory, socialism was an economic system that tried to organize society in the same way as most families are organized, trying to see that individuals get what they need. Socialism tried to take other people's needs into account and adjust people's own wants in accordance with what's available. In socialist economies, individuals were urged to look out for the other person; if individuals' inherent goodness does not make them consider the general good, government would make them. In contrast, a capitalist economy expected people to be selfish; it relied on markets and competition to direct that selfishness to the general good.[2]

Q-2 Which would be more likely to attempt to foster individualism: socialism or capitalism?

Q-3 Are there any activities in a family that you believe should be allocated by a market? What characteristics do those activities have?

Socialism is, in theory, an economic system that tries to organize society in the same way as most families are organized—all people contribute what they can and get what they need.

---

[2]As you probably surmised, the above distinction is too sharp. Even capitalist societies wanted people to be selfless, but not too selfless. Children in capitalist societies were generally taught to be selfless at least in dealing with friends and family. The difficulty parents and societies face is finding a balance between the two positions: selfless but not too selfless; selfish but not too selfish.

Tradition and Today's Economy

In a tradition-based society, the social and cultural forces create an inertia (a tendency to resist change) that predominates over economic and political forces.

"Why did you do it that way?"

"Because that's the way we've always done it."

Tradition-based societies had markets, but they were peripheral, not central, to economic life. In feudal times, what was produced, how it was produced, and for whom it was produced were primarily decided by tradition.

In today's U.S. economy, the market plays the central role in economic decisions. But that doesn't mean that tradition is dead. As I said in Chapter 1, tradition still plays a significant role in today's society, and, in many aspects of society, tradition still overwhelms the invisible hand. Consider the following:

1. The persistent view that women should be homemakers rather than factory workers, consumers rather than producers.

2. The raised eyebrows when a man is introduced as a nurse, secretary, homemaker, or member of any other profession conventionally identified as women's work.

3. Society's unwillingness to permit the sale of individuals or body organs.

4. Parents' willingness to care for their children without financial compensation.

Each of these tendencies reflects tradition's influence in Western society. Some are so deeply rooted that we see them as self-evident. Some of tradition's effects we like; others we don't—but we often take them for granted. Economic forces may work against these traditions, but the fact that they're still around indicates the continued strength of tradition in our market economy.

As I stated above, the term *socialism* originally developed as a description of a hypothetical, not an actual, economic system. Actual socialist economies came into being only in the early 1900s, and when they developed they differed enormously from the hypothetical socialist economies that writers had described earlier.

Q-4 What is the difference between socialism in theory and socialism in practice?

In practice socialist governments had to take a strong role in guiding the economy. Socialism became known as an economic system based on government ownership of the means of production, with economic activity governed by central planning. In a centrally planned socialist economy, sometimes called a command economy, government planning boards set society's goals and then directed individuals and firms as to how to achieve those goals.

For example, if government planning boards decided that whole-wheat bread was good for people, they directed firms to produce large quantities and priced it exceptionally low. Planners, not prices, coordinated people's actions. The results were often not quite what the planners desired. Bread prices were so low that pig farmers fed bread to their pigs even though pig feed would have been better for the pigs and bread was more costly to produce. At the low price, the quantity of bread demanded was so high that there were bread shortages; consumers had to stand in long lines to buy bread for their families.

As is often the case, over time the meaning of the word *socialism* expanded and evolved further. It was used to describe the market economies of Western Europe, which by the 1960s had evolved into economies that had major welfare support systems and governments that were very much involved in their market economies. For example, Sweden, even though it relied on markets as its central coordinating institution, was called a socialist economy because its taxes were high and it provided a cradle-to-grave welfare system.

When the Union of Soviet Socialist Republics (USSR) broke apart, Russia and the countries that evolved out of the USSR adopted a market economy as their organizing framework. China, which is ruled by the Communist Party, also adopted many market institutions. As they did, the terms *capitalism* and *socialism* fell out of favor. People today talk little about the differences in economic systems such as capitalism and socialism; instead they talk about the differences in institutions. Most economies today are differentiated primarily by the degree to which their economies rely on markets, not whether they are a market, capitalist, or socialist economy.

People today talk little about differences in economic systems; instead they talk about differences in institutions.

The term *socialism,* however, still shows up in the news. China, for example, continues to call itself a socialist country, even though it is relying more and more heavily on markets to organize production, and is sometimes seen as more capitalistic than many Western economies. Another example of the interest in socialism can be found in the rhetoric of Venezuelan President Hugo Chávez, who is attempting to transform Venezuela into what he calls "21st century socialism." He defines 21st century socialism as government ownership, or at least control, of major resources, and an economy dominated by business cooperatives owned and operated by workers supported by government loans and contracts. President Chávez argues that this "21st century socialism" will serve as a new economic model of egalitarianism for the entire world. Most observers are doubtful. But what is likely is that economic systems and the institutions that make them up are constantly evolving, and will likely continue to evolve.[3]

Revolutionary shifts that give rise to new economic systems are not the only way economic systems change. Systems also evolve internally, as I discussed above. For example, the U.S. economy is and has always been a market economy, but it has changed over the years, evolving with changes in social customs, political forces, and the strength of markets. In the 1930s, during the Great Depression, the U.S. economy integrated a number of what might be called socialist institutions into its existing institutions. Distribution of goods was no longer, even in theory, only according to ability; need also played a role. Governments began to play a larger role in the economy, taking control over some of the *how, what,* and *for whom* decisions. From the 1980s until recently the process has been reversed. The United States became even more market oriented and the government tried to pull back its involvement in the market in favor of private enterprise. That movement slowed, and possibly ended, with the financial crisis of 2007. Which direction the future will take remains to be seen, but we can expect institutions to continue to change.

Economic Institutions in a Market Economy

Now that we have put the U.S. economic system in historical perspective, let's consider some of its main components. The U.S. economy can be divided into three sectors: businesses, households, and government, as Figure 3-1 shows. Households supply labor and other factors of production to businesses and are paid by businesses for doing so. The market where this interaction takes place is called a *factor market.* Businesses produce goods and services and sell them to households and government. The market where this interaction takes place is called the *goods market.*

Q-5 Into what three sectors are market economies generally broken up?

Each of the three sectors is interconnected; moreover, the entire U.S. economy is interconnected with the world economy. Notice also the arrows going out to and coming in from both business and households. Those arrows represent the connection of an

---

[3]The appendix to this chapter traces the development of economic systems.

FIGURE 3-1   **Diagrammatic Representation of a Market Economy**

This circular-flow diagram of the economy is a good way to organize your thinking about the aggregate economy. As you can see, the three sectors—households, government, and business—interact in a variety of ways.

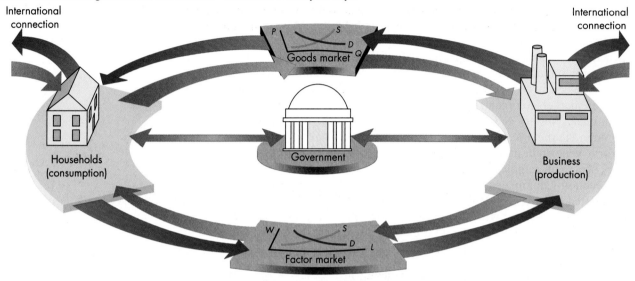

economy to the world economy. It consists of interrelated flows of goods (exports and imports) and money (capital flows). Finally, consider the arrows connecting government with households and business. Government taxes business and households. It buys goods and services from business and buys labor services from households. Then, with some of its tax revenue, it provides services (for example, roads, education) to both business and households and gives some of its tax revenue directly back to individuals. In doing so, it redistributes income. But government also serves a second function. It oversees the interaction of business and households in the goods and factor markets. Government, of course, is not independent. The United States, for instance, is a democracy, so households vote to determine who shall govern. Similarly, governments are limited not only by what voters want but also by their relationships with other countries. They are part of an international community of countries, and they must keep up relations with other countries in the world. For example, the United States is a member of many international organizations and has signed international treaties in which it has agreed to limit its domestic actions, such as its ability to tax imports.

Now let's look briefly at the individual components.

Business

www   **Web Note 3.2**
         Starting a Business

President Calvin Coolidge once said "The business of America is business." That's a bit of an overstatement, but business is responsible for over 80 percent of U.S. production. (Government is responsible for the other 20 percent.) In fact, anytime a household decides to produce something, it becomes a business. **Business** is simply the name given to *private producing units in our society.*

Businesses in the United States decide *what* to produce, *how* much to produce, and *for whom* to produce it.

Businesses in the United States decide *what* to produce, *how* much to produce, and *for whom* to produce it. They make these central economic decisions on the basis of their own self-interest, which is influenced by market incentives. Anyone who wants to can start a business, provided he or she can come up with the required cash and meet the necessary regulatory requirements. Each year, about 600,000 businesses are started.

Don't think of business as something other than people. Businesses are ultimately made up of a group of people organized together to accomplish some end. Although corporations account for about 80 percent of all sales, in terms of numbers of businesses, most are one- or two-person operations. Home-based businesses are easy to start. All you have to do is say you're in business, and you are. However, some businesses require licenses, permits, and approvals from various government agencies. That's one reason why **entrepreneurship** (*the ability to organize and get something done*) is an important part of business.

Entrepreneurship is an important part of business.

WHAT DO U.S. FIRMS PRODUCE?   Producing physical goods is only one of society's economic tasks. Another task is to provide services (activities done for others). Services do not involve producing a physical good. When you get your hair cut, you buy a service, not a good. Much of the cost of the physical goods we buy actually is not a cost of producing the good, but is a cost of one of the most important services: distribution, which includes payments associated with having the good where you want it when you want it. After a good is produced, it has to be transported to consumers, either indirectly through retailers or directly to consumers. If the good isn't at the right place at the right time, it can often be useless.

Let's consider an example: hot dogs at a baseball game. How many of us have been irked that a hot dog that costs 40 cents to fix at home costs $5.00 at a baseball game? The reason why the price can differ so much is that a hot dog at home isn't the same as a hot dog at a game and you are willing to pay the extra $4.60 to have the hot dog when and where you want it. *Distribution*—getting goods where you want them when you want them—is as important as production and is a central component of a service economy.

The importance of the service economy can be seen in modern technology companies. They provide information and methods of handling information, not physical goods. Google and Facebook produce no physical product but they provide central services to our lives. As the U.S. economy has evolved, the relative importance of services has increased. Today, services make up approximately 80 percent of the U.S. economy, compared to 20 percent in 1947, and services are likely to continue to rise in importance in the future.

CONSUMER SOVEREIGNTY AND BUSINESS   To say that businesses decide what to produce isn't to say that **consumer sovereignty** (*the consumer's wishes determine what's produced*) doesn't reign in the United States. Businesses decide what to produce based on what they believe will sell. A key question a person in the United States generally asks about starting a business is: Can I make a profit from it? **Profit** is *what's left over from total revenues after all the appropriate costs have been subtracted.* Businesses that guess correctly what the consumer wants generally make a profit. Businesses that guess wrong generally operate at a loss.

Although businesses decide what to produce, they are guided by consumer sovereignty.

People are free to start businesses for whatever purposes they want. No one asks them: "What's the social value of your term paper assistance business, your Twinkies business, your pornography business, or your textbook publishing business?" In the United States we rely on the market to channel individuals' desire to make a profit into the general good of society. That's the invisible hand at work. As long as the business violates no law and conforms to regulations, people

Q-6 True or false? In the United States, the invisible hand ensures that only socially valuable businesses are started. Why?

FIGURE 3-2 (A AND B)   Forms of Business

The charts divide firms by the type of ownership. Approximately 72 percent of businesses in the United States are sole proprietorships (**a**). In terms of annual receipts, however, corporations surpass all other forms (**b**).

Source: *Statistics of Income,* IRS, Summer 2011 (www.irs.ustreas.gov/taxstats).

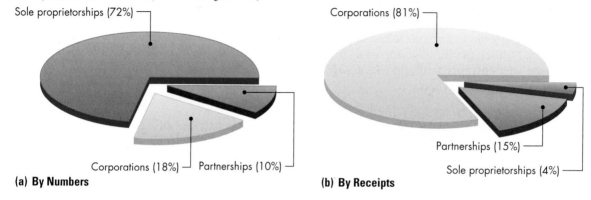

(a) By Numbers   **(b) By Receipts**

Sole proprietorships (72%)
Corporations (18%)   Partnerships (10%)

Corporations (81%)
Partnerships (15%)
Sole proprietorships (4%)

in the United States are free to start whatever business they want, if they can get the money to finance it.

Q-7 Are most businesses in the United States corporations? If not, what are most businesses?

FORMS OF BUSINESS   The three primary forms of business are sole proprietorships, partnerships, and corporations. **Sole proprietorships**—*businesses that have only one owner*—are the easiest to start and have the fewest bureaucratic hassles. **Partnerships**—*businesses with two or more owners*—create possibilities for sharing the burden, but they also create unlimited liability for each of the partners. **Corporations**—*businesses that are treated as a person, and are legally owned by their stockholders, who are not liable for the actions of the corporate "person"*—are the largest form of business when measured in terms of receipts. In corporations, ownership is separated from control of the firm. Of the 35 million businesses in the United States, approximately 72 percent are sole proprietorships, 10 percent are partnerships, and 18 percent are corporations, as we see in Figure 3-2(a). In terms of total receipts, however, we get a quite different picture, with corporations far surpassing all other business forms, as Figure 3-2(b) shows.[4]

A corporation provides the owner with limited liability.

In the past few years a number of companies—what might be *called flexible-purpose corporations or benefit corporations (B-corporations)*—have arisen that explicitly take social mission in addition to profit into consideration when making decisions. An example is Maine's Own Organic Milk Company (MOO Milk Co), which has both selling milk and educating the public about the value of local family farming as explicit goals. Some states have established a new form of corporation—the L3C, which allows companies, such as MOO Milk Co, to blend social and private goals. Unlike for-profit companies, L3Cs can receive grants and endowments otherwise reserved for nonprofits. Other companies, such as Google, are retaining their for-profit corporate status but are explicitly including social welfare in their charters.

---

[4]As laws have evolved, the sharp distinctions among forms of businesses have blurred. Today there are many types of corporations and types of partnerships that have varying degrees of limited liabilities.

The advantages and disadvantages of each form of business are summarized in the following table:

Advantages and Disadvantages of Various Forms of For-Profit Businesses

	Sole Proprietorship	Partnership	Corporation
Advantages	1. Minimum bureaucratic hassle 2. Direct control by owner	1. Ability to share work and risks 2. Relatively easy to form	1. No personal liability 2. Increasing ability to get funds 3. Ability to avoid personal income taxes
Disadvantages	1. Limited ability to get funds 2. Unlimited personal liability	1. Unlimited personal liability (even for partner's blunder) 2. Limited ability to get funds	1. Legal hassle to organize 2. Possible double taxation of income 3. Monitoring problems

FINANCE AND BUSINESS   Much of what you hear in the news about business concerns financial assets—assets that acquire value from an obligation of someone else to pay. Stocks are one example of a financial asset; bonds are another. Financial assets are traded in markets such as the New York Stock Exchange. Trading in financial markets can make people rich (or poor) quickly. Stocks and bonds also can provide a means through which corporations can finance expansions and new investments.

Trading in financial markets can make people rich (or poor) quickly.

An important tool investors use to decide where to invest is the accounting statements firms provide. From these, individuals judge how profitable firms are, and how profitable they are likely to be in the future. In the early 2000s, investors' trust in firms was shattered by a series of accounting frauds, which led government to increase the regulatory control of business accounting practices.

Households

The second classification we'll consider in this overview of U.S. economic institutions is households. **Households** (*groups of individuals living together and making joint decisions*) are the most powerful economic institution. They ultimately control government and business, the other two economic institutions. Households' votes in the political arena determine government policy; their decisions about supplying labor and capital determine what businesses will have available to work with; and their spending decisions or expenditures (the "votes" they cast with their dollars) determine what business will be able to sell.

In the economy, households vote with their dollars.

THE POWER OF HOUSEHOLDS   While the ultimate power does in principle reside with the people and households, we, the people, have assigned much of that power to representatives. As I discussed above, corporations are only partially responsive to owners of their stocks, and much of that ownership is once-removed from individuals. Ownership of 1,000 shares in a company with a total of 2 million shares isn't going to get you any influence over the corporation's activities. As a stockholder, you simply accept what the corporation does.

Who Are the 1%?

The differences between the very rich and everyone else has come to the fore with the Occupy movement. The slogan "We are the 99%" pits most people against the 1%. Who are the 1%?

When presidential candidate Mitt Romney was asked about his income in 2012, he declined to answer, but he did note that in 2011 he got speakers' fees from time to time, but that they were "not very much." Elsewhere he had listed those "not very much" speaker fees—they totaled $375,000. When you can say that $375,000 is not very much, you are definitely part of the 1%. In fact, that "not very much" alone would have almost put him in the top 1%, since a household's income needs to be at least $383,000 to be in the top 1%. That's approximately eight times the median income. $188,000 puts you in the top 5% while $90,000 put you in the top 25%.

Those numbers are an average for the country as a whole. The threshold differs a lot by state. In Flint, Michigan, $180,000 would put you in the top 1% but in the New York City area that's only the top 10%. In Stamford, Connecticut, you'd have to earn about $900,000 to be in the top 1%.

This top 1% earns about 20% of total pretax income in the United States and pays about 25% of all federal taxes. Forty percent of them inherited money as well as earning it, and they are twice as likely to be married, in part because that gives them two incomes, and in part because they are good "marriage material." They don't have more cars than middle-class, but they do tend to drive ritzier cars—you see lots of Lexus's and Mercedes's in Naples, Florida. You see a lot more clunkers in Flint.

When thinking about the 1%, it is important to realize that one can consume only so much "stuff." Capitalism may create inequalities but it also can improve the life of the poor. As economist, Joseph Schumpeter pointed out: "Electric lighting is no great boon to anyone who has money enough to buy a sufficient number of candles and to pay servants to attend them. It is the cheap cloth, the cheap cotton and rayon fabric, boots, motorcars and so on that are the typical achievements of capitalist production, and not as a rule improvements that would mean much to a rich man. Queen Elizabeth owned silk stockings. The capitalist achievement does not typically consist in providing more silk stockings for queens but in bringing them within the reach of factory girls in return for steadily decreasing amounts of effort."

A major decision that corporations make independently of their stockholders concerns what to produce. True, ultimately we, the people, decide whether we will buy what business produces, but business spends a lot of money telling us what services we want, what products make us "with it," what books we want to read, and the like. Most economists believe that consumer sovereignty reigns—that we are not fooled or controlled by advertising. Still, it is an open question in some economists' minds whether we, the people, control business or whether the business representatives control the people.

Because of this assignment of power to other institutions, in many spheres of the economy households are not active producers of output but merely passive recipients of income, primarily in their role as suppliers of labor.

Consumer sovereignty reigns, but it works indirectly by influencing businesses.

SUPPLIERS OF LABOR The largest source of household income is wages and salaries (the income households get from labor). Households supply the labor with which businesses produce and government governs. The total U.S. labor force is about 155 million people, about 8 percent of whom were unemployed in 2012. The average U.S. workweek is about 41 hours for males and about 36 hours for females. The median pay in the United States was $850 per week for males and $700 for females. The median hourly wage for all workers is about $16.50. Of course, that average represents enormous variability and depends on the occupation and region of the country where one is employed. For example, lawyers often earn $100,000 per year; physicians earn about $190,000 per year; and CEOs of large corporations often make $2 million per year or more. A beginning McDonald's employee generally makes about $13,000 per year.

The Roles of Government

The third major U.S. economic institution I'll consider is government. Government plays two general roles in the economy. It's both a referee (setting the rules that determine relations between business and households) and an actor (collecting money in taxes and spending that money on projects such as defense and education). Let's first consider government's role as an actor.

Government as an Actor

The United States has a federal government system, which means we have various levels of government (federal, state, and local), each with its own powers. Together they consume about 20 percent of the country's total output and employ about 22 million individuals. The various levels of government also have a number of programs that redistribute income through taxation and social welfare and assistance programs designed to help specific groups.

State and local governments employ over 19 million people and spend about $2.1 trillion a year. As you can see in Figure 3-3(a), state and local governments get much of their income from taxes: property taxes, sales taxes, and state and local income taxes. They spend their tax revenues on public welfare, administration, education (education through high school is available free in U.S. public schools), and transportation, as Figure 3-3(b) shows.

Probably the best way to get an initial feel for the federal government and its size is to look at the various categories of its tax revenues and expenditures in Figure 3-4(a). Notice income taxes make up about 42 percent of the federal government's revenue, and Social Security taxes make up about 35 percent. That's about 80 percent of the federal government's revenues, most of which show up as a deduction from your paycheck. In Figure 3-4(b), notice that the federal government's two largest categories of spending are income security and health and education, with expenditures on national defense close behind.

Web Note 3.3
Government Websites

Q-8 The largest percentage of federal expenditures is in what general category?

FIGURE 3-3 (A AND B)   **Income and Expenditures of State and Local Governments**

The charts give you a sense of the importance of state and local governments—where they get (**a**) and where they spend (**b**) their revenues.

Source: *State and Local Government Finance Estimates,* Bureau of the Census (www.census.gov).

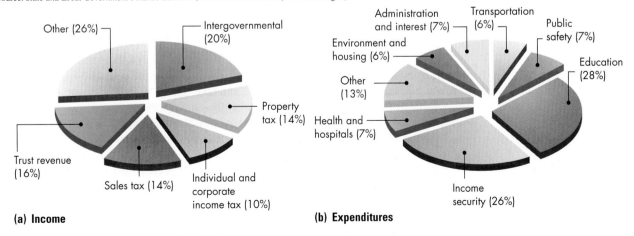

(a) **Income**

Other (26%)
Intergovernmental (20%)
Property tax (14%)
Individual and corporate income tax (10%)
Sales tax (14%)
Trust revenue (16%)

(b) **Expenditures**

Administration and interest (7%)
Transportation (6%)
Public safety (7%)
Environment and housing (6%)
Education (28%)
Other (13%)
Health and hospitals (7%)
Income security (26%)

FIGURE 3-4 (A AND B)   Income and Expenditures of the Federal Government

The pie charts show the sources and uses of federal government revenue. It is important to note that, when the government runs a deficit, expenditures exceed income and the difference is made up by borrowing, so the size of the income and expenditure pies may not be equal. In recent years expenditures have significantly exceeded income.

Source: *Survey of Current Business,* Bureau of Economic Analysis (www.bea.doc.gov).

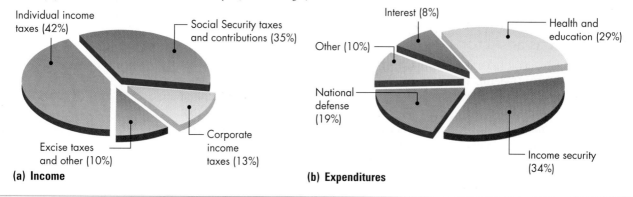

(a) Income

(b) Expenditures

Government as a Referee

Even if government spending made up only a small proportion of total expenditures, government would still be central to the study of economics. The reason is that, in a market economy, government sets the rules of interaction between households and businesses, and acts as a referee, enforcing the rules and changing them when it sees fit. Government decides whether economic forces will be allowed to operate freely.

Some examples of U.S. laws regulating the interaction between households and businesses today are:

1. Businesses are not free to hire and fire whomever they want. They must comply with equal opportunity and labor laws. Even closing a plant requires 60 days' notice for many kinds of firms.

2. Many working conditions are subject to government regulation: safety rules, wage rules, overtime rules, hours-of-work rules, and the like.

3. Businesses cannot meet with other businesses to agree on prices they will charge.

4. In some businesses, workers must join a union to work at certain jobs.

Most of these laws evolved over time. Up until the 1930s, household members, in their roles as workers and consumers, had few rights. Businesses were free to hire and fire at will and, if they chose, to deceive and take advantage of consumers.

Over time, new laws to curb business abuses have been passed, and government agencies have been formed to enforce these laws. Some people think the pendulum has swung too far the other way. They believe businesses are saddled with too many regulatory burdens.

One big question that I'll address throughout this book is: What referee role should the government play in an economy? For example, should government use its taxing powers to redistribute income from the rich to the poor? Should it allow mergers between companies? Should it regulate air traffic? Should it regulate prices? Should it attempt to stabilize fluctuations of aggregate income?

Specific Roles for Government

In its role as both an actor and a referee, government plays a variety of specific roles in the economy. These include:

1. Providing a stable set of institutions and rules.
2. Promoting effective and workable competition.
3. Correcting for externalities.
4. Ensuring economic stability and growth.
5. Providing public goods.
6. Adjusting for undesirable market results.

PROVIDE A STABLE SET OF INSTITUTIONS AND RULES   A basic role of government is to provide a stable institutional framework that includes the set of laws specifying what can and cannot be done as well as a mechanism to enforce those laws. For example, if someone doesn't pay you, you can't go take what you are owed; you have to go through the government court system. Where governments don't provide a stable institutional framework, as often happens in developing and transitional countries, economic activity is difficult; usually such economies are stagnant. Somalia in the early 2000s is an example. As various groups fought for political control, the Somalian economy stagnated.

PROMOTE EFFECTIVE AND WORKABLE COMPETITION   In a market economy, the pressure to monopolize—for one firm to try to control the market—and competition are always in conflict; the government must decide what role it is to play in protecting or promoting competition. Thus, when Microsoft gained monopolistic control of the computer operating system market with Windows, the U.S. government took the company to court and challenged that monopoly.

What makes this a difficult function for government is that most individuals and firms believe that competition is far better for the other guy than it is for themselves, that their own monopolies are necessary monopolies, and that competition facing them is unfair competition. For example, most farmers support competition, but these same farmers also support government farm subsidies (payments by government to producers based on production levels) and import restrictions. Likewise, most firms support competition, but these same firms also support tariffs, which protect them from foreign competition. Most professionals, such as architects and engineers, support competition, but they also support professional licensing, which limits the number of competitors who can enter their field. As you will see when reading the newspapers, there are always arguments for limiting entry into fields. The job of the government is to determine whether these arguments are strong enough to overcome the negative effects those limitations have on competition.

CORRECT FOR EXTERNALITIES   When two people freely enter into a trade or agreement, they both believe that they will benefit from the trade. But unless they're required to do so, traders are unlikely to take into account any effect that an action may have on a third party. Economists call *the effect of a decision on a third party not taken into account by the decision maker* an **externality.** An externality can be positive (in which case society as a whole benefits from the trade between the two parties) or negative (in which case society as a whole is harmed by the trade between the two parties).

An example of a positive externality is education. When someone educates herself or himself, all society benefits, since better-educated people usually make better citizens and

The government may be able to help correct for externalities.

are better equipped to figure out new approaches to solving problems—approaches that benefit society as a whole. An example of a negative externality involves the burning of coal, which puts sulfur dioxide, carbon dioxide, and fine particulates into the air. Sulfur dioxide contributes to acid rain, carbon dioxide contributes to global warming, and fine particulates damage people's lungs. This means that burning coal has an externality associated with it—an effect of an action that is not taken into account by market participants.

When there are externalities, there is a potential role for government to adjust the market result through taxes, subsidies, or regulation. Throughout this book we will be considering the advantages and disadvantages of each.

ENSURE ECONOMIC STABILITY AND GROWTH　　In addition to providing general stability, government has the potential role of providing economic stability. Most people would agree that if it's possible, government should prevent large fluctuations in the level of economic activity, maintain a relatively constant price level, and provide an economic environment conducive to economic growth. These aims, which became the goals of the U.S. government in 1946 when the Employment Act was passed, are generally considered macroeconomic goals. They're justified as appropriate aims for government to pursue because they involve **macroeconomic externalities** (*externalities that affect the levels of unemployment, inflation, or growth in the economy as a whole*).

Here's how a macro externality could occur. When individuals decide how much to spend, they don't take into account the effects of their decision on others; thus, there may be too much or too little spending. Too little spending often leads to unemployment. But in making their spending decision, people don't take into account the fact that spending less might create unemployment. So their spending decisions can involve a macro externality. Similarly, when people raise their price and don't consider the effect on inflation, they too might be creating a macro externality.

A macroeconomic externality is the effect of an individual decision that affects the levels of unemployment, inflation, or growth in an economy as a whole but is not taken into account by the individual decision maker.

PROVIDE PUBLIC GOODS　　Another role for government is to supply public goods. A **public good** is *a good that if supplied to one person must be supplied to all and whose consumption by one individual does not prevent its consumption by another individual*. In contrast, a **private good** is *a good that, when consumed by one individual, cannot be consumed by another individual*. An example of a private good is an apple; once I eat that apple, no one else can consume it. An example of a public good is national defense, which, if supplied to one, will also protect others. In order to supply defense, governments must require people to pay for it with taxes, rather than leaving it to the market to supply it.

ADJUST FOR UNDESIRABLE MARKET RESULTS　　A controversial role for government is to adjust the results of the market when those market results are seen as socially undesirable. Government redistributes income, taking it away from some individuals and giving it to others whom it sees as more deserving or more in need. In doing so, it attempts to see that the outcomes of trades are fair. Determining what's fair is a difficult philosophical question that economists can't answer. That question is for the people, through the government, to decide.

An example of this role involves having government decide what's best for people, independently of their desires. The market allows individuals to decide. But what if people don't know what's best for themselves? Or what if they do know but don't act on that knowledge? For example, people might know that addictive drugs are bad for them, but because of peer pressure, or because they just don't care, they may take drugs anyway. Government action prohibiting such activities through laws or high taxes may then be warranted. *Goods or activities that government believes are bad for*

Our International Competitors

The world economy is often divided into three main areas or trading blocs: the Americas, Europe and Africa, and East Asia. These trading blocs are shown in the map below.

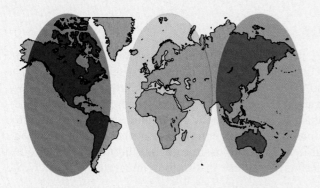

Each area has a major currency. In the Americas, it is the dollar; in Europe, it is the euro; and in East Asia, it is the Japanese yen. These areas are continually changing; the EU recently expanded to 28 countries, incorporating many of the countries of eastern Europe. China's economy has been growing fast and, given the size of its population, is likely to overtake Japan as the key Asian economy in the coming decades.

The accompanying table gives you a sense of the similarities and differences in the economies of the United States, China, and the European Union.

	United States	China	European Union
Area (square miles)	3,537,438	3,705,407	1,691,588
Population	314 million	1.3 billion	507 million
GDP*	$15.6 trillion	$13 trillion	$15.7 trillion
Percentage of world output	19%	14%	19%
GDP per capita	$50,000	$10,000	$31,000
Natural resources	Coal, copper, lead, and others	Coal, iron ore	Coal, iron ore, natural gas, fish, and others
Exports as a percentage of GDP	14%	17%	11%
Imports as a percentage of GDP	18%	15%	13%
Currency	Dollar	Yuan	Euro
Value (as of July 2012)	($1 = $1)	(¥6.36 = $1)	(€0.82 = $1)

*Calculated using purchasing power parity.

Source: *CIA World Factbook 2012* (www.cia.gov) and current exchange rate tables. Currency changes can affect GDP figures. GDP updated by the author.

people even though they choose to use the goods or engage in the activities are called **demerit goods or activities.** Illegal drugs are a demerit good and using addictive drugs is a demerit activity.

Alternatively, there are some activities that government believes are good for people, even if people may not choose to engage in them. For example, government may believe that going to the opera or contributing to charity is a good activity. But in the United States only a small percentage of people go to the opera, and not everyone in the United States contributes to charity. Similarly, government may believe that whole-wheat bread is more nutritious than white bread. But many consumers prefer white bread. Goods like whole-wheat bread and activities like contributing to charity are known as **merit goods or activities**—*goods and activities that government believes are good for you even though you may not choose to engage in the activities or to consume the goods.* Government sometimes provides support for them through subsidies or tax benefits.

With merit and demerit goods, individuals are assumed to be doing what is not in their self-interest.

Market Failures and Government Failures

The reasons for government intervention are often summed up in the phrase *market failure.* **Market failures** are *situations in which the market does not lead to a desired*

Q-9 If there is an externality, does that mean that the government should intervene in the market to adjust for that externality?

result. In the real world, market failures are pervasive—the market is always failing in one way or another. But the fact that there are market failures does not mean that government intervention will improve the situation. There are also **government failures**—*situations in which the government intervenes and makes things worse.* Government failures are pervasive in the government—the government is always failing in one way or another. So real-world policy makers usually end up choosing which failure—market failure or government failure—will be least problematic.

Global Institutions

So far in this chapter we've put the U.S. economy in historical and institutional perspective. In this last section, we briefly put it into perspective relative to the world economy. By doing so, we gain a number of insights into the U.S. economy. The U.S. economy makes up about 20 percent of world output and consumption, a percentage that is much larger than its relative size by geographic area (6 percent of the world's land mass) or by population (just over 4 percent of the world population). It is becoming more integrated; it is impossible to talk about U.S. economic institutions without considering how those institutions integrate with the world economy.

Global Corporations

Consider corporations. Most large corporations today are not U.S., German, or Japanese corporations; they are **global corporations** (*corporations with substantial operations on both the production and sales sides in more than one country*). Just because a car has a Japanese or German name doesn't mean that it was produced abroad. Many Japanese and German companies now have manufacturing plants in the United States, and many U.S. firms have manufacturing plants abroad. When goods are produced by global corporations, corporate names don't always tell much about where a good is produced. As global corporations' importance has grown, most manufacturing decisions are made in reference to the international market, not the U.S. domestic market. This means that the consumer sovereignty that guides decisions of firms is becoming less and less U.S. consumer sovereignty, and more and more global consumer sovereignty.

Global corporations offer enormous benefits for countries. They create jobs; they bring new ideas and new technologies to a country; and they provide competition for domestic companies, keeping them on their toes. But global corporations also pose a number of problems for governments. One is their implication for domestic and international policy. A domestic corporation exists within a country and can be dealt with using policy measures within that country. A global corporation exists within many countries and there is no global government to regulate or control it. If it doesn't like the policies in one country—say taxes are too high or regulations too tight—it can shift its operations to other countries.

Coordinating Global Issues

Global economic issues differ from national economic issues because national economies have governments to referee disputes among players in the economy; global economies do not; no international government exists. Some argue that we need a global government to oversee global businesses. But no such government exists. The closest institution there is to a world government is the United Nations (UN), which, according to critics, is simply a debating society. It has no ability to tax and no ability

Global corporations are corporations with substantial operations on both the production and sales sides in more than one country.

WWW Web Note 3.4
Global 500

to impose its will separate from the political and military power of its members. When the United States opposes a UN mandate, it can, and often does, ignore it. Hence, international problems must be dealt with through negotiation, consensus, bullying, and concessions.

Governments, however, have developed a variety of international institutions to promote negotiations and coordinate economic relations among countries. Besides the United Nations, these include the World Bank, the World Court, and the International Monetary Fund (IMF). These organizations have a variety of goals. For example, the World Bank, a multinational, international financial institution, works with developing countries to secure low-interest loans, channeling such loans to them to foster economic growth. The International Monetary Fund (IMF), a multinational, international financial institution, is concerned primarily with monetary issues. It deals with international financial arrangements. When developing countries encountered financial problems in the 1980s and had large international debts that they could not pay, the IMF helped work on repayment plans.

Countries also have developed global and regional organizations whose job it is to coordinate trade among countries and reduce trade barriers. On the international level, the World Trade Organization (WTO) works to reduce trade barriers among countries. On the regional level, there are the European Union (EU), which is an organization of European countries that developed out of a trade association devoted to reducing trade barriers among member countries; the North American Free Trade Agreement (NAFTA), an organization devoted to reducing trade barriers between the United States, Mexico, and Canada; and Mercosur, an organization devoted to reducing trade barriers among North, Central, and South American countries.

In addition to these formal institutions, there are informal meetings of various countries. These include the Group of Eight, which meets to promote negotiations and to coordinate economic relations among countries. The eight are Japan, Germany, Britain, France, United States, Canada, Italy, and Russia.

Since governmental membership in international organizations is voluntary, their power is limited. When the United States doesn't like a World Court ruling, it simply states that it isn't going to follow the ruling. When the United States is unhappy with what the United Nations is doing, it withholds some of its dues. Other countries do the same from time to time. Other member countries complain but can do little to force compliance. It doesn't work that way domestically. If you decide you don't like U.S. policy and refuse to pay your taxes, you'll wind up in jail.

What keeps nations somewhat in line when it comes to international rules is a moral tradition: Countries want to (or at least want to look as if they want to) do what's "right." Countries will sometimes follow international rules to keep international opinion favorable to them. But perceived national self-interest often overrides international scruples.

> Governments have developed international institutions to promote negotiations and coordinate economic relations among countries. Some are: the UN; the World Bank; the World Court; and the International Monetary Fund.

> Countries have developed global and regional organizations to coordinate trade and reduce trade barriers. Some are: the WTO; the EU; and NAFTA.

> Since governmental membership in international organizations is voluntary, their power is limited.

> Q-10 If the United States chooses not to follow a World Court decision, what are the consequences?

Conclusion

This has been a whirlwind introduction to economic institutions and their role in the economy. Each of them—business, households, and government—is important, and to understand what happens in the economy, one must have a sense of how these institutions work and the role they play. In the remainder of the book we won't discuss institutions much as we concentrate on presenting economic analysis. I rely upon you to integrate the analysis with institutions, as you apply the economic analysis and reasoning that you learn to the real world.

Summary

- A market economy is an economic system based on private property and the market. It gives private property rights to individuals and relies on market forces to solve the *what, how,* and *for whom* problems.   *(LO3-1)*

- In a market economy, price is the mechanism through which people's desires are coordinated and goods are rationed. The U.S. economy today is a market economy.   *(LO3-1)*

- The predominant market-based system during the early 1900s was capitalism, an economic system based on the market in which the ownership of production resided with a small group of individuals called capitalists.   *(LO3-1)*

- In principle, under socialism society solves the *what, how,* and *for whom* problems in the best interest of the individuals in society. It is based on individuals' goodwill toward one another.   *(LO3-1)*

- In practice, socialism is an economic system based on government ownership of the means of production, with economic activity governed by central planning. Socialism in practice is sometimes called a command economy.   *(LO3-1)*

- A diagram of the U.S. market economy shows the connections among businesses, households, and government. It also shows the U.S. economic connection to other countries.   *(LO3-2)*

- In the United States, businesses make the *what, how,* and *for whom* decisions.   *(LO3-2)*

- Although businesses decide what to produce, they succeed or fail depending on their ability to meet consumers' desires. That's consumer sovereignty.   *(LO3-2)*

- The three main forms of business are corporations, sole proprietorships, and partnerships. Each has its advantages and disadvantages.   *(LO3-2)*

- Although households are the most powerful economic institution, they have assigned much of their power to government and business. Economics focuses on households' role as the supplier of labor.   *(LO3-2)*

- Government plays two general roles in the economy: (1) as a referee and (2) as an actor.   *(LO3-3)*

- Six roles of government are to (1) provide a stable set of institutions and rules, (2) promote effective and workable competition, (3) correct for externalities, (4) ensure economic stability and growth, (5) provide public goods, and (6) adjust for undesirable market results.   *(LO3-3)*

- To understand the U.S. economy, one must understand its role in the world economy.   *(LO3-4)*

- Global corporations are corporations with significant operations in more than one country. They are increasing in importance.   *(LO3-4)*

- Global economic issues differ from national economic issues because national economies have governments. The global economy does not.   *(LO3-4)*

Key Terms

business *(56)*
capitalism *(53)*
consumer
  sovereignty *(57)*
corporation *(58)*
demerit good or
  activity *(65)*
entrepreneurship *(57)*

externality *(63)*
global corporation *(66)*
government
  failure *(66)*
households *(59)*
institutions *(51)*
macroeconomic
  externality *(64)*

market
  economy *(52)*
market failure *(65)*
merit good or
  activity *(65)*
partnership *(58)*
private good *(64)*

private property
  right *(52)*
profit *(57)*
public good *(64)*
socialism *(53)*
sole proprietorship *(58)*

Questions and Exercises

1. In a market economy, what is the central coordinating mechanism? *(LO3-1)*

2. In a centrally planned socialist economy, what is the central coordinating mechanism? *(LO3-1)*

3. How does a market economy solve the what, how, and for whom to produce problems? *(LO3-1)*

4. How does a centrally planned socialist economy solve the what, how, and for whom to produce problems? *(LO3-1)*

5. Is capitalism or socialism the better economic system? Why? *(LO3-1)*

6. Why does an economy's strength ultimately reside in its people? *(LO3-2)*

7. Why is entrepreneurship a central part of any business? *(LO3-2)*

8. List the three major forms of business. *(LO3-2)*
   a. What form is most common?
   b. What form accounts for the largest proportion of sales?

9. You're starting a software company in which you plan to sell software to your fellow students. What form of business organization would you choose? Why? *(LO3-2)*

10. What are the two largest categories of federal government expenditures? *(LO3-3)*

11. What are the six roles of government listed in the text? *(LO3-3)*

12. Say the government establishes rights to pollute so that without a pollution permit you aren't allowed to emit pollutants into the air, water, or soil. Firms are allowed to buy and sell these rights. In what way will this correct for an externality? *(LO3-3)*

13. Give an example of a merit good, a demerit good, a public good, and a good that involves an externality. *(LO3-3)*

14. Name two international organizations that countries have developed to coordinate economic actions. *(LO3-4)*

15. What are two organizations that countries can use to coordinate economic relations and reduce trade barriers? *(LO3-4)*

16. Why are international organizations limited in their effectiveness? *(LO3-4)*

Questions from Alternative Perspectives

1. Friedrich Hayek, the man quoted at the start of the chapter, is an Austrian economist who won a Nobel Prize in economics. He argued that government intervention is difficult to contain. Suppose central planners have decided to financially support all children with food vouchers, free day care, and public school.
   a. What problems might this create?
   b. How might this lead to further interference by central planners into family choices? (Austrian)

2. In his *The Social Contract,* Jean-Jacques Rousseau argued that "no State has ever been founded without a religious basis [but] the law of Christianity at bottom does more harm by weakening than good by strengthening the constitution of the State." What does he mean by that, and is he correct? (Religious)

3. In economics, a household is defined as a group of individuals making joint decisions as though acting as one person.
   a. How do you think decisions are actually made about things like consumption and allocation of time within the household?
   b. Does bargaining take place?
   c. If so, what gives an individual power to bargain effectively for his or her preferences?

   d. Do individuals act cooperatively within the family and competitively everywhere else?
   e. Does this make sense? (Feminist)

4. This chapter emphasized the importance of the relationship between how the economic system is organized and value systems. Knowing that how I raise my child will greatly shape how he or she will ultimately fit into the social and economic process, should I raise my child to be selfless, compassionate, and dedicated to advancing the well-being of others, knowing she will probably be poor; or shall I raise her to be self-centered, uncaring, and greedy to increase her chances to acquire personal fortune? Which decision is just and why? (Institutionalist)

5. The text discusses consumer sovereignty and suggests that it guides the market choices.
   a. Is consumer sovereignty a myth or reality in today's consumer culture?
   b. Do consumers "direct" the economy as suggested by the text, or has invention become the mother of necessity, as Thorstein Veblen once quipped?
   c. If the consumer is not sovereign, then who is and what does that imply for economics? (Radical)

Issues to Ponder

1. What arguments can you give for supporting a socialist organization of a family and a market-based organization of the economy?

2. Economists Edward Lazear and Robert Michael calculated that the average family spends two and a half times as much on each adult as they do on each child.
   a. Does this mean that children are deprived and that the distribution is unfair?
   b. Do you think these percentages change with family income? If so, how?
   c. Do you think that the allocation would be different in a family in a command economy than in a capitalist economy? Why?

3. One of the specific problems socialist economies had was keeping up with capitalist countries technologically.
   a. Can you think of any reason inherent in a centrally planned economy that would make innovation difficult?
   b. Can you think of any reason inherent in a capitalist economy that would foster innovation?
   c. Joseph Schumpeter, a famous Harvard economist of the 1930s, predicted that as firms in capitalist societies grew in size, they would innovate less. Can you suggest what his argument might have been?
   d. Schumpeter's prediction did not come true. Modern capitalist economies have had enormous innovations. Can you provide explanations as to why?

4. Tom Rollins heads a company called Teaching Co. He has taped lectures at the top universities, packaged the lectures on DVD and sells them for between $20 and $230 per series.
   a. Discuss whether such an idea could be expanded to include college courses that one could take at home.
   b. What are the technical, social, and economic issues involved?
   c. If it is technically possible and cost-effective, will the new venture be a success?

5. Go to a store in your community.
   a. Ask what limitations the owners faced in starting their business.
   b. Were these limitations necessary?
   c. Should there have been more or fewer limitations?
   d. Under what heading of reasons for government intervention would you put each of the limitations?
   e. Ask what kinds of taxes the business pays and what benefits it believes it gets for those taxes.
   f. Is it satisfied with the existing situation? Why? What would it change?

6. A market system is often said to be based on consumer sovereignty—the consumer determines what's to be produced. Yet business decides what's to be produced. Can these two views be reconciled? How? If not, why?

7. How might individuals disagree about the government's role in intervening in the market for merit, demerit, and public goods?

8. Discuss the concepts of market failure and government failure in relation to operas.

9. You've set up the rules for a game and started the game but now realize that the rules are unfair. Should you change the rules?

10. In trade talks with Australia, the United States proposed that Australia cannot regulate the amount of foreign content on new media without first consulting the United States. Actress Bridie Carter of *McLeod's Daughters* argued against adopting the trade agreement, arguing the agreement trades away Australia's cultural identity. This highlights one of the effects of globalization: the loss of variety based on cultural differences. How important should such cultural identity issues be in trade negotiations?

Answers to Margin Questions

1. He is wrong. Property rights are required for a market to operate. Once property rights are allocated, the market will allocate goods, but the market cannot distribute the property rights that are required for the market to operate. (*p. 52; LO3-1*)

2. Capitalism places much more emphasis on fostering individualism. Socialism tries to develop a system in which the individual's needs are placed second to society's needs. (*p. 53; LO3-1*)

3. Most families allocate basic needs through control and command. The parents do (or try to do) the controlling and commanding. Generally parents are well-intentioned, trying to meet their perception of their children's needs. However, some family activities that are not basic needs might be allocated through the market. For example, if one child wants a go-cart and is willing to do extra work at home in order to get it, go-carts might be allocated through the market, with the child earning chits that can be used for such nonessentials. (*p. 53; LO3-1*)

4. In theory, socialism is an economic system based upon individuals' goodwill. In practice, socialism involved central planning and government ownership of the primary means of production. (*p. 54; LO3-1*)

5. Market economies are generally broken up into businesses, households, and government. (*p. 55; LO3-2*)

6. False. In the United States, individuals are free to start any type of business they want, provided it doesn't violate the law. The invisible hand sees to it that only those businesses that customers want earn a profit. The others lose money and eventually go out of business, so in that sense only businesses that customers want stay in business. (*p. 57; LO3-2*)

7. As can be seen in Figure 3-2, most businesses in the United States are sole proprietorships, not corporations. Corporations, however, generate the most revenue. (*p. 58; LO3-2*)

8. The largest percentage of federal expenditures is for income security. (*p. 61; LO3-3*)

9. Not necessarily. The existence of an externality creates the possibility that government intervention might help. But there are also government failures in which the government intervenes and makes things worse. (*p. 66; LO3-3*)

10. The World Court has no enforcement mechanism. Thus, when a country refuses to follow the court's decisions, the country cannot be directly punished except through indirect international pressures. (*p. 67; LO3-4*)

APPENDIX A

The History of Economic Systems

In Chapter 1, I made the distinction between market and economic forces: Economic forces have always existed—they operate in all aspects of our lives—but market forces have not always existed. Markets are social creations societies use to coordinate individuals' actions. Markets developed, sometimes spontaneously, sometimes by design, because they offered a better life for at least some—and usually a large majority of—individuals in a society.

To understand why markets developed, it is helpful to look briefly at the history of the economic systems from which our own system descended.

Feudal Society: Rule of Tradition

Let's go back in time to the year 1000 when Europe had no nation-states as we now know them. (Ideally, we would have gone back further and explained other economic systems, but, given the limited space, I had to draw the line somewhere—an example of a trade-off.) The predominant economic system at that time was feudalism. There was no coordinated central government, no unified system of law, no national patriotism, no national defense, although a strong religious institution simply called the Church fulfilled some of these roles.

There were few towns; most individuals lived in walled manors, or "estates." These manors "belonged to" the "lord of the manor." (Occasionally the "lord" was a lady, but not often.) I say "belonged to" rather than "were owned by" because most of the empires or federations at that time were not formal nation-states that could organize, administer, and regulate ownership. No documents or deeds gave ownership of the land to an individual. Instead, tradition ruled, and in normal times nobody questioned the lord's right to the land. The land "belonged to" the lord because the land "belonged to" him—that's the way it was.

Without a central nation-state, the manor served many functions a nation-state would have served had it existed. The lord provided protection, often within a walled area surrounding the manor house or, if the manor was large enough, a castle. He provided administration and decided disputes. He also decided *what* would be done, *how* it would be done, and *who* would get what, but these decisions were limited. In the same way that the land belonged to the lord because that's the way it always had been, what people did and how they did it were determined by what they always had done. Tradition ruled the manor more than the lord did.

Problems of a Tradition-Based Society

Feudalism developed about the 8th and 9th centuries and lasted until about the 15th century, though in isolated countries such as Russia it continued well into the 19th century, and in all European countries its influence lingered for hundreds of years (as late as about 150 years ago in some parts of Germany). Such a long-lived system must have done some things right, and feudalism did: It solved the *what, how,* and *for whom* problems in an acceptable way.

But a tradition-based society has problems. In a traditional society, because someone's father was a baker, the son also must be a baker, and because a woman was a homemaker, she wouldn't be allowed to be anything but a homemaker. But what if Joe Blacksmith Jr., the son of Joe Blacksmith Sr., is a lousy blacksmith and longs to knead dough, while Joe Baker Jr. would be a superb blacksmith but hates making pastry? Tough. Tradition dictated who did what. In fact, tradition probably arranged things so that we will never know whether Joe Blacksmith Jr. would have made a superb baker.

As long as a society doesn't change too much, tradition operates reasonably well, although not especially efficiently, in holding the society together. However, when a society must undergo change, tradition does not work. Change means that the things that were done before no longer need to be done, while new things do need to get done. But if no one has traditionally done these new things, then they don't get done. If the change is important but a society can't figure out some way for the new things to get done, the society falls apart. That's what happened to feudal society. It didn't change when change was required.

The life of individuals living on the land, called *serfs,* was difficult, and feudalism was designed to benefit the lord. Some individuals in feudal society just couldn't take life on the manor, and they set off on their own. Because there was no organized police force, they were unlikely to be caught and forced to return to the manor. Going hungry, being killed, or both, however, were frequent fates of an escaped serf. One place to which serfs could safely escape, though, was a town or city—the remains of what in Roman times had been thriving and active cities. These cities, which had been decimated by plagues, plundering bands, and starvation in the preceding centuries, nevertheless remained an escape hatch for runaway serfs because they relied far less on tradition than did manors. City dwellers had to live by their wits; many became merchants who lived predominantly by trading. They were middlemen; they would buy from one group and sell to another.

Trading in towns was an alternative to the traditional feudal order because trading allowed people to have an income independent of the traditional social structure. Markets broke down tradition. Initially merchants traded using barter (exchange of one kind of good for another): silk and spices from the Orient for wheat, flour, and artisan products in Europe. But soon a generalized purchasing power (money) developed as a medium of exchange. Money greatly expanded the possibilities of trading because its use meant that goods no longer needed to be bartered. They could be sold for money, which could then be spent to buy other goods.

In the beginning, land was not traded, but soon the feudal lord who just had to have a silk robe but had no money was saying, "Why not? I'll sell you a small piece of land so I can buy a shipment of silk." Once land became tradable, the traditional base of the feudal society was undermined. Tradition that can be bought and sold is no longer tradition—it's just another commodity.

From Feudalism to Mercantilism

Toward the end of the Middle Ages (mid-15th century), markets went from being a sideshow, a fair that spiced up people's lives, to being the main event. Over time, some traders and merchants started to amass fortunes that dwarfed those of the feudal lords. Rich traders settled down; existing towns and cities expanded and new towns were formed. As towns grew and as fortunes shifted from feudal lords to merchants, power in society shifted to the towns. And with that shift came a change in society's political and economic structure.

As these traders became stronger politically and economically, they threw their support behind a king (the strongest lord) in the hope that the king would expand their ability to trade. In doing so, they made the king even stronger. Eventually, the king became so powerful that his will prevailed over the will of the other lords and even over the will of the Church. As the king consolidated his power, nation-states as we know them today evolved. *The government became an active influence on economic decision making.*

As markets grew, feudalism evolved into mercantilism. The evolution of feudal systems into mercantilism occurred in the following way: As cities and their markets grew in size and power relative to the feudal manors and the traditional economy, a whole new variety of possible economic activities developed. It was only natural that individuals began to look to a king to establish a new tradition that would determine who would do what. Individuals in particular occupations organized into groups called *guilds,* which were similar to strong labor unions today. These guilds, many of which had financed and supported the king, now expected the king and his government to protect their interests.

As new economic activities, such as trading companies, developed, individuals involved in these activities similarly depended on the king for the right to trade and for help in financing and organizing their activities. For example, in 1492, when Christopher Columbus had the wild idea that by sailing west he could get to the East Indies and trade for their riches, he went to Spain's Queen Isabella and King Ferdinand for financial support.

Since many traders had played and continued to play important roles in financing, establishing, and supporting the king, the king was usually happy to protect their interests. The government doled out the rights to undertake a variety of economic activities. By the late 1400s, western Europe had evolved from a feudal to a mercantilist economy.

The mercantilist period was marked by the increased role of government, which could be classified in two ways: by the way it encouraged growth and by the way it limited growth. Government legitimized and financed a variety of activities, thus encouraging growth. But government also limited economic activity in order to protect the monopolies of those it favored, thus limiting growth. So mercantilism allowed the market to operate, but it kept the market under its control. The market was not allowed to respond freely to the laws of supply and demand.

From Mercantilism to Capitalism

Mercantilism provided the source for major growth in western Europe, but mercantilism also unleashed new tensions within society. Like feudalism, mercantilism limited entry into economic activities. It used a different form of limitation—politics rather than social and cultural tradition—but individuals who were excluded still felt unfairly treated.

The most significant source of tension was the different roles played by craft guilds and owners of new businesses, who were called industrialists or capitalists (businesspeople who have acquired large amounts of money and use it to invest in businesses). Craft guild members were artists in their own crafts: pottery, shoemaking, and the like. New business owners destroyed the art of production by devising machines to replace hand production. Machines produced goods cheaper and faster than craftsmen.[1] The result was an increase in supply and a downward pressure on the price, which was set by the government. Craftsmen didn't want to be replaced by machines. They argued that machine-manufactured goods didn't have the same quality as hand-crafted goods, and that the new machines would disrupt the economic and social life of the community.

Industrialists were the outsiders with a vested interest in changing the existing system. They wanted the freedom to conduct business as they saw fit. Because of the enormous cost advantage of manufactured goods over crafted goods, a few industrialists overcame government opposition and succeeded within the mercantilist system. They earned their fortunes and became an independent political power.

Once again, the economic power base shifted, and two groups competed with each other for power—this time, the guilds and the industrialists. The government had to decide whether to support the industrialists (who wanted government to loosen its power over the country's economic affairs) or the craftsmen and guilds (who argued for strong government limitations and for maintaining traditional values of workmanship). This struggle raged in the 1700s and 1800s. But during this time, governments themselves were changing. This was the Age of Revolutions, and the kings' powers were being limited by democratic reform movements—revolutions supported and financed in large part by the industrialists.

The Need for Coordination in an Economy

Craftsmen argued that coordination of the economy was necessary, and the government had to be involved. If government wasn't going to coordinate economic activity, who would? To answer that question, a British moral philosopher named Adam Smith developed the concept of the invisible hand, in his famous book *The Wealth of Nations* (1776), and used it to explain how markets could coordinate the economy without the active involvement of government.

As stated in Chapter 2, Smith argued that the market's invisible hand would guide suppliers' actions toward the general good. No government coordination was necessary.

With the help of economists such as Adam Smith, the industrialists' view won out. Government pulled back from its role in guiding the economy and adopted a laissez-faire policy.

---

[1]Throughout this section I use *men* to emphasize that these societies were strongly male-dominated. There were almost no businesswomen. In fact, a woman had to turn over her property to a man upon her marriage, and the marriage contract was written as if she were owned by her husband!

The Industrial Revolution

The invisible hand worked; capitalism thrived. Beginning about 1750 and continuing through the late 1800s, machine production increased enormously, almost totally replacing hand production. This phenomenon has been given a name, the Industrial Revolution. The economy grew faster than ever before. Society was forever transformed. New inventions changed all aspects of life. James Watt's steam engine (1769) made manufacturing and travel easier. Eli Whitney's cotton gin (1793) changed the way cotton was processed. James Kay's flying shuttle (1733),[2] James Hargreaves' spinning jenny (1765), and Richard Arkwright's power loom (1769), combined with the steam engine, changed the way cloth was processed and the clothes people wore.

The need to mine vast amounts of coal to provide power to run the machines changed the economic and physical landscapes. The repeating rifle changed the nature of warfare. Modern economic institutions replaced guilds. Stock markets, insurance companies, and corporations all became important. Trading was no longer financed by government; it was privately financed (although government policies, such as colonial policies giving certain companies monopoly trading rights with a country's colonies, helped in that trading). The Industrial Revolution, democracy, and capitalism all arose in the middle and late 1700s. By the 1800s, they were part of the institutional landscape of Western society. Capitalism had arrived.

Welfare Capitalism
From Capitalism to ~~Socialism~~

Capitalism was marked by significant economic growth in the Western world. But it was also marked by human abuses—18-hour workdays; low wages; children as young as five years old slaving long hours in dirty, dangerous factories and mines—to produce enormous wealth for an elite few. Such conditions and inequalities led to criticism of the capitalist or market economic system.

---

[2]The invention of the flying shuttle frustrated the textile industry because it enabled workers to weave so much cloth that the spinners of thread from which the cloth was woven couldn't keep up. This challenge to the textile industry was met by offering a prize to anyone who could invent something to increase the thread spinners' productivity. The prize was won when the spinning jenny was invented.

Marx's Analysis

The best-known critic of this system was Karl Marx, a German philosopher, economist, and sociologist who wrote in the 1800s and who developed an analysis of the dynamics of change in economic systems. Marx argued that economic systems are in a constant state of change, and that capitalism would not last. Workers would revolt, and capitalism would be replaced by a socialist economic system.

Marx saw an economy marked by tensions among economic classes. He saw capitalism as an economic system controlled by the capitalist class (businessmen). His class analysis was that capitalist society is divided into capitalist and worker classes. He said constant tension between these economic classes causes changes in the system. The capitalist class made large profits by exploiting the proletariat class—the working class—and extracting what he called surplus value from workers who, according to Marx's labor theory of value, produced all the value inherent in goods. Surplus value was the additional profit, rent, or interest that, according to Marx's normative views, capitalists added to the price of goods. What standard economic analysis sees as recognizing a need that society has and fulfilling it, Marx saw as exploitation.

Marx argued that this exploitation would increase as production facilities became larger and larger and as competition among capitalists decreased. At some point, he believed, exploitation would lead to a revolt by the proletariat, who would overthrow their capitalist exploiters.

By the late 1800s, some of what Marx predicted had occurred, although not in the way that he thought it would. Production moved from small to large factories. Corporations developed, and classes became more distinct from one another. Workers were significantly differentiated from owners. Small firms merged and were organized into monopolies and trusts (large combinations of firms). The trusts developed ways to prevent competition among themselves and ways to limit entry of new competitors into the market. Marx was right in his predictions about these developments, but he was wrong in his prediction about society's response to them.

The Revolution That Did Not Occur

Western society's response to the problems of capitalism was not a revolt by the workers. Instead, governments stepped in to stop the worst abuses of capitalism. The hard edges of capitalism were softened.

Evolution, not revolution, was capitalism's destiny. The democratic state did not act, as Marx argued it would, as a mere representative of the capitalist class. Competing pressure groups developed; workers gained political power that offset the economic power of businesses.

In the late 1930s and the 1940s, workers dominated the political agenda. During this time, capitalist economies developed an economic safety net that included government-funded programs, such as public welfare and unemployment insurance, and established an extensive set of regulations affecting all aspects of the economy. Today, depressions are met with direct government policy. Antitrust laws, regulatory agencies, and social programs of government softened the hard edges of capitalism. Laws were passed prohibiting child labor, mandating a certain minimum wage, and limiting the hours of work. Capitalism became what is sometimes called welfare capitalism.

Due to these developments, government spending now accounts for about a fifth of all spending in the United States, and for more than half in some European countries. Were an economist from the late 1800s to return from the grave, he'd probably say socialism, not capitalism, exists in Western societies. Most modern-day economists wouldn't go that far, but they would agree that our economy today is better described as a welfare capitalist economy than as a capitalist, or even a market, economy. Because of these changes, the U.S. and Western European economies are a far cry from the competitive "capitalist" economy that Karl Marx criticized. Markets operate, but they are constrained by the government.

The concept *capitalism* developed to denote a market system controlled by one group in society, the capitalists. Looking at Western societies today, we see that domination by one group no longer characterizes Western economies. Although in theory capitalists control corporations through their ownership of shares of stock, in practice corporations are controlled in large part by managers. There remains an elite group who control business, but *capitalist* is not a good term to describe them. Managers, not capitalists, exercise primary control over business, and even their control is limited by laws or the fear of laws being passed by governments.

Governments, in turn, are controlled by a variety of pressure groups. Sometimes one group is in control; at other times, another. Government policies similarly fluctuate. Sometimes they are proworker, sometimes proindustrialist, sometimes progovernment, and sometimes prosociety.

From Feudalism to Socialism

You probably noticed that I crossed out *Socialism* in the previous section's heading and replaced it with *Welfare Capitalism.* That's because capitalism did not evolve to socialism as Karl Marx predicted it would. Instead, Marx's socialist ideas took root in feudalist Russia, a society that the Industrial Revolution had in large part bypassed. Since socialism arrived at a different place and a different time than Marx predicted it would, you shouldn't be surprised to read that socialism arrived in a different way than Marx predicted. The proletariat did not revolt to establish socialism. Instead, World War I, which the Russians were losing, crippled Russia's feudal economy and government. A small group of socialists overthrew the czar (Russia's king) and took over the government in 1917. They quickly pulled Russia out of the war, and then set out to organize a socialist society and economy.

Russian socialists tried to adhere to Marx's ideas, but they found that Marx had concentrated on how capitalist economies operate, not on how a socialist economy should be run. Thus, Russian socialists faced a huge task with little guidance. Their most immediate problem was how to increase production so that the economy could emerge from feudalism into the modern industrial world. In Marx's analysis, capitalism was a necessary stage in the evolution toward the ideal state for a very practical reason. The capitalists exploit the workers, but in doing so capitalists extract the necessary surplus—an amount of production in excess of what is consumed. That surplus had to be extracted in order to provide the factories and machinery upon which a socialist economic system would be built. But since capitalism did not exist in *Russia,* a true socialist state could not be established immediately. Instead, the socialists created *state socialism*— an economic system in which government sees to it that people work for the common good until they can be relied upon to do that on their own.

Socialists saw state socialism as a transition stage to pure socialism. This transition stage still exploited the workers; when Joseph Stalin took power in Russia in the late 1920s, he took the peasants' and small farmers' land and turned it into collective farms. The government then paid farmers low prices for their produce. When farmers balked at the low prices, millions of them were killed.

Simultaneously, Stalin created central planning agencies that directed individuals what to produce and how to produce it, and determined for whom things would be produced. During this period, *socialism* became synonymous with *central economic planning,* and Soviet-style socialism became the model of socialism in practice.

Also during this time, Russia took control of a number of neighboring states and established the Union of Soviet Socialist Republics (USSR), the formal name of the Soviet Union. The Soviet Union also installed Soviet-dominated governments in a number of eastern European countries. In 1949 most of China, under the rule of Mao Zedong, adopted Soviet-style socialist principles.

Since the late 1980s, the Soviet socialist economic and political structure has fallen apart. The Soviet Union as a political state broke up, and its former republics became autonomous. Eastern European countries were released from Soviet control. Now they faced a new problem: transition from socialism to a market economy. Why did the Soviet socialist economy fall apart? Because workers lacked incentives to work; production was inefficient; consumer goods were either unavailable or of poor quality; and high Soviet officials were exploiting their positions, keeping the best jobs for themselves and moving themselves up in the waiting lists for consumer goods. In short, the parents of the socialist family (the Communist party) were no longer acting benevolently; they were taking many of the benefits for themselves.

These political and economic upheavals in eastern Europe and the former Soviet Union suggest the kind of socialism these societies tried did not work. However, that failure does not mean that socialist goals are bad; nor does it mean that no type of socialism can ever work. The point is that all systems have problems, and it is likely that the political winds of change will lead to new forms of economic organization being tried as the problems of the existing system lead to political demands for change. Venezuela's recent attempt to establish a new form of socialism is an example. Given past experience with socialist systems, however, most economists believe that any future workable "new socialist" system will include important elements of market institutions.

chapter 4

Supply and Demand

> *Teach a parrot the terms supply and demand and you've got an economist.*
>
> —Thomas Carlyle

Supply and demand. Supply and demand. Roll the phrase around in your mouth; savor it like a good wine. *Supply* and *demand* are the most-used words in economics. And for good reason. They provide a good off-the-cuff answer for any economic question. Try it.

Why are bacon and oranges so expensive this winter? *Supply and demand.*

Why are interest rates falling? *Supply and demand.*

Why can't I find decent wool socks anymore? *Supply and demand.*

The importance of the interplay of supply and demand makes it only natural that, early in any economics course, you must learn about supply and demand. Let's start with demand.

After reading this chapter, you should be able to:

LO4-1 State the law of demand and distinguish shifts in demand from movements along a demand curve.

LO4-2 State the law of supply and distinguish shifts in supply from movements along a supply curve.

LO4-3 Explain how the law of demand and the law of supply interact to bring about equilibrium.

LO4-4 Discuss the limitations of demand and supply analysis.

Demand

People want lots of things; they "demand" much less than they want because demand means a willingness and ability to pay. Unless you are willing and able to pay for it, you may *want* it, but you don't *demand* it. For example, I want to own a Ferrari. But, I must admit, I'm not willing to do what's necessary to own one. If I really wanted one, I'd mortgage everything I own, increase my income by doubling the number of hours I work, not buy anything else, and get that car. But I don't do any of those things, so at the going price, $650,000, I do not demand a Ferrari. Sure, I'd buy one if it cost $30,000, but from my actions it's clear that, at $650,000, I don't demand it. This points to an important aspect of demand: The quantity you demand at a low price differs from the quantity you demand at a high price. Specifically, the quantity you demand varies inversely—in the opposite direction—with price.

Prices are the tool by which the market coordinates individuals' desires and limits how much people demand. When goods become scarce, the market reduces the quantity people demand; as their prices go up, people buy fewer goods. As goods become abundant, their prices go down, and people buy more of them. The invisible hand—the price mechanism—sees to it that what people demand (do what's necessary to get) matches what's available.

The Law of Demand

The ideas expressed above are the foundation of the **law of demand:**

> *Quantity demanded rises as price falls, other things constant.*

Or alternatively:

> *Quantity demanded falls as price rises, other things constant.*

This law is fundamental to the invisible hand's ability to coordinate individuals' desires; as prices change, people change how much they're willing to buy.

What accounts for the law of demand? If the price of something goes up, people will tend to buy less of it and buy something else instead. They will *substitute* other goods for goods whose relative price has gone up. If the price of MP3 files from the Internet rises, but the price of CDs stays the same, you're more likely to buy that new Coldplay recording on CD than to download it from the Internet.

To see that the law of demand makes intuitive sense, just think of something you'd really like but can't afford. If the price is cut in half, you—and other consumers—become more likely to buy it. Quantity demanded goes up as price goes down.

Just to be sure you've got it, let's consider a real-world example: demand for vanity—specifically, vanity license plates. When the North Carolina state legislature increased the vanity plates' price from $30 to $40, the quantity demanded fell from 60,334 to 31,122. Assuming other things remained constant, that is the law of demand in action.

The Demand Curve

A **demand curve** is *the graphic representation of the relationship between price and quantity demanded.* Figure 4-1 shows a demand curve.

As you can see, the demand curve slopes downward. That's because of the law of demand: As the price goes up, the quantity demanded goes down, other things constant. In other words, price and quantity demanded are inversely related.

The law of demand states that the quantity of a good demanded is inversely related to the good's price.

Web Note 4.1
Markets without Money

When price goes up, quantity demanded goes down. When price goes down, quantity demanded goes up.

Q-1 Why does the demand curve slope downward?

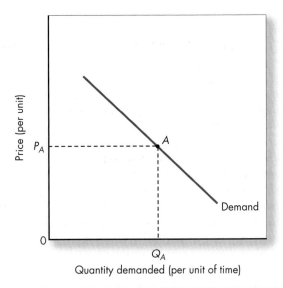

FIGURE 4-1   **A Sample Demand Curve**

The law of demand states that the quantity demanded of a good is inversely related to the price of that good, other things constant. As the price of a good goes up, the quantity demanded goes down, so the demand curve is downward-sloping.

Notice that in stating the law of demand, I put in the qualification "other things constant." That's three extra words, and unless they were important I wouldn't have included them. But what does "other things constant" mean? Say that over two years, both the price of cars and the number of cars purchased rise. That seems to violate the law of demand, since the number of cars purchased should have fallen in response to the rise in price. Looking at the data more closely, however, we see that individuals' income has also increased. Other things didn't remain the same.

The increase in price works as the law of demand states—it decreases the number of cars bought. But the rise in income increases the quantity demanded at every price. That increase in demand outweighs the decrease in quantity demanded that results from a rise in price, so ultimately more cars are sold. If you want to study the effect of price alone—which is what the law of demand refers to—you must make adjustments to hold income constant. Because other things besides price affect demand, the qualifying phrase "other things constant" is an important part of the law of demand.

The other things that are held constant include individuals' tastes, prices of other goods, and even the weather. Those other factors must remain constant if you're to make a valid study of the effect of an increase in the price of a good on the quantity demanded. In practice, it's impossible to keep all other things constant, so you have to be careful when you say that when price goes up, quantity demanded goes down. It's likely to go down, but it's always possible that something besides price has changed.

> "Other things constant" places a limitation on the application of the law of demand.

Shifts in Demand versus Movements along a Demand Curve

To distinguish between the effects of price and the effects of other factors on how much of a good is demanded, economists have developed the following precise terminology—terminology that inevitably shows up on exams. The first distinction is between demand and quantity demanded.

- **Demand** refers to *a schedule of quantities of a good that will be bought per unit of time at various prices, other things constant.*

- **Quantity demanded** refers to *a specific amount that will be demanded per unit of time at a specific price, other things constant.*

In graphical terms, the term *demand* refers to the entire demand curve. *Demand* tells us how much will be bought *at various prices. Quantity demanded* tells us how much will be bought at a specific price; it refers to a point on a demand curve, such as point *A* in Figure 4-1. This terminology allows us to distinguish between *changes in quantity demanded* and *shifts in demand.* A change in price changes the quantity demanded. It refers to a **movement along a demand curve**—*the graphical representation of the effect of a change in price on the quantity demanded.* A change in anything other than price that affects demand changes the entire demand curve. A shift factor of demand causes a **shift in demand,** *the graphical representation of the effect of anything other than price on demand.*

To make sure you understand the difference between a movement along a demand curve and a shift in demand, let's consider an example. Singapore has one of the world's highest number of cars per mile of road. This means that congestion is considerable. Singapore adopted two policies to reduce road use: It increased the fee charged to use roads and it provided an expanded public transportation system. Both policies reduced congestion. Figure 4-2(a) shows that increasing the toll charged to use roads from $1 to $2 per 50 miles of road reduces quantity demanded from 200 to 100 cars per mile

Shifts in Demand versus Movements along a Demand Curve

> **Q-2** The uncertainty caused by the terrorist attacks of September 11, 2001, made consumers reluctant to spend on luxury items. This reduced _____. Should the missing words be *demand for luxury goods* or *quantity of luxury goods demanded?*

> Change in price causes a movement along a demand curve; a change in a shift factor causes a shift in demand.

FIGURE 4-2 (A AND B)   Shift in Demand versus a Change in Quantity Demanded

A rise in a good's price results in a reduction in quantity demanded and is shown by a movement up along a demand curve from point *A* to point *B* in (**a**). A change in any other factor besides price that affects demand leads to a shift in the entire demand curve, as shown in (**b**).

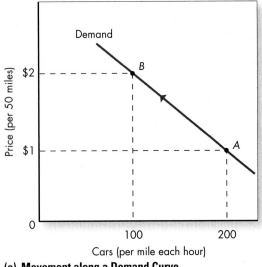

(a) Movement along a Demand Curve

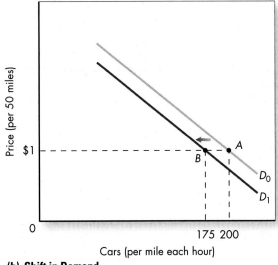

(b) Shift in Demand

every hour (a movement along the demand curve). Figure 4-2(b) shows that providing alternative methods of transportation such as buses and subways shifts the demand curve for roads in to the left so that at every price, demand drops by 25 cars per mile every hour.

Some Shift Factors of Demand

Important shift factors of demand include:

1. Society's income.
2. The prices of other goods.
3. Tastes.
4. Expectations.
5. Taxes and subsidies.

Web Note 4.2
Influencing Demand

Let's consider a couple of them. First, income. From our example above of the "other things constant" qualification, we saw that a rise in income increases the demand for goods. For most goods this is true. As individuals' income rises, they can afford more of the goods they want, such as steaks, computers, or clothing. These are normal goods. For other goods, called inferior goods, an increase in income reduces demand. An example is urban mass transit. A person whose income has risen tends to stop riding the bus to work because she can afford to buy a car and rent a parking space.

Next, let's consider the price of other goods. Because people make their buying decisions based on the price of related goods, demand will be affected by the prices of other goods. Suppose the price of jeans rises from $25 to $35, but the price of khakis remains at $25. Next time you need pants, you're apt to try khakis instead of jeans. They are substitutes. When the price of a substitute rises, demand for the good whose price has remained the same will rise. Or consider another example. Suppose the price of movie tickets falls. What will happen to the demand for popcorn? You're likely to increase the number of times you go to the movies, so you'll also likely increase the amount of popcorn you purchase. The lower cost of a movie ticket increases the demand for popcorn because popcorn and movies are complements. When the price of a good declines, the demand for its complement rises.

Let's consider taxes and subsidies as examples of shift factors. Taxes levied on consumers increase the cost of goods to consumers and therefore reduce demand for those goods. Subsidies to consumers have the opposite effect. When states host tax-free weeks during August's back-to-school shopping season, consumers load up on products to avoid sales taxes. Demand for retail goods rises during the tax holiday.

There are many other shift factors in addition to the ones I've listed. In fact anything—except the price of the good itself—that affects demand (and many things do) is a shift factor. While economists agree these shift factors are important, they believe that no shift factor influences how much of a good people buy as consistently as its price. That's why economists make the law of demand central to their analysis.

Before we move on let's test your understanding: What happens to your demand curve for CDs in the following examples: First, let's say you buy an iPod. Next, let's say that the price of CDs falls. Finally, say that you won $1 million in a lottery. What happens to the demand for CDs in each case? If you answered: It shifts in to the left; it remains unchanged; and it shifts out to the right—you've got it.

Q-3 Explain the effect of each of the following on the demand for new computers:

1. The price of computers falls by 30 percent.

2. Total income in the economy rises.

Web Note 4.3
Shifting Demand

The Demand Table

As I emphasized in Chapter 2, introductory economics depends heavily on graphs and graphical analysis—translating ideas into graphs and back into words. So let's graph the demand curve.

Figure 4-3(a), a demand table, describes Alice's demand for online movies. For example, at a price of $4, Alice will rent (buy the use of) six movies per week, and at a price of $1 she will rent nine.

Four points about the relationship between the number of movies Alice rents and the price of renting them are worth mentioning. First, the relationship follows the law of demand: As the rental price rises, quantity demanded decreases. Second, quantity demanded has a specific *time dimension* to it. In this example, demand refers to the number of movie rentals per week. Without the time dimension, the table wouldn't provide us with any useful information. Nine movie rentals per year is quite different from nine movie rentals per week. Third, the analysis assumes that Alice's movie rentals are interchangeable—the ninth movie rental doesn't significantly differ from the first, third, or any other movie rental. The fourth point is already familiar to you: The analysis assumes that everything else is held constant.

From a Demand Table to a Demand Curve

Figure 4-3(b) translates the demand table in Figure 4-3(a) into a demand curve. Point A (quantity = 9, price = $1.00) is graphed first at the (9, $1.00) coordinates. Next we plot points B, C, D, and E in the same manner and connect the resulting dots with a solid line. The result is the demand curve, which graphically conveys the same information that's in the demand table. Notice that the demand curve is downward sloping, indicating that the law of demand holds.

FIGURE 4-3 (A AND B)   From a Demand Table to a Demand Curve

The demand table in (a) is translated into a demand curve in (b). Each combination of price and quantity in the table corresponds to a point on the curve. For example, point A on the graph represents row A in the table: Alice demands nine movie rentals at a price of 50 cents. A demand curve is constructed by plotting all points from the demand table and connecting the points with a line.

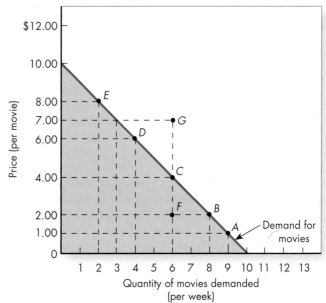

	Price per Movie	Movie Rentals Demanded per Week
A	$1.00	9
B	2.00	8
C	4.00	6
D	6.00	4
E	8.00	2

(a) A Demand Table

(b) A Demand Curve

The demand curve represents the maximum price that an individual will pay.

The demand curve represents the *maximum price* that an individual will pay for various quantities of a good; the individual will happily pay less. For example, say iTunes offers Alice six movie rentals at a price of $2 each (point *F* of Figure 4-3(b)). Will she accept? Sure; she'll pay any price within the shaded area to the left of the demand curve. But if iTunes offers her six rentals at $7 each (point *G*), she won't accept. At a price of $7 apiece, she's willing to rent only three movies.

Individual and Market Demand Curves

Normally, economists talk about market demand curves rather than individual demand curves. A **market demand curve** is *the horizontal sum of all individual demand curves*. Firms don't care whether individual A or individual B buys their goods; they only care that *someone* buys their goods.

Adding individual demand curves together to create a market demand curve is a good graphical exercise. I do that in Figure 4-4. In it I assume that the market consists of three buyers, Alice, Bruce, and Carmen, whose demand tables are given in Figure 4-4(a). Alice and Bruce have demand tables similar to the demand tables discussed previously. At a price of $6 each, Alice rents four movies; at a price of $4, she rents six. Carmen is an all-or-nothing individual. She rents one movie as long as the price is equal to or less than $2; otherwise she rents nothing. If you plot Carmen's demand curve, it's a vertical line. However, the law of demand still holds: As price increases, quantity demanded decreases.

The quantity demanded by each consumer is listed in columns 2, 3, and 4 of Figure 4-4(a). Column 5 shows total market demand; each entry is the horizontal sum of the entries in columns 2, 3, and 4. For example, at a price of $6 apiece (row *F*), Alice demands four movie rentals, Bruce demands one, and Carmen demands zero, for a total market demand of five movie rentals.

Q-4 Derive a market demand curve from the following two individual demand curves:

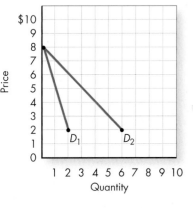

FIGURE 4-4 (A AND B) **From Individual Demands to a Market Demand Curve**

The table (**a**) shows the demand schedules for Alice, Bruce, and Carmen. Together they make up the market for movie rentals. Their total quantity demanded (market demand) for movie rentals at each price is given in column 5. As you can see in (**b**), Alice's, Bruce's, and Carmen's demand curves can be added together to get the total market demand curve. For example, at a price of $4, Carmen demands 0, Bruce demands 3, and Alice demands 6, for a market demand of 9 (point *D*).

	(1) Price (per Movie)	(2) Alice's Demand	(3) Bruce's Demand	(4) Carmen's Demand	(5) Market Demand
A	$1.00	9	6	1	16
B	2.00	8	5	1	14
C	3.00	7	4	0	11
D	4.00	6	3	0	9
E	5.00	5	2	0	7
F	6.00	4	1	0	5
G	7.00	3	0	0	3
H	8.00	2	0	0	2

(a) A Demand Table

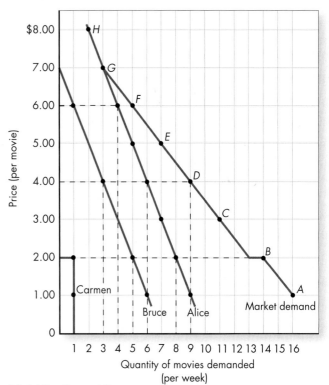

(b) Adding Demand Curves

Figure 4-4(b) shows three demand curves: one each for Alice, Bruce, and Carmen. The market, or total, demand curve is the horizontal sum of the individual demand curves. To see that this is the case, notice that if we take the quantity demanded at $2 by Alice (8), Bruce (5), and Carmen (1), they sum to 14, which is point *B* (14, $2) on the market demand curve. We can do that for each price. Alternatively, we can simply add the individual quantities demanded, given in the demand tables, prior to graphing (which we do in column 5 of Figure 4-4(a)), and graph that total in relation to price. Not surprisingly, we get the same total market demand curve.

In practice, of course, firms don't measure individual demand curves, so they don't sum them up in this fashion. Instead, they statistically estimate market demand. Still, summing up individual demand curves is a useful exercise because it shows you how the market demand curve is the sum (the horizontal sum, graphically speaking) of the individual demand curves, and it gives you a good sense of where market demand curves come from. It also shows you that, even if individuals don't respond to small changes in price, the market demand curve can still be smooth and downward sloping. That's because, for the market, the law of demand is based on two phenomena:

1. At lower prices, existing demanders buy more.

2. At lower prices, new demanders (some all-or-nothing demanders like Carmen) enter the market.

Individual and Market Demand Curves

For the market, the law of demand is based on two phenomena:

1. At lower prices, existing demanders buy more.

2. At lower prices, new demanders enter the market.

Six Things to Remember about a Demand Curve

- A demand curve follows the law of demand: When price rises, quantity demanded falls, and vice versa.

- The horizontal axis—quantity—has a time dimension.

- The quality of each unit is the same.

- The vertical axis—price—assumes all other prices remain the same.

- The demand curve assumes everything else is held constant.

- Effects of price changes are shown by movements along the demand curve. Effects of anything else on demand (shift factors) are shown by shifts of the entire demand curve.

Supply

In one sense, supply is the mirror image of demand. Individuals control the factors of production—inputs, or resources, necessary to produce goods. Individuals' supply of these factors to the market mirrors other individuals' demand for those factors. For example, say you decide you want to rest rather than weed your garden. You hire someone to do the weeding; you demand labor. Someone else decides she would prefer more income instead of more rest; she supplies labor to you. You trade money for labor; she trades labor for money. Her supply is the mirror image of your demand.

For a large number of goods and services, however, the supply process is more complicated than demand. For many goods there's an intermediate step: Individuals supply factors of production to firms.

Let's consider a simple example. Say you're a taco technician. You supply your labor to the factor market. The taco company demands your labor (hires you). The taco company combines your labor with other inputs such as meat, cheese, beans, and tables, and produces tacos (production), which it supplies to customers in the goods market. For produced goods, supply depends not only on individuals' decisions to supply factors of production but also on firms' ability to transform those factors of production into usable goods.

The supply process of produced goods is generally complicated. Often there are many layers of firms—production firms, wholesale firms, distribution firms, and retailing firms—each of which passes on in-process goods to the next layer of firms. Real-world production and supply of produced goods is a multistage process.

The supply of nonproduced goods is more direct. Individuals supply their labor in the form of services directly to the goods market. For example, an independent contractor may repair your washing machine. That contractor supplies his labor directly to you.

Thus, the analysis of the supply of produced goods has two parts: an analysis of the supply of factors of production to households and to firms and an analysis of the process by which firms transform those factors of production into usable goods and services.

The Law of Supply

There's a law of supply that corresponds to the law of demand. The **law of supply** states:

> *Quantity supplied rises as price rises, other things constant.*

Or alternatively:

> *Quantity supplied falls as price falls, other things constant.*

Price determines quantity supplied just as it determines quantity demanded. Like the law of demand, the law of supply is fundamental to the invisible hand's (the market's) ability to coordinate individuals' actions.

The law of supply is based on a firm's ability to switch from producing one good to another, that is, to substitute. When the price of a good a person or firm supplies rises, individuals and firms can rearrange their activities in order to supply more of that good to the market. They want to supply more because the opportunity cost of *not*

Supply of produced goods involves a much more complicated process than demand and is divided into analysis of factors of production and the transformation of those factors into goods.

The law of supply is based on substitution and the expectation of profits.

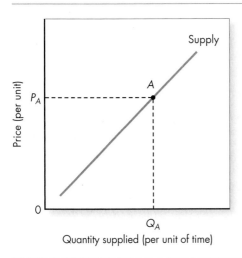

FIGURE 4-5 **A Sample Supply Curve**

The supply curve demonstrates graphically the law of supply, which states that the quantity supplied of a good is directly related to that good's price, other things constant. As the price of a good goes up, the quantity supplied also goes up, so the supply curve is upward sloping.

supplying the good rises as its price rises. For example, if the price of corn rises and the price of soybeans has not changed, farmers will grow less soybeans and more corn, other things constant.

With firms, there's a second explanation of the law of supply. Assuming firms' costs are constant, a higher price means higher profits (the difference between a firm's revenues and its costs). The expectation of those higher profits leads it to increase output as price rises, which is what the law of supply states.

The Supply Curve

A **supply curve** is *the graphical representation of the relationship between price and quantity supplied.* A supply curve is shown in Figure 4-5.

Notice how the supply curve slopes upward to the right. That upward slope captures the law of supply. It tells us that the quantity supplied varies *directly*—in the same direction—with the price.

As with the law of demand, the law of supply assumes other things are held constant. If the price of soybeans rises and quantity supplied falls, you'll look for something else that changed—for example, a drought might have caused a drop in supply. Your explanation would go as follows: Had there been no drought, the quantity supplied would have increased in response to the rise in price, but because there was a drought, the supply decreased, which caused prices to rise.

As with the law of demand, the law of supply represents economists' off-the-cuff response to the question "What happens to quantity supplied if price rises?" If the law seems to be violated, economists search for some other variable that has changed. As was the case with demand, these other variables that might change are called shift factors.

Shifts in Supply versus Movements along a Supply Curve

The same distinctions in terms made for demand apply to supply.

> **Supply** refers to *a schedule of quantities a seller is willing to sell per unit of time at various prices, other things constant.*

> **Quantity supplied** refers to *a specific amount that will be supplied at a specific price.*

amount supplied

Shifts in Supply versus Movements along a Supply Curve

different causes for a drop or rise in supply

Q-5 Assume that the price of gasoline rises, causing the demand for hybrid cars to rise. As a result, the price of hybrid cars rises. This makes _____ rise. Should the missing words be *the supply* or *the quantity supplied*?

In graphical terms, supply refers to the entire supply curve because a supply curve tells us how much will be offered for sale at various prices. "Quantity supplied" refers to a point on a supply curve, such as point *A* in Figure 4-5.

The second distinction that is important to make is between the effects of a change in price and the effects of shift factors on how much is supplied. Changes in price cause changes in quantity supplied; such changes are represented by a **movement along a supply curve**—*the graphical representation of the effect of a change in price on the quantity supplied*. If the amount supplied is affected by anything other than price, that is, by a shift factor of supply, there will be a **shift in supply**—*the graphical representation of the effect of a change in a factor other than price on supply*.

To make that distinction clear, let's consider an example: the supply of oil. In September 2005, Hurricane Katrina hit the Gulf Coast region of the United States and disrupted oil supply lines and production in the United States. U.S. production of oil declined from 4.6 to 4.1 million barrels each day. This disruption reduced the amount of oil U.S. producers were offering for sale *at every price,* thereby shifting the supply of U.S. oil to the left from S_0 to S_1, and the quantity of oil that would be supplied at the $50 price fell from point *A* to point *B* in Figure 4-6. But the price did not stay at $50. It rose to $80. In response to the higher price, other areas in the United States increased their quantity supplied (from point *B* to point *C* in Figure 4-6). That increase *due to the higher price* is called a movement along the supply curve. So if a change in quantity supplied occurs because of a higher price, it is called a *movement along the supply curve;* if a change in supply occurs because of one of the shift factors (i.e., for any reason other than a change in price), it is called a *shift in supply*.

Shift Factors of Supply

Other factors besides price that affect how much will be supplied include the price of inputs used in production, technology, expectations, and taxes and subsidies. The analysis of how these affect supply parallels the analysis of the law of demand, so we will only consider technology, leaving the analysis of other shift factors to you.

Shift factors of supply are similar to those for demand. Examples include:

1. Price of inputs.
2. Technology.
3. Expectations.
4. Taxes and subsidies.

FIGURE 4-6 **Shifts in Supply versus Movement along a Supply Curve**

A *shift in supply* results when the shift is due to any cause other than a change in price. It is a shift in the entire supply curve (see the arrow from *A* to *B*). A *movement along a supply curve* is due to a change in price only (see the arrow from *B* to *C*). To differentiate the two, movements caused by changes in price are called *changes in the quantity supplied,* not changes in supply.

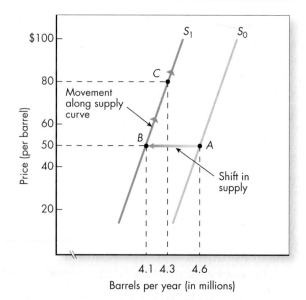

Advances in technology change the production process, reducing the number of inputs needed to produce a good, and thereby reducing its cost of production. A reduction in the cost of production increases profits and leads suppliers to increase production. Advances in technology increase supply.

Remember, as was the case with demand, a shift factor of supply is anything other than its price that affects supply. It shifts the entire supply curve. A change in price causes a movement along the supply curve.

To be sure you understand shifts in supply, explain what is likely to happen to your supply curve for labor in the following cases: (1) You suddenly decide that you absolutely need a new car. (2) You win a million dollars in the lottery. And finally, (3) the wage you earn doubles. If you came up with the answers: Shift out to the right, shift in to the left, and no change—you've got it down. If not, it's time for a review.

Do we see such shifts in the supply curve often? Yes. A good example is computers. For the past 30 years, technological changes have continually shifted the supply curve for computers out to the right.

The Supply Table

Remember Figure 4-4(a)'s demand table for movie rentals? In Figure 4-7(a), we follow the same reasoning to construct a supply table for three hypothetical movie suppliers. Each supplier follows the law of supply: When price rises, each supplies more, or at least as much as each did at a lower price.

From a Supply Table to a Supply Curve

Figure 4-7(b) takes the information in Figure 4-7(a)'s supply table and translates it into a graph of each supplier's supply curve. For instance, point C_A on Ann's supply curve corresponds to the information in columns 1 and 2, row C. Point C_A is at a price of $2 per movie and a quantity of two movies per week. Notice that Ann's supply curve is upward sloping, meaning that price is positively related to quantity. Charlie's and Barry's supply curves are similarly derived.

The supply curve represents the set of *minimum* prices an individual seller will accept for various quantities of a good. The market's invisible hand stops suppliers from charging more than the market price. If suppliers could escape the market's invisible hand and charge a higher price, they would gladly do so. Unfortunately for them, and fortunately for consumers, a higher price encourages other suppliers to begin selling movies. Competing suppliers' entry into the market sets a limit on the price any supplier can charge.

Individual and Market Supply Curves

The market supply curve is derived from individual supply curves in precisely the same way that the market demand curve was. To emphasize the symmetry, I've made the three suppliers quite similar to the three demanders. Ann (column 2) will supply two at $2; if price goes up to $4, she increases her supply to four. Barry (column 3) begins supplying at $2, and at $6 supplies five, the most he'll supply regardless of how high price rises. Charlie (column 4) has only two units to supply. At a price of $7 he'll supply that quantity, but higher prices won't get him to supply any more.

The **market supply curve** is *the horizontal sum of all individual supply curves*. In Figure 4-7(a) (column 5), we add together Ann's, Barry's, and Charlie's supplies to arrive at the market supply curve, which is graphed in Figure 4-7(b). Notice that each

Q-6 Explain the effect of each of the following on the supply of romance novels:

1. The price of paper rises by 20 percent.

2. Government provides a 10 percent subsidy to book producers.

Individual and Market
Supply Curves

FIGURE 4-7 (A AND B) From Individual Supplies to a Market Supply

As with market demand, market supply is determined by adding all quantities supplied at a given price. Three suppliers—Ann, Barry, and Charlie—make up the market of movie suppliers. The total market supply is the sum of their individual supplies at each price, shown in column 5 of (a).

Each of the individual supply curves and the market supply curve have been plotted in (b). Notice how the market supply curve is the horizontal sum of the individual supply curves.

Quantities Supplied	(1) Price (per Movie)	(2) Ann's Supply	(3) Barry's Supply	(4) Charlie's Supply	(5) Market Supply
A	$0.00	0	0	0	0
B	1.00	1	0	0	1
C	2.00	2	1	0	3
D	3.00	3	2	0	5
E	4.00	4	3	0	7
F	5.00	5	4	0	9
G	6.00	6	5	0	11
H	7.00	7	5	2	14
I	8.00	8	5	2	15

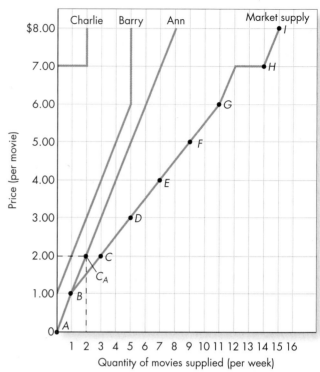

(a) A Supply Table

(b) Adding Supply Curves

point corresponds to the information in columns 1 and 5 for each row. For example, point *H* corresponds to a price of $7 and a quantity of 14.

The market supply curve's upward slope is determined by two different sources: As price rises, existing suppliers supply more and new suppliers enter the market. Sometimes existing suppliers may not be willing to increase their quantity supplied in response to an increase in prices, but a rise in price often brings brand-new suppliers into the market. For example, a rise in teachers' salaries will have little effect on the number of hours current teachers teach, but it will increase the number of people choosing to be teachers.

The law of supply is based on two phenomena:

1. At higher prices, existing suppliers supply more.

2. At higher prices, new suppliers enter the market.

The Interaction of Supply and Demand

Thomas Carlyle, the English historian who dubbed economics "the dismal science," also wrote this chapter's introductory tidbit. "Teach a parrot the terms *supply* and *demand* and you've got an economist." In earlier chapters, I tried to convince you that economics is *not* dismal. In the rest of this chapter, I hope to convince you that, while supply and demand are important to economics, parrots don't make good economists. If students think that when they've learned the terms *supply* and *demand* they've learned economics, they're mistaken. Those terms are just labels for the ideas behind supply and demand, and it's the ideas that are important. What matters about supply and demand isn't the labels but how the concepts interact. For instance, what happens if a freeze kills the blossoms on the orange trees? If price doesn't change, the quantity of oranges supplied isn't expected to equal the quantity demanded. But in the real world, prices do change, often before the frost hits, as expectations of the frost lead people to adjust. It's in understanding the interaction of supply and demand that economics becomes interesting and relevant.

Equilibrium

When you have a market in which neither suppliers nor consumers collude and in which prices are free to move up and down, the forces of supply and demand interact to arrive at an equilibrium. The concept of equilibrium comes from physics—classical mechanics. **Equilibrium** is *a concept in which opposing dynamic forces cancel each other out.* For example, a hot-air balloon is in equilibrium when the upward force exerted by the hot air in the balloon equals the downward pressure exerted on the balloon by gravity. In supply/demand analysis, equilibrium means that the upward pressure on price is exactly offset by the downward pressure on price. **Equilibrium quantity** is *the amount bought and sold at the equilibrium price.* **Equilibrium price** is *the price toward which the invisible hand drives the market.* At the equilibrium price, quantity demanded equals quantity supplied.

What happens if the market is not in equilibrium—if quantity supplied doesn't equal quantity demanded? You get either excess supply or excess demand, and a tendency for prices to change.

above equilibrium ↑

EXCESS SUPPLY   If there is **excess supply** (a surplus), *quantity supplied is greater than quantity demanded,* and some suppliers won't be able to sell all their goods. Each supplier will think: "Gee, if I offer to sell it for a bit less, I'll be the lucky one who sells my goods; someone else will be stuck with goods they can't sell." But because all suppliers with excess goods will be thinking the same thing, the price in the market will fall. As that happens, consumers will increase their quantity demanded. So the movement toward equilibrium caused by excess supply is on both the supply and demand sides.

EXCESS DEMAND   The reverse is also true. Say that instead of excess supply, there's **excess demand** (a shortage)—*quantity demanded is greater than quantity supplied.* There are more consumers who want the good than there are suppliers selling the good. Let's consider what's likely to go through demanders' minds. They'll likely call long-lost friends who just happen to be sellers of that good and tell them it's good to talk to them and, by the way, don't they want to sell that . . . ? Suppliers will be rather pleased that so many of their old friends have remembered them, but they'll also likely see the connection between excess demand and their friends' thoughtfulness. To stop their phones from ringing all the time, they'll likely raise their price. The reverse is true for excess supply. It's amazing how friendly suppliers become to potential consumers when there's excess supply.

below equilibrium ↙

PRICE ADJUSTS   This tendency for prices to rise when the quantity demanded exceeds the quantity supplied and for prices to fall when the quantity supplied exceeds

Bargain hunters can get a deal when there is excess supply.

the quantity demanded is a central element to understanding supply and demand. So remember:

When quantity demanded is greater than quantity supplied, prices tend to rise.

When quantity supplied is greater than quantity demanded, prices tend to fall.

Price Adjustment and Equilibrium

Two other things to note about supply and demand are (1) the greater the difference between quantity supplied and quantity demanded, the more pressure there is for prices to rise or fall, and (2) when quantity demanded equals quantity supplied, the market is in equilibrium.

People's tendencies to change prices exist as long as quantity supplied and quantity demanded differ. But the change in price brings the laws of supply and demand into play. As price falls, quantity supplied decreases as some suppliers leave the business (the law of supply). And as some people who originally weren't really interested in buying the good think, "Well, at this low price, maybe I do want to buy," quantity demanded increases (the law of demand). Similarly, when price rises, quantity supplied will increase (the law of supply) and quantity demanded will decrease (the law of demand).

Whenever quantity supplied and quantity demanded are unequal, price tends to change. If, however, quantity supplied and quantity demanded are equal, price will stay the same because no one will have an incentive to change.

The Graphical Interaction of Supply and Demand

Figure 4-8 shows supply and demand curves for movie rentals and demonstrates the force of the invisible hand. Let's consider what will happen to the price of movies in three cases:

1. When the price is $7 each.
2. When the price is $3 each.
3. When the price is $5 each.

1. When price is $7, quantity supplied is seven and quantity demanded is only three. Excess supply is four. Individual consumers can get all they want, but most suppliers can't sell all they wish; they'll be stuck with movies that they'd like to rent. Suppliers will tend to offer their goods at a lower price and demanders, who see plenty of suppliers out there, will bargain harder for an even lower price. Both these forces will push the price as indicated by the down arrows in Figure 4-8.

Now let's start from the other side.

2. Say price is $3. The situation is now reversed. Quantity supplied is three and quantity demanded is seven. Excess demand is four. Now it's consumers who can't get what they want and suppliers who are in the strong bargaining position. The pressures will be on price to rise in the direction of the up arrows in Figure 4-8.

3. At $5, price is at its equilibrium: Quantity supplied equals quantity demanded. Suppliers offer to sell five and consumers want to buy five, so there's no pressure on price to rise or fall. Price will tend to remain where it is (point *E* in Figure 4-8). Notice that the equilibrium price is where the supply and demand curves intersect.

What Equilibrium Isn't

It is important to remember two points about equilibrium. First, equilibrium isn't a state of the world. It's a characteristic of the model—the framework you use to look at the world. The same situation could be seen as an equilibrium in one framework and as

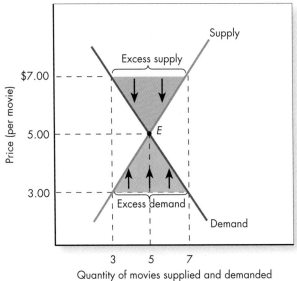

FIGURE 4-8 **The Interaction of Supply and Demand**

Combining Ann's supply from Figure 4-7 and Alice's demand from Figure 4-4, let's see the force of the invisible hand. When there is excess demand, there is upward pressure on price. When there is excess supply, there is downward pressure on price. Understanding these pressures is essential to understanding how to apply economics to reality.

Price (per Movie)	Quantity Supplied	Quantity Demanded	Surplus (+)/ Shortage (−)
$7.00	7	3	+4
$5.00	5	5	0
$3.00	3	7	−4

a disequilibrium in another. Say you're describing a car that's speeding along at 100 miles an hour. That car is changing position relative to objects on the ground. Its movement could be, and generally is, described as if it were in disequilibrium. However, if you consider this car relative to another car going 100 miles an hour, the cars could be modeled as being in equilibrium because their positions relative to each other aren't changing.

Second, equilibrium isn't inherently good or bad. It's simply a state in which dynamic pressures offset each other. Some equilibria are good—a market in competitive equilibrium is one in which people can buy the goods they really want at the best possible price. Other equilibria are awful. Say two countries are engaged in a nuclear war against each other and both sides are blown away. An equilibrium will have been reached, but there's nothing good about it.

Equilibrium is not inherently good or bad.

Political and Social Forces and Equilibrium

Understanding that equilibrium is a characteristic of the model, not of the real world, is important in applying economic models to reality. For example, in the preceding description, I said equilibrium occurs where quantity supplied equals quantity demanded. In a model where economic forces were the only forces operating, that's true. In the real world, however, other forces—political and social forces—are operating. These will likely push price away from that supply/demand equilibrium. Were we to consider a model that included all these forces—political, social, and economic—equilibrium would be likely to exist where quantity supplied isn't equal to quantity demanded. For example:

- Farmers use political pressure to obtain prices that are higher than supply/demand equilibrium prices.

- Social pressures often offset economic pressures and prevent unemployed individuals from accepting work at lower wages than currently employed workers receive.

FIGURE 4-9 (A AND B) Shifts in Supply and Demand

If demand increases from D_0 to D_1, as shown in (**a**), the quantity of movie rentals that was demanded at a price of $4.50, 8, increases to 10, but the quantity supplied remains at 8. This excess demand tends to cause prices to rise. Eventually, a new equilibrium is reached at the price of $5, where the quantity supplied and the quantity demanded are 9 (point *B*).

If supply of movie rentals decreases, then the entire supply curve shifts inward to the left, as shown in (**b**), from S_0 to S_1. At the price of $4.50, the quantity supplied has now decreased to 6 movies, but the quantity demanded has remained at 8 movies. The excess demand tends to force the price upward. Eventually, an equilibrium is reached at the price of $5 and quantity 7 (point *C*).

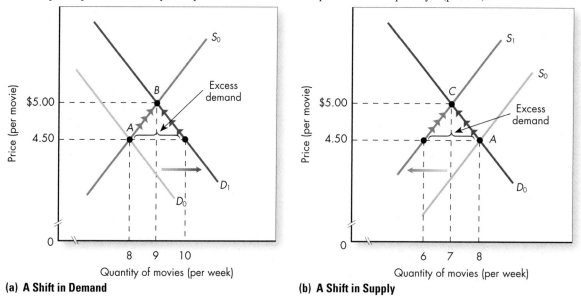

(a) **A Shift in Demand**   (b) **A Shift in Supply**

- Existing firms conspire to limit new competition by lobbying Congress to pass restrictive regulations and by devising pricing strategies to scare off new entrants.

- Renters often organize to pressure local government to set caps on the rental price of apartments.

If social and political forces were included in the analysis, they'd provide a counter–pressure to the dynamic forces of supply and demand. The result would be an equilibrium with continual excess supply or excess demand if the market were considered only in reference to economic forces. Economic forces pushing toward a supply/demand equilibrium would be thwarted by social and political forces pushing in the other direction.

Shifts in Supply and Demand

Supply and demand are most useful when trying to figure out what will happen to equilibrium price and quantity if either supply or demand shifts. Figure 4-9(a) deals with an increase in demand. Figure 4-9(b) deals with a decrease in supply.

Q-7 Demonstrate graphically the effect of a heavy frost in Florida on the equilibrium quantity and price of oranges.

Let's consider again the supply and demand for movie rentals. In Figure 4-9(a), the supply is S_0 and initial demand is D_0. They meet at an equilibrium price of $4.50 per movie and an equilibrium quantity of 8 movies per week (point *A*). Now say that the demand for movie rentals increases from D_0 to D_1. At a price of $4.50, the quantity of movie rentals supplied will be 8 and the quantity demanded will be 10; excess demand of 2 exists.

The Supply and Demand for Children

In Chapter 1, I distinguished between an economic force and a market force. Economic forces are operative in all aspects of our lives; market forces are economic forces that are allowed to be expressed through a market. My examples in this chapter are of market forces—of goods sold in a market—but supply and demand also can be used to analyze situations in which economic, but not market, forces operate. An economist who is adept at this is Gary Becker of the University of Chicago. He has applied supply and demand analysis to a wide range of issues, even the supply and demand for children.

Becker doesn't argue that children should be bought and sold. But he does argue that economic considerations play a large role in people's decisions on how many children to have. In farming communities, children can be productive early in life; by age six or seven, they can work on a farm. In an advanced industrial community, children provide pleasure but generally don't contribute productively to family income. Even getting them to help around the house can be difficult.

Becker argues that since the price of having children is lower for a farming society than for an industrial society, farming societies will have more children per family. Quantity of children demanded will be larger. And that's what we find. Developing countries that rely primarily on farming often have three, four, or more children per family. Industrial societies average fewer than two children per family.

The excess demand pushes prices upward in the direction of the small arrows, decreasing the quantity demanded and increasing the quantity supplied. As it does so, movement takes place along both the supply curve and the demand curve.

The upward push on price decreases the gap between the quantity supplied and the quantity demanded. As the gap decreases, the upward pressure decreases, but as long as that gap exists at all, price will be pushed upward until the new equilibrium price ($5) and new quantity (9) are reached (point B). At point B, quantity supplied equals quantity demanded. So the market is in equilibrium. Notice that the adjustment is twofold: The higher price brings about equilibrium by both increasing the quantity supplied (from 8 to 9) and decreasing the quantity demanded (from 10 to 9).

Figure 4-9(b) begins with the same situation that we started with in Figure 4-9(a); the initial equilibrium quantity and price are eight movies per week and $4.50 per movie (point A). In this example, however, instead of demand increasing, let's assume supply decreases—say because some suppliers change what they like to do and decide they will no longer supply movies. That means that the entire supply curve shifts inward to the left (from S_0 to S_1). At the initial equilibrium price of $4.50, the quantity demanded is greater than the quantity supplied. Two more movies are demanded than are supplied. (Excess demand = 2.)

This excess demand exerts upward pressure on price. Price is pushed in the direction of the small arrows. As the price rises, the upward pressure on price is reduced but will still exist until the new equilibrium price, $5, and new quantity, seven, are reached. At $5, the quantity supplied equals the quantity demanded. The adjustment has involved a movement along the demand curve and the new supply curve. As price rises, quantity supplied is adjusted upward and quantity demanded is adjusted downward until quantity supplied equals quantity demanded where the new supply curve intersects the demand curve at point C, an equilibrium of seven and $5.

Here is an exercise for you to try. Demonstrate graphically how the price of computers could have fallen dramatically in the past 10 years, even as demand increased. (Hint: Supply has increased even more, so even at lower prices, far more computers have been supplied than were being supplied 10 years ago.)

WWW Web Note 4.4
Changes in Equilibrium

Q-8 Demonstrate graphically the likely effect of an increase in the price of gas on the equilibrium quantity and price of hybrid cars.

A Limitation of Supply/Demand Analysis

Supply and demand are tools, and, like most tools, they help us enormously when used appropriately. Used inappropriately, however, they can be misleading. Throughout the book I'll introduce you to the limitations of the tools, but let me discuss an important one here.

Q-9 When determining the effect of a shift factor on price and quantity, in which of the following markets could you likely assume that other things will remain constant?

1. Market for eggs.
2. Labor market.
3. World oil market.
4. Market for luxury boats.

In supply/demand analysis, other things are assumed constant. If other things change, then one cannot directly apply supply/demand analysis. Sometimes supply and demand are interconnected, making it impossible to hold other things constant. Let's take an example. Say we are considering the effect of a fall in the wage rate on unemployment. In supply/demand analysis, you would look at the effect that fall would have on workers' decisions to supply labor, and on business's decision to hire workers. But there are also other effects. For instance, the fall in the wage lowers people's income and thereby reduces demand for goods. That reduction in demand for goods may feed back to firms and reduce the firms' demand for workers which might further reduce the demand for goods. If these ripple effects do occur, and are important enough to affect the result, they have to be added for the analysis to be complete. A complete analysis always includes the relevant feedback effects.

There is no single answer to the question of which ripples must be included. There is much debate among economists about which ripple effects to include, but there are some general rules. Supply/demand analysis, used without adjustment, is most appropriate for questions where the goods are a small percentage of the entire economy. That is when the other-things-constant assumption will most likely hold. As soon as one starts analyzing goods that are a large percentage of the entire economy, the other-things-constant assumption is likely not to hold true. The reason is found in the **fallacy of composition**— *the false assumption that what is true for a part will also be true for the whole.*

The fallacy of composition is the false assumption that what is true for a part will also be true for the whole.

Consider a lone supplier who lowers the price of his or her good. People will substitute that good for other goods, and the quantity of the good demanded will increase. But what if all suppliers lower their prices? Since all prices have gone down, why should consumers switch? The substitution story can't be used in the aggregate. There are many such examples.

Q-10 Why is the fallacy of composition relevant for macroeconomic issues?

An understanding of the fallacy of composition is of central relevance to macroeconomics. In the aggregate, whenever firms produce (whenever they supply), they create income (demand for their goods). So in macro, when supply changes, demand changes. This interdependence is one of the primary reasons we have a separate macroeconomics. In macroeconomics, the other-things-constant assumption central to microeconomic supply/demand analysis often does not hold.

It is to account for interdependency between aggregate supply decisions and aggregate demand decisions that we have a separate micro analysis and a separate macro analysis.

It is to account for these interdependencies that we separate macro analysis from micro analysis. In macro we use curves whose underlying foundations are much more complicated than the supply and demand curves we use in micro and in modern economics there is an active debate about how more complex structural models can extend our understanding of how markets operate.

One final comment: The fact that supply and demand may be interdependent does not mean that you can't use supply/demand analysis; it simply means that you must modify its results with the interdependency that, if you've done the analysis correctly, you've kept in the back of your head. Using supply and demand analysis is generally a step in any good economic analysis, but you must remember that it may be only a step.

Conclusion

Throughout the book, I'll be presenting examples of supply and demand. So I'll end this chapter here because its intended purposes have been served. What were those intended purposes? First, I exposed you to enough economic terminology and economic thinking to allow you to proceed to my more complicated examples. Second, I have set your mind to work putting the events around you into a supply/demand framework. Doing that will give you new insights into the events that shape all our lives. Once you incorporate the supply/demand framework into your way of looking at the world, you will have made an important step toward thinking like an economist.

Summary

- The law of demand states that quantity demanded rises as price falls, other things constant.   (LO4-1)

- The law of supply states that quantity supplied rises as price rises, other things constant.   (LO4-2)

- Factors that affect supply and demand other than price are called shift factors. Shift factors of demand include income, prices of other goods, tastes, expectations, and taxes on and subsidies to consumers. Shift factors of supply include the price of inputs, technology, expectations, and taxes on and subsidies to producers.   (LO4-1, LO4-2)

- A change in quantity demanded (supplied) is a movement along the demand (supply) curve. A change in demand (supply) is a shift of the entire demand (supply) curve.   (LO4-1, LO4-2)

- The laws of supply and demand hold true because individuals can substitute.   (LO4-1, LO4-2)

- A market demand (supply) curve is the horizontal sum of all individual demand (supply) curves.   (LO4-1, LO4-2)

- When quantity supplied equals quantity demanded, prices have no tendency to change. This is equilibrium.   (LO4-3)

- When quantity demanded is greater than quantity supplied, prices tend to rise. When quantity supplied is greater than quantity demanded, prices tend to fall.   (LO4-3)

- When the demand curve shifts to the right (left), equilibrium price rises (declines) and equilibrium quantity rises (falls).   (LO4-3)

- When the supply curve shifts to the right (left), equilibrium price declines (rises) and equilibrium quantity rises (falls).   (LO4-3)

- In the real world, you must add political and social forces to the supply/demand model. When you do, equilibrium is likely not going to be where quantity demanded equals quantity supplied.   (LO4-4)

- In macro, small side effects that can be assumed away in micro are multiplied enormously and can significantly change the results. To ignore them is to fall into the fallacy of composition.   (LO4-4)

Key Terms

demand (79)
demand curve (78)
equilibrium (89)
equilibrium price (89)
equilibrium quantity (89)
excess demand (89)
excess supply (89)

fallacy of
   composition (94)
law of demand (78)
law of supply (84)
market demand
   curve (82)
market supply curve (87)

movement along a
   demand curve (79)
movement along a supply
   curve (86)
quantity demanded (79)
quantity supplied (85)

shift in demand (79)
shift in supply (86)
supply (85)
supply curve (85)

Questions and Exercises

1. State the law of demand. Why is price inversely related to quantity demanded?   (*LO4-1*)

2. You're given the following individual demand tables for comic books.   (*LO4-1*)

Price	John	Liz	Alex
$ 2	4	36	24
4	4	32	20
6	0	28	16
8	0	24	12
10	0	20	8
12	0	16	4
14	0	12	0
16	0	8	0

   a. Determine the market demand table.
   b. Graph the individual and market demand curves.
   c. If the current market price is $4, what's total market demand? What happens to total market demand if price rises to $8?
   d. Say that an advertising campaign increases demand by 50 percent. What will happen to the individual and market demand curves?

3. List four shift factors of demand and explain how each affects demand.   (*LO4-1*)

4. Distinguish the effect of a shift factor of demand on the demand curve from the effect of a change in price on the demand curve.   (*LO4-1*)

5. State the law of supply. Why is price directly related to quantity supplied?   (*LO4-2*)

6. Mary has just stated that normally, as price rises, supply will increase. Her teacher grimaces. Why?   (*LO4-2*)

7. List four shift factors of supply and explain how each affects supply.   (*LO4-2*)

8. Derive the market supply curve from the following two individual supply curves.   (*LO4-2*)

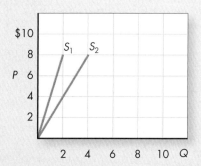

9. You're given the following demand and supply tables: (*LO4-3*)

P	Demand D₁	D₂	D₃

P	Demand D_1	D_2	D_3
$30	20	5	10
40	15	3	7
50	10	0	5
60	5	0	0

P	Supply S_1	S_2	S_3
$30	0	4	11
40	0	8	17
50	10	12	18
60	10	15	20

   a. Draw the market demand and market supply curves.
   b. What is excess supply/demand at price $30? Price $60?
   c. Label equilibrium price and quantity.

10. It has just been reported that eating red meat is bad for your health. Using supply and demand curves, demonstrate the report's likely effect on the equilibrium price and quantity of steak sold in the market.   (*LO4-3*)

11. Why does the price of airline tickets rise during the summer months? Demonstrate your answer graphically.   (*LO4-3*)

12. Why does sales volume rise during weeks when states suspend taxes on sales by retailers? Demonstrate your answer graphically assuming that the retailer pays the tax.   (*LO4-3*)

13. What is the expected impact of increased security measures imposed by the federal government on airlines fares and volume of travel? Demonstrate your answer graphically.   (*LO4-3*)

14. Explain what a sudden popularity of "Economics Professor" brand casual wear would likely do to prices of that brand.   (*LO4-3*)

15. In a flood, usable water supplies ironically tend to decline because the pumps and water lines are damaged. What will a flood likely do to prices of bottled water?   (*LO4-3*)

16. OPEC announces it will increase oil production by 20 percent. What is the effect on the price of oil? Demonstrate your answer graphically.   (*LO4-3*)

17. Draw hypothetical supply and demand curves for tea. Show how the equilibrium price and quantity will be affected by each of the following occurrences: (*LO4-3*)
    a. Bad weather wreaks havoc with the tea crop.
    b. A medical report implying tea is bad for your health is published.
    c. A technological innovation lowers the cost of producing tea.
    d. Consumers' income falls. (Assume tea is a normal good.)

18. You're a commodity trader and you've just heard a report that the winter wheat harvest will be 2 billion bushels, a 40 percent jump, rather than an expected 30 percent jump. (*LO4-3*)
    a. What would you expect would happen to wheat prices?
    b. Demonstrate graphically the effect you suggested in part *a*.

19. In the United States, say gasoline costs consumers about $2.50 per gallon. In Italy, say it costs consumers about $6 per gallon. What effect does this price differential likely have on: (*LO4-3*)
    a. The size of cars in the United States and in Italy?
    b. The use of public transportation in the United States and in Italy?
    c. The fuel efficiency of cars in the United States and in Italy?
    d. What would be the effect of raising the price of gasoline in the United States to $5 per gallon?

20. Assume that Argentina imposes a 20 percent tax on natural gas exports. (*LO4-3*)
    a. Demonstrate the likely effect of that tax on gas exports using supply and demand curves.
    b. What does it likely do to the price of natural gas in Argentina?

21. In most developing countries, there are long lines of taxis at airports, and these taxis often wait two or three hours. What does this tell you about the price in that market? Demonstrate with supply and demand analysis. (*LO4-3*)

22. Define the fallacy of composition. How does it affect the supply/demand model? (*LO4-4*)

23. In which of the following three markets are there likely to be the greatest feedback effects: market for housing, market for wheat, market for manufactured goods? (*LO4-4*)

24. State whether the "other things constant" is likely to hold in the following supply/demand analyses: (*LO4-3*)
    a. The impact of an increase in the demand for pencils on the price of pencils.
    b. The impact of an increase in the supply of labor on the quantity of labor demanded.
    c. The impact of an increase in aggregate savings on aggregate expenditures.
    d. The impact of a new method of producing CDs on the price of CDs.

Questions from Alternative Perspectives

1. In a centrally planned economy, how might central planners estimate supply or demand? (Austrian)

2. In the late 19th century, Washington Gladden said, "He who battles for the Christianization of society, will find their strongest foe in the field of economics. Economics is indeed the dismal science because of the selfishness of its maxims and the inhumanity of its conclusions."
    a. Evaluate this statement.
    b. Is there a conflict between the ideology of capitalism and the precepts of Christianity?
    c. Would a society that emphasized a capitalist mode of production benefit by a moral framework that emphasized selflessness rather than selfishness? (Religious)

3. Economics is often referred to as the study of choice.
    a. In U.S. history, have men and women been equally free to choose the amount of education they receive even within the same family?
    b. What other areas can you see where men and women have not been equally free to choose?
    c. If you agree that men and women have not had equal rights to choose, what implications does that have about the objectivity of economic analysis? (Feminist)

4. Knowledge is derived from a tautology when something is true because you assume it is true. In this chapter, you have learned the conditions under which supply and demand explain outcomes. Yet, as your text author cautions, these conditions may not hold. How can you be sure if they ever hold? (Institutionalist)

5. Do you think consumers make purchasing decisions based on general rules of thumb instead of price?
    a. Why would consumers do this?
    b. What implication might this have for the conclusions drawn about markets? (Post-Keynesian)

6. Some economists believe that imposing international labor standards would cost jobs. In support of this argument, one economist said, "Either you believe labor demand curves are downward sloping, or you don't." Of course, not to believe that demand curves are negatively sloped would be tantamount to declaring yourself an economic illiterate. What else about the nature of labor demand curves might help a policy maker design policies that could counteract the negative effects of labor standards employment? (Radical)

Issues to Ponder

1. Oftentimes, to be considered for a job, you have to know someone in the firm. What does this observation tell you about the wage paid for that job?

2. In the early 2000s, the demand for housing increased substantially as low interest rates increased the number of people who could afford homes.
   a. What was the likely effect of this on housing prices? Demonstrate graphically.
   b. In 2005, mortgage rates began increasing. What was the likely effect of this increase on housing prices? Demonstrate graphically.
   c. In a period of increasing demand for housing, would you expect housing prices to rise more in Miami suburbs, which had room for expansion and fairly loose laws about subdivisions, or in a city such as San Francisco, which had limited land and tight subdivision restrictions?

3. In 1994, the U.S. postal service put a picture of rodeo rider Ben Pickett, not the rodeo star Bill Pickett, whom it meant to honor, on a stamp. It printed 150,000 sheets. Recognizing its error, it recalled the stamp, but it found that 183 sheets had already been sold.
   a. What would the recall likely do to the price of the 183 sheets that were sold?
   b. When the government recognized that it could not recall all the stamps, it decided to issue the remaining ones. What would that decision likely do?
   c. What would the holders of the misprinted sheet likely do when they heard of the government's decision?

4. What would be the effect of a 75 percent tax on lawsuit punitive awards that was proposed by California Governor Arnold Schwarzenegger in 2004 on:
   a. The number of punitive awards. Demonstrate your answer using supply and demand curves.
   b. The number of pretrial settlements.

5. Why is a supply/demand analysis that includes only economic forces likely to be incomplete?

Answers to Margin Questions

1. The demand curve slopes downward because price and quantity demanded are inversely related. As the price of a good rises, people switch to purchasing other goods whose prices have not risen by as much. (*p. 78; LO4-1*)

2. *Demand for luxury goods.* The other possibility, *quantity of luxury goods demanded,* is used to refer to movements along (not shifts of) the demand curve. (*p. 79; LO4-1*)

3. (1) The decline in price will increase the quantity of computers demanded (movement down along the demand curve). (2) With more income, demand for computers will rise (shift of the demand curve out to the right). (*p. 81; LO4-1*)

4. When adding two demand curves, you sum them horizontally, as in the accompanying diagram. (*p. 82; LO4-1*)

5. *The quantity supplied* rises because there was a movement along the supply curve. The supply curve itself remains unchanged. (*p. 85; LO4-2*)

6. (1) The supply of romance novels declines since paper is an input to production (supply shifts in to the left); (2) the supply of romance novels rises since the subsidy decreases the cost to the producer (supply shifts out to the right). (*p. 87; LO4-2*)

7. A heavy frost in Florida will decrease the supply of oranges, increasing the price and decreasing the quantity demanded, as in the accompanying graph. (*p. 92; LO4-3*)

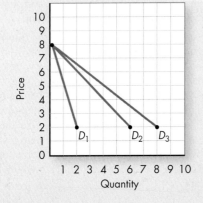

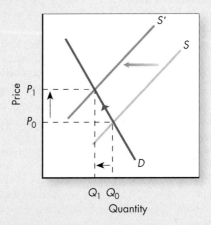

8. An increase in the price of gas will likely increase the demand for hybrid cars, increasing their price and increasing the quantity supplied, as in the accompanying graph. (*p. 93; LO4-3*)

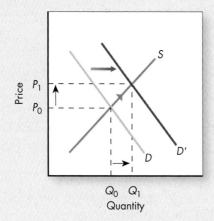

9. Other things are most likely to remain constant in the egg and luxury boat markets because each is a small percentage of the whole economy. Factors that affect the world oil market and the labor market will have ripple effects that must be taken into account in any analysis. (*p. 94; LO4-4*)

10. The fallacy of composition is relevant for macroeconomic issues because it reminds us that, in the aggregate, small effects that are immaterial for micro issues can add up and be material. (*p. 94; LO4-4*)

chapter 5

Using Supply and Demand

> *It is by invisible hands that we are bent and tortured worst.*
>
> —Nietzsche

Supply and demand give you a lens through which to view the economy. That lens brings into focus issues that would otherwise seem like a muddle. In this chapter, we use the supply/demand lens to consider real-world events.

Real-World Supply and Demand Applications

Let's begin by giving you an opportunity to apply supply/demand analysis to real-world events. Below are three events. After reading each, try your hand at explaining what happened, using supply and demand curves. To help you in the process Figure 5-1 provides some diagrams. *Before* reading my explanation, try to match the shifts to the examples. In each, be careful to explain which curve, or curves, shifted and how those shifts affected equilibrium price and quantity.

1. In the summer of 2011 Hurricane Irene damaged farms in the northeastern United States, destroying a significant portion of the apple crop. As a result apple prices rose. Market: Apples in the United States.

2. When the price of gas rose so that it cost as much as $100 to fill a tank of gas, Americans switched from SUVs to more fuel-efficient cars. The number of people shopping for used SUVs fell over 30 percent and the price of used SUVs fell an average of 10 percent. Market: Used SUVs in the United States.

3. A growing middle class in China and India has increased the demand for many food products, particularly edible oils such as soy and palm. At the same time, to meet the increasing demand for ethanol, U.S. farmers have chosen to grow less soy (from which soy oil is made) and more corn. The result? Dramatic increases in the price of edible oil worldwide. Market: Global edible oils.

Now that you've matched them, let's see if your analysis matches mine.

After reading this chapter, you should be able to:

LO5-1 Apply the supply and demand model to real-world events.

LO5-2 Demonstrate the effect of a price ceiling and a price floor on a market.

LO5-3 Explain the effect of excise taxes and tariffs on a market.

LO5-4 Explain the effect of quantity restrictions on a market.

LO5-5 Explain the effect of a third-party payer system on equilibrium price and quantity.

FIGURE 5-1 (A, B, AND C)

In this exhibit, three shifts of supply and demand are shown. Your task is to match them with the events listed in the text.

Answers: 1–b; 2–a; 3–c.

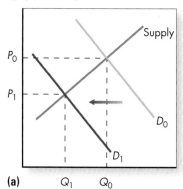
(a)

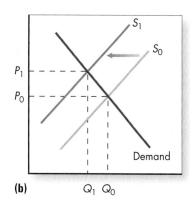
(b)

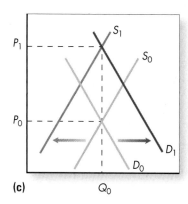
(c)

HURRICANE IRENE   Weather is a shift factor of supply. The hurricane shifted the supply curve for apples to the left, as shown in Figure 5-1(b). At the original price (shown by P_0), quantity demanded exceeded quantity supplied and the invisible hand of the market pressured the price to rise until quantity demanded equaled quantity supplied (shown by P_1).

Q-1   True or false? If supply rises, price will rise.

SALES OF SUVS   Gas is a significant cost of driving a car. To reduce their automotive gas bills, Americans reduced their demand for gas-guzzling SUVs, both new and used. Figure 5-1(a) shows that the demand curve for SUVs in the used-car market shifted from D_0 to D_1. At the original price P_0, sellers were unable to sell the SUVs they wanted to sell and began to lower their price. Buyers of used SUVs were able to purchase them at a 10 percent lower price, shown by P_1.

EDIBLE OILS   Increases in the size of the middle class in developing countries such as China and India have increased the demand for food and edible oils used to prepare those foods. This is represented by a shift in the demand for edible oils out to the right from D_0 to D_1. At the same time, increases in the price of crude oil have led U.S. farmers to grow less soy and more corn, which has shifted the supply curve from S_0 to S_1. The result has been a dramatic increase in the price of edible oils, shown in Figure 5-1(c) as an increase from P_0 to P_1.

Now that we've been through some examples, let's review. Remember: Anything that affects demand and supply other than price of the good will shift the curves. Changes in the price of the good result in movements along the curves. Another thing to recognize is that when both curves are shifting, you can get a change in price but little change in quantity, or a change in quantity but little change in price.

To test your understanding Table 5-1 gives you six generic results from the interaction of supply and demand. Your job is to decide what shifts produced those results. This exercise is a variation of the one with which I began the chapter. It goes over the same issues, but this time without the graphs. On the left-hand side of Table 5-1, I list combinations of movements of observed prices and quantities, labeling them 1–6. On the right I give six shifts in supply and demand, labeling them *a–f*.

Web Note 5.1
Fair Trade Coffee

Anything other than price that affects demand or supply will shift the curves.

Q-2   Say a hormone has been discovered that increases cows' milk production by 20 percent. Demonstrate graphically what effect this discovery would have on the price and quantity of milk sold in a market.

Supply and Demand in Action

Sorting out the effects of the shifts of supply or demand or both can be confusing. Here are some helpful hints to keep things straight:

- Draw the initial demand and supply curves and label them. The equilibrium price and quantity is where these curves intersect. Label them.

- If only price has changed, no curves will shift and a shortage or surplus will result.

- If a nonprice factor affects demand, determine the direction demand has shifted and add the new demand curve. Do the same for supply.

- Equilibrium price and quantity is where the new demand and supply curves intersect. Label them.

- Compare the initial equilibrium price and quantity to the new equilibrium price and quantity.

See if you can describe what happened in the three graphs below.

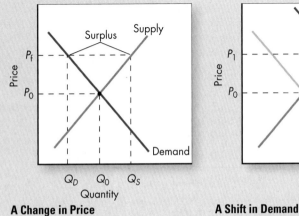

A Change in Price

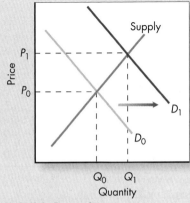

A Shift in Demand

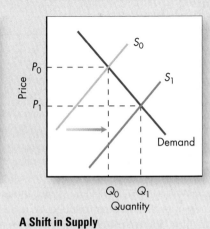

A Shift in Supply

If you don't confuse your "shifts of" with your "movements along," supply and demand provide good off-the-cuff answers for many economic questions.

You are to match the shifts with the price and quantity movements that best fit each described shift, using each shift and movement only once. My recommendation to you is to draw the graphs that are described in *a–f*, decide what happens to price and quantity, and then find the match in 1–6.

TABLE 5-1

Price and Quantity Changes		Shifts in Supply and Demand
1.	$P\uparrow$ $Q\uparrow$	a. No change in demand. Supply shifts in.
2.	$P\uparrow$ $Q\downarrow$	b. Demand shifts out. Supply shifts in.
3.	$P\uparrow$ $Q?$	c. Demand shifts in. No change in supply.
4.	$P\downarrow$ $Q?$	d. Demand shifts out. Supply shifts out.
5.	$P?$ $Q\uparrow$	e. Demand shifts out. No change in supply.
6.	$P\downarrow$ $Q\downarrow$	f. Demand shifts in. Supply shifts out.

	No Change in Supply	Supply Increases	Supply Decreases
No change in demand	P same Q same	P down Q up	P up Q down
Demand increases	P up Q up	P ambiguous Q up	P up Q ambiguous
Demand decreases	P down Q down	P down Q ambiguous	P ambiguous Q down

TABLE 5-2 Diagram of Effects of Shifts of Demand and Supply on Price and Quantity

This table provides a summary of the effects of shifts in supply and demand on equilibrium price and equilibrium quantity. Notice that when both curves shift, the effect on either price or quantity depends on the relative size of the shifts.

Now that you've worked them, let me give you the answers I came up with. They are: 1–*e;* 2–*a;* 3–*b;* 4–*f;* 5–*d;* 6–*c.* How did I come up with the answers? I did what I suggested you do—took each of the scenarios on the right and predicted what happens to price and quantity. For case *a,* supply shifts in to the left and there is a movement up along the demand curve. Since the demand curve is downward-sloping, the price rises and quantity declines. This matches number *2* on the left. For case *b,* demand shifts out to the right. Along the original supply curve, price and quantity would rise. But supply shifts in to the left, leading to even higher prices but lower quantity. What happens to quantity is unclear, so the match must be number *3.* For case *c,* demand shifts in to the left. There is movement down along the supply curve with lower price and lower quantity. This matches number *6.* For case *d,* demand shifts out and supply shifts out. As demand shifts out, we move along the supply curve to the right and price and quantity rise. But supply shifts out too, and we move out along the new demand curve. Price declines, erasing the previous rise, and the quantity rises even more. This matches number *5.*

I'll leave it up to you to confirm my answers to *e* and *f.* Notice that when supply and demand both shift, the change in either price or quantity is uncertain—it depends on the relative size of the shifts. As a summary, I present a diagrammatic of the combinations in Table 5-2.

Q-3 If both demand and supply shift in to the left, what happens to price and quantity?

Q-4 If price and quantity both fell, what would you say was the most likely cause?

Government Intervention: Price Ceilings and Price Floors

People don't always like the market-determined price. If the invisible hand were the only factor that determined prices, people would have to accept it. But it isn't; social and political forces also determine price. For example, when prices fall, sellers look to government for ways to hold prices up; when prices rise, buyers look to government for ways to hold prices down. Let's now consider the effect of such actions in the supply/demand model.[1] Let's start with an example of the price being held down.

---

[1]Modern economists use many different models. No model precisely fits reality, and when I discuss a real-world market as fitting a model, I am using pedagogical license. As I have emphasized in previous chapters, the propositions that come out of a model are theorems–logical conclusions given the assumptions. To extend the theorem to a policy precept requires considering which assumptions of the model fit the situation one is describing.

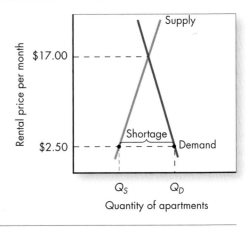

FIGURE 5-2 Rent Control in Paris

A price ceiling imposed on housing rent in Paris during World War II created a shortage of housing when World War II ended and veterans returned home. The shortage would have been eliminated if rents had been allowed to rise to $17 per month.

Price Ceilings

When government wants to hold prices down, it imposes a **price ceiling**—*a government-imposed limit on how high a price can be charged.* That limit is generally below the equilibrium price. (A price ceiling that is above the equilibrium price will have no effect at all.) From Chapter 4, you already know the effect of a price that is below the equilibrium price—quantity demanded will exceed quantity supplied and there will be excess demand. Let's now look at an example of **rent control**—*a price ceiling on rents, set by government*—and see how that excess demand shows up in the real world.

Rent controls exist today in a number of American cities as well as other cities throughout the world. Many of the laws governing rent were first instituted during the two world wars in the first half of the 20th century. Consider Paris, for example. In World War II, the Paris government froze rent to ease the financial burden of those families whose wage earners were sent to fight in the war. When the soldiers returned at the end of the war, the rent control was continued; removing it would have resulted in an increase in rents from $2.50 to $17 a month, and that was felt to be an unfair burden for veterans.

Figure 5-2 shows this situation. The below-market rent set by government created an enormous shortage of apartments. Initially this shortage didn't bother those renting apartments, since they got low-cost apartments. But it created severe hardships for those who didn't have apartments. Many families moved in with friends or extended families. Others couldn't find housing at all and lived on the streets. Eventually the rent controls started to cause problems even for those who did have apartments. The reason is that owners of buildings cut back on maintenance. More than 80 percent of Parisians had no private bathrooms and 20 percent had no running water. Since rental properties weren't profitable, no new buildings were being constructed and existing buildings weren't kept in repair. It was even harder for those who didn't have apartments.

Since the market price was not allowed to ration apartments, alternative methods of rationing developed. People paid landlords bribes to get an apartment, or watched the obituaries and then simply moved in their furniture before anyone else did. Eventually the situation got so bad that rent controls were lifted.

Web Note 5.2
Rent Control

Price Ceilings

Q-5 What is the effect of the price ceiling, P_c, shown in the graph below on price and quantity?

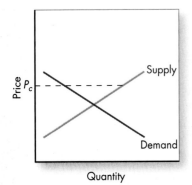

The system of rent controls is not only of historical interest. Below I list some phenomena that existed in New York City recently.

1. A couple paid $350 a month for a two-bedroom Park Avenue apartment with a solarium and two terraces, while another individual paid $1,200 a month for a studio apartment shared with two roommates.

2. The vacancy rate for apartments in New York City was 3.5 percent. Anything under 5 percent is considered a housing emergency.

3. The actress Mia Farrow paid $2,900 a month (a fraction of the market-clearing rent) for 10 rooms on Central Park West. It was an apartment her mother first leased 70 years ago.

4. Would-be tenants made payments, called key money, to current tenants or landlords to get apartments.

Your assignment is to explain how these phenomena might have come about, and to demonstrate, with supply and demand, the situation that likely caused them. (Hint: New York City had rent control.)

Now that you have done your assignment (you have, haven't you?), let me give you my answers so that you can check them with your answers.

The situation is identical with that presented above in Figure 5-2. Take the first item. The couple lived in a rent-controlled apartment while the individual with roommates did not. If rent control were eliminated, rent on the Park Avenue apartment would rise and rent on the studio would most likely decline. Item 2: The housing emergency was a result of rent control. Below-market rent resulted in excess demand and little vacancy. Item 3: That Mia Farrow rents a rent-controlled apartment was the result of nonprice rationing. Instead of being rationed by price, other methods of rationing arose. These other methods of rationing scarce resources are called *nonprice rationing*. In New York City, strict rules determined the handing down of rent-controlled apartments from family member to family member. Item 4: New residents searched for a long time to find apartments to rent, and many discovered that illegal payments to landlords were the only way to obtain a rent-controlled apartment. Key money is a black market payment for a rent-controlled apartment. Because of the limited supply of apartments, individuals were willing to pay far more than the controlled price. Landlords used other methods of rationing the limited supply of apartments—instituting first-come, first-served policies, and, in practice, selecting tenants based on gender, race, or other personal characteristics, even though such discriminatory selection was illegal. In some cases in New York City the rent was so far below the market that developers paid thousands of dollars—in one case $400,000—to a tenant to vacate an apartment so the developer could buy the building from the landlord, tear it down, and replace it with a new building.

If rent controls had only the bad effects described above, no community would institute them. They are, however, implemented with good intentions—to cope with sudden increases in demand for housing that would otherwise cause rents to explode and force many poor people out of their apartments. The negative effects occur over time as buildings begin to deteriorate and the number of people looking to rent and unable to find apartments increases. As this happens, people focus less on the original renters and more on new renters excluded from the market and on the inefficiencies of price ceilings. Since politicians tend to focus on the short run, we can expect rent control to continue to be used when demand for housing suddenly increases.

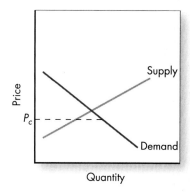

Q-6 What is the effect of the price ceiling, P_c, shown in the graph below on price and quantity?

With price ceilings, existing goods are no longer rationed entirely by price. Other methods of rationing existing goods arise called nonprice rationing.

Q-7 What is the effect of the price floor, P_f, shown in the graph below, on price and quantity?

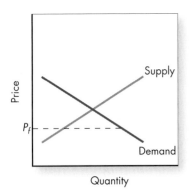

Web Note 5.3
Minimum Wage

Price Floors

The minimum wage helps some people and hurts others.

Price Floors

Sometimes political forces favor suppliers, sometimes consumers. So let us now go briefly through a case when the government is trying to favor suppliers by attempting to prevent the price from falling below a certain level. **Price floors**—*government-imposed limits on how low a price can be charged*—do just this. The price floor is generally above the existing price. (A price floor below equilibrium price would have no effect.) When there is an effective price floor, quantity supplied exceeds quantity demanded and the result is excess supply.

An example of a price floor is the minimum wage. Both individual states and the federal government impose **minimum wage laws**—*laws specifying the lowest wage a firm can legally pay an employee*. The U.S. federal government first instituted a minimum wage of 25 cents per hour in 1938 as part of the Fair Labor Standards Act. It has been raised many times since. As of 2012 the federal minimum wage was $7.25. (With inflation, that's a much smaller increase than it looks.) In 2011 about 1.7 million hourly wage earners received the minimum wage, or about 2 percent of hourly paid workers, most of whom are unskilled and/or part-time. The market-determined equilibrium wage for most full-time adult workers is generally above the minimum wage.

The effect of a minimum wage on the unskilled labor market is shown in Figure 5-3. The government-set minimum wage is above equilibrium, as shown by W_{min}. At the market-determined equilibrium wage W_e, the quantity of labor supplied and demanded equals Q_e. At the higher minimum wage, the quantity of labor supplied rises to Q_1 and the quantity of labor demanded declines to Q_2. There is an excess supply of workers (a shortage of jobs) represented by the difference $Q_1 - Q_2$. This represents people who are looking for work but cannot find it.

Who wins and who loses from a minimum wage? The minimum wage improves the wages of the Q_2 workers who are able to find work. Without the minimum wage, they would have earned W_e per hour. The minimum wage hurts those, however, who cannot find work at the minimum wage but who are willing to work, and would have been hired, at the market-determined wage. These workers are represented by the distance $Q_e - Q_2$ in Figure 5-3. The minimum wage also hurts firms that now must

FIGURE 5-3   **A Minimum Wage**

A minimum wage, W_{min}, above equilibrium wage, W_e, helps those who are able to find work, shown by Q_2, but hurts those who would have been employed at the equilibrium wage but can no longer find employment, shown by $Q_e - Q_2$. A minimum wage also hurts producers who have higher costs of production and consumers who may face higher product prices.

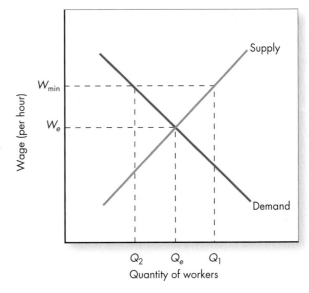

pay their workers more, increasing the cost of production, and consumers to the extent that firms are able to pass that increase in production cost on in the form of higher product prices.

All economists agree that the above analysis is logical and correct. But they disagree about whether governments should have minimum wage laws. One reason is that the empirical effects of minimum wage laws are relatively small; in fact, some studies have found them to be negligible. (There is, however, much debate about these estimates, since "other things" never remain constant.) A second reason is that some real-world labor markets are not sufficiently competitive to fit the supply/demand model. A third reason is that the minimum wage affects the economy in ways that some economists see as desirable and others see as undesirable. I point this out to remind you that the supply/demand framework is a tool to be used to analyze issues. It does not provide final answers about policy. (In microeconomics, economists explore the policy issues of interferences in markets much more carefully.)

Because the federal minimum wage is low, and not binding for most workers, a movement called the living-wage movement has begun. The living-wage movement focuses on local governments, calling on them to establish a minimum wage at a *living wage*—a wage necessary to support a family at or above the federally determined poverty line. In 2012, about 125 local governments had passed living-wage laws, with living wages ranging from $10.29 an hour in Santa Fe, NM, to $17 in Richmond, California. The analysis of these living-wage laws is the same as that for minimum wages.

Government Intervention: Excise Taxes and Tariffs

Web Note 5.4
Taxing Our Sins

Let's now consider an example of a tax on goods. An **excise tax** is *a tax that is levied on a specific good.* The luxury tax on expensive cars that the United States imposed in 1991 is an example. A **tariff** is *an excise tax on an imported good.* What effect will excise taxes and tariffs have on the price and quantity in a market?

To lend some sense of reality, let's take the example from the 1990s, when the United States taxed the suppliers of expensive boats. Say the price of a boat before the luxury tax was $60,000, and 600 boats were sold at that price. Now the government taxes suppliers $10,000 for every luxury boat sold. What will the new price of the boat be, and how many will be sold?

If you were about to answer "$70,000," be careful. Ask yourself whether I would have given you that question if the answer were that easy. By looking at supply and demand curves in Figure 5-4, you can see why $70,000 is the wrong answer.

To sell 600 boats, suppliers must be fully compensated for the tax. So the tax of $10,000 on the supplier shifts the supply curve up from S_0 to S_1. However, at $70,000, consumers are not willing to purchase 600 boats. They are willing to purchase only 420 boats. Quantity supplied exceeds quantity demanded at $70,000. Suppliers lower their prices until quantity supplied equals quantity demanded at $65,000, the new equilibrium price.

The new equilibrium price is $65,000, not $70,000. The reason is that at the higher price, the quantity of boats people demand is less. Some people choose not to buy boats and others find substitute vehicles or purchase their boats outside the United States. The tax causes a movement up along a demand curve to the left. Excise taxes reduce the quantity of goods demanded. That's why boat manufacturers were up in arms after the tax was imposed and why the revenue generated from the tax was less than expected. Instead of collecting $10,000 × 600 ($6 million), revenue collected was only $10,000 × 510 ($5.1 million). (The tax was repealed three years after it was imposed.)

A tax on suppliers shifts the supply curve up by the amount of the tax.

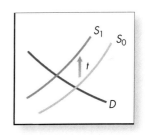

Q-8 Your study partner, Umar, has just stated that a tax on demanders of $2 per unit will raise the equilibrium price from $4 to $6. How do you respond?

FIGURE 5-4   **The Effect of an Excise Tax**

An excise tax on suppliers shifts the entire supply curve up by the amount of the tax. Since at a price equal to the original price plus the tax there is excess supply, the price of the good rises by less than the tax.

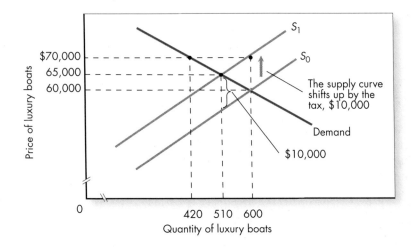

Excise Taxes

A tariff has the same effect on the equilibrium price and quantity as an excise tax. The difference is that only foreign producers sending goods into the United States pay the tax. An example is the 30 percent tariff imposed on steel imported into the United States in the early 2000s. The government instituted the tariffs because U.S. steelmakers were having difficulty competing with lower-cost foreign steel. The tariff increased the price of imported steel, making U.S. steel more competitive to domestic buyers. As expected, the price of imported steel rose by over 15 percent, to about $230 a ton, and the quantity imported declined. Tariffs don't hurt just the foreign producer. Tariffs increase the cost of imported products to domestic consumers. In the case of steel, manufacturing companies such as automakers faced higher production costs. The increase in the cost of steel lowered production in those industries and increased the cost of a variety of goods to U.S. consumers.

Government Intervention: Quantity Restrictions

Q-9 What is the effect of the quantity restrictions, Q_R, shown in the graph below, on equilibrium price and quantity?

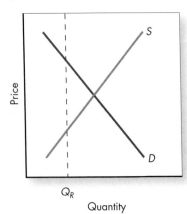

Another way in which governments often interfere with, or regulate, markets is with licenses, which limit entry into a market. For example, to be a doctor you need a license; to be a vet you need a license; and in some places to be an electrician, a financial planner, or a cosmetologist, or to fish, you need a license. There are many reasons for licenses, and we will not consider them here. Instead, we will simply consider what effect licenses have on the price and quantity of the activity being licensed. Specifically, we'll look at a case where the government issues a specific number of licenses and holds that number constant. The example we'll take is licenses to drive a taxi. In New York City, these are called taxi medallions because the license is an aluminum plate attached to the hood of a taxi. Taxi medallions were established in 1937 as a way to increase the wages of licensed taxi drivers. Wages of taxi drivers had fallen from $26 a week in 1929 to $15 a week in 1933. As wages fell, the number of taxi drivers fell from 19,000 to about 12,000. The remaining 12,000 taxi drivers successfully lobbied New York City to grant drivers with current licenses who met certain requirements permanent rights to drive taxis—medallions. (It wasn't until the early 2000s that the number of medallions was increased slightly.) The restriction had the desired effect. As the economy grew, demand for taxis grew (the demand for taxis shifted out) as shown in Figure 5-5(a) and because the supply of taxis remained at about 12,000, the wages of the taxi drivers owning medallions increased.

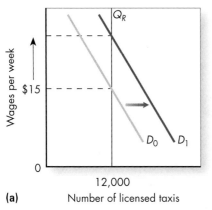 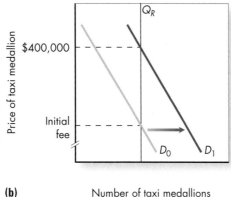

(a) Number of licensed taxis   (b) Number of taxi medallions

FIGURE 5-5 (A AND B) Quantity Restrictions in the Market for Taxi Licenses

When the demand for taxi services increased, because the number of taxi licenses was limited to 12,000, wages increased to above $15 an hour, as (**a**) shows. Because taxi medallions were limited in supply, as demand for taxi services rose, so did the demand for medallions. Their price rose significantly, as (**b**) shows.

Issuing taxi medallions had a secondary effect. Because New York City also granted medallion owners the right to sell their medallions, a market in medallions developed. Those fortunate enough to have been granted a medallion by the city found that they had a valuable asset. A person wanting to drive a taxi, and earn those high wages, had to buy a medallion from an existing driver. This meant that while new taxi drivers would earn a higher wage once they had bought a license, their wage after taking into account the cost of the license would be much lower.

As the demand for taxis rose, the medallions became more and more valuable. The effect on the price of medallions is shown in Figure 5-5(b). The quantity restriction, Q_R, means that any increases in demand lead only to price increases. Although the initial license fee was minimal, increases in demand for taxis quickly led to higher and higher medallion prices.

> Quantity restrictions tend to increase price.

The demand for taxi medallions continues to increase each year as the New York City population grows more than the supply is increased. The result is that the price of a taxi medallion continues to rise. Even with the slight increase in the number of medallions, today taxi medallions for individuals cost about $400,000, giving anyone who has bought that license a strong reason to oppose an expansion in the number of licenses being issued.[2]

Third-Party-Payer Markets

As a final example for this chapter, let's consider third-party-payer markets. In **third-party-payer markets,** *the person who receives the good differs from the person paying for the good.* An example is the health care market where many individuals have insurance. They generally pay a co-payment for health care services and an HMO or other insurer pays the remainder. Medicare and Medicaid are both third-party payers. Figure 5-6 shows what happens in the supply/demand model when there is a third-party-payer market and a small co-payment. In the normal case, when the individual demander pays for the good, equilibrium quantity is where quantity demanded equals quantity supplied—in this case at an equilibrium price of $25 and an equilibrium quantity of 10.

---

[2]As is usually the case, the analysis is more complicated in real life. New York issues both individual and corporate licenses. But the general reasoning carries through: Effective quantity restrictions increase the value of a license.

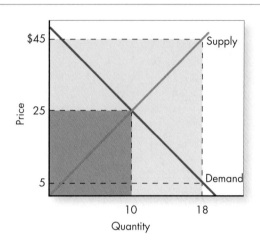

FIGURE 5-6 Third-Party-Payer Markets

In a third-party-payer system, the person who chooses the product doesn't pay the entire cost. Here, with a co-payment of $5, consumers demand 18 units. Sellers require $45 per unit for that quantity. Total expenditures, shown by the entire shaded region, are much greater compared to when the consumer pays the entire cost, shown by just the dark shaded region.

In third-party-payer markets, equilibrium quantity and total spending are much higher.

Under a third-party-payer system, the person who chooses how much to purchase doesn't pay the entire cost. Because the co-payment faced by the consumer is much lower, quantity demanded is much greater. In this example with a co-payment of $5, the consumer demands 18. Given an upward-sloping supply curve, the seller requires a higher price, in this case $45 for each unit supplied to provide that quantity. Assuming the co-payment is for each unit, the consumers pay $5 of that price for a total out-of-pocket cost of $90 ($5 times 18). The third-party payer pays the remainder, $40, for a cost of $720 ($40 times 18). Total spending is $810. This compares to total spending of only $250 (25 times 10) if the consumer had to pay the entire price. Notice that with a third-party-payer system, total spending, represented by the large shaded rectangle, is much higher than total spending if the consumer paid, represented by the small darker rectangle.

The third-party-payer system describes much of the health care system in the United States today. Typically, a person with health insurance makes a fixed co-payment for an office visit, regardless of procedures and tests provided. Given this payment system, the insured patient has little incentive to limit the procedures offered by the doctor. The doctor charges the insurance company, and the insurance company pays. The rise in health care costs over the past decades can be attributed in part to the third-party-payer system.

A classic example of how third-party-payer systems can affect choices is a case where a 70-year-old man spent weeks in a hospital recovering from surgery to address abdominal bleeding. The bill, to be paid by Medicare, was nearing $275,000 and the patient wasn't recovering as quickly as expected. The doctor finally figured out that the patient's condition wasn't improving because ill-fitting dentures didn't allow him to eat properly. The doctor ordered the hospital dentist to fix the dentures, but the patient refused the treatment. Why? The patient explained: "Seventy-five dollars is a lot of money." The $75 procedure wasn't covered by Medicare.

Q-10 If the cost of textbooks were included in tuition, what would likely happen to their prices? Why?

Third-party-payer systems are not limited to health care. (Are your parents or the government paying for part of your college? If you were paying the full amount, would you be demanding as much college as you currently are?) Anytime a third-party-payer system exists, the quantity demanded will be higher than it otherwise would be. Market forces will not hold down costs as much as they would otherwise because the person using the service doesn't have an incentive to hold down costs. Of course, that doesn't mean that there are no pressures. The third-party payers—parents, employers, and government—will respond to this by trying to limit both the quantity of the good individuals consume and the amount they pay for it. For example, parents will put pressure on their kids to get through school quickly rather than lingering for five or six years, and government will place limitations on what procedures Medicare and Medicaid patients can use. The goods will be rationed through social and political means. Such effects are not unexpected; they are just another example of supply and demand in action.

Conclusion

I began this chapter by pointing out that supply and demand are the lens through which economists look at reality. It takes practice to use that lens, and this chapter gave you some practice. Focusing the lens on a number of issues highlighted certain aspects of those issues. The analysis was simple but powerful and should, if you followed it, provide you with a good foundation for understanding the economist's way of thinking about policy issues.

Summary

- By minding your *P*s and *Q*s—the shifts of and movements along curves—you can describe almost all events in terms of supply and demand.   *(LO5-1)*

- A price ceiling is a government-imposed limit on how high a price can be charged. Price ceilings below market price create shortages.   *(LO5-2)*

- A price floor is a government-imposed limit on how low a price can be charged. Price floors above market price create surpluses.   *(LO5-2)*

- Taxes and tariffs paid by suppliers shift the supply curve up by the amount of the tax or tariff. They raise the equilibrium price (inclusive of tax) and decrease the equilibrium quantity.   *(LO5-3)*

- Quantity restrictions increase equilibrium price and reduce equilibrium quantity.   *(LO5-4)*

- In a third-party-payer market, the consumer and the one who pays the cost differ. Quantity demanded, price, and total spending are greater when a third party pays than when the consumer pays.   *(LO5-5)*

Key Terms

excise tax *(107)*
minimum wage law *(106)*

price ceiling *(104)*
price floor *(106)*

rent control *(104)*
tariff *(107)*

third-party-payer
market *(109)*

Questions and Exercises

1. Say that the equilibrium price and quantity both rose. What would you say was the most likely cause?   *(LO5-1)*

2. Say that equilibrium price fell and quantity remained constant. What would you say was the most likely cause?   *(LO5-1)*

3. The technology is now developing so that road use can be priced by computer. A computer in the surface of the road picks up a signal from your car and automatically charges you for the use of the road. How would this affect bottlenecks and rush-hour congestion?   *(LO5-1)*

4. Demonstrate the effect on price and quantity of each of the following events: (*LO5-1*)
   a. In a recent popularity test, Elmo topped Cookie Monster in popularity (this represents a trend in children's tastes). Market: cookies.
   b. The Atkins Diet that limits carbohydrates was reported to be very effective. Market: bread.

5. In 2011 oil production in Libya was interrupted by political unrest. At the same time, the demand for oil by China continued to rise. (*LO5-1*)
   a. Demonstrate the impact on the quantity of oil bought and sold.
   b. Oil production in Libya returned to its original levels by the end of 2012. What was the likely effect on equilibrium oil price and quantity? Demonstrate your answer graphically.

6. Kennesaw University Professor Frank A. Adams III and Auburn University Professors A. H. Barnett and David L. Kaserman recently estimated the effect of legalizing the sale of cadaverous organs, which currently are in shortage at zero price. What are the effects of the following two possibilities on the equilibrium price and quantity of transplanted organs if their sale were to be legalized? Demonstrate your answers graphically. (*LO5-1*)
   a. Many of those currently willing to donate the organs of a deceased relative at zero price are offended that organs can be bought and sold and therefore withdraw from the donor program.
   b. People are willing to provide significantly more organs.

7. In 2008 a drought in Australia's rice-growing regions raised the world price of rice from 12 to 24 cents a pound. Demonstrate graphically the effect of the drought on equilibrium price and quantity in the world rice market. (*LO5-1*)

8. Demonstrate graphically the effect of an effective price ceiling. (*LO5-2*)

9. Demonstrate graphically why rent controls might increase the total payment that new renters pay for an apartment. (*LO5-2*)

10. Demonstrate graphically the effect of a price floor. (*LO5-2*)

11. Graphically show the effects of a minimum wage on the number of unemployed. (*LO5-2*)

12. Taxes can be levied on consumers or producers. (*LO5-3*)
   a. Demonstrate the effect of a $4 per unit tax on suppliers on equilibrium price and quantity.
   b. Demonstrate the effect of a $4 per unit tax on consumers on equilibrium price and quantity.
   c. How does the impact on equilibrium prices (paid by consumers and received by producers) and quantity differ between *a* and *b*?

13. Draw the supply and demand curves associated with the tables below. (*LO5-3*)

Price	Q_S	Q_D
$0.00	50	200
.50	100	175
1.00	150	150
1.50	200	125
2.00	250	100

   a. What is equilibrium price and quantity?
   b. What is equilibrium price and quantity with a $.75 per unit tax levied on suppliers? Demonstrate your answer graphically.
   c. How does your answer change to *b* if the tax were levied on consumers not producers? Demonstrate your answer graphically.
   d. What conclusion can you draw about the difference between levying a tax on suppliers and consumers?

14. Quotas are quantity restrictions on imported goods. Demonstrate the effect of a quota on the price of imported goods. (*LO5-4*)

15. The City of Pawnee issues a fixed number of fishing licenses each year. (*LO5-4*)
   a. Using the accompanying graph, demonstrate the effect of a limit of 100 fishing licenses at a cost of $20 per license.
   b. Is there excess supply or demand for licenses? Label the excess supply or demand on the graph.
   c. What is the maximum amount a person would be willing to pay on the black market for a license?
   d. How much would Pawnee need to charge to eliminate the excess supply or demand?

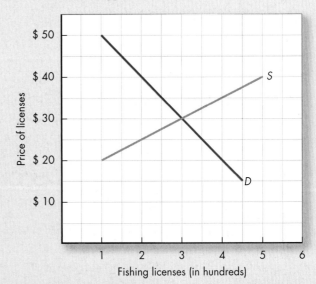

16. In what ways is the market for public post-secondary education an example of a third-party-payer market?

What's the impact of this on total educational expenditures? (*LO5-5*)

17. You're given the following supply and demand tables: (*LO5-5*)

Demand		Supply	
P	**Q**	**P**	**Q**
$ 0	1,200	$ 0	0
2	900	2	0
4	600	4	150
6	300	6	300
8	0	8	600
10	0	10	600
12	0	12	750
14	0	14	900

a. What is equilibrium price and quantity in a market system with no interferences?
b. If this were a third-party-payer market where the consumer pays $2, what is the quantity demanded? What is the price charged by the seller?
c. What is total spending in the two situations described in *a* and *b*?

Questions from Alternative Perspectives

1. Some economists believe minimum wages create distortions in the labor market. If you are an employer and unable to hire the one willing and able to work for the lowest wage, how else might you choose a worker? Is this fair? Why or why not? (Austrian)

2. On average, women are paid less than men. What are the likely reasons for that? Should the government intervene with a law that requires firms to pay equal wages to those with comparable skills? (Feminist)

3. Biological evolution occurs very slowly; cultural evolution occurs less slowly, but still slowly compared to institutional and market evolution.
   a. Give some examples of these observations about the different speeds of adjustment.
   b. Explain the relevance of these observations to economic reasoning. (Institutionalist)

4. Most religions argue that individuals should not fully exploit market positions. For example, the text makes it sound as if allowing prices to rise to whatever level clears the market is the best policy to follow. That means that if, for example, someone were stranded in the desert and were willing to pay half his or her future income for life for a drink of water, charging him or her that price would be appropriate. Is it appropriate? Why or why not? (Religious)

5. Rent control today looks far different from the rent freeze New York City enacted after World War II. Most rent controls today simply restrict annual rent increases and guarantee landlords a "fair return" in return for maintaining their properties.
   a. How would the economic effects of today's rent controls differ from the rent control programs depicted in your textbook?
   b. Do you consider them an appropriate mechanism to address the disproportionate power that landlords hold over tenants?
   c. If not, what policies would you recommend to address that inequity and the lack of affordable housing in U.S. cities? (Radical)

Issues to Ponder

1. In the late 1990s, the television networks were given $70 billion worth of space on public airways for broadcasting high-definition television rather than auctioning it off.
   a. Why do airways have value?
   b. After the airway had been given to the network, would you expect that the broadcaster would produce high-definition television?

2. About 10,000 tickets for the 2005 Men's Final Four college basketball games at the St. Louis Edward Jones Dome were to be sold in a lottery system for between $110 and $130 apiece. Typically applications exceed available tickets by 100,000. A year before the game, scalpers were already offering to sell tickets for between $200 and $2,000 depending on seat location, even though the practice is illegal.
   a. Demonstrate the supply and demand for Final Four tickets. How do you know that there is an excess demand for tickets at $130?

b. Demonstrate the scalped price of between $200 and $2,000.

c. What would be the effect of legalizing scalping on the resale value of Final Four tickets?

3. In some states and localities "scalping" is against the law, although enforcement of these laws is spotty.
   a. Using supply/demand analysis and words, demonstrate what a weakly enforced antiscalping law would likely do to the price of tickets.
   b. Using supply/demand analysis and words, demonstrate what a strongly enforced antiscalping law would likely do to the price of tickets.

4. In 1938 Congress created a Board of Cosmetology in Washington, D.C., to license beauticians. To obtain a license, people had to attend a cosmetology school. In 1992 this law was used by the board to close down a hair-braiding salon specializing in cornrows and braids operated by unlicensed Mr. Uqdah, even though little was then taught in cosmetology schools about braiding and cornrows.
   a. What possible reason can you give for why this board exists?
   b. What options might you propose to change the system?
   c. What will be the political difficulties of implementing those options?

5. In the Oregon health care plan for rationing Medicaid expenditures, therapy to slow the progression of AIDS and treatment for brain cancer were covered, while liver transplants and treatment for infectious mononucleosis were not covered.
   a. What criteria do you think were used to determine what was covered and what was not covered?
   b. Should an economist oppose the Oregon plan because it involves rationing?
   c. How does the rationing that occurs in the market differ from the rationing that occurs in the Oregon plan?

6. Airlines and hotels have many frequent flyer and frequent visitor programs in which individuals who fly the airline or stay at the hotel receive bonuses that are the equivalent to discounts.
   a. Give two reasons why these companies have such programs rather than simply offering lower prices.
   b. Can you give other examples of such programs?
   c. What is a likely reason why firms whose employees receive these benefits do not require their employees to give the benefits to the firm?

7. Since 1981, the U.S. government has supported the U.S. price of sugar by limiting sugar imports into the United States. Restricting imports is effective because the United States consumes more sugar than it produces.
   a. Using supply/demand analysis, demonstrate how import restrictions increase the price of domestic sugar.
   b. What other import policy could the government implement to have the same effect as the import restriction?

c. Under the Uruguay Round of the General Agreement on Tariffs and Trade, the United States agreed to permit at least 1.25 million tons of sugar to be imported into the United States. How does this affect the U.S. sugar price support program?

8. Apartments in New York City are often hard to find. One of the major reasons is rent control.
   a. Demonstrate graphically how rent controls could make apartments hard to find.
   b. Often one can get an apartment if one makes a side payment to the current tenant. Can you explain why?
   c. What would be the likely effect of eliminating rent controls?
   d. What is the political appeal of rent controls?

9. Until recently, angora goat wool (mohair) has been designated as a strategic commodity (it used to be utilized in some military clothing). Because of that, in 1992 for every dollar's worth of mohair sold to manufacturers, ranchers received $3.60.
   a. Demonstrate graphically the effect of eliminating this designation and subsidy.
   b. Why was the program likely kept in existence for so long?
   c. Say that a politician has suggested that the government should pass a law that requires all consumers to pay a price for angora goat wool high enough so that the sellers of that wool would receive $3.60 more than the market price. Demonstrate the effect of the law graphically. Would consumers support it? How about suppliers?

10. Supply/demand analysis states that equilibrium occurs where quantity supplied equals quantity demanded, but in U.S. agricultural markets quantity supplied almost always exceeds quantity demanded. How can this be?

11. Nobel Prize–winning economist Bill Vickrey suggested that automobile insurance should be paid as a tax on gas, rather than as a fixed fee per year per car. How would that change likely affect the number of automobiles that individuals own?

12. The United States imposes substantial taxes on cigarettes but not on loose tobacco. When the tax went into effect, what effect did it likely have for cigarette rolling machines?

13. In Japan, doctors prescribe drugs and sell the drugs to the patient, receiving a 25 percent markup. In the United States, doctors prescribe drugs, but, generally, they do not sell them.
   a. Which country prescribes the most drugs? Why?
   b. How would a plan to limit the price of old drugs, but not new drugs to allow for innovation, likely affect the drug industry?
   c. How might a drug company in the United States encourage a doctor in the United States, where doctors receive nothing for drugs, to prescribe more drugs?

14. In the early 2000s, Whole Foods Market Inc. switched to a medical care plan that had a high deductible, which meant that employees were responsible for the first $1,500 of care, whereas after that they received 80 percent coverage. The firm also put about $800 in an account for each employee to use for medical care. If they did not use this money, they could carry it over to the next year.
    a. What do you expect happened to medical claim costs?
    b. What do you believe happened to hospital admissions?
    c. Demonstrate graphically the reasons for your answers in *a* and *b*.

Answers to Margin Questions

1. False. When supply rises, supply shifts out to the right. Price falls because demand slopes downward. (*p. 101; LO5-1*)

2. A discovery of a hormone that will increase cows' milk production by 20 percent will increase the supply of milk, pushing the price down and increasing the quantity demanded, as in the accompanying graph. (*p. 101; LO5-1*)

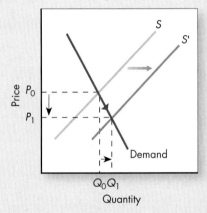

3. Quantity decreases but it is unclear what happens to price. (*p. 103; LO5-1*)

4. It is likely demand shifted in and supply remained constant. (*p. 103; LO5-1*)

5. Since the price ceiling is above the equilibrium price, it will have no effect on the market-determined equilibrium price and quantity. (*p. 104; LO5-2*)

6. The price ceiling will result in a lower price and quantity sold. There will be excess demand $Q_D - Q_S$. (*p. 105; LO5-2*)

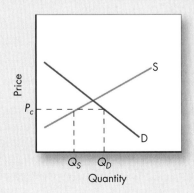

7. Since the price floor is below the equilibrium price, it will have no effect on the market-determined equilibrium price and quantity. (*p. 106; LO5-2*)

8. I would respond that the tax will most likely raise the price by less than $2 since the tax will cause the quantity demanded to decrease. This will decrease quantity supplied, and hence decrease the price the suppliers receive. In the diagram below, Q falls from Q_0 to Q_1 and the price the supplier receives falls from $4 to $3, making the final price $5, not $6. (*p. 107; LO5-3*)

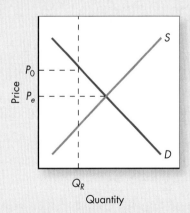

9. Given the quantity restriction, equilibrium quantity will be Q_R and equilibrium price will be P_0, which is higher than the market equilibrium price of P_e. (*p. 108; LO5-4*)

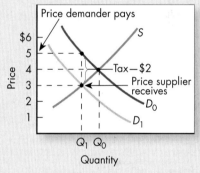

10. Universities would probably charge the high tuition they do now, but they would likely negotiate with publishers for lower textbook prices because they are both demanding and paying for the textbook. (*p. 110; LO5-5*)

Algebraic Representation of Supply, Demand, and Equilibrium

In this chapter and Chapter 4, I discussed demand, supply, and the determination of equilibrium price and quantity in words and graphs. These concepts also can be presented in equations. In this appendix I do so, using straight-line supply and demand curves.

The Laws of Supply and Demand in Equations

Since the law of supply states that quantity supplied is positively related to price, the slope of an equation specifying a supply curve is positive. (The quantity intercept term is generally less than zero since suppliers are generally unwilling to supply a good at a price less than zero.) An example of a supply equation is

$$Q_S = -5 + 2P$$

where Q_S is units supplied and P is the price of each unit in dollars per unit. The law of demand states that as price rises, quantity demanded declines. Price and quantity are negatively related, so a demand curve has a negative slope. An example of a demand equation is

$$Q_D = 10 - P$$

where Q_D is units demanded and P is the price of each unit in dollars per unit.

Determination of Equilibrium

The equilibrium price and quantity can be determined in three steps using these two equations. To find the equilibrium price and quantity for these particular demand and supply curves, you must find the quantity and price that solve both equations simultaneously.

Step 1: Set the quantity demanded equal to quantity supplied:

$$Q_S = Q_D \rightarrow -5 + 2P = 10 - P$$

Step 2: Solve for the price by rearranging terms. Doing so gives:

$$3P = 15$$
$$P = \$5$$

116

FIGURE A5-1 Supply and Demand Equilibrium

The algebra in this appendix leads to the same results as the geometry in the chapter. Equilibrium occurs where quantity supplied equals quantity demanded.

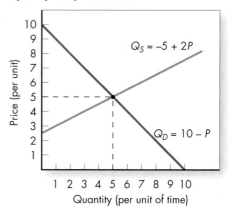

Thus, equilibrium price is $5.

Step 3: To find equilibrium quantity, you can substitute $5 for P in either the demand or supply equation. Let's do it for supply: $Q_S = -5 + (2 \times 5) = 5$ units. I'll leave it to you to confirm that the quantity you obtain by substituting $P = \$5$ in the demand equation is also 5 units.

The answer could also be found graphically. The supply and demand curves specified by these equations are depicted in Figure A5-1. As you can see, demand and supply intersect; quantity demanded equals quantity supplied at a quantity of 5 units and a price of $5.

Movements along a Demand and Supply Curve

The demand and supply curves above represent schedules of quantities demanded and supplied at various prices. Movements along each can be represented by selecting various prices and solving for quantity demanded and supplied. Let's create a supply and demand table using the above equations—supply: $Q_S = -5 + 2P$; demand: $Q_D = 10 - P$.

P	$Q_S = -5 + 2P$	$Q_D = 10 - P$
$ 0	−5	10
1	−3	9
2	−1	8
3	1	7
4	3	6
5	5	5
6	7	4
7	9	3
8	11	2
9	13	1
10	15	0

As you move down the rows, you are moving up along the supply schedule, as shown by increasing quantity supplied, and moving down along the demand schedule, as shown by decreasing quantity demanded. Just to confirm your equilibrium quantity and price calculations, notice that at a price of $5, quantity demanded equals quantity supplied.

Shifts of a Demand and Supply Schedule

What would happen if suppliers changed their expectations so that they would be willing to sell more goods at every price? This shift factor of supply would shift the entire supply curve out to the right. Let's say that at every price, quantity supplied increases by 3. Mathematically the new equation would be $Q_S = -2 + 2P$. The quantity intercept increases by 3. What would you expect to happen to equilibrium price and quantity? Let's solve the equations mathematically first.

Step 1: To determine equilibrium price, set the new quantity supplied equal to quantity demanded:

$$10 - P = -2 + 2P$$

Step 2: Solve for the equilibrium price:

$$12 = 3P$$
$$P = \$4$$

Step 3: To determine equilibrium quantity, substitute P in either the demand or supply equation:

$$Q_D = 10 - (1 \times 4) = 6 \text{ units}$$
$$Q_S = -2 + (2 \times 4) = 6 \text{ units}$$

Equilibrium price declined to $4 and equilibrium quantity rose to 6, just as you would expect with a rightward shift in a supply curve.

Now let's suppose that demand shifts out to the right. Here we would expect both equilibrium price and

equilibrium quantity to rise. We begin with our original supply and demand curves—supply: $Q_S = -5 + 2P$; demand: $Q_D = 10 - P$. Let's say at every price, the quantity demanded rises by 3. The new equation for demand would be $Q_D = 13 - P$. You may want to solve this equation for various prices to confirm that at every price, quantity demanded rises by 3. Let's solve the equations for equilibrium price and quantity.

Step 1: Set the quantities equal to one another:

$$13 - P = -5 + 2P$$

Step 2: Solve for equilibrium price:

$$18 = 3P$$
$$P = \$6$$

Step 3: Substitute P in either the demand or supply equation:

$$Q_D = 13 - (1 \times 6) = 7 \text{ units}$$
$$Q_S = -5 + (2 \times 6) = 7 \text{ units}$$

Equilibrium price rose to $6 and equilibrium quantity rose to 7 units, just as you would expect with a rightward shift in a demand curve.

Just to make sure you've got it, I will do two more examples. First, suppose the demand and supply equations for wheat per year in the United States can be specified as follows (notice that the slope is negative for the demand curve and positive for the supply curve):

$$Q_D = 500 - 2P$$
$$Q_S = -100 + 4P$$

P is the price in dollars per thousand bushels and Q is the quantity of wheat in thousands of bushels. Remember that the units must always be stated. What are the equilibrium price and quantity?

Step 1: Set the quantities equal to one another:

$$500 - 2P = -100 + 4P$$

Step 2: Solve for equilibrium price:

$$600 = 6P$$
$$P = \$100$$

Step 3: Substitute P in either the demand or supply equation:

$$Q_D = 500 - (2 \times 100) = 300$$
$$Q_S = -100 + (4 \times 100) = 300$$

Equilibrium quantity is 300 thousand bushels.

As my final example, take a look at Alice's demand curve depicted in Figure 4-4(b) in Chapter 4. Can you write an equation that represents the demand curve in that figure? It is $Q_D = 10 - 2P$. At a price of zero, the quantity of movie rentals Alice demands is 10, and for every increase in price of $1, the quantity she demands falls by 2. Now look at Ann's supply curve shown in Figure 4-7(b) in Chapter 4. Ann's supply curve mathematically is $Q_S = 2P$. At a zero price, the quantity Ann supplies is zero, and for every $1 increase in price, the quantity she supplies rises by 2. What are the equilibrium price and quantity?

Step 1: Set the quantities equal to one another:

$$10 - 2P = 2P$$

Step 2: Solve for equilibrium price:

$$4P = 10$$
$$P = \$2.5$$

Step 3: Substitute P in either the demand or supply equation:

$$Q_D = 10 - (2 \times 2.5) = 5, \text{ or}$$
$$Q_S = 2 \times 2.5 = 5 \text{ movies per week}$$

Ann is willing to supply five movies per week at $2.50 per rental and Alice demands five movies at $2.50 per movie rental. Remember that in Figure 4-8 in Chapter 4, I showed you graphically the equilibrium quantity and price of Alice's demand curve and Ann's supply curve. I'll leave it up to you to check that the graphic solution in Figure 4-8 is the same as the mathematical solution we came up with here.

Price Ceilings and Price Floors

Let's now consider a price ceiling and price floor. We start with the supply and demand curves:

$$Q_S = -5 + 2P$$
$$Q_D = 10 - P$$

This gave us the solution

$$P = 5$$
$$Q = 5$$

Now, say that a price ceiling of $4 is imposed. Would you expect a shortage or a surplus? If you said "shortage," you're doing well. If not, review the chapter before continuing with this appendix. To find out how much the shortage is, we must find out how much will be supplied and how much will be demanded at the price ceiling. Substituting $4 for price in both equations lets us see that $Q_S = 3$ units and $Q_D = 6$ units. There will be a shortage of three units. Next, let's consider a price floor of $6. To determine the surplus, we follow the same exercise. Substituting $6 into the two equations gives a quantity supplied of seven units and a quantity demanded of four units, so there is a surplus of three units.

Taxes and Subsidies

Next, let's consider the effect of a tax of $1 placed on the supplier. That tax would decrease the price received by suppliers by $1. In other words,

$$Q_S = -5 + 2(P - 1)$$

Multiplying the terms in parentheses by 2 and collecting terms results in

$$Q_S = -7 + 2P$$

This supply equation has the same slope as in the previous case, but a new intercept term—just what you'd expect. To determine the new equilibrium price and quantity, follow steps 1 to 3 discussed earlier. Setting this new equation equal to demand and solving for price gives

$$P = 5\tfrac{2}{3}$$

Substituting this price into the demand and supply equations tells us equilibrium quantity:

$$Q_S = Q_D = 4\tfrac{1}{3} \text{ units}$$

Of that price, the supplier must pay $1 in tax, so the price the supplier receives net of tax is $4\tfrac{2}{3}$.

Next, let's say that the tax were put on the demander rather than on the supplier. In that case, the tax increases the price for demanders by $1 and the demand equation becomes

$$Q_D = 10 - (P + 1), \text{ or}$$
$$Q_D = 9 - P$$

Again solving for equilibrium price and quantity requires setting the demand and supply equations equal to one another and solving for price. I leave the steps to you. The result is

$$P = 4\tfrac{2}{3}$$

This is the price the supplier receives. The price demanders pay is $5\tfrac{2}{3}$. The equilibrium quantity will be $4\tfrac{1}{3}$ units.

These are the same results we got in the previous cases showing that, given the assumptions, it doesn't matter who actually pays the tax: The effect on equilibrium price and quantity is identical no matter who pays it.

Quotas

Finally, let's consider the effect of a quota of $4\tfrac{1}{3}$ placed on the market. Since a quota limits the quantity supplied, as long as the quota is less than the market equilibrium quantity, the supply equation becomes

$$Q_S = 4\tfrac{1}{3}$$

where Q_S is the actual amount supplied. The price that the market will arrive at for this quantity is determined by the demand curve. To find that price, substitute the quantity $4\frac{1}{3}$ into the demand equation ($Q_D = 10 - P$):

$$4\frac{1}{3} = 10 - P$$

and solve for P:

$$P = 5\frac{2}{3}$$

Since consumers are willing to pay $\$5\frac{2}{3}$, this is what suppliers will receive. The price that suppliers would have been willing to accept for a quantity of $4\frac{1}{3}$ is $\$4\frac{2}{3}$. This can be found by substituting the amount of the quota in the supply equation:

$$4\frac{1}{3} = -5 + 2P$$

and solving for P:

$$2P = 9\frac{1}{3}$$
$$P = 4\frac{2}{3}$$

Notice that this result is very similar to the tax. For demanders it is identical; they pay $\$5\frac{2}{3}$ and receive $4\frac{1}{3}$ units. For suppliers, however, the situation is much preferable; instead of receiving a price of $\$4\frac{2}{3}$, the amount they received with the tax, they receive $5\frac{2}{3}$. With a quota, suppliers receive the "implicit tax revenue" that results from the higher price.

Questions and Exercises

1. Suppose the demand and supply for milk are described by the following equations: $Q_D = 600 - 100P$; $Q_S = -150 + 150P$, where P is price in dollars, Q_D is quantity demanded in millions of gallons per year, and Q_S is quantity supplied in millions of gallons per year.
   a. Create demand and supply tables corresponding to these equations.
   b. Graph supply and demand and determine equilibrium price and quantity.
   c. Confirm your answer to b by solving the equations mathematically.

2. Beginning with the equations in question 1, suppose a growth hormone is introduced that allows dairy farmers to offer 125 million more gallons of milk per year at each price.
   a. Construct new demand and supply curves reflecting this change. Describe with words what happened to the supply curve and to the demand curve.
   b. Graph the new curves and determine equilibrium price and quantity.
   c. Determine equilibrium price and quantity by solving the equations mathematically.
   d. Suppose the government set the price of milk at $3 a gallon. Demonstrate the effect of this regulation on the market for milk. What is quantity demanded? What is quantity supplied?

3. Write demand and supply equations that represent demand, D_0, and supply, S_0, in Figure A5-1 in this appendix.
   a. Solve for equilibrium price and quantity mathematically. Show your work.
   b. Rewrite the demand equation to reflect an increase in demand of 3 units. What happens to equilibrium price and quantity?
   c. Rewrite the supply equation to reflect a decrease in supply of 3 units at every price level. What happens to equilibrium price and quantity using the demand curve from b?

4. a. How is a shift in demand reflected in a demand equation?
   b. How is a shift in supply reflected in a supply equation?
   c. How is a movement along a demand (supply) curve reflected in a demand (supply) equation?

5. Suppose the demand and supply for wheat are described by the following equations: $Q_D = 10 - P$; $Q_S = 2 + P$, where P is the price in dollars, Q_D is quantity demanded in millions of bushels per year, and Q_S is quantity supplied in millions of bushels per year.
   a. Solve for equilibrium price and quantity of wheat.
   b. Would a government-set price of $5 create a surplus or a shortage of wheat? How much? Is $5 a price ceiling or a price floor?

6. Suppose the U.S. government imposes a $1 per gallon of milk tax on dairy farmers. Using the demand and supply equations from question 1:
   a. What is the effect of the tax on the supply equation? The demand equation?
   b. What are the new equilibrium price and quantity?
   c. How much do dairy farmers receive per gallon of milk after the tax? How much do demanders pay?

7. Repeat question 6 assuming the tax is placed on the buyers of milk. Does it matter who pays the tax?

8. Repeat question 6 assuming the government pays a subsidy of $1 per gallon of milk to farmers.

9. Suppose the demand for movies is represented by $Q_D = 15 - 4P$, and the supply of movies is represented by $Q_S = 4P - 1$. Determine if each of the following is a price floor, price ceiling, or neither. In each case, determine the shortage or surplus.
   a. $P = \$3$
   b. $P = \$1.50$
   c. $P = \$2.25$
   d. $P = \$2.50$

Microeconomics

In my vacations, I visited the poorest quarters of several cities and walked through one street after another, looking at the faces of the poorest people. Next I resolved to make as thorough a study as I could of Political Economy.

You may remember having already seen this quotation from Alfred Marshall. It began the first chapter. I chose this beginning for two reasons. First, it gives what I believe to be the best reason to study economics. Second, the quotation is from a hero of mine, one of the economic giants of all times. His *Principles of Economics* was the economists' bible in the late 1800s and early 1900s. How important was Marshall? It was Marshall who first used the supply and demand curves as an engine of analysis.

I repeat this quotation here because, for Marshall, economics was microeconomics, and it is his vision of economics that underlies this book's approach to microeconomics. For Marshall, economics was an art that was meant to be applied—used to explain why things were the way they were, and what we could do about them. He had little use for esoteric theory that didn't lead to a direct application to a real-world problem. Reflecting on the state of economics in 1906, Marshall wrote to a friend:

> I had a growing feeling in the later years of my work at the subject that a good mathematical theorem dealing with economic hypotheses was very unlikely to be good economics: and I went more and more on the rules—(1) Use mathematics as a shorthand language, rather than as an engine of inquiry. (2) Keep to them until you have done. (3) Translate into English. (4) Then illustrate by examples that are important in real life. (5) Burn the mathematics. (6) If you can't succeed in (4), burn (3). This last I did often. (From a letter from Marshall to A. L. Bowley, reprinted in A. C. Pigou, *Memorials of Alfred Marshall*, p. 427.)

Marshall didn't feel this way about mathematical economics because he couldn't do mathematics. He was trained as a formal mathematician, and he was a good one. But, for him, mathematics wasn't economics, and the real world was too messy to have applied to it much of the fancy mathematical economic work that some of his fellow economists were doing. Marshall recognized the influence of market, political, and social forces and believed that all three had to be taken into account in applying economic reasoning to reality.

You won't see much highfalutin mathematical economics in these microeconomic chapters. The chapters follow the Marshallian methodology and present the minimum of formal theory necessary to apply the concepts of economics to the real world, and then they do just that: start talking about real-world issues.

Section I, The Power of Traditional Economic Models (Chapters 6, 7, 8, and 8W), develops the supply/demand model and shows you how it can be used to analyze policy issues. Section II, International Economic Policy Issues (Chapters 9 and 10), extends economic reasoning to international issues. Section III, Production and Cost Analysis (Chapters 11 and 12), shows the foundation of cost analysis and how it relates to firms.

Section IV, Market Structure (Chapters 13–16), introduces you to various market structures, and antitrust policy.

Section V, Factor Markets (Chapters 17, 17W, and 18), looks at a particular set of markets—factor markets. These markets play a central role in determining the distribution of income. These chapters won't tell you how to get rich (you'll have to wait for the sequel for that), but they will give you new insights into how labor markets work.

Section VI, Choice and Decision Making (Chapters 19 and 20), presents both the traditional and modern theories of choice, including the game theoretic foundations of modern economic thinking and new developments in behavioral economics.

Section VII, Modern Economic Thinking (Chapters 21–23), discusses some new developments that are changing the nature of modern microeconomics.

chapter 6

Describing Supply and Demand: Elasticities

> *The master economist must understand symbols and speak in words. He must contemplate the particular in terms of the general, and touch abstract and concrete in the same flight of thought.*
>
> —J. M. Keynes

After reading this chapter, you should be able to:

LO6-1 Use *elasticity* to describe the responsiveness of quantities to changes in price and distinguish five elasticity terms.

LO6-2 Explain the importance of substitution in determining elasticity of supply and demand.

LO6-3 Relate price elasticity of demand to total revenue.

LO6-4 Define and calculate income elasticity and cross-price elasticity of demand.

LO6-5 Explain how the concept of *elasticity* makes supply and demand analysis more useful.

When JetBlue entered the airline industry, it decided to set its fares about 50 percent lower than what other airlines were charging. That decision was based on the prediction that lowering price would entice a large number of travelers to switch carriers and book travel with JetBlue. That is, JetBlue was hoping that the quantity demanded was very responsive to a change in price, or, in economic terminology, that the demand for air travel was price elastic.

Information about elasticity is extremely important to firms in making their pricing decisions, and to economists in their study of the economy. That's one reason why grocery stores like shoppers to use their preferred customer cards. These cards provide them with data about shopper behavior such as how sensitive shoppers are to price changes. Whenever a firm is thinking of changing its prices, it has a strong interest in elasticity.

Price Elasticity

The most commonly used elasticity concept is price elasticity of demand and supply. **Price elasticity of demand** is *the percentage change in quantity demanded divided by the percentage change in price:*

$$E_D = \frac{\text{Percentage change in quantity demanded}}{\text{Percentage change in price}}$$

Price elasticity of supply is *the percentage change in quantity supplied divided by the percentage change in price:*

$$E_S = \frac{\text{Percentage change in quantity supplied}}{\text{Percentage change in price}}$$

Let's consider some numerical examples. Say the price of a good rises by 10 percent and, in response, quantity demanded falls by 20 percent. The price elasticity of demand is 2 (−20 percent/10 percent). Notice that I said 2, not −2. Because quantity demanded is inversely related to price, the calculation for the price elasticity of demand comes out negative. Despite this fact, economists talk about price elasticity of demand as a positive number. (Those of you who remember some math can think of elasticity as an *absolute value* of a number, rather than a simple number.) Using this convention makes it easier to remember that a *larger* number for price elasticity of demand means quantity demanded is *more responsive* to price.

To make sure you have the idea down, let's consider two more examples. Say that when price falls by 5 percent, quantity supplied falls by 2 percent. In this case, the price elasticity of supply is 0.4 (2 percent/5 percent). And, finally, say the price goes up by 10 percent and in response the quantity demanded falls by 15 percent. Price elasticity of demand is 1.5 (15 percent/10 percent).

What Information Price Elasticity Provides

Price elasticity of demand and supply tells us exactly how quantity responds to a change in price. A price elasticity of demand of 0.3 tells us that a 10 percent rise in price will lead to a 3 percent decline in quantity demanded. If the elasticity of demand were a larger number, say 5, the same 10 percent rise in price will lead to a 50 percent decline in quantity demanded. As elasticity increases, quantity responds more to price changes.

Classifying Demand and Supply as Elastic or Inelastic

It is helpful to classify elasticities by relative responsiveness. Economists usually describe supply and demand by the terms *elastic* and *inelastic*. Formally, demand or supply is **elastic** if *the percentage change in quantity is greater than the percentage change in price* ($E > 1$). Conversely, demand or supply is **inelastic** if *the percentage change in quantity is less than the percentage change in price* ($E < 1$). In the last two examples, an elasticity of demand of 0.3 means demand is inelastic ($E_D < 1$), and an elasticity of demand of 5 means demand is elastic ($E_D > 1$).

The commonsense interpretation of these terms is the following: An *inelastic* supply means that the quantity supplied doesn't change much with a change in price. For example, say the price of land rises. The amount of land supplied won't change much, so the supply of land is inelastic. An *elastic* supply means that quantity supplied changes by a larger percentage than the percentage change in price. For example, say the price of pencils doubles. What do you think will happen to the quantity of pencils supplied? I suspect it will more than double, which means that the supply of pencils is elastic.

The same terminology holds with demand. Consider a good such as Hulu, which has a close substitute, Netflix. If Hulu's price rises, the quantity demanded will fall a lot as people shift to the substitute (Netflix). So the demand for Hulu would be highly elastic. Alternatively, consider table salt, which has no close substitute, at least at current prices. Demand for table salt is highly inelastic. That is, a rise in the price of table salt does not result in a large decline in quantity demanded.

Elasticity Is Independent of Units

Before continuing, notice that elasticity measures the percentage, not the unit, change in variables. Using percentages allows us to measure responsiveness independent of units, making comparisons among different goods easier. Say a $1

Price elasticity is the percentage change in quantity divided by the percentage change in price.

Q-1 If when price rises by 4 percent, quantity supplied rises by 8 percent, what is the price elasticity of supply?

Price Elasticity

Elastic: $E > 1$
Inelastic: $E < 1$

Elasticity Classifications

Q-2 If price elasticity of demand is greater than 1, what would we call demand: elastic or inelastic?

Percentages allow us to have a measure of responsiveness that is independent of units, making comparisons of responsiveness among different goods easier.

increase in the price of a $1,000 computer decreases the quantity demanded by 1, from 10 to 9. Say also that a $1 increase in the price of a pen, from $1 to $2, decreases quantity demanded by 1—from 10,000 to 9,999. Using unit changes, the $1 price increase reduced the quantities demanded for both pens and computers by 1. But such a comparison of unit changes is not very helpful. To see that, ask yourself if you were planning on raising your price, which good you'd rather be selling.

The computer price increased by 1/1,000 of its original price, a relatively small percentage increase, and quantity demanded declined by 1/10 of original sales, a large percentage decline. The percentage decline in quantity demanded exceeded the percentage rise in price, so your total revenue (Price × Quantity) would decrease. The percentage increase in price of pens was relatively large—100 percent—and the percentage decline in quantity demanded was relatively small—1/100 of 1 percent. So if you raise the price of pens, total revenue increases. Clearly, if you're raising your price in these examples, you'd rather be selling pens than computers.

By using percentages, this is made clear: With computers, a 0.1 percent increase in price decreases quantity demanded by 10 percent, so the elasticity is 100. With pens, a 100 percent increase in price decreases quantity demanded by 0.01 percent—an elasticity of 0.0001.

Calculating Elasticities

To see that you've got the analysis down, calculate price elasticity of demand or supply in the following three real-world examples:

Case 1: When the City of London raised the daily toll motorists pay to drive in central London by 46 percent the number of motorists driving in central London fell by 3 percent.

Case 2: In the 1980s, when gasoline prices rose by 10 percent in Washington, D.C., the quantity of gasoline demanded there fell by 40 percent.

Case 3: When the minimum wage in Vermont rose by 11 percent, the quantity of labor supplied for relevant jobs increased by about 1.7 percent.

In the first case, price elasticity of demand is 0.07. The quantity of motorists in London did not change much when the toll was increased. Elasticity was less than 1, so demand was inelastic. In the second case, price elasticity of demand is 4. The quantity of gas demanded in Washington, D.C., responded by a lot to a relatively small change in gas prices. Elasticity was greater than 1, so demand was elastic. The price elasticity of supply in the third case is 0.15. The quantity of labor supplied did not respond much to the change in wage. Elasticity was less than 1, so supply was inelastic.

Let's now calculate some elasticities graphically. Let's begin by determining the price elasticity of demand between points *A* and *B* in Figure 6-1(a).

The demand curve in the figure is a hypothetical demand for WolfPack Simulation Software. You can see that as the price of the software rises from $20 to $26, the quantity demanded falls from 14,000 to 10,000 units a year. To determine the price elasticity of demand, we need to determine the percentage change in quantity and the percentage change in price. In doing so, there is a small problem that is sometimes called the *endpoint problem:* The percentage change differs depending on whether you view the change as a rise or a decline. For example, say you calculate the rise in price from $20 to $26, starting from $20. That gives you a percentage increase in price of $[(20 - 26)/20] \times 100 = 30$ percent. If, however, you calculate that same change

FIGURE 6-1 (A AND B)   **Graphs of Elasticities**

In **(a)** we are calculating the elasticity of the demand curve between *A* and *B*. We essentially calculate the midpoint and use that midpoint to calculate percentage changes. This gives us a percentage change in price of 26 percent and a percentage change in quantity of 33 percent, for an elasticity of 1.27. In **(b)** the percentage change in price is 10.53 percent and the percentage change in quantity is 1.87 percent, giving an elasticity of 0.18.

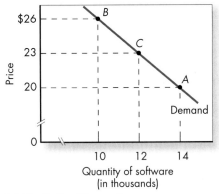

(a) Elasticity of Demand

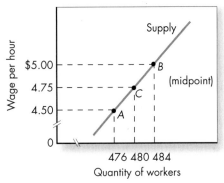

(b) Elasticity of Supply

in price, $6, as a fall in price from $26 to $20, the percentage decrease in price is $[(26 - 20)/26] \times 100 = 23$ percent. The easiest way to solve this problem is to use the average of the two end values to calculate percentage change. In our example, instead of using 20 or 26 as a starting point, you use $(20 + 26)/2$, or 23. So the percentage change in price is

Economists use the average of the two end values to get around the endpoint problem.

$$\frac{P_2 - P_1}{\frac{1}{2}(P_1 + P_2)} = \frac{(26 - 20)}{23} \times 100 = 26 \text{ percent}$$

Similarly, the percentage change in quantity is

$$\frac{Q_2 - Q_1}{\frac{1}{2}(Q_1 + Q_2)} = \frac{(10 - 14)}{12} \times 100 = -33 \text{ percent}$$

Having done this, we can calculate elasticity as usual by dividing the percentage change in quantity by the percentage change in price:[1]

$$\text{Elasticity} = \frac{\text{Percentage change in quantity}}{\text{Percentage change in price}} = \frac{-33}{26} = 1.27$$

The elasticity of demand between points *A* and *B* is approximately 1.3. This means that a 10 percent increase in price will cause a 13 percent fall in quantity demanded. Thus, demand between *A* and *B* is elastic.

---

[1] I drop the negative sign because, as discussed earlier, economists talk about price elasticity of demand as a positive number.

Q-3 What is the approximate elasticity between points *A* and *B* on the graph below?

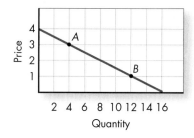

Other Examples

In Figure 6-1(b) I go through another example, this time using the supply elasticity from case 3 on p. 124. Initially, the Vermont minimum wage was $4.50 an hour; it was then raised to $5 an hour. The average of the two end points is $4.75 and so the percentage change in price is (0.50/4.75) × 100 = 10.53 percent. The initial quantity of labor supplied I estimated for my area in Vermont was 476; the rise in the minimum wage increased that number to 484, which gives us a percentage change in quantity of (8/480) × 100 = 1.67 percent. To calculate the elasticity of supply, divide the percentage change in quantity by the percentage change in price to get 1.67/10.53 = 0.16. A 10 percent rise in the minimum wage will bring about a 1.6 percent increase in quantity of labor supplied. The labor supply at the minimum wage in Vermont is inelastic.

Learning the mechanics of calculating elasticities takes some practice, so in the figure to the left are three additional examples, leaving the calculations for you.

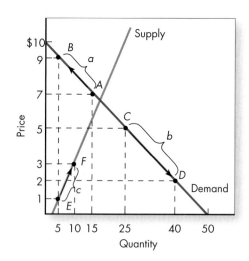

    a. Move from *A* to *B* on the demand curve.
    b. Move from *C* to *D* on the demand curve.
    c. Move from *E* to *F* on the supply curve.

Now that you've calculated them (you have, haven't you?), here are the answers upside down: a = 4; b = 0.54; c = 0.67

Elasticity Is Not the Same as Slope

There are two important points to remember about elasticity and supply and demand curves. The first is that elasticity is related to (but is not the same as) slope, and the second is that elasticity changes along straight-line demand and supply curves.

Let's begin with the first point. The relationship between elasticity and slope is the following: The steeper the curve becomes at a given point, the less elastic is supply or demand. The limiting examples of this are a vertical curve (most steep), shown in Figure 6-2(a), and a horizontal (least steep) curve, shown in Figure 6-2(b).

The vertical demand curve shown in Figure 6-2(a) demonstrates how a change in price leads to no change in quantity demanded. Economists describe this curve as **perfectly inelastic**—*quantity does not respond at all to changes in price* ($E = 0$). Curves that are vertical are perfectly inelastic. The demand curve shown in Figure 6-2(b), in contrast, is horizontal. A change in price from above or below P_0 results in an infinitely large increase in quantity demanded. This curve is **perfectly elastic,** reflecting the fact that *quantity responds enormously to changes in price* ($E = \infty$). Horizontal curves are perfectly elastic. From these extreme cases, you can see that steeper (more vertical) curves at a given point are more *in*elastic and less steep (more horizontal) curves at a given point are more elastic. Elasticity, however, is not the same as slope. The second point illustrates this well.

Elasticity Is Not the Same as Slope

Elasticity Changes along Straight-Line Curves

On straight-line supply and demand curves, slope does not change, but elasticity does. Figure 6-2(c and d) shows how elasticity changes along demand and supply curves. At the price intercept of the demand curve in Figure 6-2(c), demand is perfectly elastic ($E_D = \infty$); elasticity becomes smaller as price declines until it becomes perfectly inelastic ($E_D = 0$) at the quantity intercept. At one point along the demand curve, between an elasticity of infinity and zero, demand is **unit elastic**—*the percentage*

Q-4 Your study partner, Nicole, has just stated that a straight-line demand curve is inelastic. How do you respond?

FIGURE 6-2 (A–D) **Elasticities and Supply and Demand Curves**

In **(a)** and **(b)**, two special elasticity cases are shown. A perfectly inelastic curve is vertical; a perfectly elastic curve is horizontal. In **(c)** and **(d)**, I show how elasticity generally varies along both supply and demand curves. Along demand curves, it always goes from infinity at the vertical axis intercept to zero at the horizontal axis intercept. How elasticity of supply varies depends on which axis the supply curve intersects. If it intersects the vertical axis, elasticity starts at infinity and declines, and eventually approaches 1. If it intersects the horizontal axis, it starts at zero and increases, and eventually approaches 1. The one exception is when the supply curve intersects the origin. A good exercise is to determine what happens to elasticity in that case.

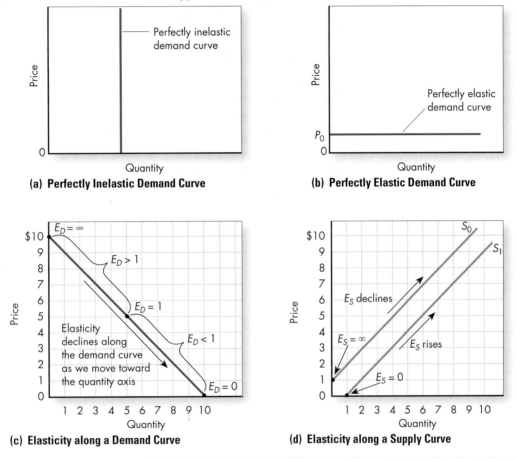

(a) Perfectly Inelastic Demand Curve

(b) Perfectly Elastic Demand Curve

(c) Elasticity along a Demand Curve

(d) Elasticity along a Supply Curve

change in quantity equals the percentage change in price ($E = 1$). In Figure 6-2(c) demand is unit elastic at a price of $5. To confirm this, calculate elasticity of demand between $4 and $6. The percentage change in price is $(2/5) \times 100 = 40$ percent, and the percentage change in quantity is $(2/5) \times 100 = 40$ percent. The point at which demand is unit elastic divides the demand curve into two sections—an elastic portion ($E_D > 1$) above the point at which demand is unit elastic and an inelastic portion ($E_D < 1$) below the point at which demand is unit elastic.

The change in elasticity along a supply curve is less dramatic. At the point on a straight-line supply curve that intercepts the price axis, supply is perfectly elastic ($E_S = \infty$). Points become less elastic as you move out along the supply curve. At the point on a straight-line supply curve that intercepts the quantity axis, supply is perfectly inelastic ($E_S = 0$); it becomes more elastic as you move out along the

Thinking Like a Modern Economist

Why Do So Many Prices End in 99 Cents?

The traditional economic assumption is that a 1 percent change in price, say from $1.01 to $1.00, is the close equivalent to a 1 percent change in price, say from $1.00 to 99 cents. Both should have almost identical effects. Behavioral economists have found that that is not the case; people react more to a fall in price from $1.00 to 99 cents than they do to a fall in price from $1.01 to $1.00. That's why we see so many prices that end in 99 cents. People perceive a $4.00 price as much higher than a $3.99 price, and they buy much more at $3.99. So the elasticity is much greater for price declines from $1.00 to $0.99 than from $1.01 to $1.00. This is a predictably irrational behavior.

Another predictably irrational behavior involves a zero price—when goods are free. People seem to react quite differently to a zero price than to other prices. In

an experiment, behavioral economists Kristina Shampanies and Dan Ariely offered to sell people one of two chocolates—a ritzy Lindt Chocolate truffle for 15 cents or a Hershey kiss for 1 cent. Seventy-three percent chose the truffle and 27 percent chose the Kiss. Then they reduced the price of both chocolates by a penny—the Lindt chocolate to 14 cents and the Kiss to FREE. The effect on demand was enormous. Now only 31 percent chose the Lindt and 69 percent chose the Hershey Kiss. A zero price seems to have a big effect on the quantity demanded.

Firms know that people react to zero prices in this manner, and they try to take advantage of it all the time. For example, they offer "free" goods that aren't really free; *buy one, and get one free* sells a lot more goods than cutting price by 50 percent.

---

supply curve. These changes are labeled in Figure 6-2(d). I leave it to you to determine what happens to the elasticity of the supply curve if the supply curve intercepts the origin. (Hint: See the Added Dimension box "Geometric Tricks for Estimating Price Elasticity.")

As a review, the five terms to describe elasticity along a curve are listed here from most to least elastic:

> Five elasticity terms are:
> 1. perfectly elastic ($E = \infty$);
> 2. elastic ($E > 1$);
> 3. unit elastic ($E = 1$);
> 4. inelastic ($E < 1$); and
> 5. perfectly inelastic ($E = 0$).

1. *Perfectly elastic:* Quantity responds enormously to changes in price ($E = \infty$).
2. *Elastic:* The percentage change in quantity exceeds the percentage change in price ($E > 1$).
3. *Unit elastic:* The percentage change in quantity is the same as the percentage change in price ($E = 1$).
4. *Inelastic:* The percentage change in quantity is less than the percentage change in price ($E < 1$).
5. *Perfectly inelastic:* Quantity does not respond at all to changes in price ($E = 0$).

Now that you have seen that elasticity changes along straight-line supply and demand curves, the first point—that elasticity is related to but not the same as slope—should be clear. Whereas elasticity changes along a straight-line curve, slope does not.

Geometric Tricks for Estimating Price Elasticity

There are a couple of useful tricks to determine whether a point on a straight-line supply or demand curve is elastic or inelastic. The trick with demand is the following: (1) Determine where the demand curve intersects the price and quantity axes. (2) At a point midway between the origin and the quantity line intersection, draw a vertical line back up to the demand curve. The point where it intersects the demand curve will have an elasticity of 1; it will be unit elastic; all points to the left of that line (a price above $4) will be elastic, and all points to the right of that (a price below $4) will be inelastic.

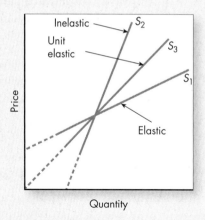

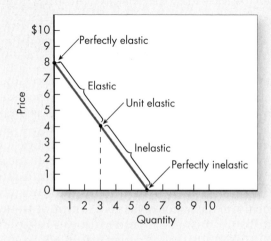

To determine whether a straight-line supply curve is elastic or inelastic you simply extend it to one of the axes, as in the following graph. The point at which this extension intersects the axes indicates the elasticity of the supply curve:

- If the extension intersects the vertical (price) axis, as does S_1, all points on the supply curve have an elasticity greater than 1; the supply curve is elastic.

- If the extension intersects the horizontal (quantity) axis, as does S_2, all points on the supply curve have an elasticity less than 1; the supply curve is inelastic.

- If the extension intersects the two axes at the origin, the supply curve has an elasticity of 1; the supply curve has unit elasticity.

If you combine these tricks with a knowledge that a perfectly elastic supply or demand curve is horizontal and crosses the price axis, and a perfectly inelastic supply or demand curve is vertical and crosses the quantity axis, you can even remember which is which. If a straight-line supply curve crosses the quantity axis, all points on it are inelastic; if it crosses the price axis, all points on it are elastic. Similarly, the top half of the demand curve (the part that crosses the price axis) is elastic; the bottom half (the part that crosses the quantity axis) is inelastic.

Substitution and Elasticity

Now that you know how to measure elasticity, let's consider some of the factors that are likely to make demand more or less elastic, that is, more or less responsive to price.

How responsive quantity demanded will be to changes in price can be summed up in one word: substitution. As a general rule, the more substitutes a good has, the more elastic is its demand.

The reasoning is as follows: If a good has substitutes, a rise in the price of that good will cause the consumer to shift consumption to those substitute goods. Put another way, when a satisfactory substitute is available, a rise in that good's price will have a large effect on the quantity demanded. For example, I think a Whopper is a satisfactory substitute for a Big Mac. If most people agree with me, when the price of Big Macs rises people will switch from Big Macs to Whoppers. The demand for Big Macs would be very elastic.

The most important determinant of price elasticity of demand is the number of substitutes for the good.

Substitution and Demand

The number of substitutes a good has is affected by several factors. Four of the most important are:

1. The time period being considered.
2. The degree to which a good is a luxury.
3. The market definition.
4. The importance of the good in one's budget.

These four reasons are derivatives of the substitution factor. Let's consider each to see why.

The more substitutes, the more elastic the demand and the more elastic the supply.

1. *The time period being considered.*   The larger the time interval considered, or the longer the run, the more elastic is the good's demand. There are more substitutes in the long run than in the short run. That's because the long run provides more alternatives. Consider when the price of rubber went up significantly during World War II. In the short run, rubber had few substitutes; the demand for rubber was inelastic. In the long run, however, the rise in the price of rubber stimulated research for alternatives. Today automobile tires, which were made of all rubber when World War II broke out, are made from almost entirely synthetic materials. In the long run, demand was very elastic.

2. *The degree to which a good is a luxury.*   The less a good is a necessity, the more elastic is its demand. Because by definition one cannot do without necessities, they tend to have fewer substitutes than do luxuries. Insulin for a diabetic is a necessity; the demand is highly inelastic. Chocolate Ecstasy cake, however, is a luxury. A variety of other luxuries can be substituted for it (for example, cheesecake or a ball game).

Q-5 What are four important factors affecting the number of substitutes a good has?

3. *The market definition.*   As the definition of a good becomes more specific, demand becomes more elastic. If the good we're talking about is broadly defined (say, transportation), it has few substitutes and demand will be inelastic. If you want to get from A to B, you need transportation. If the definition of the good is narrowed—say, to "transportation by bus"—there are more substitutes. Instead of taking a bus, you can walk, ride your bicycle, or drive your car. In that case, demand is more elastic.

4. *The importance of the good in one's budget.*   Demand for goods that represent a large proportion of one's budget is more elastic than demand for goods that represent a small proportion of one's budget. Goods that cost very little relative to your total expenditures aren't worth spending a lot of time figuring out whether there's a good substitute. An example is pencils. Their low price means most people would buy just as many even if their price doubled. Their demand is inelastic. It is, however, worth spending lots of time looking for substitutes for goods that take a large portion of one's income. The demand for such goods tends to be more elastic. Many colleges have discovered this as they tried to raise tuition when other colleges did not. The demand curve they faced was elastic.

How Substitution Factors Affect Specific Decisions

Let's consider how some of the substitution factors affect a specific decision. Let's say you've been hired by two governments (the city of Washington, D.C., and the U.S. government) to advise them about the effect that raising the gas tax by 10 percent will have on tax revenues. You look at the three factors that affect elasticity of demand.

In your report to the two governments, you would point out that in the short run demand is less elastic than in the long run, since people aren't going to trade in their gas-guzzling cars for fuel-efficient cars immediately in response to a 10 percent rise in gas taxes—partly because they can't afford to, partly because they don't want to, and partly because not that many fuel-efficient cars are available to buy at the moment.

When the time comes, however, that they would ordinarily purchase a new car, they're likely to switch to cars that are more fuel-efficient than their old cars, and to switch as much as they can to forms of transportation that are more fuel-efficient than cars. In the long run the demand will be far more elastic.

In the long run, demand generally becomes more elastic.

The second point you'd note is that gasoline is generally considered a necessity, although not all driving is necessary. However, since gasoline is only a small part of the cost of driving a car, demand will probably tend to be inelastic.

The third factor (how specifically the good is defined) requires special care. It makes your recommendations for the government of the city of Washington, D.C., and the U.S. government quite different from each other. For the U.S. government, which is interested in the demand for gasoline in the entire United States, gasoline has a relatively inelastic demand. The general rule of thumb is that a 1-cent rise in tax will raise tax revenues by $1 billion. That inelasticity can't be carried over to the demand for gasoline in a city such as Washington, D.C. Because of the city's size and location, people in Washington have a choice. A large proportion of the people who buy gas in Washington can as easily buy gas in the adjacent states of Maryland or Virginia. Gasoline in Washington is a narrowly defined good and therefore has a quite elastic demand. A rise in price will mean a large fall in the quantity of gas demanded.

www   Web Note 6.1
Price Elasticity of
Gas Demand

I mention this point because someone forgot about it when the city of Washington, D.C., raised the tax on a gallon of gasoline by 8 cents, a rise at that time of about 10 percent (this was case 2 in our discussion of calculating elasticities on p. 124). In response, monthly gasoline sales in Washington fell from 16 million gallons to less than 11 million gallons, a 40 percent decrease! The demand for gas in Washington was not inelastic, as it was for the United States as a whole; it was very elastic ($E_D = 4$). Washingtonians went elsewhere to buy gas.

The fact that smaller geographic areas have more elastic demands limits how highly state and local governments can tax goods relative to their neighboring localities or states. Where there are tax differences, new stores open all along the border and existing stores expand to entice people to come over that border and save on taxes. For example, the liquor tax is higher in Vermont than in New Hampshire, so it isn't surprising that right across the border from Vermont, New Hampshire has a large number of liquor stores. Here's one final example: If you look at license plates in Janzen Beach, Oregon (right across the Washington state border), you'll see a whole lot of Washington license plates. Why? If you answered that it likely has something to do with differential sales taxes in Washington and Oregon, you've got the idea.

Elasticity, Total Revenue, and Demand

Knowing elasticity of demand is useful to firms because from it they can tell whether the total revenue will go up or down when they raise or lower their prices. The total revenue a supplier receives is the price he or she charges times the quantity he or she sells. (Total revenue equals total quantity sold multiplied by the price of the good.) Elasticity tells sellers what will happen to total revenue if their price changes. Specifically:

- If demand is elastic ($E_D > 1$), a rise in price lowers total revenue. (Price and total revenue move in opposite directions.)
- If demand is unit elastic ($E_D = 1$), a rise in price leaves total revenue unchanged.
- If demand is inelastic ($E_D < 1$), a rise in price increases total revenue. (Price and total revenue move in the same direction.)

Q-6 If demand is inelastic and a firm raises price, what happens to total revenue?

The relationship between elasticity and total revenue is no mystery. There's a very logical reason why they are related, which can be seen most neatly by recognizing that total revenue ($P \times Q$) is represented by the area under the demand curve at

FIGURE 6-3 (A, B, AND C)   Elasticity and Total Revenue

Total revenue is measured by the rectangle produced by extending lines from the demand curve to the price and quantity axes. The change in total revenue resulting from a change in price can be estimated by comparing the sizes of the before and after rectangles. If price is being raised, total revenue increases by rectangle C and decreases by rectangle B. As you can see, the effect of a price rise on total revenue differs significantly at different points on a demand curve; **(a)** shows an almost unitary elastic range, **(b)** shows an inelastic range, and **(c)** shows an elastic range.

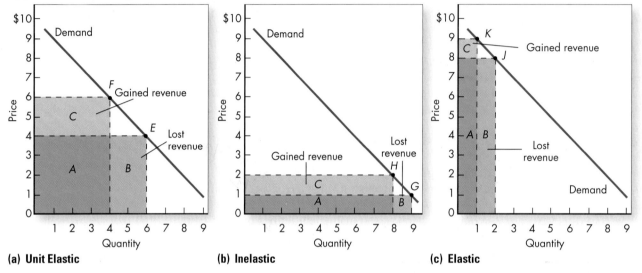

(a) Unit Elastic   **(b) Inelastic**   **(c) Elastic**

Elasticity and the
Total Revenue Rule

that price and quantity. For example, at point *E* on the demand curve in Figure 6-3(a), the total revenue at price $4 and quantity 6 is the area designated by the *A* and *B* rectangles, $24.

If we increase price to $6, quantity demanded decreases to 4, so total revenue is still $24. Total revenue has remained constant, so the demand curve from point *E* to point *F* is unit elastic. The new total revenue is represented by the *A* and *C* rectangles. The difference between the old total revenue (*A* and *B*) and the new total revenue (*A* and *C*) is the difference between the rectangles *B* and *C*. Comparing these rectangles provides us with a visual method of estimating elasticities.

Figure 6-3(b) shows an inelastic range; Figure 6-3(c) shows a highly elastic range. While in Figure 6-3(b) the slope of the demand curve is the same as in Figure 6-3(a), we begin at a different point on the demand curve (point *G*). If we raise our price from $1 to $2, quantity demanded falls from 9 to 8. The gained area (rectangle *C*) is much greater than the lost area (rectangle *B*). In other words, total revenue increases significantly, so the demand curve between points *H* and *G* is highly inelastic.

In Figure 6-3(c) the demand curve is again the same, but we begin at still another point, *J*. If we raise our price from $8 to $9, quantity demanded falls from 2 to 1. The gained area (rectangle *C*) is much smaller than the lost area (rectangle *B*). In other words, total revenue decreases significantly, so the demand curve from points *J* to *K* is highly elastic.

Total Revenue along a Demand Curve

The way in which elasticity changes along a demand curve and its relationship to total revenue can be seen in Figure 6-4. When output is zero, total revenue is zero; similarly, when price is zero, total revenue is zero. That accounts for the two endpoints of the total revenue curve in Figure 6-4(b). Let's say we start at a price of zero, where demand

With elastic demands, a rise in price decreases total revenue. With inelastic demands, a rise in price increases total revenue.

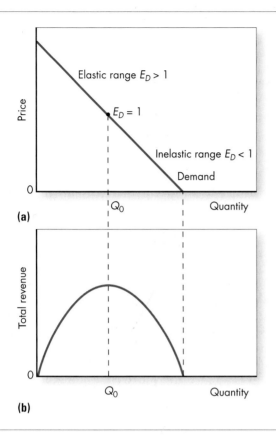

(a)

(b)

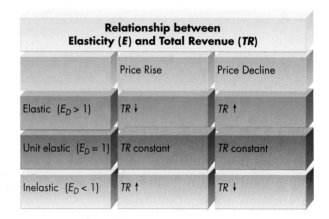

FIGURE 6-4 (A AND B)   How Total Revenue Changes

Total revenue is at a maximum when elasticity equals 1, as you can see in (**a**) and (**b**). When demand is elastic, total revenue decreases with an increase in price. When demand is inelastic, total revenue increases with an increase in price.

Relationship between Elasticity (*E*) and Total Revenue (*TR*)		
	Price Rise	Price Decline
Elastic ($E_D > 1$)	*TR* ↓	*TR* ↑
Unit elastic ($E_D = 1$)	*TR* constant	*TR* constant
Inelastic ($E_D < 1$)	*TR* ↑	*TR* ↓

is perfectly inelastic. As we increase price (decrease quantity demanded), total revenue increases significantly. As we continue to do so, the increases in total revenue become smaller until finally, after output of Q_0, total revenue actually starts decreasing. It continues decreasing at a faster and faster rate until finally, at zero output, total revenue is zero.

As an example of where such calculations might come in handy, recall the vanity license plates that we used to illustrate the law of demand in Chapter 4. A rise in the price of vanity plates of about 29 percent, from \$30 to \$40, decreased the quantity demanded about 64 percent, from 60,334 to 31,122, so the price elasticity of demand was about 0.64/0.29 = 2.2. Since demand was elastic, total revenue fell. Specifically, total revenue fell from \$1,810,020 (\$30 × 60,334) to \$1,244,880 (\$40 × 31,122).

Elasticity of Individual and Market Demand

In thinking about elasticity of demand, keep in mind the point made in Chapter 4: The market demand curve is the horizontal summation of individual demand curves. Some individuals have highly inelastic demands and others have highly elastic demands. A slight rise in the price of a good will cause some people to stop buying the good; the slight increase won't affect other people's quantity demanded for the good at all. Market demand elasticity is influenced both by how many people drop out totally and by how much an existing consumer marginally changes his or her quantity demanded.

If a firm can somehow separate the people with less elastic demand from those with more elastic demand, it can charge more to the individuals with inelastic demands and less to individuals with elastic demands. Economists call this *price discrimination.*

Web Note 6.2
Elasticity and Cartels

Firms have a strong incentive to separate out people with less elastic demand and charge them a higher price.

We see firms throughout the economy trying to use price discrimination. Let's consider three examples:

1. Airlines pricing. If you buy a ticket at the last minute, it will likely cost more than if you buy it two weeks ahead of time. The reason is that businesspeople have inelastic demands and frequently have to make last-minute flights, while pleasure travelers have more elastic demands. By charging individuals more for last-minute flights, airlines can separate out businesspeople and charge them more.

2. The phenomenon of selling new cars. Most new cars don't sell at the listed price. They sell at a discount. Salespeople are trained to separate out comparison shoppers (who have more elastic demands) from impulse buyers (who have inelastic demands). By not listing the selling price of cars so that the discount can be worked out in individual negotiations, salespeople can charge more to customers who have inelastic demands.

3. The almost-continual-sale phenomenon. Some items, such as washing machines, go on sale rather often. Why don't suppliers sell them at a low price all the time? Because some buyers whose washing machines break down have inelastic demands. They can't wait, so they'll pay the "unreduced" price. Others have elastic demands; they can wait for the sale. By running sales (even though they're frequent sales), sellers can separate consumers with inelastic demand curves from consumers with elastic demand curves.

Q-7 Why might museums offer different admission prices for youth, students, adults, and seniors?

Income and Cross-Price Elasticity

Other Elasticities

There are many elasticity concepts besides the price elasticity of demand and the price elasticity of supply. Since these other elasticities can be useful in specifying the effects of shift factors on the demand for a good, I will introduce you to two of them: income elasticity of demand and cross-price elasticity of demand.

Income Elasticity of Demand

The most commonly used of these other elasticity terms is *income elasticity of demand.* **Income elasticity of demand** is defined as *the percentage change in demand divided by the percentage change in income.* Put another way,

$$\text{Income elasticity of demand} = \frac{\text{Percentage change in demand}}{\text{Percentage change in income}}$$

Income elasticity of demand shows the responsiveness of demand to changes in income.

It tells us the responsiveness of demand to changes in income. (Notice I used *demand,* not *quantity demanded,* to emphasize that in response to a change in anything but the price of that good, the entire demand curve shifts; there's no movement along the demand curve.) An increase in income generally increases one's consumption of almost all goods, although the increase may be greater for some goods than for others. **Normal goods**—*goods whose consumption increases with an increase in income*—have income elasticities greater than zero.

Q-8 If a good's consumption increases with an increase in income, what type of good would you call it?

Normal goods are sometimes divided into luxuries and necessities. **Luxuries** are *goods that have an income elasticity greater than 1*—their percentage increase in demand is greater than the percentage increase in income. For example, say your income goes up 10 percent and you buy 20 percent more songs from iTunes. The income elasticity of iTunes music is 2; thus, iTunes music is a luxury good. Economist Robert Fogel estimates income elasticity for health care to be 1.6 and, therefore, it is a luxury. Alternatively, say your income goes up by 100 percent and your demand for

Empirically Measuring Elasticities

Where do firms get the information they need to calculate elasticities? Think of the grocery store where you can get a special buyer's card; the checkout clerk scans it and you get all the discounts. And the card is free! Those grocery stores are not just being nice. When the clerk scans your purchases, the store gets information that is forwarded to a central processing unit that can see how people react to different prices. This information allows firms to fine-tune their pricing—raising prices on goods for which the demand is inelastic and lowering prices on goods for which the demand is elastic.

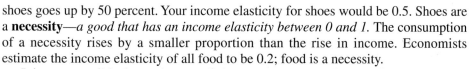

Alternatively, think of the warranty cards that you send in when you buy a new computer or a new TV. The information goes into the firms' databases and is used by their economists in future price-setting decisions.

How do stores use this information? One way is that they develop user profiles, and run promotions on items such as laundry products, carbonated soft drinks, cereal, and several other items for which consumers are most responsive to price (i.e., the demand is elastic). This attracts shoppers to their store. Then, the stores place high-profit novelty items that consumers generally do not compare across stores, but for which demand is inelastic, in prominent in-store displays. It's not quite a bait-and-switch strategy, but it is a strategy to lure shoppers into a store for a "deal" but still end up selling higher-priced products than their competitors. Another way stores calculate the elasticity of demand for goods is to initially charge different prices in different stores, and then, once they have determined the elasticity, they choose a price that maximizes total profit.

---

shoes goes up by 50 percent. Your income elasticity for shoes would be 0.5. Shoes are a **necessity**—*a good that has an income elasticity between 0 and 1*. The consumption of a necessity rises by a smaller proportion than the rise in income. Economists estimate the income elasticity of all food to be 0.2; food is a necessity.

It is even possible that an increase in income can cause a *decrease* in the consumption of a particular good. These goods have a negative income elasticity of demand. The term applied to such goods is **inferior goods**—*goods whose consumption decreases when income increases.* In some circumstances, potatoes could be an example of an inferior good. As income goes up, people might so significantly shift their consumption toward meat and away from potatoes that their total consumption of potatoes decreases. A recent study by a Stanford economist found tortillas to be an inferior good in Mexico.

Income elasticity for most goods is different in the short run than in the long run. The income elasticity for foreign travel, for example, is estimated to be 0.2 in the short run and 3.0 in the long run. Short-run decisions to travel abroad may be motivated by factors other than income such as business trips or family emergencies. Foreign travel decisions in the long run are likely to be part of vacation plans and people choose from a variety of locations, both domestic and foreign. In the short run, people often save high proportions of their increases in income, so most goods, other than impulse goods, such as furniture, have low short-run income elasticities. To avoid this problem, economists generally focus on long-run income elasticities.

www Web Note 6.3
Inferior Goods

Q-9 Label each of the following goods as a luxury, necessity or inferior good. Elasticity is given for each.

a. Dental services: 1.6

b. Beer: 0.8

c. Farm goods: −0.6

Cross-Price Elasticity of Demand

Cross-price elasticity of demand is another frequently used elasticity concept. It tells us the responsiveness of demand to the change in prices of related goods.

Cross-price elasticity of demand
shows the responsiveness of demand
to changes in prices of related goods.

Cross-price elasticity of demand is defined as *the percentage change in demand divided by the percentage change in the price of a related good.* Put another way,

$$\text{Cross-price elasticity of demand} = \frac{\text{Percentage change in demand}}{\text{Percentage change in price of a related good}}$$

Let's consider an example. Say the price of Apple iPhones rises. What is likely to happen to the demand for Android phones? It is likely to rise, so the cross-price elasticity between the two is positive. Positive cross-price elasticities of demand mean the goods are **substitutes**—*goods that can be used in place of one another.* When the price of a good goes up, the demand for the substitute goes up. Another example is the demand for beef and pork, with an estimated cross-price elasticity of 0.1. When the price of beef rises, consumers will switch to pork. Yet another is domestic cars and foreign cars, with a cross-price elasticity of 0.3.

Web Note 6.4
Calculating Elasticity

Most goods have substitutes, so most cross-price elasticities are positive. But not all. To see that, let's consider another example: Say the price of hot dogs rises; what is likely to happen to the demand for ketchup? If you're like me and use lots of ketchup on your hot dogs, as you cut your consumption of hot dogs, you will also cut your consumption of ketchup. Ketchup and hot dogs are not substitutes but rather complements. **Complements** are *goods that are used in conjunction with other goods.* A fall in the price of a good will increase the demand for its complement. The cross-price elasticity of complements is negative. As practice, list pairs of goods that are complements, make another list of substitutes, and compare lists with a study partner. On the list might be name and generic brands of the same product. If you've identified these as substitutes, you're on the right track.

Substitutes have positive cross-price
elasticities; complements have
negative cross-price elasticities.

Some Examples

To make sure you've got these concepts down, see Figure 6-5, which demonstrates two examples. In Figure 6-5(a), income has risen by 20 percent, increasing demand at price P_0 from 20 to 26. To determine the income elasticity, we must first determine the percentage change in demand. We calculate the percentage demand to be $6/[(20 + 26)/2] = (6/23) \times 100 = 26$ percent. The percentage change in income is 20, so the income elasticity is 26/20, or 1.3.

In Figure 6-5(b), a 33 percent fall in the price of pork has caused the demand for beef to fall by 3.8 percent—from 108 to 104 at a price of P_0. The cross-price elasticity of demand is 3.8/33 = 0.12.

FIGURE 6-5 (A AND B)

Calculating Elasticities

Shift factors, such as income or the price of another good, shift the entire demand curve. To calculate these elasticities, we see how much demand will shift at a constant price and then calculate the relevant elasticities.

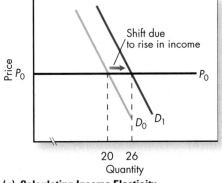

(a) Calculating Income Elasticity

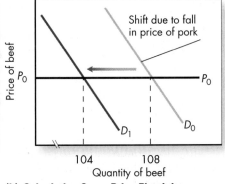

(b) Calculating Cross-Price Elasticity

The Power of Supply/Demand Analysis

Now that you've got the elasticity terms down, let's consider some examples that demonstrate the power of supply/demand analysis when it is combined with the concept of elasticity. Let's start with some easy cases.

When Should a Supplier Not Raise Price?

First, let's say a firm is trying to increase its profits and hires you to tell it whether it should raise or lower its price. The firm knows that it faces an inelastic demand. Should it raise its price?

I hope your answer was: Definitely yes. How can I be so sure the correct answer is yes? Because I remembered the discussion of the relationship between price elasticity of demand and total revenue. With an inelastic demand, the percentage change in quantity is less than the percentage change in price, so total revenue must increase with an increase in price. Total costs also will decrease, so profits—total revenues minus total costs—also must increase.

Along those same lines, consider a university president thinking of raising tuition. Say that raising tuition by 10 percent will decrease the number of students by 1 percent. What's the price elasticity? The percentage change in quantity is 1 percent; the percentage change in price is 10. Dividing the percentage change in quantity by the percentage change in price, we have an elasticity of 0.1. That's an inelastic demand ($E_D < 1$), so raising tuition will increase the university's total revenue.

But if a 10 percent rise in tuition will decrease the enrollment by 25 percent, the elasticity will be large (2.5). In response to an increase in tuition, the university's total revenue will decrease significantly. When you have an elastic demand, you should hesitate to increase price. To make sure you're following the argument, explain the likely effect an elastic demand will have on lowering tuition. (Your argument should involve the *possibility* of increasing profit.) If you're not following the argument, go back to the section on elasticity and total revenue, especially Figure 6-3.

When the long-run and short-run elasticities differ, the analysis becomes somewhat more complicated. Consider the case of a local transit authority that, faced with a budget crisis, increased its fares from $1.50 to $2.50. The rise in revenue during the first year helped the authority balance its books. But in the two years following, ridership declined so much that total revenue fell. What happened? In the short-run, commuters had few substitutes to taking the bus—demand was relatively inelastic, so that total revenue rose when fares were increased. But, as time went on, commuters found alternative ways to get to work. Long-run demand was more elastic in this case, so much so that total revenue declined.

A REMINDER

A Review of the Alternative Elasticity Terms

Income elasticity of demand is defined as *the percentage change in demand divided by the percentage change in income.*

$$\text{Income elasticity of demand} = \frac{\text{Percentage change in demand}}{\text{Percentage change in income}}$$

Cross-price elasticity of demand is defined as *the percentage change in demand divided by the percentage change in the price of a related good.*

$$\text{Cross-price elasticity of demand} = \frac{\text{Percentage change in demand}}{\text{Percentage change in price of a related good}}$$

Complement: Cross-price elasticity of demand is negative.

Substitute: Cross-price elasticity of demand is positive.

Normal good: Income elasticity of demand is positive.

Luxury: Income elasticity is greater than 1.

Necessity: Income elasticity is less than 1.

Inferior good: Income elasticity of demand is negative.

Q-10 A firm faces an elastic demand for its product. It has come to an economist to advise it on whether to lower its price. The answer she gives is: Maybe. Why is this the right answer?

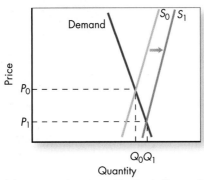

(a) Inelastic Supply and Inelastic Demand

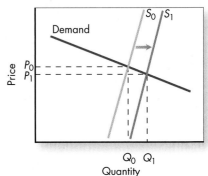

(b) Inelastic Supply and Elastic Demand

Elasticity and Shifting Supply and Demand

Let's now turn to shifts in supply and demand. Knowing the elasticity of the supply and demand curves allows us to be more specific about the effects of shifts in supply and demand.

Figure 6-6 demonstrates the relative effects of supply shifts on equilibrium price and quantity under different assumptions about elasticity. As you can see, the more elastic the demand, the greater the effect of a supply shift on quantity, and the smaller the effect on price. Going through a similar exercise for demand shifts with various supply elasticities is also a useful exercise. If you do so, you will see that the more elastic the supply, the greater the effect of a demand shift on quantity, and the smaller the effect on price.

To be sure that you have understood elasticity, consider the following three observations about price and quantity and match them with the three descriptions of supply and demand:

a. Price rises significantly; quantity hardly changes at all.

b. Price remains almost constant; quantity increases enormously.

c. Price falls significantly; quantity hardly changes at all.

1. Demand is highly elastic; supply shifts out.

2. Supply is highly inelastic; demand shifts out.

3. Demand is highly inelastic; supply shifts out.

The answers are ˙Ɛ–ɔ ‘Ɩ–q ‘ᄅ–ɐ

Conclusion

I'll stop the exercises here. As you can see, the elasticity concept is important. Economists use it all the time when discussing supply and demand.

However, the elasticity concept is not easy to remember, or to calculate, so working with it takes some practice. It becomes a bit less forbidding if you remember that elasticity is what your shorts lose when they've been through the washer and drier too many times. If a relationship is elastic, price (for price elasticity) exerts a strong pull on quantity. If it's inelastic, there's little pull on quantity.

Summary

- Elasticity is defined as percentage change in quantity divided by percentage change in some variable that affects demand (or supply) or quantity demanded (or supplied). The most common elasticity concept used is price elasticity.   *(LO6-1)*

$$E_D = \frac{\text{Percentage change in quantity demanded}}{\text{Percentage change in price}}$$

$$E_S = \frac{\text{Percentage change in quantity supplied}}{\text{Percentage change in price}}$$

- Elasticity is a better descriptor than is slope because it is independent of units of measurement.   *(LO6-1)*

- To calculate percentage changes in prices and quantities, use the average of the end values.   *(LO6-1)*

- Five elasticity terms are *elastic* ($E > 1$); *inelastic* ($E < 1$); *unit elastic* ($E = 1$); *perfectly inelastic* ($E = 0$); and *perfectly elastic* ($E = \infty$).   *(LO6-1)*

- The more substitutes a good has, the greater its elasticity.   *(LO6-2)*

- Factors affecting the number of substitutes in demand are (1) time period considered, (2) the degree to which the good is a luxury, (3) the market definition, and (4) the importance of the good in one's budget.   *(LO6-2)*

- The most important factor affecting the number of substitutes for supply is time. As the time interval lengthens, supply becomes more elastic.   *(LO6-2)*

- Elasticity changes along straight-line demand and supply curves. Demand becomes less elastic as we move down along a demand curve.   *(LO6-3)*

- When a supplier raises price, if demand is inelastic, total revenue increases; if demand is elastic, total revenue decreases; if demand is unit elastic, total revenue remains constant.   *(LO6-3)*

- Other important elasticity concepts are income elasticity and cross-price elasticity of demand.   *(LO6-4)*

$$\frac{\text{Income}}{\text{elasticity of demand}} = \frac{\text{Percentage change in demand}}{\text{Percentage change in income}}$$

$$\frac{\text{Cross-price}}{\text{elasticity of demand}} = \frac{\text{Percentage change in demand}}{\text{Percentage change in price of a related good}}$$

- Knowing elasticities allows us to be more precise about the qualitative effects that shifts in demand and supply have on prices and quantities.   *(LO6-5)*

- The more elastic the demand, the greater the effect of a supply shift on quantity and the smaller the effect on price.   *(LO6-5)*

- The more elastic the supply, the greater the effect of a demand shift on quantity and the smaller the effect on price.   *(LO6-5)*

Key Terms

complement *(136)*
cross-price elasticity of demand *(136)*
elastic *(123)*
income elasticity of demand *(134)*

inelastic *(123)*
inferior good *(135)*
luxury *(134)*
necessity *(135)*
normal good *(134)*
perfectly elastic *(126)*

perfectly inelastic *(126)*
price elasticity of demand *(122)*
price elasticity of supply *(122)*

substitute *(136)*
unit elastic *(126)*

Questions and Exercises

1. Determine the price elasticity of demand if, in response to an increase in price of 10 percent, quantity demanded decreases by 20 percent. Is demand elastic or inelastic? (*LO6-1*)

2. A firm has just increased its price by 5 percent over last year's price, and it found that quantity sold remained the same. (*LO6-1*)
   a. The firm comes to you and wants to know its price elasticity of demand.
   b. How would you calculate it?
   c. What additional information would you search for before you did your calculation?

3. When tolls on the Dulles Airport Greenway were reduced from $1.75 to $1.00, traffic increased from 10,000 to 26,000 trips a day. Assuming all changes in quantity were due to the change in price, what is the price elasticity of demand for the Dulles Airport Greenway? (*LO6-1*)

4. One football season Domino's Pizza, a corporate sponsor of the Washington Redskins (a football team), offered to reduce the price of its medium-size pizza by $1 for every touchdown scored by the Redskins during the previous week. Until that year, the Redskins weren't scoring many touchdowns. Much to the surprise of Domino's, in one week in 1999, the Redskins scored six touchdowns. (Maybe they like pizza.) Domino's pizzas were selling for $2 a pie! The quantity of pizzas demanded soared the following week from 1 pie an hour to 100 pies an hour. What was price elasticity of demand for Domino's pizza? (*LO6-1*)

5. Which has greater elasticity: a supply curve that goes through the origin with slope of 1 or a supply curve that goes through the origin with slope of 4? (*LO6-1*)

6. Calculate the elasticity of the designated ranges of supply and demand curves on the following graph. (*LO6-1*)

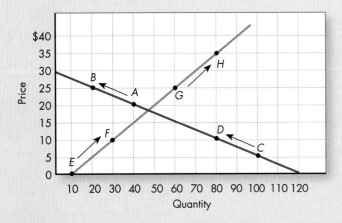

7. Which of the pairs of goods would you expect to have a greater price elasticity of demand? (*LO6-2*)
   a. Cars, transportation.
   b. Housing, leisure travel.
   c. Rubber during World War II, rubber during the entire 20th century.

8. Economists have estimated the following transportation elasticities. For each pair, explain possible reasons why the elasticities differ. (*LO6-2*)
   a. Elasticity of demand for buses is 0.23 during peak hours and 0.42 during off-peak hours.
   b. Elasticity of demand for buses is 0.7 in the short run and 1.5 in the long run.
   c. Elasticity of demand for toll roads is 4.7 for low-income commuters and 0.63 for high-income commuters.

9. Kean University Professor Henry Saffer and Bentley University Professor Dave Dhaval estimated that if the alcohol industry increased the prices of alcoholic beverages by 100 percent underage drinking would fall by 28 percent and underage binge drinking would fall by 51 percent. (*LO6-2*)
   a. What is the elasticity of demand of underage drinking and binge drinking?
   b. What might explain the difference in elasticities?

10. A newspaper recently lowered its price from 50 cents to 30 cents. As it did, the number of newspapers sold increased from 240,000 to 280,000. (*LO6-3*)
    a. What was the newspaper's elasticity of demand?
    b. Given that elasticity, did it make sense for the newspaper to lower its price?
    c. What would your answer be if much of the firm's revenue came from advertising and the higher the circulation, the more it could charge for advertising?

11. Once a book has been written, would an author facing an inelastic demand curve for the book prefer to raise or lower the book's price? Why? (*LO6-3*)

12. University of Richmond Professor Erik Craft analyzed the states' pricing of vanity plates. He found that in California, where vanity plates cost $28.75, the elasticity of demand was 0.52. In Massachusetts, where vanity plates cost $50, the elasticity of demand was 3.52. (*LO6-3*)
    a. Assuming vanity plates have zero production cost and his estimates are correct, was each state collecting the maximum revenue it could from vanity plates? Explain your reasoning.
    b. What recommendation would you have for each state to maximize revenue?
    c. If these estimates are correct, which state was most likely to be following a politically unsupportable policy?

d. Assuming the demand curves were linear, graphically demonstrate your reasoning in *a* and *b*.

13. How is elasticity related to the revenue from a sales tax? (*LO6-3*)

14. According to Exhibitor Relations Co., in 2006 average movie ticket prices were $6.55 and attendance was 1.4 billion; in 2007 ticket prices were $6.88 and attendance was 1.41 billion. (*LO6-3*)
   a. What happened to total revenue from 2006 to 2007?
   b. If you were to estimate elasticity from these figures, what would your estimate be?
   c. What provisos would you offer about your estimate of elasticity?

15. Which of the following producers would you expect to support a tax on beer? Which would not? Explain your answer. (*LO6-4*)
   a. Producers of hard liquor. Cross-price elasticity with beer: −0.11.
   b. Producers of wine. Cross-price elasticity with beer: 0.23.

16. For each of the following goods, state whether it is a normal good, a luxury, a necessity, or an inferior good. Explain your answers. (*LO6-4*)
   a. Vodka.   d. Perfume.
   b. Table salt.   e. Beer.
   c. Furniture.   f. Sugar.

17. For each of the following pairs of goods, state whether the cross-price elasticity is likely positive, negative, or zero. Explain your answers. (*LO6-4*)
   a. Lettuce, carrots.
   b. Housing, furniture.

   c. Nike sneakers, Puma sneakers.
   d. Jeans, formal suits.

18. When the price of ketchup rises by 15 percent, the demand for hot dogs falls by 1 percent. (*LO6-4*)
   a. Calculate the cross-price elasticity of demand.
   b. Are the goods complements or substitutes?
   c. In the original scenario, what would have to happen to the demand for hot dogs for us to conclude that hot dogs and ketchup are substitutes?

19. Calculate the income elasticities of demand for the following: (*LO6-4*)
   a. Income rises by 20 percent; demand rises by 10 percent.
   b. Income rises from $30,000 to $40,000; demand increases (at a constant price) from 16 to 19.

20. Would you expect a shift in supply to have a greater effect on equilibrium quantity in the short run or in the long run? Explain your answer. (*LO6-5*)

21. Would a shift in demand have a greater effect on the percentage change in equilibrium quantity for a straight-line supply curve that intersects the quantity axis or the price axis? (*LO6-5*)

22. For each of the following assume that the supply curve shifts while the demand curve remains constant. What is the direction of the supply shift and relative elasticity of demand? (*LO6-5*)
   a. Price remains nearly constant. Quantity increases enormously.
   b. Price falls enormously. Quantity does not change.
   c. Price rises slightly. Quantity remains nearly constant.

Questions from Alternative Perspectives

1. The text tells us that there are long-run elasticities and short-run elasticities.
   a. How long is the long run and how long is the short run?
   b. What meaning do the elasticity measures have if you don't know those lengths? (Austrian)

2. In this chapter, we learn that most new cars aren't sold at their list price but are sold at a discount and that this allows dealerships to charge more to customers with inelastic demand. At the same time, studies have shown that retail car dealerships systematically offer substantially better prices on identical cars to white men than they do to blacks or women. (Source: Ian Ayres, "Fair Driving: Gender and Race Discrimination in Retail Car Negotiations," *Harvard Law Review* 104 (1991): 817–72.)
   a. Why do you think this happens?
   b. In this example, does the existence of price discrimination allow for racial or sexual discrimination? (Feminist)

3. Early economists made a distinction between needs and wants. Needs were economists' concern; wants were of far less importance.
   a. Is such a distinction useful?
   b. Would making such a distinction change the nature of economic analysis?
   c. Does the fact that the book makes no distinction between luxuries and necessities other than in their elasticity of demand reflect a bias in economic analysis? (Religious)

4. In the chapter, you saw that an increase in Vermont's minimum wage stimulated a small quantity response.
   a. What does this tell you about the nature of the labor market in Vermont? (Hint: Think carefully and critically about the conditions shaping worker options and their responses to changes in wages.)
   b. What policy implications does your answer to *a* suggest? (Institutionalist)

5. If elasticities are constantly changing as the time period gets longer, how do managers use a measure of elasticity of demand to determine the price they charge? If they don't use elasticities, how do they set price? (Post-Keynesian)

6. Price elasticity is not just a technical economic concept. It also reflects the distribution of economic power—the bargaining power and economic opportunities of buyers and sellers.
   a. When suppliers (for example, landlords or energy companies) hold disproportionate power over buyers, or consumers (for example, employers in low-wage labor markets) hold disproportionate power over sellers, what meaning do elasticities have?
   b. Should anything be done about those inequities? (Radical)

Issues to Ponder

1. In the box "Geometric Tricks for Estimating Price Elasticity," there are three statements about the elasticities of straight-line supply curves. One of those statements is that supply curves intersecting the quantity axis are inelastic. Can you prove that that is true by algebraic manipulation of the elasticity formula?

2. In the 1960s, coffee came in 1-pound cans. Today, most coffee comes in 11-ounce cans.
   a. Can you think of an explanation why?
   b. Can you think of other products besides coffee whose standard size has shrunk? (Often the standard size is supplemented by a "supersize" alternative.)

3. Why would an economist be more hesitant about making an elasticity estimate of the effect of an increase in price of 1 percent rather than an increase in price of 50 percent?

4. A major cereal producer decides to lower price from $3.60 to $3 per 15-ounce box.
   a. If quantity demanded increases by 18 percent, what is the price elasticity of demand?
   b. If, instead of lowering its price, the cereal producer increases the size of the box from 15 to 17.8 ounces, what would you expect that the response would have been? Why?

5. Economists have estimated the demand elasticity for motor fuel to be between 0.4 and 0.85.
   a. If the price rises 10 percent and the initial quantity sold is 10 million gallons, what is the range of estimates of the new quantity demanded?
   b. In carrying out their estimates, they came up with different elasticity estimates for rises in price than for falls in price, with an increase in price having a larger elasticity than a decrease in price. What hypothesis might you propose for their findings?

6. Demand for "prestige" college education is generally considered to be highly inelastic. What does this suggest about tuition increases at prestige schools in the future? Why don't colleges raise tuition by amounts even greater than they already do?

7. In 2004, Congress allocated over $20 billion to fight illegal drugs. About 60 percent of the funds was directed at reducing the supply of drugs through domestic law enforcement and interdiction. Some critics of this approach argue that supply-side approaches to reduce the drug supply actually help drug producers.
   a. Demonstrate graphically the effect of supply-side measures on the market for illegal drugs.
   b. Explain how these measures affect drug producers. (Hint: Consider the elasticity of demand.)
   c. Demonstrate the effect of demand-side measures such as treatment and prevention on the market for illegal drugs.
   d. How does the shift in demand affect the profitability of producers?

8. In the discussion of elasticity and raising and lowering prices, the text states that if you have an elastic demand, you should hesitate to raise your price, and that lowering price can *possibly* increase profits (total revenue minus total cost). Why is the word *possibly* used?

9. Colleges have increasingly used price sensitivity to formulate financial aid. The more eager the student, the less aid he or she can expect to get. Use elasticity to explain this phenomenon. Is this practice justified?

10. If there were only two goods in the world, can you say whether they would be complements or substitutes? Explain your answer.

Answers to Margin Questions

1. Price elasticity of supply = Percentage change in quantity supplied divided by percentage change in price = 8/4 = 2. (*p. 123; LO6-1*)

2. If price elasticity of demand is greater than 1, by definition demand is elastic. (*p. 123; LO6-1*)

3. The percentage change in quantity is 100 (8/8 × 100) and the percentage change in price is 100 (2/2 × 100). Elasticity, therefore, is approximately 1 (100/100). (*p. 126; LO6-1*)

4. I tell her that she is partially right (for the bottom part of the curve), but that elasticity on a straight-line demand curve changes from perfectly elastic at the vertical axis intersection to perfectly inelastic at the horizontal axis intersection. (*p. 126; LO6-1*)

5. Four factors affecting the number of substitutes in demand are (1) time period considered, (2) the degree to which the good is a luxury, (3) the market definition, and (4) importance of the good in one's budget. (*p. 130; LO6-2*)

6. If demand is inelastic, total revenue increases with an increase in price. (*p. 131; LO6-3*)

7. Museums set different prices for different age groups for a variety of reasons. If a motivation is to maximize revenue, it would charge lower prices for those with greater elasticities, such as youth and seniors, and higher prices for adults. (*p. 134; LO6-3*)

8. If consumption increases with an increase in income, the good is a normal good. (*p. 134; LO6-4*)

9. a. Luxury
   b. Necessity
   c. Inferior good. (*p. 135; LO6-4*)

10. With an elastic demand, lowering price will increase total revenue because it will increase sales by more than the change in price. But producing more also will increase costs, so information about total revenue is not enough to answer the question. (*p. 137; LO6-5*)

Taxation and Government Intervention

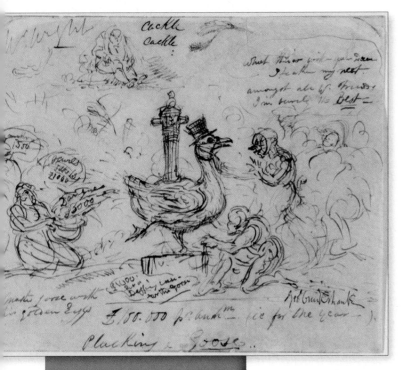

John Baptiste Colbert, finance minister for Louis XIV, once said that the art of taxation consists of plucking the goose so as to obtain the largest amount of feathers with the least amount of squawk. In figuring out what taxes will bring about the least amount of squawk, politicians have turned to economists, who, in turn, turn to their models. Previous chapters introduced you to those models; in this chapter, we apply the models to taxation. As we do that, you'll see that when combined with the concept of elasticity, supply and demand become powerful tools. We'll see how by considering the burden of taxation and government intervention into markets.

Producer and Consumer Surplus

We begin our discussion of the effects of taxation and government intervention by looking at how economists measure the benefits of the market to consumers and producers; the benefit can be seen by considering what the supply and demand curves are telling us. Each of these curves tells us how much individuals are willing to pay (in the case of demand) or accept (in the case of supply) for a good. Thus, in Figure 7-1(a), a consumer is willing to pay $8 each for 2 units of the good. The supplier is willing to sell 2 units for $2 apiece.

If the consumer pays less than what he's willing to pay, he ends up with a net gain—the value of the good to him minus the price he actually paid for the good. Thus, the distance between the demand curve and the price he pays is the net gain for the consumer. Economists call this net benefit **consumer surplus**—*the value the consumer gets from buying a product less its price*. It is represented by the area underneath the demand curve and above the price that an individual pays. Thus, with the price at equilibrium ($5), consumer surplus is represented by the blue area.

Similarly, if a producer receives more than the price she would be willing to sell it for, she too receives a net benefit. Economists call this gain

FIGURE 7-1 (A AND B)   Consumer and Producer Surplus

Market equilibrium price and quantity maximize the combination of consumer surplus (shown in blue) and producer surplus (shown in brown) as demonstrated in (**a**). When price deviates from its equilibrium, as in (**b**), combined consumer and producer surplus falls. The gray shaded region shows the loss of total surplus when price is $1 higher than equilibrium price.

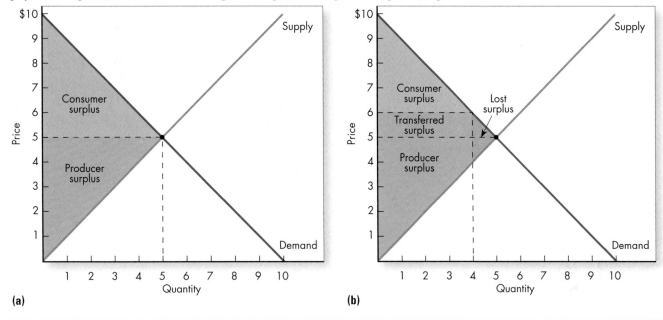

(a)

(b)

producer surplus—*the price the producer sells a product for less the cost of producing it.* It is represented by the area above the supply curve but below the price the producer receives. Thus, with the price at equilibrium ($5), producer surplus is represented by the brown area.

What's good about market equilibrium is that it makes the combination of consumer and producer surpluses as large as it can be. To see this, say that for some reason the equilibrium price is held at $6. Consumers will demand only 4 units of the good, and some suppliers are not able to sell all the goods they would like. The combined producer and consumer surplus will decrease, as shown in Figure 7-1(b). The gray triangle represents lost consumer and producer surplus. In general, a deviation of price from equilibrium lowers the combination of producer and consumer surplus. This is one of the reasons economists support markets and why we teach the supply/demand model. It gives us a visual sense of what is good about markets: By allowing trade, markets maximize the combination of consumer and producer surplus.

For straight-line demand curves, the amount of surplus can be determined by calculating the area of the relevant triangle or rectangle. For example, in Figure 7-1(a), the consumer surplus triangle has a base of 5 and a height of 5 (10 − 5). Since the area of a triangle is ½ (base × height), the consumer surplus is 12.5 units. Alternatively, in Figure 7-1(b), the lost surplus from a price above equilibrium price is 1. This is calculated by determining that the height of the triangle (looked at sideways) is 1 (5 − 4) and the base is 2 (6 − 4), making the area of lost surplus ½ × 2 × 1 = 1. In this case, the consumer and producer share in the loss equally. The higher price transfers 4 units of surplus from consumer to producer, calculated by determining the area of the rectangle (base × height) created by the origin and output, 4, and

Q-1 If price moves from disequilibrium to equilibrium, what happens to the combination of producer and consumer surplus in the market?

Producer and Consumer Surplus

The Ambiguity of Total Surplus

The consumer and producer surplus concepts do not treat all wants equally. How much importance your surplus is given depends on how much income you have. People with lots of income generate lots of surplus; people with little income generate little. So if Mr. Rich likes gold-plated toilets but dislikes bread, while Mr. Poor likes bread but has little money to spend on bread, it is gold-plated toilets, not bread, that will generate the most consumer surplus.

What this means is that if income were distributed differently, our measure of consumer surplus would change. Let's consider an extreme example to show the problems this can present. Say we have two individuals, Jules and Jim, and two goods, apples and oranges. Jules likes only oranges and Jim likes only apples. If Jim has all the income, only apples will provide any consumer surplus. Now, say that Jules has all the income. In that case, only oranges will provide any consumer surplus. More generally, when two individuals have different tastes, the way in which income is distributed between them can change the measure of consumer surplus.

Economists get around part of the problem theoretically either by assuming individuals have the same tastes or by assuming that income can be costlessly redistributed. This separates the issue of equity from the issue of efficiency. In practice, economists recognize that these conditions do not hold. They know that, in the real world, it is extraordinarily difficult to redistribute income. You can't go up to Bill Gates and tell him, "Hey, you need to give $10 billion to some poor people," although he might choose to do it on his own, as he has done.

For this reason economists are careful to apply the producer and consumer surplus analysis only to those cases where the conditions are "reasonable" approximations of reality—where distributional and taste issues do not play a big role in a policy recommendation. Of course, economists may disagree on what are "reasonable" approximations of reality. That is why economic policy is an art, not a science.

prices 5 and 6, which equals $(6 - 5) \times (4 - 0) = 4$. This leaves the consumer with 8 units of surplus.[1]

To fix the ideas of consumer and producer surplus in your mind, let's consider a couple of real-world examples. Think about the water you drink. What does it cost? Almost nothing. Given that water is readily available, it has a low price. But since you'd die from thirst if you had no water, you are getting an enormous amount of consumer surplus from that water. Next, consider a ballet dancer who loves the ballet so much he'd dance for free. But he finds that people are willing to pay to see him and that he can receive $4,000 a performance. He is receiving producer surplus.

Burden of Taxation

Now that you have seen how market equilibrium can provide benefits to producers and consumers, as measured by producer and consumer surplus, let's see how taxes affect that surplus. You already know that taxes on suppliers shift the supply curve up. In most cases, equilibrium price (including the tax) rises and equilibrium quantity declines. Taxes on consumers shift the "after-tax" demand curve down, lowering equilibrium quantity and also lowering the price paid to suppliers. But the price demanders pay inclusive of the tax rises (which is why the equilibrium quantity demanded falls). In both cases, taxes reduce, or limit, trade. Economists often talk about the limitations that taxes place on trade as the *burden of taxation*. Figure 7-2 provides the basic framework for understanding the burden of taxation. For a given good, a per-unit tax *t* paid by the supplier increases the price at which suppliers are

A tax paid by the supplier shifts the supply curve up by the amount of the tax.

---

[1]Additional explanations of how to calculate consumer and producer surplus can be found on the web at www.mhhe.com/colander9e.

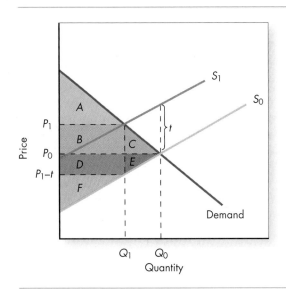

FIGURE 7-2   The Costs of Taxation

A per-unit tax t paid by the supplier shifts the supply curve up from S_0 to S_1. Equilibrium price rises from P_0 to P_1, and equilibrium quantity falls from Q_0 to Q_1. Consumer surplus is represented by areas A, B, and C before the tax and area A after the tax. Producer surplus is represented by areas D, E, and F before the tax and area F after the tax. Government collects tax shown by areas B and D. The tax imposes a deadweight loss, represented by the welfare loss triangle of areas C and E.

willing to sell that good. The effect of the tax is shown by a shift upward of the supply curve from S_0 to S_1. The equilibrium price of the good rises and the quantity sold declines.

Before the tax, consumers pay P_0 and producers keep P_0. Consumer surplus is represented by areas $A + B + C$, and producer surplus is represented by areas $D + E + F$. With the tax t, equilibrium price rises to P_1 and equilibrium quantity falls to Q_1. Consumers now pay a higher price P_1, but producers keep less, only $P_1 - t$. Tax revenue paid equals the tax t times equilibrium quantity Q_1, or areas B and D.

The total cost to consumers and producers is taxes they pay *plus* lost surplus because of fewer trades. Consumers pay area B in tax revenue and lose area C in consumer surplus. Producers pay area D in tax revenue and lose area E in producer surplus. The triangular area $C + E$ represents a cost of taxation over and above the taxes paid to government. It is lost consumer and producer surplus that is not gained by government. *The loss of consumer and producer surplus from a tax* is known as **deadweight loss.** Deadweight loss is shown graphically by the **welfare loss triangle**——*a geometric representation of the welfare cost in terms of misallocated resources caused by a deviation from a supply/demand equilibrium.* Keep in mind that with the tax, quantity sold declines. The loss of welfare, therefore, represents a loss for those consumers and producers who, because of the tax, no longer buy or sell goods.

The deadweight loss from taxes shows up in a variety of other ways. Say the government establishes a property tax that increases with the number of floors a building has, as Paris did in the 1700s. A three-story building was taxed a third higher than a two-story building. That will lead people to build in a way to minimize what are counted as floors. The Mansard roof—as shown in the photo in the margin—does this; it hides the top floor so that it looks like an attic, not a floor. Such roofs can be found throughout Paris. They are building in a style that is less efficient (in terms of the building's function) than they would build without the tax. Building in a style that is less efficient in terms of function is another consequence of a tax, and is a type of deadweight loss.[2]

Costs and Incidence of Taxation

Q-2 Demonstrate the welfare loss of a tax when the supply is highly elastic and the demand is highly inelastic.

Mansard roofs

---

[2]Interestingly, in terms of aesthetics, people have come to like the style of Paris roofs; it is one of the many things that makes Paris distinct. Including aesthetics complicates the analysis enormously. Economic reasoning is based on the architectural view that form follows function.

What Goods Should Be Taxed?

What goods should be taxed depends on the goal of government. If the goal is to fund a program with as little loss as possible in consumer and producer surplus, then the government should tax a good whose supply or demand is inelastic. If the goal is to change behavior, taxes will be most effective if demand or supply is elastic. In 2011 Denmark implemented a "fat tax" to reduce consumption of goods with saturated fat to raise overall health among Danes. The effectiveness of the tax depends on the elasticity of demand for fatty foods. As a quick review, use the following table:

Distributional issues also must be considered when determining what goods are to be taxed. In general, the group with the relatively more inelastic supply or demand will bear a greater portion of the tax. The following table reviews these conclusions:

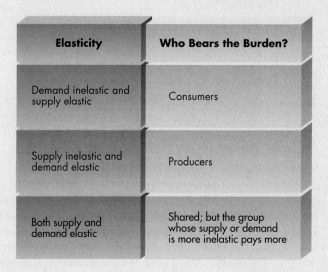

Goal of Government	Most Effective When
Raise revenue, limit deadweight loss	Demand or supply is inelastic
Change behavior	Demand or supply is elastic

Elasticity	Who Bears the Burden?
Demand inelastic and supply elastic	Consumers
Supply inelastic and demand elastic	Producers
Both supply and demand elastic	Shared; but the group whose supply or demand is more inelastic pays more

The cost of taxation includes the direct cost of revenue paid, lost surplus, and administrative cost.

The costs of taxation don't end there. Resources must be devoted by government to administer the tax code and by individuals to comply with it. Firms and individuals either spend hours filling out income tax forms or pay others to do so. Firms hire accountants and lawyers to take full advantage of any tax-code allowances. Administration costs are often as much as 5 percent or more of the total tax revenue paid to government. Like the tax itself, these costs increase the price at which producers are willing to sell their goods, reducing quantity sold and further increasing welfare loss.

Who Bears the Burden of a Tax?

Taxes are like hot potatoes: Everyone wants to pass them on to someone else. Nobody wants to pay taxes, and there are usually large political fights about whom government should tax. For example, should the Social Security tax (mandated by the Federal Insurance Contributions Act, or FICA) be placed on workers or on the company that hires them? As you will see, the supply/demand framework gives an unexpected answer to this question.

The person who physically pays the tax is not necessarily the person who bears the burden of the tax.

BURDEN DEPENDS ON RELATIVE ELASTICITY Let's consider the issue of who bears the burden of a tax by looking at the example involving excise taxes introduced in Chapter 5. There I defined an **excise tax** as *a tax levied on a specific good* and gave the example of a luxury tax on expensive boats that the United States imposed in 1990. An excise tax can be levied on (physically paid by) the consumer or the seller.

The person who *physically pays* the tax, however, is not necessarily the person who *bears the burden* of the tax. Who bears the burden of the tax (also known as tax incidence)

FIGURE 7-3 (A, B, AND C) **Who Bears the Burden of a Tax?**

In the general case, the burden of a tax is determined by the relative elasticities of supply and demand. The blue shaded area shows the burden on the consumer; the brown shaded area shows the burden on the supplier. This split occurs regardless of who actually pays the tax, as can be seen by noticing that the burden of the tax is equal in (**a**), where the supplier pays the tax, and in (**c**), where the consumer pays the tax. In (**b**) you can see how consumers with an inelastic demand bear a greater burden of the tax.

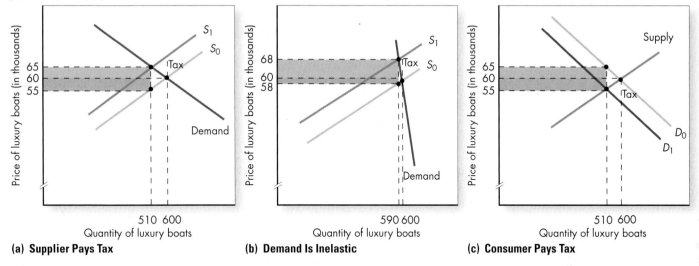

(a) **Supplier Pays Tax**   (b) **Demand Is Inelastic**   (c) **Consumer Pays Tax**

depends on who is best able to change his or her behavior in response to the tax, or who has the greater elasticity. Elasticity and supply/demand analysis let us answer the question "Who will end up bearing the burden of the tax?" (More technically: "What is the incidence of the tax?")

Figure 7-3(a) shows the case I considered in Chapter 5. A $10,000 per-unit tax levied on the supplier shifts the supply curve up from S_0 to S_1. That reduces quantity supplied and quantity demanded by 90—from 600 to 510. The equilibrium price rises from $60,000 to $65,000. Suppliers are able to shift $5,000 of the total $10,000 per-unit tax onto consumers, leaving the suppliers the burden of the remaining $5,000.

Had we known elasticities at the market equilibrium, we could have stated, without additional calculations, that the tax burden would be shared equally. Specifically, suppliers sold and consumers purchased 90 fewer boats, an approximate 15 percent reduction. The suppliers' price fell by about 8 percent while the consumers' price rose by about 8 percent, meaning the elasticity of both supply and demand was approximately 1.9.[3] With equal elasticities, the tax burden will be divided equally.

In reality, the tax burden is rarely shared equally because elasticities are rarely equal. The relative burden of the tax follows this general rule: *The more inelastic one's relative supply and demand, the larger the burden of the tax one will bear.* If demand were more inelastic, sellers would have been able to sell the boats at a higher price and could have passed more of the tax along to the buyers.

Figure 7-3(b) shows what the divisions would have been had the demand curve been highly inelastic. In this case, the price would rise more, the supplier would pay a lower proportion of the tax (the brown area), and the consumer would pay a much larger proportion (the blue area). The general rule about elasticities and the tax burden

Q-3 If a person has a highly elastic demand, will he likely bear a large or small percentage of the burden of a tax?

Tax burden is allocated by relative elasticities.

---

[3]There will be slight variations in the measured elasticities depending on how they are calculated.

is this: If demand is more inelastic than supply, consumers will pay a higher percentage of the tax; if supply is more inelastic than demand, suppliers will pay a higher share. This rule makes sense—*elasticity is a measure of how easy it is for the supplier and consumer to change behavior and substitute another good.*

More specifically, we can calculate the fraction of the tax actually borne by the demander by dividing the price elasticity of supply by the sum of the price elasticities of supply and demand:

$$\text{Fraction of tax borne by demander} = \frac{E_S}{E_D + E_S}$$

Q-4 How much of a $100 tax would a consumer pay if elasticity of demand is .2 and elasticity of supply is 1.8?

Similarly, we can calculate the fraction of the tax borne by the supplier by dividing the price elasticity of demand by the sum of the price elasticities of supply and demand:

$$\text{Fraction of tax borne by supplier} = \frac{E_D}{E_D + E_S}$$

For example, say the price elasticity of supply is 4 and the price elasticity of demand is 1. In that case, the supplier will pay one-fifth [1/(1 + 4)] of the tax and the consumer will pay four-fifths [4/(1 + 4)] of the tax. This situation is shown in Figure 7-3(b).

The rule about the elasticities and the tax burden can lead to some unexpected consequences of taxation. For example, the U.S. luxury tax on boats was initially implemented as a way to tax the wealthy. It turned out, however, that the wealthy found substitutes for American-made boats; their demand was relatively elastic. They either purchased other luxury items or purchased their boats from foreign firms. U.S. boat manufacturers, however, couldn't easily switch to producing other products. Their supply was inelastic. As a result, when they tried to pass on the cost increase to consumers, their sales plummeted. They had to lower their price by almost as much as the tax, which meant that they were bearing most of the burden of the tax. As noted in Chapter 5, pressured by boat manufacturers, the government repealed the luxury tax on boats three years after it was instituted.

WHO PAYS A TAX IS NOT NECESSARILY WHO BEARS THE BURDEN   The allocation of tax burden by relative elasticity means that it doesn't matter who actually pays the tax and that, as I said earlier, the person who bears the burden can differ from the person who pays. To assure yourself that it doesn't matter who pays the tax, ask yourself how your answer would have differed if the tax of $10,000 had been paid by the consumer. Figure 7-3(c) shows this case. Because the tax is paid by the consumer, the demand curve shifts down by the amount of the tax. As you can see, the results of the tax are identical. The percentage of the tax paid by the supplier and the consumer, after adjusting for the changes in supply and demand price, is independent of who actually makes the physical payment of the tax.

The burden is independent of who physically pays the tax.

Tax Incidence and Current Policy Debates

Now let's consider two policy questions in relation to what we have learned about tax incidence.

Q-5 If Social Security taxes were paid only by employees, what would likely happen to workers' pretax pay?

SOCIAL SECURITY TAXES   The first policy question concerns the Social Security (or payroll) tax, which accounts for 35 percent of federal government revenue. In 2012, the standard Social Security and Medicare tax rate was 12.4 percent on wages up to an annual maximum wage of $110,100, and another 2.9 percent on all wages, no matter how high. As a political compromise, half of Social Security taxes are placed on the employee and half on the employer. (In recent years the tax has been temporarily lowered on workers so that the combined rate was 10.4 percent.) But the fact that the law places the tax

College Newspaper Editors Should Take More Economics

In almost all towns and counties, nearly every year property taxes rise. College and university towns are no different. In 2006, the Orange County Board of Commissioners imposed an annual 7-cent property tax increase per $100 assessed value on properties in Orange County, the county where the University of North Carolina is located. UNC's student newspaper, the *Daily Tar Heel,* covered the story and suggested that off-campus rents would surely rise.

Based on the tools you've learned in this chapter, you know that the answer to that is not "surely" but is, rather, that the answer depends on elasticities. In the short run, the supply of housing tends to be very inelastic. The

demand for housing by students, however, is generally quite elastic; they just haven't got much money, and often can choose to live on campus in a dorm. So who will likely pay almost all the property tax? The owner of the house, which means that rents are unlikely to be significantly affected by the tax. To put some numbers on it, economists who study the tax incidence of property taxes have found that for every $1 increase in property taxes, about 88 cents is paid by landlords and 12 cents is paid by renters, which means that the renter's share of the 7-cent per $100 tax increase on an apartment valued at $100,000 amounts to about 70 cents a month.

equally on both does not mean that the burden of the tax is shared equally between employees and employers. On average, labor supply tends to be less elastic than labor demand. This means that the Social Security tax burden is primarily on the employees, even though employees see only their own statutory portion of the Social Security tax on their pay stub.

Now, let's say that you are advising a person running for Congress who has come up with the idea to place the entire tax on the employer and eliminate the tax on the employee. What will the effect of that be? Our tax incidence analysis tells us that, ultimately, it will have no effect. Wages paid to employees will fall to compensate employers for the cost of the tax. This example shows that who is assessed the tax can be quite different than who actually bears the burden, or incidence, of the tax. The burden will be borne by those with the most inelastic supply or demand because they are less able to get out of paying the tax by substitution.

So what do you tell the candidate? Is the idea a good one or not? Although economically it will not make a difference who pays the tax, politically it may be a popular proposal because individuals generally look at statutory assessment, not incidence. The candidate may gain significant support from workers, since they would no longer see a Social Security tax on their pay stub. The moral, then, is this: Politics often focuses on surface appearance; economics tries to get under the surface, and what is good economics is not always good politics.

SALES TAXES Our second policy question concerns sales taxes paid by retailers on the basis of their sales revenue. Say, for example, that the general sales tax is 6 cents on the dollar. Since sales taxes are broadly defined, consumers have little ability to substitute. Demand is inelastic and consumers bear the greater burden of the tax. Although stores could simply incorporate the tax into the price of their goods, most stores add the tax onto the bill after the initial sale is calculated, to make you aware of the tax. So even though economically, it doesn't matter whether the tax is assessed on the store or on you, psychologically, it matters a lot.

Web Note 7.1
Debating Social
Security

What makes sense politically is not always what makes sense economically.

151

Recently, however, the Internet has given consumers a substitute to shopping at actual retail stores. Retail sales over the Internet are over $200 billion annually and are continuing to grow. States have found it very difficult to tax Internet sales because the supplier has no retail address. The point of sale is in cyberspace. Technically in these cases, the buyer is required to pay the tax to the state where he or she lives, but in practice that seldom happens. How to tax Internet sales will be heavily debated over the next few years. The federal government currently has placed a moratorium on new Internet sales taxes. As Internet sales grow, states will lose more and more sales tax revenue and retail shops will bear a larger portion of the tax levied on their sales, which together will invite strong pressure to end the moratorium, and to establish procedures in which the tax on Internet sales is automatically assessed and paid.

Government Intervention as Implicit Taxation

Taxes are not the only way government affects our lives. For example, government establishes laws that dictate what we can do, what prices we can charge for goods, and what working conditions are and are not acceptable. This second part of the chapter continues the discussion of such issues, which began in Chapter 5. I show how the elasticity concept can help us talk about such interventions and how, using the producer and consumer surplus framework, such interventions can be seen as a combination tax and subsidy that does not show up on government books.

To see how government intervention in the market can be viewed as a combination tax and subsidy, let's first consider the two types of price controls mentioned in Chapter 5: price ceilings and price floors.

Price Ceilings and Floors

Q-6 Demonstrate the effect of an effective price ceiling on producer and consumer surplus when both supply and demand are highly inelastic.

As discussed in Chapter 5, an effective **price ceiling** is *a government-set price below the market equilibrium price*. It is in essence an implicit tax on producers and an implicit subsidy to consumers. Consider the effect of a price ceiling on producer and consumer surplus, shown in Figure 7-4(a).

FIGURE 7-4 (A AND B)   **Effect of Price Controls on Consumer and Producer Surplus**

Price floors and price ceilings create deadweight loss just as taxes do. In (**a**) we see how a price ceiling, P_1, transfers surplus D from producers to consumers. Price ceilings are equivalent to a tax on producers and a subsidy to consumers. In (**b**) we see how a price floor, P_2, transfers surplus B from consumers to producers. With either a price floor or a price ceiling, areas C and E represent the welfare loss triangle.

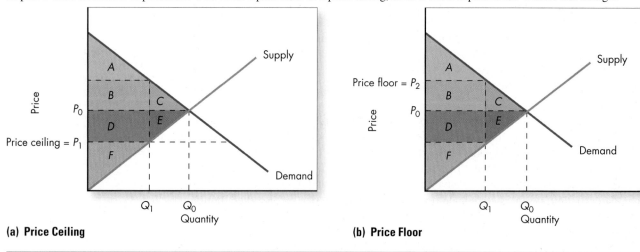

(a) **Price Ceiling**   (b) **Price Floor**

If the price were at the market equilibrium price, the total surplus would be the combination of the areas *A* through *F.* But with an effective price ceiling P_1, the quantity supplied falls from Q_0 to Q_1. The combined producer and consumer surplus is reduced by triangles *C* and *E.* The loss of surplus represents those individuals who would like to make trades—the individuals represented by the demand and supply curves between Q_1 and Q_0—but cannot do so because of the price ceiling.

This loss of consumer and producer surplus includes the welfare loss from taxation. That is not a coincidence. The price ceiling is a combination implicit tax on suppliers, shown by area *D,* and implicit subsidy to consumers of that same area. It is as if government places a tax on suppliers when they sell the good, and then gives that tax revenue to consumers when they purchase the good.

A price ceiling is a combination implicit tax on suppliers and implicit subsidy to consumers.

Price floors have the opposite effect on the distribution of consumer and producer surplus. Effective **price floors**—*government-set prices above equilibrium price*—transfer consumer surplus to producers. They can be seen as a tax on consumers of area *B* and a subsidy to producers of that same area, as shown in Figure 7-4(b). Price floors also impose a deadweight loss, shown by the welfare loss triangle, areas *C* and *E.*

The Difference between Taxes and Price Controls

While the effects of taxation and controls are similar, there is an important difference: *Price ceilings create shortages; taxes do not.* The reason is that taxes leave people free to choose how much they want to supply and consume as long as they pay the tax. Taxes create a wedge between the price the consumers pay and the price the suppliers receive just large enough to equate quantity demanded with quantity supplied.

Price ceilings create shortages; taxes do not.

Since with price ceilings the price consumers pay is the same as the price suppliers receive, as long as the price ceiling is below equilibrium price, the desired quantity demanded will exceed the quantity supplied. Some method of rationing—limiting the demand or increasing the supply in the case of price ceilings, and limiting the supply or increasing the demand in the case of price floors—must be found. Because so far we have assumed that suppliers can choose how much or how little they want to supply, there are shortages. Such shortages create black markets—markets in which individuals buy or sell illegally. (Taxes also may create black markets if buyers and sellers attempt to evade the tax.)

www   Web Note 7.2   Sin Taxes

Rent Seeking, Politics, and Elasticities

If price controls reduce total producer and consumer surplus, why do governments institute them? The answer is that *people care about their own surplus and how the surplus is distributed more than they do about total surplus.* As we have seen, price ceilings redistribute surplus from producers to consumers, so if the consumers have the political power, there will be strong pressures to create price ceilings. Alternatively, if the suppliers have the political power, there will be strong pressures to create price floors.

The possibility of transferring surplus from one set of individuals to another causes people to spend time and resources on doing so. For example, if criminals know that $1 million ransoms are commonly paid for executives, it will be worthwhile for them to figure out ways to kidnap executives—which happens in some developing and transitional economies. (That's why all countries state that they will never pay ransoms; however, not all countries follow their stated policies.)

The possibility of kidnapping, in turn, causes executives to hire bodyguards, which in turn causes kidnappers to think of ingenious ways to kidnap (which in turn . . .). The result is that, as one group attempts to appropriate surplus from another group, enormous amounts of resources are spent on activities that benefit no one.

The same reasoning holds for lobbying government. Individuals have an incentive to spend resources to lobby government to institute policies that increase their own surplus.

www   Web Note 7.3   Lobbying for Rent

The Excess Burden of a Draft

One way to deal with shortages is to require by law that suppliers supply all the goods demanded at the ceiling price. The military draft is an example. A draft is a law that requires some people to serve a set period in the armed forces at whatever pay the government chooses. It has often been used as a way of meeting the military's need for soldiers. The draft is a price ceiling combined with forced supply.

The effects of a draft are shown in the graph. A draft must be imposed when the wage offered by the army is below equilibrium because the quantity of soldiers demanded exceeds the quantity supplied. In the graph, the offered wage W_0 is below the equilibrium wage W_e. The market answer to the shortage would be to increase the wage to W_e, which would both reduce the quantity of soldiers demanded by government and increase the quantity of people willing to become soldiers. How much the wage would need to be increased to bring about equilibrium depends on the elasticity of supply and demand. If both supply and demand are inelastic, then the pay will need to be increased enormously; if both are elastic, the pay will need to be increased only slightly.

The people who are proposing the draft suspect that both supply and demand are inelastic, in which case the market solution would be very expensive to the government, requiring large increases in taxes. They argue that a draft is much cheaper, and requires lower taxes.

Our supply/demand analysis reveals the fallacy in that reasoning. It's true that with a draft the government does not have to collect as much revenue as it would have to if it raised the wage to a market-clearing wage. But that doesn't mean it's costless because the draft places an implicit hidden tax on the draftees. By paying a lower-than-equilibrium wage and instituting a draft, which requires draftees to serve in the military whether they want to or not, the supply curve effectively becomes the horizontal line at W_0. Individuals drafted are implicitly taxed by the difference between the wage they would have received, W_e, in their alternative private employment and the military wage, W_0. For example, when Elvis Presley was drafted, he gave up a wage of

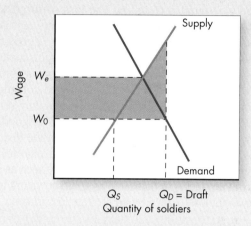

Quantity of soldiers

over a million dollars a year for a wage of about $5,000 a year. That is a large implicit tax on him. So, the draft imposes an implicit tax on draftees that doesn't show up on the government books.

Who, you ask, gets the proceeds of the tax? Those proceeds are implicitly given to those who consume defense services. Specifically, in the graph, the brown shaded area is transferred from suppliers to consumers of national defense. In this case, the welfare loss triangle is the shaded triangle to the right of the market equilibrium. It represents the opportunities that the suppliers lose but that the demanders do not receive.

The welfare loss triangle shows only the minimum loss that the ceiling will create. The analysis assumes that the individuals drafted will be those whose opportunity cost of being drafted is lowest. In fact, that is not the case. The actual amount of loss depends on how the draft selects individuals. If it selects individuals totally randomly (which, in principle, is how drafts are structured), it will draft some into the armed forces who would not consider serving even at the equilibrium wage (Elvis Presley, for example). Thus, the welfare loss is larger for interferences in the market such as the draft than it is for an equivalent tax, although it is difficult to specify precisely how much larger.

Q-7 Would a firm's research and development expenditures be classified as rent seeking?

Others have an incentive to spend money to counteract those lobbying efforts. *Activities designed to transfer surplus from one group to another* are called **rent-seeking activities.** Rent-seeking activities require resources, and the net result is unproductive. **Public choice economists**—*economists who integrate an economic analysis of politics with their analysis of the economy*—argue that rent seeking through government is significant, and that much of the transfer of surplus that occurs through government intervention creates an enormous waste of resources. They argue that the taxes and the benefits of government programs offset each other and do not help society significantly, but they do cost resources. These economists point out that much of the redistribution through government is from one group of the middle class to another group of the middle class.

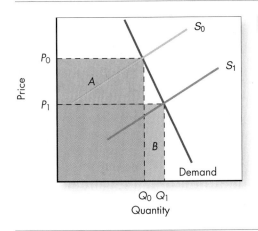

FIGURE 7-5   Inelastic Demand and the Incentive to Restrict Supply

When demand is inelastic, increases in productivity that shift the supply curve to the right result in lower revenue for suppliers. Although suppliers gain area *B*, they lose the much larger area *A*. Suppliers have an incentive to restrict supply when demand is inelastic because, by doing so, they will increase their revenues.

Inelastic Demand and Incentives to Restrict Supply

To understand the rent-seeking process a bit better, let's look more carefully at the incentives that consumers and producers have to lobby government to intervene in the market. We'll begin with suppliers. A classic example of the political pressures to limit supply is found in agricultural markets. Within the past century, new machinery, new methods of farming, and hybrid seeds have increased the productivity of farmers tremendously. You might think that because farmers can now produce more at a lower cost, they'd be better off. But if you think that, you're ignoring the interaction of supply and demand. As advances in productivity increase supply, they do increase the quantity sold, but they also result in lower prices. Farmers sell more but they get less for each unit they sell. Because food is a necessity and has few substitutes, the demand for many agricultural goods is inelastic. Since demand is inelastic, the price declines by a greater proportion than the rise in quantity sold, meaning that total revenue declines and the farmers are actually worse off. The situation is shown in Figure 7-5.

Because of the increase in supply, price declines from P_0 to P_1 and quantity sold increases from Q_0 to Q_1. The farmer's revenue rises by area *B* but also falls by the larger area *A*. To counteract this trend, farmers have an incentive to get government to restrict supply or create a price floor, thereby raising their revenue. In fact, that's what they did in the 1930s. Farmers then were instrumental in getting the government to establish the Farm Board, a federal agency whose job was to manage productivity of agricultural goods. The benefits of limiting competition are greatest for suppliers when demand is inelastic because price will rise proportionately more than quantity will fall.

Farmers have been very successful in lobbying government to restrict the supply of agricultural goods. Public choice economists have suggested that the reasons for farm groups' success involve the nature of the benefits and costs. The groups that are hurt by agricultural subsidies are large, but the negative effect on each individual in that group is relatively small. Large groups that experience small costs per individual don't provide a strong political opposition to a small group that experiences large gains. This seems to reflect a **general rule of political economy** in a democracy: *When small groups are helped by a government action and large groups are hurt by that same action, the small group tends to lobby far more effectively than the large group; thus, policies tend to reflect the small group's interest, not the interest of the large group.*

This simple example provides us with an important insight about how markets work and how the politics of government intervention work. Inelastic demand creates an enormous incentive for suppliers either to pressure government to limit the quantity

Q-8 How can an increase in productivity harm suppliers?

The general rule of political economy states that small groups that are significantly affected by a government policy will lobby more effectively than large groups that are equally affected by that same policy.

The central problem of political
economy is that you need
government to ensure that
competition works, but government
also can be used to prevent
competition.

Q-9 If supply is perfectly inelastic,
will price controls cause a large
shortage?

supplied or to get together and look for other ways to limit the quantity supplied. The
more inelastic demand is, the more suppliers have to gain by restricting supply.

Sometimes sellers can get government to limit quantity supplied through licensing;
other times they can limit supply by force. A well-placed threat ("If you enter this market,
I will blow up your store") is often effective. In some developing economies, such threats
are common. What stops existing suppliers from making good on such threats? Government.
But the government also creates opportunities for individuals to prevent others from entering the market. Therein lies a central problem of political economy. You need government
to see that competition works—to ensure that existing suppliers don't prevent others from
entering the market—but government can also be used to prevent competition and protect
existing suppliers. Government is part of both the problem and the solution.

Inelastic Supplies and Incentives to Restrict Prices

Firms aren't the only ones who can lobby government to intervene. Consider consumers.
When supply is inelastic, consumers can face significant price increases if their demand
increases. Thus, when the supply of a good is inelastic and the demand for that good rises,
prices will rise significantly and consumers will scream for price controls.

This is what happened in the New York City rent-control example (price ceilings
imposed on apartments) in Chapter 5. During World War II, an influx of short-term workers
into New York City increased demand for apartments. Because supply was inelastic, rents
rose tremendously. To keep apartments affordable, the city capped rents.

Such controls are not costless. One of the results of rent control is an ongoing
shortage of apartments. As we noted earlier, effective price ceilings will cause a shortage
unless suppliers are forced to supply a market-clearing quantity. With the knowledge of
elasticities, you also know whether a large or small shortage will develop with a price
ceiling and whether a large or small surplus will develop with a price floor.

To make sure you understand how elasticity can tell you the relative size of a
surplus or shortage when there are price controls, look at Figure 7-6, which shows
three cases of price floors, each with different elasticities of supply and demand.

FIGURE 7-6 (A, B, AND C)   Price Floors and Elasticity of Demand and Supply

A price floor above equilibrium market price will always create a surplus. The extent of the surplus created depends on the elasticity of the
curves. With elastic curves, a large surplus is created by price controls; with inelastic curves, a small surplus is created. Thus, in (**a**) the
intersection of supply and demand occurs where the curves are more elastic and the result is a larger surplus. In (**b**) demand and supply
intersect where the demand curve is less elastic and the surplus declines. In (**c**) demand and supply intersect where supply and demand are
most inelastic and the result is the smallest surplus.

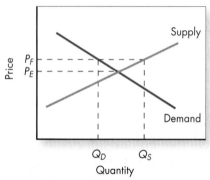

(a) **Price Floor with Elastic
Supply and Demand**

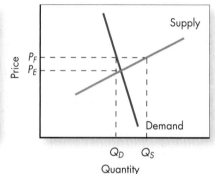

(b) **Price Floor with Elastic Supply
and Inelastic Demand**

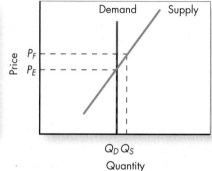

(c) **Price Floor with Inelastic Supply
and Demand**

As you can see, all three cases create excess supply—surpluses—but the proportional amount of excess supply depends on the elasticity. In Figure 7-6(a), supply and demand intersect at P_E, where they are relatively elastic. There, the price floor, P_F, leads to a relatively large surplus. Figure 7-6(b) represents an intermediate case: The intersection is where supply is elastic and demand is highly inelastic, and a relatively smaller surplus is created by the price floor. In Figure 7-6(c), where the demand and supply curves intersect at relatively inelastic portions, the surplus created by the price floor is relatively small. A good exercise is to go through the same analysis for price ceilings.

> The more elastic supply and demand, the larger the surplus or shortage created by price controls.

The Long-Run/Short-Run Problem of Price Controls

Now let's combine our analysis of price controls with another insight from the elasticity chapter—that in the long run, supply tends to be much more elastic than in the short run. This means that price controls will cause only relatively small shortages or surpluses in the short run, but large ones in the long run. Let's consider how this would play out in our rent-control example—see Figure 7-7. In the short run, supply is inelastic; thus, if demand shifts from D_0 to D_1, and the government allows landlords to charge the price they want, they will raise their price significantly, from P_0 to P_1.

In the long run, however, additional apartments will be built and other existing buildings will be converted into apartments. Supply becomes more elastic, rotating from S_0 to S_1. Faced with additional competition, landlords will lower their price to P_2. In the long run, price will fall and the number of apartments rented will increase.

Herein lies another political policy problem. In large part, it is the rise in price that brings in new competitors and increases in output. But if the government imposes price controls, keeping prices at P_0, the long-run incentives for competitors to enter the market will be eliminated. Landlords would not build additional apartments, and the shortage resulting from the price controls ($Q_3 - Q_0$) would remain. The political problems arise

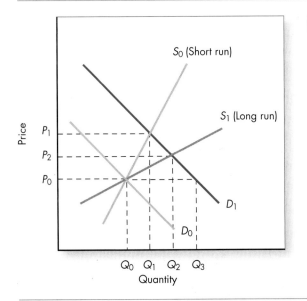

FIGURE 7-7 Long-Run and Short-Run Effects of Price Controls

This exhibit shows how lower long-run elasticities result in smaller price increases when demand increases. Price ceilings keep the long-run supply from lowering price impacts of shocks to housing markets.

Thinking Like a Modern Economist

How to Get Students to Be Responsible

Traditional economic policy focuses on getting the incentives right. If you want people to do less of something, raise its price. Behavioral economists take a broader view of policy and argue that economists' policy should go beyond incentives. For example, they point out that at times being in a state of high emotion "makes" people act irrationally (at least when compared to the choices they would make when not emotional). To demonstrate this tendency, Duke University economist Dan Ariely tested people's reactions under different emotional states. In one experiment, students answered the following questions in two different states: a normal state of calm and an emotionally excited state. (To get them into an emotional state, he showed students erotic photos.)

- Could you enjoy sex with someone you hate?
- Would you slip a person a drug to increase the chance that he or she would have sex with you?
- Would you always use a condom?

He found that students in an emotional state were often twice as likely to answer "yes, yes, and no" than when they were calm and collected. Behavioral economists argue that these and similar results suggest that policies

designed around rational responses to incentives in situations that involve emotion likely will not work. Instead, policy makers must design policies that take into account people's emotional self, which is far less likely to respond to incentives. Dan Ariely writes, "If we don't teach our young people how to deal with sex when they are half out of their minds, we are not only fooling them; we are fooling ourselves as well."

Policy makers include not only governments. They also include parents. And emotions don't affect just sexual decisions, they affect other high-risk behavior such as driving. To help parents deal with situations where their teenagers' emotions lead them to drive too fast, Ariely suggests that if parents provide their teenagers with cars, those cars should be equipped with a radio that automatically switches from playing 2Pac to Schumann's Second Symphony (and a phone that automatically calls his or her parents) whenever the student exceeds 65 miles an hour. I leave it to you to figure out if the policy makes sense, and whether some similar plan could be designed to get teenagers to abstain from sex, or at least practice safe sex.

Q-10 Why do price controls tend to create ongoing shortages or surpluses in the long run?

because politics generally responds to short-run pressures. In the short run, demand and supply are generally inelastic, making it look as if the price ceiling will not create significant problems. But in the long run, supply is usually elastic. Price controls that might alleviate the short-run problem cause fewer new apartments to be built. In the long run, the shortage becomes even more severe. As we noted in Chapter 5, the rent-control laws in New York City were initially written to be effective whenever the vacancy rate was below 5 percent, which was the vacancy rate at the time. But the rent controls stopped new apartments from being built and old ones from being maintained. Today, the vacancy rate is less than 4 percent and many rent-controlled apartments have deteriorated. The government's imposition of a price ceiling prevents the market from achieving a more desirable long-run equilibrium, at which output has expanded and price has fallen from its initially high level.

Conclusion

Government is a part of our life and, therefore, so too are taxes. Economic theory doesn't say government should or shouldn't play any particular role in the economy or what the taxes should be. Those decisions depend on normative judgments and the relevant costs and benefits. What economic theory does is to help point out the costs and benefits. For example, in the case of taxes, economists can show that the cost of taxation in terms of lost surplus is independent of who physically pays the tax.

In thinking about taxes and government involvement, the public often perceives economic theory and economists as suggesting the best policy is one of laissez-faire, or government noninvolvement in the economy. Many economists do suggest a laissez-faire policy, but that suggestion is based on empirical observations of government's role in the past, not on economic theory.

Still, economists as a group generally favor less government involvement than does the general public. I suspect this is because economists are taught to look below the surface at the long-run effect of government actions. They've discovered that the effects often aren't the intended effects, and that programs frequently have long-run consequences that make the problems worse, not better. Economists, both liberal and conservative, speak in the voice of reason: "Look at all the costs; look at all the benefits. Then decide whether government should or should not intervene." The supply/demand framework and the elasticity concept are extremely useful tools in making those assessments.

Economists' suggestions for laissez-faire policy are based on empirical observations of government's role in the past, not on economic theory.

Summary

- Equilibrium maximizes the combination of consumer surplus and producer surplus. Consumer surplus is the net benefit a consumer gets from purchasing a good, while producer surplus is the net benefit a producer gets from selling a good. (LO7-1)

- Taxes create a loss of consumer and producer surplus known as deadweight loss, which graphically is represented by the welfare loss triangle. (LO7-2)

- The cost of taxation to consumers and producers includes the actual tax paid, the deadweight loss, and the costs of administering the tax. (LO7-2)

- Who bears the burden of the tax depends on the relative elasticities of demand and supply. The more inelastic one's relative supply and demand, the larger the burden of the tax one will bear. (LO7-2)

- Price ceilings and price floors, like taxes, result in loss of consumer and producer surplus. (LO7-3)

- Price ceilings transfer producer surplus to consumers and therefore are equivalent to a tax on producers and a subsidy to consumers. Price floors have the opposite effect; they are a tax on consumers and a subsidy to producers. (LO7-3)

- Rent-seeking activities are designed to transfer surplus from one group to another. Producers facing inelastic demand for their product will benefit more from rent-seeking activities than producers facing elastic demand. Consumers facing inelastic supply for a product benefit more from rent-seeking activities such as lobbying for price ceilings than consumers facing an elastic supply. (LO7-4)

- The more elastic supply and/or demand is, the greater the surplus is with an effective price floor and the greater the shortage is with an effective price ceiling. (LO7-4)

- The general rule of political economy is that policies tend to reflect small groups' interests, not the interests of large groups. (LO7-4)

- The negative aspects of price controls worsen as the length of time considered rises because elasticity rises as time progresses. (LO7-4)

Key Terms

consumer surplus *(144)*
deadweight loss *(147)*
excise tax *(148)*
general rule of political
   economy *(155)*

price ceiling *(152)*
price floor *(153)*
producer
   surplus *(145)*

public choice
   economist *(154)*
rent-seeking
   activity *(154)*

welfare loss
   triangle *(147)*

Questions and Exercises

1. Why isn't the combination of consumer and producer surplus maximized if there is either excess demand or supply? *(LO7-1)*

2. Why does nearly every purchase you make provide you with consumer surplus? *(LO7-1)*

3. How is elasticity related to the revenue from a sales tax? *(LO7-2)*

4. Minneapolis Federal Reserve Bank economist Edward Prescott estimates the elasticity of the U.S. labor supply to be 3. Given this elasticity, what would be the impact of funding the Social Security program with tax increases on the number of hours worked and on the amount of taxes collected to fund Social Security? *(LO7-2)*

5. Demonstrate the welfare loss of: *(LO7-2)*
   a. A restriction on output when supply is perfectly elastic.
   b. A tax *t* placed on suppliers.
   c. A subsidy *s* given to suppliers.
   d. A restriction on output when demand is perfectly elastic.

6. Use the graph below that shows the effect of a $4 per-unit tax on suppliers to answer the following questions: *(LO7-2)*

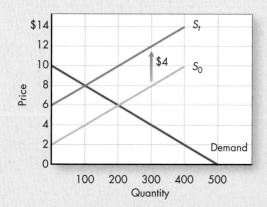

   a. What are equilibrium price and quantity before the tax? After the tax?

   b. What is producer surplus when the market is in equilibrium before the tax? After the tax?
   c. What is consumer surplus when the market is in equilibrium before the tax? After the tax?
   d. What is total tax revenue collected after the tax is implemented?

7. If the federal government wanted to tax a good and suppliers were strong lobbyists, but consumers were not, would government prefer supply or demand to be more inelastic? Why? *(LO7-2)*

8. What types of goods would you recommend that the government tax if it wants the tax to result in no welfare loss? Name a few examples. *(LO7-2)*

9. Suppose demand for cigarettes is inelastic and the supply of cigarettes is elastic. Who would bear the larger share of the burden of a tax placed on cigarettes? *(LO7-2)*

10. If the demand for a good is perfectly elastic and the supply is elastic, who will bear the larger share of the burden of a tax on the good where the tax is paid by consumers? *(LO7-2)*

11. What percentage of a tax will the demander pay if price elasticity of supply is 0.3 and price elasticity of demand is 0.7? What percentage will the supplier pay? *(LO7-2)*

12. Which good would an economist normally recommend taxing if government wanted to minimize welfare loss and maximize revenue: a good with an elastic or inelastic supply? Why? *(LO7-2)*

13. Should tenants who rent apartments worry that increases in property taxes will increase their rent? Does your answer change when considering the long run? *(LO7-2)*

14. Calculate the percentage of the tax borne by the demander and supplier in each of the following cases: *(LO7-2)*
    a. $E_D = 0.3, E_S = 1.2$
    b. $E_D = 3, E_S = 2$
    c. $E_D = 0.5, E_S = 1$
    d. $E_D = 0.5, E_S = 0.5$
    e. Summarize your findings regarding relative elasticity and tax burden.

15. In which case would the shortage resulting from a price ceiling be greater: when supply is inelastic or elastic? Explain your answer. (*LO7-3*)

16. Demonstrate how a price floor is like a tax on consumers and a subsidy to suppliers. Label the following: tax on consumers, transfer of surplus to suppliers, and welfare loss. (*LO7-3*)
    a. Who gets the revenue in the case of a tax?
    b. Who gets the revenue in the case of a price floor?

17. Suppose government imposed a minimum wage above equilibrium wage. (*LO7-3*)
    a. Assuming nothing else changes, what do you expect to happen to the resulting shortage of jobs as time progresses?
    b. What do you expect to happen to the producer surplus transferred to minimum wage earners as time progresses?

18. Use the graph below to answer the following questions: (*LO7-3*)

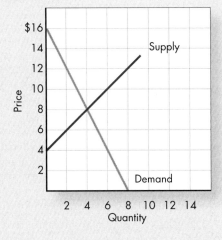

a. What are equilibrium price and quantity?
b. What is producer surplus when the market is in equilibrium?
c. What is consumer surplus when the market is in equilibrium?
d. If price were held at $12 a unit, what are consumer and producer surplus?

19. A political leader comes to you and wonders from whom she will get the most complaints if she institutes a price ceiling when demand is inelastic and supply is elastic. (*LO7-3*)
    a. How do you respond?
    b. Demonstrate why your answer is correct.

20. Define rent seeking. Do firms have a greater incentive to engage in rent-seeking behavior when demand is elastic or when it is inelastic? (*LO7-4*)

21. What is the general rule of political economy? Give an example from the real world. (*LO7-4*)

22. Given the graph below, up to how much would suppliers be willing to spend to restrict supply to Q_1? (*LO7-4*)

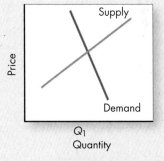

Questions from Alternative Perspectives

1. The quotation from Calvin Coolidge at the beginning of the chapter equates taxation to robbery.
   a. Is that a reasonable position to take?
   b. What alternatives to taxation could a country consider to collect the revenue it needs to operate? (Austrian)

2. The chapter frames the issue of the effects of taxation in terms of its effects on producer and consumer surplus.
   a. What does that framework leave out of the analysis?
   b. How might one frame the analysis differently?
   c. If women are discriminated against and receive less income than men on average, do they get less weight than men in consumer surplus? (Feminist)

3. Do Pierre, a software engineer earning $200,000 a year, and Sally, a single mother whose welfare benefits are about to expire, get equal weight in the measure of consumer surplus? (Institutionalist)

4. The elasticity of the supply of labor in part determines who bears the burden of Social Security taxes. Those taxes are typically levied in matching 6.2 percent shares on workers' wages and wages paid out by employers. Economists treat the two shares as one tax and then consider two cases. In competitive labor markets, the supply of labor is taken to be totally inelastic. In noncompetitive labor markets, workers' bargaining power matches that

of employers and the supply and demand curves for labor have similar elasticities. Who bears the burden of Social Security taxes in each case? Illustrate your answer with two labor market diagrams. (Hint: Empirical evidence indicates that in the noncompetitive case, the employer's share of Social Security taxes is passed on to consumers in the form of higher prices.) (Radical)

5. God sees all individuals as equal, and that what one does to the least of God's children, one does to all. How does that approach to thinking about issues fit with the economic analysis that focuses on consumer and producer surplus? (Religious)

Issues to Ponder

1. Many of the buildings in Paris have Mansard roofs, such as those shown in the photograph on page 147.
   a. What property tax structure would bring this about?
   b. Could you imagine a change in the property tax that would reduce the number of Mansard roofs built?
   c. Can you think of other design elements that reflect tax structure?

2. Because of the negative incentive effect that taxes have on goods with elastic supply, in the late 1980s Margaret Thatcher (then prime minister of Great Britain) changed the property tax to a poll tax (a tax at a set rate that every individual must pay).
   a. Show why the poll tax is preferable to a property tax in terms of consumer and producer surplus.
   b. What do you think the real-life consequences of the poll tax were?

3. Can you suggest a tax system that led to this building style, which was common in old eastern European cities?

4. The Pure Food and Drug Act of 1906 is known as "Dr. Wiley's Law." It is generally regarded by non-economic historians as representing the triumph of consumer interests over producer interests.
   a. Why might an economist likely be somewhat wary of this interpretation?

   b. What evidence would a skeptical economist likely look for to determine the motives behind the passage of this law?
   c. What would be the significance of the fact that the Pure Food and Drug Act was passed in 1906, right when urbanization and technological change were fostering new products that competed significantly with existing producers' interests?

5. The president of Lebanon Valley College proposed the following tuition program: provide a 50 percent tuition reduction for those graduating in the top 10 percent of their high school class, 33 percent reduction for those in the top 20 percent, and 25 percent reduction for those in the top 30 percent. All scholarship recipients were also required to maintain a minimum GPA. The comptroller estimated that the elasticity of demand for these students was greater than 1.
   a. Economics Professor Paul Heise recommended that the president institute the program, arguing that it would increase revenues. What was his argument?
   b. Why did the program distinguish among top-performing students?
   c. Why didn't the president reduce tuition for all students?

6. In 2004, the University of California education system drastically cut enrollment due to significant state budget cuts and asked 7,600 applicants to defer enrollment for two years after completing two years at a community college. Tuition costs remained fixed by the state.
   a. Demonstrate the situation described in 2004 with supply and demand curves, carefully labeling any excess supply or demand for college admissions.
   b. What is the market solution to the excess demand for college?
   c. What is a possible reason the market solution was not pursued?

Answers to Margin Questions

1. The combination of consumer and producer surplus will increase since there will be no lost surplus at the equilibrium price. (*p. 145; LO7-1*)

2. Welfare loss when supply is highly elastic and demand is highly inelastic is shown by the shaded triangle in the graph below. The supply curve shifts up by the amount

of the tax. Since equilibrium quantity changes very little, from Q_0 to Q_1, welfare loss is very small. (*p. 147; LO7-2*)

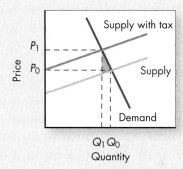

3. If a person's demand is highly elastic, he would bear a small percentage of the burden of a tax. (*p. 149; LO7-2*)

4. The percentage of the tax borne by the consumer equals price elasticity of supply divided by the sum of the price elasticities of demand and supply, or

$$\frac{1.8}{(0.2 + 1.8)} = 0.9.$$

The consumer pays $90 of the tax. (*p. 150; LO7-2*)

5. If the entire amount of the tax were levied on employees, their before-tax income would rise because employers would have to compensate their employees for the increased taxes they would have to physically pay. The burden of the taxation does not depend on who pays the tax. It depends on relative elasticities. (*p. 150; LO7-2*)

6. The effect of a price ceiling below equilibrium price when demand and supply are inelastic is shown in the following graph. Quantity demanded exceeds quantity supplied, but because demand and supply are both inelastic, the shortage is not big. Likewise, the welfare

loss triangle, shown by the shaded area in the gra[ph] not large. (*p. 152; LO7-3*)

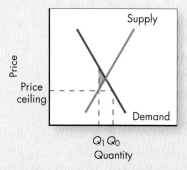

7. No. Research and development expenditures are an effort to increase technology to either lower production costs or discover a new product that can be marketed. If the firm can get a patent on that new product, the firm will have a monopoly and be able to restrict supply, transferring surplus from consumers to itself, but this is not rent seeking. Rent-seeking activities are designed to transfer surplus from one group to another given current technology. They are unproductive. (*p. 154; LO7-4*)

8. If suppliers are selling a product for which demand is inelastic, increases in productivity would result in a drop in price that would be proportionately greater than the rise in equilibrium quantity. Total revenue would decline for suppliers. (*p. 155; LO7-4*)

9. With a perfectly inelastic supply, price controls will cause a smaller shortage compared to other supply elasticities. (*p. 156; LO7-4*)

10. Price controls tend to create ongoing shortages and surpluses in the long run because they prevent market forces from working. (*p. 158; LO7-4*)

Chapter 8

Market failure versus Government Failure

> *The business of government is to keep the government out of business—that is unless business needs government aid.*
>
> —Will Rogers

There is an ongoing (indeed unending) debate: Should the government intervene in markets such as health care or agriculture? The supply/demand framework you learned in the previous chapters was created to provide some insight into answering that question, and those chapters began exploring the issues. In this chapter we explore economic policy questions more deeply and develop a fuller understanding of some of the roles of government first presented in Chapter 3.

The economic analysis of policy is set in the economic framework, which can also be called the *invisible hand framework*. It says that if markets are perfectly competitive, they will lead individuals to make voluntary choices that are in the society's interest. It is as if individuals are guided by an invisible hand to do what society wants them to do.

For the invisible hand to guide private actions toward the social good, a number of conditions must be met. When they are not met, economists say that there is a **market failure**—*a situation in which the invisible hand pushes in such a way that individual decisions do not lead to socially desirable outcomes.* In this chapter we consider three sources of market failures: externalities, public goods, and imperfect information.

Any time there is a market failure, it is possible that government intervention could improve the outcome. But it is important to remember that even if a market failure exists, it is not clear that government action will improve the result since the politics of implementing the solution often lead to further problems. These problems of government intervention are often called **government failures**—*when the government intervention in the market to improve the market failure actually makes the situation worse.* After discussing the three sources of market failures, we will discuss government failures. The economic policy debate can be best thought of as choosing which failure is likely to be the lesser of two evils.

Externalities

An important requirement for the invisible hand to guide markets in society's interest is that market transactions have no side effects on anyone not involved in the transactions. As discussed in Chapter 3, such side effects are called

After reading this chapter, you should be able to:

LO8-1 Explain what an externality is and show how it affects the market outcome.

LO8-2 Describe three methods of dealing with externalities.

LO8-3 Define *public good* and explain the problem with determining the value of a public good to society.

LO8-4 Explain how informational and moral hazard problems can lead to market failure.

LO8-5 Explain why market failure is not necessarily a reason for government intervention.

Pareto Optimality and the Perfectly Competitive Benchmark

Perfect competition serves as a benchmark for judging policies. A foundation for this benchmark is in the work of Stanford economist Kenneth Arrow, who showed that the market translates self-interest into society's interest. (Arrow was given a Nobel Prize in 1972 for this work.) Arrow's ideas are based on many assumptions that can only be touched on in an introductory book. I will, however, discuss one here—the interpretation of the term *society's welfare*. In the economic framework, society's welfare is interpreted as coming as close as one can to a *Pareto optimal position*—a position from which no person can be made better off without another being made worse off.

Let's briefly consider what Arrow proved. He showed that if the market was perfectly competitive, and if there was a complete set of markets (a market for every possible good now and in the future), the invisible hand would guide the economy to a Pareto optimal position. If these assumptions hold true, the supply curve (which represents the marginal cost to the suppliers) would represent the marginal cost to society. Similarly, the demand curve (which represents the marginal benefit to consumers) would represent the marginal benefit to society. In a supply/demand equilibrium, not only would an individual be as well off as he or she possibly could be, given where he or she started from, but so too would society. A perfectly competitive market equilibrium would be a Pareto optimal position.

A number of criticisms exist to using perfect competition as a benchmark:

1. *The nirvana criticism:* A perfectly competitive equilibrium is highly unstable. It's usually in some person's interest to restrict entry by others, and, when a market is close to a competitive equilibrium, it is in few people's interest to stop such restrictions. Thus, perfect competition will never exist in the real world. Comparing reality to a situation that cannot occur (i.e., to nirvana) is unfair and unhelpful because it leads to attempts to achieve the unachievable. A better benchmark would be workable competition—a state of competition that one might reasonably hope could exist.

2. *The second-best criticism:* The conditions that allow us to conclude that perfect competition leads to a Pareto optimal position are so restrictive that they are never even approached in reality. If the economy deviates in hundreds of ways from perfect competition, how are we to know whether a movement toward more competition will improve people's welfare?

3. *The normative criticism:* Even if the previous two criticisms didn't exist, the perfect competition benchmark still isn't appropriate because there is nothing necessarily wonderful about Pareto optimality. A Pareto optimal position could be horrendous. For example, say one person has all the world's revenues and all the other people are starving. If that rich person would be made worse off by taking some money from him and giving it to the starving poor, that starting position would be Pareto optimal. By most people's normative criteria, it would also be a lousy place to remain.

Critics of the use of the perfect competition benchmark argue that society has a variety of goals. Pareto optimality may be one of them, but it's only one. They argue that economists should take into account all of society's goals—not just Pareto optimality—when determining a benchmark for judging policies.

---

externalities—*the effects of a decision on a third party that are not taken into account by the decision maker.* Externalities can be either positive or negative. Secondhand smoke and carbon monoxide emissions are examples of **negative externalities,** which occur *when the effects of a decision not taken into account by the decision maker are detrimental to others.* **Positive externalities** occur *when the effects of a decision not taken into account by the decision maker are beneficial to others.* An example is education. When you purchase a college education, it benefits not only you but others as well. Innovation is another example. The invention of the personal computer has had significant beneficial effects on society, which were not taken into account by the inventors. When there are externalities, the supply and/or demand curves no longer represent the marginal cost and marginal benefit curves to society.

An externality is an effect of a decision on a third party not taken into account by the decision maker.

Web Note 8.1
The Invisible Hand

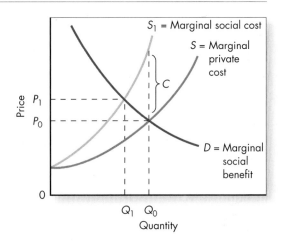

FIGURE 8-1   A Negative Externality

When there is a negative externality, the marginal private cost will be below the marginal social cost and the competitive price will be too low to maximize social welfare.

A Negative Externality Example

Say that you and I agree that I'll produce steel for you. I'll build my steel plant on land I own, and start producing. We both believe our welfare will improve. But what about my plant's neighbors? The resulting smoke will pollute the air they breathe. The people involved in the market trade (you and I) are made better off, but people external to the trade are made worse off. Thus, there is a negative externality. My production of steel has a cost to society that neither you nor I take into account.

The effect of a negative externality is shown in Figure 8-1. The supply curve S represents the marginal private cost to society of producing steel. The demand curve D represents the marginal social benefit of consuming the steel. With no externalities, the marginal private costs and benefits represent the marginal social costs and benefits, so the supply/demand equilibrium (P_0, Q_0) represents where the marginal social benefit equals the marginal social cost. At that point society is as well off as possible.

But now consider what happens when production results in negative externalities. In that case people not involved in production also incur costs. This means that the supply curve no longer represents both the marginal private and marginal social costs of supplying the good. Marginal social cost is greater than the marginal private cost. This case can be represented by adding a curve in Figure 8-1 called the *marginal social cost curve*. The **marginal social cost** includes all the marginal costs that society bears—or *the marginal private costs of production plus the cost of the negative externalities associated with that production.*

Since in this case the externality represents an additional cost to society, the marginal social cost curve lies above the marginal private cost curve. The distance between the two curves represents the additional cost of the externality. For example, at quantity Q_0, the private marginal cost faced by the firm is P_0. The marginal cost from the externality at quantity Q_0 is shown by distance C. The optimal price and quantity for society is P_1 and Q_1. When the externality is not taken into account, the supply/demand equilibrium is at too high a quantity, Q_0, and at too low a price, P_0.

Notice that the market solution results in a level of steel production that exceeds the level that equates the marginal social costs with the marginal social benefits. If the market is to maximize welfare, some type of government intervention may be needed to reduce production from Q_0 to Q_1 and raise price from P_0 to P_1.

When there are externalities, the marginal social cost differs from the marginal private cost.

Q-1 Why does the existence of an externality prevent the market from working properly?

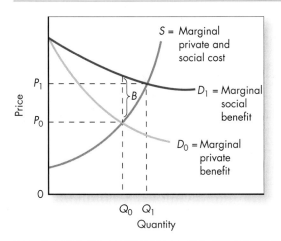

FIGURE 8-2 **A Positive Externality**

When there is a positive externality, the marginal social benefit will be above the marginal private benefit and the market price will be too low to maximize social welfare.

A Positive Externality Example

Private trades can also benefit third parties not involved in the trade. These are positive externalities. Again, an example is education. Consider a person who is working and takes a class at night. He or she will bring the knowledge from class back to co-workers through day-to-day interaction on projects. The co-workers will be learning the material from the class indirectly. They are outside the initial decision to take the class, but they benefit nonetheless.

In the case of positive externalities, the market will not provide enough of the good. Let's see how. In Figure 8-2, we start again with the standard demand and supply curves. The supply curve S represents the marginal private cost of the course. The demand curve D_0 is the marginal private benefit to those who take the course. Since others not taking the course also benefit, the marginal social benefit, shown by D_1, is above the marginal private benefit. The **marginal social benefit** equals *the marginal private benefit of consuming a good plus the benefits of the positive externalities resulting from consuming that good.* The vertical distance between D_0 and D_1 is the additional benefit that others receive at each quantity. At quantity Q_0, the market equilibrium, the marginal benefit of the externality, is shown by distance B. At this quantity, the marginal social benefit exceeds the marginal social cost. The market provides too little of the good. The optimal price and quantity for society are P_1 and Q_1, respectively. Again, some type of intervention to increase quantity may be warranted.

Q-2 If a positive externality exists, does that mean that the market works better than if no externality exists?

Positive externalities make the marginal private benefit below the marginal social benefit.

Alternative Methods of Dealing with Externalities

Ways to deal with externalities include (1) direct regulation, (2) incentive policies (tax incentive policies and market incentive policies), and (3) voluntary solutions.

Externalities can be dealt with via
1. Direct regulation.
2. Incentive policies.
3. Voluntary solutions.

Direct Regulation

In a program of **direct regulation,** *the amount of a good people are allowed to use is directly limited by the government.* Let's consider an example. Say we have two individuals, Ms. Thrifty, who uses 10 gallons of gasoline a day, and Mr. Big, who uses 20 gallons a day. Say we have decided that we want to reduce total daily gas consumption by 10 percent, or 3 gallons. The regulatory solution might require both individuals to reduce consumption by

Common Resources and the Tragedy of the Commons

Individuals tend to overuse commonly owned goods. Let's consider an example—say that grazing land is held in common. Individuals are free to bring their sheep to graze on the land. What is likely to happen? Each grazing sheep will reduce the amount of grass for other sheep. If individuals don't have to pay for grazing, when deciding how much to graze their sheep they will not take into account the cost to others of their sheep's grazing. The result may be overgrazing—killing the grass and destroying the grazing land. This is known as the *tragedy of the commons*. A more contemporary example of the tragedy of the commons is fishing. The sea is a common resource; no one owns it, and whenever people catch fish, they reduce the number of fish that others can catch. The result will likely be overfishing.

The tragedy of the commons is an example of the problems posed by externalities. Catching fish imposes a negative externality—fewer fish for others to catch. Because of the negative effect on others, the social cost of catching a fish is greater than the private cost. Overfishing has been a problem in the United States and throughout the world. Thus, the tragedy of the commons is caused by individuals not taking into account the negative externalities of their actions.

Why doesn't the market solve the externality problem? Some economists argue that in the tragedy of the commons examples it would, if given a chance. The problem is a lack of property rights (lack of ownership). If rights to all goods were defined, the tragedy of the commons would disappear. In the fishing example, if someone owned the sea, he or she would charge individuals to fish. By charging for fishing rights, the owner would internalize the externality and thus avoid the tragedy of the commons.

Nobel Prize winning political economist, Elinor Ostrom, has studied common resources in a number of cultures, and has found that different societies have used a wide variety of institutional arrangements to deal with the tragedy of the commons. Her work has shown that there is no single answer to these problems, and that the answer chosen needs to reflect cultural mores of the society.

---

some specified amount. Likely direct regulatory strategies would be to require an equal quantity reduction (each consumer reducing consumption by 1.5 gallons) or an equal percentage reduction (each consumer reducing consumption by 10 percent).

Both of those strategies would reduce consumption, but neither would be **efficient** *(achieving a goal at the lowest cost in total resources without consideration as to who pays those costs)*. This is because direct regulation does not take into account that the costs of reducing consumption may differ among individuals. Say, for example, that Ms. Thrifty could almost costlessly reduce consumption by 3 gallons while Mr. Big would find it very costly to reduce consumption by even 0.5 gallon. In that case, either regulatory solution would be **inefficient** *(achieving a goal in a more costly manner than necessary)*. It would be less costly (more efficient) to have Ms. Thrifty undertake most of the reduction. A policy that would automatically make the person who has the lower cost of reduction *choose* (as opposed to being *required*) to undertake the most reduction would achieve the same level of reduction at a lower cost. In this case, the efficient policy would get Ms. Thrifty to choose to undertake the majority of the reduction.

Incentive Policies

Two types of incentive policies would each get Ms. Thrifty to undertake the larger share of reduction. One is to tax consumption; the other is to issue certificates to individuals who reduce consumption and to allow them to trade those certificates with others.

TAX INCENTIVE POLICIES Let's say that the government imposes a tax on gasoline consumption of 50 cents per gallon. This would be an example of a **tax incentive**

Q-3 It is sometimes said that there is a trade-off between fairness and efficiency. Explain one way in which that is true and one way in which that is false.

Economists tend to like incentive policies to deal with externalities.

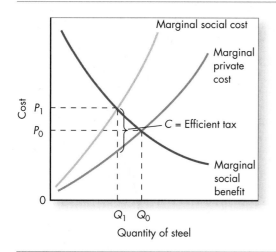

FIGURE 8-3

Regulation through Taxation

If the government sets a tax sufficient to take into account a negative externality, individuals will respond by reducing the quantity of the pollution-causing activity supplied to a level that individuals would have supplied had they included the negative externality in their decision.

program *(a program using a tax to create incentives for individuals to structure their activities in a way that is consistent with the desired ends).* Since Ms. Thrifty can almost costlessly reduce her gasoline consumption, she will likely respond to the tax by reducing gasoline consumption, say, by 2.75 gallons. She pays only $3.63 in tax but undertakes most of the conservation. Since Mr. Big finds it very costly to reduce his consumption of gasoline, he will likely respond by reducing gasoline consumption by very little, say by 0.25 gallon. He pays $9.88 in tax but does little of the conservation.

In this example, the tax has achieved the desired end in a more efficient manner than would the regulatory solution—the person for whom the reduction is least costly cuts consumption the most. Why? Because the incentive to reduce is embodied in the price, and individuals are forced to choose how much to change their consumption. The tax has made them internalize the externality. The solution also has a significant element of fairness about it. The person who conserves the most pays the least tax.

Let's now consider how the tax incentive solution will solve the problem in our earlier example of steel production. Figure 8-3 shows the situation. Say the government determines that the additional cost to society of producing steel equals C. If the government sets the pollution tax on steel production at C, the firm will reduce its output to Q_1 on its own. Such taxes on externalities are often called **effluent fees**—*charges imposed by government on the level of pollution created.* The efficient tax equals the additional cost imposed on society and not taken into account by the decision maker. With such a tax, the cost the suppliers face is the social cost of supplying the good. With the tax, the invisible hand guides the traders to equate the marginal social cost to the marginal social benefit and the equilibrium is socially optimal.

MARKET INCENTIVE POLICIES   A second incentive policy that gets individuals to internalize an externality is a **market incentive plan** *(a plan requiring market participants to certify that they have reduced total consumption—not necessarily their own individual consumption—by a specified amount).* Such a program would be close to the regulatory solution but involves a major difference. If individuals choose to reduce consumption by more than the required amount, they will be given a marketable certificate that they can sell to someone who has chosen to reduce consumption by less than the required amount. By buying that certificate, the person who has not personally reduced consumption by the requisite amount will have met the program's requirements. Let's see how the program would work with Mr. Big and Ms. Thrifty.

Negative Externalities and the Excise Tax Solution

Q-4 In what sense is the tax incentive approach to externalities fair?

In our example, Mr. Big finds it very costly to reduce consumption while Ms. Thrifty finds it easy. So we can expect that Mr. Big won't reduce consumption much and will instead buy certificates from Ms. Thrifty, who will choose to undertake significant reduction in her consumption to generate the certificates, assuming she can sell them to Mr. Big for a high enough price to make that reduction worth her while. So, as was the case in the tax incentive program, Ms. Thrifty undertakes most of the conservation—but she reaps a financial benefit for it.

Incentive policies are more efficient than direct regulatory policies.

Obviously there are enormous questions about the administrative feasibility of these types of proposals, but what's important to understand here is not the specifics of the proposals but the way in which incentive policies are *more efficient* than the regulatory policy. As I stated before, *more efficient* means *less costly* in terms of resources, with no consideration paid to who is bearing those costs. Incorporating the incentive into a price and then letting individuals choose how to respond to that incentive lets those who find it least costly undertake most of the adjustment.

More and more, governments are exploring incentive policies for solving problems. Sin taxes (taxes on goods government believes to be harmful) are an example of the tax incentive approach. (These will be discussed further in Chapter 23, "Microeconomic Policy, Economic Reasoning, and Beyond.") Marketable permits for pollution and for CO_2 emissions are an example of the marketable certificate approach. You can probably see more examples discussed in the news.

Voluntary Reductions

A third alternative method of dealing with externalities is to make the reduction voluntary, leaving individuals free to choose whether to follow a socially optimal or a privately optimal path. Let's consider how a voluntary program might work in our Mr. Big and Ms. Thrifty example. Let's say that Ms. Thrifty has a social conscience and undertakes most of the reduction while Mr. Big has no social conscience and reduces consumption hardly at all. It seems that this is a reasonably efficient solution. But what if the costs were reversed and Mr. Big had the low cost of reduction and Ms. Thrifty had the high cost? Then the voluntary solution would not be so efficient. Of course, it could be argued that when people do something voluntarily, it makes them better off. So one could argue that even when Ms. Thrifty has a high cost of reduction and voluntarily undertakes most of the reduction, she also has a high benefit from reducing her consumption.

Web Note 8.2
Free Riders and Union Shops

Q-5 What are two reasons to be dubious of solutions based on voluntary action that is not in people's self-interest?

The largest problem with voluntary solutions is that a person's willingness to do things for the good of society generally depends on that person's belief that others will also be helping. If a socially conscious person comes to believe that a large number of other people won't contribute, he or she will often lose that social conscience: Why should I do what's good for society if others won't? This is an example of the **free rider problem** (*individuals' unwillingness to share in the cost of a public good*), which economists believe will often limit, and eventually undermine, social actions based on voluntary contributions. A small number of free riders will undermine the social consciousness of many in the society and eventually the voluntary policy will fail.

Economists believe that a small number of free riders will undermine the social consciousness of many in the society and that eventually a voluntary policy will fail.

There are exceptions. During times of war and extreme crisis, voluntary programs are often successful. For example, during World War II the war effort was financed in part through successful voluntary programs. But generally the results of voluntary programs for long-term social problems that involve individuals significantly changing their actions haven't been positive.

The Optimal Policy

An **optimal policy** is *one in which the marginal cost of undertaking the policy equals the marginal benefit of that policy*. If a policy isn't optimal (that is, the marginal cost exceeds the marginal benefit or the marginal benefit exceeds the marginal cost), resources are being wasted because the savings from reducing expenditures on a program will be worth more than the gains that would be lost from reducing the program, or the benefit from spending more on a program will exceed the cost of expanding the program.

Let's consider an example of this latter case. Say the marginal benefit of a program significantly exceeds its marginal cost. That would seem good. But that would mean that we could expand the program by decreasing some other program or activity whose marginal benefit doesn't exceed its marginal cost, with a net gain in benefits to society. To spend too little on a beneficial program is as inefficient as spending too much on a nonbeneficial program.

This concept of optimality carries over to economists' view of most problems. For example, some environmentalists would like to completely rid the economy of pollution. Most economists believe that doing so is costly and that since it's costly, one would want to take into account those costs. That means that society should reduce pollution only to the point where the marginal cost of reducing pollution equals the marginal benefit. That point is called the *optimal level of pollution*—the amount of pollution at which the marginal benefit of reducing pollution equals the marginal cost. To reduce pollution below that level would make society as a whole worse off.

> If a policy isn't optimal, resources are being wasted because the savings from reducing expenditures on a program will be worth more than the gains that will be lost from reducing the program.

> Some environmentalists want to rid the world of all pollution, while most economists want to reduce pollution to the point where the marginal cost of reducing pollution equals the marginal benefit.

Public Goods

A **public good** is *a good that is nonexclusive (no one can be excluded from its benefits) and nonrival (consumption by one does not preclude consumption by others)*. As I discussed in Chapter 3, in reality there is no such thing as a pure public good, but many of the goods that government provides—education, defense, roads, and legal systems—have public-good aspects to them. Probably the closest example we have of a pure public good is national defense. A single individual cannot protect himself or herself from a foreign invasion without protecting his or her neighbors as well. Protection for one person means that many others are also protected. Governments generally provide goods with significant public aspects to them because private businesses will not supply them, unless they transform the good into a mostly private good.

What is and is not considered a public good depends on technology. Consider roads—at one point roads were often privately supplied since with horses and buggies the road owners could charge tolls relatively easily. Then, with the increased speed of the automobile, collecting tolls on most roads became too time-consuming. At that point the nonexclusive public-good aspect of roads became dominant—once a road was built, it was most efficiently supplied to others at a zero cost—and government became the provider of most roads. Today, with modern computer technology, sensors that monitor road use can be placed on roads and in cars. Charging for roads has once again become more feasible. In the future we may again see more private provision of roads. Some economists have even called for privatization of existing roads, and private roads are being built in California and in Bangkok, Thailand.

> A public good is a good that is nonexclusive and nonrival.

> **Web Note 8.3**
> **Charging for Roads**

The Market Value of a Public Good

One of the reasons that pure public goods are sufficiently interesting to warrant a separate discussion is that the supply/demand model can be modified to neatly contrast the efficient quantity of a private good with the efficient quantity of a public good. The key to understanding the difference is to recognize that once a pure public good is supplied to one individual, it is simultaneously supplied to all, whereas a private good is supplied only to the individual who purchased it. For example, if the price of an apple is 50 cents, the efficient purchase rule is for individuals to buy apples until the marginal benefit of the last apple consumed is equal to 50 cents. The analysis focuses on the individual. If the equilibrium price is 50 cents, the marginal benefit of the last apple sold in the market is equal to 50 cents. That benefit is paid for by one individual and is enjoyed by one individual.

Market Demand for a Public Good

FIGURE 8-4 **The Market Value of a Public Good**

Since a public good is enjoyed by many people without diminishing its value to others, the market demand curve is constructed by adding the marginal benefit each individual receives from the public good at each quantity. For example, the value of the first unit to the market is $1.10, the sum of individual A's value ($0.50) and individual B's value ($0.60).

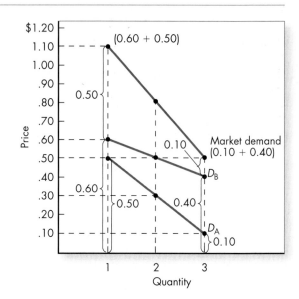

Now consider a public good. Say that the marginal benefit of an additional missile for national defense is 50 cents to one individual and 25 cents to another. In this case the value of providing one missile provides 75 cents (25 + 50) of total social benefit. With a public good the focus is on the group. The societal benefit in the case of a public good is the *sum* of the individual benefits (since each individual gets the benefit of the good). With private goods, we count only the benefit to the person buying the good since only one person gets it.

The above reasoning can be translated into supply and demand curves. The market demand curve represents the marginal benefit of a good to society. As we saw in Chapter 4, in the case of a private good, the market demand curve is the *horizontal sum* of the individual demand curves. The total amount of a private good supplied is split up among many buyers. While the market demand curve for a private good is constructed by adding all the quantities demanded at every price, the market demand curve in the case of public goods is the *vertical sum* of the individual demand curves at every quantity. The quantity of the good supplied is not split up; the full benefit of the total output is received by everyone.

Figure 8-4 gives an example of a public good. In it we assume that society consists of only two individuals—A and B, with demand curves D_A and D_B. To arrive at the market demand curve for the public good, we vertically add the price that each individual is willing to pay for each unit since both receive a benefit when the good is supplied. Thus, at quantity 1 we add $0.60 to $0.50. We arrive at $1.10, the marginal benefit of providing the first missile. By adding together the willingness to pay by individuals A and B for quantities 2 and 3, we generate the market demand curve for missiles. Extending this example from two individuals to the economy as a whole, you can see that, even though the benefit of a public good is small to each person, the total benefit is large. With about 320 million people in the United States, the benefit of that missile would be $160 million even if each person valued it on average at 50 cents.

Adding demand curves vertically is easy to do in textbooks, but not in practice. With private-good demand curves, individuals reveal their demand when they buy a good. If they don't buy it, it wasn't worth the price. Since public goods are free of charge, individuals do not purchase public goods; their demand is not revealed by their

With private goods you sum demand curves horizontally; with public goods you sum them vertically.

Q-6 Why is it so difficult for government to decide the efficient quantity of a public good to provide?

actions. Government must guess how much people are willing to pay. If a public good is to be financed by a tax on the citizens who benefit from it, individuals have an incentive to conceal their willingness to pay for it. The self-interested citizen wants to benefit from the public good without bearing the cost of providing it. Similarly, if people think they will not be taxed but will benefit from the public good, they have an incentive to exaggerate their willingness to pay. That is, people have an incentive to be free riders.

Excludability and the Costs of Pricing

The public/private good differentiation is seldom clear-cut since many goods are somewhat public and somewhat private in nature, with the degree of publicness in large part determined by available technology. As technology changes, the degree of publicness of a good changes. For example, radio signals were previously classified as public goods because it was technologically impossible to exclude listeners, but when encoded satellite broadcasting was developed, exclusion became relatively easy. Today companies such as SIRIUS Satellite Radio supply radio broadcasts as private goods.

The public/private good differentiation is seldom clear-cut.

To capture the complicated nature of goods, economist Paul Romer suggested that instead of categorizing goods as purely public or private, it is better to divide them by their degree of publicness and privateness, which means by their degree of rivalry in consumption, and their degree of excludability in their pricing. This division gives us the following categories:

True private goods, such as an apple (if you eat it, no one else can, and you can easily exclude others from consuming it), which are both rival in consumption and 100 percent excludable, are in the upper-left corner; they are most efficiently supplied privately. True public goods, such as basic research and development (sometimes called the development of general-purpose technology), which are nonrival in consumption and 0 percent excludable, are in the lower-right corner; they must be supplied publicly. Goods in other positions in the box can be provided either publicly or privately. How they are supplied depends on political decisions made by the government. An example of a debate about how to supply a good that is somewhat excludable is music. It is nonrival in consumption (after you've listened to a song, that song is still available to others to hear) but is excludable (those not owning CDs or concert tickets cannot listen), although the ease of excludability depends on the nature and level of enforcement of the property rights for music. For example, at one time Napster offered free music downloads, but because of pressure by the music industry, Napster, along with a variety of other providers such as iTunes, now sells music downloads and pays royalties to those who own the songs. Because technology has changed with the development of digital recording and the Internet, the nature of supply of music has become contested, as the fights about Napster and other online sharing services demonstrate.

Informational and Moral Hazard Problems

The final case of market failure I want to address is caused by imperfect information. The perfectly competitive model assumes that individuals have perfect information about what they are buying. So, if they voluntarily buy a good, it is a reasonable presumption that they expect that they are making themselves better off by doing so. But what if the buyer doesn't know everything there is to know about the product or service— that is, they don't have perfect information? Say someone convinces you that he is selling an expensive diamond and you buy it, only to find out later that it is actually just glass. Alternatively, say someone convinces you her used car is a cherry (in perfect condition). You buy it only to discover later that it is a lemon (faulty) and won't run no matter what you do to it.

Real-world markets often involve deception, cheating, and inaccurate information. For example, car dealers often know about defects in the cars they sell but do not always reveal those defects to consumers. Another example is when consumers who want health insurance do not reveal their health problems to the insurance company. In both cases, it is in the interest of the knowledgeable person not to reveal information that the other person or firm would need to know to make an informed decision about the transaction. Hence, imperfect information can be a cause of market failure.

Markets in goods where there is a lack of information or when buyers and sellers don't have equal information may not work well. Let's consider the used-car example more carefully to make the point. Let's say that owners of used cars know everything about their cars, but buyers know nothing. If sellers are profit maximizers, they will reveal as little as possible about the cars' defects; they will reveal as much as they can about the cars' good qualities.

To make the example specific, let's say also that only two types of cars exist: "lemons" that are worth $4,000 and "cherries" that are worth $8,000. The market initially consists of equal quantities of lemons and cherries. Say also that the buyers cannot distinguish between lemons and cherries. What will happen? Individuals, knowing that they have a 50 percent chance of buying a lemon, may well offer around $6,000 (the average of $4,000 and $8,000). Given that price, individuals with cherries will be very hesitant to sell and individuals with lemons will be eager to sell. Eventually, buyers will recognize that the sellers of cherries have left the market. In the end only lemons will be offered for sale, and buyers will offer only $4,000 with the expectation that cars offered will be lemons. When the market for cherries—good used cars—has disappeared, the result is a market failure.

Such a market failure is called an **adverse selection problem**—*a problem that occurs when buyers and sellers have different amounts of information about the good for sale and use that information to the detriment of the other.* In the case of adverse selection, only lemons—those with the most problems—remain in the market. Take the example of medical insurance. Insurance providers need to make a profit. To do so, they set rates that reflect their estimate of the costs of providing health care. The problem is that individuals have better information about their health than do the insurance providers. Health insurers want a diverse group to spread out the costs, but they face a greater demand among those with the worst health problems. Seeing that their customers have more health problems than

Imperfect information can be a cause of market failure.

Adverse selection problems can occur when buyers and sellers have different amounts of information about the good for sale.

average, medical insurance providers raise the rates. Those who are in good health find those charges to be too high and reduce the quantity of health insurance they purchase. The providers are therefore left with a group with an even higher incidence of health problems and higher medical costs than the general population. Less than the desired amount of low-cost insurance exists for people in good health. In addition to the adverse selection problem there is also a **moral hazard problem**—*a problem that arises when people don't have to bear the negative consequences of their actions.* In insurance this means that individuals tend to change their behavior to the detriment of the insurer because they have insurance. Put simply, people with insurance tend to be less careful, because the consequences of not being careful are reduced. So not only do those with more medical problems choose to be insured, but once insured they will be less careful.

Q-7 How would you expect medical insurance rates to change if medical insurers could use information contained in DNA to predict the likelihood of major medical illnesses?

Signaling and Screening

Informational problems can be partially resolved by signaling. **Signaling** refers to *an action taken by an informed party that reveals information to an uninformed party that offsets the false signal that caused the adverse selection problem in the first place.* Take the lemon problem with used cars. The adverse selection problem occurred because the individual's act of selling the used car provided a signal to the buyer that the car was a lemon. Lowering the offering price of a car would provide an even stronger signal that the car is a lemon—buyers reasonably would equate low prices with low quality. But the false signal can be partially offset by a seller warranty—a guarantee to the buyer that the car is not a lemon. That's why many used cars come with warranties. The warranty offers a signal to the buyer that the car is not a lemon.

In other cases it is harder to offset a false signal. Consider the plight of an unemployed worker. This person may be an excellent worker who, because she is unemployed, is willing to work for a low wage because she really needs the job. However, if she offers to work for a low wage, the firm may think that she must not be a very good worker. The knowledge that the firm may think that way may prevent her from offering to work at a low wage. So she remains unemployed even though, if there were full information, there is a wage at which she would like to work and at which the firm would like to hire her.

The informational problem can also be partially resolved by screening. **Screening** refers to *an action taken by the uninformed party that induces the informed party to reveal information.* Whereas signaling is an action taken by the informed party, screening is an action taken by the uninformed party. Take the car example. The person buying the car could ask the seller's permission to take the car to a mechanic. If the seller says "no," the car is likely a lemon. Another example is asking job applicants for references even if a company isn't going to contact them.

Signaling refers to an action taken by an informed party that reveals information to an uninformed party and thereby partially offsets adverse selection.

Policies to Deal with Informational Problems

What should society do about informational problems that lead to market failures? One answer is to regulate the market and see that individuals provide the right information. An example of regulation is government licensing of individuals in the market, requiring those with licenses to reveal full information about the good being sold. Government has set up numerous regulatory commissions and passed laws that require full disclosure of information. The Federal Trade Commission, the Consumer Product Safety Commission, the Occupational Safety and Health Administration, the Food and Drug Administration, and state licensing boards are all examples of regulatory solutions designed to partially offset informational market failures.

But these regulatory solutions have problems of their own. The commissions and their regulations introduce restrictions that can slow down the economic process and prevent trades that people want to make. Consider as an example the Food and Drug Administration (FDA). It restricts what drugs may be sold until sufficient information about the drugs' effects can be disclosed. The FDA testing and approval process can take 5 to 10 years, is extraordinarily costly, and raises the price of drugs. The delays have caused some people to break the law by buying the drugs before they are approved.

A MARKET IN INFORMATION   Economists who lean away from government regulation suggest that the problem presented by the information examples above is not really a problem of market failure but instead a problem of the lack of a market. Information is valuable and is an economic product in its own right. Left on their own, markets will develop to provide the information that people need and are willing to pay for. (For example, a large number of consumer magazines provide such information.) In the car example, the buyer can hire a mechanic who can test the car with sophisticated diagnostic techniques and determine whether it is likely a cherry or a lemon. Firms can offer guarantees that will provide buyers with assurance that they can either return the car or have it fixed if the car is a lemon. There are many variations of such market solutions. If the government regulates information, these markets may not develop; people might rely on government instead of markets. Thus, the informational problem can be seen as a problem of government regulation not a problem of the market.

Information problems may be a problem of the lack of a market.

LICENSING OF DOCTORS   Let's consider another informational problem that contrasts the market approach with the regulatory approach: medical licensing.[1] Currently all doctors in the United States are required to be licensed to practice, but this was not always the case.

In the early 1800s, medical licenses were not required by law, so anyone who wanted to could set up shop as a physician. Today, however, it is illegal to practice medicine without a license. Licensing of doctors can be justified by information problems since individuals often don't have an accurate way of deciding whether a doctor is good. Licensing requires that all doctors have at least a minimum competency. Because people see the license framed and hanging on the doctor's office wall, they have the *information* that a doctor must be competent.

A small number of economists, of whom Milton Friedman is the best known, have proposed that licensure laws be eliminated, leaving the medical field unlicensed. Specifically, critics of medical licensure raise these questions:

Some economists argue that licensure laws were established to restrict supply, not to help the consumer.

Why, if licensed medical training is so great, do we even need formal restrictions to keep other types of medicine from being practiced?

Whom do these restrictions benefit: the general public or the doctors who practice mainstream medicine?

What have been the long-run effects of licensure?

Even the strongest critics of licensure agree that, in the case of doctors, the informational argument for government intervention is strong. But the question is whether licensure is the right form of government intervention. Why doesn't the government simply provide the public with information about doctors' training and about which treatments work and which don't? That would give the freest rein to *consumer sovereignty* (the right of the individual to make choices about what is consumed and produced). The same argument applies to pharmaceuticals. If people have the necessary information but still choose to treat cancer with laetrile, why should the government tell them they can't?

---

[1]The arguments presented here about licensing doctors also apply to dentists, lawyers, college professors, cosmetologists (in some states, cosmetologists must be licensed), and other professional groups.

Licensure and Surgery

Surgery should be the strongest case for licensure. Would you want an untrained butcher to operate on you? Of course not. But opponents of licensure point out that it's not at all clear how effectively licensure prevents butchery. Ask a doctor, "Would you send your child to any board-certified surgeon picked at random?" The honest answer you'd get is "No way. Some of them are butchers." How do they know that? Being around hospitals, they have access to information about various surgeons' success and failure rates; they've seen them operate and know whether or not they have manual dexterity.

Advocates of the informational alternative suggest that you ask yourself, "What skill would you want in a surgeon?" A likely answer would be "Manual dexterity. Her fingers should be magic fingers." Does the existing system of licensure ensure that everyone who becomes a surgeon has magic fingers? No. To become licensed as a surgeon requires a grueling seven-year residency after four years of medical school, but manual dexterity, as such, is never explicitly tested or checked!

The informational alternative wouldn't necessarily eliminate the seven-year surgical residency. If the public believed that a seven-year residency was necessary to create skilled surgeons, many potential surgeons would choose that route. But there would be other ways to become a surgeon. For example, in high school, tests could be given for manual dexterity. Individuals with superb hand/eye coordination could go to a one-year technical college to train to be "heart technicians," who would work as part of a team doing heart surgery.

Clearly open-heart surgery is the extreme case, and most people will not be convinced that it can be performed by unlicensed medical personnel. But what about minor surgery? According to informational alternative advocates, many operations could be conducted more cheaply and better (since people with better manual dexterity would be doing the work) if restrictive licensing were ended. Or, if you don't accept the argument for human medical treatments, how about for veterinarians? For cosmetologists? For plumbers? Might the informational alternatives work in these professions?

If the informational alternative is preferable to licensure, why didn't the government choose it? Friedman argues that government didn't follow that path because the licensing was done as much for the doctors as for the general public. Licensure has led to a monopoly position for doctors. They can restrict supply and increase price and thereby significantly increase their incomes.

Let's now take a closer look at the informational alternative that critics say would be preferable.

THE INFORMATIONAL ALTERNATIVE TO LICENSURE The informational alternative would allow anyone to practice medicine but would have the government certify doctors' backgrounds and qualifications. The government would require that doctors' backgrounds be made public knowledge. Each doctor would have to post the following information prominently in his or her office:

1. Grades in college.
2. Grades in medical school.
3. Success rate for various procedures.
4. References.
5. Medical philosophy.
6. Charges and fees.

According to supporters of the informational alternative, these data would allow individuals to make informed decisions about their medical care. Like all informed decisions, they would be complicated. For instance, doctors who only take patients

Q-8 Who would benefit and who would lose if an informational alternative to licensing doctors were used?

with minor problems can show high "success rates," while doctors who are actually more skilled but who take on problem patients may have to provide more extensive information so people can see why their success rates shouldn't be compared to those of the doctors who take just easy patients. But despite the problems, supporters of the informational alternative argue that it's better than the current situation.

Current licensure laws don't provide any of this information to the public. All a patient knows is that a doctor has managed to get through medical school and has passed the medical board exams (which are, after all, only sets of multiple-choice questions). The doctor may have done all this 30 years ago, possibly by the skin of his or her teeth, but, once licensed, a doctor is a doctor for life. (A well-known doctor joke is the following: What do you call the person with the lowest passing grade point average in medical school? Answer: Doctor.) The informational alternative would provide much more useful data to the public than the current licensing procedure does. There are, of course, arguments on both sides. A key issue of debate is whether people have the ability to assess the information provided. Supporters of licensing argue that people do not have ability; supporters of the informational alternative argue that they do.

Government Failure and Market Failures

The above three types of market failure—externalities, public goods, and informational problems—give you a good sense of how markets can fail. They could be extended almost infinitely; all real-world markets in some way fail. But the point was to provide you not only with a sense of the way in which markets fail but also with a sense that economists know that markets fail and many of them support markets and oppose regulation anyway. Simply to point out a market failure is not necessarily to call for government to step in and try to rectify the situation. Why? The reason can be called *government failure,* which we defined above as happening when the government intervention in the market to improve the market failure actually makes the situation worse.

Why are there government failures? Let's briefly list some important reasons:

1. *Government doesn't have an incentive to correct the problem.* Government reflects politics, which reflects individuals' interests in trying to gain more for themselves. Political pressures to benefit some group or another will often dominate over doing the general good.

2. *Governments don't have enough information to deal with the problem.* Regulating is a difficult business. To intervene effectively, even if it wants to, government must have good information, but just as the market often lacks adequate information, so does the government.

3. *Intervention in markets is almost always more complicated than it initially seems.* Almost all actions have unintended consequences. Government attempts to offset market failures can prevent the market from dealing with the problem more effectively. The difficulty is that generally the market's ways of dealing with problems work only in the long run. As government deals with the short-run problems, it eliminates the incentives that would have brought about a long-run market solution.

4. *The bureaucratic nature of government intervention does not allow fine-tuning.* When the problems change, the government solution often responds far more slowly. An example is the Interstate Commerce Commission, which continued to exist years after its regulatory job had been eliminated.

5. *Government intervention leads to more government intervention.* Given the nature of the political process, opening the door in one area allows government to enter into other areas where intervention is harmful. Even in those cases

Q-9 Would an economist necessarily believe that we should simply let the market deal with a pollution problem?

WWW Web Note 8.4 Unintended Consequences

Q-10 If one accepts the three reasons for market failure, why might one still oppose government intervention?

Global Warming and Economic Policy

An issue in which almost all the dimensions of economic policy analysis come into play is global warming. The issue is enormous, and a recent expert consensus estimate of the cost of global warming in terms of lost income was a 1 percent decline in global economic activity, which for the United States comes out to about $150 billion, or $470 per person. As discussed in the box in Chapter 1 on global warming, the framework within which the debate is taking place is the economic framework. Economists have done numerous studies of the costs and benefits of various policies, which have led to a consensus that global warming should be seen as an issue of market failure; that is, that the market places no price on emitting carbon-dioxide gas into the atmosphere even though emissions impose a cost on society.

The policy problems of dealing with global warming are formidable. The first is a major free rider problem. Because there is no world government that can force countries to comply with any global effort to address carbon emissions, any policy has to be voluntary, making it easy for one country to opt out (free ride). A second problem is that global warming is not a pure public bad. Some countries and areas within countries actually benefit from global warming. For example, significant global warming will extend the growing season in northern countries and make areas that previously were almost uninhabitable much more pleasant. The costs of global warming are highly concentrated in low-lying coastal areas. This diversity of costs makes arriving at a voluntary agreement much less likely.

A third problem is that the largest expected benefits to stopping global warming are in the future, while many of the costs are *now,* and people tend to discount future costs and benefits. A fourth problem is the lack of a clear cost/benefit

analysis for various policy alternatives and the uncertainty of the success of various technologies. Cost estimates of various policies to become largely free of fossil fuel emissions by 2100 vary from 1 percent to 16 percent of total world output. (Were a cost-competitive fuel-cell-powered car or a fusion nuclear reactor developed, the use of fossil fuel would decrease significantly, and the cost estimate would be much less.)

All these problems suggest that the debate about global warming policy will likely be a lively one. Over the coming years, we can expect to see three types of policies implemented: (1) the lowest-cost/highest-benefit policies that are easy to implement such as more use of energy-efficient light bulbs, improved insulation standards on new buildings, and reduced standby power requirements on electronic devices; (2) the politically high-profile policies instituted on a state or country basis, rather than on a global basis, that don't really do much to solve the problem but that sound good in a sound bite; and (3) those policies that do not make much sense in an economic framework but that help certain firms and geographic areas, and that make sense within a political framework.

Many economists believe that increased corn-based ethanol production is an example; the carbon-dioxide emissions from producing ethanol from corn are almost as great as the reduction in carbon-dioxide emissions resulting from the use of ethanol as a fuel, but the programs significantly help farmers, so they have political support. In December of 2011, the U.S. government ended the large subsidy for the production of corn based ethanol, but the requirement that refiners use a certain portion of renewable fuels such as ethanol remained.

where government action may seem to be likely to do some good, it might be best not to intervene, if that intervention will lead to additional government action in cases where it will not likely do good.

The above list is only a brief introduction to government failures. Much more could be said about each of them. But exploring them would take us away from economics and into political science. The important point to remember is that government failures exist and must be taken into account before making any policy recommendation. That's why real-world economic policy falls within the art of economics, and policy conclusions cannot be drawn from the models of positive economics.

Conclusion

As a textbook writer, I wish I could say that some conclusions can be drawn about whether the government should, or should not, enter into the economy. I certainly have views about particular instances (in case you haven't guessed, I'm a highly opinionated individual), but to lay out arguments and information that would convince a reasonable person to agree with me would take an entire book for each area in which government might intervene.

What I can do in this textbook is to stimulate your interest in discovering for yourself the information and the subtleties of the debates for and against government intervention. Just about every time you read, hear, or are asked the question "Should the government intervene in a market?" the answer is "It depends." If your first impulse is to give any answer other than that one, you may have trouble maintaining the appropriate objectivity when you start considering the costs and benefits of government intervention.

Should the government intervene in the market? It depends.

Summary

- An externality is the effect of a decision on a third party that is not taken into account by the decision maker. Positive externalities provide benefits to third parties. Negative externalities impose costs on third parties. (LO8-1)

- The markets for goods with negative externalities produce too much of the good for too low a price. The markets for goods with positive externalities produce too little of the good for too great a price. (LO8-1)

- Economists generally prefer incentive-based programs to regulatory programs because incentive-based programs are more efficient. An example of an incentive-based program is to tax the producer of a good that results in a negative externality by the amount of the externality. (LO8-2)

- Voluntary solutions are difficult to maintain for long periods of time because people have an incentive to be free riders—to enjoy the benefits of others' volunteer efforts without putting forth effort themselves. (LO8-2)

- An optimal policy is one in which the marginal cost of undertaking the policy equals its marginal benefit. (LO8-2)

- Public goods are nonexclusive and nonrival. It is difficult to measure the benefits of public goods because people do not reveal their preferences by purchasing them in the marketplace. (LO8-3)

- Theoretically, the market value of a public good can be calculated by summing the value that each individual places on every quantity. This is vertically summing individual demand curves. (LO8-3)

- Individuals have an incentive to withhold information that will result in a lower price if one is a seller and a higher price if one is a consumer. Because of this incentive to withhold information, the markets for some goods disappear. Such market failures are known as adverse selection problems. (LO8-4)

- The health insurance market suffers from both adverse selection problems and moral hazard problems. (LO8-4)

- Licensure and full disclosure are two solutions to the information problem. (LO8-4)

- Government intervention may worsen the problem created by the market failure. Government failure occurs because: (1) governments don't have an incentive to correct the problem, (2) governments don't have enough information to deal with the problem, (3) intervention is more complicated than it initially seems, (4) the bureaucratic nature of government precludes fine-tuning, and (5) government intervention often leads to more government intervention. (LO8-5)

Key Terms

adverse selection problem *(174)*	free rider problem *(170)*	market failure *(164)*	positive externality *(165)*
direct regulation *(167)*	government failure *(164)*	market incentive plan *(169)*	public good *(171)*
efficient *(168)*	inefficient *(168)*	moral hazard problem *(175)*	screening *(175)*
effluent fee *(169)*	marginal social benefit *(167)*	negative externality *(165)*	signaling *(175)*
externality *(165)*	marginal social cost *(166)*	optimal policy *(170)*	tax incentive program *(168)*

Questions and Exercises

1. State three reasons for a potentially beneficial role of government intervention. *(LO8-1)*

2. Is the marginal social benefit of a good that exhibits positive externalities greater or less than the private social benefit of that good? Why? *(LO8-1)*

3. How would an economist likely respond to the statement "There is no such thing as an acceptable level of pollution"? *(LO8-1)*

4. Would a high tax on oil significantly reduce the amount of pollution coming from the use of oil? Why or why not? *(LO8-2)*

5. The marginal cost, marginal social cost, and demand for fish are represented by the curves in the graph below. Suppose that there are no restrictions on fishing. *(LO8-1)*
   a. Assuming perfect competition, demonstrate graphically what the catch is going to be, and at what price will it be sold.
   b. What are the socially efficient price and output?

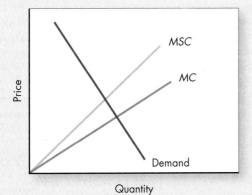

6. Which is more efficient: a market incentive program or a direct regulatory program? Why? *(LO8-2)*

7. There's a gas shortage in Gasland. You're presented with two proposals that will achieve the same level of reduction in the use of gas. Proposal A would force everybody to reduce their gas consumption by 5 percent. Proposal B would impose a 50-cent tax on the consumption of a gallon of gas, which would also achieve a 5 percent reduction.

Consumers of gas can be divided into two groups—one group whose demand is elastic and another group whose demand is inelastic. *(LO8-2)*
   a. How will the proposals affect each group?
   b. Which group would support a regulatory policy?
   c. Which would support a tax policy?

8. Economists Don Fullerton and Thomas C. Kinnaman studied the effects of Charlottesville, Virginia's change from charging a flat fee for garbage collection to charging $0.80 per 32-gallon bag and found the following results: *(LO8-2)*
   The weight of garbage collected fell by 14 percent. The volume of garbage collected fell by 37 percent. The weight of recycling rose by 16 percent.
   a. Why did recycling increase and garbage collection decrease?
   b. Why did the weight of garbage fall by less than the volume of garbage collected?
   c. Demonstrate, using supply and demand curves, the effect of the change in pricing on the volume of garbage collected.

9. List the public-good aspects (if any) of the following goods: safety, street names, and a steak dinner. *(LO8-3)*

10. Why are both nonexcludability and nonrivalry important elements of public goods? *(LO8-3)*

11. Why are voluntary contributions to provide for public goods such as city parks unlikely to lead to an efficient quantity of parks in a city? *(LO8-3)*

12. Use the table below, which shows the demand for a public good in an economy consisting of two households, A and B, to answer *a* to *d* below. *(LO8-3)*

Price	$0.00	$0.50	$1.00	$1.50	$2.00	$2.50	$3.00
Quantity A	12	10	8	6	4	2	0
demanded B	4	3	2	1	0	0	0

   a. Graph the individual demand curves and the market demand curve.

b. What would make you doubt that the table is an accurate reporting of the individual demand curves?

c. If the marginal cost of providing one unit of the good is $2.00, what is the socially optimal amount of the public good?

d. Given the free rider problem, is your answer to *c* most likely an underestimate or an overestimate?

13. If you are willing to pay $1,000 for a used stereo that is a "cherry" and $200 for a used stereo that is a "lemon," how much will you be willing to offer to purchase a stereo if there is a 50 percent chance that the stereo is a lemon? If owners of cherry stereos want $700 for their cherries, how will your estimate of the chance of getting a cherry change?   (*LO8-4*)

14. Give three examples of signaling in the real world.   (*LO8-4*)

15. Automobile insurance companies offer low-premium contracts with a high deductible and high-premium contracts with low deductibles. How is this an example of screening?   (*LO8-4*)

16. What is the adverse selection problem?   (*LO8-4*)

17. If neither buyers nor sellers could distinguish between "lemons" and "cherries" in the used-car market, what would you expect to be the mix of lemons and cherries for sale?   (*LO8-4*)

18. Automobile insurance companies charge lower rates to married individuals than they do to unmarried individuals. What economic reason is there for such a practice? Is it fair?   (*LO8-4*)

19. An advanced degree is required to teach at most colleges. In what sense is this a form of restricting entry through licensure?   (*LO8-4*)

20. Who would benefit and who would lose if an informational alternative to licensing doctors were introduced?   (*LO8-4*)

21. What is the effect of the moral hazard problem on insurance premiums? Explain your answer.   (*LO8-4*)

22. Economics professors Thomas Hopkins and Arthur Gosnell of the Rochester Institute of Technology estimated that in the year 2000, regulations cost the United States $662 billion, or about $5,700 per family.   (*LO8-5*)

a. Do their findings mean that the United States had too many regulations?

b. How would an economist decide which regulations to keep and which to do away with?

23. When Ben wears his red shirt, it bothers Sally, who hates the color red. Since Ben's wearing of a red shirt imposes a cost on Sally, it involves an externality. Would it therefore be correct to have the government intervene and forbid Ben from wearing a red shirt?   (*LO8-5*)

24. True or false? Burning fossil fuels contributes to global warming. Thus, it makes sense for the government to place a tax on the burning of fossil fuels. Why?   (*LO8-5*)

Questions from Alternative Perspectives

1. The book titles this chapter "Market Failure versus Government Failure."

a. Does the fact that the author spends most of the chapter discussing market failure rather than government failure suggest an ideological bias in the book?

b. If so, how would you characterize that bias? (Austrian)

2. In the late 19th century, Washington Gladden said, "He who battles for the Christianization of society will find their strongest foe in the field of economics. Economics is indeed the dismal science because of the selfishness of its maxims and the inhumanity of its conclusions."

a. Evaluate this statement.

b. Is there a conflict between the ideology of the market and the precepts of Christianity?

c. Would a society that emphasized a market mode of production benefit from having a moral framework that emphasized selflessness rather than selfishness? (Religious)

3. Institutional economists define economics as the study of how people use institutions to socially interact in the process of extracting materials from the biophysical world to produce and exchange goods and services to reproduce culture and better the human condition. If you accept this definition of economics, under what conditions is government intervention in the market acceptable? (Institutionalist)

4. Post-Keynesians suggest that contractual agreements might be a way to deal with asymmetric information.

a. Name a business or consumer transaction where asymmetric information might occur.

b. How could a contractual agreement overcome the problems of asymmetric information in that market?

c. Would that contractual agreement arise without government intervention? (Post-Keynesian)

5. Water privatization in South Africa has been guided by what the World Bank calls the "cost recovery" approach: Water should be made available to people only if the company providing it can recover its costs plus a profit. In 1995, private companies began taking over the provision of water in South Africa. By the early 2000s some cities saw water prices increase fourfold, millions

of people had their water cut off, and outbreaks of cholera returned for the first time in decades.

a. Which of your textbook's list of market failures apply to the privatization of water utilities in South Africa?

b. Is the failure so serious that it makes the private provision of water bad public policy?

c. If not, why not? If so, what policies would make more economic sense? (Radical)

Issues to Ponder

1. More than half of 30 economists polled recently stated that the federal gasoline tax should be raised to $1 or higher. What do you suppose were their reasons?

2. In his book *At the Hand of Man*, Raymond Bonner argues that Africa should promote hunting, charging large fees for permits to kill animals (for example, $7,500 for a permit to shoot an elephant).
   a. What are some arguments in favor of this proposal?
   b. What are some arguments against?

3. Suppose an air-quality law is passed that requires 3.75 percent of all the cars sold to emit zero pollution.
   a. What would be the likely impact of this law?
   b. Can you think of any way in which this law might actually increase pollution rather than decrease it?
   c. How might an economist suggest modifying this law to better achieve economic efficiency?

4. Economist Robert W. Turner suggested three market failures that could justify government provision of national parks. What three failures did he likely discuss and what is the cause of the failure?

5. Should government eliminate the Food and Drug Administration's role in restricting which drugs may be marketed? Why or why not?

6. Financial analysts are not currently required to be licensed. Should they be licensed? Why or why not?

7. Recently scientists identified a gene that accounts for 5 percent of thrill-seeking behavior. People with this gene are likely to take more risks such as smoking and bungee jumping in search of the next thrill. Provide two arguments—one for and one against—requiring people to undergo testing to find out if they have this gene before a company agrees to provide life insurance.

8. List five ways you are affected on a daily basis by government intervention in the market. For what reason might government be involved? Is that reason justified?

9. Would a high tax on oil significantly reduce the total amount of pollution in the environment?

10. A debate about dairy products concerns the labeling of milk produced from cows that have been injected with the hormone BST, which significantly increases milk production. Since the FDA has determined that this synthetically produced copy of a milk hormone is indistinguishable from the hormone produced naturally by the cow, and also has determined that milk from cows treated with BST is indistinguishable from milk from untreated cows, some people have argued that no labeling requirement is necessary. Others argue that the consumer has a right to know.
    a. Where do you think most dairy farmers stand on this labeling issue?
    b. If consumers have a right to know, should labels inform them of other drugs, such as antibiotics, normally given to cows?
    c. Do you think dairy farmers who support BST labeling also support the broader labeling law that would be needed if other drugs were included? Why?

Answers to Margin Questions

1. An externality is an effect of a decision not taken into account by the decision maker. When there are externalities, the private price no longer necessarily reflects the social price, and therefore the market may not work properly. (*p. 166; LO8-1*)

2. No. The existence of a positive externality does not mean that the market works better than if no externality existed. It means that the market is not supplying a sufficient amount of the resource or activity, and insufficient supply can be as inefficient as an oversupply. (*p. 167; LO8-1*)

3. Because efficiency does not take into account who pays the costs, there may be a trade-off between fairness and efficiency. For example, a tax on gasoline would be efficient, but because the poor tend to drive older, less fuel-efficient cars, they will end up paying more of the tax, which some may believe to be unfair. The tax could be seen as both fair and efficient because consumers choose to reduce their gas use based on the new price, so the solution is efficient. The solution has an element of fairness in it since those causing the pollution are those paying more. (*p. 168; LO8-2*)

4. The tax incentive approach to deal with externalities is fair in the following sense: Individuals whose actions result in more pollution pay more. Individuals whose actions result in less pollution pay less. In some broader sense this may not be fair if one takes into account the initial positions of those polluting. For example, people who live in less-populated states often have to drive farther to work and would pay a higher tax than others. (*p. 169; LO8-2*)

5. Voluntary actions that are not in people's self-interest may not work in large groups because individuals will rely on others to volunteer. There is also a potential lack of efficiency in voluntary solutions since the person who voluntarily reduces consumption may not be the person who faces the least cost of doing so. (*p. 170; LO8-2*)

6. It is difficult for government to decide the efficient quantity of a public good because public goods are not purchased by individuals in markets. Therefore, individuals do not reveal the value they place on public goods. Individuals also face incentives to overstate the value they place on public goods if they do not have to pay for them, and to understate the value if they do have to share the cost. (*p. 177; LO8-3*)

7. Since adverse selection is a problem in the medical insurance industry, with fuller information, I would expect that average medical rates would decline since the adverse selection problem would disappear. Medical insurers would be able to offer lower-cost insurance to people who are less likely to get sick and who perhaps choose not to be covered at today's high rates. (*p. 175; LO8-4*)

8. If an informational alternative to licensing doctors were introduced, existing doctors would suffer a significant monetary loss, and students who would likely go on to medical school in existing institutions would face lower potential incomes when they entered practice. Those who benefit would likely be (1) those who did not want to go through an entire medical school schedule but were willing to learn a specialty that required far less education and in which they had a particular proclivity to do well and (2) consumers, who would get more for less. (*p. 177; LO8-4*)

9. An economist would not necessarily believe that we should simply let the market deal with the pollution problem. Pollution clearly involves externalities. Where economists differ from many laypeople is in how to handle the problem. An economist is likely to look more carefully into the costs, try to build price incentives into whatever program is designed, and make the marginal private cost equal the marginal social cost. (*p. 178; LO8-5*)

10. One can accept all three explanations for market failure and still oppose government intervention if one believes that government intervention will cause worse problems than the market failure causes. (*p. 178; LO8-5*)

Politics and Economics:
The Case of Agricultural Markets

American farmers have become welfare addicts, protected and assisted at every turn by a network of programs paid for by their fellow citizens. If Americans still believe in the virtue of self-reliance, they should tell Washington to get out of the way and let farmers practice it.

—Stephen Chapman

This web chapter can be found at: www.mhhe.com/colander9e

After reading this chapter, you should be able to:

LO8W-1 Explain the good/bad paradox in farming and how it can be avoided.

LO8W-2 Explain how a price support system works and show the distributional consequences of four alternative methods of price support.

LO8W-3 Discuss real-world pressures politicians face when designing agricultural policy.

chapter 9

Comparative Advantage, Exchange Rates, and Globalization

One of the purest fallacies is that trade follows the flag. Trade follows the lowest price current. If a dealer in any colony wished to buy Union Jacks, he would order them from Britain's worst foe if he could save a sixpence.

—Andrew Carnegie

If economists had a mantra, it would be "Trade is good." Trade allows specialization and division of labor and thereby promotes economic growth. Much of economists' support for trade comes from their theory of comparative advantage. In this chapter we consider how the theory of comparative advantage relates to the U.S. economy. We also explore the role exchange rates play in the theory of comparative advantage and international trade.

The Principle of Comparative Advantage

The reason countries trade is the same reason that people trade: Trade can make both better off. The reason that this is true is the principle of comparative advantage to which you were introduced in Chapter 2. It is, however, important enough to warrant an in-depth review. The basic idea of the principle of **comparative advantage** is that *as long as the relative opportunity costs of producing goods (what must be given up of one good in order to get another good) differ among countries, then there are potential gains from trade.* Let's review this principle by considering the story of I.T., an imaginary international trader, who convinces two countries to enter into trades by giving both countries some of the advantages of trade; he keeps the rest for himself.

The Gains from Trade

Here's the situation. On his trips to the United States and Saudi Arabia, I.T. noticed that the two countries did not trade. He also noticed that the opportunity cost of producing a ton of food in Saudi Arabia was 10 barrels of oil and that the opportunity cost for the United States of producing a ton of food was 1/10 of a barrel of oil. At the time, the United States' production was 60 barrels of oil and 400 tons of food, while Saudi Arabia's production was 400 barrels of oil and 60 tons of food.

The choices for the United States can be seen in Figure 9-1(a), and the choices for Saudi Arabia can be seen in Figure 9-1(b). The tables give the numerical choices and the figures translate those numerical choices into graphs.

These graphs represent the two countries' production possibility curves. Each combination of numbers in the table corresponds to a point on the curve. For example, point *B* in each graph corresponds to the entries in row *B*, columns 2 and 3, in the relevant table.

Let's assume that the United States has chosen point *C* (production of 60 barrels of oil and 400 tons of food) and Saudi Arabia has chosen point *D* (production of 400 barrels of oil and 60 tons of food).

The principle of comparative advantage states that as long as the relative opportunity costs of producing goods differ among countries, then there are potential gains from trade.

Q-1 If the opportunity cost of oil for food were the same for both the United States and Saudi Arabia, what should I.T. do?

FIGURE 9-1 (A AND B)   Comparative Advantage: The United States and Saudi Arabia

Looking at tables (**a**) and (**b**), you can see that if Saudi Arabia devotes all its resources to oil, it can produce 1,000 barrels of oil, but if it devotes all of its resources to food, it can produce only 100 tons of food. For the United States, the story is the opposite: Devoting all of its resources to oil, the United States can only produce 100 barrels of oil—10 times less than Saudi Arabia—but if it devotes all of its resources to food, it can produce 1,000 tons of food—10 times more than Saudi Arabia. Assuming resources are comparable, Saudi Arabia has a comparative advantage in the production of oil, and the United States has a comparative advantage in the production of food. The information in the tables is presented graphically below each table. These are the countries' production possibility curves. Each point on each country's curve corresponds to a row on that country's table.

Percentage of Resources Devoted to Oil	Oil Produced (barrels)	Food Produced (tons)	Row
100%	100	0	A
80	80	200	B
60	60	400	C
40	40	600	D
20	20	800	E
0	0	1,000	F

United States' Production Possibility Table

Percentage of Resources Devoted to Oil	Oil Produced (barrels)	Food Produced (tons)	Row
100%	1,000	0	A
80	800	20	B
60	600	40	C
40	400	60	D
20	200	80	E
0	0	100	F

Saudi Arabia's Production Possibility Table

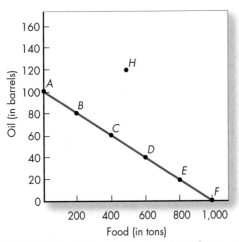

(a) United States' Production Possibility Curve

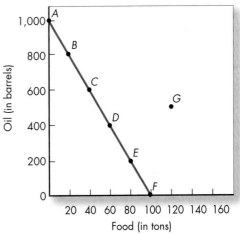

(b) Saudi Arabia's Production Possibility Curve

Now I.T., who understands the principle of comparative advantage, comes along and offers the following deal to the United States:

> If you produce 1,000 tons of food and no oil (point *F* in Figure 9-1(a)) and give me 500 tons of food while keeping 500 tons for yourself, I'll guarantee you 120 barrels of oil, double the amount you're now getting. I'll put you on point *H,* which is totally above your current production possibility curve. You'll get more oil and have more food. It's an offer you can't refuse.

I.T. then flies off to Saudi Arabia, to whom he makes the following offer:

> If you produce 1,000 barrels of oil and no food (point *A* in Figure 9-1(b)) and give me 500 barrels of oil while keeping 500 barrels for yourself, I guarantee you 120 tons of food, double the amount of food you're now getting. I'll put you on point *G,* which is totally above your current production possibility curve. You'll get more oil and more food. It's an offer you can't refuse.

Both countries accept; they'd be foolish not to. So the two countries' final consumption positions are as follows:

	Oil (barrels)	Food (tons)
Total production	1,000	1,000
U.S. consumption	120	500
U.S. gain in consumption	+60	+100
Saudi consumption	500	120
Saudi gain in consumption	+100	+60
I.T.'s profit	380	380

For arranging the trade, I.T. makes a handsome profit of 380 tons of food and 380 barrels of oil. I.T. has become rich because he understands the principle of comparative advantage.

Now obviously this hypothetical example significantly overemphasizes the gains a trader makes. Generally the person arranging the trade must compete with other traders and offer both countries a better deal than the one presented here. But the person who first recognizes a trading opportunity often makes a sizable fortune. The second and third persons who recognize the opportunity make smaller fortunes. Once the insight is generally recognized, the possibility of making a fortune is gone. Traders still make their normal returns, but the instantaneous fortunes are not to be made without new insight. In the long run, benefits of trade go to the producers and consumers in the trading countries, not the traders, but the long run can be years, and even decades, in coming.

Dividing Up the Gains from Trade

As the above story suggests, when countries avail themselves of comparative advantage, there are high gains of trade to be made. Who gets these gains is unclear. The principle of comparative advantage doesn't determine how those gains of trade will be divided up among the countries involved and among traders who make the trade possible. While there are no definitive laws determining how real-world gains from trade will be apportioned, economists have developed some insights into how those gains are likely to be divided up. The first insight concerns how much the trader gets. The general rule is:

> *The more competition that exists among traders, the less likely it is that the trader gets big gains of trade; more of the gains from trade will go to the citizens in the two countries, and less will go to the traders.*

What this insight means is that where entry into trade is unimpaired, most of the gains of trade will pass from the trader to the countries. Thus, the trader's big gains from trade occur in markets that are newly opened or if the product is unique and cannot be easily copied.

This insight isn't lost on trading companies. Numerous import/export companies exist whose business is discovering possibilities for international trade in newly opened markets. Individuals representing trading companies go around hawking projects or goods to countries. For example, at the end of the 1999 NATO bombing campaign in Kosovo, what the business world calls the *import/export contingent* flew to Kosovo with offers of goods and services to sell. Many of these same individuals had been in Iraq and Iran in the early 1990s, in Saudi Arabia when oil prices rose in the 1970s, and in the Far East when China opened its doors to international trade in the 1980s.

A second insight is:

> *Once competition prevails, smaller countries tend to get a larger percentage of the gains of trade than do larger countries.*

The reason, briefly, is that more opportunities are opened up for smaller countries by trade than for larger countries. The more opportunities, the larger the relative gains. Say, for instance, that the United States begins trade with Mali, a small country in Africa. Enormous new consumption possibilities are opened up for Mali—prices of all types of goods will fall. Assuming Mali has a comparative advantage in fish, before international trade began, cars were probably extraordinarily expensive in Mali, while fish were cheap. With international trade, the price of cars in Mali falls substantially, so Mali gets the gains. Because the U.S. economy is so large compared to Mali's, the U.S. price of fish doesn't change noticeably. Mali's fish are just a drop in the bucket. The price ratio of cars to fish doesn't change much for the United States, so it doesn't get much of the gains of trade. Mali gets almost all the gains from trade.

There's an important catch to this gains-from-trade argument. The argument holds only if competition among traders prevails. That means that Mali residents are sold cars at the same price (plus shipping costs) as U.S. residents. International traders in small countries often have little competition from other traders and keep large shares of the gains from trade for themselves. In the earlier food/oil example, the United States and Saudi Arabia didn't get a large share of the benefits. It was I.T. who got most of the benefits. Since the traders often come from the larger country, the smaller country doesn't get this share of the gains from trade; the larger country's international traders do.

A third insight is:

> *Gains from trade go to the countries producing goods that exhibit economies of scale.*

Trade allows an increase in production. If there are economies of scale, that increase can lower the average cost of production of a good. Hence, an increase in production can lower the price of the good in the producing country. The country producing the good with the larger economies of scale has its costs reduced by more, and hence gains more from trade than does its trading partner.

Three determinants of the terms of trade are:

1. The more competition, the less the trader gets.
2. Smaller countries get a larger proportion of the gain than larger countries.
3. Countries producing goods with economies of scale get a larger gain from trade.

Q-2 In what circumstances would a small country not get the larger percentage of the gains from trade?

Why Economists and Laypeople Differ in Their Views of Trade

The comparative advantage model conveys a story with the theme of "trade is good"; trade benefits both parties to the trade. This story doesn't fit much of the lay public's view of trade, nor the fear of outsourcing. If trade is good, why do so many people oppose it, and what accounts for the difference between economists' view of trade and the lay public's view? I suggest four reasons.

Gains Are Often Stealth

Gains from trade are often stealth gains.

One reason for the difference is that laypeople often do not recognize the gains of trade—the gains are often stealth gains such as a decline in prices—while they easily identify the loss of jobs caused by the trade adjustments as countries shift production to take advantage of trade. For example, consider the price of clothing: A shirt today costs far less in real terms (in terms of the number of hours you have to work to buy it) than it did a decade or two ago. Much of the reason for that is trade. But how many people attribute that fall in price of shirts to trade? Not many; they just take it for granted. But the reality is that much of our current lifestyle in the United States has been made possible by trade.

Much of our current lifestyle is made possible by trade.

Opportunity Cost Is Relative

A second reason for the difference between the lay view of trade and economists' view is that the lay public often believes that since countries such as China have lower wages, they must have a comparative advantage in just about everything so that if we allow free trade, eventually we will lose all U.S. jobs. This belief is a logical contradiction; by definition comparative advantage refers to relative cost. If one country has a comparative advantage in one set of goods, the other country must have a comparative advantage in another set.

The comparative advantage model assumes that a country's imports and exports are equal.

That said, economists also must admit that the lay public does have a point. The comparative advantage model assumes that a country's imports and exports are equal. That is, its **balance of trade**—*the difference between the value of exports and the value of imports*—is zero. But U.S. imports and exports are not equal. Currently, the United States imports much more than it exports; it pays for the excess of imports over exports with IOU's. As long as foreign countries are willing to accept U.S. promises to pay some time in the future, they can have a comparative advantage in the production of many more goods than the United States.[1] Currently, people in other countries finance the U.S. trade deficit by buying U.S. assets. Once the other countries decide that it is no longer in their interests to finance the U.S. trade deficit, economic forces such as the adjustment of exchange rates will be set in motion to restore a more equal division of comparative advantages.

Trade Is Broader Than Manufactured Goods

Q-3 What are four reasons for the difference between laypeople's and economists' views of trade?

A third reason accounting for the difference between the lay view of trade and the economists' view is that laypeople often think of trade as trade in just manufactured goods. Trade is much broader, and includes the services that traders provide. Countries can have comparative advantages in trade itself, and the gains the trader makes can account for the seeming differences in countries' comparative advantages.

---

[1]One could make the model fit reality if one thinks of the United States as having a comparative advantage in producing IOUs that other people will accept.

Notice in my example that the international traders who brought the trade about benefited significantly from trade. I included traders because trade does not take place on its own—markets and trade require entrepreneurs. The market is not about abstract forces; it is about real people working to improve their position. Many of the gains from trade do not go to the countries producing or consuming the good but rather to the trader. And the gains that traders get can be enormous.

Consider, for example, the high-priced sneakers ($190) that many "with-it" students wear. Those sneakers are likely made in China, costing about $8 to make. So much of the benefits of trade do not go to the producer or the consumer; they go to the trader. However, not all of the difference is profit. The trader has other costs, such as the costs of transportation and advertising—someone has to convince you that you need those "with-it" sneakers. (Just do it, right?) A portion of the benefits of the trade accrues to U.S. advertising firms, which can pay more to creative people who think up those crazy ads.

The United States currently has a large comparative advantage in facilitating trade and many trade companies are U.S.-based. These companies buy many of the goods and services that support trade from their home country—the United States. What this means is that goods manufactured in China, India, and other Asian countries are creating demand for advertising, management, and distribution, and are therefore creating jobs and income in the United States. That's one reason for the large increase in service jobs in the U.S. economy. These are jobs that laypeople often do not associate with trade.

Trade with China and India has been generating jobs in the United States.

Trade Has Distributional Effects

A fourth reason most economists see international trade differently than do most laypeople involves distributional issues. The economists' model doesn't take into account trade's effect on the distribution of income. Most laypeople, however, are extremely concerned with the distribution of income, which means that they look at the effects of trade differently. The problem is that while trade tends to benefit society as a whole, the benefits are often highly unevenly distributed. In the short run (which can last for 10 or 20 years), trade can hurt some a lot. Specifically, when trade is opened among countries, as it has been during the period of globalization, those producers whose goods are both tradable and internationally competitive benefit; those producers whose goods are both tradable and not internationally competitive lose. On the consumer's side, most people generally benefit since they now can get tradable goods at the lower international prices.

For the United States, this has meant that with globalization many people who worked in manufacturing either lost their jobs or saw their wages fall to make U.S. production competitive. The same was true for those holding less-skilled jobs that could be outsourced. Blue-collar America was hard hit by globalization. The problems facing these groups were multiplied by immigration of workers who were willing to work at physically difficult jobs for lower wages than Americans were unwilling to work for. This immigration is another aspect of globalization that put further downward pressure on wages in those sectors.

On the high end of the income distribution were people with intellectual property rights who suddenly had billions more people to whom to sell their products. Their income shot up; instead of being multimillionaires, they were now billionaires. Similarly, demand for the services of those in high-tech and managerial and organizational jobs increased enormously because their work could not (yet) be duplicated in low-wage countries. Both finance and high-level management fell into these categories. So while the share of U.S. jobs in the manufacturing sector fell from 25 percent in 1970 to 10 percent, the share of U.S. jobs in the professional service sector rose from 7 percent to 24 percent. The income going to those sectors also rose significantly. Finance in the economy rose from about 4 percent of the economy in the 1980s to over

Web Note 9.1
Blue-Collar America

9 percent in 2010, which is an enormous increase, and the financial sector accounted for much of the profits in the U.S. economy. Salaries in the financial sector went up to astronomical levels, even as manufacturing wages were falling. Put another way, the international traders, and those associated with them, (those who got many of the gains from trade in our comparative advantage example) thrived as a result of globalization. The gains from trade from which to take their share of the trade grew. So with every switch of business from the United States to China, U.S. international traders benefited.

Workers in the education, health care, and government sectors also felt little or no downward pressure on their wages from globalization, because these sectors produce goods and services that cannot be easily traded on the global market. They are non-tradables. In fact, these sectors grew; just as in the financial sector, the share of employment in the government, education, and health industries rose significantly, and wages in these sectors rose relative to manufacturing wages. The reason these work-ers' pay could rise is that their wages are determined by institutional factors that kept wages increasing as they had before globalization.

People in these nontradable sectors benefited not just as producers but also as consumers—earning more and getting manufactured and tradable agricultural goods such as televisions, iPads, automobiles, shirts, shoes, and grapes—at lower and lower prices. Thus, the workers in these sectors got the gains of trade as consumers—lower prices—and kept their jobs and higher wages.

In contrast, manufacturing wages in the United States have not risen for 20 years; lower-paid individuals in these sectors have been able to keep up their consump-tion only by borrowing and by increasing workloads (e.g., as in two-income fami-lies). When you put all these effects together, you can see that globalization played a major role in increasing the income disparity in the United States. It created a group of haves—those who worked in nontradable and trade-organization sectors—and of have nots—those who worked in sectors facing brutal global competition. Much of the lay public's concern about globalization and international trade is rooted in these distributional effects. True, on average, trade may have benefited the United States, but that is of little comfort to those whose pay has fallen, and who have lost a job, because of it.

These distributional effects within the United States are important, and it is true that economists' comparative advantage model doesn't focus on them. Instead it focuses on the aggregate effects of trade. In the aggregate the many U.S. workers who have been hurt by trade are counterbalanced by the billions of people in developing countries who have been pulled out of poverty by trade. Outsourced U.S. jobs often go to people who earn one-tenth of what a U.S. worker earns, and that job sometimes means that they can feed their family. On a global perspective, if one believes in global income equality, trade is the way it comes about. Trade also leads to greater world economic growth. That world growth increases income and wealth abroad, thereby creating additional demand for U.S. goods. Two billion consumers whose incomes are increasing offer many new growth opportunities for U.S. firms. Trade expands the total pie, and even when a country gets a smaller proportion of the new total pie, the absolute amount it gets can increase.

Sources of U.S. Comparative Advantage

When thinking about how the theory of comparative advantage relates to the current debate about outsourcing—what jobs are outsourced and what jobs are created in the United States—it is important to remember that comparative advantage is not determined by wages alone. Many other factors enter into comparative advantage and these other factors give the United States a comparative advantage in a variety of goods and services. Some of those other sources of U.S. comparative advantage include:

1. *Skills of the U.S. labor force.* Our educational system and experience in production (learning by doing) have created a U.S. workforce that is highly productive, which means that it can be paid more and still be competitive.

2. *U.S. governmental institutions.* The United States has a stable, relatively noncorrupt government, which is required for effective production. These institutions give firms based in the United States a major comparative advantage.

3. *U.S. physical and technological infrastructure.* The United States has probably the best infrastructure for production in the world. This infrastructure includes extensive road systems, telecommunications networks, and power grids.

4. *English is the international language of business.* U.S. citizens learn English from birth. Chinese and Indian citizens must learn it as a second language. One is seldom as comfortable or productive working in one's second language as in one's first language.

5. *Wealth from past production.* The United States is extraordinarily wealthy, which means that the United States is the world's largest consumer. Production that supports many aspects of consumption cannot be easily transferred geographically, and thus the United States will maintain a comparative advantage in producing these nontransferable goods.

6. *U.S. natural resources.* The United States is endowed with many resources: rich farmland, a pleasant and varied climate, beautiful scenery for tourism, minerals, and water. These give it comparative advantages in a number of areas.

7. *Cachet.* The United States continues to be a cultural trendsetter. People all over the world want to watch U.S. movies, want to have U.S. goods, and are influenced by U.S. advertising agencies to favor U.S. goods. As long as that is the case, the United States will have a comparative advantage in goods tied to that cachet.

8. *Inertia.* It takes time and costs money to change production. Companies will not move production to another country for a small cost differential. The difference has to be large, it has to be expected to continue for a long time, and it must be large enough to offset the risk of the unknown. Thus, the current place of production has an advantage over other potential places for production simply because the current location is known.

9. *U.S. intellectual property rights.* Currently, U.S. companies and individuals hold a large number of intellectual property rights, which require other countries that use their patented goods or methods to pay U.S. patent holders. Every time someone (legally) buys the Windows operating system for his or her computer, a portion of the purchase price covers a payment to a U.S. company. America's culture of embracing new ideas and questioning authority cultivates an environment of innovation that will likely continue to generate new intellectual property rights.

10. *A relatively open immigration policy.* Many of the brightest, most entrepreneurial students of developing countries immigrate and settle in the United States. They create jobs and help maintain U.S. comparative advantages in a number of fields, especially high-technology fields. More than 50 percent of the engineering degrees, for example, go to foreign students, many of whom remain in the United States.

The United States has numerous sources of comparative advantage.

Web Note 9.2
Immigration Programs

Combined, these other sources of comparative advantage will maintain the United States' competitiveness in a variety of types of production for the coming decades.

Some Concerns about the Future

The above discussion of the sources of U.S. comparative advantage should have made those of you who are U.S. citizens feel a bit better about the future of the U.S. economy; the United States is not about to lose all its jobs to outsourcing. But that does not mean that there are not real issues of concern. The typical layperson's concern that the comparative advantage story does not capture what is going on with trade and outsourcing has some real foundations, and deserves to be considered seriously.

Inherent and Transferable Sources of Comparative Advantages

When David Ricardo first made the comparative advantage argument in the early 1800s, he was talking about an economic environment that was quite different from today's. His example was Britain and Portugal, with Britain producing wool and Portugal producing wine. What caused their differing costs of production was climate; Britain's climate was far less conducive to growing grapes than Portugal's but more conducive to raising sheep. Differing technologies or labor skills in the countries did not play a key role in their comparative advantages, and it was highly unlikely that the climates, and therefore comparative advantages, of the countries could change. Put another way, both countries had inherent sources of comparative advantages, which we will call **inherent comparative advantages**—*comparative advantages that are based on factors that are relatively unchangeable,* rather than transferable sources of comparative advantages, which we will call **transferable comparative advantages**—*comparative advantages based on factors that can change relatively easily.*

As the theory of comparative advantage developed, economists applied it to a much broader range of goods whose sources of comparative advantage were not due to climate. For example, some countries had land, specific resources, capital, types of labor, or technology as sources of comparative advantage. Extending the analysis to these other sources of comparative advantage makes sense, but it is important to keep in mind that only some of these comparative advantages are inherent; others are transferable. Comparative advantages due to resources or climate are unlikely to change; comparative advantages that depend on capital, technology, or education, however, can change. In fact, we would expect them to change.

The Law of One Price

Whether a country can maintain a much higher standard of living than another country in the long run depends in part on whether its sources of comparative advantage are transferable or inherent. Saudi Arabia will maintain its comparative advantage in producing oil, but the United States' comparative advantage based on better education is likely to be more fleeting. In cases where sources of comparative advantage are not inherent, economic forces will push to eliminate that comparative advantage. The reason is the *law of one price*—in a competitive market, there will be pressure for equal factors to be priced equally. If factor prices aren't equal, firms can reduce costs by redirecting production to countries where factors are priced lower. The tendency of economic forces to eliminate transferable comparative advantage is sometimes called the *convergence hypothesis.* Even seemingly inherent comparative advantages can be changed by technology. Consider oil. The development of cost-effective fuel cells may leave Saudi Arabia with a comparative advantage in oil but not necessarily with a comparative advantage in producing energy.

When markets are working, any country with a comparative advantage due only to transferable capital and technology will lose that comparative advantage as capital and technology spread to other countries. Ultimately, in the case of transferable comparative advantage, production will shift to the lower-wage country that has equivalent institutional

Q-5 Will transferable or inherent comparative advantages be more impacted by the law of one price? Why?

structures. This is the law of one price in action: The same good—including equivalent labor—must sell for the same price, unless trade is restricted or other differences exist. That is what's happening now with the United States and outsourcing. Skills needed in the information technology sector, for example, are transferable. Because an information technology professional with three to five years' experience earns about $75,000 in the United States and only $26,000 in India, those jobs are moving abroad. As long as wages differ, and the workers' productivities in countries are comparable, transferable comparative advantages of U.S. production will continue to erode, and as they erode, production and jobs will be moved abroad.

Transferable comparative advantages will tend to erode over time.

The question, therefore, is not: Why is outsourcing to China and India occurring today? The questions are: Why didn't it happen long ago, and how did U.S. productivity, and hence their standard of living, come to so exceed China's and India's productivity? Or alternatively: How did the United States get in its current high-wage position, and is it likely to maintain that position into the indefinite future?

How the United States Gained and Is Now Losing Sources of Comparative Advantage

To better understand the current U.S. position, let's look at it historically. The United States developed its highly favorable position from the 1920s until the late 1940s when the two world wars directed production toward the United States. Those wars, the entrepreneurial spirit of the U.S. population, U.S. institutions conducive to production, and the flow of technology and capital (financial assets) into the United States gave the United States a big boost both during the two world wars and after. Coming out of World War II, at the then-existing exchange rates, the United States had a major cost advantage in producing a large majority of goods, just as China has a cost advantage in producing the large majority of goods today.

Such cost advantages in a majority of areas of production are not sustainable because the balance of trade will be highly imbalanced. In the absence of specific policy by governments, or large private flows of capital to pay for those imports, eventually that imbalance will right itself. After World War II, the trade balance that favored the United States was maintained temporarily by U.S. companies, which invested heavily in Europe, and by the U.S. government, which transferred funds to Europe with programs such as the Marshall Plan—a program to aid Europe in rebuilding its economy. These flows of capital financed Europe's **trade deficits**—*when imports exceed exports*—and allowed the United States to run large **trade surpluses**—*when exports exceed imports*—just as current flows of capital into the United States from a variety of countries, and the explicit policy of buying U.S. bonds by Chinese and Japanese central banks, are financing the U.S. trade deficits now, and allowing large Chinese trade surpluses with the United States.

In the absence of specific policy by governments, or large private flows of capital, eventually any large trade imbalance will right itself.

Methods of Equalizing Trade Balances

Capital flows that sustain trade imbalances eventually stop, and when they do, adjustments in sources of comparative advantages must take place so that the trade surplus countries—such as China today—become less competitive (lose sources of comparative advantage) and the trade deficit countries—in this case, the United States—become more competitive (gain sources of comparative advantage). This adjustment can occur in a number of ways. The two most likely adjustments today are that wages in China rise relative to wages in the United States, or the U.S. exchange rate (discussed in the next section) falls. Both adjustments will make Chinese goods relatively more expensive and U.S. goods relatively cheaper, just as these adjustments did with countries such as Japan, Taiwan, and Korea in previous decades. Neither of these is especially pleasant for us, which is why we will likely hear continued calls for trade restrictions in the coming decade.

Q-6 What are two likely adjustments that will reduce the wage gap between China and the United States?

Unfortunately, as I will discuss in the next chapter, the trade restriction policies that governments can undertake will generally make things worse. In a globalized free-trade economy, the U.S. wage advantage can be maintained only to the degree that the total cost of production of a good in the United States (with all the associated costs) is no more expensive than the total cost of producing that same good abroad (with all the associated costs). The degree to which production shifts because of lower wages abroad depends on how transferable are the U.S. comparative advantages that we listed above. Some of them are generally nontransferable, and thus will support sustained higher relative U.S. wages. English as the language of business; the enormous wealth of the United States gained earlier; inertia; and U.S. political, social, and capital infrastructure will keep much production in the United States, and will maintain a comparative advantage for U.S. production even with significantly higher U.S. wages.

But in the coming decades, we can expect a narrowing of the wage gap between the United States and China and India. Given these strong market forces that cannot be prevented without undermining the entire international trading system, about the only available realistic strategy for the United States is to adapt to this new situation. Its best strategy is to work toward maintaining existing comparative advantages through investment in education and infrastructure, while continuing to provide an environment conducive to innovation so that we develop comparative advantages in new industries.

Determination of Exchange Rates and Trade

Web Note 9.3
Exchange Rate Data

As mentioned above, transferable sources of comparative advantage aren't the only way to eliminate trade imbalances. Exchange rates are another. The market for foreign currencies is called the foreign exchange (forex) market. It is this market that determines the **exchange rates**—*the rate at which one country's currency can be traded for another country's currency*— that newspapers report daily in tables such as the table below, which shows the cost of various currencies in terms of dollars and the cost of dollars in terms of those currencies.

Exchange Rates, July 6, 2012

	U.S. $ Equivalent	Currency per U.S. $
Argentina (peso)	0.22	4.53
Canada (dollar)	0.98	1.02
China (renminbi)	0.16	6.37
Denmark (krone)	0.17	6.01
European Union (euro)	1.23	0.81
Israel (shekel)	0.25	3.94
Japan (yen)	0.01	79.81
Pakistan (rupee)	0.01	94.11
Philippines (peso)	0.02	41.86
Russia (ruble)	0.03	32.77
Saudi Arabia (riyal)	0.27	3.75
U.K. (pound)	1.55	0.64

The second column in this table reports the price of foreign currencies in terms of dollars. For example, one Argentinean peso costs about 22 cents. The third column tells you the price of dollars in terms of the foreign currency. For example, one U.S. dollar costs 4.5 Argentinean pesos.

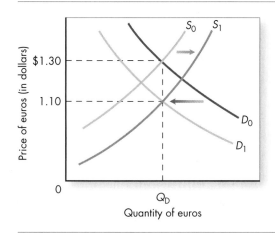

FIGURE 9-2 **The Supply of and Demand for Euros**

As long as you keep quantities and prices of *what* straight, the determination of exchange rates is easy. Just remember that if you're talking about the supply of and demand for euros, the price will be measured in dollars and the quantity will be in euros.

People exchange currencies to buy goods or assets in other countries. For example, an American who wants to buy stock of a company that trades on the EU stock exchange first needs to buy euros with dollars. If the stock costs 150 euros, he will need to buy 150 euros. With an exchange rate of $1.30 for 1 euro, he will need to pay $195 to buy 150 euros ($1.30 × 150). Only then can he buy the stock.

Let's now turn to a graphical analysis of the forex market. At first glance, the graphical analysis of foreign exchange rates seems simple: You have an upward-sloping supply curve and a downward-sloping demand curve. But what goes on the axes? Obviously price and quantity, but what price? And what quantity? Because you are talking about the prices of currencies relative to each other, you have to specify which currencies you are using.

Figure 9-2 presents the supply of and demand for euros in terms of dollars. Notice that the quantity of euros goes on the horizontal axis and the dollar price of euros goes on the vertical axis. When you are comparing currencies of only two countries, the supply of one currency equals the demand for the other currency. To demand one currency, you must supply another. In this figure, I am assuming that there are only two trading partners: the United States and the European Union. This means that the supply of euros is equivalent to the demand for dollars. The Europeans who want to buy U.S. goods or assets supply euros to buy dollars. Let's consider an example. Say a European wants to buy a Dell computer made in the United States. She has euros, but Dell wants dollars. So, to buy the computer, she or Dell must somehow exchange euros for dollars. She is *supplying* euros in order to *demand* dollars.

The supply curve of euros is upward-sloping because the more dollars European citizens get for their euros, the cheaper U.S. goods and assets are for them and the greater the quantity of euros they want to supply for those goods. Say, for example, that the dollar price of one euro rises from $1.30 to $1.35. That means that the price of a dollar to a European has fallen from 0.78 euro to 0.74 euro. For a European, a good that cost $100 now falls in price from 78 euros to 74 euros. U.S. goods are cheaper, so the Europeans buy more U.S. goods and more dollars, which means they supply more euros.

The demand for euros comes from Americans who want to buy European goods or assets. The demand curve is downward-sloping because the lower the dollar price of euros, the more euros U.S. citizens want to buy, using the same reasoning I just described.

The market is in equilibrium when the quantity supplied equals the quantity demanded. In my example, when supply is S_0 and demand is D_0, equilibrium occurs at a dollar price of $1.30 for one euro.

To demand one currency, you must supply another currency.

Q-7 Show graphically the effect on the price of euros of an increase in the demand for dollars by Europeans.

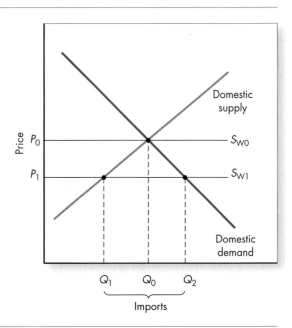

FIGURE 9-3

The exchange rate plays an important role in international trade. If the world price of goods is less than the domestic price of tradable goods, domestic producers must match the world price level. If the world price level is P_1, domestic producers will sell Q_1 and domestic consumers demand Q_2. The difference is made up by imports shown by the difference between Q_2 and Q_1. A country will have a zero trade balance when the world price level equals the domestic price level, P_0.

Suppose forces shift the supply and demand for euros; for example, say people lose faith in the euro, leading them to want to hold their assets in dollar denominated assets. The supply of euros rises from S_0 to S_1. At the same time, Americans also lose faith in the euro and decide to buy fewer euros. This shifts the demand for euros from D_0 to D_1. Combined, the two shifts lead to a fall in the price of the euro as shown in Figure 9-2, decreasing the price from $1.30 to $1.10.

Because it takes more euros to buy dollars, we say the euro has depreciated in value. A **currency depreciation** is *a change in the exchange rate so that one currency buys fewer units of a foreign currency.* The dollar, on the other hand appreciated in value because one dollar can be exchanged for more euros. A **currency appreciation** is *a change in the exchange rate so that one currency buys more units of a foreign currency.*

Q-8 Interest rates and income rise in Britain. Would you expect the British currency, the pound, to appreciate or depreciate? Explain your answer using supply and demand curves.

Exchange Rates and Trade

The exchange rate plays an important role in the demand for a country's domestic goods. We can see that by considering both the domestic supply of tradable goods—those goods that can be produced in one country and sold in another—and the international supply of tradable goods on the same graph. We do so in Figure 9-3. In it, for simplicity we assume that the world supply of goods is perfectly elastic (horizontal) at P_1. That is, foreign countries are willing to sell as much as is demanded at a single price. With free trade, if domestic producers of tradable goods want to sell any goods, they must match this world price. If consumers can buy all the goods they want at the world price, why pay more?

Domestic supply of tradable goods is determined by the wage and the productivity of workers in the United States—as quantity supplied rises, suppliers have to charge higher prices to cover higher costs of production. The supply curve, therefore, reflects the comparative advantages of U.S. producers with respect to world producers. It is upward sloping because as output increases, the cost of production rises relative to the cost of world production. If the world supply is S_{W1}, the United States has a comparative advantage for goods up until Q_1, where the domestic supply intersects the world supply. World producers have a comparative advantage in the production of goods to the right of Q_1.

Trade for an economy that faces global competition needs to take into account world supply, which is horizontal at the world price for tradable goods.[2] If the world supply curve intersects domestic supply and demand at the domestic equilibrium price as it does when the world supply curve is S_{W0}, imports will be exactly offset by exports. If the world price is below the domestic equilibrium, as it is when the world supply curve is S_{W1}, a country is running a trade deficit. In this figure the world price is P_1, which results in a trade deficit is $Q_2 - Q_1$. Indefinite trade deficits are not sustainable. A decrease in the domestic economy's exchange rates, relative declines in wages, or improvements in comparative advantage can eliminate the trade deficit.

Let's consider how exchange rates adjustment can eliminate a U.S. trade deficit with China. (We are using China to represent the rest of the world.)

Exchange rates affect a trade balance through their impact on relative comparative advantages. The reason is that as the exchange rate changes the price of a country's goods to people in other countries changes. In the case of dollars and yuan, if the dollar depreciates U.S. citizens will pay more U.S. dollars for each good they buy from China, which means that the relative price of foreign goods rises. So, a depreciation of the domestic country's currency will shift the world supply curve up, making it easier for U.S. producers to compete. Similarly, an appreciation will shift the world supply curve down, making it harder for a country to compete globally.

In theory, the exchange rate adjustment can bring two countries' comparative advantages into alignment, eliminating any trade imbalance. The assumption that exchange rates will adjust to bring trade into balance underlies the story economists tell about comparative advantages. That story assumes that comparative advantages net out so the trade deficit of both countries is zero.

Some Complications in Exchange Rates

If the supply and demand for currencies applied only to tradable goods, trade among countries would generally be in balance, and countries would have roughly equal sectors of comparative advantages in producing goods. However, that doesn't always happen. A major reason why is that the demand for a country's currency reflects not only the demand for a country's produced goods but also reflects a demand for its assets.

When the demand for a country's assets is high, the value of its currency will also be high. With a higher exchange rate, the world price of produced goods will be low and the domestic country will have a comparative advantage in relatively fewer sectors compared to other countries. That has been the case in the United States over the past 20 years, and is one of the reasons so much manufacturing production has fared so poorly.

Another source of differences in comparative advantage is what is called the **resource curse**—*the paradox that countries with an abundance of resources tend to have lower economic growth and more unemployment than countries with fewer natural resources.* What happens is that the country that has a comparative advantage in resources finds that the demand for its resources pushes its exchange rate up. A higher exchange rate reduces the comparative advantage of other tradable goods, shifting the world supply curve, and hence domestic production, of these goods, down. In terms of Figure 9-3, world supply for goods other than resources falls from S_{W0} to S_{W1} and

Q-9 If the world supply of goods is at the domestic price level, will there be a trade deficit or trade surplus? Explain your answer.

Q-10 How can the discovery of a highly valuable resource lead to the appreciation of a currency and loss of comparative advantage in other goods?

---

[2]This is a discussion for a composite good. Actual trade is in many different types of goods and services, and this position is consistent with significant imports and exports of particular goods, as long as in the aggregate they balance out. It is the trade balance, not total trade, that is captured by the graph.

domestic production falls from Q_0 to Q_1. The resource curse also tends to reduce employment because a decline in employment in these other goods is not offset by an increase in employment in the resource sector. While the production of the resource often pays well, it does not require large numbers of workers. Because the Netherlands experienced this phenomenon when it discovered offshore oil, it is also sometimes called the Dutch disease.

When one sector of an economy gains a comparative advantage, other sectors must either lose their comparative advantage or there will be a trade imbalance.

The resource curse is not tied to natural resources. It happens whenever there is a large increase in global demand for one sector of an economy's goods. When one sector of an economy gains a comparative advantage, other sectors must either lose their comparative advantage or there will be a trade imbalance. This happened in the United States during the rise in globalization for technology, business organization, and finance sectors. Globalization increased the demand for people providing logistical support, marketing, and financial expertise. These were high paying jobs and, on average, it was an enormous boon to the United States economy. But that increase in demand meant that the low-wage U.S. workers in globally competitive industries lost their comparative advantage since the U.S. dollar did not depreciate to maintain it. So total income in the United States rose, but income and employment in the low-wage manufacturing tradable sector fell, causing significant hardship and unemployment in these sectors.

Conclusion

International trade, and changing comparative advantages, has become more and more important for the United States in recent decades. With international transportation and communication becoming faster and easier, and with other countries' economies growing, the U.S. economy will inevitably become more interdependent with the other economies of the world. Ultimately, this international trade will improve the lives for most Americans, and even more so for the world. However, the path there will likely be very difficult for those U.S. citizens in the competitive global sector.

Summary

- According to the principle of comparative advantage, as long as the relative opportunity costs of producing goods (what must be given up in one good in order to get another good) differ among countries, there are potential gains from trade. *(LO9-1)*

- Three insights into the terms of trade are:
  1. The more competition exists in international trade, the less the trader gets and the more the involved countries get.
  2. Once competition prevails, smaller countries tend to get a larger percentage of the gains from trade than do larger countries.
  3. Gains from trade go to countries that produce goods that exhibit economies of scale. *(LO9-1)*

- Economists and laypeople differ in their views on trade. *(LO9-2)*

- The gains from trade in the form of low consumer prices tend to be widespread and not easily recognized, while the costs in jobs lost tend to be concentrated and readily identifiable. *(LO9-2)*

- The United States has comparative advantages based on its skilled workforce, its institutions, and its language, among other things. *(LO9-3)*

- Inherent comparative advantages are based on factors that are relatively unchangeable. They are not subject to the law of one price. *(LO9-3)*

- Transferable comparative advantages are based on factors that can change relatively easily. The law of one price can eliminate these comparative advantages. *(LO9-3)*

- Concerns about trade for the United States are that U.S. relative wages will decline and the value of the dollar will decline as well.   (*LO9-3*)

- The prices of currencies—foreign exchange rates—can be analyzed with the supply and demand model in the same way as any other good can be. An appreciation of the dollar occurs when a single dollar can buy more foreign currency. A depreciation of the dollar occurs when a single dollar buys less foreign currency.   (*LO9-4*)

- An appreciation of a currency will shift the world supply of a good down and increase that country's trade deficit.   (*LO9-4*)

- The depreciation of a country's currency makes that country's goods more competitive.   (*LO9-4*)

- The resource curse occurs when a significant amount of natural resources are discovered. This raises foreign demand for the resource, raising the value of the domestic country's currency, making other sectors less competitive. A variation of the resource curse is one reason for a greater inequality of income distribution in the United States.   (*LO9-4*)

Key Terms

balance of trade *(190)*
comparative
  advantage *(186)*
currency
  appreciation *(198)*

currency
  depreciation *(198)*
exchange rate *(196)*
inherent comparative
  advantage *(194)*

resource curse *(199)*
trade deficit *(195)*
trade surplus *(195)*

transferable comparative
  advantage *(194)*

Questions and Exercises

1. Will a country do better importing or exporting a good for which it has a comparative advantage? Why?   (*LO9-1*)

2. Widgetland has 60 workers. Each worker can produce 4 widgets or 4 wadgets. Each resident in Widgetland currently consumes 2 widgets and 2 wadgets. Wadgetland also has 60 workers. Each can produce 3 widgets or 12 wadgets. Wadgetland's residents consume 1 widget and 9 wadgets. Is there a basis for trade? If so, offer the countries a deal they can't refuse.   (*LO9-1*)

3. Suppose there are two states that do not trade: Iowa and Nebraska. Each state produces the same two goods: corn and wheat. For Iowa the opportunity cost of producing 1 bushel of wheat is 3 bushels of corn. For Nebraska the opportunity cost of producing 1 bushel of corn is 3 bushels of wheat. At present, Iowa produces 20 million bushels of wheat and 120 million bushels of corn, while Nebraska produces 20 million bushels of corn and 120 million bushels of wheat.   (*LO9-1*)
   a. Explain how, with trade, Nebraska can end up with 40 million bushels of wheat and 120 million bushels of corn while Iowa can end up with 40 million bushels of corn and 120 million bushels of wheat.
   b. If the states ended up with the numbers given in *a*, how much would the trader get?

4. Suppose that two countries, Machineland and Farmland, have the following production possibility curves: (*LO9-1*)

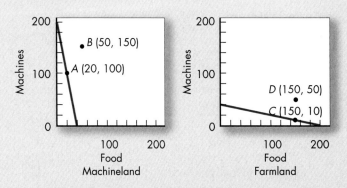

   a. Explain how these two countries can move from points *A* and *C*, where they currently are, to points *B* and *D*.
   b. If possible, state by how much total production for the two countries has risen.
   c. If you were a trader, how much of the gains from trade would you deserve for discovering this trade?
   d. If the per unit cost of production falls as output rises, how would the analysis change?

5. Suppose there are two countries, Busytown and
    Lazyasiwannabe, with the following production
    possibility tables: (*LO9-1*)

Busytown

% of Resources Devoted to Cars	Cars Produced (thousands)	Gourmet Meals Produced (thousands)
100%	60	0
80	48	10
60	36	20
40	24	30
20	12	40
0	0	50

Lazyasiwannabe

% of Resources Devoted to Cars	Cars Produced (thousands)	Gourmet Meals Produced (thousands)
100%	50	0
80	40	10
60	30	20
40	20	30
20	10	40
0	0	50

a. Draw the production possibility curves for each country.
b. Which country has the comparative advantage in
    producing cars? In producing gourmet meals?
c. Suppose each country specializes in the production of
    one good. Explain how Busytown can end up with
    36,000 cars and 22,000 meals and Lazyasiwannabe
    can end up with 28,000 meals and 24,000 cars.

6. Why does competition among traders affect how much of
    the gains from trade are given to the countries involved in
    the trade? (*LO9-1*)

7. Why do smaller countries usually get most of the gains
    from trade? (*LO9-1*)

8. What are some reasons why a small country might not get
    the gains of trade? (*LO9-1*)

9. Country A can produce, at most, 40 olives or 20 pickles,
    or some combination of olives and pickles such as
    the 20 olives and 10 pickles it is currently producing.
    Country B can produce, at most, 120 olives or
    60 pickles, or some combination of olives and pickles
    such as the 100 olives and 50 pickles it is currently
    producing. (*LO9-1*)
    a. Is there a basis for trade? If so, offer the two countries
        a deal they can't refuse.

b. How would your answer change if you knew that the
    per unit cost of producing pickles and olives falls as
    more of each is produced? Why? Which country
    would you have produce which good?

10. What are four reasons why economists' and laypeople's
    view of trade differ? (*LO9-2*)

11. True or false? Wages in China are lower than those
    in the United States. This means that China has a
    comparative advantage in everything. Explain your
    answer. (*LO9-2*)

12. How does the outsourcing of manufacturing production
    benefit production in the United States? (*LO9-2*)

13. How has globalization made the rich richer and poor
    poorer in the United States? (*LO9-2*)

14. List at least three sources of comparative advantage that
    the United States has and will likely maintain over the
    coming decade. (*LO9-3*)

15. How do inherent comparative advantages differ from
    transferable comparative advantages? (*LO9-3*)

16. From the standpoint of adjustment costs to trade, which
    would a country prefer—inherent or transferable compar-
    ative advantage? Why? (*LO9-3*)

17. The dollar price of the South African rand fell from
    29 cents to 22 cents in 1996, the same year the country
    was rocked by political turmoil. Using supply/demand
    analysis, explain why the turmoil led to a decline in the
    price of the rand. (*LO9-4*)

18. How does a depreciation of a currency change the price of
    imports and exports? Explain using the U.S. dollar and
    the Chinese yuan. (*LO9-4*)

19. Using the graph below, indicate domestic production and
    imports. (*LO9-4*)

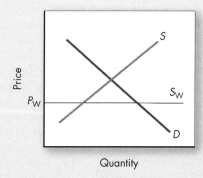

a. Would the United States want to raise or lower the
    world supply of the good? Why?
b. How might that happen?

20. Would you expect the resource curse to improve or
    worsen the distribution of income in a country? (*LO9-4*)

Questions from Alternative Perspectives

1. Evaluate the following statement: Comparative advantage will benefit all people because everyone has a comparative advantage in something. Therefore, trade based on comparative advantage should be facilitated without undue government intervention. (Austrian)

2. In the 10th century B.C., King Solomon brought the Israelites into great economic wealth through specialization and trade. It was difficult when faced with the practices and beliefs of their trading partners, however, for Israel to maintain its identity as a people of one God. King Solomon, for example, provided a place for each of his wives to worship the gods of her own people. If such syncretism (adoption of foreign practices and beliefs) is inevitable with increased globalization, should trade be encouraged, even today? (Religious)

3. Global outsourcing has cost the U.S. economy far more than one million jobs since 2001, or somewhere between 15 and 35 percent of the total decline in employment since the onset of the 2001 recession.
   a. How does outsourcing affect the bargaining power of U.S. workers and the bargaining power of U.S. employers?
   b. What will it likely do to the overall level of U.S. workers' wages?
   c. What will it likely do to lawyers' wages?
   d. If you stated that it affected lawyers' wages differently, do you believe that the U.S. policy response to outsourcing would be different? (Post-Keynesian)

4. In David Ricardo's original example of comparative advantage in his *Principles of Political Economy*, written in 1817, Portugal possesses an absolute advantage in both the production of cloth and the production of wine. But England has a comparative advantage in the production of cloth, while Portugal's comparative advantage is in wine production. According to Ricardo, an English political economist, England should specialize in the production of cloth and Portugal in wine making.
   a. Was Ricardo's advice self-serving?
   b. Knowing that light manufacturing, such as clothing and textile production, has led most industrialization processes, would you have advised 19th-century Portugal to specialize in wine making? (Radical)

5. In the *Wealth of Nations* Adam Smith claimed, "Servants, labourers and workmen of different kinds, make up the far greater part of every great political society. But what improves the circumstances of the greater part can never be regarded as an inconvenience to the whole. No society can surely be flourishing and happy, of which the far greater part of the members are poor and miserable. It is but equity, besides, that they who feed, clothe and lodge the whole body of the people, should have such a share of the produce of their own labour as to be themselves tolerably well fed, cloathed and lodged." In light of today's economy, what argument can you give that supports this claim? What argument can you give that disputes this claim? (Austrian and Post-Keynesian)

Issues to Ponder

1. How is outsourcing to China and India today different from U.S. outsourcing in the past?

2. One of the basic economic laws is the "law of one price." Does it imply that the U.S. wage level will have to equal the Chinese wage level if free trade is allowed? Why or why not?

3. The normal textbook presentation of international trade does not include the international trader. How does including the trader in the model provide a different view of trade than one would get from a model that did not include the trader?

4. One way to equalize imports and exports would be to pass a law that (1) in order to import, importers must provide a certificate certifying that an equal value of exports had occurred; and (2) in order to export, exporters must provide a certificate certifying that an equal value of imports had occurred.
   a. If the trade is balanced, what would the price of these certificates be?
   b. In the current U.S. situation, what would the price of these certificates be?
   c. In the current Chinese situation, what would the price of these certificates be?
   d. Would such a law make exchange rate adjustment more or less likely?

5. Assuming a law such as the one suggested in question 4 were passed in the mid-1990s in the U.S., what subgroups of U.S. workers would have likely been helped, and what subgroups of U.S. workers would have likely been hurt?

Answers to Margin Questions

1. He should walk away because there is no basis for trade. (*p. 187; LO9-1*)

2. The percentage of gains from trade that goes to a country depends upon the change in the price of the goods being traded. If trade led to no change in prices in a small country, then that small country would get no gains from trade. Another case in which a small country gets a small percentage of the gains from trade would occur when its larger trading partner was producing a good with economies of scale and the small country was not. A third case is when the traders who extracted most of the surplus or gains from trade come from the larger country, then the smaller country would end up with few of the gains from trade. (*p. 189; LO9-1*)

3. Four reasons for the difference are: (1) gains from trade are often stealth gains, (2) comparative advantage is determined by more than wages, (3) nations trade more than just manufactured goods, and (4) trade has distributional effects. (*p. 190; LO9-2*)

4. The manufacturing sector produces tradable goods, which has made it vulnerable to international trade. Foreign producers could produce these goods at a lower cost, putting downward pressure on wages and employment. Production in the education, health care, and government sectors is less tradable, making it less subject to pressure from globalization. (*p. 192; LO9-2*)

5. Transferable comparative advantage will be more affected because it is an advantage that is not tied to a particular country. Countries where prices are higher will face outflow of capital and technology to bring prices back in balance. This will transfer comparative advantage from the high-price countries to low-price countries. (*p. 194; LO9-3*)

6. Two likely adjustments that will reduce the wage gap are a fall in the value of the dollar (U.S. exchange rate) and a rise in Chinese wages relative to U.S. wages. (*p. 195; LO9-3*)

7. An increase in the demand for dollars is the equivalent to an increase in the supply of euros, so an increase in the demand for dollars pushes down the price of euros in terms of dollars, as in the following diagram. (*p. 197; LO9-4*)

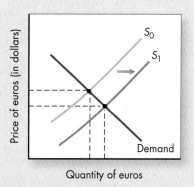

8. The pound would be expected to appreciate because the demand for pounds would shift to the right as foreign investors bought more British bonds and other assets. The supply curve would shift to the left because British citizens would shift their investments back to Britain. This is shown in the graph below. (*p. 198; LO9-4*)

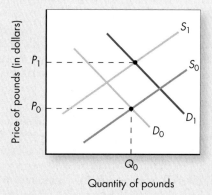

9. There would be neither a trade surplus nor deficit since imports cost the same as domestic goods. American consumers would be indifferent between buying foreign and domestic goods. (*p. 199; LO9-4*)

10. The discovery of the resource will increase the demand for the domestic currency, which leads to an appreciation of the currency. This appreciation makes domestic goods more expensive to foreigners, which leads to a loss in the comparative advantage in those goods. (*p. 199; LO9-4*)

chapter 10

International Trade Policy

Manufacturing and commercial monopolies owe their origin not to a tendency imminent in a capitalist economy but to governmental interventionist policy directed against free trade.

—Ludwig von Mises

Based on the theory of comparative advantage, most economists oppose trade restrictions. Not everyone agrees with economists; almost every day we hear calls from some sector of the economy to restrict foreign imports to save U.S. jobs and protect U.S. workers from unfair competition. In this chapter we consider the pattern and nature of trade, the variety of trade restrictions that governments impose, and why economists generally oppose trade restrictions.

The Nature and Patterns of Trade

Let's begin with some numbers to get a sense of the nature and dimensions of international trade.

Increasing but Fluctuating World Trade

In 1928, total world trade was about $640 billion (in today's dollars). U.S. gross domestic product (GDP) was about $1,070 billion, so world trade as a percentage of U.S. GDP was almost 60 percent. In 1935, that ratio had fallen to less than 30 percent. In 1950 it was only 20 percent. Then it started rising. Today it is about 240 percent, with world trade amounting to about $35 trillion. As you can see, international trade has been growing, but with significant fluctuations in that growth. Sometimes international trade has grown rapidly; at other times it has grown slowly or has even fallen.

In part, fluctuations in world trade result from fluctuations in world output. When output rises, international trade rises; when output falls, international trade falls. Fluctuations in world trade are also in part explained by trade restrictions that countries have imposed from time to time. For example,

After reading this chapter, you should be able to:

LO10-1 Summarize some important data of trade.

LO10-2 Explain policies countries use to restrict trade.

LO10-3 Summarize the reasons for trade restrictions and why economists generally oppose trade restrictions.

LO10-4 Explain how free trade associations both help and hinder international trade.

decreases in world income during the Depression of the 1930s caused a large decrease in trade, but that decrease was exacerbated by a worldwide increase in trade restrictions.

Differences in the Importance of Trade

The importance of international trade to countries' economies differs widely, as we can see in the table below, which presents the importance of the shares of exports (the value of goods and services sold abroad) and imports (the value of goods and services purchased abroad) for various countries.

	Total Output[*]	Export Ratio	Import Ratio
Netherlands	$ 844	78%	71%
Germany	3,695	47	41
Canada	1,706	29	31
Italy	2,180	27	29
France	2,825	26	28
United Kingdom	2,462	30	33
Japan	6,078	15	14
United States	15,094	13	16

[*]Numbers in billions.

Source: *World Development Indicators, 2012,* The World Bank.

Among the countries listed, the Netherlands has the highest exports compared to total output; the United States has the lowest. The Netherlands' imports are also the highest as a percentage of total output. U.S. exports are close to the lowest. The relationship between a country's imports and its exports is no coincidence. For most countries, imports and exports roughly equal one another, though in any particular year that equality can be rough indeed. For the United States in recent years, imports have generally significantly exceeded exports, which means that a trade imbalance can continue for a long time. But that situation can't continue forever, as I'll discuss.

Total trade figures provide us with only part of the international trade picture. We must also look at what types of goods are traded and with whom that trade is conducted.

What and with Whom the United States Trades

The majority of U.S. exports and imports involve significant amounts of manufactured goods. This isn't unusual, since much of international trade is in manufactured goods.

The primary trading partners of the United States are Canada, Mexico, the European Union, and the Pacific Rim countries.

Figure 10-1 shows the regions with which the United States trades. Exports to Canada and Mexico made up the largest percentage of total U.S. exports to individual countries in 2012. The largest regions to whom the U.S. exports are the Pacific Rim and the European Union. Countries from which the United States imports major quantities include Canada and Mexico and the regions of the European Union and the Pacific Rim. Thus, the countries we export to are also the countries we import from.

THE CHANGING NATURE OF TRADE   The nature of trade is continually changing, both in terms of the countries with which the United States trades and the goods and services traded. For example, U.S. imports from China, India, and other East Asian countries have increased substantially in recent years. In the late 1980s goods from

FIGURE 10-1 (A AND B)   U.S. Exports and Imports by Region

Major regions that trade with the United States include Canada, Mexico, the European Union, and the Pacific Rim.

Source: FT900 U.S. International Trade in Goods and Services 2012, U.S. Census Bureau (www.census.gov).

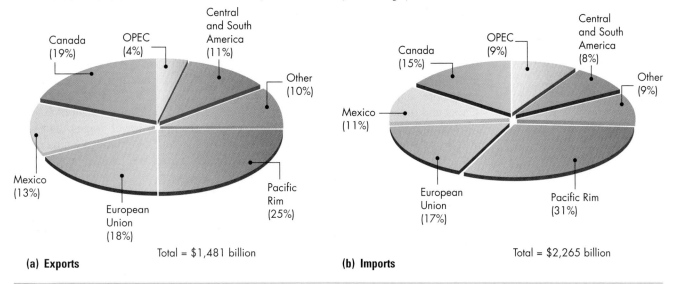

(a) **Exports**   (b) **Imports**

China accounted for 2.5 percent of all U.S. merchandise imports. Today they account for 17 percent. Imports from India have increased twentyfold over that time—from 0.1 percent to 2 percent of all goods imported.

The kind of goods and services the United States imports also has changed. Thirty years ago, the goods the United States imported from China and India were primarily basic manufacturing goods and raw commodities. Technologically advanced goods were produced here in the United States. Today we are importing high-tech manufactured goods from these countries, and they are even developing their own new products that require significant research and development.

The change in the nature of the goods that a country produces and exports up the technological ladder is typical for developing countries. It characterized Japan, Korea, and Singapore in the post–World War II era, and today characterizes China and India. As this movement up the technological ladder occurs, foreign companies that had been subcontractors for U.S. companies become direct competitors of the U.S. companies. For example, the automaker Kia and the electronics producer Samsung have developed into major global firms, and in the future you can expect numerous Chinese companies to become household names.

We can expect the nature of trade to change even more in the future as numerous technological changes in telecommunications continue to reduce the cost of both voice and data communications throughout the world and expand the range of services that can be provided by foreign countries. Production no longer needs to occur in the geographic area where the goods are consumed. For example, financial accounting, compositing (typesetting) of texts, and research can now be done almost anywhere, and transferred with the click of a mouse. The customer service calls for a U.S. company can be answered almost anywhere in India, which has a sizable well-educated, English-speaking population, and much lower wage rates. India even trains its employees to speak with a Midwest U.S. accent to make it less apparent to customers that the

Q-1 How has the nature of U.S. imports from China changed in recent years?

We can expect the nature of trade to change even more in the future.

call is being answered in India. This trade in services is what the press often refers to as *outsourcing,* but it is important to remember that outsourcing is simply a description of some aspects of trade.

IS CHINESE AND INDIAN OUTSOURCING DIFFERENT FROM PREVIOUS OUTSOURCING?

There has been a lot of discussion about outsourcing to China and India recently, and thus it is worthwhile to consider what is, and what is not, different about trade with China and India. First, what isn't different is the distance of outsourcing. Manufacturers have used overseas suppliers for years. What is different about outsourcing to China and India today compared to earlier outsourcing to Japan, Singapore, and Korea in the 1980s and 1990s is the potential size of that outsourcing. China and India have a combined population of 2.5 billion people, a sizable number of whom are well educated and willing to work for much lower wages than U.S. workers. As technology opens up more areas to trade, and as India and China move up the technology ladder, U.S.-based firms will likely experience much more competition than they have experienced to date. How U.S. companies deal with this competition will likely be the defining economic policy issue for the next decade. If they develop new technologies and new industries in which the United States has comparative advantages, then the United States' future can be bright. If they don't, significant, difficult adjustment will need to occur.

> How U.S. companies deal with new high-tech competition will likely be the defining economic policy issue for the next decade.

The rising competitiveness of Asian economies with the U.S. economy is manifested in the large deficit the United States is running on its balance of trade, as shown in Figure 10-2(a). A trade deficit means that U.S. imports exceed U.S. exports. The United States has been running trade deficits since the 1970s, and in 2008 the U.S. trade deficit reached over $820 billion. It has decreased slightly since then, but it remains high.

The trade deficit looks a little less threatening when considered as a percentage of GDP, as is shown in Figure 10-2(b), but it is still of concern. The U.S. trade deficit means that the United States is consuming a lot more than it is producing, and paying for current consumption with promises to pay in the future.

FIGURE 10-2 (A AND B) **The U.S. Trade Balance**

The United States has been running trade deficits since the 1970s. Panel (**a**) shows the trade deficit in billions of dollars. As (**b**) shows, the trade deficit looks slightly less threatening when considered as a percentage of GDP.

Source: U.S. Department of Commerce: Bureau of Economic Analysis *International Transactions* (www.bea.gov).

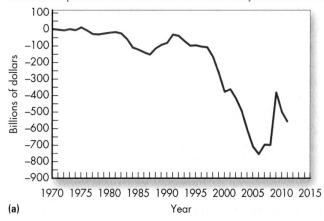

(a)

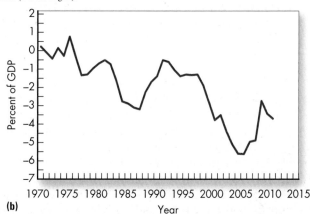

(b)

International Issues in Perspective

Since the 1970s, international issues have become increasingly important for the U.S. economy. That statement would be correct even if the reference period went back as far as the late 1800s. From the late 1800s through the first 40 years of the 1900s, the United States was in an isolationist period in which the country turned inward in both economic and foreign policies.

The statement would not be correct if the reference period were earlier than the late 1800s. In the 1600s, 1700s, and most of the 1800s, international trade was vital to the American economy—even more vital than now. The American nation grew from colonial possessions of England, France, and Spain. These "new world" colonial possessions were valued for their gold, agricultural produce, and natural resources. From a European standpoint, international trade was the colonies' reason for being.*

A large portion of the U.S. government's income during much of the 1800s came from tariffs. Our technology was imported from abroad, and international issues played a central role in wars fought here. (Many historians believe that the most important cause of the U.S. Civil War was the difference of views about tariffs on manufactured goods. The South opposed them because it wanted cheap manufactured goods, while the North favored them because it wanted to protect its manufacturing industries.) Up until the 1900s, no one would have studied the U.S. economy independently of international issues. Not only was there significant international trade; there was also significant immigration. The United States is a country of immigrants.

Only in the late 1800s did the United States adopt an isolationist philosophy in both politics and trade. So in reference to that isolationist period, the U.S. economy has become more integrated with the world economy. However, in a broader historical perspective, that isolationist period was an anomaly, and today's economy is simply returning international issues to the key role they've usually played.

Another important insight is that international trade has social and cultural dimensions. While much of the chapter deals with specifically economic issues, we must also remember the cultural and social implications of trade.

Let's consider an example from history. In the Middle Ages, Greek ideas and philosophy were lost to Europe when hordes of barbarians swept over the continent. These ideas and that philosophy were rediscovered in the Renaissance only as a by-product of trade between the Italian merchant cities and the Middle East. (The Greek ideas that had spread to the Middle East were protected from European upheavals.) *Renaissance* means rebirth: a rebirth in Europe of Greek learning. Many of our traditions and sensibilities are based on those of the Renaissance, and that Renaissance was caused, or at least significantly influenced, by international trade. Had there been no trade, our entire philosophy of life might have been different.

In economics courses we do not focus on these broader cultural issues but instead focus on relatively technical issues such as the reasons for trade and the implications of tariffs. But keep in the back of your mind these broader implications as you go through the various components of international economics. They add a dimension to the story that otherwise might be forgotten.

---

*The Native American standpoint was, I suspect, somewhat different.

Debtor and Creditor Nations

Running a trade deficit isn't necessarily bad. In fact, while you're doing it, it's rather nice. If you were a country, you probably would be running a trade deficit now since, most likely, you're consuming (importing) more than you're producing (exporting). How can you do that? By living off past savings, getting support from your parents or a spouse, or borrowing.

Countries have the same options. They can live off foreign aid, past savings, or loans. The U.S. economy is currently financing its trade deficit by selling off assets—financial assets such as stocks and bonds, or real assets such as real estate and corporations. Since the assets of the United States total many trillions of dollars, it can continue to run trade deficits of a similar size for years to come, but in doing so it is reducing its wealth each year.

Running a trade deficit isn't necessarily bad.

Q-2 Will a debtor nation necessarily be running a trade deficit?

The United States has not always run a trade deficit. Following World War II it ran trade surpluses—an excess of exports over imports—with other countries, so it was an international lender. Thus, it acquired large amounts of foreign assets. Because of the large trade deficits the United States has run since the 1980s, now the United States is a large debtor nation. The United States has borrowed more from abroad than it has lent abroad.

As the United States has gone from being a large creditor nation to being the world's biggest debtor, international considerations have been forced on the nation. The cushion of being a creditor—of having a flow of interest income—has been replaced by the trials of being a debtor and having to pay out interest every year without currently getting anything for it when they pay that interest.

One way countries try to reduce trade deficits is to reduce imports by restricting trade. These trade restrictions can keep a country from having to face the adjustments associated with improving its comparative advantage either by reducing wages or, as we saw in the last chapter, by allowing its currency to depreciate.

Varieties of Trade Restrictions

Three policies used to restrict trade are

1. Tariffs (taxes on internationally traded goods).

2. Quotas (quantity limits placed on imports).

3. Regulatory trade restrictions (government-imposed procedural rules that limit imports).

The policies countries can use to restrict trade include tariffs and quotas, voluntary restraint agreements, embargoes, regulatory trade restrictions, and nationalistic appeals. I'll consider each in turn and also review the geometric analysis of each.

Tariffs and Quotas

A **tariff** is a *tax that governments place on internationally traded goods*—generally imports. (Tariffs are also called *customs duties*.) Tariffs are the most-used and most-familiar type of trade restriction. Tariffs operate in the same way a tax does: They make imported goods relatively more expensive than they otherwise would have been, and thereby encourage the consumption of domestically produced goods. On average, U.S. tariffs raise the price of imported goods by less than 3 percent. Figure 10-3(a) presents average tariff rates for industrial goods for a number of countries and Figure 10-3(b) shows the tariff rates imposed by the United States since 1920.

FIGURE 10-3 (A AND B)   Selected Tariff Rates

The tariff rates in **(a)** will be continually changing as the changes negotiated by the World Trade Organization come into effect. In **(b)** you see tariff rates for the United States since 1920.

Source: General Agreement on Tariffs and Trade (GATT) and the World Bank (www.worldbank.org).

Country	%	Country	%
Argentina	12.2	Norway	3.1
Australia	3.9	Philippines	2.8
Canada	3.4	Poland	2.0
Colombia	11.6	Singapore	0
Czech Rep.	2.0	South Africa	5.7
Hungary	2.0	Sri Lanka	9.0
India	6.9	Thailand	4.8
Indonesia	2.4	United States	2.1
Japan	2.7	Venezuela	12.2
Mexico	8.4	Zimbabwe	17.1

(a) Tariff Rates by Country

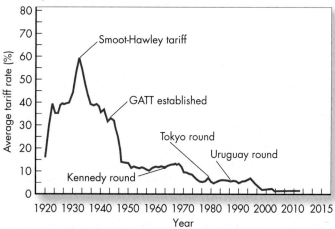

(b) U.S. Tariff Rates since 1920

Probably the most infamous tariff in U.S. history is the Smoot-Hawley Tariff of 1930, which raised tariffs on imported goods to an average of 60 percent. It was passed at the height of the Great Depression in the United States in the hope of protecting American jobs. It didn't work. Other countries responded with similar tariffs. Partly as a result of these trade wars, international trade plummeted from $60 billion in 1928 to $25 billion in 1938, unemployment worsened, and the international depression deepened. These effects of the tariff convinced many, if not most, economists that free trade is preferable to trade restrictions.

The dismal failure of the Smoot-Hawley Tariff was the main reason the **General Agreement on Tariffs and Trade (GATT)**, *a regular international conference to reduce trade barriers,* was established in 1947 immediately following World War II. In 1995 GATT was replaced by the **World Trade Organization (WTO)**, *an organization whose functions are generally the same as GATT's were—to promote free and fair trade among countries.* Unlike GATT, the WTO is a permanent organization with an enforcement system (albeit weak). Since its formation, rounds of negotiations have resulted in a decline in worldwide tariffs.

A **quota** is a *quantity limit placed on imports.* They have the same effect on equilibrium price and quantity as the quantity restrictions discussed in Chapter 5, and their effect in limiting trade is similar to the effect of a tariff. Both increase price and reduce quantity. Tariffs, like all taxes on suppliers, shift the supply curve up by the amount of the tax, as Figure 10-4 shows. A tariff, *T*, raises equilibrium price from P_0 to P_1 by an amount that is less than the tariff, and equilibrium quantity declines from Q_0 to Q_1. With a quota, Q_1, the equilibrium price also rises to P_1.

There is, however, a difference between tariffs and quotas. In the case of the tariff, the government collects tariff revenue represented by the shaded region. In the case of a quota, the government collects no revenue. The benefit of the increase in price goes to the importer as additional corporate revenue. So which of the two do you think import companies favor? The quota, of course—it means more profits as long as your company is the one to receive the rights to fill those quotas. In fact, once quotas are instituted, firms compete intensely to get them.

Tariffs affect trade patterns. For example, since the 1960s the United States has imposed a tariff on light trucks from Japan. The result is that the United States imports few light trucks from Japan. You will see Japanese-named trucks, but most of these are produced in the United States. Many similar examples exist, and by following the tariff structure, you can gain a lot of insight into patterns of trade.

The issues involved with tariffs and quotas can be seen in a slightly different way by assuming that the country being considered is small relative to the world economy and that imports compete with domestic producers. The small-country assumption means that the supply from the world to this country is perfectly elastic (horizontal) at the world price, $2, as in Figure 10-5(a).

The world price of the good is unaffected by this country's supply. This assumption allows us to distinguish the world supply from domestic supply. In the absence of any trade restrictions, the world price of $2 would be the domestic price. Domestic low-cost suppliers would supply 100 units of the good at $2. The remaining 100 units demanded are being imported.

In Figure 10-5(a) I show the effect of a tariff of 50 cents placed on all imports. Since the world supply curve is perfectly elastic, all of this tax, shown by the shaded region, is borne by domestic consumers. Price rises to $2.50 and quantity demanded falls to 175. With a tariff, the rise in price will increase domestic quantity supplied from 100 to 125 and will reduce imports to 50. Now let's compare this situation with a quota of 50, shown in Figure 10-5(b). Under a quota of 50, the final price would be the same, but higher revenue would accrue to foreign and domestic producers rather than to the government. One final difference: Any increase in demand under a quota would

Q-3 How are tariffs like taxes? Demonstrate with a supply and demand curve.

FIGURE 10-4   The Effects of Tariffs and Quotas

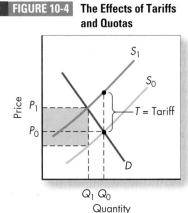

Tariffs and Quotas

Q-4 Why do importers prefer a quota to a tariff? Why does government prefer a tariff?

FIGURE 10-5 (A AND B)   **Tariffs and Quotas When the Domestic Country Is Small**

This exhibit shows the effects of a tariff in (**a**) and of a quota in (**b**) when the domestic country is small. The small-country assumption means that the world supply is perfectly elastic, in this case at $2.00 a unit. With a tariff of 50 cents, world supply shifts up by 50 cents. Domestic quantity demanded falls to 175 and domestic quantity supplied rises to 125. Foreign suppliers are left supplying the difference, 50 units. The domestic government collects revenue shown in the shaded area. The figure in (**b**) shows how the same result can be achieved with a quota of 50. Equilibrium price rises to $2.50. Domestic firms produce 125 units and consumers demand 175 units. The difference between the tariff and the quota is that, with a tariff, the domestic government collects the revenue from the higher price. With a quota, the benefits of the higher price accrue to the foreign and domestic producers.

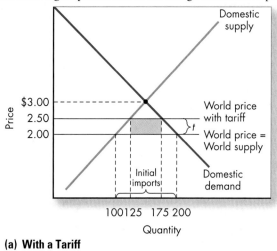

(a) With a Tariff

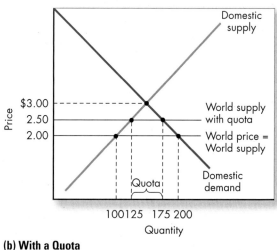

(b) With a Quota

result in higher prices because it would have to be filled by domestic producers. Under a tariff, any increase in demand would not affect price.

Voluntary Restraint Agreements

Voluntary restraint agreements are often not all that voluntary.

Imposing new tariffs and quotas is specifically ruled out by the WTO, but foreign countries know that WTO rules are voluntary and that, if a domestic industry brought sufficient political pressure on its government, the WTO rules would be forgotten. To avoid the imposition of new tariffs on their goods, countries often voluntarily restrict their exports. That's why Japan has, at times, agreed informally to limit the number of cars it exports to the United States.

The effect of such voluntary restraint agreements is similar to the effect of quotas: They directly limit the quantity of imports, increasing the price of the good and helping domestic producers. For example, when the United States encouraged Japan to impose "voluntary" quotas on exports of its cars to the United States, Toyota benefited from the quotas because it could price its limited supply of cars higher than it could if it sent in a large number of cars, so profit per car would be high. Since they faced less competition, U.S. car companies also benefited. They could increase their prices because Toyota had done so. As Chinese car companies develop in the next decade, we can expect similar pushes for Chinese voluntary restraints.

Embargoes

An embargo is a total restriction on import or export of a good.

An **embargo** is *a total restriction on the import or export of a good.* Embargoes are usually established for international political reasons rather than for primarily economic reasons.

An example was the U.S. embargo of trade with Iraq prior to the U.S. invasion in 2001. The U.S. government hoped that the embargo would so severely affect Iraq's economy that Saddam Hussein would lose political power. It did make life difficult for Iraqis, but it did not bring about the downfall of the Hussein government. The United States has imposed embargoes on Cuba, Iran, and Libya.

Regulatory Trade Restrictions

Tariffs, quotas, and embargoes are the primary *direct* methods to restrict international trade. There are also indirect methods that restrict trade in not-so-obvious ways; these are called **regulatory trade restrictions** (*government-imposed procedural rules that limit imports*). One type of regulatory trade restriction has to do with protecting the health and safety of a country's residents. For example, a country might restrict imports of all vegetables grown where certain pesticides are used, knowing full well that all other countries use those pesticides. The effect of such a regulation would be to halt the import of vegetables. Another example involves building codes. U.S. building codes require that plywood have fewer than, say, three flaws per sheet. Canadian building codes require that plywood have fewer than, say, five flaws per sheet. The different building codes are a nontariff barrier that makes trade in building materials between the United States and Canada difficult.

A second type of regulatory restriction involves making import and customs procedures so intricate and time-consuming that importers simply give up. For example, at one time France required all imported electronics to be individually inspected in Toulouse. Since Toulouse is a provincial city, far from any port and outside the normal route for imports after they enter France, the inspection process took months.

Some regulatory restrictions are imposed for legitimate reasons; others are designed simply to make importing more difficult and hence protect domestic producers from international competition. It's often hard to tell the difference. A good example of this difficulty began in 1988, when the EU disallowed all imports of meat from animals that had been fed growth-inducing hormones. As the box "Hormones and Economics" details, the debate continues.

Nationalistic Appeals and "Buy Domestic" Requirements

Finally, nationalistic appeals can help to restrict international trade. "Buy American" campaigns and Japanese xenophobia[1] are examples. Many Americans, given two products of equal appeal, except that one is made in the United States and one is made in a foreign country, would buy the U.S. product. To get around this tendency, foreign and U.S. companies often go to great lengths to get a MADE IN THE U.S.A. classification on goods they sell in the United States. For example, components for many autos are made in Japan but shipped to the United States and assembled in Ohio or Tennessee so that the finished car can be called an American product. These "Buy American" policies can even be requirements. For example, the U.S. government stimulus package of 2009 included a "Buy American" clause that required recipients to spend the money they received on American, not foreign, goods.

Reasons for Trade Restrictions

Let's now turn to a different question: If trade is beneficial, as it is in our example of I.T. in the previous chapter why do countries restrict trade?

---

[1]*Xenophobia* is a Greek word meaning "fear of foreigners." Pronounce the *x* like *z*.

Web Note 10.1
Sugar Regulation

Q-5 How might a country benefit from having an inefficient customs agency?

Some regulatory restrictions are imposed for legitimate reasons; others are designed simply to make importing more difficult.

Web Note 10.2
Buy American

Hormones and Economics

Trade restrictions, in practice, are often much more complicated than they seem in textbooks. Seldom does a country say, "We're limiting imports to protect our home producers." Instead the country explains the restrictions in a more politically acceptable way. Consider the fight between the European Union (EU) and the United States over U.S. meat exports. In 1988 the EU, in line with Union-wide internal requirements, banned imports of any meat from animals treated with growth-inducing hormones, which U.S. meat producers use extensively. The result: the EU banned the meat exported from the United States.

The EU claimed that it had imposed the ban only because of public health concerns. The United States claimed that the ban was actually a trade restriction, pointing out that its own residents ate this kind of meat with confidence because a U.S. government agency had certified that the levels of hormones in the meat were far below any danger level.

The United States retaliated against the EU by imposing 100 percent tariffs on Danish and West German hams, Italian tomatoes, and certain other foods produced by EU member nations. The EU threatened to respond by placing 100 percent tariffs on $100 million worth of U.S. walnuts and dried fruits, but instead entered into bilateral meetings with the United States. Those meetings allowed untreated meats into the EU for human consumption and treated meats that would be used as dog food. In response, the United States removed its retaliatory tariff on hams and tomato sauce, but retained its tariffs on many other goods. In the 1990s, Europe's dog population seemed to be growing exponentially as Europe's imports of "dog food" increased by leaps and bounds. In 1996 the United States asked the WTO to review the EU ban. It did so in 1997, finding in favor of the United States. The EU appealed and in 1999 the WTO stood by its earlier ruling and the United States reimposed the 100 percent tariffs. Since then, the EU has stood firm and has conducted studies that, it says, show the use of growth hormones to be unsafe, but the WTO continues to rule that they are safe. In 2004, the EU replaced its ban on U.S. beef with a provisional ban until it collects more information, and argued that this provisional ban met the WTO rules. The United States disagreed and continued its retaliatory tariffs. In January 2009, for example, the U.S. government placed a 300 percent tariff on Roquefort cheese as one of its retaliatory measures but quickly removed it temporarily. So the dispute continues more than 25 years after it started.

Which side is right in this dispute? The answer is far from obvious. Both the United States and the EU have potentially justifiable positions. As I said, trade restrictions are more complicated in reality than in textbooks.

Unequal Internal Distribution of the Gains from Trade

One reason is that the gains of trade are not equally distributed. In the example of the argument for trade discussed in a previous chapter, I.T. persuaded Saudi Arabia to specialize in the production of oil rather than food, and persuaded the United States to produce more food than oil. That means, of course, that some U.S. oil workers will have to become farmers, and in Saudi Arabia some farmers will have to become oil producers.

Often people don't want to make radical changes in the kind of work they do—they want to keep on producing what they're already producing. So when these people see the same kinds of goods that they produce coming into their country from abroad, they lobby to prevent the foreign competition.

Had I.T. been open about the difficulties of trading, he would have warned the countries that change is hard. It has very real costs that I.T. didn't point out when he made his offers. Economists generally favor free trade because the costs of trade are temporary, whereas gains from trade are permanent. Once the adjustment has been made, the costs will be gone but the benefits will still be there.

For most goods, the benefits for the large majority of the population so outweigh the costs to some individuals that, decided on a strict cost/benefit basis, international trade is still a deal you can't refuse. The table below lists economists' estimates of the cost to consumers of saving a job in some industries through trade restrictions.

Industry	Cost of Production (per job saved)
Footwear	$505,000
Sugar	213,000
Apparel	181,000
Dairy	167,000
Canned tuna	43,000

Source: *Economic Effects of Significant Import Restraints,* U.S. International Trade Commission (www.usitc.gov).

With benefits so outweighing costs, it would seem that transition costs could be forgotten. But they can't.

Benefits of trade are generally widely scattered among the entire population. In contrast, costs of free trade often fall on small groups of people who loudly oppose the particular free trade that hurts them. This creates a political push against free trade.

It isn't only in the United States that the push for trade restrictions focuses on the small costs and not on the large benefits. For example, the European Union (EU) places large restrictions on food imports from nonmember nations. If the EU were to remove those barriers, food prices in EU countries would decline significantly—it is estimated that meat prices alone would fall by about 65 percent. Consumers would benefit, but farmers would be hurt. The farmers, however, have the political clout to see that the costs are considered and the benefits aren't. The result: The EU places high duties on foreign agricultural products.

The cost to society of relaxing trade restrictions has led to a number of programs to assist those who are hurt. Such programs are called **trade adjustment assistance programs**—*programs designed to compensate losers for reductions in trade restrictions.*

Governments have tried to use trade adjustment assistance to facilitate free trade, but they've found that it's enormously difficult to limit the adjustment assistance to those who are actually hurt by international trade. As soon as people find that there's assistance for people injured by trade, they're likely to try to show that they too have been hurt and deserve assistance. Losses from free trade become exaggerated and magnified. Instead of only a small portion of the gains from trade being needed for trade adjustment assistance, much more is demanded—often even more than the gains.

Telling people who claim to be hurt that they aren't really being hurt isn't good politics. That's why offering trade adjustment assistance as a way to relieve the pressure to restrict trade is a deal many governments can refuse.

Haggling by Companies over the Gains from Trade

Many naturally advantageous bargains aren't consummated because each side is pushing for a larger share of the gains from trade than the other side thinks should be allotted.

To see how companies haggling over the gains of trade can restrict trade, let's reconsider the original deal that I.T. proposed in an earlier chapter explaining comparative advantage. I.T. got 380 tons of food and 380 barrels of oil. The United States got an additional 100 tons of food and 60 barrels of oil. Saudi Arabia got an additional 100 barrels of oil and 60 tons of food.

Benefits of trade are generally widely scattered among the entire population. In contrast, costs of free trade often fall on specific small groups.

Q-6　Who is likely to be more vocal when lobbying government to impose trade restrictions: producers or consumers? Explain your answer.

Telling people who claim to be hurt that they aren't really being hurt isn't good politics.

Suppose the Saudis had said, "Why should we be getting only 100 barrels of oil and 60 tons of food when I.T. is getting 380 barrels of oil and 380 tons of food? We want an additional 300 tons of food and another 300 barrels of oil, and we won't deal unless we get them." Similarly, the United States might have said, "We want an additional 300 tons of food and an additional 300 barrels of oil, and we won't go through with the deal unless we get them." If either the U.S. or the Saudi Arabian company that was involved in the trade for its country (or both) takes this position, I.T. might just walk—no deal. Tough bargaining positions can make it almost impossible to achieve gains from trade.

Strategic bargaining can lead to higher gains from trade for the side that drives the hardest bargain, but it also can make the deal fall through.

The side that drives the hardest bargain gets the most gains from the bargain, but it also risks making the deal fall through. Such strategic bargaining goes on all the time. **Strategic bargaining** means *demanding a larger share of the gains from trade than you can reasonably expect.* If you're successful, you get the lion's share; if you're not successful, the deal falls apart and everyone is worse off.

Haggling by Countries over Trade Restrictions

Another type of trade bargaining that often limits trade is bargaining between countries. Trade restrictions and the threat of trade restrictions play an important role in that kind of haggling. Sometimes countries must go through with trade restrictions that they really don't want to impose, just to make their threats credible.

Q-7 True or false? In strategic trade bargaining, it is sometimes reasonable to be unreasonable. Explain.

Once one country has imposed trade restrictions, other countries attempt to get those restrictions reduced by threatening to increase their own restrictions. Again, to make the threat credible, sometimes countries must impose or increase trade restrictions simply to show they're willing to do so. For example, China allowed significant illegal copying of U.S. software without paying royalties. The United States put pressure on China to stop such copying and felt that China was not responding effectively. To force compliance, the United States made a list of Chinese goods that it threatened with 100 percent tariffs unless China complied. The United States did not want to put on these restrictions but felt that it would have more strategic bargaining power if it threatened to do so. Hence the name **strategic trade policies**—*threatening to implement tariffs to bring about a reduction in tariffs or some other concession from the other country.*

Strategic trade policies are threats to implement tariffs to bring about a reduction in tariffs or some other concession from the other country.

Ultimately, strategic bargaining power depends on negotiators' skills and the underlying gains from trade that a country would receive. A country that would receive only a small portion of the gains from trade is in a much stronger bargaining position than a country that would receive significant gains. It's easier for the former to walk away from trade.

The potential problem with strategic trade policies is that they can backfire. One rule of strategic bargaining is that the other side must believe that you'll go through with your threat. Thus, strategic trade policy can lead a country that actually supports free trade to impose trade restrictions, just to show how strongly it believes in free trade.

Specialized Production

My discussion of comparative advantage took as a given that one country was inherently more productive than another country in producing certain goods. But when one looks at trading patterns, it's often not at all clear why particular countries have a productive advantage in certain goods. There's no inherent reason for Switzerland to specialize in the production of watches or for South Korea to specialize in the production of cars. Much in trade cannot be explained by inherent comparative advantages due to resource endowments. If they don't have inherent advantages, why are countries and places often so good at producing what they specialize in? Two important explanations are *learning by doing* and *economies of scale.*

The Antiglobalization Forces

Often when the World Trade Organization or a similar type of organization promoting free trade hosts a meeting, protests (sometimes violent ones) are held by a loosely organized collection of groups opposing globalization. The goals of these groups are varied. Some argue that trade hurts developed countries such as the United States; others argue that it hurts developing countries by exploiting poor workers so that Westerners can get luxuries cheaply. Still others argue against a more subtle Western economic imperialism in which globalization spreads Western cultural values and undermines developing countries' social structures.

Each of these arguments has some appeal, although making the first two simultaneously is difficult because it says that voluntary trade hurts both parties to the trade. But the arguments have had little impact on the views of most policy makers and economists.

Supporting free trade does not mean that globalization has no costs. It does have costs, but many of the costs associated with free trade are really the result of technological changes. The reality is that technological developments, such as those in telecommunications and transportation, are pushing countries closer together and will involve difficult social and cultural changes, regardless of whether trade is free or not. Restricting trade might temporarily slow these changes but is unlikely to stop them.

Most empirical studies have found that, with regard to material goods, the workers in developing countries involved in trade are generally better off than those not involved in trade. That's why most developing countries work hard to encourage companies to move production facilities into their countries. From a worker's perspective, earning $4 a day can look quite good when the alternative is earning $3 a day. Would the worker rather earn $10 a day? Of course, but the higher the wages in a given country, the less likely it is that firms are going to locate production there.

Many economists are sympathetic to various antiglobalization arguments, but they often become frustrated at the lack of clarity of the antiglobalization groups' views. To oppose something is not enough; to effect positive change, one must both (1) understand how the thing one opposes works and (2) have a realistic plan for a better alternative.

LEARNING BY DOING   **Learning by doing** means *becoming better at a task the more often you perform it.* Take watches in Switzerland. Initially production of watches in Switzerland may have been a coincidence; the person who started the watch business happened to live there. But then people in the area became skilled in producing watches. Their skill made it attractive for other watch companies to start up. As additional companies moved in, more and more members of the labor force became skilled at watchmaking and word went out that Swiss watches were the best in the world. That reputation attracted even more producers, so Switzerland became the watchmaking capital of the world. Had the initial watch production occurred in Austria, not Switzerland, Austria might be the watch capital of the world.

When there's learning by doing, it's much harder to attribute inherent comparative advantage to a country. One must always ask: Does country A have an inherent comparative advantage, or does it simply have more experience? Once country B gets the experience, will country A's comparative advantage disappear? If it will, then country B has a strong reason to limit trade with country A in order to give its own workers time to catch up as they learn by doing.

ECONOMIES OF SCALE   In determining whether an inherent comparative advantage exists, a second complication is **economies of scale**—*the situation in which costs per unit of output fall as output increases.* Many manufacturing industries (such as steel and autos) exhibit economies of scale. The existence of significant economies of

Learning by doing means becoming better at a task the more you perform it.

In economies of scale, costs per unit of output go down as output increases.

217

Q-8 Is it efficient for a country to maintain a trade barrier in an industry that exhibits economies of scale?

The infant industry argument says that with initial protection, an industry will be able to become competitive.

scale means that it makes sense (that is, it lowers costs) for one country to specialize in one good and another country to specialize in another good. But who should specialize in what is unclear. Producers in a country can, and generally do, argue that if only the government would establish barriers, they would be able to lower their costs per unit and eventually sell at lower costs than foreign producers.

Most countries recognize the importance of learning by doing and economies of scale. A variety of trade restrictions are based on these two phenomena. The most common expression of the learning-by-doing and economies-of-scale insights is the **infant industry argument,** which is that *with initial protection, an industry will be able to become competitive.* Countries use this argument to justify many trade restrictions. They argue, "You may now have a comparative advantage, but that's simply because you've been at it longer, or are experiencing significant economies of scale. We need trade restrictions on our _____ industry to give it a chance to catch up. Once an infant industry grows up, then we can talk about eliminating the restrictions."

This infant industry argument also has been used to justify tariffs on new high-tech products such as solar panels. U.S. firms have pushed for tariffs on Chinese solar panels so that they can develop the technology here in the United States rather than have the technology developed in China.

Macroeconomic Costs of Trade

The comparative advantage argument for free trade assumes that a country's resources are fully utilized. When countries don't have full employment, imports can decrease domestic aggregate demand and increase unemployment. Exports can stimulate domestic aggregate demand and decrease unemployment. Thus, when an economy is in a recession, there is a strong macroeconomic reason to limit imports and encourage exports. These macroeconomic effects of free trade play an important role in the public's view of imports and exports. When a country is in a recession, pressure to impose trade restrictions increases substantially. We saw this in 2009 when, faced with the job losses due to the serious recession, there was serious pressure to design programs to keep spending in the United States where it would create jobs and not be spent on imports that would create jobs for other countries.

National Security

Countries often justify trade restrictions on grounds of national security. These restrictions take two forms:

1. Export restrictions on strategic materials and defense-related goods.
2. Import restrictions on defense-related goods. For example, in a war we don't want to be dependent on oil from abroad.

For a number of goods, national security considerations make sense. For example, the United States restricts the sale of certain military items to countries that may be fighting the United States someday. The problem is where to draw the line about goods having a national security consideration. Should countries protect domestic agriculture? All high-technology items, since they might be useful in weapons? All chemicals? Steel? When a country makes a national security argument for trade, we must be careful to consider whether a domestic political reason may be lurking behind that argument.

International Politics

International politics frequently provides another reason for trade restrictions. Over the past decades, the United States restricted trade with Cuba to punish that country for trying to extend its Marxist political and economic policies to other Latin American

Reasons for restricting trade include:

1. Unequal internal distribution of the gains from trade.
2. Haggling by companies over the gains from trade.
3. Haggling by countries over trade restrictions.
4. Specialized production: learning by doing and economies of scale.
5. Macroeconomic aspects of trade.
6. National security.
7. International politics.
8. Increased revenue brought in by tariffs.

countries. The United States also has trade restrictions on Iran for its reluctance to limit its nuclear enrichment activities. The list can be extended, but you get the argument: Trade helps you, so we'll hurt you by stopping trade until you do what we want. So what if it hurts us too? It'll hurt you more than it hurts us.

Increased Revenue Brought in by Tariffs

A final argument made for one particular type of trade restriction—a tariff—is that tariffs bring in revenues. In the 19th century, tariffs were the U.S. government's primary source of revenue. They are less important as a source of revenue today for many developed countries because those countries have instituted other forms of taxes. However, tariffs remain a primary source of revenue for many developing countries. They're relatively easy to collect and are paid by people rich enough to afford imports. These countries justify many of their tariffs with the argument that they need the revenues.

Why Economists Generally Oppose Trade Restrictions

Each of the preceding arguments for trade restrictions has some validity, but most economists discount them and support free trade. The reason is that, in their considered judgment, the harm done by trade restrictions outweighs the benefits. This is true, even though, from the U.S. perspective, transferable comparative advantages are likely to place significant pressures on firms to outsource U.S. jobs abroad, and hold down U.S. wages in the coming decades. Most economists believe that the United States will be better off if it allows free trade.

Economists generally oppose trade restrictions because:

1. From a global perspective, free trade increases total output.
2. International trade provides competition for domestic companies.
3. Restrictions based on national security are often abused or evaded.
4. Trade restrictions are addictive.

FREE TRADE INCREASES TOTAL OUTPUT   Economists' first argument for free trade is that, viewed from a global perspective, free trade increases total output. From a national perspective, economists agree that particular instances of trade restrictions may actually help one nation, even as most other nations are hurt. But they argue that the country imposing trade restrictions can benefit *only if the other country doesn't retaliate* with trade restrictions of its own. Retaliation is the rule, not the exception, however, and when there is retaliation, trade restrictions cause both countries to lose. Thus, if the United States were to place a tariff on goods from China, those aspects of production that depend on Chinese goods would be hurt, and, as I discussed above, there are many such goods. Moreover, China would likely place tariffs on goods from the United States, hurting both countries. Such tariffs would cut overall production, making both countries worse off.

INTERNATIONAL TRADE PROVIDES COMPETITION   A second reason most economists support free trade is that trade restrictions reduce international competition. International competition is desirable because it forces domestic companies to stay on their toes. If trade restrictions on imports are imposed, domestic companies don't work as hard and therefore become less efficient.

For example, in the 1950s and 1960s, the United States imposed restrictions on imported steel. U.S. steel industries responded to this protection by raising their prices and channeling profits from their steel production into other activities. By the 1970s, the U.S. steel industry was using outdated equipment to produce overpriced steel. Instead of making the steel industry stronger, restrictions made it a flabby, uncompetitive industry.

In the 1980s and 1990s, the U.S. steel industry became less and less profitable. Larger mills closed or consolidated, while nonunion minimills, which made new steel out of scrap steel, did well. By the late 1990s, minimills accounted for 45 percent of total U.S. steel production. In 2002 it looked as if a number of larger mills were going to declare bankruptcy, and enormous pressure was placed on the federal government to bail them out by taking over their pension debt and instituting tariffs. The U.S. government responded by imposing 20–30 percent tariffs on foreign steel imports. Most economists opposed the tariffs and pointed out that they were unlikely to lead to a rebuilding of the U.S. steel industry because other countries had a comparative advantage in steel production. Moreover, other countries would retaliate with tariffs on U.S. goods. Despite their opposition, the tariffs were instituted. Major U.S. trading partners—including EU countries, Japan, and China—responded by threatening to implement tariffs on U.S. goods worth about $335 million; in 2003, the U.S. government withdrew the tariffs. That same year. U.S. Steel, which was the number two producer of steel in the United States, closed. Today, U.S. steel companies produce about 6 percent of total world steel, down from 20 percent in 1970.

The benefits of international competition are not restricted to mature industries like steel; they can also accrue to young industries wherever they appear. Economists dispose of the infant industry argument by referencing the historical record. In theory the argument makes sense. But very few of the infant industries protected by trade restrictions have ever grown up. What tends to happen instead is that infant industries become dependent on the trade restrictions and use political pressure to keep that protection. As a result, they often remain immature and internationally uncompetitive. Most economists would support the infant industry argument only if the trade restrictions included definite conditions under which the restrictions would end.

RESTRICTIONS BASED ON NATIONAL SECURITY ARE OFTEN ABUSED OR EVADED

Most economists agree with the national security argument for export restrictions on goods that are directly war related. Selling bombs to Iran, whom the United States has called a member of the Axis of Evil, doesn't make much sense. Economists point out that the argument is often carried far beyond goods directly related to national security. For example, in the 1980s the United States restricted exports of sugar-coated cereals to the Soviet Union purportedly for reasons of national security. Sugar-frosted flakes may be great, but they were unlikely to help the Soviet Union in a war.

Another argument that economists give against the national security rationale is that trade restrictions on military sales can often be evaded. Countries simply have another country buy the goods for them. Such third-party sales—called *transshipments*—are common in international trade and limit the effectiveness of any absolute trade restrictions for national security purposes.

Economists also argue that by fostering international cooperation, international trade makes war less likely—a significant contribution to national security.

TRADE RESTRICTIONS ARE ADDICTIVE

Economists' final argument against trade restrictions is: Yes, some restrictions might benefit a country, but almost no country can limit its restrictions to the beneficial ones. Trade restrictions are addictive—the more you have, the more you want. Thus, a majority of economists take the position that the best response to such addictive policies is "Just say no."

Institutions Supporting Free Trade

As I have stated throughout the text, economists generally like markets and favor trade being as free as possible. They argue that trade allows specialization and the division of labor. When each country follows its comparative advantage, production is more efficient and the production possibility curve shifts out. These views mean that most economists, liberal and conservative alike, generally oppose international trade restrictions.

Very few of the infant industries protected by trade restrictions have ever grown up.

www Web Note 10.3
Thumbs Up or
Down?

Yes, some restrictions might benefit a country, but almost no country can limit its restrictions to the beneficial ones.

www Web Note 10.4
Promoting Trade

Dumping

The WTO allows countries to impose trade restrictions on imports if they can show that the goods are being dumped. *Dumping* is selling a good in a foreign country at a lower price than in the country where it's produced. On the face of it, who could complain about someone who wants to sell you a good cheaply? Why not just take advantage of the bargain price? The first objection is the learning-by-doing argument. To stay competitive, a country must keep on producing. Dumping by another country can force domestic producers out of business. Having eliminated the competition, the foreign producer has the field to itself and can raise the price. Thus, dumping can be a form of predatory pricing.

The second argument against dumping involves the short-term macroeconomic and political effects it can have on the importing country. Even if one believes that dumping is not a preliminary to predatory pricing, it can displace workers in the importing country, causing political pressure on that government to institute trade restrictions. If that country's economy is in a recession, the resulting unemployment will have substantial macroeconomic repercussions, so pressure for trade restrictions will be amplified.

Despite political pressures to restrict trade, governments have generally tried to follow economists' advice and have entered into a variety of international agreements and organizations. The most important is the World Trade Organization (WTO), which has over 150 members, and is the successor to the General Agreement on Tariffs and Trade (GATT). You will still occasionally see references to GATT, even though the WTO has taken its place. One of the differences between the WTO and GATT is that the WTO includes some enforcement mechanisms.

Q-9 What are two important international economic organizations?

Achieving agreement on trade barrier reductions is politically difficult, as is demonstrated by the latest WTO negotiations, called the Doha Development Round. Begun in 2001, it was meant to lead to fairer trade rules for developing countries, especially in agriculture. The Round did not go well; the United States and Europe were unwilling to eliminate subsidies to their farmers that the developing countries said made it impossible for them to compete fairly, and hence would not reduce their tariffs on manufactured goods. The Round was never concluded.

The push for free trade has a geographic dimension, which includes **free trade associations**—*groups of countries that have reduced or eliminated trade barriers among themselves.* The European Union (EU) is the most famous free trade association. All barriers to trade among the EU's member countries were removed in 1992, and over the next 20 years the EU expanded significantly. In 1993, the United States and Canada agreed to enter into a similar free trade union, and they, together with Mexico, created the North American Free Trade Association (NAFTA). Under NAFTA, tariffs and other trade barriers among these countries are being gradually reduced. Some other trading associations include Mercosur (among South American countries) and ASEAN (among Southeast Asian countries).

A free trade association is a group of countries that allows free trade among its members and puts up common barriers against all other countries' goods.

Economists have mixed reactions to free trade associations. They see free trade as beneficial, but they are concerned about the possibility that these regional free trade associations will impose significant trade restrictions on nonmember countries. They also believe that bilateral negotiations between member nations will replace multilateral efforts among members and nonmembers. Whether the net effect of these bilateral negotiations is positive or negative remains to be seen.

Q-10 What is economists' view of limited free trade associations such as the EU or NAFTA?

Groups of other countries have loose trading relationships because of cultural or historical reasons. These loose trading relationships are sometimes called trading zones. For example, many European countries maintain close trading ties with many of their former colonies in Africa where they fit into a number of overlapping trading zones. European companies tend to see that central area as their turf. The United States has close ties in Latin America, making the Western hemisphere another trading zone. Another example of a trading zone is that of Japan and its economic ties with other Far East countries; Japanese companies often see that area as their commercial domain.

These trading zones overlap, sometimes on many levels. For instance, Australia and England, Portugal and Brazil, and the United States and Saudi Arabia are tied together for historical or political reasons, and those ties lead to increased trade between them that seems to deviate from the above trading zones. Similarly, as companies become more and more global, it is harder and harder to associate companies with particular countries. Let me give an example: Do you know who the largest exporters of cars from the United States are? The answer is: Japanese automobile companies! Thus, there is no hard-and-fast specification of trading zones, and knowing history and politics is important to understanding many of the relationships.

One way countries strengthen trading relationships among groups of countries is through a most-favored-nation status. The term **most-favored nation** refers to *a country that will be charged as low a tariff on its exports as any other country.* Thus, if the United States lowers tariffs on goods imported from Japan, which has most-favored-nation status with the United States, it must lower tariffs on those same types of goods imported from any other country with most-favored-nation status.

A most-favored nation is a country that will pay as low a tariff on its exports as will any other country.

Conclusion

The difficulties that globalization and trade bring to a country—the effect on income distribution, and the wrenching structural changes it requires—lead many laypeople to support trade restrictions such as tariffs, quotas, and indeed anything to protect domestic jobs. Such policies might alleviate some short-run problems, but they ultimately will be unlikely to work. Not only will other countries retaliate; they will also take advantage of trade. So if the United States closes off trade with China, other countries will emerge as competitors.

The problem comes when we don't face up to those problems and don't deal with the political problems that an expansion of trade creates. The United States has avoided dealing with these problems for the last 20 years, and the problems have built up. The result is the current high unemployment and sluggish economic growth in the United States. The large trade deficits run up over the past 20 years have given us great benefits, but those eventually will end. How we deal with that ending will play a key role in determining the course of the U.S. economy over the next decade.

Summary

- The nature of trade is continually changing. The United States is importing more and more high-tech goods and services from India and China and other East Asian countries.   *(LO10-1)*

- Outsourcing is a type of trade. Outsourcing is a larger phenomenon today compared to 30 years ago because China and India are so large, enormous outsourcing is possible.   *(LO10-1)*

- Trade restrictions include tariffs and quotas, embargoes, voluntary restraint agreements, regulatory trade restrictions, and nationalistic appeals.   *(LO10-2)*

- Reasons that countries impose trade restrictions include unequal internal distribution of the gains from trade, haggling by companies over the gains from trade, haggling by countries over trade restrictions, learning by doing and economies of scale, macroeconomic costs of trade, national security, international political reasons, and increased revenue brought in by tariffs.   *(LO10-3)*

- Economists generally oppose trade restrictions because of the history of trade restrictions and their understanding of the advantages of free trade. *(LO10-3)*
- The World Trade Organization is an international organization committed to reducing trade barriers. *(LO10-4)*

- Free trade associations help trade by reducing barriers to trade among member nations. Free trade associations could hinder trade by building up barriers to trade with nations outside the association; negotiations among members could replace multilateral efforts to reduce trade restrictions among members and nonmembers. *(LO10-4)*

Key Terms

economies of scale *(217)*
embargo *(212)*
free trade association *(221)*
General Agreement on Tariffs and Trade (GATT) *(211)*

infant industry argument *(218)*
learning by doing *(217)*
most-favored nation *(222)*
quota *(211)*

regulatory trade restriction *(213)*
strategic bargaining *(216)*
strategic trade policy *(216)*
tariff *(210)*

trade adjustment assistance program *(215)*
World Trade Organization (WTO) *(211)*

Questions and Exercises

1. How important is international trade in terms of its relationship to total U.S. production? What does this suggest about the importance of trade policies relative to other countries? *(LO10-1)*

2. Which countries are the two greatest trading partners for the United States? With which countries is trade rapidly increasing? *(LO10-1)*

3. Demonstrate graphically how the effects of a tariff differ from the effects of a quota. *(LO10-2)*

4. How do the effects of voluntary restraint agreements differ from the effects of a tariff? *(LO10-2)*

5. The world price of textiles is P_w, as in the accompanying figure of the domestic supply and demand for textiles.

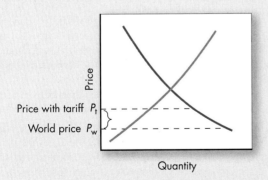

The government imposes a tariff t, to protect the domestic producers. For this tariff: *(LO10-2)*
a. Label the revenue gains to domestic producers.
b. Label the revenue to government.
c. Label the costs to domestic producers.
d. Are the gains to domestic producers greater than the costs? Why?

6. In 1964 President Lyndon B. Johnson imposed the Chicken Tax—a 25 percent tax on all imported light trucks in retaliation for a tariff placed by Germany on chickens imported from the United States. The light-truck tariff hurt Volkswagen van sales. Were these tariffs good or bad from the following perspectives? *(LO10-2)*
a. The U.S. government.
b. German consumers of chickens.
c. U.S. chicken producers.
d. U.S. light truck producers.
e. Economists.

7. On January 1, 2005, quotas on clothing imports to the United States first instituted in the 1960s to protect the U.S. garment industry were eliminated. *(LO10-2)*
a. Demonstrate graphically how this change affected equilibrium price and quantity of imported garments.
b. Demonstrate graphically how U.S. consumers benefited from the end of the quota system.
c. What was the likely effect on profits of foreign companies that sold clothing in the U.S. market?

8. What are three reasons countries restrict trade? Are they justified? *(LO10-3)*

9. Why would a country have trade assistance programs? What makes them difficult to implement? *(LO10-3)*

10. How would a credible threat of trade restrictions lead to lower trade restrictions? *(LO10-3)*

11. How are economies of scale, comparative advantage, and trade restrictions related? *(LO10-3)*

12. Name three reasons economists support free trade. *(LO10-3)*

13. Why would a country want to be a most-favored nation? Why might it not want to be a most-favored nation? (*LO10-4*)

14. What is the relationship between GATT and WTO? (*LO10-4*)

Questions from Alternative Perspectives

1. Federic Bastiat wrote that "government is the great fiction through which everybody endeavors to live at the expense of everybody else." Is this a correct way to understand the fight about tariffs? (Austrian)

2. Federic Bastiat wrote: "It seems to me that this is theoretically right, for whatever the question under discussion— whether religious, philosophical, political, or economic; whether it concerns prosperity, morality, equality, right, justice, progress, responsibility, cooperation, property, labor, trade, capital, wages, taxes, population, finance, or government—at whatever point on the scientific horizon I begin my researches, I invariably reach this one conclusion: The solution to the problems of human relationships is to be found in liberty." What is problematic with this view? (Radical)

3. Federic Bastiat wrote "when goods do not cross borders, soldiers will." Discuss. (Religious)

4. Who has benefited most from free trade? Who has been hurt most by it? Does that match the positions the various groups have about their support for free trade? Which group do economists align themselves with? Why? (Post-Keynesian)

5. The text presents free trade as advantageous for developing countries. However, in its period of most rapid development, the half century following the Civil War, the United States imposed tariffs on imports that averaged around 40 percent, a level higher than those in all but one of today's developing economies.
   a. Why did so many of today's industrialized countries not follow those policies as they were developing?
   b. What does this insight into economic history suggest about the doctrine of free trade and whose interests it serves? (Radical)

Issues to Ponder

1. How does considering trade in the broader cultural context change one's analysis?

2. One of the basic economic laws is "the law of one price." It says that given certain assumptions one would expect that if free trade is allowed, the price of goods in countries should converge.
   a. Can you list what three of those assumptions likely are?
   b. Should the law of one price hold for labor also? Why or why not?
   c. Should it hold for capital more so or less so than for labor? Why?

3. Suggest an equitable method of funding trade adjustment assistance programs.
   a. Why is it equitable?
   b. What problems might a politician have in implementing such a method?

4. When the United States placed a temporary price floor on tomatoes imported from Mexico, U.S. trade representative Mickey Kantor said, "The agreement will provide strong relief to the tomato growers in Florida and other states, and help preserve jobs in the industry." What costs did Americans bear from the price floor?

5. Mexico exports many vegetables to the United States. These vegetables are grown using chemicals that are not allowed in U.S. vegetable agriculture. Should the United States restrict imports of Mexican vegetables? Why or why not?

6. The U.S. government taxes U.S. companies for their overseas profits, but it allows them to deduct from their U.S. taxable income the taxes that they pay abroad and interest on loans funding operations abroad, with no limits on the amount deducted.
   a. Is it possible that the overseas profit tax produces no net revenue?
   b. What would you suggest to the government about this tax if its purpose were to increase corporate income tax revenue?
   c. Why might the government keep this tax even if it were not collecting any net revenue?

7. In the 1930s Clair Wilcox of Swarthmore College organized a petition by economists "that any measure which provided for a general upward revision of tariff rates be denied passage by Congress, or if passed, be vetoed." It was signed by one-third of all economists in the United States at the time, of all political persuasions. A month later, the Smoot-Hawley Tariff was passed.
   a. Why did economists oppose the tariff?
   b. Demonstrate the effect of the tariff on the price of goods.

c. How would the tariff help the economy if other countries did not institute a retaliatory tariff?

d. What would be the effect on the macroeconomy if other countries did institute a retaliatory tariff?

8. If you were economic adviser to a country that was following your advice about trade restrictions and that country fell into a recession, would you change your advice? Why, or why not?

Answers to Margin Questions

1. The type of goods being imported has changed from primarily low-tech goods to technologically advanced goods. (*p. 207; LO10-1*)

2. A debtor nation will not necessarily be running a trade deficit. *Debt* refers to accumulated past deficits. If a country had accumulated large deficits in the past, it could run a surplus now but still be a debtor nation. (*p. 210; LO10-1*)

3. Like tariffs, taxes shift the supply of a good up by the amount of the tariff. Equilibrium quantity falls and equilibrium price rises. (*p. 211; LO10-2*)

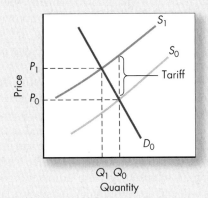

4. Importers prefer quotas because they receive higher prices. Government prefers a tariff because the tariff brings in revenue for government. (*p. 211; LO10-2*)

5. An inefficient customs agency can have the same effect as a trade restriction, and if trade restrictions would help the country, then it is possible that an inefficient customs agency could also help the country. (*p. 213; LO10-2*)

6. Production is concentrated among a small number of firms that stand to benefit from trade restrictions and thus are more likely to combine efforts to lobby government. Because the number of consumers is large and the cost of trade restrictions to each relatively small, consumers have less incentive to take joint action. (*p. 215; LO10-3*)

7. True. In strategic trade bargaining it is sometimes reasonable to be unreasonable. The belief of the other bargainer that you will be unreasonable leads you to be able to extract larger gains from trade. Of course, this leads to the logical paradox that if "unreasonable" is "reasonable," unreasonable really is reasonable, so it is only reasonable to be reasonable. Sorting out that last statement can be left for a philosophy or logic class. (*p. 216; LO10-3*)

8. Whether or not it is efficient for a country to maintain barriers to trade in an industry that exhibits economies of scale depends upon the marginal costs and marginal benefits of maintaining those barriers. Having significant economies of scale does mean that average costs of production will be lower at higher levels of production; however, trade restrictions might mean that the industry is able to inflate its costs. (*p. 218; LO10-3*)

9. Two important international economic organizations are the WTO and GATT, which was replaced by the WTO. (*p. 221; LO10-4*)

10. Most economists have a mixed view of limited free trade associations such as NAFTA or the EU. While they see free trade as beneficial, they are concerned about the possibility that these limited trade associations will impose trade restrictions on nonmember countries. Whether the net effect of these will be positive or negative is a complicated issue. (*p. 221; LO10-4*)

Production and Cost Analysis I

After reading this chapter, you should be able to:

LO11-1 Explain the role of the firm in economic analysis.

LO11-2 Describe the production process in the short run.

LO11-3 Calculate fixed costs, variable costs, marginal costs, total costs, average fixed costs, average variable costs, and average total costs.

LO11-4 Distinguish the various cost curves and describe the relationships among them.

The ability of market economies to supply material goods and services to members of their societies is one of the strongest arguments for using the market as a means of organizing society. Just consider the coordination needed to provide you a freshly brewed Starbucks latte in the morning. Trees had to be harvested and made into paper; the paper had to be processed and made into cups and printed with the Starbucks logo. Coffee beans had to be grown, picked, roasted, and ground. The espresso maker parts had to be made and assembled. The ingredients were produced in 20 different countries and shipped to a Starbucks near you at the right time and in the right quantities. Finally, a barista had to be paid enough to prepare coffee when people want it—on the way to *their* jobs, in which they were producing goods that people from many other countries will end up consuming. Somehow markets are able to channel individuals' imagination, creativity, and drive into the production of material goods and services that other people want. They do this by giving people incentives to supply goods and services to the market.

Ultimately all supply comes from individuals. Individuals control the factors of production such as land, labor, and capital. Why do individuals supply these factors to the market? Because they want something in return. This means that industry's ability to supply goods depends on individuals' willingness to supply the factors of production they control. This connection was obvious in the formerly socialist countries such as Russia when consumer goods were often unavailable. People in those countries stopped working (supplying their labor). They reasoned: Why supply our labor if there's nothing to get in return?

The analysis of supply is more complicated than the analysis of demand. In the supply process, people first offer their factors of production to the market. Then the factors are transformed by firms, such as GM or IBM, into goods that consumers want. **Production** is the name given to that *transformation of factors into goods and services.*

To simplify the analysis, economists separate out the consideration of the supply of factors of production (considered in detail in a later chapter) from the supply of produced goods. This allows us to assume that the prices of factors of production are constant, which simplifies the analysis of the supply of produced goods enormously. There's no problem with doing this as long as you remember that behind any produced good are individuals' factor supplies. Ultimately people, not firms, are responsible for supply.

Even with the analysis so simplified, there's still a lot to cover—so much, in fact, that we devote two chapters (this chapter and the next) to considering production, costs, and supply. In this chapter, I introduce you to the production process and short-run cost analysis. Then, in the next chapter, I focus on long-run costs and how cost analysis is used in the real world.

The Role of the Firm

With goods that already exist, such as housing and labor, the law of supply is rather intuitive. Their supply to the market depends on people's opportunity costs of keeping their houses and time for themselves and of supplying them to the market. But many of the things we buy (such as cell phones, cars, and jackets) don't automatically exist; they must be produced. The supply of such goods depends on production.

A key concept in production is the firm. A **firm** is *an economic institution that transforms factors of production into goods and services.* A firm (1) organizes factors of production and/or (2) produces goods and/or (3) sells produced goods to individuals, businesses, or government.

Which combination of activities a firm will undertake depends on the cost of undertaking each activity relative to the cost of subcontracting the work out to another firm. Some firms don't have a physical location and don't "produce" anything; they simply subcontract out all production. An example is Perdue chickens. Perdue does not grow any chickens itself. It hires farmers to grow chickens. It provides the farmers with chicks and a detailed set of directions about how to raise them into chickens. Perdue then hires another company to pick up the adult chickens for slaughter, puts its label on the processed chickens, and ships them to supermarkets. While most firms are not totally virtual, more and more of the organizational structures of businesses are being separated from the production process. As cost structures change because of technological advances such as the Internet, an increasing number of well-known firms will likely concentrate on organizational instead of production activities.

> Firms:
> 1. Organize factors of production, and/or
> 2. Produce goods and services, and/or
> 3. Sell produced goods and services.

> **Web Note 11.1**
> **Virtual Firms**

> More and more of the organizational structures of business are being separated from the production process.

Firms Maximize Profit

Economists assume that firms maximize profit. Profit is defined as follows:

Profit = *Total revenue − Total cost*

In accounting, total revenue equals total sales times price; if a firm sells 1,000 pairs of earrings at $5 each, its total revenue is $5,000. For an accountant, total costs are the wages paid to labor, rent paid to owners of capital, interest paid to lenders, and actual payments to other factors of production. If the firm paid $2,000 to employees to make the earrings and $1,000 for the materials, rent, and interest, total cost is $3,000.

In determining what to include in total revenue and total costs, accountants focus on such explicit revenues and explicit costs. That's because they must have quantifiable measures that go into a firm's income statement. For this reason, you can think of *accounting profit* as explicit revenue less explicit cost. The accounting profit for the earring firm described above is $2,000.

Economists have different measures of revenues and costs and hence have a different measure of profit. Economists include in revenue and costs both explicit and implicit costs and revenues. Their measure of profit is both explicit and implicit revenue less both explicit and implicit costs.

> Accounting focuses on explicit costs and revenues; economics focuses on both explicit and implicit costs and revenues.

Transaction Costs and the Internet

In Chapter 3, we discussed the types of firms that exist in real life, and explained how they are one of the most important of the economic institutions. They are the organizations that translate factors of production into consumer goods. Types of real-world firms include sole proprietorships, partnerships, corporations, for-profit firms, nonprofit firms, and cooperatives. Each type has its own problems, and organizational theory is a key area of research in economics. One of those areas of research considers why the nature of firms changes over time.

Much of the research in organizational theory is based upon the work of Chicago economist Ronald Coase, who pointed out that in order to understand the firm, one must understand that how activities are organized in firms depends on the transaction costs (costs of undertaking trades through the market) it faces. Production internal to the firm reduces transaction costs but also can increase costs since internal-to-the-firm production involves command and control and is not subject to the competition of the market. (Coase won a Nobel Prize for his work in 1991.)

The Internet has lowered transaction costs, significantly changing how firms are organized. It used to be that firms hired employees for the long term. The most significant transactions

cost was the hiring—finding an employee who matched a need, negotiating pay, paying for the employee to move, and then training one employee. After hiring, transactions costs were pretty low; when a firm had a need, it assigned the project in-house, providing additional training when necessary. The original transactions cost could be spread over a number of projects.

Now a firm can identify a need and outsource the work by posting it on Internet sites such as outsourcemyproject.com for freelancers to bid on. The firm has no obligation to the freelancer other than to pay for the service, which lowers the transactions cost enormously. The freelancer can be anywhere in the world, working in any time zone, and project managers can oversee the work through online communications such as Skype. Setting up a clothing line and need a fashion designer? Need to develop a website? Post the project online.

The key point to remember is that as transactions costs change, the efficient structure of firms changes, which brings about a change in the nature of firms. Whereas large command and control companies such as IBM once arose to lower transactions costs, now in some industries the efficient firms are small, fragmenting production into ever smaller parts.

Economic Profit

Implicit costs include the opportunity costs of the factors of production provided by the owners of the business. Say that the owner of our earring firm could have earned $1,500 working elsewhere if she did not own the earring firm. The opportunity cost of working in her own business is $1,500. It is an implicit cost of doing business and would be included as a cost. For economists, **total cost** is *explicit payments to the factors of production plus the opportunity cost of the factors provided by the owners of the firm.* Total cost of the earring firm is $3,000 in explicit cost and $1,500 in implicit cost, or $4,500. Generally, implicit costs must be estimated and are not directly measurable, which is why accountants do not include them.

www Web Note 11.2
Economic vs
Accounting Costs

Implicit revenues include the increase in the value of assets. Say the earring firm owns a kiosk whose market value rises from $10,000 to $11,000. The economic concept of revenue would include the $1,000 increase in the value of the kiosk as part of total revenue. For economists, **total revenue** is *the amount a firm receives for selling its product or service plus any increase in the value of the assets owned by the firm.* Total revenue of the earring firm is $5,000 in explicit revenue plus $1,000 in implicit revenue, or $6,000. For economists,

Economic profit = *(Explicit and implicit revenue)* − *(Explicit and implicit cost)*

Q-1 What distinguishes accounting profit from economic profit?

So in this case, economic profit is ($5,000 + $1,000) − ($3,000 + $1,500) = $1,500. The difference really has to do with measurability. Implicit costs must be estimated, and the estimations can sometimes be inexact. General accounting rules do not permit such

Value Added and the Calculation of Total Production

This book (like all economics textbooks) treats production as if it were a one-stage process—as if a single firm transforms a factor of production into a consumer good. Economists write like that to keep the analysis manageable. (Believe me, it's complicated enough.) But you should keep in mind that reality is more complicated. Most goods go through a variety of stages of production.

For example, consider the production of desks. One firm transforms raw materials into usable raw materials (iron ore into steel); another firm transforms usable raw materials into more usable inputs (steel into steel rods, bolts, and nuts); another firm transforms those inputs into desks, which it sells wholesale to a general distributor, which then sells them to a retailer, which sells them to consumers. Many goods go through five or six stages of production and distribution. As a result, if you added up all the sales of all the firms, you would overstate how much total production was taking place.

To figure out how much total production is actually taking place, economists use the concept *value added*. Value added is the contribution that each stage of production makes to the final value of a good. A firm's value added is the firm's total

output less the cost of the inputs bought from other firms. For example, if a desk assembly firm spends $4,000 on component parts and sells its output for $6,000, its value added is $2,000, or $33\frac{1}{3}$ percent of its revenue.

When you add up all the stages of production, the value added of all the firms involved must equal 100 percent, and no more, of the total output. When I discuss "a firm's" production of a good in this book, to relate that discussion to reality, you should think of that firm as a composite of all the firms contributing to the production and distribution of that product.

Why is it important to remember that there are various stages of production? Because it brings home to you how complicated producing a good is. If any one stage gets messed up, the good doesn't get to the consumer. Producing a better mousetrap isn't enough. The firm also must be able to get it out to consumers and let them know that it's a better mousetrap. The traditional economic model doesn't bring home this point. But if you're ever planning to go into business for yourself, you'd better remember it. Many people's dreams of supplying a better product to the market have been squashed by this reality.

inexactness because it might allow firms to misstate their profit, something accounting rules are designed to avoid.

The Production Process

As I stated at the beginning of the chapter, supply is the key to the market's ability to provide the goods people want. Underlying supply is production; firms are important because they control the production process.

The Long Run and the Short Run

The production process is generally divided into a *long-run* planning decision, in which a firm chooses the least expensive method of producing from among all possible methods, and a *short-run* adjustment decision, in which a firm adjusts its long-run planning decision to reflect new information.

In a **long-run decision**, *a firm chooses among all possible production techniques.* This means that it can choose the size of the plant it wants, the type of machines it wants, and the location it wants. The firm has fewer options in a **short-run decision,** in which *the firm is constrained in regard to what production decisions it can make.*

The terms *long run* and *short run* do not necessarily refer to specific periods of time independent of the nature of the production process. They refer to the degree of flexibility the firm has in changing its inputs. In the long run, by definition, the firm can vary the inputs as much as it wants. In the short run, some of the flexibility that existed in the long run no longer exists. In the short run, some inputs are so costly to adjust that they are treated as fixed. *So in the long run, all inputs are variable; in the short run, some inputs are fixed.*

Production Tables and Production Functions

How a firm combines factors of production to produce goods and services can be presented in a **production table** (*a table showing the output resulting from various combinations of factors of production or inputs*).

Real-world production tables are complicated. They often involve hundreds of inputs, hundreds of outputs, and millions of possible combinations of inputs and outputs. Studying these various combinations and determining which is best requires expertise and experience. Business schools devote entire courses to it (operations research and production analysis); engineering schools devote entire specialties to it (industrial engineering).

Studying the problems and answering the questions that surround production is much of what a firm does: What combination of outputs should it produce? What combination of inputs should it use? What combination of techniques should it use? What new techniques should it explore? To answer these questions, the managers of a firm look at a production table.

Production tables are so complicated that in introductory economics we concentrate on short-run production analysis in which one of the factors is fixed. Doing so allows us to capture some important technical relationships of production without getting too tied up in numbers. The relevant part of a production table of earrings appears in Figure 11-1(c). In it the number of the assumed fixed inputs (machines) has already been determined. Columns 1 and 2 of the table tell us how output of earrings varies as the variable input (the number of workers) changes. For example, you can see that with 3 workers the firm can produce 17 pairs of earrings. Column 3 tells us workers' **marginal product** (*the additional output that will be forthcoming from an additional worker, other inputs constant*). Column 4 tells us workers' **average product** (*output per worker*).

It is important to distinguish marginal product from average product. Workers' average product is the total output divided by the number of workers. For example, let's consider the case of 5 workers. Total output is 28, so average product is 5.6 (28 divided by 5). To find the marginal product, we must ask how much additional output will be forthcoming if we change the number of workers. For example, if we change from 4 to 5 workers, the additional worker's marginal product will be 5; if we change from 5 to 6, the additional worker's marginal product will be 3. That's why the marginal products are written between each level of output.

The information in a production table is often summarized in a production function. A **production function** is *the relationship between the inputs (factors of production) and outputs.* Specifically, the production function tells the maximum amount of output that can be derived from a given number of inputs. Figure 11-1(a) is the production function

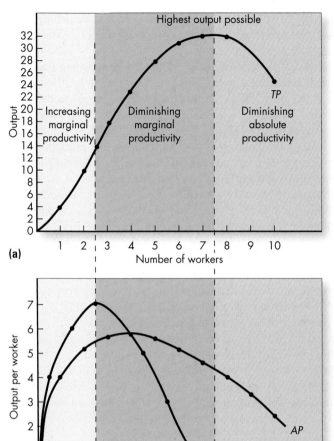

(a)

(b)

FIGURE 11-1 (A, B, AND C) **A Production Table and Production Function**

The production function in (**a**) is a graph of the production table in (**c**). Its shape reflects the underlying production technology. The graph in (**b**) shows the marginal and average product. Notice that when marginal product is increasing, the production function is bowed upward; when marginal product is decreasing, the production function is bowed downward; when marginal product is zero, the production function is at its highest point. Firms are interested in producing where both average product and marginal product are positive and falling, which starts at 4 workers and ends at 7.5 workers.

Number of Workers	Total Output	Marginal Product (Change in Total Output)	Average Product (Total Product/ Number of Workers)	
1	4		4	Increasing marginal productivity
		4		
2	10	6	5	
		7		
3	17		5.7	Diminishing marginal productivity
		6		
4	23	5	5.8	
5	28		5.6	
		3		
6	31	1	5.2	
7	32		4.6	
		0		
8	32		4.0	Diminishing absolute productivity
		−2		
9	30	−5	3.3	
10	25		2.5	

(c)

that displays the information in the production table in Figure 11-1(c). The number of workers is on the horizontal axis and the output of earrings is on the vertical axis.

The Law of Diminishing Marginal Productivity

Figure 11-1(b) graphs the workers' average and marginal productivities from the production function in Figure 11-1(a). (Alternatively you can determine those graphs by plotting columns 3 and 4 from the table in Figure 11-1(c).) Notice that both marginal and average productivities are initially increasing, but that eventually they both decrease. Between 7 and 8 workers, the marginal productivity of workers actually becomes negative.

This means that initially this production function exhibits increasing marginal productivity and then it exhibits *diminishing marginal productivity*. Eventually it exhibits negative marginal productivity.

The same information can be gathered from Figure 11-1(a), but it's a bit harder to interpret.[1] Notice that initially the production function is bowed upward. Where it's bowed upward there is increasing marginal productivity, as you can see if you extend

Marginal Product and the Law of Diminishing Marginal Productivity

Q-2 What are the normal shapes of marginal productivity and average productivity curves?

---

[1]Technically the marginal productivity curve is a graph of the slope of the total product curve.

a line down to Figure 11-1(b). Then, between 2.5 and 7.5 workers, the production function is bowed downward but is still rising. In this range, there's diminishing marginal productivity, as you can see by extending a line down to Figure 11-1(b). Finally marginal productivity is negative.

The most important area of these relationships is the area of diminishing marginal productivity and falling average product (between 4 and 7.5 workers). Why? Because a firm is most likely to operate in that area. If it's in the first range and marginal productivity is increasing, a firm can increase its existing workers' output by hiring more workers; it will have a strong incentive to do so and get out of that range. Similarly, if hiring an additional worker actually cuts total output (as it does when marginal productivity is negative), the firm would be crazy to hire that worker. So it stays out of that range.

This range of the relationship between fixed and variable inputs is so important that economists have formulated a law that describes what happens in production processes when firms reach this range—when more and more of one input is added to a fixed amount of another input. The **law of diminishing marginal productivity** states that *as more and more of a variable input is added to an existing fixed input, eventually the additional output one gets from that additional input is going to fall.*

The law of diminishing marginal productivity is sometimes called the *flowerpot law* because if it didn't hold true, the world's entire food supply could be grown in one flowerpot. In the absence of diminishing marginal productivity, we could take a flowerpot and keep adding seeds to it, getting more and more food per seed until we had enough to feed the world. In reality, however, a given flowerpot is capable of producing only so much food no matter how many seeds we add to it. At some point, as we add more and more seeds, each additional seed will produce less food than did the seed before it. That's the law of diminishing marginal productivity in action. Eventually the pot reaches a stage of diminishing absolute productivity, in which the total output, not simply the output per unit of input, decreases as inputs are increased.

The Costs of Production

In any given firm, owners and managers probably discuss costs far more than anything else. Invariably costs are too high and the firm is trying to figure out ways to lower them. But the concept *costs* is ambiguous; there are many different types of costs and it's important to know what they are. Let's consider some of the most important categories of costs in reference to Table 11-1, which shows costs associated with making between 3 and 32 pairs of earrings.

Fixed Costs, Variable Costs, and Total Costs

Fixed costs are *costs that are spent and cannot be changed in the period of time under consideration.* There are no fixed costs in the long run since all inputs are variable and hence their costs are variable. In the short run, however, a number of costs will be fixed. For example, say you make earrings. You buy a machine for working with silver, but suddenly there's no demand for silver earrings. Assuming that machine can't be modified and used for other purposes, the money you spent on it is a fixed cost. So within this model, all fixed costs are assumed to be sunk costs.

Fixed costs are shown in column 2 of Table 11-1. Notice that fixed costs remain the same ($50) regardless of the level of production. As you can see, it doesn't matter whether output is 3 or 32; fixed costs are always $50.

Besides buying the machine, the silversmith must also hire workers. These workers are the earring firm's **variable costs**—*costs that change as output changes.* The earring firm's variable costs are shown in column 3. Notice that as output increases,

Q-3 Firms are likely to operate on what portion of the marginal productivity curve?

The law of diminishing marginal productivity states that as more and more of a variable input is added to an existing fixed input, after some point the additional output one gets from the additional input will fall.

Web Note 11.3 What's Fixed? What's Variable?

variable costs increase. For example, when the firm produces 9 pairs of earrings, variable costs are $100; when it produces 10, variable costs rise to $108.

All costs are either fixed or variable in the standard model, so the *total cost* is the sum of the fixed and variable costs:

$$TC = FC + VC$$

$TC = FC + VC$

The earring firm's total costs are presented in column 4. Each entry in column 4 is the sum of the entries in columns 2 and 3 in the same row. For example, to produce 16 pairs of earrings, fixed costs are $50 and variable costs are $150, so total cost is $200.

Average Costs

Total cost, fixed cost, and variable cost are important, but much of a firm's discussion is about average cost. So the next distinction we want to make is between total cost and average cost. To arrive at the earring firm's average cost, we simply divide the total amount of whatever cost we're talking about by the quantity produced. Each of the three costs we've discussed has a corresponding average cost.

For example, **average total cost** (often called average cost) equals *total cost divided by the quantity produced.* Thus:

Average cost equals total cost divided by quantity.

$$ATC = TC/Q$$

Average fixed cost equals *fixed cost divided by quantity produced:*

$$AFC = FC/Q$$

Average variable cost equals *variable cost divided by quantity produced:*

$$AVC = VC/Q$$

Q-4 If total costs are $400, fixed costs are 0, and output is 10, what are average variable costs?

TABLE 11-1 **The Cost of Producing Earrings**

1	2	3	4	5	6	7	8
				Marginal Costs (MC) (Change in Total Costs/			
	Fixed	**Variable**	**Total Costs (TC)**	**Change in**	**Average Fixed Costs (AFC)**	**Average Variable Costs (AVC)**	**Average Total Costs (ATC)**
Output	Costs (FC)	Costs (VC)	(FC + VC)	Output)	(FC/Output)	(VC/Output)	(AFC + AVC)
3	$50	$ 38	$ 88		$16.67	$12.66	$29.33
4	50	50	100	$12	12.50	12.50	25.00
9	50	100	150		5.56	11.11	16.67
10	50	108	158	8	5.00	10.80	15.80
16	50	150	200		3.12	9.38	12.50
17	50	157	207	7	2.94	9.24	12.18
22	50	200	250		2.27	9.09	11.36
23	50	210	260	10	2.17	9.13	11.30
27	50	255	305		1.85	9.44	11.29
28	50	270	320	15	1.79	9.64	11.43
32	50	400	450		1.56	12.50	14.06

Thinking Like a Modern Economist

What "Goods" Do Firms Produce? The Costs of Producing Image

The textbook economic models are implicitly structured around the production of physical goods that require physical inputs. Such physical goods have become less important in the modern economy. In today's economy, many of the goods that firms produce involve intangibles such as image and perception. For example, Starbucks is not only producing coffee; it is also producing an image of luxury, so when you buy a Frappuccino, you are actually buying something that makes you feel good about yourself—you see yourself as a quality person. Or when you buy a car—you are not just buying a car—you are buying an image for yourself. Modern firms spend enormous time and effort trying to associate whatever they are selling with an image that people want to associate with themselves.

Image is real, and has real effects. For example, experimental economists have shown that people respond better to medicine with a high price than to that same medicine with a low price. (This is a variation of the well-known placebo effect in medicine; people get better from taking a sugar pill if they think it is a medicine that is going to help them.)

Producing "image" rather than physical products affects both the structure of costs and how costs are analyzed. Specifically, producing image tends to require large expenditures not directly related to production of any specific good that the firm produces. It might involve:

- Advertising that has little to do with the product. ("Just do it" could apply to any number of goods, not just sneakers.)
- Buying only the highest-price coffee bean even though lower-price coffee might taste just as good, or better. (Do you buy Dunkin' Donuts or Starbucks brand?)
- Associating the firm's name with something positive, that is, underwriting the cost of a stadium. (Think of Busch Stadium in St. Louis.)
- Supporting a local sports team or public radio station. (According to one study, 88 percent of public radio listeners say their opinion of a company is more positive when they discover the company supports public radio.)

These expenditures might seem inconsistent with profit maximizing until one recognizes that the firm is selling its image. These nondirect costs of creating image are not quite fixed costs—since they must be made continually if the firm is to maintain its good's image—but they are not variable costs either, since they do not vary with output of the product. Modern economists' more advanced models of costs capture these distinctions.

Average fixed cost and average variable cost are shown in columns 6 and 7 of Table 11-1. The most important average cost concept, average total cost, is shown in column 8. Average total cost also can be thought of as the sum of average fixed cost and average variable cost:

$$ATC = AFC + AVC$$

As you can see, the average total cost of producing 16 pairs of earrings is $12.50. It can be calculated by dividing total cost ($200) by output (16).

Marginal Cost

All these costs are important to our earring firm, but they are not the most important costs it considers when deciding how many pairs of earrings to produce. That distinction goes to marginal cost, which appears in column 5.[2] **Marginal cost** is *the increase*

---

[2]Since only selected output levels are shown, not all entries have marginal costs. For a marginal cost to exist, there must be a marginal change, a change by only one unit.

(decrease) in total cost from increasing (decreasing) the level of output by one unit. Let's find marginal cost by considering what happens if our earring firm increases production by one unit—from 9 to 10. Looking again at Table 11-1, we see that the total cost rises from $150 to $158. In this case, the marginal cost of producing the 10th unit is $8.

Graphing Cost Curves

Average Total Cost, Average Variable Cost, and Marginal Cost

Let's say that the owner of the earring firm sees things better in pictures and asks you (an economic consultant) to show her what all those numbers in Table 11-1 mean. To do so, you first draw a graph, putting quantity on the horizontal axis and a dollar measure of various costs on the vertical axis.

Total Cost Curves

Figure 11-2(a) graphs the total cost, total fixed cost, and total variable costs for all the levels of output given in Table 11-1.[3] The total cost curve is determined by plotting the entries in column 1 and the corresponding entries in column 4. For example, point *L* corresponds to a quantity of 10 and a total cost of $158. Notice that the total cost curve is upward-sloping: Increasing output increases total cost.

Web Note 11.4
Short-Run Cost Curves

The total fixed cost curve is determined by plotting column 1 and column 2 on the graph. The total variable cost curve is determined by plotting column 1 and column 3. As you can see, the total variable cost curve has the same shape as the total cost curve: Increasing output increases variable cost. This isn't surprising, since the total cost curve is the vertical summation of total fixed cost and total variable cost. For example,

---

FIGURE 11-2 (A AND B) **Total and Per-Unit Output Cost Curves**

Total fixed costs, shown in (**a**), are always constant; they don't change with output. All other total costs increase with output. As output gets high, the rate of increase has a tendency to increase. The average fixed cost curve, shown in (**b**), is downward-sloping; the average variable cost curve and average total cost curve are U-shaped. The U-shaped *MC* curve goes through the minimum points of the *AVC* and *ATC* curves. (The *AFC* curve is often not drawn since *AFC* is also represented by the distance between the *AVC* and *ATC*.)

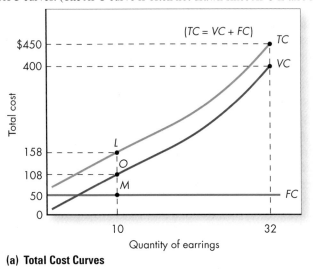

(a) Total Cost Curves

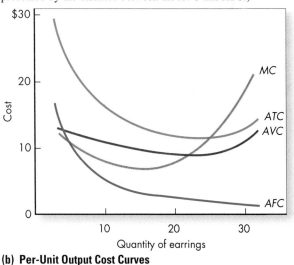

(b) Per-Unit Output Cost Curves

---

[3]To keep the presentation simple, we focus only on the most important part of the total cost curve, that part that follows the simplest rules. Other areas of the total cost curve can be bowed downward rather than bowed upward.

at output 10, total fixed cost equals $50 (point *M*); total variable cost equals $108 (point *O*); and total cost equals $158 (point *L*).

Average and Marginal Cost Curves

The marginal cost curve goes through the minimum point of the average total cost curve and average variable cost curve; each of these curves is U-shaped. The average fixed cost curve slopes down continuously.

Figure 11-2(b) presents the average fixed cost curve, average total cost curve (or average cost curve, as it's generally called), average variable cost curve, and marginal cost curve associated with the cost figures in Table 11-1. As was the case with the total cost curves, all the firm's owner need do is look at this graph to find the various costs associated with different levels of output, since the graphical visualization of cost curves provides a good sense of what happens to costs as we change output. Let's start our consideration with average fixed cost. Average fixed cost is decreasing throughout.

Downward-Sloping Shape of the Average Fixed Cost Curve

The average fixed cost curve looks like a child's slide: It starts out with a steep decline; then it becomes flatter and flatter. What this tells us about production is straightforward: As output increases, the same fixed cost can be spread over a wider range of output, so average fixed cost falls. Average fixed cost initially falls quickly but then falls more and more slowly. As the denominator gets bigger while the numerator stays the same, the increase has a smaller and smaller effect.

The U Shape of the Average Cost Curves

Q-5 Draw a graph of both the marginal cost curve and the average cost curve.

Let's now move on to the average cost curves. Why do they have the shapes they do? Or, expressed another way, how does our analysis of production relate to our analysis of costs? You may have already gotten an idea of how production and costs relate if you remembered Figure 11-1 and recognized the output numbers that we presented were similar output numbers to those that we used in the cost analysis. Cost analysis is simply another way of considering production analysis. The laws governing costs are the same laws governing productivity.

As more and more of a variable input is added to a fixed input, the law of diminishing marginal productivity causes marginal and average productivities to fall. As these fall, marginal and average costs rise.

In the short run, output can be raised only by increasing the variable input. But as more and more of a variable input is added to a fixed input, the law of diminishing marginal productivity enters in. Marginal and average productivities fall. The key insight here is that when marginal productivity falls, marginal cost must rise, and when average productivity falls, average variable cost must rise. So to say that productivity falls is equivalent to saying that cost rises.

It follows that if eventually the law of diminishing marginal productivity holds true, then eventually both the marginal cost curve and the average cost curve must be upward-sloping. And, indeed, in our examples they are. It's also generally assumed that at low levels of production, marginal and average productivities are increasing. This means that marginal cost and average variable cost are initially falling. If they're falling initially and rising eventually, at some point they must be neither rising nor falling. This means that both the marginal cost curve and the average variable cost curve are U-shaped.

Q-6 What determines the distance between the average total cost and the average variable cost?

As you can see in Figure 11-2(b), the average total cost curve has the same general U shape as the average variable cost curve. It has the same U shape because it is the vertical summation of the average fixed cost curve and the average variable cost curve. Its minimum, however, is to the right of the minimum of the average variable cost curve. We'll discuss why after we cover the shape of the average variable cost curve.

Average total cost initially falls faster and then rises more slowly than average variable cost. If we increased output enormously, the average variable cost curve and the average total cost curve would almost meet. Average total cost is of key importance to the firm's owner. She wants to keep it low.

The Relationship between the Marginal Productivity and Marginal Cost Curves

Let's now consider the relationship between marginal product and marginal cost. In Figure 11-3(a), I draw a marginal cost curve and average variable cost curve. Notice their U shape. Initially costs are falling. Then there's some minimum point. After that, costs are rising.

In Figure 11-3(b), I graph the average and marginal productivity curves similar to those that I presented in Figure 11-1(b), although this time I relate average and marginal productivities to output, rather than to the number of workers. This allows us to relate output per worker and output. Say, for example, that we know that the average

If $MP > AP$, then AP is rising.
If $MP < AP$, then AP is falling.

FIGURE 11-3 (A AND B)   **The Relationship between Productivity and Costs**

The shapes of the cost curves are mirror-image reflections of the shapes of the corresponding productivity curves. (The corresponding productivity curve is an implicit function in which marginal productivity is related to output rather than inputs. At each output there is an implicit number of workers who would supply that output.) When one is increasing, the other is decreasing; when one is at a minimum, the other is at a maximum.

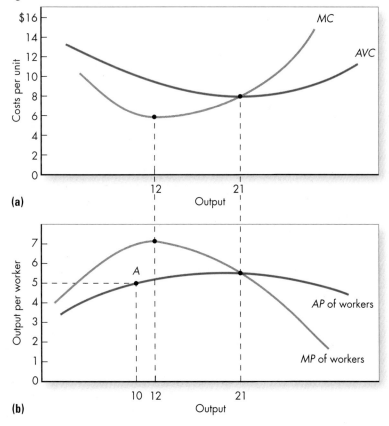

When marginal cost exceeds average cost, average cost must be rising. When marginal cost is less than average cost, average cost must be falling. This relationship explains why marginal cost curves always intersect the average cost curve at the minimum of the average cost curve.

Q-7 When marginal cost equals the minimum point of average variable cost, what is true about the average productivity and marginal productivity of workers?

When the productivity curves are falling, the corresponding cost curves are rising.

product of 2 workers is 5, and that 2 workers can produce an output of 10. This means that when output is 10, the workers' average productivity is 5. By continuing this reasoning, we can construct the curves. Point A corresponds to an output of 10 and average productivity of 5.

Now let's compare the graphs in Figure 11-3 (a and b). If you look at the two graphs carefully, you'll see that one is simply the mirror image of the other. The minimum point of the average variable cost curve (output = 21) is at the same level of output as the maximum point of the average productivity curve; the minimum point of the marginal cost curve (output = 12) is at the same level of output as the maximum point on the marginal productivity curve. When the productivity curves are falling, the corresponding cost curves are rising. Why is that the case? Because as productivity falls, costs per unit increase; and as productivity increases, costs per unit decrease.

The Relationship between the Marginal Cost and Average Cost Curves

Now that we've considered the shapes of each cost curve, let's consider some of the important relationships among them—specifically the relationships between the marginal cost curve on the one hand and the average variable cost and average total cost curves on the other. These general relationships are shown graphically in Figure 11-4.

Let's first look at the relationship between marginal cost and average total cost. In the green shaded and yellow shaded areas (areas A and B) at output below Q_1, even though marginal cost is rising, average total cost is falling. Why? Because, in areas A and B, the marginal cost curve is below the average total cost curve. At point B, where average total cost is at its lowest, the marginal cost curve intersects the average total cost curve. In area C, above output Q_1, where average total cost is rising, the marginal cost curve is above the *ATC* curve.

Web Note 11.5
Marginal Costs in the
Information Economy

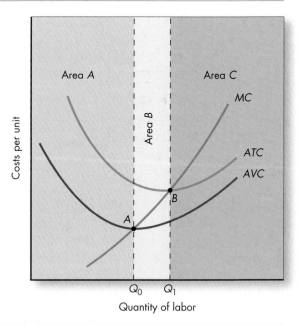

FIGURE 11-4

The Relationship of Marginal Cost Curve to Average Variable Cost and Average Total Cost Curves

The marginal cost curve goes through the minimum points of both the average variable cost curve and the average total cost curve. Thus, there is a small range where average total costs are falling and average variable costs are rising.

The positioning of the marginal cost curve is not happenstance. The position of marginal cost relative to average total cost tells us whether average total cost is rising or falling.

If $MC > ATC$, then ATC is rising.

If $MC = ATC$, then ATC is at its low point.

If $MC < ATC$, then ATC is falling.

Q-8 If marginal costs are increasing, what is happening to average total costs?

To understand why this is, think of it in terms of your grade point average. If you have a B average and you get a C on the next test (that is, your marginal grade is a C), your grade point average will fall below a B. Your marginal grade is below your average grade, so your average grade is falling. If you get a C+ on the next exam (that is, your marginal grade is a C+), *even though your marginal grade has risen from a C to a C+,* your grade point average will fall. Why? Because your marginal grade is still below your average grade. To make sure you understand the concept, explain the next two cases:

1. If your marginal grade is above your average grade, your average grade will rise.
2. If your marginal grade and average grade are equal, the average grade will remain unchanged.

Q-9 If marginal costs are decreasing, what must be happening to average variable costs?

Marginal and average reflect a general relationship that also holds for marginal cost and average variable cost.

If $MC > AVC$, then AVC is rising.

If $MC = AVC$, then AVC is at its low point.

If $MC < AVC$, then AVC is falling.

Q-10 Why does the marginal cost curve intersect the average variable cost curve at the minimum point?

This relationship is best seen in the yellow shaded area (area B) of Figure 11-4, when output is between Q_0 and Q_1. In this area, the marginal cost curve is above the average variable cost curve, so average variable cost is rising; but the MC curve is below the average total cost curve, so average total cost is falling. The intuitive explanation for the relationship in this area is that average total cost includes average variable cost, but it also includes average fixed cost, which is falling. As long as short-run marginal cost is only slightly above average variable cost, the average total cost will continue to fall. Put another way: Once marginal cost is above average variable cost, as long as average variable cost doesn't rise by more than average fixed cost falls, average total cost will still fall.

Intermission

At this point I'm going to cut off the chapter, not because we're finished with the subject, but because there's only so much that anyone can absorb in one chapter. It's time for a break.

Those of you with significant others, go out and do something significant. Those of you with parents bearing the cost of this education, give them a call and tell them that you appreciate their expenditure on your education. Think of the opportunity cost of that education to them; it's not peanuts. Those of you who are married should go out and give your spouse a big kiss; tell him or her that the opportunity cost of being away for another minute was so high that you couldn't control yourself. Those of you with kids, go out and read them a Dr. Seuss book. (My favorite is about Horton.) Let's face it—Seuss is a better writer than I, and if you've been conscientious about this course, you may not have paid your kids enough attention. We'll return to the grind in the next chapter.

Dr. Seuss books are often more interesting than economics books.

A Review of Costs

Term	Definition	Equation
Marginal cost	The additional cost resulting from a one-unit increase in output.	$MC = \Delta TC$
Total cost	The sum of all costs of inputs used by a firm in production.	$TC = FC + VC$
Average total cost	Total cost per unit of production.	$ATC = AFC + AVC$ $= TC/Q$
Fixed cost	Cost that is already spent and cannot be recovered. It exists only in the short run.	FC
Average fixed cost	Fixed costs per unit of production.	$AFC = FC/Q$
Variable cost	Costs that vary with production.	VC
Average variable cost	Variable costs per unit of production.	$AVC = VC/Q$

Summary

- Accounting profit is explicit revenue less explicit cost. Economists include implicit revenue and cost in their determination of profit. (*LO11-1*)

- Implicit revenue includes the increases in the value of assets owned by the firm. Implicit costs include opportunity cost of time and capital provided by the owners of the firm. (*LO11-1*)

- In the long run, a firm can choose among all possible production techniques; in the short run, the firm is constrained in its choices. (*LO11-2*)

- The law of diminishing marginal productivity states that as more and more of a variable input is added to a fixed input, the additional output the firm gets will eventually be decreasing. (*LO11-2*)

- Costs are generally divided into fixed costs, variable costs, and total costs.   *(LO11-3)*

- $TC = FC + VC$; $MC =$ Change in TC; $AFC = FC/Q$; $AVC = VC/Q$; $ATC = AFC + AVC$. *(LO11-3)*

- The average variable cost curve and marginal cost curve are mirror images of the average product curve and the marginal product curve, respectively.   *(LO11-4)*

- The law of diminishing marginal productivity causes marginal and average costs to rise.   *(LO11-4)*

- If $MC > ATC$, then ATC is rising.
  If $MC = ATC$, then ATC is constant.
  If $MC < ATC$, then ATC is falling.   *(LO11-4)*

- The marginal cost curve goes through the minimum points of the average variable cost curve and average total cost curve.   *(LO11-4)*

Key Terms

average fixed cost *(233)*
average product *(230)*
average total cost *(233)*
average variable
   cost *(233)*
economic profit *(228)*

firm *(227)*
fixed cost *(232)*
law of diminishing
   marginal
   productivity *(232)*
long-run decision *(230)*

marginal cost *(234)*
marginal product *(230)*
production *(226)*
production
   function *(230)*
production table *(230)*

profit *(227)*
short-run decision *(230)*
total cost *(228)*
total revenue *(228)*
variable cost *(232)*

Questions and Exercises

1. What costs and revenues do economists include when calculating profit that accountants don't include? Give an example of each.   *(LO11-1)*

2. Peggy-Sue's cookies are the best in the world, or so I hear. She has been offered a job by Cookie Monster, Inc., to come to work at $125,000 per year. Currently, she is producing her own cookies, and she has revenues of $260,000 per year. Her costs are $40,000 for labor, $10,000 for rent, $35,000 for ingredients, and $5,000 for utilities. She has $100,000 of her own money invested in the operation, which, if she leaves, can be sold for $40,000 that she can invest at 10 percent per year.   *(LO11-1)*
   a. Calculate her accounting and economic profits.
   b. Advise her as to what she should do.

3. Economan has been infected by the free enterprise bug. He sets up a firm on extraterrestrial affairs. The rent of the building is $4,000, the cost of the two secretaries is $40,000, and the cost of electricity and gas comes to $5,000. There's a great demand for his information, and his total revenue amounts to $100,000. By working in the firm, though, Economan forfeits the $50,000 he could earn by working for the Friendly Space Agency and the $4,000 he could have earned as interest had he

saved his funds instead of putting them in this business.   *(LO11-1)*
   a. What is his profit or loss by an accountant's definitions?
   b. What is his profit or loss by an economist's definitions?

4. What distinguishes the short-run from the long run?   *(LO11-2)*

5. What is the difference between marginal product and average product?   *(LO11-2)*

6. Explain how studying for an exam is subject to the law of diminishing marginal productivity.   *(LO11-2)*

7. Find *TC, AFC, AVC, AC,* and *MC* from the following table.   *(LO11-3)*

Units	FC	VC
0	$100	$ 0
1	100	40
2	100	60
3	100	70
4	100	85
5	100	130

8. For each of the following indicate what costs are being calculated: *(LO11-3)*
   a. FC + VC
   b. TC/Q
   c. FC/Q
   d. VC/Q
   e. AFC + AVC

9. Classify each of the following as fixed or variable costs: *(LO11-3)*
   a. Outsourced payroll services.
   b. Leased offices.
   c. Company-owned building.
   d. Payroll taxes.

10. Which of the costs discussed in the chapter is the most important when a firm is deciding how much to produce? *(LO11-3)*

11. Explain how each of the following will affect the average fixed cost, average variable cost, average total cost, and marginal cost curves faced by a steel manufacturer: *(LO11-3)*
    a. New union agreement increases hourly pay.
    b. Local government imposes an annual lump-sum tax per plant.
    c. Federal government imposes a "stack tax" on emission of air pollutants by steel mills.
    d. New steel-making technology increases productivity of every worker.

12. Graph the following table. *(LO11-4)*

Number of Workers	Total Output
0	0
1	20
2	60
3	150
4	260
5	350
6	420
7	455
8	420
9	375
10	300

   a. What is marginal product and average product at each level of production?
   b. Graph marginal product and average product.
   c. Label the areas of increasing marginal productivity, diminishing marginal productivity, and diminishing absolute productivity.

13. If average product is falling, what is happening to short-run average variable cost? *(LO11-4)*

14. If marginal cost is increasing, what do we know about average cost? *(LO11-4)*

15. A firm has fixed costs of $100 and variable costs of the following: *(LO11-4)*

Output	1	2	3	4	5	6	7	8	9
Variable costs	$35	75	110	140	175	215	260	315	390

   a. Show *AFC, ATC, AVC,* and *MC* in a table.
   b. Graph the *AFC, ATC, AVC,* and *MC* curves.
   c. Explain the relationship between the *MC* curve and the *AVC* and *ATC* curves.
   d. Say fixed costs dropped to $50. Which curves shifted? Why?

16. If average productivity falls, will marginal cost necessarily rise? How about average cost? *(LO11-4)*

17. An economic consultant is presented with the following total product table and asked to derive a table for average variable costs. The price of labor is $15 per hour. *(LO11-4)*

Labor	TP
1	5
2	15
3	30
4	36
5	40

   a. Help him do so.
   b. Show that the graph of the average productivity curve and average variable cost curve are mirror images of each other.
   c. Show the marginal productivity curve for labor inputs between 1 and 5.
   d. Show that the marginal productivity curve and marginal cost curve are mirror images of each other.

18. Say that a firm has fixed costs of $100 and constant average variable costs of $25. *(LO11-4)*
    a. Show *AFC, VC, AVC,* and *MC* in a table.
    b. Graph the *AFC, ATC, AVC,* and *MC* curves.
    c. Explain why the curves have the shapes they do.
    d. What law is not operative for this firm?

19. Say a firm has $100 in fixed costs and average variable costs increase by $5 for each unit, so that the cost of 1 is $25, the cost of 2 is $30, the cost of 3 is $35, and so on. *(LO11-4)*
    a. Show *VC, AFC, AVC,* and *MC* in a table.
    b. Graph the *AFC, ATC, AVC,* and *MC* curves associated with these costs.
    c. Explain how costs would have to increase in order for the curves to have the "normal" shapes of the curves presented in the text.

Questions from Alternative Perspectives

1. The text presents very detailed cost tables when it considers the decisions of firms.
   a. Do entrepreneurs have such cost tables available to them when they enter a business?
   b. If not, how do they gather such information?
   c. If such information is gathered through trial and error, what implications does that have for government intervention in the marketplace? (Austrian)

2. Say that a drug firm could increase its profit by marketing a drug that it knows might have serious side effects. Say also that it knows that it can never be prosecuted for doing so.
   a. Would it?
   b. Should it? (Religious)

3. The analysis in the book suggests that firms hire inputs so that they hold costs as low as possible. Yet, as Gloria Steinem has pointed out, looking at reality one sees men selling refrigerators and women selling men's underwear.
   a. Do you believe that that allocation of jobs reflects firms trying to minimize costs because of the relative expertise of women and men?
   b. If not, what does it reflect? (Feminist)

4. The text does not emphasize firms' role in shaping the tastes and preferences of consumers even though this is a very important role with firms spending about $150 billion a year on advertising. If it is true that firms are shaping consumer preferences, whose welfare are people maximizing when they make consumption decisions? (Institutionalist)

5. Walmart, the nation's largest retailer, has perfected a "just-in-time competitive strategy." This retail giant relies on barcodes for instant inventory, distribution centers that purchase supplies at the last minute and deliver only when needed, a small core of suppliers that Walmart can pressure for large discounts, routinized work that requires on average seven hours of training, and part-time workers who often work full-time hours without getting corresponding benefits. How does this "just-in-time" approach change the mix of fixed and variable costs to the advantage of Walmart? (Radical)

Issues to Ponder

1. "There is no long run; there are only short and shorter runs." Evaluate that statement.

2. If you increase production to an infinitely large level, the average variable cost and the average total cost will merge. Why?

3. The following cell-phone offer by Sprint is typical of what one can get on a cell phone plan: 4,000 free minutes for $39.99 a month. The fine print says that only 350 of those minutes are anytime minutes; the remaining are restricted to evening and weekend usage. If you go over your allotted time, you are charged 35 cents per minute for any additional minutes.
   a. What is your marginal cost? Graph it.
   b. What would your average variable cost curve for peak time usage look like?

   c. If you do not keep track of your usage, how would you figure your marginal cost?
   d. Why do firms offer such confusing plans?
   e. Were firms that charged this way in favor of or against portability of phone numbers?

4. Say that neither labor nor machines are fixed but that there is a 50 percent quick-order premium paid to both workers and machines for delivery of them in the short run. Once you buy them, they cannot be returned, however. What do your short-run marginal cost and short-run average total cost curves look like?

5. If machines are variable and labor fixed, how will the general shapes of the short-run average cost curve and marginal cost curve change?

Answers to Margin Questions

1. Accounting profit measures explicit costs and revenues; economic profit includes implicit costs and revenues as well. (*p. 228; LO11-1*)

2. Normally the marginal productivity curve and average productivity curve are both inverted U shapes. (*p. 231; LO11-2*)

3. Firms are likely to operate on the downward-sloping portion of the marginal productivity curve because on the upward-sloping portion, firms could increase workers' output by hiring more workers. A firm will continue to hire more workers at least to the point where diminishing marginal productivity sets in. (*p. 232; LO11-2*)

4. Average variable costs would be $40. (*p. 233; LO11-3*)

5. As you can see in the graph, both these curves are U-shaped and the marginal cost curve goes through the average cost curve at the minimum point of the average cost curve. (*p. 236; LO11-4*)

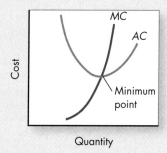

6. The distance between the average total cost and the average variable cost is determined by the average fixed cost at that quantity. As quantity increases, the average fixed cost decreases, so the two curves get closer and closer together. (*p. 236; LO11-4*)

7. Since the average productivity and marginal productivity of workers are the mirror images of average costs and marginal costs, and when the marginal costs and average costs intersect the two are equal, it follows that the average productivity and marginal productivity of workers must also be equal at that point. (*p. 238; LO11-4*)

8. It is impossible to say what is happening to average total costs on the basis of what is happening to marginal costs. It is the magnitude of marginal costs relative to average total costs that is important. (*p. 239; LO11-4*)

9. It is impossible to say because it is the magnitude of marginal cost relative to average variable cost that determines what is happening to average variable cost. (*p. 239; LO11-4*)

10. The marginal cost curve intersects the average variable cost curve at the minimum point because once the marginal cost exceeds average variable costs, the average variable costs must necessarily begin to rise, and vice versa. (*p. 239; LO11-4*)

chapter 12

Production and Cost Analysis II

Economic efficiency consists of making things that are worth more than they cost.

—J. M. Clark

Welcome back from your intermission. I hope you've reestablished your relationship with the real world and are ready to return, with renewed vigor, to the world of economics. When we took our intermission last chapter, we had worked our way through the various short-run costs. That short run is a time period in which some inputs are fixed. In the first part of this chapter, we consider firms' long-run decisions and the determinants of the long-run cost curves. Then, in the second part, we'll talk about applying cost analysis to the real world.

Firms have many more options in the long run than they do in the short run. They can change any input they want. Plant size is not given; neither is the technology available given.

To make their long-run decisions, firms look at the costs of the various inputs and the technologies available for combining those inputs, and then decide which combination offers the lowest cost.

Say you're opening a hamburger stand. One decision you'll have to make is what type of stove to buy. You'll quickly discover that many different types are available. Some use more gas than others but cost less to buy; some are electric; some are self-cleaning and hence use less labor; some are big; some are little; some use microwaves; some use convection. Some have long-term guarantees; some have no guarantees. Each has a colorful brochure telling you how wonderful it is. After studying the various detailed specifications and aspects of the production technology, you choose the stove that has the combination of characteristics that you believe best fits your needs.

Next you decide on workers. Do you want bilingual workers, college-educated workers, part-time workers, experienced workers . . . ? You get the idea: Even simple production decisions involve complicated questions. These decisions are made on the basis of the expected costs, and expected usefulness, of inputs.

After reading this chapter, you should be able to:

LO12-1 Distinguish technical efficiency from economic efficiency.

LO12-2 Explain how economies and diseconomies of scale influence the shape of long-run cost curves.

LO12-3 Explain the role of the entrepreneur in translating cost of production to supply.

LO12-4 Discuss some of the problems of using cost analysis in the real world.

Technical Efficiency and Economic Efficiency

When choosing among existing technologies in the long run, firms are interested in the lowest cost, or most economically efficient, methods of production. They consider all technically efficient methods and compare their costs. The terms *economically efficient* and *technically efficient* differ in meaning. Here's how: **Technical efficiency** in production means that *as few inputs as possible are used to produce a given output.*

Web Note 12.1
Cheap Labor

Many different production processes can be technically efficient. For example, say you know that to produce 100 tons of wheat, you can use 10 workers and 1 acre or 1 worker and 100 acres. Which of these two production techniques is more efficient? Both can be technically efficient since neither involves more of both inputs. But that doesn't mean that both are equally economically efficient. That question can't be answered unless you know the relative costs of the two inputs. If an acre of land rents for $1 million and each worker costs $10 a day, our answer likely will be different than if land rents for $40 an acre and each worker costs $100 a day. The **economically efficient** method of production is *the method that produces a given level of output at the lowest possible cost.*

Q-1 True or false? If a process is economically efficient, it is also technically efficient. Explain your answer.

In long-run production decisions, firms will look at all available production technologies and choose the technology that, given the available inputs and their prices, is the economically efficient way to produce. These choices will reflect the prices of the various factors of production. Those prices, in turn, will reflect the factors' relative scarcities.

Q-2 Why does China use production techniques that require more workers per acre of land than does the United States?

Consider the use of land by firms in the United States and in Japan. The United States has large amounts of land (8 acres) per person, so the price of land is lower than in Japan, which has only 0.73 acre per person. An acre of rural land in the United States might cost about $1,300; in Japan it costs over $10,000. Because of this difference in the price of inputs, production techniques use land much more intensively in Japan than in the United States. Similarly with China: Labor is more abundant and capital is scarcer, so production techniques in China use capital much more intensively than it is used in the United States. Whereas China would use hundreds of workers and very little machinery to build a road, the United States would use three or four people along with three machines. Both countries are being economically efficient, but because costs of inputs differ, the economically efficient method of production differs. Thus, the economically efficient method of production is the technically efficient method of production that has the lowest cost. (For a further, graphical analysis of economic efficiency, see Appendix A.)

The Shape of the Long-Run Cost Curve

In the last chapter, we saw that the law of diminishing marginal productivity accounted for the shape of the short-run average cost curve. The firm was adding more of a variable input to a fixed input. The law of diminishing marginal productivity doesn't apply to the long run since, in the long run, all inputs are variable. The most important determinants of what is economically efficient in the long run are economies and diseconomies of scale. Let's consider each of these in turn and see what effect they will have on the shape of the long-run average cost curve.

The shape of the long-run cost curve is due to the existence of economies and diseconomies of scale.

Economies of Scale

We say that production exhibits **economies of scale** *when long-run average total costs decrease as output increases.* For example, if producing 40,000 high definition TVs costs a firm $16 million ($400 each), but producing 200,000 costs the firm

Changing Technology in Automobile Production

In the late 1980s, the normal production run of a U.S. auto-maker was 200,000 units. Why was it so high? Because of indivisible setup costs of the then-current production technology. In order to reduce those indivisible setup costs to an acceptable level, the production level per year had to equal at least 200,000, or the car was considered an economic failure. Small-sports-car sales did not meet that sales level, and so, in the 1980s, small, low-cost sports cars faded from the scene. For example, the Pontiac Fiero, a small American sports car, was dropped in 1988.

But what is an indivisible setup cost depends on the structure of production. In the 1980s, Japanese companies changed the nature of automobile production by organizing assembly lines so that many cars with different sizes and shapes could share the same assembly line,

allowing economies of scope (discussed later in the chapter). This redesign lowered the indivisible setup costs for each type of car, and made the Japanese companies' minimum profitable production level 30,000, not 200,000. The Mazda Miata was one of the first cars developed using this new assembly-line approach, and it was a big success. In response to the challenge, other car companies switched their assembly lines to this alternative, and, over the past 20 years, there has been an enormous increase in the number of reasonably priced sporty two-seaters.

These changes are ongoing. Auto companies are designing their various lines of cars so that the components of one are easily interchangeable with the components of another, allowing more shared assembly lines and lower indivisible setup costs.

$40 million ($200 each), between 40,000 and 200,000 units, production exhibits significant economies of scale. One can also say that there are increasing returns to scale.

In real-world production processes, at low levels of production, economies of scale are extremely important because many production techniques require a certain minimum level of output to be useful. For example, say you want to produce a pound of steel. You can't just build a mini blast furnace, stick in some coke and iron ore, and come out with a single pound of steel. The smallest technically efficient blast furnaces have a production capacity measured in tons per hour, not pounds per year. The cost of the blast furnace is said to be an **indivisible setup cost** (*the cost of an indivisible input for which a certain minimum amount of production must be undertaken before the input becomes economically feasible to use*).

Indivisible setup costs are important because they create many real-world economies of scale: As output increases, the costs per unit of output decrease. As an example, consider this book. Preparing the book for publishing is an indivisible setup cost; it is a cost that must be incurred if any production is to take place, but it is not a cost that increases with the number of books produced. That means that the more copies of the book that are produced, the lower the cost per book. That's why it costs more per book to produce a textbook for an upper-level, low-enrollment course than it does for a lower-level, high-enrollment course. The same amount of work goes into both (both need to be written, edited, and composited), and the printing costs differ only slightly. The actual print-run costs of printing a book are only about $3 to $8 per book. The other costs are indivisible setup costs. Prices of produced goods, including books, reflect their costs of production. As you move to upper-level academic courses, where print runs are smaller, you'll likely discover that the books are smaller and less colorful but are priced the same as, or more than, this introductory text.

Web Note 12.2
Economies of Scale

In the production of steel, the cost of a blast furnace is an indivisible setup cost that requires a minimum level of production to be economically feasible.

Q-3 Why are larger production runs often cheaper per unit than smaller production runs?

FIGURE 12-1 (A AND B)   A Typical Long-Run Average Total Cost Table and Curve

In the long run, average costs initially fall because of economies of scale; then they are constant for a while, and finally they tend to rise due to diseconomies of scale.

Quantity	Total Costs of Labor	Total Costs of Machines	Total Costs = $TC_L + TC_M$	Average Total Costs = TC/Q
11	$381	$254	$ 635	$58
12	390	260	650	54
13	402	268	670	52
14	420	280	700	50
15	450	300	750	50
16	480	320	800	50
17	510	340	850	50
18	549	366	915	51
19	600	400	1,000	53
20	666	444	1,110	56

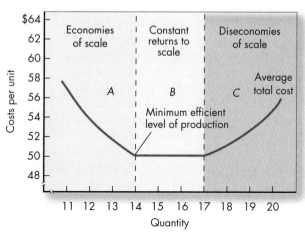

(a) Long-Run Production Table

(b) Long-Run Average Cost Curve

In the long-run planning decisions about the cost of producing this book, the expected number of copies to be sold was an important element. That figure influenced the number of books produced, which in turn affected the expected cost per unit. This will be the case any time there are economies of scale. With economies of scale, cost per unit of a small production run is higher than cost per unit of a large production run.

Figure 12-1(a) demonstrates a long-run production table; Figure 12-1(b) shows the related typical shape of a long-run average cost curve. (Notice that there are no fixed costs. Because we're in the long run, all costs are variable.) Economies of scale account for the downward-sloping part. Cost per unit of output is decreasing.

In the long run, all inputs are variable, so only economies of scale can influence the shape of the long-run cost curve.

Because of the importance of economies of scale, businesspeople often talk of a minimum efficient level of production. What they mean by minimum efficient level of production is that, given the price at which they expect to be able to sell a good, the indivisible setup costs are so high that production runs of less than a certain size don't make economic sense. Thus, the **minimum efficient level of production** is *the amount of production that spreads setup costs out sufficiently for a firm to undertake production profitably*. At this point, the market has expanded to a size large enough for firms to take advantage of all economies of scale. The minimum efficient level of production is where the average total costs are at a minimum.

Diseconomies of Scale

Diminishing marginal productivity refers to the decline in productivity caused by increasing units of a variable input being added to a fixed input. Diseconomies of scale refer to the decreases in productivity that occur when there are equal percentage increases of all inputs (no input is fixed).

Notice that on the right side of Figure 12-1(b) the long-run average cost curve is upward-sloping. Average cost is increasing. We say that production exhibits **diseconomies of scale** *when long-run average total costs increase as output increases*. For example, if producing 200,000 high definition TVs costs the firm $40 million ($200 each) and producing 400,000 high definition TVs costs the firm $100 million ($250 each), there are diseconomies of scale associated with choosing to produce 400,000 rather than 200,000. One also can say there are decreasing

Travels of a T-Shirt and Economies of Scale

The T-shirt said "MADE IN CHINA," but when economist Pietra Rivoli, in her delightful book *The Travels of a T-Shirt in the Global Economy,* tracked down the process of making the T-shirt that she bought in Florida, she discovered that it's a lot more complicated than that. True, the company that sewed the shirt was in Shanghai, China. But guess where the cotton for the shirt came from? West Texas, USA, at a farm like the Reinsch family farm that is highlighted in Rivoli's book.

Now here's an exam question for you: Why, if China's labor cost is 1/20 that of U.S. labor costs, is the cotton for a T-shirt grown in the United States, shipped across the ocean to China to be woven and sewn into a T-shirt, and shipped back again to the United States to be sold?

Answer: Economies of scale (and some U.S. subsidies, but you aren't expected to know that yet). In fact, the United States leads the world in the production of cotton, and has done so for over 200 years. Farms in Africa average 8 acres and in China average less than 1 acre. The Reinsch's farm is 1,000 acres and can produce about 500,000 pounds of cotton, enough for 1.3 million T-shirts. Size makes a difference; cotton farmers outside the United States almost exclusively handpick their cotton. Because U.S. farmers have such large farms, they can use large machinery to do all the picking, and thereby take advantage of economies of scale, countering the much higher labor costs in the United States.

returns to scale. Diseconomies of scale usually, but not always, start occurring as firms get large.

Diseconomies of scale could not occur if production relationships were only technical relationships. If that were the case, the same technical process could be used over and over again at the same per-unit cost. In reality, however, production relationships have social dimensions, which introduce the potential for important diseconomies of scale into the production process in two ways:

1. As the size of the firm increases, monitoring costs generally increase.

2. As the size of the firm increases, team spirit or morale generally decreases.

Monitoring costs are *the costs incurred by the organizer of production in seeing to it that the employees do what they're supposed to do.* If you're producing something yourself, the job gets done the way you want it done; monitoring costs are zero. However, as the scale of production increases, you have to hire people to help you produce. This means that if the job is to be done the way you want it done, you have to monitor (supervise) your employees' performance. The cost of monitoring can increase significantly as output increases; it's a major contributor to diseconomies of scale. Most big firms have several layers of bureaucracy devoted simply to monitoring employees. The job of middle managers is, to a large extent, monitoring.

The other social dimension that can contribute to diseconomies of scale is the loss of **team spirit** (*the feelings of friendship and being part of a team that bring out people's best efforts*). Most types of production are highly dependent on team spirit. When the team spirit or morale is lost, production slows considerably. The larger the firm is, the more difficult it is to maintain team spirit.

An important reason diseconomies of scale can come about is that the bigger things get, the more checks and balances are needed to ensure that the right hand and the left hand are coordinated. The larger the organization, the more checks and balances and the more paperwork.

Q-4 If production involved only technical relationships and had no social dimension, what would the long-run average total cost curve look like?

As firms become larger, monitoring costs increase and achieving team spirit is more difficult.

Some large firms manage to solve these problems and avoid diseconomies of scale. But problems of monitoring and loss of team spirit often limit the size of firms. They underlie diseconomies of scale in which less additional output is produced for a given increase in inputs, so that per-unit costs of output increase.

Constant Returns to Scale

Sometimes in a range of output, a firm does not experience either economies of scale or diseconomies of scale. In this range, there are **constant returns to scale** *where long-run average total costs do not change with an increase in output.* Constant returns to scale are shown by the flat portion of the average total cost curve in Figure 12-1(b). Constant returns to scale occur when production techniques can be replicated again and again to increase output. This occurs before monitoring costs rise and team spirit is lost.

The long-run and the short-run average cost curves have similar U shapes. But it's important to remember that the reasons why they have this U shape are quite different. The assumption of initially increasing and then eventually diminishing marginal productivity (as a variable input is added to a fixed input) accounts for the shape of the short-run average cost curve. Economies and diseconomies of scale account for the shape of the long-run average total cost curve.

The Importance of Economies and Diseconomies of Scale

Economies and diseconomies of scale play important roles in real-world long-run production decisions. Economies of scale are an important reason why firms attempt to expand their markets either at home or abroad. If they can make and sell more at lower per-unit costs, they will make more profit. Diseconomies of scale prevent a firm from expanding and can lead corporate raiders to buy the firm and break it up in the hope that the smaller production units will be more efficient, thus eliminating some of the diseconomies of scale.

Envelope Relationship

Since in the long run all inputs are flexible, while in the short run some inputs are not flexible, long-run cost will always be less than or equal to short-run cost at the same level of output. To see this, let's consider a firm that had planned to produce 100 units but now adjusts its plan to produce more than 100. We know that in the long run the firm chooses the lowest-cost method of production. In the short run, it faces an additional constraint: All expansion must be done by increasing only the variable input. That constraint must increase average cost (or at least not decrease it) compared to what average cost would have been had the firm planned to produce that level to begin with. If it didn't, the firm would have chosen that new combination of inputs in the long run. Additional constraints increase cost. The *envelope relationship* is the relationship between long-run and short-run average total costs. It is shown in Figure 12-2.

Why it is called an envelope relationship should be clear from the figure. Each short-run average total cost curve touches (is tangent to) the long-run average total cost curve at one, and only one, output level; at all other output levels, short-run average cost exceeds long-run average cost. The long-run average total cost curve is an envelope of short-run average total cost curves.

The intuitive reason why the short-run average total cost curves always lie above or tangent to the long-run average cost curve is simple. In the short run, you have chosen a plant; that plant is fixed, and its costs for that period are part of your average fixed

Q-5 Why is the short-run average cost curve a U-shaped curve?

Q-6 Why is the long-run average total cost curve generally considered to be a U-shaped curve?

Economies and diseconomies of scale play important roles in real-world long-run production decisions.

The envelope relationship is the relationship explaining that, at the planned output level, short-run average total cost equals long-run average total cost, but at all other levels of output, short-run average total cost is higher than long-run average total cost.

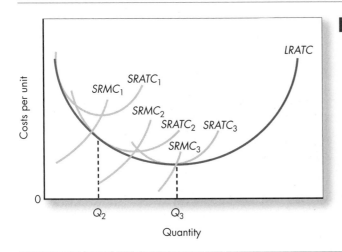

FIGURE 12-2

Envelope of Short-Run Average Total Cost Curves

The long-run average total cost curve is an envelope of the short-run average total cost curves. Each short-run average total cost curve touches the long-run average total cost curve at only one point. (*SR* stands for short run; *LR* stands for long run.)

More on the Envelope Relationship

costs. Changes must be made within the confines of that plant. In the long run, you can change everything, choosing the combination of inputs in the most efficient manner. The more options you have to choose from, the lower the costs of production. Put another way: Constraints always raise costs (or at least won't lower them). So in the long run, costs must be the same or lower.

Another insight to note about this envelope relationship is the following: When there are economies of scale and you have chosen an efficient plant size for a given output, your short-run average costs will fall as you increase production. Technically, this must be the case because the short-run marginal cost (*SRMC*) curve goes through the minimum point of the short-run average total cost (*SRATC*) curve, and the minimum point of the *SRATC* curve is to the right of the efficient level of production in the long run. That means that at output Q_2, $SRMC_2$ has to be below $SRATC_2$ and short-run average total cost has to be falling. Intuitively, what's happening is that at output Q_2, your fixed costs are high. Now demand increases and you increase production. Your average fixed costs are high; your marginal costs are low; and initially the fall in average fixed costs more than offsets the increased marginal cost. Once marginal cost exceeds *SRATC*, that no longer is the case.[1]

Only when the firm is at the minimum point of the long-run average total cost (*LRATC*) curve (at output Q_3) is the $SRATC_3$ curve tangent to the *LRATC* curve at a point where the *SRMC* curve intersects both the curves. For large markets, this point is the least-cost production level of a firm.

---

[1]The above reasoning depends on the curves being smooth (i.e., having no kinks), a standard assumption of the model. If we give up the smoothness assumption, the *SRATC* curve could be kinked and the *SRMC* curve could be discontinuous. In that case, the *SRATC* curve might be tangent to the *LRATC* curve from the left, but not from the right, and it might not decrease. This would make movement from the long to the short run a discrete jump, whereas the existing model and smoothness assumption make it a smooth continuous movement. So if your intuition doesn't lead you to understand the model, you are probably thinking of a model with different assumptions. You'll be in good company, too. When an economist by the name of Jacob Viner first created this model, his intuition led him to a different result because his intuition was basing the analysis on different assumptions than he was using in his formal model.

Why Are Textbooks So Long?

Understanding costs and their structure will help you understand why intro economics textbooks are so long—and why their length is to your advantage.

The majority of the costs of a book are fixed costs in relation to the length of the book. The initial costs in terms of length are about 20 percent of the total price of the book. So increasing the length of the book increases costs slightly. But the longer length allows the writer to include more issues that some professors want and many professors require to even consider using the book. That means that greater length can allow publishers to sell more books, allowing the fixed costs to be divided over more output. This decrease in fixed cost per unit can lower average total cost more than increasing the length of the book increases average total costs per unit. So if

the added length increases the number of users, the additional length can lower the average cost of the book.

Length does lower the costs of the book—up to a point. Textbook publishers are continually looking for that point. They direct authors to shorten their books but also to include almost all issues that various groups want. The latter direction—in favor of inclusion—often takes precedence, which is why textbooks are so long. This doesn't mean that textbooks will always be longer. Recently, economics textbooks have become smaller because students began to complain that the texts were getting too heavy to carry. There has also been technological change; books are now placing more and more of the less-used chapters on the web, and some are becoming ebooks.

Entrepreneurial Activity and the Supply Decision

In this chapter and the preceding one, we have discussed the technical nature of costs and production. In the next chapter, we will formally relate costs of production to the supply of goods. As a bridge between the two chapters, let's consider the entrepreneur, who establishes the relationship between costs and the supply decision, and discuss some of the problems of using cost analysis in the real world.

In thinking about the connection between cost and supply, one fundamental insight is that the revenue received for a good must be greater than the planned cost of producing it. Otherwise why would anyone supply it? The difference between the expected price of a good and the expected average total cost of producing it is the supplier's expected economic profit per unit. It's profit that underlies the dynamics of production in a market economy.

Cost curves do not become supply curves through some magic process. To move from cost to supply, entrepreneurial initiative is needed. An **entrepreneur** is *an individual who sees an opportunity to sell an item at a price higher than the average cost of producing it.* The entrepreneur is the organizer of production and the one who visualizes the demand and convinces the individuals who own the factors of production that they want to produce that good. Businesses work hard at maintaining the entrepreneurial spirit in their employees. The greater the difference between price and average total cost, the greater the entrepreneur's incentive to tackle the organizational problems and supply the good.

The role of the entrepreneur is not easily captured in models but should not be underestimated. Entrepreneurs are the visionaries who turn new technologies into usable goods and services. They are the hidden element of supply that is essential to the

The expected price must exceed the average total costs of supplying the good for a good to be supplied.

www Web Note 12.3
Entrepreneurship

Q-7 Why is the role of the entrepreneur central to the production process in the economy?

continued growth of an economy. While financial reward plays a role in entrepreneurial effort, it is not always the central motivation. People are motivated by many desires, including recognition, fame, and just the pleasure of seeing something done efficiently and well.

In recent years we have seen an increase of social entrepreneurship—where entrepreneurs turn their focus on achieving social, rather than just economic, ends. These social entrepreneurs are blending profit motives with other motives into the charters of the corporations, making them *for-benefit,* not *for-profit,* corporations. Novo Nordisk is an example. It is a pharmaceutical company whose goal is more than just profit. Instead of a profit bottom line, it has what it calls a triple bottom line. It tries to be profitable, responsible, and valuable for patients, employees, and society. For-benefit institutions provide a way in which people can join together to simultaneously fulfill their social goals as well as their material welfare goals. Advocates argue that for-benefit corporations will become a new "fourth sector" in the U.S. economy.

In recent years there has been an increase in social entrepreneurship.

Using Cost Analysis in the Real World

All too often, students walk away from an introductory economics course thinking that cost analysis is a relatively easy topic. Memorize the names, shapes, and relationships of the curves, and you're home free. In the textbook model, that's right. In real life, it's not because actual production processes are marked by economies of scope, learning by doing and technological change, many dimensions, unmeasured costs, joint costs, indivisible costs, uncertainty, asymmetries, and multiple planning and adjustment periods with many different short runs. And this is the short list!

Web Note 12.4
Increasing the Scope

Economies of Scope

The cost of production of one product often depends on what other products a firm is producing. Economists say that in the production of two goods, there are **economies of scope** *when the costs of producing products are interdependent so that it's less costly for a firm to produce one good when it's already producing another.* For example, once a firm has set up a large marketing department to sell cereal, the department might be able to use its expertise in marketing a different product—say, dog food. A firm that sells gasoline can simultaneously use its gas station attendants to sell soda, milk, and incidentals. The minimarts so common along our highways and neighborhood streets developed because gasoline companies became aware of economies of scope.

Economies of scope play an important role in firms' decisions about what combination of goods to produce. They look for both economies of scope and

Thinking Like a Modern Economist

Social Norms and Production

The traditional economic model presents the production decision as a cost-based decision. The firm calculates the cost of inputs and chooses the lowest-price input. Modern economists believe that these costs are important, but they also believe that a number of other elements come into play. They are working to devise models that incorporate them. One of the most important of those other elements is social norms, and the choices a firm makes so that they fit the social norms of society. Behavioral economist Dan Ariely argues that social norms play a far greater role in a firm's decisions than the traditional economic model includes. He argues both that firms should include social norms in their decision making and that economists should develop new models of the firms that incorporate social norms in their decision process. He writes:

> If corporations started thinking in terms of social norms, they would realize that these norms build loyalty and—more important—make people want to extend themselves to the degree that corporations need today: to be flexible, concerned, and willing to pitch in. That's what a social relationship delivers.

Q-8 What is the difference between an economy of scope and an economy of scale?

Economies of Scale
and Economies of Scope

economies of scale. When you read about firms' mergers, think about whether the combination of their products will generate economies of scope. Many otherwise unexplainable mergers between seemingly incompatible firms can be explained by economies of scope.

By allowing firms to segment the production process, globalization has made economies of scope even more important to firms in their production decisions. Low-cost labor in other countries has led U.S. firms to locate their manufacturing processes in those countries and to concentrate domestic activities on other aspects of production. As I have stressed throughout this book, production is more than simply manufacturing; the costs of marketing, advertising, and distribution are often larger components of the cost of a good than are manufacturing costs. Each of these involves special knowledge and expertise, and U.S. companies are specializing in the marketing, advertising, and distribution aspects of the production process. By concentrating on those aspects, and by making themselves highly competitive by taking advantage of low-cost manufacturing elsewhere, U.S. firms become more competitive and expand, increasing demand for U.S. labor. Often they expand into new areas, taking advantage of economies of scope in distribution and marketing.

Consider Nike—it produces shoes, right? Wrong. It is a U.S. marketing and distribution company; it outsources all its production to affiliate companies. Nike is expanding, but not in the production of shoes. It is expanding into leisure clothing, where it hopes economies of scope in its marketing and distribution specialties will bring it success.

Nike is only one of many examples. The large wage differentials in the global economy are causing firms to continually reinvent themselves—to shed aspects of their business where they do not have a comparative advantage, and to add new businesses where their abilities can achieve synergies and economies of scope.

Learning by Doing and Technological Change

The production terminology that we've been discussing is central to the standard economic models. In the real world, however, other terms and concepts are also important. The production techniques available to real-world firms are constantly changing because of *learning by doing* and *technological change*. These changes occur over time and cannot be accurately predicted.

Unlike events in the standard economic model, all events in the real world are influenced by the past; people learn by doing. But to keep the model simple, learning by doing isn't a part of the traditional economic model. **Learning by doing** simply means that *as we do something, we learn what works and what doesn't, and over time we become more proficient at it.* Practice may not make perfect, but it certainly makes better and more efficient. Many firms estimate that output per unit of input will increase by 1 or 2 percent a year, even if inputs or technologies do not change, as employees learn by doing.

The concept of learning by doing emphasizes the importance of the past in trying to predict performance. Let's say a firm is deciding between two applicants for the job of managing its restaurant. One was a highly successful student but has never run a restaurant; the other was an OK student who has run a restaurant that failed. Which one does the firm hire? The answer is unclear. The first applicant may be brighter, but the lack of experience will likely mean that the person won't be hired. Businesses give enormous weight to experience. So this firm may reason that in failing, the second applicant will have learned lessons that make her the better candidate. U.S. firms faced such a choice when they were invited to expand into the new market

Q-9 Does learning by doing cause the average cost curve to be downward-sloping?

Many firms estimate worker productivity to grow 1 to 2 percent a year because of learning by doing.

The nature of production has changed considerably in the last 70 years. The picture on the left shows a 1933 production line in which people did the work as the goods moved along the line. The picture on the right shows a modern production line. Robots do much of the work.

economies of Eastern Europe in the early 1990s. Should they hire the former communist managers who had failed to produce efficiently, or should they hire the reformers? (Generally they decided on the former communist managers, hoping they had learned by failing.)

Technological change is *an increase in the range of production techniques that leads to more efficient ways of producing goods as well as the production of new and better goods.* That is, technological change offers an increase in the known range of production. For example, at one point automobile tires were made from rubber, clothing was made from cotton and wool, and buildings were made of wood. As a result of technological change, many tires are now made from petroleum distillates, much clothing is made from synthetic fibers (which in turn are made from petroleum distillates), and many buildings are constructed from steel.

The standard long-run model takes technology as a given. From our experience, we know that technological change affects firms' decisions and production. Technological change can fundamentally alter the nature of production costs.

In some industries, technological change is occurring so fast that it overwhelms all other cost issues. The digital electronics industry is a good example. The expectation of technological change has been built into the plans of firms in that industry. The industry has followed Moore's law, which states that the cost of computing will fall by half every 18 months. Indeed, that has happened since the computer was first offered to the mass retail market. With costs falling that fast because of learning by doing and technological change, all other cost components are overwhelmed, and, instead of costs increasing as output rises significantly, as might be predicted because of diseconomies of scale, costs keep going down.

Increased computational power (decreased cost) has affected other industries as well. Technological change has been so dramatic that we no longer talk about changes in a good, but rather the development of entirely new goods and ways of doing things. Consider consumer goods. Telephone land lines have been replaced by cell phones that are effectively computers with voice and messaging capabilities. VCRs have been

Technological change can fundamentally alter the nature of production costs.

Web Note 12.5
Moore's Law

replaced by wireless video streaming on appliances such as the iPod. Music isn't played from CDs but is streamed online, chosen by you or for you by programs such as Pandora. You don't buy paper books but download bits and bytes transformed into words on a digital page.

Computational technology has also revolutionized automobiles, making them more reliable and of much higher quality per dollar spent. In the 1960s, I could work on my own car, changing the points or modifying the carburetor. Modern cars have no such parts; they have been replaced by electronic parts. When a car isn't running right, its owner must now take it to a garage, which hooks up the car to a diagnostic computer that reports what is wrong. No more lifting the hood. My point is that automobiles have fundamentally changed; they are much more efficient and reliable and their price has fallen because of the introduction of computer technology. Technological change drives costs down and can overwhelm diseconomies of scale, causing prices to fall more and more.

Don't think of technological change as occurring only in high-tech industries. Consider chicken production. The price of chickens has fallen enormously over the past 50 years. Why? Because of technological change. At one time, chickens were raised in farmyards. They walked around, ate scraps and feed, and generally led a chicken's life. Walking around had definite drawbacks—it took space (which cost money); it made standardization (a requirement of taking advantage of economies of scale) difficult, which prevented lowering costs; it used energy, which meant more feed per pound of chicken; and sometimes it led to disease, since chickens walked in their own manure.

Technological change occurs in all industries, not only high-tech industries.

The technological change was to put the chickens in wire cages so that the manure falls through to a conveyor belt and is transferred outside. Another conveyor belt feeds the chickens food laced with antibiotics to prevent disease. Soft music is played to keep them calm (they burn fewer calories). Once they reach the proper weight, they are slaughtered in a similar automated process. How the chickens feel about this technological change is not clear. (When I asked them, all they had to say was *cluck.*)

This method of raising chickens will likely be replaced in the next couple of decades by another technological change—genetic engineering that will allow chicken parts to be produced directly from single cells. Only the breasts and drumsticks will be produced (and wings if you live in Buffalo) as what is known as "in vitro meat." All low-efficiency, low-profit-margin parts such as necks, feet, and heads will be eliminated from the "efficient chicken."

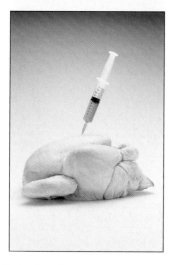

Technological change and learning by doing are intricately related.

In many businesses, the effect of learning by doing and technological change on prices is built into the firm's pricing structure. If they expect their costs to fall with more experience, or if they expect technological advances to lower costs in the future, businesses might bid low for a big order to give themselves the chance to lower their costs through learning by doing or technological change.

Technological change and learning by doing are intricately related. The efficient chicken production we now have did not come about overnight. It occurred over a 20-year period as firms learned how to do it. Chickens respond to Mozart better than to hip-hop. That had to be learned. Similarly, genetic reproduction of chicken parts will evolve as scientists and firms learn more about cloning and DNA.

Many Dimensions

The only dimension of output in the standard model is how much to produce. Many, if not most, decisions that firms make are not the one-dimensional decisions of the traditional model, such as "Should we produce more or less?" They're multidimensional questions such as "Should we change the quality? Should we change the wrapper? Should we improve our shipping speed? Should we increase our inventory?" Each of these questions relates to a different dimension of the production decision and each has its own marginal costs. Thus, there isn't just one marginal cost; there are 10 or 20 of them. Good economic decisions take all relevant margins into account.

Good economic decisions take all relevant margins into account.

The reason that the traditional model is important is that each of these questions can be analyzed by applying the same reasoning used in the traditional model. But you must remember, *in applying the analysis, it's the reasoning, not the specific model, that's important.*

Unmeasured Costs

If asked "In what area of decision making do businesses most often fail to use economic insights?" most economists would say costs. The relevant costs are generally not the costs you'll find in a firm's accounts.

Why the difference? Economists operate conceptually; they include in costs exactly what their theory says they should. They include all opportunity costs. Accountants who have to measure firms' costs in practice and provide the actual dollar figures take a much more pragmatic approach; their concepts of costs must reflect only explicit costs—those costs that are reasonably precisely measurable.

To highlight the distinction, let me review the difference between explicit and implicit costs (discussed in the previous chapter) and introduce another difference—how economists and accountants measure depreciation of capital.

ECONOMISTS INCLUDE OPPORTUNITY COST   First, say that a business produces 1,000 widgets[2] that sell at $4 each for a total revenue of $4,000. To produce these widgets, the business had to buy $1,200 worth of widgetgoo, which the owner has hand-shaped into widgets. An accountant would say that the total cost of producing 1,000 widgets was $1,200 and that the firm's profit was $2,800. That's because an accountant uses explicit costs that can be measured.

Economic profit is different. An economist, looking at that same example, would point out that the accountant's calculation doesn't take into account the time and effort that the owner put into making the widgets. While a person's time involves no explicit cost in money, it does involve an opportunity cost, the forgone income that the owner could have made by spending that time working in another job. If the business takes 400 hours of the person's time and the person could have earned $8 an hour working for someone else, then the person is forgoing $3,200 in income. Economists include that implicit cost in their concept of cost. When that implicit cost is included, what looks like a $2,800 profit becomes a $400 economic loss.

Q-10 As the owner of the firm, Jim pays himself $1,000. All other expenses of the firm add up to $2,000. What would an economist say are the total costs for Jim's firm?

ECONOMIC DEPRECIATION VERSUS ACCOUNTING DEPRECIATION
Depreciation is *a measure of the decline in value of an asset that occurs over time.* Say a firm buys a machine for $10,000 that's meant to last 10 years. After 1 year,

---

[2]What's a widget? It's a wonderful little gadget that's the opposite of a wadget. (No one knows what they look like or what they are used for.) Why discuss widgets? For the same reason that scientists discuss fruit flies—their production process is simple, unlike most real-world production processes.

machines like that become in short supply, so instead of falling, its value rises to $12,000. An accountant, looking at the firm's costs that year, would use historical cost (what the machine cost in terms of money actually spent) depreciated at, say, 10 percent per year, so the machine's depreciation for each of its 10 years of existence would be $1,000. An economist would say that since the value of the machine is rising, the machine has no depreciation; it has appreciation and provides a revenue of $2,000 to the firm. The standard model avoids such messy, real-world issues of measuring depreciation costs and instead assumes that all costs are measurable in a single time period.

The Standard Model as a Framework

Despite its limitations, the standard model provides a good framework for cost analysis.

The standard model can be expanded to include these real-world complications. Modern production is data intensive and, as computing and information processing costs fall, cost accounting and production decisions are becoming more and more integrated with the economist's analysis. Just about every industry has industry-specific software that tailors economic analysis to its particular needs. For example, Robert Kaplan of the Harvard Business School argues that cost accounting systems based on traditional concepts of fixed and variable costs lead firms consistently to make the wrong decisions. He argues that in today's manufacturing, direct labor costs have fallen substantially—in many industries to only 2 or 3 percent of the total cost—and overhead costs have risen substantially. This change in costs facing firms requires a much more careful division among types of overhead costs, and a recognition that what should and should not be assigned as a cost to a particular product differs with each decision.

I don't discuss these real-world complications because I suspect that even with its simplifications, the standard model has been more than enough to learn in an introductory course. Learning the standard model, however, provides you with only the rudiments of cost analysis, in the same way that learning the rules of mechanics provides you with only the basics of mechanical engineering. In addition to a knowledge of the laws of mechanics, building a machine requires years of experience. Similarly for economics and cost analysis. Introductory economics provides you with a superb framework for starting to think about real-world cost measurement, but it can't make you an expert cost analyst.

Conclusion

We've come to the end of our discussion of production, cost, and supply. The two chapters we spent on them weren't easy; there's tons of material here, and, quite frankly, it will likely require at least two or three reads and careful attention to your professor's lecture before your mind can absorb it. So if you're planning to sleep through a lecture, the ones on these chapters aren't the ones for that.

These chapters will provide a framework for considering costs, and as long as you remember that it is only a framework, it will allow you to get into interesting real-world issues. But you've got to know the basics to truly understand those issues. So, now that you've come to the end of these two chapters, unless you really feel comfortable with the analysis, it's probably time to review them from the beginning. (Sorry, but remember, there ain't no such thing as a free lunch.)

Summary

- An economically efficient production process must be technically efficient, but a technically efficient process need not be economically efficient. *(LO12-1)*

- The long-run average total cost curve is U-shaped. Economies of scale initially cause average total cost to decrease; diseconomies eventually cause average total cost to increase. *(LO12-2)*

- Production is a social, as well as a technical, phenomenon; that's why concepts like team spirit are important—and that's why diseconomies of scale occur. *(LO12-2)*

- The marginal cost and short-run average cost curves slope upward because of diminishing marginal productivity. The long-run average cost curve slopes upward because of diseconomies of scale. *(LO12-2)*

- There is an envelope relationship between short-run average cost curves and long-run average cost curves. The short-run average cost curves are always above the long-run average cost curve. *(LO12-2)*

- An entrepreneur is an individual who sees an opportunity to sell an item at a price higher than the average cost of producing it. *(LO12-3)*

- Once we start applying cost analysis to the real world, we must include a variety of other dimensions of costs that the traditional model does not cover. *(LO12-4)*

- Costs in the real world are affected by economies of scope, learning by doing and technological change, the many dimensions to output, and unmeasured costs such as opportunity costs. *(LO12-4)*

Key Terms

constant returns to
  scale *(250)*
depreciation *(257)*
diseconomies of
  scale *(248)*

economically
  efficient *(246)*
economies of scale *(246)*
economies of scope *(253)*
entrepreneur *(252)*

indivisible setup
  cost *(247)*
learning by doing *(254)*
minimum efficient level
  of production *(248)*

monitoring cost *(249)*
team spirit *(249)*
technical efficiency *(246)*
technological
  change *(255)*

Questions and Exercises

1. What is the difference between technical efficiency and economic efficiency? *(LO12-1)*

2. One farmer can grow 1,000 bushels of corn on 1 acre of land with 200 hours of labor and 20 pounds of seed. Another farmer can grow 1,000 bushels of corn on 1 acre of land with 100 hours of labor and 20 pounds of seed. *(LO12-1)*
   a. Could both methods be technically efficient?
   b. Is it possible that both of these production processes are economically efficient?

3. A dressmaker can sew 800 garments with 160 bolts of fabric and 3,000 hours of labor. Another dressmaker can sew 800 garments with 200 bolts of fabric and 2,000 hours

of identical labor. Fabric costs $100 a bolt and labor costs $10 an hour. *(LO12-1)*
   a. Is it possible for both methods to be technically efficient? Why or why not?
   b. Is it possible for both methods to be economically efficient? Why or why not?

4. A student has just written on an exam that, in the long run, fixed cost will make the average total cost curve slope downward. Why will the professor mark it incorrect? *(LO12-2)*

5. Why could diseconomies of scale never occur if production relationships were only technical relationships? *(LO12-2)*

6. In the early 2000s car makers began to design vehicles' chassis, engine, and transmissions so that different models could be produced on the same assembly line. Within the first year of implementing the plan, Ford cut production costs by $240 per car.   (*LO12-2*)
   a. What cost concept was Ford taking advantage of to produce its savings?
   b. What effect did the plan likely have on Ford's short-run average total cost curve?

7. Draw a long-run average total cost curve.   (*LO12-2*)
   a. Why does it slope downward initially?
   b. Why does it eventually slope upward?
   c. How would your answers to *a* and *b* differ if you had drawn a short-run cost curve?
   d. How large is the fixed-cost component of the long-run cost curve?
   e. If there were constant returns to scale everywhere, what would the long-run cost curve look like?

8. Sea lions have been depleting the stock of steelhead trout. One idea to scare sea lions off the Washington state coast was to launch fake killer whales, predators of sea lions. The cost of making the first whale is $16,000—$5,000 for materials and $11,000 for the mold. The mold can be reused to make additional whales, so additional whales would cost $5,000 apiece.   (*LO12-2*)
   a. Make a table showing the total cost and average total cost of producing 1 to 10 fake killer whales.
   b. Does production of fake whales exhibit diseconomies of scale, economies of scale, or constant returns to scale?

c. What is the fixed cost of producing fake whales?
d. What is the variable cost of producing fake whales?

9. Why are long-run costs always less than or equal to than short-run costs?   (*LO12-2*)

10. Draw a short-run marginal cost curve, short-run average cost curve, and long-run average total cost curve for an efficient firm producing where there are diseconomies of scale.   (*LO12-2*)

11. Where along the long-run average total cost curve will an efficient firm try to produce in the long run?   (*LO12-2*)

12. What is the role of the entrepreneur in translating cost of production into supply?   (*LO12-3*)

13. Your average total cost is $40; the price you receive for the good is $12. Should you keep on producing the good? Why?   (*LO12-3*)

14. True or false? Because entrepreneurs are motivated by opportunities to sell an item at a price higher than the average cost of producing it, they do not start for-benefit firms. Explain your answer.   (*LO12-3*)

15. A student has just written on an exam that technological change will mean that the cost curve is downward-sloping. Why did the teacher mark it wrong?   (*LO12-4*)

16. How does learning by doing affect average total costs?   (*LO12-4*)

17. If a firm is experiencing learning by doing, what is likely true about the long-run average total cost curve? Explain your answer.   (*LO12-4*)

Questions from Alternative Perspectives

1. The text presents costs as if a firm could look them up in a book.
   a. How do you believe a firm's true costs are revealed?
   b. Is this an optimal method of finding out costs? (Austrian)

2. The chapter points out that "businesses give enormous weight to experience," or learning by doing. Empirical evidence suggests that, in surveys and applications, women tend to report the nature of their jobs in far less detail than do men.
   a. How might this contribute to differences in "experience" between men and women?
   b. In what other ways might women's real-world experiences be undervalued when they go to look for jobs? (Feminist)

3. Adam Smith argued that at birth most people were similarly talented, and that differences in individual abilities, and hence productivity, are largely the effect of the division of labor, not its cause. What implications does that insight have for economic policy, and for the way we

should treat others who receive less income than we do? (Religious)

4. Firms have an incentive to "externalize" their costs, that is, to make others face the opportunity costs of their actions while firms reduce their own accounting costs.
   a. Give some examples of firms doing this.
   b. What implications for policy does it have? (Institutionalist)

5. A major survey conducted by economists David Levine and Laura Tyson found that "In most reported cases the introduction of substantive shop floor participation (job redesign and participatory work groups) leads to some combination of an increase in satisfaction, commitment, quality and productivity, and a reduction in turnover and absenteeism." Despite that evidence of real cost savings of participatory work groups, only a few U.S. corporate employers (for instance, Xerox and Scott Paper) have taken this high road to labor relations, while many continue to pursue the low road Walmart-like approach to cost saving. Why is that? (Radical)

Issues to Ponder

1. A pair of shoes that wholesales for $28.79 has approximately the following costs:

Manufacturing labor	$ 2.25
Materials	4.95
Factory overhead, operating expenses, and profit	8.50
Sales costs	4.50
Advertising	2.93
Research and development	2.00
Interest	.33
Net income to producer	3.33
Total	$28.79

   a. Which of these costs would likely be a variable cost?
   b. Which would likely be a fixed cost?
   c. If output were to rise, what would likely happen to average total costs? Why?

2. What inputs do you use in studying this book? What would the long-run average total cost and marginal cost curves for studying look like? Why?

3. If you were describing the marginal cost of an additional car driving on a road, what costs would you look at? What is the likely shape of the marginal cost curve?

4. A major issue of contention at many colleges concerns the cost of meals that is rebated when a student does not sign up for the meal plan. The administration usually says that it should rebate only the marginal cost of the food alone, which it calculates at, say, $1.25 per meal. Students say that the marginal cost should include more costs, such as the saved space from fewer students using the facilities and the reduced labor expenses on food preparation. This can raise the marginal cost to $6.00.
   a. Who is correct, the administration or the students?
   b. How might your answer to *a* differ if this argument were being conducted in the planning stage, before the dining hall is built?
   c. If you accept the $1.25 figure of a person not eating, how could you justify using a higher figure of about $6.00 for the cost of feeding a guest at the dining hall, as many schools do?

5. When economist Jacob Viner first developed the envelope relationship, he told his draftsman to make sure that all the marginal cost curves went through both (1) the minimum point of the short-run average cost curve and (2) the point where the short-run average total cost curve was tangent to the long-run average total cost curve. The draftsman told him it couldn't be done. Viner told him to do it anyhow. Why was the draftsman right?

6. The cost of setting up a steel mill is enormous. For example, a Gary, Indiana, hot-strip mill would cost an estimated $1.5 billion to build. Using this information and the cost concepts from the chapter, explain the following quotation: "To make operations even marginally profitable, big steelmakers must run full-out. It's like a car that is more efficient at 55 miles an hour than in stop-and-go traffic at 25."

Answers to Margin Questions

1. True. Since an economically efficient method of production is that method that produces a given level of output at the lowest possible cost, it also must use as few inputs as possible. It is also technically efficient. (*p. 246; LO12-1*)

2. China uses more labor-intensive techniques than does the United States because the price of labor is much lower in China relative to the United States. Both countries are producing economically efficiently. (*p. 246; LO12-1*)

3. Larger production runs are generally cheaper per unit than smaller production runs because of indivisible setup costs, which do not vary with the size of the run. (*p. 247; LO12-2*)

4. Because the same technical process could be used over and over again at the same cost, the long-run average cost curve would never become upward-sloping. (*p. 249; LO12-2*)

5. The short-run average cost curve initially slopes downward because of increasing marginal productivity and large average fixed costs, then begins sloping upward because of diminishing marginal productivity, giving it a U shape. (*p. 250; LO12-2*)

6. The long-run average total cost curve is generally considered to be U-shaped because initially there are economies of scale and, for large amounts of production, there are diseconomies of scale. (*p. 250; LO12-2*)

7. Economic activity does not just happen. Some dynamic, driven individual must instigate production. That dynamic individual is called an entrepreneur. (*p. 252; LO12-3*)

8. Economies of scale are economies that occur because of increases in the amount of one good a firm is producing. Economies of scope occur when producing different

types of goods lowers the cost of each of those goods. (*p. 254; LO12-4*)

9. Learning by doing causes a shift in the cost curve because it is a change in the technical characteristics of production. It does not cause the cost curve to be downward-sloping—it causes it to shift downward. (*p. 254; LO12-4*)

10. An economist would say that he doesn't know what total cost is without knowing what Jim could have earned if he had undertaken another activity besides running his business. Just because he paid himself $1,000 doesn't mean that $1,000 is his opportunity cost. (*p. 257; LO12-4*)

APPENDIX A

Isocost/Isoquant Analysis

In the long run, a firm can vary more than one factor of production. One of the decisions firms face in this long run is which combination of factors of production to use. Economic efficiency involves choosing those factors to minimize the cost of production.

In analyzing this choice of which combination of factors to use, economists have developed a graphical technique called *isocost/isoquant analysis.* In this technique, the analyst creates a graph placing one factor of production, say labor, on one axis and another factor, say machines, on the other axis, as I have done in Figure A12-1. Any point on that graph represents a combination of machines and labor that can produce a certain amount of output, say 8 pairs of earrings. For example, point *A* represents 3

machines and 4 units of labor being used to produce 8 pairs of earrings. Any point in the blue shaded area represents more of one or both factors and any point in the brown shaded area represents less of one or both factors.

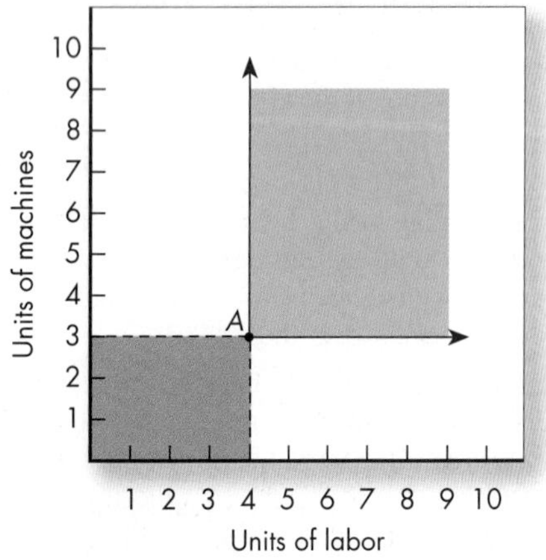

The Isoquant Curve

The firm's problem is to figure out how to produce its output—let's say it has chosen an output of 60 pairs of earrings—at as low a cost as possible. That means somehow we must show graphically the combinations of machines and labor that can produce 60 pairs of earrings as cheaply as possible. We do so with what is called an isoquant curve. An **isoquant curve** is *a curve that represents combinations of factors of production that result in equal amounts of output.* (*Isoquant* is a big name for an "equal quantity.") At all points on an isoquant curve, the firm can produce the same amount of output. So, given a level of output, a firm can find out what combinations of the factors of production will produce that output. Suppose a firm can produce 60 pairs of earrings with the following combination of labor and machines:

FIGURE A12-1 The Isocost/Isoquant Graph

	Labor	Machines	Pairs of Earrings
A	3	20	60
B	4	15	60
C	6	10	60
D	10	6	60
E	15	4	60
F	20	3	60

This table shows the technical limits of production. It shows that the firm can use, for example, 3 units of labor and 20 machines or 20 units of labor and 3 machines to produce 60 pairs of earrings. The isoquant curve is a graphical representation of the table. I show the isoquant curve for producing 60 pairs in Figure A12-2. Points A to F represent rows A to F in the table.

To be sure you understand it, let's consider some points on the curve. Let's start at point A. At point A, the firm is producing 60 pairs of earrings using 20 machines and 3 workers. If the firm wants to reduce the number of machines by 5, it must increase the number of units of labor by 1 to keep output constant. Doing so moves the firm to point B. At point B, the firm is also producing 60 pairs of earrings, but is doing it with 15 machines and 4 workers. Alternatively, if the firm were at point D, and it wants to reduce the number of machines from 6 to 4, it must increase the number of units of labor from 10 to 15 to keep output constant at 60. At any point on this isoquant curve, the firm is being technically efficient—it is using as few resources as possible to produce 60 pairs of earrings. It would never want to produce 60 at a point like G because that point uses more inputs. It is a technically inefficient method of production.

The numbers in the production table and the shape of the curve were not chosen randomly. They were chosen to be consistent with the law of diminishing marginal productivity, which means the curve is bowed inward. That is because as the firm increases the use of one factor more and more, it must use fewer and fewer units of the other factor to keep output constant. This reflects the technical considerations embodied in the law of diminishing marginal productivity. Thus, the chosen numbers

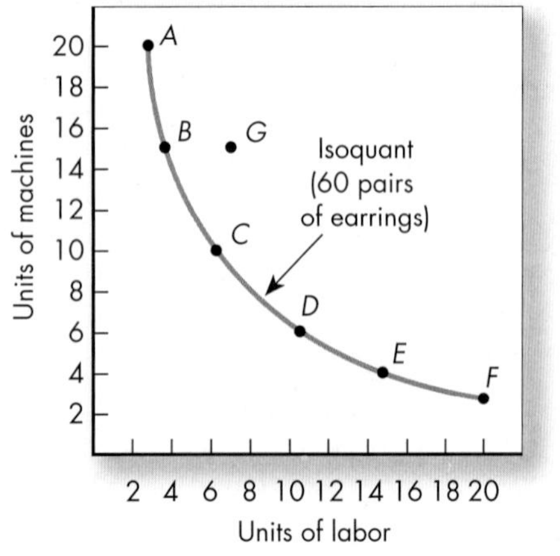

tell us that if a firm wants to keep output constant, as it adds more and more of one factor (and less of the other factor), it has to use relatively more of that factor. For example, initially it might add 1 machine to replace 1 worker, holding output constant. If it continues, it will have to use 1.5 machines, then 2 machines, and so on.

The rate at which one factor must be added to compensate for the loss of another factor, to keep output constant, is called the **marginal rate of substitution.** To say that there is diminishing marginal productivity is to say that there is a diminishing marginal rate of substitution. It is because the table assumes a diminishing marginal rate of substitution that the isoquant curve is bowed inward.

Graphically, the slope of the isoquant curve is the marginal rate of substitution. To be exact, the absolute value of the slope at a point on the isoquant curve equals the ratio of the marginal productivity of labor to the marginal productivity of machines:

$$| \text{ Slope } | = \frac{MP_{\text{labor}}}{MP_{\text{machines}}} = \frac{\text{Marginal rate of substitution}}{}$$

With this equation, you can really see why the isoquant is downward-sloping. As the firm moves from point A to point F, it is using more labor and fewer machines. Because of the law of diminishing marginal productivity, as the firm moves from A to F, the marginal productivity of labor decreases and the marginal productivity of machines increases. The slope of the isoquant falls since the marginal rate of substitution is decreasing.

Let's consider a specific example. Say in Figure A12-2 the firm is producing at point B. If it cuts its input by 5 machines but also wants to keep output constant, it must increase labor by 2 (move from point B to point C). So the marginal rate of substitution of labor for machines between points B and C must be 5/2, or 2.5.

The firm can complete this exercise for many different levels of output. Doing so will result in an **isoquant map,** *a set of isoquant curves that shows technically efficient combinations of inputs that can produce different levels of output.* Such a map for output levels of 40, 60, and 100 is shown in Figure A12-3.

Each curve represents a different level of output. Isoquant I is the lowest level of output, 40, and isoquant III is the highest level of output. When a firm chooses an output level, it is choosing one of those isoquants. The chosen isoquant represents the technically efficient combinations of resources that can produce the desired output.

FIGURE A12-2 **Isoquant Curve for 60 Pairs of Earrings**

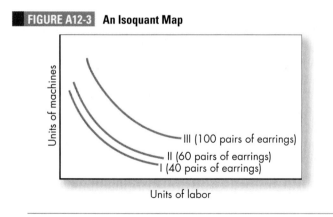

FIGURE A12-3   An Isoquant Map

Units of machines

III (100 pairs of earrings)
II (60 pairs of earrings)
I (40 pairs of earrings)

Units of labor

The Isocost Line

So far I have only talked about technical efficiency. To move to economic efficiency, we have to bring in the costs of production. We do so with the **isocost line**—*a line that represents alternative combinations of factors of production that have the same costs.* (*Isocost* is a fancy name for "equal cost.") Each point on the isocost line represents a combination of factors of production that, in total, cost the firm an equal amount.

To draw the isocost line, you must know the cost per unit of each input as well as the amount the firm has chosen to spend on production. Say labor costs $5 a unit, machinery costs $3 a unit, and the firm has chosen to spend $60. What is the greatest number of earrings it can produce with that $60? To answer that question, we need to create a curve representing the various amounts of inputs a firm can get with that $60. We do so in the following manner. Say the firm decides to spend the entire $60 on labor. Since labor costs $5 a unit, it can buy 12 units of labor. This alternative is represented by point *A* in Figure A12-4.

Alternatively, since machines cost $3 a unit, if the firm chooses to spend all of the $60 on machines, it can buy 20 machines (point *B* in Figure A12-4). This gives us two points on the isocost curve. Of course, the assumption of diminishing marginal rates of substitution makes it highly unlikely that the firm would want to produce at either of these points. Instead, it would likely use some combination of inputs. But these extreme points are useful nonetheless because by connecting them (the line that goes from *A* to *B* in Figure A12-4), we can see the various combinations of inputs that also cost $60.

To see that this is indeed the case, say the firm starts with 20 machines and no labor. If the firm wants to use some combination of labor and machinery, it can give up some machines and use the money it saves by using fewer machines to purchase units of labor. Let's say it gives up 5 machines, leaving it with 15. That means it has $15 to spend on labor, for which it can buy 3 units of labor. That means 15 machines and 3 units of labor is another combination of labor and machines that cost the firm $60. This means that point *C* is also a point on the isocost line. You can continue with this exercise to prove to yourself that the line connecting points *A* and *B* does represent various combinations of labor and machinery the firm can buy with $60. Thus, the line connecting *A* and *B* is the $60 isocost line.

To see that you understand the isocost line, it is useful to go through a couple of examples that would make it shift. For example, what would happen to the isocost line if the firm chooses to increase its spending on production to $90? To see the effect, we go through the same exercise as before: If it spent it all on labor, it could buy 18 units of labor. If it spent it all on machines, it could buy 30 units of machinery. Connecting these points will give us a curve to the right of and parallel to the original curve. It has the same slope because the relative prices of the factors of production, which determine the slope, have not changed.

Now ask yourself, What happens to the isocost line if the price of labor rises to $10 a unit? If you said the isocost curve becomes steeper, shifting along the labor axis to point *D* while remaining anchored along the machinery axis until the slope is −10/3, you've got it. In general, the

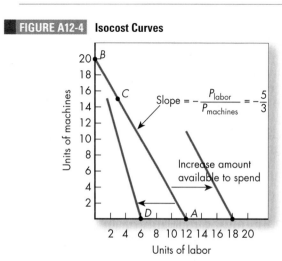

FIGURE A12-4   Isocost Curves

$$\text{Slope} = -\frac{P_{labor}}{P_{machines}} = -\frac{5}{3}$$

Increase amount available to spend

Units of machines

Units of labor

absolute value of the slope of the isocost curve is the ratio of the price of the factor of production on the *x*-axis to the price of the factor of production on the *y*-axis. That means that as the price of a factor rises, the end point of the isocost curve shifts in on the axis on which that factor is measured.

Choosing the Economically Efficient Point of Production

Now let's move on to a consideration of the economically efficient combination of resources to produce 60 pairs of earrings with $60. To do that, we must put the isoquant cost curve from Figure A12-2 and the isocost curve from Figure A12-4 together. We do so in Figure A12-5.

The problem for the firm is to produce as many pairs of earrings as possible with the $60 it has to spend. Or, put another way, given a level of production it has chosen, it wants to produce at the least-cost combination of the factors of production.

Let's now find the least-cost combination of inputs to produce 60 pairs of earrings. Let's say that, initially, the firm chooses point A on its isoquant curve—that's at 15 machines and 4 workers. That produces 60 pairs of earrings, but has a cost of $45 + $20 = $65. The firm can't produce 60 pairs of earrings unless it is willing to spend more than $60. If it fires a worker to bring its cost in line, moving it to point B, it moves down to a lower isoquant—it is producing only 40 pairs.

If the firm has a less-than-competent manager, that manager will conclude that you can't produce 60 for $60.

But say the firm has an efficient manager—one who has taken introductory economics. As opposed to *reducing* the number of workers as the other manager did, she *increases* the number of workers to 6 and reduces the number of machines to 10. Doing so still produces 60 pairs of earrings, since C is a point on the isoquant curve, but the strategy reduces the cost from $65 at point A to $60 (10 machines at $3 = $30 and 6 workers at $5 = $30). So she is producing 60 pairs of earrings at a cost of $60. She is operating at the economically efficient point—point C.

Let's talk about the characteristics of point C. Point C is the point where the isoquant curve is tangent to the isocost curve—the point at which the slope of the isoquant curve ($-MP_L/MP_M$) equals the slope of the isocost curve ($-P_L/P_M$). That is, $-MP_L/MP_M = -P_L/P_M$. This can be rewritten as

$$MP_L/P_L = MP_M/P_M$$

What this equation says is that when the additional output per dollar spent on labor equals the additional output per dollar spent on machines, the firm is operating efficiently. It makes sense. If the additional output per dollar spent on labor exceeded the additional output per dollar spent on machines, the firm would do better by increasing its use of labor and decreasing its use of machines.

Point C represents the combination of labor and machines that will result in the highest output given the isocost curve facing the firm. To put it in technical terms, the firm is operating at an economically efficient point where the marginal rate of substitution equals the ratio of the factor prices. Any point other than C on the isocost curve will cost $60 but produce fewer than 60 pairs of earrings. Any other point than C on the isoquant curve will produce 60 pairs of earrings but cost more than $60. Only C is the economically efficient point given the factor costs.

To see that you understand the analysis, say that the price of labor falls to $3 and you still want to produce 60. What will happen to the amount of labor and machines you hire? Alternatively, say that the price of machines rises to $5 and you want to spend only $60. What will happen to the amount of labor and machines you hire?

If your answers are (1) you hire more workers and fewer machines and (2) you reduce production using fewer machines and, maybe, less labor, you've got the analyses down. If you didn't give those answers, I suggest rereading this appendix, if it is to be on the exam, and working through the questions and exercises.

FIGURE A12-5   Combining Isoquant and Isocost Curves

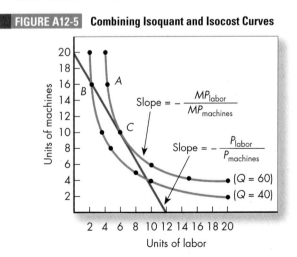

Key Terms

isocost line *(264)*   isoquant map *(263)*   marginal rate of substitution *(263)*
isoquant curve *(262)*

Questions and Exercises

1. What happens to the marginal rate of substitution as a firm increases the use of one input, keeping output constant? What accounts for this?

2. Draw an isocost curve for a firm that has $100 to spend on producing jeans. Input includes labor and materials. Labor costs $8 and materials cost $4 a unit. How does each of the following affect the isocost curve? Show your answer graphically.
   a. Production budget doubles.
   b. Cost of materials rises to $10 a unit.
   c. Cost of labor and materials each rises by 25 percent.

3. Show, using isocost/isoquant analysis, how firms in the United States use relatively less labor and relatively more land than Japan for the production of similar goods, yet both are behaving economically efficiently.

4. Demonstrate the difference between economic efficiency and technical efficiency, using isocost/isoquant analysis.

5. Draw a hypothetical isocost curve and an isoquant curve tangent to the isocost curve. Label the combination of inputs that represents an economically efficient use of resources.
   a. How does a technological innovation affect your analysis?
   b. How does the increase in the price of the input on the *x*-axis affect your analysis?

6. Show graphically the analysis of the example in Figure A12-5 if the price of labor falls to $3. Demonstrate that the firm can increase production given the same budget.

7. Show graphically the analysis of the example in Figure A12-5 if the price of machines rises to $5. Demonstrate that the firm must reduce production if it keeps the same budget.

chapter 13

Perfect Competition

> *There's no resting place for an enterprise in a competitive economy.*
>
> —Alfred P. Sloan

The concept *competition* is used in two ways in economics. One way is as a process. *Competition as a process* is a rivalry among firms and is prevalent throughout our economy. It involves one firm trying to figure out how to take away market share from another firm. An example is my publishing firm giving me a contract to write a great book like this in order for the firm to take market share away from other publishing firms that are also selling economics textbooks. The other use of *competition* is as a *perfectly competitive market structure.* It is this use that is the subject of this chapter.

Perfect Competition as a Reference Point

Although perfect competition has highly restrictive assumptions, it provides us with a reference point for thinking about various market structures and competitive processes. Why is such a reference point important? Think of the following analogy.

In physics when you study the laws of gravity, you initially study what would happen in a vacuum. Perfect vacuums don't exist, but talking about what would happen if you dropped an object in a perfect vacuum makes the analysis easier. So too with economics. Our equivalent of a perfect vacuum is perfect competition. In perfect competition, the invisible hand of the market operates unimpeded. In this chapter, we'll consider how perfectly competitive markets work and see how to apply the cost analysis developed in the previous two chapters.

Conditions for Perfect Competition

A **perfectly competitive market** is *a market in which economic forces operate unimpeded.* For a market to be called *perfectly competitive,* it must meet some stringent conditions. Some of them are: Both buyers and sellers are price takers. The number of firms is large. There are no barriers to entry. Firms' products are identical. There is complete information. Selling firms are profit-maximizing entrepreneurial firms. These and other similar conditions

After reading this chapter, you should be able to:

LO13-1 Explain how perfect competition serves as a reference point.

LO13-2 Explain why producing an output at which marginal cost equals price maximizes total profit for a perfect competitor.

LO13-3 Determine the output and profit of a perfect competitor graphically and numerically.

LO13-4 Explain the adjustment process from short-run equilibrium to long-run equilibrium.

are needed to ensure that economic forces operate instantaneously and are unimpeded by political and social forces.

To give you a sense of these conditions, let's consider some of these conditions a bit more carefully.

1. *Both buyers and sellers are price takers.* A **price taker** is *a firm or individual who takes the price determined by market supply and demand as given.* When you buy, say, toothpaste, you go to the store and find that the price of toothpaste is, say, $2.33 for the medium-size tube; you're a price taker. The firm, however, is a price maker since it set the price at $2.33. So even though the toothpaste industry is highly competitive, it's not a perfectly competitive market. In a perfectly competitive market, market supply and demand determine the price; both firms and consumers take the market price as given.

2. *There are no barriers to entry.* **Barriers to entry** are *social, political, or economic impediments that prevent firms from entering a market.* They might be legal barriers such as patents for products or processes. Barriers might be technological, such as when the minimum efficient level of production allows only one firm to produce at the lowest average total cost. Or barriers might be created by social forces, such as when bankers will lend only to individuals with specific racial characteristics. Perfect competition can have no barriers to entry.

3. *Firms' products are identical.* This requirement means that each firm's output is indistinguishable from any other firm's output. Corn bought by the bushel is relatively homogeneous. One kernel is indistinguishable from any other kernel. In contrast, you can buy 30 different brands of many goods—soft drinks, for instance: Pepsi, Coke, 7UP, and so on. They are all slightly different from one another and thus not identical.

Generally these conditions aren't met and firms are less than perfectly competitive.

Demand Curves for the Firm and the Industry

The market demand curve is downward sloping, but each individual firm in a competitive industry is so small that it perceives that its actions will not affect the price it can get for its product. Price is the same no matter how much the firm produces. Think of an individual firm's actions as removing one piece of sand from a beach. Does that lower the level of the beach? For all practical, and even most impractical, purposes, we can assume it doesn't. Similarly for a perfectly competitive firm. That is why we consider the demand curve facing the firm to be perfectly elastic (horizontal).

The price the firm can get is determined by the market, and the competitive firm takes the market price as given. This difference in perception is extremely important. It means that firms will increase their output in response to an increase in market demand even though that increase in output will cause the market price to fall and can make all firms collectively worse off. But since, by the assumptions of perfect competition, they don't act collectively, each firm follows its self-interest. Let's now consider that self-interest in more detail.

The Profit-Maximizing Level of Output

The goal of a firm is assumed to be maximizing profits—to get as much for itself as possible. So when it decides what quantity to produce, it will continually ask, "What will changes in how much I produce do to profit?" Since profit is the difference between total revenue and total cost, what happens to profit in response to a change in output is determined by **marginal revenue** *(MR), the change in total revenue associated with a change in quantity,* and **marginal cost** *(MC), the change in total cost associated with*

Q-1 Why is the assumption of no barriers to entry important for the existence of perfect competition?

WWW Web Note 13.1
Barriers to Entry

Q-2 How can the demand curve for the market be downward-sloping but the demand curve for a competitive firm be perfectly elastic?

Market vs. Firm Demand

a change in quantity. That's why marginal revenue and marginal cost are key concepts in determining the profit-maximizing or loss-minimizing level of output of any firm.

To emphasize the importance of *MR* and *MC,* those are the only cost and revenue figures shown in Figure 13-1. Notice that we don't illustrate profit at all. We'll calculate profit later. All we want to determine now is the profit-maximizing level of output. To do this, you need only know *MC* and *MR.* Specifically, a firm maximizes profit when *MC* = *MR.* To see why, let's look at *MC* and *MR* more closely.

> To determine the profit-maximizing output, all you need to know is *MC* and *MR*. Firms maximize profits where *MC* = *MR*.

Marginal Revenue

Let's first consider marginal revenue. Since a perfect competitor accepts the market price as given, marginal revenue is simply the market price. In the example shown in Figure 13-1, if the firm increases output from 2 to 3, its revenue rises by $35 (from $70 to $105). So its marginal revenue is $35, the price of the good. Since at a price of $35 it can sell as much as it wants, for a competitive firm, *MR* = *P.* Marginal revenue is given in column 1 of Figure 13-1(a). As you can see, *MR* equals $35 for all levels of output.

> For a competitive firm, *MR* = *P*.

Marginal Cost

Now let's move on to marginal cost. I'll be brief since I discussed marginal cost in detail in an earlier chapter. Marginal cost is the change in total cost that accompanies a change in output. Figure 13-1(a) shows marginal cost in column 3. Notice that initially in this example, marginal cost is falling, but after the fifth unit of output, it's increasing. This is consistent with our discussion in earlier chapters.

Notice also that the marginal cost figures are given for movements from one quantity to another. That's because marginal concepts tell us what happens when there's a change in something, so marginal concepts are best defined between numbers. The numbers in column 3 are the marginal costs. So the marginal cost of increasing output from 1 to 2 is $20, and the marginal cost of increasing output from 2 to 3 is $16. The marginal cost right at 2 (which the marginal cost graph shows) would be between $20 and $16, at approximately $18.

FIGURE 13-1 (A AND B) **Marginal Cost, Marginal Revenue, and Price**

The profit-maximizing output for a firm occurs where marginal cost equals marginal revenue. Since for a competitive firm *P* = *MR,* its profit-maximizing output is where *MC* = *P.* At any other output, it is forgoing profit.

Price = MR	Quantity Produced	Marginal Costs
$35.00	0	
		$28.00
35.00	1	
		20.00
35.00	2	
		16.00
35.00	3	
		14.00
35.00	4	
		12.00
35.00	5	
		17.00
35.00	6	
		22.00
35.00	7	
		30.00
35.00	8	
		40.00
35.00	9	
		54.00
35.00	10	

(a) *MC*/Price Table

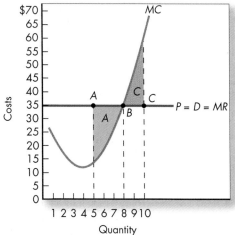

(b) *MC*/Price Graph

The Internet and the Perfectly Competitive Model

Recent technological developments are making the perfectly competitive model more directly relevant to our economy. Specifically, the Internet has eliminated the spatial dimension of competition (except for shipping), allowing individuals to compete globally rather than locally. When you see a bid on the Internet, you don't care where the supplier is (as long as you do not have to pay shipping fees). Because it allows access to so many buyers and sellers, the Internet reduces the number of seller-set posted price markets (such as found in retail stores), and replaces them with auction markets.

The Internet has had its biggest impact in firms' buying practices. Today, when firms want to buy standardized products, they will often post their technical requirements for desired components on the Net and allow suppliers from all over the world to bid to fill their orders. Firms have found that buying in this fashion over the

Internet has, on average, lowered the prices they pay by over 10 percent.

Similar changes are occurring in consumer markets. With sites like Priceline.com, individuals can set the price they are willing to pay for goods and services (such as hotel rooms and airline tickets) and see if anyone wants to supply them. (Recently, I successfully bid $150 for a $460 retail price hotel room in New York City.) With sites such as eBay, you can buy and sell almost anything. The Internet even has its own payment systems, such as PayPal.

In short, with the Internet, entry and exit are much easier than in traditional brick-and-mortar business, and that makes the market more like a perfectly competitive market. As Internet search engines become better designed for commerce, and as more people become Internet savvy, the economy will more and more closely resemble the perfectly competitive model.

Profit Maximization: MC = MR

As I noted above, to maximize profit, a firm should produce where marginal cost equals marginal revenue. Looking at Figure 13-1(b), we see that a firm following that rule will produce at an output of 8, where $MC = MR = \$35$. Now let me try to convince you that 8 is indeed the profit-maximizing output. To do so, let's consider three different possible quantities the firm might look at.

Q-3 What are the two things you must know to determine the profit-maximizing output?

Let's say that initially the firm decides to produce 5 widgets, placing it at point A in Figure 13-1(b). The firm receives $35 for each widget, so the marginal revenue for producing the fifth unit is $35. The marginal cost of doing so is $12. By producing five rather than four units, profit has increased by $23 ($35 − $12). So it makes sense to have produced 5 units rather than four. Notice that we don't know total profit, just the change in total profit as we change production levels. Should the firm increase production to 6? Again, marginal revenue is $35. This time marginal cost is $17. Profit increases by $18. Again it makes sense to increase production. As long as $MC <$ MR, it makes sense to increase production. The green shaded area (A) represents the entire increase in profit the firm can get by increasing output beyond 5 units.

Now let's say that the firm decides to produce 10 widgets, placing it at point C. Here the firm gets $35 for each widget. The marginal cost of producing that 10th unit is $54. So, $MC > MR$. If the firm decreases production by one unit, its cost decreases by $54 and its revenue decreases by $35. Profit increases by $19 ($54 − $35 = $19), so at point C, it makes sense to decrease output. This reasoning holds true as long as the marginal cost is above the marginal revenue. The brown shaded area (C) represents the increase in profits the firm can get by decreasing output.

At point B (output = 8) the firm gets $35 for each widget, and its marginal cost is $35, as you can see in Figure 13-1(b). The marginal cost of increasing output by one unit is $40 and the marginal revenue of selling one more unit is $35, so its profit falls by $5. If the firm decreases output by one unit, its *MC* is $30 and its *MR* is $35, so its profit falls by $5. Either increasing or decreasing production will decrease profit, so at point *B,* an output of 8, the firm is maximizing profit.

Since *MR* is just market price, we can state the **profit-maximizing condition** of a competitive firm as *MC = MR = P.* So, if *MR > MC,* increase production; if *MR < MC,* decrease production. If *MR = MC,* the firm is maximizing profit.

> Profit-maximizing condition for a competitive firm: *MC = MR = P.*

You should commit this profit-maximizing condition to memory. You should also be sure that you understand the intuition behind it. If marginal revenue isn't equal to marginal cost, a firm obviously can increase profit by changing output. If that isn't obvious, the marginal benefit of an additional hour of thinking about this condition will exceed the marginal cost (whatever it is), meaning that you should . . . right, you guessed it . . . study some more.

> If marginal revenue does not equal marginal cost, a firm can increase profit by changing output.

The Marginal Cost Curve Is the Supply Curve

Now let's consider again the definition of the supply curve as a schedule of quantities of goods that will be offered to the market at various prices. Notice that the upward-sloping portion of the marginal cost curve fits that definition. It tells how much the firm will supply at a given price. Figure 13-2 shows the various quantities the firm will supply at different market prices beginning at the upward-sloping portion at point *A*. If the price is $35, we showed that the firm would supply 8 (point *C*). If the price had been $19.50, the firm would have supplied 6 (point *B*); if the price had been $61, the firm would have supplied 10 (point *D*). Because the marginal cost curve tells us how much of a produced good a firm will supply at a given price, *the marginal cost curve is the firm's supply curve.* The *MC* curve tells the competitive firm how much it should produce at a given price. (As you'll see later, there's an addendum to this statement. Specifically, the marginal cost curve is the firm's supply curve only if price exceeds average variable cost.)

> Because the marginal cost curve tells us how much of a produced good a firm will supply at a given price, the marginal cost curve is the firm's supply curve.

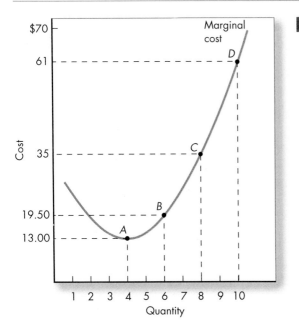

FIGURE 13-2 **The Marginal Cost Curve Is a Firm's Supply Curve**

Since the marginal cost curve tells the firm how much to produce, the marginal cost curve is the perfectly competitive firm's supply curve. This exhibit shows four points on a firm's supply curve; as you can see, the quantity the firm chooses to supply depends on the price. For example, if market price is $19.50, the firm produces 6 units.

Firms Maximize Total Profit

Q-4 Why do firms maximize total profit rather than profit per unit?

Notice that when you talk about maximizing profit, you're talking about maximizing *total profit,* not profit per unit. Profit per unit would be maximized at a much lower output level than is total profit. Profit-maximizing firms don't care about profit per unit; as long as an increase in output will increase total profits, a profit-maximizing firm should increase output. That's difficult to grasp, so let's consider a concrete example.

Say two people are selling T-shirts that cost $4 each. One sells 2 T-shirts at a price of $6 each and makes a profit per shirt of $2. His total profit is $4. The second person sells 8 T-shirts at $5 each, making a profit per unit of only $1 but selling 8. Her total profit is $8, twice as much as the fellow who had the $2 profit per unit. In this case, $5 (the price with the lower profit per unit), not $6, yields more total profit.

An alternative method of determining the profit-maximizing level of output is to look at the total revenue and total cost curves directly. Figure 13-3 shows total cost and total revenue for the firm we're considering so far. The table in Figure 13-3(a) shows total revenue in column 2, which is just the number of units sold times market price. Total cost is in column 3. Total cost is the cumulative sum of the marginal costs from Figure 13-1(a) plus a fixed cost of $40. Total profit (column 4) is the difference between total revenue and total cost. Looking down column 4 of Figure 13-3(a), you can quickly see that the profit-maximizing level of output is 8, as it was using the *MR = MC* rule, since total profit is highest at an output of 8.

In Figure 13-3(b) we plot the firm's total revenue and total cost curves from the table in Figure 13-3(a). The total revenue curve is a straight line; each additional unit sold increases revenue by the same amount, $35. The total cost curve is bowed upward at most quantities, reflecting the increasing marginal cost at different levels of output. The firm's profit is represented by the distance between the total revenue curve and the total cost curve. For example, at output 5, the firm makes $45 in profit.

FIGURE 13-3 (A AND B)   **Determination of Profits by Total Cost and Total Revenue Curves**

The profit-maximizing output level also can be seen by considering the total cost curve and the total revenue curve. Profit is maximized at the output where total revenue exceeds total cost by the largest amount. This occurs at an output of 8.

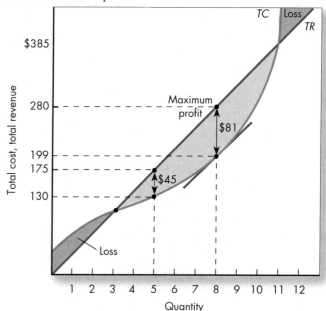

Quantity	Total Revenue	Total Cost	Total Profit
0	$ 0	$ 40	$-40
1	35	68	-33
2	70	88	-18
3	105	104	1
4	140	118	22
5	175	130	45
6	210	147	63
7	245	169	76
8	280	199	81
9	315	239	76
10	350	293	57

(a) Total Revenue and Total Cost Table

(b) Total Revenue and Total Cost Curves

Total profit is maximized where the vertical distance between total revenue and total cost is greatest. In this example, total profit is maximized at output 8, just as in the alternative approach. At that output, marginal revenue (the slope of the total revenue curve) and marginal cost (the slope of the total cost curve) are equal.

Total Profit at the Profit-Maximizing Level of Output

In the initial discussion of the firm's choice of output, given price, I carefully presented only marginal cost and price. We talked about maximizing profit, but nowhere did I mention what profit, average total cost, average variable cost, or average fixed cost was. I mentioned only marginal cost and price to emphasize that marginal cost is all that's needed to determine a competitive firm's supply curve (and a competitive firm is the only firm that has a supply curve) and to determine the output that will maximize profit. Now that you know that, let's turn our attention more closely to profit.

Marginal cost is all that is needed to determine a competitive firm's supply curve.

Determining Profit from a Table of Costs and Revenue

The $P = MR = MC$ condition tells us how much output a competitive firm should produce to maximize profit. It does not tell us the profit the firm makes. *Profit is determined by total revenue minus total cost.* Table 13-1 expands Figure 13-1(a) and presents a table of all the costs relevant to the firm. Going through the columns and reminding yourself of the definition of each is a good review of the two previous chapters. If the definitions don't come to mind immediately, you need a review. If you don't know the definitions of *MC, AVC, ATC, FC,* and *AFC,* go back and reread those chapters.

Profit is determined by total revenue minus total cost.

The firm is interested in maximizing profit. Looking at Table 13-1, you can quickly see that the profit-maximizing position is 8, as it was before, since at an output of 8, total profit is highest.

Using the $MC = MR = P$ rule, you can also see that the profit-maximizing level of output is 8. Increasing output from 7 to 8 has a marginal cost of $30, which is less than $35, so it makes sense to do so. Increasing output from 8 to 9 has a marginal cost of $40, which is more than $35, so it does not make sense to do so. The output 8 is the profit-maximizing output. At that profit-maximizing level of output, the profit the firm earns is $81, which is calculated by subtracting total cost of $199 from total revenue of

TABLE 13-1 Costs Relevant to a Firm

Price = Marginal Revenue	1 Quantity Produced	2 Total Fixed Cost	3 Average Fixed Cost	4 Total Variable Cost	5 Average Variable Cost	6 Total Cost	7 Marginal Cost	8 Average Total Cost	9 Total Revenue	10 Total Profit
$35.00	0	$40.00	—	0	—	$ 40.00		—	0	$−40.00
35.00	1	40.00	$40.00	$ 28.00	$28.00	68.00	$28.00	$68.00	$ 35.00	−33.00
35.00	2	40.00	20.00	48.00	24.00	88.00	20.00	44.00	70.00	−18.00
35.00	3	40.00	13.33	64.00	21.33	104.00	16.00	34.67	105.00	1.00
35.00	4	40.00	10.00	78.00	19.50	118.00	14.00	29.50	140.00	22.00
35.00	5	40.00	8.00	90.00	18.00	130.00	12.00	26.00	175.00	45.00
35.00	6	40.00	6.67	107.00	17.83	147.00	17.00	24.50	210.00	63.00
35.00	7	40.00	5.71	129.00	18.43	169.00	22.00	24.14	245.00	76.00
35.00	8	40.00	5.00	159.00	19.88	199.00	30.00	24.88	280.00	81.00
35.00	9	40.00	4.44	199.00	22.11	239.00	40.00	26.56	315.00	76.00
35.00	10	40.00	4.00	253.00	25.30	293.00	54.00	29.30	350.00	57.00

FIGURE 13-4 (A, B, AND C) Determining Profits Graphically

The profit-maximizing output depends *only* on where the *MC* and *MR* curves intersect. The total amount of profit or loss that a firm makes depends on the price it receives and its average total cost of producing the profit-maximizing output. This exhibit shows the case of (**a**) a profit, (**b**) zero profit, and (**c**) a loss.

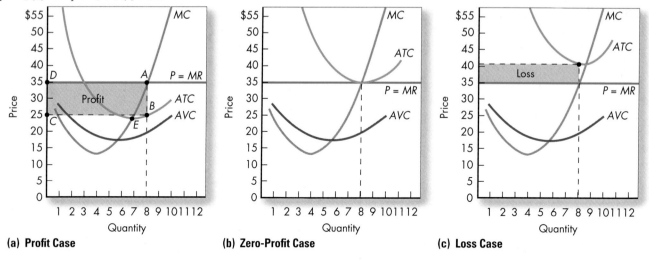

(a) Profit Case

(b) Zero-Profit Case

(c) Loss Case

$280. Notice also that average total cost is lowest at an output of about 7, and the average variable cost is lowest at an output of about 6.[1] Thus, the profit-maximizing position (which is 8) is *not* necessarily a position that minimizes either average variable cost or average total cost. It is only the position that maximizes total profit.

Determining Profit from a Graph

These relationships can be seen in a graph. In Figure 13-4(a) I add the average total cost and average variable cost curves to the graph of marginal cost and price first presented in Figure 13-1. Notice that the marginal cost curve goes through the lowest points of both average cost curves. (If you don't know why, it would be a good idea to go back and review the previous chapters.)

FIND OUTPUT WHERE *MC* = *MR*   The way you find profit graphically is first to find the point where *MC* = *MR* (point A). That intersection determines the quantity the firm will produce if it wants to maximize profit. Why? Because the vertical distance between a point on the marginal cost curve and a point on the marginal revenue curve represents the additional profit the firm can make by changing output. For example, if it increases production from 6 to 7, its marginal cost is $22 and its marginal revenue is $35. By increasing output it can increase profit by $13 (from $63 to $76). The same reasoning holds true for any output less than 8. For outputs higher than 8, the opposite reasoning holds true. Marginal cost exceeds marginal revenue, so it pays to decrease output. So, to maximize profit, the firm must see that there is no distance between the two curves—it must see where they intersect.

The profit-maximizing output can be determined in a table (as in Table 13-1) or in a graph (as in Figure 13-4).

Q-5 If the firm described in Figure 13-4 is producing 4 units, what would you advise it to do, and why?

---

[1] I say "about 6" and "about 7" because the table gives only whole numbers. The actual minimum point occurs at 5.55 for average variable cost and 6.55 for average total cost. The nearest whole numbers to these are 6 and 7.

FIND PROFIT PER UNIT WHERE MC = MR

After having determined the profit-maximizing quantity, drop a vertical line down to the horizontal axis and see what average total cost is at that output level (point *B*). Next extend a line back to the vertical axis (point *C*). That tells us that the average total costs per unit are $25. Next go up the price axis to the price that the firm receives (point *D*). For a competitive firm, that price is the marginal revenue as well as its average revenue, since the price is constant. The difference between this price and average cost is profit per unit. Connecting these points gives us the shaded rectangle, *ABCD,* which is the total profit earned by the firm (the total quantity times the profit per unit).

Notice that at the profit-maximizing position, the profit per unit isn't at its highest because average total cost is *not* at its minimum point. Profit per unit of output would be highest at point *E*. A common mistake that students make is to draw a line up from point *E* when they are finding profits. That is wrong. It is important to remember: *To determine maximum profit, you must first determine what output the firm will choose to produce by seeing where* MC *equals* MR *and then determine the average total cost at that quantity by dropping a line down to the* ATC *curve.* Only then can you determine what maximum profit will be.

Thinking Like a Modern Economist

Profit Maximization and Real-World Firms

Most real-world firms do not have profit as their only goal. The reason is that, in the real world, the decision maker's income is part of the cost of production. For example, a paid manager has an incentive to hold down costs but has little incentive to hold down his income, which, for the firm, is a cost. Alternatively, say that a firm is a worker-managed firm. If workers receive a share of the profits, they'll push for higher profits, but they'll also see to it that in the process of maximizing profits they don't hurt their own interest—maximizing their wages.

A manager-managed firm will push for high profits but will see to it that it doesn't achieve those profits by hurting the manager's interests. Managers' pay will be high. In short, real-world firms will hold down the costs of factors of production *except* the cost of the decision maker.

In real life, this problem of the lack of incentives to hold down costs is important. For example, firms' managerial expenses often balloon even as firms are cutting "costs." Similarly, CEOs and other high-ranking officers of the firm often have enormously high salaries. How and why the lack of incentives to hold down costs affects the economy is best seen by first considering the nature of an economy with incentives to hold down all costs. That's why we use as our standard model the traditional profit-maximizing firm. (*Standard model* means the model that economists use as our basis of reasoning; from it, we branch out.) Using what are called game theory models, modern economists work with firms to devise incentive-compatible contracts that align the goals of decision makers in the firm with the goals of the owners of firms.

ZERO PROFIT OR LOSS WHERE MC = MR

Notice also that as the curves in Figure 13-4(a) are drawn, *ATC* at the profit-maximizing position is below the price, so the firm makes a profit. The choice of short-run average total cost curves was arbitrary and doesn't affect the firm's profit-maximizing condition: *MC = MR*. It could have been assumed that fixed cost was higher, which would have shifted the *ATC* curve up. In Figure 13-4(b) it's assumed that fixed cost is $81 higher than in Figure 13-4(a). Instead of $40, it's $121. The appropriate average total cost curve for a fixed cost of $121 is drawn in Figure 13-4(b). Notice that in this case economic profit is zero and the marginal cost curve intersects the minimum point of the average total cost curve at an output of 8 and a price of $35. (Remember from the last chapter that even though economic profit is zero, all resources, including entrepreneurs, are being paid their opportunity cost.)

In Figure 13-4(c), fixed cost is even higher. Profit-maximizing output is still 8, but now at an output of 8 average total cost is $41 and the firm is making an economic

When the *ATC* curve is below the marginal revenue curve, the firm makes a profit. When the *ATC* curve is above the marginal revenue curve, the firm incurs a loss.

Q-6 What is wrong with the following diagram?

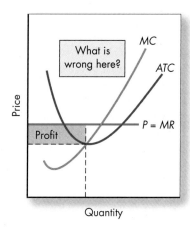

Q-7 In the early 2000s, many airlines were making losses, yet they continued to operate. Why?

The shutdown point is the point below which the firm will be better off if it shuts down than it will if it stays in business.

If $P >$ minimum of AVC, the firm will continue to produce in the short run. If $P <$ minimum of AVC, the firm will shut down.

loss of $6 on each unit sold. The loss is given by the shaded rectangle. In this case, the profit-maximizing condition is actually a loss-minimizing condition. So $MC = MR = P$ is both a *profit-maximizing condition* and a *loss-minimizing condition*.

I draw these three cases to emphasize to you that determining the profit-maximizing output level doesn't depend on fixed cost or average total cost. It depends only on where marginal cost equals price.

The Shutdown Point

Earlier I stated the supply curve of a competitive firm is its marginal cost curve. More specifically, the supply curve is the part of the marginal cost curve that is above the average variable cost curve. Considering why this is the case should help the analysis stick in your mind.

Let's consider Figure 13-5(a)—a reproduction of Figure 13-4(c)—and the firm's decision at various prices. At a price of $35, it's incurring a loss of $6 per unit. If it's making a loss, why doesn't it shut down? The answer lies in the fixed costs. There's no use crying over spilt milk. In the short run, a firm knows these fixed costs are sunk costs; it must pay them regardless of whether or not it produces. The firm considers only the costs it can save by stopping production, and those costs are its variable costs. As long as a firm is covering its variable costs, it pays to keep on producing. By producing, its loss is $48; if it stopped producing, its loss would be all the fixed costs ($169). So it makes a smaller loss by producing.

However, once the price falls below average variable costs (below $17.80), it will pay to shut down (point *A* in Figure 13-5(a)). In that case, the firm's loss from producing would be more than $169, and it would do better to simply stop producing temporarily and avoid paying the variable cost. Thus, the point at which price equals *AVC* is the **shutdown point** (*that point below which the firm will be better off if it temporarily shuts down than it will if it stays in business*). When price falls below the shutdown point, the average variable cost the firm can avoid paying by shutting down exceeds the price it would get for selling the good. When price is above average variable cost, in the short run a firm should keep on producing even though it's making a loss. As long as a firm's total revenue is covering its total variable cost, temporarily producing at a loss is the firm's best strategy because it's making a smaller loss than it would make if it were to shut down.

Short-Run Market Supply and Demand

Most of the preceding discussion focused on supply and demand analysis of a firm. Now let's consider supply and demand in an industry. We've already discussed industry demand. Even though the demand curve faced by the firm is perfectly elastic, the industry demand curve is downward-sloping.

How about the industry supply curve? We previously demonstrated that the supply curve for a competitive firm is that portion of a firm's marginal cost curve that is above the average variable cost curve. To discuss the industry supply curve, we must use a market supply curve. In the short run when the number of firms in the market is fixed, the **market supply curve** is just the *horizontal sum of all the firms' marginal cost curves, taking account of any changes in input prices that might occur*. To move from individual firms' marginal cost curves or supply curves to the market supply curve, we add the quantities all firms will supply at each possible price. Since all firms in a competitive market have identical marginal cost curves, a quick way of summing the quantities is to multiply the quantities from the marginal cost curve of a representative firm at each price by the number of firms in the market. As the short run evolves into the long run, the number of firms in the market can change. As more firms enter the

The market supply curve is the horizontal sum of all the firms' marginal cost curves, taking account of any changes in input prices that might occur.

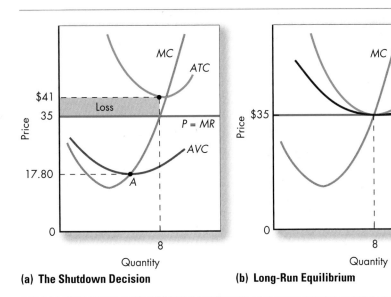

FIGURE 13-5 **The Shutdown Decision and Long-Run Equilibrium**

A firm should continue to produce as long as price exceeds average variable cost. Once price falls below that, it will do better by temporarily shutting down and saving the variable costs. This occurs at point A in (**a**). In (**b**), the long-run equilibrium position for a firm in a competitive industry is shown. In that long-run equilibrium, only normal profits are made.

market, the market supply curve shifts to the right because more firms are supplying the quantity indicated by the representative marginal cost curve. Likewise, as the number of firms in the market declines, the market supply curve shifts to the left. Knowing how the number of firms in the market affects the market supply curve is important to understanding long-run equilibrium in perfectly competitive markets.

Long-Run Competitive Equilibrium: Zero Profit

The analysis of the competitive firm consists of two parts: the short-run analysis just presented and the long-run analysis. In the short run, the number of firms is fixed and the firm can either earn economic profit or incur economic loss. In the long run, firms enter and exit the market and neither economic profits nor economic losses are possible. In the long run, firms make zero economic profit. Thus, in the long run, only the zero-profit equilibrium shown in Figure 13-5(b) is possible. As you can see, at that long-run equilibrium, the firm is at the minimum of both the short-run and the long-run average total cost curves.

Why can't firms earn economic profit or make economic losses in the long run? Because of the entry and exit of firms: If there are economic profits, firms will enter the market, shifting the market supply curve to the right. As market supply increases, the market price will decline and reduce profits for each firm. Firms will continue to enter the market and the market price will continue to decline until the incentive of economic profits is eliminated. At that price, all firms are earning zero profit. Similarly, if the price is lower than the price necessary to earn a profit, firms incurring losses will leave the market and the market supply curve will shift to the left. As market supply shifts to the left, market price will rise. Firms will continue to exit the market and market price will continue to rise until all remaining firms no longer incur losses and earn zero profit. Only at zero profit do entry and exit stop.

Zero profit does not mean that entrepreneurs get nothing for their efforts. The entrepreneur is an input to production just like any other factor of production. In order to stay in the business, the entrepreneur must receive the opportunity cost, or **normal profit** (*the amount the owners of business would have received in the next-best alternative*). That normal profit is built into the costs of the firm; economic profits are profits above normal profits.

Since profits create incentives for new firms to enter, output will increase, and the price will fall until zero profits are being made.

Web Note 13.2
Shutdown and Exit

Q-8 If a competitive firm makes zero profit, why does it stay in business?

Finding Output, Price, and Profit

To find a competitive firm's price, level of output, and profit given a firm's marginal cost curve and average total cost curve, use the following four steps:

1. Determine the market price at which market supply and demand curves intersect. This is the price the competitive firm accepts for its products.

2. Draw the horizontal marginal revenue (MR) curve at the market price.

3. Determine the profit-maximizing level of output by finding the level of output where the MR and MC curves intersect.

4. Determine profit by subtracting average total costs at the profit-maximizing level of output from the price and multiplying by the firm's output.

If you are demonstrating profit graphically, find the point at which $MC = MR$. Extend a line down to the ATC curve. Extend a line from this point to the vertical axis. To complete the box indicating profit, go up the vertical axis to the market price.

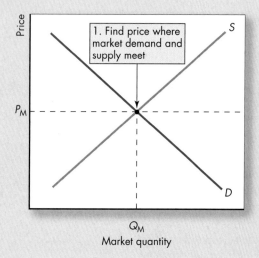

Market quantity

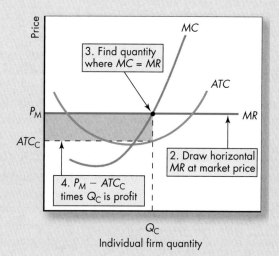

Individual firm quantity

Another aspect of the zero profit position deserves mentioning. What if one firm has superefficient workers or machinery? Won't the firm make a profit in the long run? The answer is, again, no. In a long-run competitive market, other firms will see the value of those workers and machines and will compete to get them for themselves. As firms compete for the superefficient factors of production, the prices of those specialized inputs will rise until all profits are eliminated. Those factors will receive what are called rents for their specialized ability. For example, say the average worker receives $400 per week, but Sarah, because she's such a good worker, receives $600. So $200 of the $600 she receives is a rent for her specialized ability. Either her existing firm matches that $600 wage or she will change employment.

The zero-profit condition is enormously powerful; it makes the analysis of competitive markets far more applicable to the real world than can a strict application of the assumption of perfect competition. If economic profit is being made, firms will enter and compete that profit away. Price will be pushed down to the average total cost of production as long as there are no barriers to entry. As we'll see in later chapters, in

The zero-profit condition is enormously powerful; it makes the analysis of competitive markets far more applicable to the real world than would otherwise be the case.

their analysis of whether markets are competitive, many economists focus primarily on whether barriers to entry exist.

Adjustment from the Short Run to the Long Run

Now that we've been through the basics of the perfectly competitive supply and demand curves, we're ready to consider the two together and to see how the adjustment to long-run equilibrium will likely take place for the firm and in the market.

An Increase in Demand

First, in Figure 13-6(a and b), let's consider a market that's in equilibrium but that suddenly experiences an increase in demand. Figure 13-6(a) shows the market reaction. Figure 13-6(b) shows a representative firm's reaction. Originally market equilibrium occurs at a price of $7 and market quantity supplied of 700 thousand units (point A in (a)), with each of 70 firms producing 10 thousand units (point a in (b)). Firms are making zero profit because they're in long-run equilibrium. If demand increases from D_0 to D_1, the firms will see the market price increasing and will increase their output until they're once again at a position where $MC = P$. This occurs at point B at a market output of 840 thousand units in (a) and at point b at a firm output of 12 thousand in (b). In the short run, the 70 existing firms each makes an economic profit (the shaded area in Figure 13-6(b)). Price has risen to $9, but average cost is only $7.10, so if the price remains $9, each firm is making a profit of $1.90 per unit. But price cannot remain at $9 since new firms will have an incentive to enter the market.

FIGURE 13-6 (A AND B)   **Market Response to an Increase in Demand**

Faced with an increase in demand, which it sees as an increase in price and hence profits, a competitive firm will respond by increasing output (from A to B) in order to maximize profit. The market response is shown in (a); the firm's response is shown in (b). As all firms increase output and as new firms enter, price will fall until all profit is competed away. Thus, the long-run market supply curve will be perfectly elastic, as is S_{LR} in (a). The final equilibrium will be the original price but a higher output. The original firms return to their original output (A), but since there are more firms in the market, the market output increases to C.

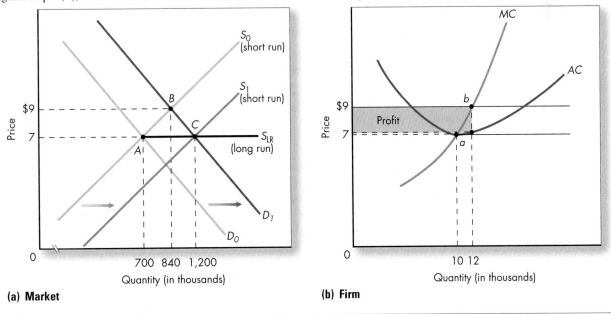

(a) Market   **(b) Firm**

The Shutdown Decision and the Relevant Costs

The previous two chapters emphasized that it is vital to choose the relevant costs to the decision at hand. Discussing the shutdown decision gives us a chance to demonstrate the importance of those choices. Say the firm leases a large computer it needs to operate. The rental cost of that computer is a fixed cost for most decisions, if, as long as the firm keeps the computer, the rent must be paid whether or not the computer is used. However, if the firm can end the rental contract at any time, and thereby save the rental cost, the computer is not a fixed cost. But neither is it your normal variable cost. Since the firm can end the rental contract and save the cost only if it shuts down, that rental cost of the computer is an *indivisible setup cost*. For the shutdown decision, the computer cost is a variable cost. For other decisions about changing quantity, it's a fixed cost.

The moral: The relevant cost can change with the decision at hand, so when you apply the analysis to real-world situations, be sure to think carefully about what the *relevant cost* is.

Consider the problem facing GM and other U.S. auto producers before they were reorganized after a government bailout. In their contracts with their workers, they had agreed to pay their workers whether they worked or not, making labor costs, in large part, fixed. This meant that GM actually saved much less when cutting production than it would if it did not have to pay idle workers. The implication of these contracts was that when demand fell, GM had a strong incentive to keep on producing, and then to sell the cars at a loss. Why sell at a loss? Because the loss was less than if GM had shut down production. GM ultimately restructured its contracts when the government bailed the company out. This restructuring changed many of its fixed costs to variable costs, so that its production can respond more quickly to changes in demand.

Q-9 If berets suddenly became the "in" thing to wear, what would you expect to happen to the price in the short run? In the long run?

As new firms enter, if input prices remain constant, the short-run market supply curve shifts from S_0 to S_1 and the market price returns to $7. The entry of 50 new firms provides the additional output in this example, bringing market output to 1.2 million units sold for $7 apiece. The final equilibrium will be at a higher market output but at the same price.

In the long run, firms earn zero profits.

Long-Run Market Supply

The long-run market supply curve is a schedule of quantities supplied when firms are no longer entering or exiting the market. This occurs when firms are earning zero profit. In this case, the long-run supply curve is created by extending to the right the line connecting points A and C. Since equilibrium price remains at $7, the long-run supply curve is perfectly elastic. The long-run supply curve is horizontal because factor prices are constant and there are constant returns to scale. That is, factor prices do not increase as industry output increases. Economists call this market a *constant-cost industry*. Two other possibilities exist: an *increasing-cost industry* (in which factor prices rise as more firms enter the market and existing firms expand production) and a *decreasing-cost industry* (in which factor prices fall as industry output expands).

Factor prices are likely to rise when industry output increases if the factors of production are specialized. An increase in the demand for the factors of production that accompanies an increase in output, in this case, will bid up factor prices. The effect on long-run supply is the following: The rise in factor prices forces costs up for each individual firm and increases the price at which firms earn zero profit. Firms will stop entering the market and expanding production at a higher equilibrium price since the price at which zero profit is made has risen. Therefore, in increasing-cost industries, the long-run supply curve is upward-sloping. In the extreme case, in which all firms in an industry are competitively supplying a perfectly inelastic resource or factor input, the long-run market supply curve is perfectly inelastic (vertical). Any increase in demand would increase the price of that factor. Costs would rise in response to the increase in demand; output would not. Input costs would also rise if there are diseconomies of scale in the input-supplying industry. In both cases, the long-run equilibrium price would have been higher and output would have been lower than if input prices remained constant.[2]

The other possibility is a decreasing-cost industry. If factor prices decline when industry output expands, individual firms' cost curves shift down. As they do, the price at which the zero-profit condition falls and the price at which firms cease to enter the market also falls. In this case, the long-run market supply curve is downward-sloping. Factor prices may decline as output rises when new entrants make it more cost-effective for other firms to provide services to all firms in the area. The supply of factors of production expands and reduces the price of inputs to production.

Notice that in the long-run equilibrium, once again zero profit is being made. Long-run equilibrium is defined by zero economic profit. Notice also that the long-run supply curve is more elastic than the short-run supply curve. That's because output changes are much less costly in the long run than in the short run. *In the short run, the price does more of the adjusting. In the long run, more of the adjustment is done by quantity.*

A REMINDER

A Summary of a Perfectly Competitive Industry

Four things to remember when considering a perfectly competitive industry are

1. The profit-maximizing condition for perfectly competitive firms is $MC = MR = P$.

2. To determine profit or loss at the profit-maximizing level of output, subtract the average total cost at that level of output from the price and multiply the result by the output level.

3. Firms will shut down production if price falls below the minimum of their average variable costs.

4. A perfectly competitive firm is in long-run equilibrium only when it is earning zero economic profit, or when price equals the minimum of long-run average total costs.

An Example in the Real World

The perfectly competitive model and the reasoning underlying it are extremely powerful. With them you have a simple model to use as a first approach to predict the effect of an event, or to explain why an event occurred. For example, consider the decision of the owners of the Blockbuster chain of video rental stores to close over 2,000 of its stores after experiencing years of losses.

Figure 13-7 shows what happened. Initially, Blockbuster saw the losses it was suffering as temporary. In the years prior to the shutdown decision, Blockbuster's cost curves looked like those in Figure 13-7. Since price exceeded average variable cost, Blockbuster continued to produce even though it was making a loss.

Q-10 In the early 2000s, demand for burkhas (the garment the Taliban had required Afghani women to wear) declined when the Taliban were ousted. In the short run, what would you expect to happen to the price of burkhas? How about in the long run?

WWW Web Note 13.3 Is It Perfect Competition or Not?

---

[2]To check your understanding, ask yourself the following question: What if there had been economies of scale? If you answered, "There couldn't have been," you're really into economic thinking. (For those of you who aren't all that heavily into economic thinking, the reason is that if there had been economies of scale, the market structure would not have been perfectly competitive. One firm would have kept expanding and expanding and, as it did, its costs would have kept falling.)

FIGURE 13-7 **A Real-World Example: A Shutdown Decision**

Supply/demand analysis can be applied to a wide variety of real-world examples. This exhibit shows one, but there are many more. As you experience life today, a good exercise is to put on your supply/demand glasses and interpret everything you see in a supply/demand framework.

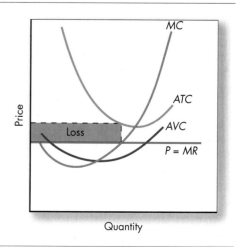

But after years of losses, Blockbuster's perspective changed. The company moved from the short run to the long run. Blockbuster began to believe that the demand wasn't temporarily low but rather permanently low. It began to ask: What costs are truly fixed and what costs are simply indivisible costs that we can save if we close down completely, selling our buildings and reducing our overhead? Since in the long run all costs are variable, the *ATC* became its relevant *AVC*. Blockbuster recognized that prices had fallen below these long-run average costs. At that point, it shut down those stores for which $P < AVC$.

There are hundreds of other real-world examples to which the perfectly competitive model adds insight. That's one reason why it's important to keep it in the back of your mind.

Conclusion

We've come to the end of the presentation of perfect competition. It was tough going, but if you went through it carefully, it will serve you well, both as a basis for later chapters and as a reference point for how real-world economies work. But like many good things, a complete understanding of the chapter doesn't come easy.

Summary

- The necessary conditions for perfect competition include: buyers and sellers are price takers, there are no barriers to entry, and firms' products are identical. (*LO13-1*)

- The profit-maximizing position of a competitive firm is where marginal revenue equals marginal cost. (*LO13-2*)

- The supply curve of a competitive firm is its marginal cost curve. Only competitive firms have supply curves. (*LO13-2*)

- To find the profit-maximizing level of output for a perfect competitor, find that level of output where $MC = MR$. Profit is price less average total cost times output at the profit-maximizing level of output. (*LO13-3*)

- In the short run, competitive firms can make a profit or loss. In the long run, they make zero profits. *(LO13-3)*

- Profit equals total revenue less total cost. Graphically, profit is the vertical distance between the price of the good and the ATC curve at the maximizing level of output times that level of output. *(LO13-3)*

- The shutdown price for a perfectly competitive firm is a price below average variable cost. *(LO13-3)*

- The short-run market supply curve is the horizontal summation of the marginal cost curves for all firms in the market. An increase in the number of firms in the market shifts the market supply curve to the right, while a decrease shifts it to the left. *(LO13-3)*

- Perfectly competitive firms make zero profit in the long run because if profit were being made, new firms would enter and the market price would decline, eliminating the profit. If losses were being made, firms would exit and the market price would rise. *(LO13-3)*

- The long-run supply curve is a schedule of quantities supplied where firms are making zero profit. *(LO13-4)*

- The slope of the long-run supply curve depends on what happens to factor prices when output increases. *(LO13-4)*

- Constant-cost industries have horizontal long-run supply curves. Increasing-cost industries have upward-sloping long-run supply curves, and decreasing-cost industries have downward-sloping long-run supply curves. *(LO 13-4)*

Key Terms

barriers to entry *(268)*
marginal cost
   (MC) (268)

marginal revenue
   (MR) (268)
market supply
   curve *(276)*

normal profit *(277)*
perfectly competitive
   market *(267)*
price taker *(268)*

profit-maximizing
   condition *(271)*
shutdown point *(276)*

Questions and Exercises

1. Why must buyers and sellers be price takers for a market to be perfectly competitive? *(LO13-1)*

2. List three conditions for perfect competition. *(LO13-1)*

3. If the conditions for perfect competition are generally not met, why do economists use the model? *(LO13-1)*

4. You're thinking of buying one of two firms. One has a profit margin of $8 per unit; the other has a profit margin of $4 per unit. Which should you buy? Why? (Difficult) *(LO13-2)*

5. A perfectly competitive firm sells its good for $20. If marginal cost is four times the quantity produced, how much does the firm produce? Why? (Difficult) *(LO13-2)*

6. Draw marginal cost, marginal revenue, and average total cost curves for a typical perfectly competitive firm and indicate the profit-maximizing level of output and total profit for that firm. Is the firm in long-run equilibrium? Why or why not? *(LO13-3)*

7. State what is *wrong* with each of the graphs. *(LO13-3)*

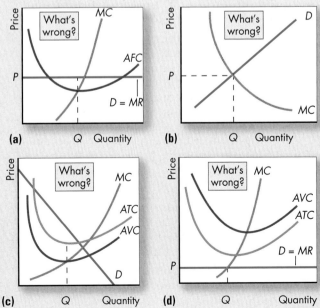

8. What will be the effect of a technological development that reduces marginal costs in a competitive market on short-run price, quantity, and profit?   (*LO13-3*)

9. Draw marginal cost, marginal revenue, and average total cost curves for a typical perfectly competitive firm in long-run equilibrium and indicate the profit-maximizing level of output and total profit for that firm.   (*LO13-3*)

10. Each of 10 firms in a given industry has the costs given in the left-hand table. The market demand schedule is given in the right-hand table.   (*LO13-3*)

Quantity	Total Cost	Price	Quantity Demanded
0	12	2	110
1	24	4	100
2	27	6	90
3	31	8	80
4	39	10	70
5	53	12	60
6	73	14	50
7	99	16	40

a. What is the market equilibrium price and the price each firm gets for its product?

b. What is the equilibrium market quantity and the quantity each firm produces?

c. What profit is each firm making?

d. Below what price will firms begin to exit the market?

11. Graphically demonstrate the quantity and price of a perfectly competitive firm.   (*LO13-3*)

a. Why is a slightly larger quantity not preferred?

b. Why is a slightly lower quantity not preferred?

c. Label the shutdown point in your diagram.

d. You have just discovered that shutting down means that you would lose your land zoning permit, which is required to start operating again. How does that change your answer to *c*?

12. How is a firm's marginal cost curve related to the market supply curve?   (*LO13-3*)

13. Draw the *ATC, AVC,* and *MC* curves for a typical firm. Label the price at which the firm would shut down temporarily and the price at which the firm would exit the market in the long run.   (*LO13-3*)

14. Under what cost condition is the shutdown point the same as the point at which a firm exits the market?   (*LO13-3*)

15. A profit-maximizing firm is producing where *MR = MC* and has an average total cost of $4, but it gets a price of $3 for each good it sells.   (*LO13-3*)

a. What would you advise the firm to do?

b. What would you advise the firm to do if you knew average variable costs were $3.50?

16. A farmer is producing where *MC = MR*. Say that half of the cost of producing wheat is the rental cost of land (a fixed cost) and half is the cost of labor and machines (a variable cost). If the average total cost of producing wheat is $8 and the price of wheat is $6, what would you advise the farmer to do? ("Grow something else" is not allowed.)   (*LO13-3*)

17. Based on the following table: (*LO13-4*)

Output	Price	Total Costs
0	$10	$ 31
1	10	40
2	10	45
3	10	48
4	10	55
5	10	65
6	10	80
7	10	100
8	10	140
9	10	220
10	10	340

a. What is the profit-maximizing output?

b. What will happen to the market price in the long run?

18. Why is the long-run market supply curve upward-sloping in an increasing-cost industry?   (*LO13-4*)

19. Why is the long-run market supply curve downward-sloping in a decreasing-cost industry?   (*LO13-4*)

20. Why is the long-run market supply curve horizontal in a constant-cost industry?   (*LO13-4*)

21. Use the accompanying graph, which shows the marginal cost and average total cost curves for the shoe store Zapateria, a perfectly competitive firm.   (*LO13-4*)

a. How many pairs of shoes will Zapateria produce if the market price of shoes is $70 a pair?

b. What is the total profit Zapateria will earn if the market price of shoes is $70 a pair?

c. Should Zapateria expect more shoe stores to enter this market? Why or why not?

d. What is the long-run equilibrium price in the shoe market assuming it is a constant-cost industry?

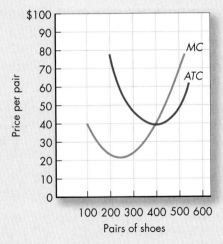

22. Suppose an increasing-cost industry is in both long-run and short-run equilibrium. Explain what will happen to the following in the long run if the demand for that product declines: (LO13-4)
    a. Price.   c. Number of firms in the market.
    b. Quantity. d. Profit.

23. A *Wall Street Journal* headline states: "A Nation of Snackers Snubs Old Favorite: The Beloved Cookie." As U.S. consumers adopted more carbohydrate-conscious diets, the number of cookie boxes sold declined 5.4 percent that year, the third consecutive year of decline.   (LO13-4)
    a. Assuming the cookie industry is perfectly competitive, demonstrate using market supply and demand curves the effect of this decline in demand on equilibrium price and quantity in the short run.
    b. Assuming a cookie firm was in equilibrium before the change in demand, and that it is a constant-cost industry, demonstrate the effect of the decline on equilibrium price for an individual cookie firm in the short run.
    c. How might your answer to *a* change if you are considering the long run?

24. Demonstrate the effect of the following on demand and supply in the short run and the long run.   (LO13-4)
    a. Assume that a textile quota expires, reducing demand for textiles imported from Mexico. The biggest competition Mexico faces is from the Chinese textile market. Market: Mexican textile market. (Assume this is an increasing-cost industry.)
    b. The European Union harmonized all taxes, which raised taxes on French restaurants. Assume restaurants are a constant-cost industry.

Questions from Alternative Perspectives

1. The book presents the perfectly competitive model as the foundation for economic analysis.
   a. How well does the theory of perfect competition reflect the real world?
   b. What role, if any, does the government have in promoting perfectly competitive markets?
   c. What is the danger in the government's intervening to promote competitive markets? (Austrian)

2. This chapter discusses perfect competition as a benchmark to think about the economy.
   a. Can labor market discrimination—hiring someone on the basis of race or gender rather than capability— exist in a perfectly competitive industry?
   b. Can the elimination of discrimination increase efficiency? (Feminist)

3. Perfect competition is analytically elegant.
   a. What percentage of an economy's total production do you think is provided by perfectly competitive firms?
   b. Based on your answer to *a,* why does the text spend so much time on perfect competition? (Institutionalist)

4. The perfectly competitive model assumes that firms know when marginal revenue equals marginal costs.
   a. If a firm doesn't have this information, can it produce at the profit-maximizing level of output?
   b. If firms don't have such knowledge, how might the theory of perfect competition be changed to better reflect reality? (Post-Keynesian)

5. As the chapter points out, the Internet has made the U.S. economy more competitive by lowering barriers to entry and exit from industries.
   a. To what extent is the Internet itself competitive?
   b. Can competitive conditions develop from information technology, a technology that was created initially by centralized planning, that depends on agreed-upon rules to conduct business, and that has notoriously low marginal costs? (Think of the cost of downloading a song off the Internet.) (Radical)

Issues to Ponder

1. If a firm is owned by its workers but otherwise meets all the qualifications for a perfectly competitive firm, will its price and output decisions differ from the price and output decisions of a perfectly competitive firm? Why?

2. The milk industry has a number of interesting aspects. Provide economic explanations for the following:
   a. Fluid milk is 87 percent water. It can be dried and reconstituted so that it is almost indistinguishable from fresh milk. What is a likely reason that such reconstituted milk is not produced?
   b. The United States has regional milk-marketing regulations whose goals are to make each of the regions self-sufficient in milk. What is a likely reason for this?
   c. A U.S. senator from a milk-producing state has been quoted as saying, "I am absolutely convinced . . . that simply bringing down dairy price supports is not a way to cut production." Is it likely that he is correct? What is a probable reason for his statement?

3. A California biotechnology firm submitted a tomato that will not rot for weeks to the U.S. Food and Drug Administration. It designed such a fruit by changing the genetic structure of the tomato. What effect will this technological change have on:
   a. The price of tomatoes?
   b. Farmers who grow tomatoes?
   c. The geographic areas where tomatoes are grown?
   d. Where tomatoes are generally placed on salad bars in winter?

4. Hundreds of music stores have been closing in the face of stagnant demand for CDs and new competitors—online music vendors and discount retailers.
   a. How would price competition from these new sources cause a retail store to close?
   b. In the long run, what effect will new entrants have on the price of CDs?

5. In 2004 FAO Schwartz closed its 89 Zany Brainy stores.
   a. Demonstrate graphically the relationship between *ATC, AVC,* and price faced by Zany Brainy stores when they decided to close.
   b. Assuming the market is perfectly competitive and is a constant-cost industry, what will happen in this market in the long run? Demonstrate with market supply and demand curves.

Answers to Margin Questions

1. Without the assumption of no barriers to entry, firms could make a profit by raising price; hence, the demand curve they face would not be perfectly elastic and, hence, perfect competition would not exist. (*p. 268; LO13-1*)

2. The competitive firm is such a small portion of the total market that it can have no effect on price. Consequently it takes the price as given, and, hence, its perceived demand curve is perfectly elastic. (*p. 268; LO13-1*)

3. To determine the profit-maximizing output of a competitive firm, you must know price and marginal cost. (*p. 270; LO13-2*)

4. Firms are interested in getting as much for themselves as they possibly can. Maximizing total profit does this. Maximizing profit per unit might yield very small total profits. (*p. 272; LO13-2*)

5. If the firm in Figure 13-4 were producing 4 units, I would explain to it that the marginal cost of increasing output is only $12 and the marginal revenue is $35, so it should significantly expand output until 8, where the marginal cost equals the marginal revenue, or price. (*p. 274; LO13-3*)

6. The diagram is drawn with the wrong profit-maximizing output and, hence, the wrong profit. Output is determined where marginal cost equals price and profit is the difference between the average total cost and price at that output, not at the output where marginal cost equals average total cost. The correct diagram is shown here. (*p. 276; LO13-3*)

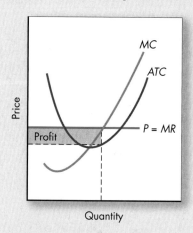

7. The marginal cost for airlines is significantly below average total cost. Since they're recovering their average variable cost, they continue to operate. In the long run, if this continues, some airlines will be forced out of business. (*p. 276; LO13-3*)

8. The costs for a firm include the normal costs, which in turn include a return for all factors of production. Thus, it is worthwhile for a competitive firm to stay in business, since it is doing better than, or at least as well as, it could in any other activity. (*p. 277; LO13-3*)

9. Suddenly becoming the "in" thing to wear would cause the demand for berets to shift out to the right, pushing the price up in the short run. In the long run, the market is probably not perfectly competitive and it would likely push the price down because there probably are considerable economies of scale in the production of berets. (*p. 280; LO13-4*)

10. A decline in demand pushed the short-run price of these burkhas down. In the long run, however, once a number of burkha makers go out of business, the price of burkhas should eventually move back to approximately where it was before the decline, assuming constant input prices. (*p. 281; LO13-4*)

chapter 14

Monopoly and Monopolistic Competition

Monopoly is business at the end of its journey.

—Henry Demarest Lloyd

In the last chapter we considered perfect competition. We now move to the other end of the spectrum: monopoly. **Monopoly** is *a market structure in which one firm makes up the entire market.* It is the polar opposite to competition. It is a market structure in which the firm faces no competitive pressure from other firms.

Monopolies exist because of barriers to entry into a market that prevent competition. These can be legal barriers (as in the case where a firm has a patent that prevents other firms from entering); sociological barriers, where entry is prevented by custom or tradition; natural barriers, where the firm has a unique ability to produce what other firms can't duplicate; or technological barriers, where the size of the market can support only one firm.

After reading this chapter, you should be able to:

LO14-1 Summarize how and why the decisions facing a monopolist differ from the collective decisions of competing firms.

LO14-2 Determine a monopolist's price, output, and profit graphically and numerically.

LO14-3 Show graphically the welfare loss from monopoly.

LO14-4 Explain why there would be no monopoly without barriers to entry.

LO14-5 Explain how monopolistic competition differs from monopoly and perfect competition.

The Key Difference between a Monopolist and a Perfect Competitor

A key question we want to answer in this chapter is: How does a monopolist's decision differ from the collective decision of competing firms (i.e., from the competitive solution)? Answering that question brings out a key difference between a competitive firm and a monopoly. Since a competitive firm is too small to affect the price, it does not take into account the effect of its output decision on the price it receives. A competitive firm's marginal revenue (the additional revenue it receives from selling an additional unit of output) is the given market price. A monopolistic firm takes into account that its output decision can affect price; its marginal revenue is not its price. A monopolistic firm will reason: "If I increase production, the price I can get for each unit sold will fall, so I had better be careful about how much I increase production."

Let's consider an example. Say your drawings in the margins of this book are seen by a traveling art critic who decides you're the greatest thing since Rembrandt, or at least since Andy Warhol. Carefully he tears each page out of the book, mounts them on special paper, and numbers them: Doodle Number 1

(Doodle While Contemplating Demand), Doodle Number 2 (Doodle While Contemplating Production), and so on.

All told, he has 100. He figures, with the right advertising and if you're a hit on the art circuit, he'll have a monopoly in your doodles. He plans to sell them for $20,000 each: He gets 50 percent, you get 50 percent. That's $1 million for you. You tell him, "Hey, man! I can doodle my way through the entire book. I'll get you 500 doodles. Then I get $5 million and you get $5 million."

The art critic has a pained look on his face. He says, "You've been doodling when you should have been studying. Your doodles are worth $20,000 each only if they're rare. If there are 500, they're worth $1,000 each. And if it becomes known that you can turn them out that fast, they'll be worth nothing. I won't be able to limit quantity at all, and my monopoly will be lost. So obviously we must figure out some way that you won't doodle anymore—and study instead. Oh, by the way, did you know that the price of an artist's work goes up significantly when he or she dies? Hmm?" At that point you decide to forget doodling and to start studying, and to remember always that increasing production doesn't necessarily make suppliers better off.

As we saw in the last chapter, competitive firms do not take advantage of that insight. Each individual competitive firm, responding to its self-interest, is not doing what is in the interest of the firms collectively. In competitive markets, as one supplier is pitted against another, consumers benefit. In monopolistic markets, the firm faces no competitors and does what is in its best interest. Monopolists can see to it that the monopolists, not the consumers, benefit; perfectly competitive firms cannot.

Doodle Number 27: Contemplating Costs

Q-1 Why should you study rather than doodle?

Monopolists see to it that monopolists, not consumers, benefit.

A Model of Monopoly

How much should the monopolistic firm choose to produce if it wants to maximize profit? To answer that we have to consider more carefully the effect that changing output has on the total profit of the monopolist. That's what we do in this section. First, we consider a numerical example; then we consider that same example graphically. The relevant information for our example is presented in Table 14-1.

Determining the Monopolist's Price and Output Numerically

Table 14-1 shows the price, total revenue, marginal revenue, total cost, marginal cost, average total cost, and profit at various levels of production. It's similar to the table in

TABLE 14-1 Monopolistic Profit Maximization

1 Quantity	2 Price	3 Total Revenue	4 Marginal Revenue	5 Total Cost	6 Marginal Cost	7 Average Total Cost	8 Profit
0	$36	$ 0		$ 47			$−47
			$33		$ 1		
1	33	33		48		$48.00	−15
			27		2		
2	30	60		50		25.00	10
			21		4		
3	27	81		54		18.00	27
			15		8		
4	24	96		62		15.50	34
			9		16		
5	21	105		78		15.60	27
			3		24		
6	18	108		102		17.00	6
			−3		40		
7	15	105		142		20.29	−37
			−9		56		
8	12	96		198		24.75	−102
			−15		80		
9	9	81		278		30.89	−197

the last chapter where we determined a competitive firm's output. The big difference is that marginal revenue changes as output changes and is not equal to the price. Why?

First, let's remember the definition of marginal revenue: Marginal revenue is the change in total revenue associated with a change in quantity. In this example, if a monopolist increases output from 4 to 5, the price it can charge falls from $24 to $21 and its revenue increases from $96 to $105, so marginal revenue is $9. Marginal revenue of increasing output from 4 to 5 for the monopolist reflects two changes: a $21 gain in revenue from selling the 5th unit and a $12 decline in revenue because the monopolist must lower the price on the previous 4 units it produces by $3 a unit, from $24 to $21. This highlights the key characteristic of a monopolist—its output decision affects its price. Because an increase in output lowers the price on all previous units, a monopolist's marginal revenue is always below its price. Comparing columns 2 and 4, you can confirm that this is true.

> A monopolist's marginal revenue is always below its price.

Now let's see if the monopolist will increase production from 4 to 5 units. The marginal revenue of increasing output from 4 to 5 is $9, and the marginal cost of doing so is $16. Since marginal cost exceeds marginal revenue, increasing production from 4 to 5 will reduce total profit and the monopolist will not increase production. If it decreases output from 4 to 3, where *MC* < *MR,* the revenue it loses ($15) exceeds the reduction in costs ($8). It will not reduce output from 4 to 3. Since it cannot increase total profit by increasing output to 5 or decreasing output to 3, it is maximizing profit at 4 units.

> Q-2 In Table 14-1, explain why 4 is the profit-maximizing output.

As you can tell from the table, profits are highest ($34) at 4 units of output and a price of $24. At 3 units of output and a price of $27, the firm has total revenue of $81 and total cost of $54, yielding a profit of $27. At 5 units of output and a price of $21, the firm has a total revenue of $105 and a total cost of $78, also for a profit of $27. The highest profit it can make is $34, which the firm earns when it produces 4 units. This is its profit-maximizing level.

Determining Price and Output Graphically

The monopolist's output decision also can be seen graphically. Figure 14-1 graphs the table's information into a demand curve, a marginal revenue curve, and a marginal cost

---

FIGURE 14-1 **Determining the Monopolist's Price and Output Graphically**

The profit-maximizing output is determined where the *MC* curve intersects the *MR* curve. To determine the price (at which *MC* = *MR*) that would be charged if this industry were a monopolist with the same cost structure as that of firms in a competitive market, we first find that output and then extend a line to the demand curve, in this case finding a price of $24. This price is higher than the competitive price, $20.50, and the quantity, 4, is lower than the competitor's quantity, 5.17.

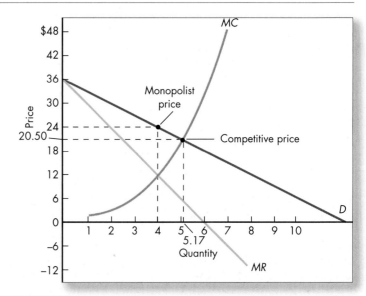

A Trick in Graphing the Marginal Revenue Curve

Here's a trick to help you graph the marginal revenue curve. The *MR* line starts at the same point on the price axis as does a linear demand curve, but it intersects the quantity axis at a point half the distance from where the demand curve intersects the quantity axis. (If the demand curve isn't linear, you can use the same trick if you use lines tangent to the curved demand curve.) So you can extend the demand curve to the two axes and measure halfway on the quantity axis (3 in the graph on the right). Then draw a line from where the demand curve intersects the price axis to that halfway mark. That line is the marginal revenue curve.

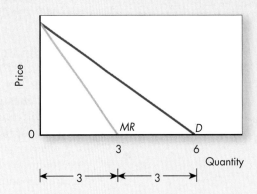

curve. The marginal cost curve is a graph of the change in the firm's total cost as it changes output. It's the same curve as we saw in our discussion of perfect competition. The marginal revenue curve tells us the change in total revenue when quantity changes. It is graphed by plotting and connecting the points given by quantity and marginal revenue in Table 14-1.

The marginal revenue curve for a monopolist is new, so let's consider it a bit more carefully. It tells us the additional revenue the firm will get by expanding output. It is a downward-sloping curve that begins at the same point as the demand curve but has a steeper slope. In this example, marginal revenue is positive up until the firm produces 6 units. Then marginal revenue is negative; after 6 units the firm's total revenue decreases when it increases output.

Notice specifically the relationship between the demand curve (which is the average revenue curve) and the marginal revenue curve. Since the demand curve is downward-sloping, the marginal revenue curve is below the average revenue curve. (Remember, if the average curve is falling, the marginal curve must be below it.)

Having plotted these curves, let's ask the same questions as we did before: What output should the monopolist produce, and what price can it charge? In answering those questions, the key curves to look at are the marginal cost curve and the marginal revenue curve.

Q-3 In the graph below, indicate the monopolist's profit-maximizing level of output and the price it would charge.

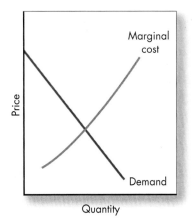

***MR = MC* DETERMINES THE PROFIT-MAXIMIZING OUTPUT** The monopolist uses the general rule that any firm must follow to maximize profit: Produce the quantity at which *MC* = *MR*. If you think about it, it makes sense that the point where marginal revenue equals marginal cost determines the profit-maximizing output. If the marginal revenue is below the marginal cost, it makes sense to reduce production. Doing so decreases marginal cost and increases marginal revenue. When *MR* < *MC*, reducing output increases total profit. If marginal cost is below marginal revenue, you should increase production because total profit will rise. If the marginal revenue is equal to marginal cost, it does not make sense to increase or reduce production. So the monopolist should produce at the output level where *MC* = *MR*. As you can see, the

MR and Profit
Maximization in Monopoly

output the monopolist chooses is 4 units, the same output that we determined numerically.[1] This leads to the following insights:

The general rule that any firm must follow to maximize profit is: Produce at an output level at which *MC* = *MR*.

If *MR* > *MC,* the monopolist gains profit by increasing output.

If *MR* < *MC,* the monopolist gains profit by decreasing output.

If *MC* = *MR,* the monopolist is maximizing profit.

Thus, *MR* = *MC* is the profit-maximizing rule for a monopolist.

THE PRICE A MONOPOLIST WILL CHARGE   The *MR* = *MC* condition determines the quantity a monopolist produces; in turn, that quantity determines the price the firm will charge. A monopolist will charge the maximum price consumers are willing to pay for that quantity. Since the demand curve tells us what consumers will pay for a given quantity, to find the price a monopolist will charge, you must extend the quantity line up to the demand curve. We do so in Figure 14-1 and see that the profit-maximizing output level of 4 allows a monopolist to charge a price of $24.

Comparing Monopoly and Perfect Competition

Q-4 Why does a monopolist produce less output than would perfectly competitive firms in the same industry?

For a competitive industry, the horizontal summation of firms' marginal cost curves is the market supply curve.[2] Output for a perfectly competitive industry would be 5.17, and price would be $20.50, as Figure 14-1 shows. The monopolist's output was 4 and its price was $24. So, if a competitive market is made into a monopoly, you can see that output would be lower and price would be higher. The reason is that the monopolist takes into account the effect that restricting output has on price.

Equilibrium output for the monopolist, like equilibrium output for the competitor, is determined by the *MC* = *MR* condition, but because the monopolist's marginal revenue is below its price, its equilibrium output is different from a competitive market.

An Example of Finding Output and Price

We've covered a lot of material quickly, so it's probably helpful to go through an example slowly and carefully review the reasoning process. Here's the problem:

> Say that a monopolist with marginal cost curve *MC* faces a demand curve *D* in Figure 14-2(a). Determine the price and output the monopolist would choose.

The first step is to draw the marginal revenue curve, since we know that a monopolist's profit-maximizing output level is determined where *MC* = *MR*. We do that in Figure 14-2(b), remembering the trick in the box on page 291 of extending our demand curve back to the vertical and horizontal axes and then bisecting the horizontal axis (half the distance from where the demand curve intersects the *x*-axis).

The second step is to determine where *MC* = *MR*. Having found that point, we extend a line up to the demand curve and down to the quantity axis to determine the output the monopolist chooses, Q_M. We do this in Figure 14-2(c). Finally we see where the quantity line intersects the demand curve. Then we extend a horizontal line from that point to the price axis, as in Figure 14-2(d). This determines the price the monopolist will charge, P_M.

---

[1]This could not be seen precisely in Table 14-1 since the table is for discrete jumps and does not tell us the marginal cost and marginal revenue exactly at 4; it only tells us the marginal cost and marginal revenue ($8 and $15, respectively) of moving from 3 to 4 and the marginal cost and marginal revenue ($16 and $9, respectively) of moving from 4 to 5. If small adjustments (1/100 of a unit or so) were possible, the marginal cost and marginal revenue precisely at 4 would be $12.

[2]The above statement has some qualifications best left to intermediate classes.

FIGURE 14-2 (A, B, C, AND D) **Finding the Monopolist's Price and Output**

Determining a monopolist's price and output can be tricky. The text discusses the steps shown in this figure. To make sure you understand, try to go through the steps on your own, and then check your work with the text.

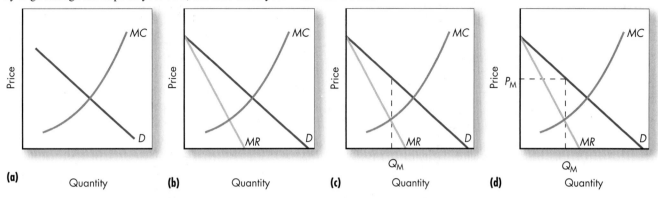

Profits and Monopoly

The monopolist's profit can be determined only by comparing average total cost to price. So before we can determine profit, we need to add another curve: the average total cost curve. As we saw with a perfect competitor, it's important to follow the correct sequence when finding profit:

- First, draw the firm's marginal revenue curve.
- Second, determine the output the monopolist will produce by the intersection of the marginal cost and marginal revenue curves.
- Third, determine the price the monopolist will charge for that output. (Remember, the price it will charge depends on the demand curve.)
- Fourth, determine the monopolist's profit (loss) by subtracting average total cost from average revenue (P) at that level of output and multiplying by the chosen output.

If price exceeds average total cost at the output it chooses, the monopolist will make a profit. If price equals average total cost, the monopolist will make no profit (but it will make a normal return). If price is less than average cost, the monopolist will incur a loss: Total cost exceeds total revenue.

A MONOPOLIST MAKING A PROFIT   I consider the case of a monopolist making a profit in Figure 14-3, going through the steps slowly. The monopolist's demand, marginal cost, and average total cost curves are presented in Figure 14-3(a). Our first step is to draw the marginal revenue curve, which has been added in Figure 14-3(b). The second step is to find the output level at which marginal cost equals marginal revenue. From that point, draw a vertical line to the horizontal (quantity) axis. That intersection tells us the monopolist's output, Q_M in Figure 14-3(b). The third step is to find what price the monopolist will charge at that output. We do so by extending the vertical line to the demand curve (point A) and then extending a horizontal line over to the price axis. Doing so gives price, P_M. Our fourth step is to determine the average total cost at that quantity. We do so by seeing where our vertical line at the chosen output intersects the average total cost curve (point B). That tells us the monopolist's average cost at its chosen output.

Q-5 Indicate the profit that the monopolist shown in the graph below earns.

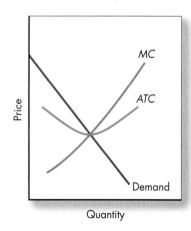

Finding a Monopolist's Output, Price, and Profit

To find a monopolist's level of output, price, and profit, follow these four steps:

1. Draw the marginal revenue curve.

2. Determine the output the monopolist will produce: The profit-maximizing level of output is where the MR and MC curves intersect.

3. Determine the price the monopolist will charge: Extend a line from where $MR = MC$ up to the demand curve. Where this line intersects the demand curve is the monopolist's price.

4. Determine the profit the monopolist will earn: Subtract the ATC from price at the profit-maximizing level of output to get profit per unit. Multiply profit per unit by quantity of output to get total profit.

To determine profit, we extend lines from where the quantity line intersects the demand curve (point A) and the average total cost curve (point B) to the price axis in Figure 14-3(c). The resulting shaded rectangle in Figure 14-3(c) represents the monopolist's profit.

A MONOPOLIST BREAKING EVEN AND MAKING A LOSS

A monopolist doesn't always make a profit. In Figure 14-4 we consider two other average total cost curves to show you that a monopolist may make a loss or no profit as well as an economic profit. In Figure 14-4(a) the monopolist is making zero profit; in Figure 14-4(b) it's making a loss. Whether a firm is making a profit, zero profit, or a loss depends on average total costs relative to price. So clearly, in the short run, a monopolist can be making either a profit or a loss, or it can be breaking even.

Most of you, if you've been paying attention, will say, "Sure, in the model monopolists might not make a profit, but in the real world monopolists are making a killing." And it is true that numerous monopolists make a killing. But many more monopolists just break even or lose money. Each year the U.S. Patent Office issues about 400,000 patents. A **patent** is *legal protection of a technical innovation that gives the person holding it sole right to use that innovation*—in other words, it gives the holder a monopoly to produce a good. Most patented goods make a loss; in fact, the cost of getting the patent often exceeds the revenues from selling the product.

Let's consider an example—the self-stirring pot, a pot with a battery-operated stirrer attached to its lid. The stirrer was designed to prevent the bottom of the pot from burning. The inventor tried to get the Home Shopping Network to sell it. Unfortunately for the inventor, HSN considered the cost (even after economies of scale were taken into account) far more than what people would be willing to pay and therefore decided not to include the pot in its offerings. The inventor had a monopoly on

---

FIGURE 14-3 (A, B, AND C) Determining Profit for a Monopolist

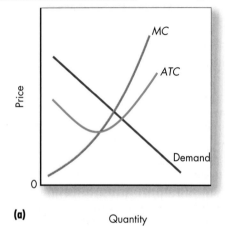

(a)

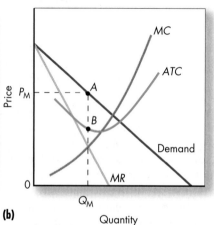

(b)

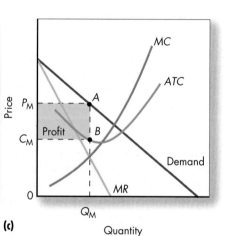

(c)

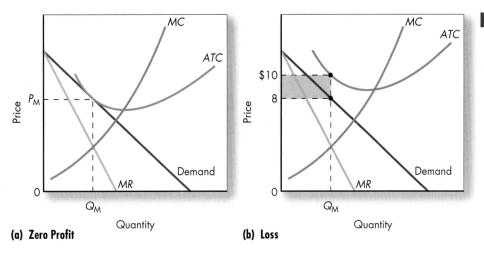

(a) Zero Profit

(b) Loss

FIGURE 14-4 (A AND B)
Other Monopoly Cases

Depending on where the *ATC* curve falls, a monopolist can make a profit, break even (as in (**a**)), or make a loss (as in (**b**)) in the short run. In the long run, a monopolist who is making a loss will go out of business.

the production and sale of the self-stirring pot, but only a loss to show for it. Examples like this can be multiplied by the thousands. The reality for many monopolies is that their costs exceed their revenues, so they make a loss.

Welfare Loss from Monopoly

As we saw above, monopolists aren't guaranteed a profit. Thus, profits can't be the primary reason that the economic model we're using sees monopoly as bad. If not because of profits, then what standard is the economic model using to conclude that monopoly is undesirable? One reason can be seen by looking at consumer and producer surplus for the normal monopolist equilibrium and perfectly competitive equilibrium.

The Normal Monopolist

Producer and consumer surplus for both monopoly and perfect competition is shown in Figure 14-5. In a competitive equilibrium, the total consumer and producer surplus is the area below the demand curve and above the marginal cost curve up to market equilibrium quantity Q_C. The monopolist reduces output to Q_M and raises price to P_M. The benefit lost to society from reducing output from Q_C to Q_M is measured by the area under the demand curve between output levels Q_C and Q_M. That area is represented by the shaded areas labeled *A, B,* and *D*. Area *A*, however, is regained by society. Society gains the opportunity cost of the resources that are freed up from reducing production—the value of the resources in their next-best use indicated by the shaded area *A*. So the net cost to society of decreasing output from Q_C to Q_M is represented by areas *B* and *D*. (Area *C* simply represents a transfer of surplus from consumers to the monopolist. It is neither a gain nor a loss to society. Since both monopolist and consumer are members of society, the gain and loss net out.) The triangular areas *B* and *D* are the net cost to society from the existence of monopoly.

As discussed in an earlier chapter, the area designated by *B* and *D* is often called the *deadweight loss* or *welfare loss triangle*. That welfare cost of monopoly is one of the reasons economists oppose monopoly. That cost can be summarized as follows: Because monopolies charge a price that is higher than marginal cost, people's decisions don't reflect the true cost to society. Price exceeds marginal cost. Because price exceeds marginal cost, people's choices are distorted; they choose to consume less of

The welfare loss from monopoly is a triangle, as in the graph below. It is not the loss that most people consider. They are often interested in normative losses that the graph does not capture.

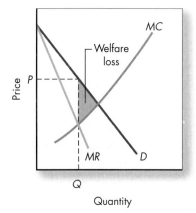

FIGURE 14-5

The Welfare Loss from Monopoly

The welfare loss from a monopoly is represented by the triangles B and D. The rectangle C is a transfer from consumer surplus to the monopolist. The area A represents the opportunity cost of diverted resources. This is not a loss to society since the resources will be used in producing other goods.

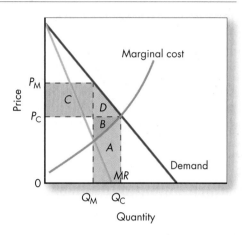

Q-6 Why is area C in Figure 14-5 not considered a loss to society from monopoly?

the monopolist's output and more of some other output than they would if markets were competitive. That distinction means that the marginal cost of increasing output is lower than the marginal benefit of increasing output, so there's a welfare loss.

The Price-Discriminating Monopolist

So far we've considered monopolists that charge the same price to all consumers. Let's consider what would happen if our monopolist suddenly gained the ability to **price-discriminate**—*to charge different prices to different individuals or groups of individuals* (for example, students as compared to businesspeople). If a monopolist can identify groups of customers who have different elasticities of demand, separate them in some way, and limit their ability to resell its product between groups, it can charge each group a different price. Specifically, it could charge consumers with less elastic demands a higher price and individuals with more elastic demands a lower price. By doing so, it will increase total profit. Suppose, for instance, Megamovie knew that at $10 it would sell 1,000 movie tickets and at $5 a ticket it would sell 1,500 tickets. Assuming Mega-movie could show the film without cost, it would maximize profits by charging $10 to 1,000 moviegoers, earning a total profit of $10,000. If, however, it could somehow attract the additional 500 viewers at $5 a ticket without reducing the price to the first 1,000 moviegoers, it could raise its profit by $2,500, to $12,500. As you can see, the ability to price-discriminate allows a monopolist to increase its profit.

When a monopolist price-discriminates, it charges individuals high up on the demand curve higher prices and those low on the demand curve lower prices.

Web Note 14.1
Divide and Conquer

We see many examples of price discrimination in the real world:

1. *Movie theaters give discounts to senior citizens and children.* Movie theaters charge senior citizens and children a lower price because they have a more elastic demand for movies.

2. *Airlines charge more to fly on Fridays and Sundays.* Businesspeople who work far from home fly out on Sunday and back on Friday. Their demand is inelastic. Tourists and leisure travelers are far more flexible in their travel plans and can fly any day of the week. Tuesday, Wednesday, and Saturday flights are the cheapest.

3. *Tracking consumer information and pricing accordingly.* Two people buying something on the Internet are not necessarily presented with the same price. Firms collect data about individuals with tracking devices called cookies,

Automobiles are seldom sold at list price.

FIGURE 14-6

A price-discriminating monopolist produces the same output as the combination of all firms in a competitive market. Total surplus is maximized in both cases. The differences is that the price-discriminating monopolist captures all of the surplus represented by areas *A* and *B* while all firms in the perfectly competitive market capture only area *B*.

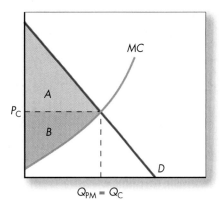

which are deposited on buyers' computer hard drives, and offer prices according to their estimated elasticity of demand. Thus, when you are searching the Internet for something to buy, you might be presented with a different price than someone else visiting the same site.

It might seem unfair for a monopolist to charge different people different prices, but doing so eliminates welfare loss from monopoly. The reason is that for a price-discriminating monopolist, the marginal revenue curve is the demand curve. So it will produce where $MC = MR = D$; in other words, it will produce the same output as would be produced in a perfectly competitive market. You can see this in Figure 14-6. The monopolist chooses to produce Q_{PM}. Since the supply curve in a perfectly competitive market is the sum of all marginal cost curves and equilibrium is where the supply and demand curves intersect, output in a competitive market will also be Q_{PM}. Both are producing where quantity supplied equals quantity demanded and there is no welfare loss.

What could be seen as unfair is what happens to consumer and producer surplus. In a perfectly competitive market, consumers pay and producers receive one price, P_C. Consumer surplus is the area above market price (area *A*) and producer surplus is the area below market price above the marginal cost curve (area *B*). For a price-discriminating monopolist, because it can charge what consumers are willing to pay, all consumer surplus is captured by the monopolist. Producer surplus for a price-discriminating monopolist is areas *A* and *B*.

Q-7 Why does a price-discriminating monopolist make a higher profit than a normal monopolist?

Barriers to Entry and Monopoly

The standard model of monopoly just presented is simple, but, like many simple things, it hides some issues. One issue the standard model of monopoly hides is in this question: What prevents other firms from entering the monopolist's market? You should be able to answer that question relatively quickly. If a monopolist exists, it must exist due to some type of barrier to entry (a social, political, or economic impediment that prevents firms from entering the market). Three important barriers to entry are natural ability, economies of scale, and government restrictions. In the absence of barriers to entry, the monopoly would face competition from other firms, which would erode its monopoly. Studying how these barriers to entry are established enriches the standard model and lets us distinguish different types of monopoly.

Web Note 14.2
Diamonds Are Forever

If there were no barriers to entry, profit-maximizing firms would always compete away monopoly profits.

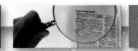

Can Price Controls Increase Output and Lower Market Price?

In an earlier chapter, you learned how effective price ceilings increase market price, reduce output, and reduce the welfare of society. With any type of price control in a competitive market, some trades that individuals would like to have made are prevented. Thus, with competitive markets, price controls of any type are seen as generally bad (though they might have some desirable income distribution effects).

When there is monopoly, the argument is not so simple. The monopoly price is higher than the marginal cost and society loses out; monopolies create their own deadweight loss. In the monopoly case, price controls can actually lower price, increase output, and reduce deadweight loss. Going through the reasoning why provides a good review of the tools.

The figure below shows you the argument.

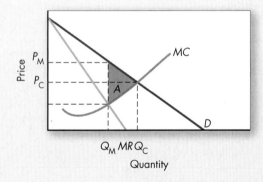

The monopoly sets its quantity where $MR = MC$. Output is Q_M and price is P_M; the welfare loss is the blue shaded triangle A. Now say that the government comes in and places a price ceiling on the monopolist at the competitive price, P_C. Since the monopolist is compelled by law to charge price P_C, it no longer has an incentive to restrict output. Put another way, the price ceiling—the dashed line P_C—becomes the monopolist's demand curve and marginal revenue curve. (Remember, when the demand curve is horizontal, the marginal revenue curve is identical to the demand curve.) Given the law, the monopolist's best option still is to produce where $MC = MR$, but that

means charging price P_C and increasing output to Q_C. As you can see from the figure, the price ceiling causes output to rise and price to fall.

If, when there is monopoly, price controls can increase efficiency, why don't economists advocate price controls more than they do? Let's review four reasons why.

1. For price controls to increase output and lower price, the price has to be set within the right price range—below the monopolist's price and above the price where the monopolist's marginal cost and marginal revenue curves intersect. It is unclear politically that such a price will be chosen. Even if regulators could pick the right price initially, markets may change. Demand may increase or decrease, putting the controlled price outside the desired range.

2. All markets are dynamic. The very existence of monopoly profits will encourage other firms in other industries to try to break into that market, keeping the existing monopolist on its toes. Because of this dynamic element, in some sense no market is ever a pure textbook monopoly.

3. Price controls create their own deadweight loss in the form of rent seeking. Price controls do not eliminate monopoly pressures. The monopolist has a big incentive to regain its ability to set its own price and will lobby hard to remove price controls. Economists see resources spent to regain their monopoly price as socially wasteful.

4. Economists distrust government. Governments have their own political agendas—there is no general belief among economists that governments will try to set the price at the competitive level. Once one opens up the price control gates in cases of monopoly, it will be difficult to stop government from using price controls in competitive markets.

The arguments are, of course, more complicated, and will be discussed in more detail in later chapters, but this should give you a good preview of some of the policy arguments that occur in real life.

Natural Ability

A barrier to entry that might exist is that a firm is better at producing a good than anyone else. It has unique abilities that make it more efficient than all other firms. The barrier to entry in such a case is the firm's natural ability. The defense attorneys in the Microsoft antitrust case argued that it was Microsoft's superior products that led to its capture of 90 percent of the market.

Monopolies based on ability usually don't provoke the public's ire. Often in the public's mind such monopolies are "just monopolies." The standard economic model doesn't distinguish between a "just" and an "unjust" monopoly. The just/unjust distinction raises the question of whether a firm has acquired a monopoly based on its ability or on certain unfair tactics such as initially pricing low to force competitive companies out of business but then pricing high. Many public debates over monopoly focus on such normative issues, about which the economists' standard model has nothing to say.

Natural Monopolies

An alternative reason why a barrier to entry might exist is that there are significant economies of scale. If sufficiently large economies of scale exist, it would be inefficient to have two producers since if each produced half of the output, neither could take advantage of the economies of scale. Such industries are called natural monopolies. A **natural monopoly** is *an industry in which a single firm can produce at a lower cost than can two or more firms.* A natural monopoly will occur when the technology is such that indivisible setup costs are so large that average total costs fall within the range of possible outputs. I demonstrate that case in Figure 14-7(a).

In a natural monopoly, a single firm can produce at a lower cost than can two or more firms.

If one firm produces Q_1, its cost per unit is C_1. If two firms each produces half that amount, $Q_{1/2}$, so that their total production is Q_1, the cost per unit will be C_2, which is significantly higher than C_1. In cases of natural monopoly, as the number of firms in the industry increases, the average total cost of producing a fixed number of units increases. For example, if each of three firms in an industry had a third of the market, each firm would have an average cost of C_3.

Until the 1990s local telephone service was a real-world example of such a natural monopoly. It made little sense to have two sets of telephone lines going into people's

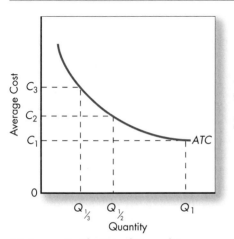

(a) Average Cost for Natural Monopolist

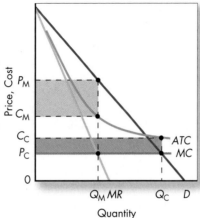

(b) Profit of Natural Monopolist

FIGURE 14-7 (A AND B)

A Natural Monopolist

The graph in (**a**) shows the average cost curve for a natural monopoly. One firm producing Q_1 would have a lower average cost than a combination of firms would have. For example, if three firms each produced $Q_{1/3}$, the average cost for each would be C_3.

The graph in (**b**) shows that a natural monopolist would produce Q_M and charge a price P_M. It will earn a profit shown by the orange shaded box. If the monopolist were required to charge a price equal to marginal cost, P_C, it would incur a loss shown by the blue shaded box.

Monopolizing Monopoly

Have you ever played Monopoly? Probably you have. And in the process, you have made money for Parker Brothers, the firm that has the monopoly on Monopoly. How they got it is an interesting story of actual events following games and vice versa. The beginnings of the Monopoly game go back to a Quaker woman named Lizzie Magie, who was part of the one-tax movement of popu- list economist Henry George. That move- ment, which was a central populist idea in the late 1800s, wanted to put a tax on all land rent to finance government. George argued that there would be no need for an income tax; the tax on the land monopoly would finance it all. Lizzie Magie created a game, called the Landlord's Game, as a way of teaching George's ideas, and showing how monopoly caused problems. She patented the game in 1904.

Despite the patent, people copied the game with her ap- proval, since her desire was to spread George's ideas. As the game spread, it kept changing form and rules, and eventually acquired the property names associated with Atlantic City,

A new invention would have undercut your most profitable item. You bought the invention and kept it off the market.

COLLECT **$75** FROM TREASURER

NEW INVENTION R.I.P.

© 1977, 1985, 1989, 2005 by Ralph Anspach. Patent 4136881

which the game now uses, and came to be called Monopoly. A number of variations of the game developed.

In the 1930s Charles Darrow was taught the game and had some friends write up the rules, which they copyrighted. (They couldn't patent the game because they didn't invent it.) In 1935 Darrow made an agreement with Parker Brothers, a firm that sold games, that gave them the right to produce this monopoly game in exchange for royalties. As Parker Brothers discovered the history of the monopoly game and of the particular games that preceded it, Parker Brothers bought the right to the previous games so that they would secure their full rights to Monopoly. It paid the various people between $500 and $10,000 for those rights. In 1974, an economics professor, Ralph Anspach, created an "Anti-Monopoly" game that pitted monopolists against competitors. That game led to suits and countersuits between Anspach and General Mills Fun Group, which had bought Parker Brothers in the interim, as they at- tempted to protect their monopoly.

---

houses. I say "until recently" because technology changes and now, with wireless communications and cable connections, the technical conditions that made local tele- phone service a natural monopoly are changing. Such change is typical; natural mo- nopolies are only natural given a technology.

A natural monopoly also can occur when a single industry standard is more efficient than multiple standards, even when that standard is owned by one firm. An example is the operating system for computers. A single standard is much more ef- ficient than multiple standards because the communication among computer users is easier.

From a welfare standpoint, natural monopolies are different from other types of monopolies. In the case of a natural monopoly, even if a single firm makes some mo- nopoly profit, the price it charges may still be lower than the price two firms making normal profit would charge because its average total costs will be lower. In the case of a natural monopoly, not only is there no welfare loss from monopoly, but there can actually be a welfare gain since a single firm producing is so much more efficient than many firms producing. Such natural monopolies are often organized as public utilities. For example, most towns have a single water department supplying water to residents.

Figure 14-7(b) shows the profit-maximizing level of output and price that a natural monopolist would choose. To show the profit-maximizing level of output, I've added a marginal cost curve that is below the average total cost curve. (If you don't know why this must be the case, a review of costs is in order.) A natural monopolist uses the same $MC = MR$ rule that a monopolist uses to determine output. The natural monopolist will produce Q_M and charge a price P_M. Average total costs are C_M and the natural monopolist earns a profit shown by the orange shaded box.

Normative Views of Monopoly

Many laypeople's views of government-created monopoly reflect the same normative judgments that Classical economists made. Classical economists considered, and much of the lay public considers, such monopolies unfair and inconsistent with liberty. Monopolies prevent people from being free to enter whatever business they want and are undesirable on normative grounds. In this view, government-created monopolies are simply wrong.

This normative argument against government-created monopoly doesn't extend to all types of government-created monopolies. The public accepts certain types of government-created monopoly that it believes have overriding social value. An example is patents. To encourage research and development of new products, government gives out patents for a wide variety of innovations, such as genetic engineering, Xerox machines, and cans that can be opened without a can opener.

A second normative argument against monopoly is that the public doesn't like the income distributional effects of monopoly. Although, as we saw in our discussion of monopoly, monopolists do not always earn an economic profit, they often do, which means that the monopoly might transfer income in a way that the public (whose normative views help determine society's policy toward monopoly) doesn't like. This distributional effect of monopoly based on normative views of who deserves income is another reason many laypeople oppose monopoly: They believe it transfers income from "deserving" consumers to "undeserving" monopolists.

A third normative reason people oppose government-created monopoly that isn't captured by the standard model of monopoly is that the possibility of government-created monopoly encourages people to spend a lot of their time in political pursuits trying to get the government to favor them with a monopoly, and less time doing "productive" things. It causes *rent-seeking* activities in which people spend resources to gain monopolies for themselves.

Each of these arguments probably plays a role in the public's dislike of monopoly. As you can see, these real-world arguments blend normative judgments with objective analysis, making it difficult to arrive at definite conclusions. Most real-world problems require this blending, making applied economic analysis difficult. The economist must interpret the normative judgments about what people want to achieve and explain how public policy can be designed to achieve those desired ends.

Where a natural monopoly exists, the perfectly competitive solution is impossible, since average total costs are not covered where $MC = P$. A monopolist required by government to charge the competitive price P_C, where $P = MC$, will incur a loss shown by the blue shaded box because marginal cost is always below average total cost. Either a government subsidy or some output restriction is necessary in order for production to be feasible. In such cases, monopolies are often preferred by the public as long as they are regulated by government. I will discuss the issues of regulating natural monopolies in the chapter on real-world competition.

Q-8 Why is the competitive price impossible for an industry that exhibits strong economies of scale?

Government-Created Monopolies

A final reason monopolies can exist is that they're created by government. The support of laissez-faire by Classical economists such as Adam Smith and their opposition to monopoly arose in large part in reaction to those government-created monopolies, not in reaction to any formal analysis of welfare loss from monopoly.

Government Policy and Monopoly: AIDS Drugs

Let's now consider how economic theory might be used to analyze monopoly and to suggest how government might deal with that monopoly. Specifically, let's consider the problem of acquired immune deficiency syndrome (AIDS) and the combination of medicinal drugs to fight AIDS. These drugs were developed by a small group of pharmaceutical companies, which own patents on them, giving the companies a monopoly. Patents are given on medicine to encourage firms to find cures for various diseases. The monopoly the patent gives them lets them charge a high price so that the firms can

www Web Note 14.3
The Best Monopoly
in America

Possible economic profits from monopoly lead potential monopolists to spend money to get government to give them a monopoly.

expect to make a profit from their research. Whether such patents are in the public interest isn't an issue, since the patent has already been granted.

The issue is what to do about these drugs. Currently demand for them is highly inelastic, so the price pharmaceutical companies can charge is high even though their marginal cost of producing them is low. Whether they are making a profit depends on their cost of development. But since that cost is already spent, that's irrelevant to the current marginal cost; development cost affects their *ATC* curve, not their marginal cost curve. Thus, the pharmaceutical companies are charging an enormously high price for drugs that may help save people's lives and that cost the companies a very small amount to produce.

What, if anything, should the government do? Some people have suggested that the government regulate the price of the drugs, requiring the firms to charge only their marginal cost. This would make society better off. But most economists point out that doing so will significantly reduce the incentives for drug companies to research new drugs. One reason drug companies spend billions of dollars for drug research is their expectation that they'll be able to make large profits if they're successful. If drug companies expect the government to come in and take away their monopoly when they're successful, they won't search for cures. So forcing these pharmaceutical companies to charge a low price for their AIDS drugs would help AIDS victims, but it would hurt people suffering from diseases that are currently being researched and that might be researched in the future. So there's a strong argument not to regulate.

But the thought of people dying when a cheap cure—or at least a partially effective treatment—is available is repulsive to me and to many others. In the 1990s Sub-Saharan African countries, which account for more than 75 percent of all AIDS deaths in the world, threatened to license production of these drugs to local manufacturers and make the drugs available at cost. U.S. pharmaceutical companies initially pressured the United States to cut off foreign aid if the African countries carried out their threat, but because of the bad public relations that the drug firms were getting, they stopped enforcing their patents in developing countries, making drugs for AIDS available to AIDS patients in poor nations at a much lower price than they do to others (an example of price discrimination).

An alternative policy suggested by economic theory to deal with such drug problems is for the government to buy the patents and allow anyone to make the drugs so their price would approach their marginal cost. Admittedly, this would be expensive. It would cause negative incentive effects because the government would have to increase taxes to cover the buyout's costs. But this approach would avoid the problem of the regulatory approach and achieve the same ends. However, it also would introduce new problems, such as determining which patents the government should buy.

Whether such a buyout policy makes sense remains to be seen, but in debating such issues the power of the simple monopoly model becomes apparent.

Monopolistic Competition

So far I have introduced you to the two extremes of market structure: perfect competition and monopoly. Most real-world market structures fall somewhere between the two—in what is called monopolistic competition and oligopoly. In this section I discuss monopolistic competition. In the next chapter I discuss oligopoly.

Characteristics of Monopolistic Competition

Monopolistic competition is *a market structure in which there are many firms selling differentiated products and few barriers to entry.*

The four distinguishing characteristics of monopolistic competition are:

1. Many sellers.
2. Differentiated products.
3. Multiple dimensions of competition.
4. Easy entry of new firms in the long run.

Let's consider each in turn.

MANY SELLERS   When there are only a few sellers, it's reasonable to explicitly take into account your competitors' reaction to the price you set. When there are many sellers, it isn't. In monopolistic competition, firms don't take into account rivals' reactions. Here's an example. There are many types of soap: Ivory, Irish Spring, Yardley's Old English, and so on. So when Ivory decides to run a sale, it won't spend a lot of time thinking about Old English's reaction. There are so many firms that one firm can't concern itself with the reaction of any specific firm. The soap industry is characterized by monopolistic competition.

PRODUCT DIFFERENTIATION   The "many sellers" characteristic gives monopolistic competition its competitive aspect. Product differentiation gives it its monopolistic aspect. In a monopolistically competitive market, the goods that are sold aren't homogeneous, as in perfect competition; they are differentiated slightly. Irish Spring soap is slightly different from Ivory, which in turn is slightly different from Yardley's Old English.

So in one sense each firm has a monopoly in the good it sells. But that monopoly is fleeting; it is based on advertising to convince people that one firm's good is different from the goods of competitors. The good may or may not really be different. Bleach differs little from one brand to another, yet buying Clorox makes many people feel that they're getting pure bleach. I generally don't buy it; I generally buy generic bleach. Ketchup, however, while made from the same basic ingredients, differs among brands (in my view). For me, only Heinz ketchup is real ketchup. (However, recently, my wife switched and put Hunt's ketchup in a Heinz bottle, and pointed out to me that I didn't notice. She's right; I didn't notice. But I still want Heinz ketchup; it's what my mother gave me, and seeing the Heinz bottle and believing that there is Heinz ketchup in it, makes me feel good—so much for my economist's rationality.)

Because a monopolistic competitor has some monopoly power, advertising to increase that monopoly power (and hence increase the firm's profits) makes sense as long as the marginal benefit of advertising exceeds the marginal cost. Despite the fact that their goods are similar but differentiated, to fit economists' monopolistically competitive model, firms must make their decisions as if they had no effect on other firms.

MULTIPLE DIMENSIONS OF COMPETITION   In perfect competition, price is the only dimension on which firms compete; in monopolistic competition, competition takes many forms. Product differentiation reflects firms' attempt to compete on perceived attributes; advertising is another form competition takes. Other dimensions of competition include service and distribution outlets. These multiple dimensions of competition make it much harder to analyze a specific industry, but the alternative methods of competition follow the same two general decision rules as price competition:

- Compare marginal costs and marginal benefits; and
- Change that dimension of competition until marginal costs equal marginal benefits.

Web Note 14.4
Product Differentiation

In monopolistic competition, competition takes many forms.

EASE OF ENTRY OF NEW FIRMS IN THE LONG RUN   The last condition a monopolistically competitive market must meet is that entry must be relatively easy; that is, there must be no significant entry barriers. Barriers to entry create the potential for long-run economic profit and prevent competitive pressures from pushing price down to average total cost. In monopolistic competition, if there were long-run economic profits, other firms would enter until no economic profit existed.

Output, Price, and Profit of a Monopolistic Competitor

Although a full analysis of the multiple dimensions of monopolistic competition cannot be compressed into two dimensions, a good introduction can be gained by considering it within the standard two-dimensional (price, quantity) graph.

To do so we simply consider the four characteristics of monopolistic competition and see what implication they have for the analysis. The firm has some monopoly power; therefore, a monopolistic competitor faces a downward-sloping demand curve. The downward-sloping demand curve means that in making decisions about output, the monopolistic competitor will, as will a monopolist, face a marginal revenue curve that is below price. At its profit-maximizing output, marginal cost will be less than price (not equal to price as it would be for a perfect competitor). We consider that case in Figure 14-8(a).

The monopolistic competitor faces the demand curve D, marginal revenue curve MR, and marginal cost curve MC. This demand curve is its portion of the total market demand curve. Using the $MC = MR$ rule discussed in the last chapter, you can see that the firm will choose output level Q_M (because that's the level of output at which marginal revenue intersects marginal cost). Having determined output, we extend a dotted line up to the demand curve and see that the firm will set a price equal to P_M. This price exceeds marginal cost. So far all we've done is reproduce the monopolist's decision.

Q-9 How does the equilibrium for a monopoly differ from that for a monopolistic competitor?

Where does the competition come in? Competition implies zero economic profit in the long run. (If there's profit, a new competitor will enter the market, decreasing the existing firms' demand [shifting it to the left].) In long-run equilibrium, a perfect competitor makes only a normal profit. Economic profits are determined by ATC, not by MC, so the competition part of monopolistic competition tells us where the average total cost curve must be at the long-run equilibrium output. It must be equal to price, and it will be equal to price only if the ATC curve is tangent to (just touching) the

---

FIGURE 14-8 (A AND B)
Monopolistic Competition

In (**a**) you can see that a monopolistically competitive firm prices in the same manner as a monopolist. It sets quantity where marginal revenue equals marginal cost. In (**b**) you can see that the monopolistic competitor is not only a monopolist but also a competitor. Competition implies zero economic profit in the long run.

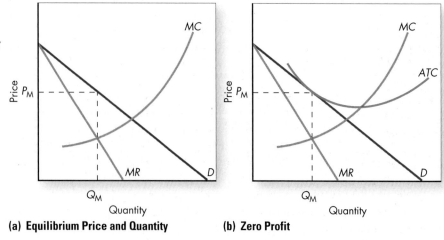

(a) **Equilibrium Price and Quantity**   (b) **Zero Profit**

demand curve at the output the firm chooses. We add that average total cost curve to the *MC, MR,* and demand curves in Figure 14-8(b). Profit or loss, I hope you remember, is determined by the difference between price and average total cost at the quantity the firm chooses.

To give this condition a little more intuitive meaning, let's say, for instance, that the monopolistically competitive firm is making a profit. This profit would set two adjustments in motion. First, it would attract new entrants. Some of the firm's customers would then defect, and its portion of the market demand curve would decrease. Second, to try to protect its profits, the firm would likely increase expenditures on product differentiation and advertising to offset that entry. (There would be an All New, Really New, Widget campaign.) These expenditures would shift its average total cost curve up. These two adjustments would continue until the profits disappeared and the new demand curve is tangent to the new average total cost curve. A monopolistically competitive firm can make no long-run economic profit.

Comparing Monopolistic Competition with Perfect Competition

If both the monopolistic competitor and the perfect competitor make zero economic profit in the long run, it might seem that, in the long run at least, they're identical. They aren't, however. The perfect competitor perceives its demand curve as perfectly elastic, and the zero economic profit condition means that it produces at the minimum of the average total cost curve where the marginal cost curve equals price. We demonstrate that case in Figure 14-9(a).

The monopolistic competitor faces a downward-sloping demand curve for its differentiated product. It produces where the marginal cost curve equals the marginal revenue curve, and not where *MC* equals price. In equilibrium, price exceeds marginal cost. The average total cost curve of a monopolistic competitor is tangent to the

---

FIGURE 14-9 (A AND B)   A Comparison of Perfect and Monopolistic Competition

The perfect competitor perceives its demand curve as perfectly elastic, and zero economic profit means that it produces at the minimum of the *ATC* curve, as represented in (**a**). A monopolistic competitor, on the other hand, faces a downward-sloping demand curve and produces where marginal cost equals marginal revenue, as represented in (**b**). In long-run equilibrium, the *ATC* curve is tangent to the demand curve at that level, which is *not* at the minimum point of the *ATC* curve. The monopolistic competitor sells Q_M at price P_M. A perfect competitor with the same marginal cost curve would produce Q_C at price P_C.

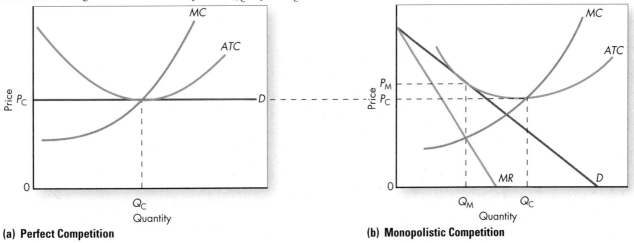

(a) Perfect Competition   **(b) Monopolistic Competition**

demand curve at the profit maximizing level of output, which cannot be at the minimum point of the average total cost curve since the demand curve is sloping downward. The minimum point of the average total cost curve (where a perfect competitor produces) is at a higher output (Q_C) than that of the monopolistic competitor (Q_M). I demonstrate the monopolistically competitive equilibrium in Figure 14-9(b) to allow you to compare monopolistic competition with perfect competition.

The perfect competitor in long-run equilibrium produces at a point where $MC = P = ATC$. At that point, ATC is at its minimum. A monopolistic competitor produces at a point where $MC = MR$. Price is higher than marginal cost. For a monopolistic competitor in long-run equilibrium:

$$(P = ATC) \geq (MC = MR)$$

At that point, ATC is *not* at its minimum.

What does this distinction between a monopolistically competitive industry and a perfectly competitive industry mean in practice? It means that for a monopolistic competitor, since increasing output lowers average cost, increasing market share is a relevant concern. If only the monopolistic competitor could expand its market, it could raise its profit. For a perfect competitor, increasing output offers no benefit in the form of lower average cost. A perfect competitor would have no concern about market share (the firm's percentage of total sales in the market).

Comparing Monopolistic Competition with Monopoly

An important difference between a monopolist and a monopolistic competitor is in the position of the average total cost curve in long-run equilibrium. For a monopolist, the average total cost curve can be, but need not be, at a position below price so that the monopolist makes a long-run economic profit. In contrast, the average total cost curve for a monopolistic competitor must be tangent to the demand curve at the price and output chosen by the monopolistic competitor. No long-run economic profit is possible.

Advertising and Monopolistic Competition

While firms in a perfectly competitive market have no incentive to advertise (since they can sell all they want at the market price), monopolistic competitors have a strong incentive. That's because their products are differentiated from the others; advertising plays an important role in providing that differentiation.

GOALS OF ADVERTISING   Goals of advertising include shifting the firm's demand curve to the right and making it more inelastic (less responsive to price increases). Advertising works by providing consumers with information about the firm's product and by making people want only a specific brand. That allows the firm to sell more, to charge a higher price, or to enjoy a combination of the two.

When many firms are advertising, the advertising might be done less to shift the demand curve out than to keep the demand curve where it is—to stop consumers from shifting to a competitor's product. In either case, firms advertise to move the demand curve further out and to make it more inelastic than it would be if the firms weren't advertising.

Advertising has another effect; it shifts the average total cost curve up. Thus, in deciding how much to advertise, a firm must consider advertising's effect on both revenue and cost. It is advantageous to the firm if the marginal revenue of advertising exceeds the marginal cost of advertising.

DOES ADVERTISING HELP OR HURT SOCIETY? Our perception of products (the degree of trust we put in them) is significantly influenced by advertising. Think of the following pairs of goods:

Rolex	Cheerios	Clorox bleach	Bayer
Timex	Oat Circles	generic bleach	generic aspirin

Web Note 14.5
Brand Names

Each of these names conveys a sense of what it is and how much trust we put in the product, and that determines how much we're willing to pay for it. For example, most people would pay more for Cheerios than for Oat Circles. Each year firms in the United States spend about $150 billion on advertising. A 30-second commercial during the Super Bowl can cost more than $3.5 million. That advertising increases firms' costs but also differentiates their products.

Are we as consumers better off or worse off with differentiated products? That's difficult to say. There's a certain waste in much of the differentiation. That waste shows up in the graph by the fact that monopolistic competitors don't produce at the minimum point of their average total cost curve. But there's also a sense of trust that we get from buying names we know and in having goods that are slightly different from one another. I'm a sophisticated consumer who knows that there's little difference between generic aspirin and Bayer aspirin. Yet sometimes I buy Bayer aspirin even though it costs more.

Edward Chamberlin, who, together with Joan Robinson, was the originator of the description of monopolistic competition, believed that the difference between the cost of a perfect competitor and the cost of a monopolistic competitor was the cost of what he called "differentness."[3] If consumers are willing to pay that cost, then it's not a waste but, rather, it's a benefit to them.

We must be careful about drawing any implications from this analysis. Average total cost for a monopolistically competitive firm includes the cost of advertising and product of differentiation. Whether we as consumers are better off with as much differentiation as we have, or whether we'd all be better off if all firms produced a generic product at a lower cost, is debatable.

Conclusion

We've come to the end of the presentation of the formal models of perfect competition, monopoly, and monopolistic competition. As you can see, the real world gets very complicated very quickly. I'll show you just how complicated in the chapter on real-world competition and technology. But don't let the complicated real world get you down on the theories presented here. It's precisely because the real world is so complicated that we need some framework, like the one presented in this chapter. That framework lets us focus on specific issues—and hopefully the most important.

Working through the models takes a lot of effort, but it's effort well spent. In Chapter 1, I quoted Einstein: "A theory should be as simple as possible, but not more so." This chapter's analysis isn't simple; it takes repetition, working through models, and doing thought experiments to get it down pat. But it's as simple as possible. Even so, it's extremely easy to make a foolish mistake, as I did in my Ph.D. oral examination when I was outlining an argument on the blackboard. ["*What* did you say the output would be for this monopolist, Mr. Colander?"] As I learned then, it takes long hours of working through the models again and again to get them right.

---

[3]Joan Robinson, a Cambridge, England, economist, called this the theory of imperfect competition, rather than the theory of monopolistic competition.

Summary

- A monopolist takes into account how its output affects price; a perfect competitor does not. *(LO14-1)*

- The price a monopolist charges is higher than that of a competitive market due to the restriction of output; a monopolist can make a profit in the long run. *(LO14-2)*

- A monopolist's profit-maximizing output is where marginal revenue equals marginal cost. *(LO14-2)*

- A monopolist can charge the maximum price consumers are willing to pay for the quantity the monopolist produces. *(LO14-2)*

- To determine a monopolist's profit, first determine its output (where $MC = MR$). Then determine its price and average total cost at that output level. The difference between price and average total cost at the profit-maximizing level of output is profit per unit. Multiply this by output to find total profit. *(LO14-2)*

- Because monopolists reduce output and charge a price that is higher than marginal cost, monopolies create a welfare loss to society. *(LO14-3)*

- If a monopolist can (1) identify groups of customers who have different elasticities of demand, (2) separate them in some way, and (3) limit their ability to resell its product between groups, it can price-discriminate. *(LO14-3)*

- A price-discriminating monopolist earns more profit than a normal monopolist because it can charge a higher price to those with less elastic demands and a lower price to those with more elastic demands. *(LO14-3)*

- Price discrimination eliminates welfare loss from monopoly. *(LO14-3)*

- Three important barriers to entry are natural ability, economies of scale, and government restrictions. *(LO14-4)*

- Natural monopolies exist in industries with strong economies of scale. Because their average total costs are always falling, it is more efficient for one firm to produce all the output. *(LO14-4)*

- The competitive price is impossible in a natural monopoly because marginal cost is always below average total cost. No firm would enter an industry where not even normal (zero economic) profit can be made. *(LO14-4)*

- Monopolistic competition is characterized by (1) many sellers, (2) differentiated products, (3) multiple dimensions of competition, and (4) ease of entry for new firms. *(LO14-5)*

- Monopolistic competitors differ from perfect competitors in that the former face a downward-sloping demand curve. *(LO14-5)*

- A monopolistic competitor differs from a monopolist in that a monopolistic competitor makes zero economic profit in long-run equilibrium. *(LO14-5)*

Key Terms

monopolistic
competition *(302)*

monopoly *(288)*
natural monopoly *(299)*

patent *(294)*

price-discriminate *(296)*

Questions and Exercises ☐ connect
ECONOMICS

1. What is the key difference between a monopolist and a perfect competitor? *(LO14-1)*

2. Does a monopolist take market price as given? Why or why not? *(LO14-1)*

3. Why is marginal revenue below average revenue for a monopolist? *(LO14-2)*

4. State what's wrong with the following graphs: (*LO14-2*)

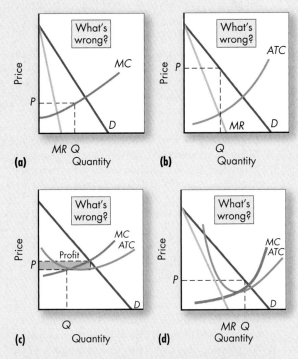

(a)

(b)

(c)

(d)

5. Say you place a lump-sum tax (a tax that is treated as a fixed cost) on a monopolist. How will that affect its output and pricing decisions? (*LO14-2*)

6. A monopolist is selling fish. But if the fish don't sell, they rot. What will be the likely elasticity at the point on the demand curve at which the monopolist sets the price? (Difficult) (*LO14-2*)

7. Demonstrate graphically the profit-maximizing positions for a perfect competitor and a monopolist. How do they differ? (*LO14-2*)

8. True or false? Monopolists differ from perfect competitors because monopolists make a profit. Why? (*LO14-2*)

9. A monopolist with a straight-line demand curve finds that it can sell two units at $12 each or 12 units at $2 each. Its fixed cost is $20 and its marginal cost is constant at $3 per unit. (*LO14-2*)
   a. Draw the *MC, ATC, MR,* and demand curves for this monopolist.
   b. At what output level would the monopolist produce?
   c. At what output level would a perfectly competitive firm produce?

10. Demonstrate the welfare loss created by a monopoly. (*LO14-3*)

11. Will the welfare loss from a monopolist with a perfectly elastic marginal cost curve be greater or less than the welfare loss from a monopolist with an upward-sloping marginal cost curve? (*LO14-3*)

12. What three things must a firm be able to do to price-discriminate? (*LO14-3*)

13. In the late 1990s, the Government Accounting Office reported that airlines block new carriers at major airports. (*LO14-4*)
    a. What effect does this have on fares and the number of flights at those airports?
    b. How much are airlines willing to spend to control the use of gates to block new carriers?

14. How is efficiency related to the number of firms in an industry characterized by strong economies of scale? (*LO14-4*)

15. During the 2001 anthrax scare, the U.S. government threatened to disregard Bayer's patent of ciprofloxacin, the most effective drug to fight anthrax, and license the production of the drug to American drug companies to stockpile the drug in case of an anthrax epidemic. While the policy would lower costs to the U.S. government of stockpiling the drug, it also would have other costs. What are those costs? (Difficult) (*LO14-4*)

16. Econocompany is under investigation by the U.S. Department of Justice for violating antitrust laws. The government decides that Econocompany has a natural monopoly and that, if it is to keep the government's business, it must sell at a price equal to marginal cost. Econocompany says that it can't do that and hires you to explain to the government why it can't. (*LO14-4*)
    a. You do so in reference to the following graph.
    b. What price would it charge if it were unregulated?
    c. What price would you advise that it should be allowed to charge?

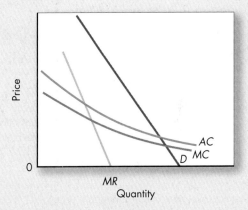

17. What are the ways in which a firm can differentiate its product from that of its competitors? What is the overriding objective of product differentiation? (*LO14-5*)

18. What are the "monopolistic" and the "competitive" elements of monopolistic competition? (*LO14-5*)

19. Suppose a monopolistic competitor in long-run equilibrium has a constant marginal cost of $6 and faces the demand curve given in the following table: (*LO14-5*)

Q	20	18	16	14	12	10	8	6
P	$ 2	4	6	8	10	12	14	16

a. What output will the firm choose?

b. What will be the monopolistic competitor's average fixed cost at the output it chooses?

20. If a monopolistic competitor is able to restrict output, why doesn't it earn economic profits?   (*LO14-5*)

21. You're the manager of a firm that has constant marginal cost of $6. Fixed cost is zero. The market structure is monopolistically competitive. You're faced with the following demand curve: (*LO14-5*)

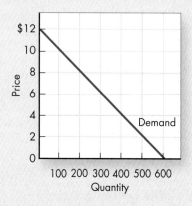

a. Determine graphically the profit-maximizing price and output for your firm in the short run. Demonstrate what profit or loss you'll be making.

b. What happens in the long run?

22. Manufacturers often pay "slotting fees," payments to retailers to provide their product prime shelf space. These fees range from $25,000 for one item in one store to $3 million for a chain of stores. An example is placing Doritos within a football display before Super Bowl Sunday.   (*LO14-5*)

a. In what type of market structure would this behavior likely be prevalent?

b. What does this behavior accomplish for the firm? Relate your answer to the observation that a typical supermarket stocks about 30,000 products.

c. Demonstrate the likely long-term profit in this market structure.

d. Firms have complained to the FTC that this practice is unfair. What is their likely argument?

e. What is an argument on the other side of that presented in *d*?

23. Both a perfect competitor and a monopolistic competitor choose output where *MC = MR,* and neither makes a profit in the long run. How is it, then, that the monopolistic competitor produces less than a perfect competitor?   (*LO14-5*)

Questions from Alternative Perspectives

1. Austrian economists observe that most lasting monopolies are the result of government and that any attempt to make government strong enough to control monopolies may result in an abuse of government power to protect and create more monopolies. What cautionary advice could we draw from this observation? (Austrian)

2. Do men have a monopoly over the best jobs in the United States? If so, how is that monopoly protected? (Feminist)

3. When analyzing the conduct of "modern" industry, Thorstein Veblen argued that captains of industry succeeded by eliminating their rivals through predatory exploitation and thus sabotaging production efficiency for personal fortune.

a. How does John D. Rockefeller's late 19th-century view that he liked to give competitors "a good sweating" and Bill Gates's "We will crush them" approach to Java fit into Veblen's argument?

b. What are the policy implications of predatory exploitation? (Institutionalist)

4. Large pharmaceutical firms use monopoly power granted by patents to sell drugs at prices that far exceed marginal costs. Evidence from countries without effective patent protections suggests that these drugs could sell for as little as 25 percent of their patent-protected prices. That difference costs U.S. consumers (including the government) nearly four times what pharmaceutical corporations spend on research each year.

a. How should we deal with these disturbing abuses of the patent system?

b. Should the government buy back patents as your textbook discusses, or should it not issue them in the first place?

c. Should patents be granted in some industries but not others?

d. If so, how should we encourage research in areas with no patent protection? (Radical)

5. The original language for patent law comes from Thomas Jefferson. He wrote that patents can be obtained for "any new and useful art, machine, manufacture, or composition of matter, or any new or useful improvement thereof." These words remain at the core of U.S. patent law.

a. Do they allow life forms to be patented?

b. Should they?

c. If humans can create life forms, does that undermine the existence of God? (Religious)

6. Firms in a monopolistically competitive market depend on differentiating their products.
    a. How do firms differentiate their products?
    b. Aside from commodities such as gold and grain, how many homogeneous products can you name?
    c. What does your answer to *b* suggest about market structure in the real world?
    d. Does the existence of monopolistically competitive markets imply that government should intervene in these markets? (Austrian)

7. Any large grocery store carries at least seven different kinds of corn chips—baked, fried, salsa-flavored, white, yellow, blue, and lime-flavored.
    a. When is product differentiation real and when is it an illusion?
    b. Is there an objective universal answer to *a*?
    c. Are there any individually objective answers to *a* and *b*?
    d. Does your answer to *c* tell you anything about the economic implication of the benefit of markets? (Hint: Is the assumption of rational consumers with well-ordered preference functions necessary to the arguments that markets benefit society?) (Institutionalist)

Issues to Ponder

1. Explain the effects on college education of the development of a teaching machine that you plug into a student's brain and that makes the student understand everything. How would your answer differ if a college could monopolize production of this machine?

2. Assume your city government has been contracting with a single garbage collection firm that has been granted an exclusive franchise, the sole right, to pick up trash within the entire city limits. However, it has been proposed that companies be allowed to compete for business with residents on an individual basis. The city government has estimated the price residents are willing to pay for various numbers of garbage collections per month and the total costs facing the garbage collector per resident as shown in the following table.

Pickup (Q)	Price per Pickup (Demand)	Total Revenue (TR)	Marginal Revenue (MR)	Total Cost (TC)	Marginal Cost (MC)	Average Total Cost (ATC)
0	$4.20	0	—	$3.20	—	—
1	3.80	___	___	4.20	___	___
2	3.40	___	___	5.60	___	___
3	3.00	___	___	7.80	___	___
4	2.60	___	___	10.40	___	___
5	2.20	___	___	13.40	___	___
6	1.90	___	___	16.80	___	___

   a. What are the fixed costs per month of garbage collection per resident?
   b. Considering that the current garbage collection firm the city has contracted with has a monopoly in garbage collection services, what is the current number of collections residents receive per month and the price charged residents for each collection? What is the economic profit received from each resident by the monopoly firm?
   c. If competitive bidding were allowed and therefore a competitive market for garbage collection services developed, what would be the number of collections per month and the price charged residents per collection? What is the economic profit received from each resident by the competitive firms?
   d. Based on the above analysis, should the city government allow competitive bidding? Why? Would you expect there to be any quality differences between the monopolistic and competitive trash collection firms?

3. When you buy a cheap computer printer or home fax, you can sometimes get it for free after the rebate. Why would a firm sell you something for a zero price? (The answer isn't that it wants to be nice.)

4. Oftentimes, gas stations a couple of miles apart will differ in price by as much as 5 to 10 cents per gallon because oil companies use a pricing system called zone pricing. For example, gas is sold wholesale to stations in Pleasanton, California, at about a 13 percent discount from the wholesale price in nearby Palo Alto.
    a. Why might oil companies do this?
    b. The FTC has been reviewing the practice. What policies might you suggest for them to consider to stop the practice, and what are the potential problems with those policies?
    c. Would such a policy lower the overall price of gas?

5. Most magazines offer enormous subscription deals for college students. For example, *Time* magazine offers a one-year subscription for $29.95, when the cover price is $3.95 per issue. This is an 85 percent discount.
    a. Why do they do this?

b. How would your answer change if you are told that most subscribers get enormous discounts, and that *Time*'s subscription revenue does not cover its costs?

c. What is a likely reason why magazines sell their subscriptions so cheaply?

6. Copyrights provide authors with a monopoly.
a. What effect would eliminating copyrights have on the price and output of textbooks?
b. Should copyrights be eliminated?

7. Colleges give financial aid to certain students. Is this price discrimination? If so, should it be against the law?

8. A best-selling horror book, *Duma Key* by Stephen King, was sold in hardback for $28 when it was first released. One year later, the publisher issued a soft-cover edition for $9.99. What accounts for the difference in price? (Note: The marginal cost of printing a book with a soft cover is not much less than the cost of a hardcover book.)

9. Does the product differentiation in monopolistic competition make us better or worse off? Why?

Answers to Margin Questions

1. If you doodle too much, your doodles will become worthless. Besides, if you want to pass the next test, you have to study. (*p. 289; LO14-1*)

2. At output 4, the marginal cost of $12 (between $8 and $16) equals the marginal revenue of $12 (between $15 and $9), making it the profit-maximizing output. It has the highest total profit, $34. (*p. 290; LO14-2*)

3. To determine the profit-maximizing price and output, one must determine where the marginal revenue curve equals marginal cost. So one must first draw the marginal revenue curve and see where it intersects marginal cost. That intersection determines the quantity, as in the accompanying graph. Carrying the line up to the demand curve determines the price. (*p. 291; LO14-2*)

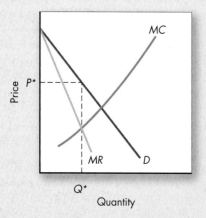

4. A monopolist produces less output than a perfectly competitive firm because a monopolist takes into account the fact that increasing output will lower the price of all previous units. (*p. 292; LO14-2*)

5. To determine profit, follow the following four steps: (1) draw the marginal revenue curve, (2) find the level of output where $MC = MR$ indicated in the graph below by Q^*, (3) find the price the monopolist would charge indicated by P^* and extend a horizontal line from the demand curve at

that price to the price axis, (4) determine the average total cost at Q^* shown by C^* and extend a horizontal line from the *ATC* curve at that cost to the price axis. The box created is the monopolist's profit. The profit is the shaded box shown in the graph below. (*p. 293; LO14-2*)

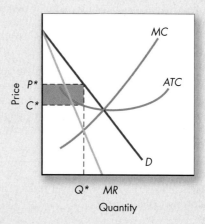

6. Area C represents the profit going to a monopolist. It is not considered a loss to society since, while consumers lose it, monopolists gain it. It is a redistribution of resources rather than an efficiency loss. (*p. 296; LO14-3*)

7. A price-discriminating monopolist makes a greater profit than a normal monopolist because a price-discriminating monopolist is able to charge a higher price to those consumers who have less elastic demands. (*p. 297; LO14-3*)

8. The marginal cost curve for an industry that exhibits strong economies of scale is always below average total costs. Therefore, the competitive price, where $P = MC$, will always result in losses for firms. Firms would not enter into such an industry and there would be no supply. (*p. 301; LO14-4*)

9. Both a monopoly and a monopolistic competitor produce where marginal cost equals marginal revenue. The difference is the position of the average total cost curve. For a monopolistic competitor, the average total cost curve

must be tangent to the demand curve because a monopolistic competitor makes no economic profits in the long run. A monopoly can make economic profits in the long run, so its average total cost can be below the price. (*p. 304; LO14-5*)

10. Monopolistically competitive firms advertise because their products are differentiated from others. Advertising

can convince people that a firm's product is better than that of other firms and increase demand for its product. Perfect competitors, in contrast, have no incentive to advertise since their products are the same as every other firm's product and they can sell all they want at the market price. (*p. 306; LO14-5*)

APPENDIX A

The Algebra of Competitive and Monopolistic Firms

In the appendix to Chapter 5, I presented the algebra relevant to supply and demand. To relate that algebra to competitive firms, all you must remember is that the market supply curve equals the marginal cost curve for the competitive industry. Let's review it briefly.

Say that marginal costs, and thus market supply, for the industry is given by

$$P = 2Q_S + 4$$

Let's also say that the market demand curve is:

$$Q_D = 28 - \frac{1}{4}P$$

To determine equilibrium price and quantity in a competitive market, you must equate quantity supplied and quantity demanded and solve for price. First, rewrite the marginal cost equation with quantity supplied on the left:

$$Q_S = \frac{1}{2}MC - 2$$

Then set quantity demanded equal to quantity supplied and $MC = P$. Then solve for equilibrium price:

$$Q_S = Q_D \Rightarrow 28 - \frac{1}{4}P = \frac{1}{2}P - 2$$
$$112 - P = 2P - 8$$
$$3P = 120$$
$$P = 40$$

Thus, the equilibrium price is $40. Competitive firms take this price as given and produce up until their marginal cost equals price. The industry as a whole produces 18 units.

Now let's consider the algebra relevant for a monopolistic firm. In the monopolistic case, supply and demand are not enough to determine where the monopolist will

produce. The monopolist will produce where marginal revenue equals marginal cost. But, for the monopolist, the industry demand curve is the demand curve, which means that in order to determine where the monopolist will produce, we must determine the marginal revenue curve that goes along with the above demand curve. There are two ways to do that.

First, if you know calculus, you can determine the marginal revenue curve in the following manner: Since marginal revenue tells us how much total revenue will change with each additional unit produced, you first specify the demand curve in terms of quantity produced.

$$P = 112 - 4Q$$

Since $TR = PQ$ we can multiply this by Q to get total revenue. Doing so gives us:

$$TR = PQ = 112Q - 4Q^2$$

To find marginal revenue, take the first derivative of total revenue with respect to Q:

$$P = 112 - 8Q$$

Second, if you don't know calculus, all you need to remember is the trick shown in a box in the chapter on how to graph the marginal revenue curve. Remember, the marginal revenue curve starts at the same price as the demand curve and bisects the quantity axis at one-half the value of the quantity axis intercept of the demand curve. The marginal revenue curve, because it bisects the quantity axis at one-half the value of the quantity axis intercept of the accompanying demand curve, must fall twice as fast as the market demand curve. That is, its slope is twice the slope of the market demand curve.

Knowing that its slope is twice the market demand curve slope, you can write the marginal revenue curve with the same price axis intercept as the demand curve and a slope of two times the slope of the demand curve. (Warning: this only works with linear demand curves.) The price-axis intercept of the demand curve is the value of P where Q equals 0: 112. The quantity-axis intercept of the demand curve is the value of Q where P equals 0: 28. So, the marginal revenue curve has a price-axis intercept at 112 and a quantity-axis intercept at 14. Mathematically, such a curve is represented by:

$$P = 112 - (112/14)P$$

or

$$P = 112 - 8Q$$

Now that we've determined the monopolist's marginal revenue curve, we can determine its equilibrium quantity by setting $MR = MC$ and solving for Q. Doing so gives us:

$$112 - 8Q = 2Q + 4$$
$$-10Q = -108$$
$$Q = 10.8$$

The monopolist then charges the price consumers are willing to pay for that quantity. Mathematically, substitute 10.8 into the demand equation and solve for price:

$$P = 112 - 4(10.8)$$
$$P = \$68.80$$

Comparing the price and quantity produced by a monopolist and those of a competitive industry shows that the monopolist charges a higher price and produces a lower output.

Questions and Exercises

1. The market demand curve is $Q_D = 50 - P$. The marginal cost curve is $MC = 4Q + 6$.
   a. Assuming the marginal cost curve is for a competitive industry as a whole, find the profit-maximizing level of output and price.
   b. Assuming the marginal cost curve is for only one firm that comprises the entire market, find the profit-maximizing level of output and price.
   c. Compare the two results.

2. The market demand curve is $Q_D = 160 - 4P$. A monopolist's total cost curve is $TC = 6Q^2 + 15Q + 50$.
   a. Find the profit-maximizing level of output and price for a monopolist.
   b. Find its average cost at that level of output.
   c. Find its profit at that level of output.

3. Suppose fixed costs for the monopolist in Question 2 increase by 52.
   a. Find the profit-maximizing level of output and price for a monopolist.
   b. Find its average cost at that level of output.
   c. Find its profit at that level of output.

4. The market demand curve is $Q_D = 12 - \frac{1}{3}P$. Costs do not vary with output.
   a. Find the profit-maximizing level of output and price for a monopolist.
   b. Find the profit-maximizing level of output and price for a competitive industry.

chapter 15

Oligopoly and Antitrust Policy

> *In business, the competition will bite you if you keep running; if you stand still, they will swallow you.*
>
> —Victor Kiam

In the last chapter we discussed competition, monopoly, and a blend of the two—monopolistic competition. In this chapter we discuss another blend: **oligopoly**—*a market structure in which there are only a few firms and firms explicitly take other firms' likely response into account.*

The Distinguishing Characteristics of Oligopoly

The central element of oligopoly is that there are a small number of firms in an industry so that, when making decisions, a firm must take into account the expected reaction of other firms. Oligopolistic firms are mutually interdependent and can be collusive or noncollusive.

This mutual interdependence is the big difference between monopolistic competition and oligopoly. In oligopoly, firms explicitly take other firms' actions into account. In monopolistic competition, there are so many firms that individual firms tend not to explicitly take into account rival firms' likely responses to their decisions. Collusion is difficult. In oligopoly there are fewer firms, and each firm is more likely to explicitly engage in **strategic decision making**—*taking explicit account of a rival's expected response to a decision you are making.* In oligopolies all decisions, including pricing decisions, are strategic decisions. Also, in oligopolies collusion is much easier. Thus, one distinguishes between monopolistic competition and oligopoly by whether or not firms explicitly take into account competitors' reactions to their decisions.

Why is the distinction important? Because it determines whether economists can model and predict the price and output of an industry. Nonstrategic decision making can be predicted relatively accurately if individuals behave rationally. Strategic decision making is much more difficult to predict, even if people behave rationally. What one person does depends on what he or she expects other people to do, which in turn depends on what others expect the one

After reading this chapter, you should be able to:

LO15-1 Explain the distinguishing characteristics of oligopoly.

LO15-2 Distinguish two models of oligopoly.

LO15-3 Describe two empirical methods of measuring market structure.

LO15-4 Explain what antitrust policy is and give a brief history of it.

Oligopolistic firms are mutually interdependent.

Oligopolies take into account the reactions of other firms; monopolistic competitors do not.

Q-1 Your study partner, Jean, has just said that monopolistic competitors use strategic decision making. How would you respond?

Models of Oligopoly

If oligopolies can limit the entry of other firms and form a cartel, they increase the profits going to the combination of firms in the cartel.

Web Note 15.1
Price-Fixing

person to do. Consistent with this distinction, economists' model of monopolistic competition has a definite prediction. A model of monopolistic competition will tell us: Here's how much will be produced and here's how much will be charged. Economists' models of oligopoly don't have a definite prediction. There are no unique price and output decisions at which an oligopoly will rationally arrive; there are a variety of rational oligopoly decisions, and a variety of oligopoly models.

Most industries in the United States have some oligopolistic elements. If you ask almost any businessperson whether he or she directly takes into account rivals' likely response, the answer you'll get is "In certain cases, yes; in others, no."

Most retail stores that you deal with are oligopolistic in your neighborhood or town, although by national standards they may be quite competitive. For example, how many grocery stores do you shop at? Do you think they keep track of what their competitors are doing? You bet. They keep a close eye on their competitors' prices and set their own accordingly.

Models of Oligopoly Behavior

No single general model of oligopoly behavior exists. The reason is that an oligopolist can decide on pricing and output strategy in many possible ways, and there are no compelling grounds to characterize any of them as *the* oligopoly strategy. Although there are five or six formal models, I'll focus on two informal models of oligopoly behavior that give you insight into real-world problems. The two models we'll consider are the cartel model and the contestable market model. These should give you a sense of how real-world oligopolistic pricing takes place.

Why, you ask, can't economists develop a simple formal model of oligopoly? The reason lies in the interdependence of oligopolists. Since there are few competitors, what one firm does specifically influences what other firms do, so an oligopolist's plan must always be a contingency or strategic plan. If my competitors act one way, I'll do X, but if they act another way, I'll do Y. Strategic interactions have a variety of potential outcomes rather than a single outcome such as in the formal models we discussed. An oligopolist spends enormous amounts of time guessing what its competitors will do, and it develops a strategy of how it will act accordingly. As we will discuss in Chapter 20, an entire theory called game theory has developed that considers interdependent decisions. The appendix to Chapter 20 shows how game theory can be applied to oligopoly decisions.

The Cartel Model

A **cartel** is *a combination of firms that acts as if it were a single firm;* a cartel is a shared monopoly. If oligopolies can limit entry by other firms, they have a strong incentive to cartelize the industry and to act as a monopolist would, restricting output to a level that maximizes profit for the combination of firms. Thus, the **cartel model of oligopoly** is *a model that assumes that oligopolies act as if they were monopolists that have assigned output quotas to individual member firms of the oligopoly so that total output is consistent with joint profit maximization.* All firms follow a uniform pricing policy that serves their collective interest.

Since a monopolist makes the most profit that can be squeezed from a market, cartelization is the best strategy for an oligopoly. It requires each oligopolist to hold its production below what would be in its own interest were it not to collude with the others. Such explicit formal collusion is against the law in the United States, but informal collusion is allowed and oligopolies have developed a variety of methods to collude implicitly. Thus, the cartel model has some relevance.

The model has some problems, however. For example, various firms' interests often differ, so the collective interest of the firms in the industry isn't clear. In many cases a single firm, often the largest or dominant firm, takes the lead in pricing and output decisions, and the other firms (which are often called *fringe firms*) follow suit, even though they might have preferred to adopt a different strategy.

This dominant-firm cartel model works only if the smaller firms face barriers to entry, or the dominant firm has significantly lower cost conditions. If that were not the case, the smaller firms would pick up an increasing share of the market, eliminating the dominant firm's monopoly. An example of such a dominant-firm market was the copier market in the 1960s and 1970s, in which Xerox set the price and other firms followed. That copier market also shows the temporary nature of such a market. As the firms became more competitive on cost and quality, Xerox's market share fell and the company lost its dominant position. The copier market is far more competitive today than it used to be.

Q-2 Why is it difficult for firms in an industry to maintain a cartel?

In other cases the various firms meet—sometimes only by happenstance, at the golf course or at a trade association gathering—and arrive at a collective decision. In the United States, meetings for this purpose are illegal, but they do occur. In yet other cases, the firms engage in **implicit collusion**—*multiple firms make the same pricing decisions even though they have not explicitly consulted with one another.* They "just happen" to come to a collective decision.

In some cases, firms collude implicitly—they just happen to make the same pricing decisions. This is not illegal.

IMPLICIT PRICE COLLUSION   Implicit price collusion, in which firms just happen to charge the same price but didn't meet to discuss price strategy, isn't against the law. Oligopolies often operate as close to the fine edge of the law as they can. For example, many oligopolistic industries allow a price leader to set the price, and then the others follow suit. The airline and steel industries take that route. Firms just happen to charge the same price or very close to the same price.

It isn't only in major industries that you see such implicit collusion. In small towns, you'll notice that most independent carpenters charge the same price. There's no explicit collusion, but were a carpenter to offer to work for less than the others, he or she would feel unwelcome at the local breakfast restaurant.

Or let's take another example: the Miami fish market, where sport fishermen sell their catch at the dock. When I lived in Miami, I often went to the docks to buy fresh fish. There were about 20 stands, all charging the same price. Price fluctuated, but it was by subtle agreement, and close to the end of the day the word would go out that the price could be reduced.

I got to know some of the sellers and asked them why they priced like that when it would be in their individual interest to set their own price. Their answer: "We like our boat and don't want it burned." They may have been talking in hyperbole, but social pressures play an important role in stabilizing prices in an oligopoly.

CARTELS AND TECHNOLOGICAL CHANGE   Even if all firms in the industry cooperate, other firms, unless they are prevented from doing so, can always enter the market with a technologically superior new product at the same price or with the same good at a lower price. It is important to remember that technological changes are constantly occurring, and that a successful cartel with high profits will provide incentives for significant technological change, which can eliminate demand for its monopolized product.

WHY ARE PRICES STICKY?   Informal collusion happens all the time in U.S. businesses. One characteristic of informal collusive behavior is that prices tend to be sticky—they don't change frequently. Informal collusion is an important reason why prices are sticky. But it's not the only reason.

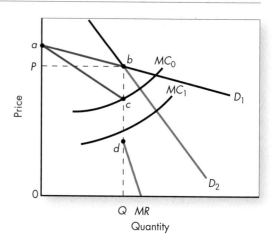

FIGURE 15-1 The Kinked Demand Curve

One explanation for why prices are sticky is that firms face a kinked demand curve. When we draw the relevant marginal revenue curve for the kinked demand, we see that the corresponding *MR* curve is discontinuous. It has a gap in it. Shifts in marginal costs between *c* and *d* will not change the price or the output that maximizes profits.

Another possible reason is that firms don't collude, but do have certain expectations of other firms' reactions, which changes their perceived demand curves. Specifically, they perceive that the demand curve they face is kinked. This kinked demand curve is used especially to explain why firms often do not use lower-price strategies to increase sales.

Let's go through the reasoning behind the kinked demand curve. If a firm increases its price, and the firm believes that other firms won't go along, its perceived demand curve for increasing price will be very elastic (D_1 in Figure 15-1). It will lose lots of business to the other firms that haven't raised their price. The relevant portions of its demand curve and its marginal revenue curve are shown in blue in Figure 15-1.

Q-3 Is the demand curve as perceived by an oligopolist likely to be more or less elastic for a price increase or a price decrease?

If it decreases its price, however, the firm assumes that all other firms would immediately match that decrease, so it would gain very few, if any, additional sales. A large fall in price would result in only a small increase in sales, so its demand is very inelastic (D_2 in Figure 15-1). This less elastic portion of the demand curve and the corresponding marginal revenue curve are shown in orange in Figure 15-1.

Notice that when you put these two curves together, you get a rather strange demand curve (it's kinked) and an even stranger marginal revenue curve (one with a gap). I didn't make a mistake in drawing the curves; that's the way they come out given the assumptions. When the demand curve has a kink, the marginal revenue curve must have a gap. Shifts in marginal cost (such as MC_0 to MC_1) will not change the firm's profit maximization position. A large shift in marginal cost is required before firms will change their price. Why should this be the case? The intuitive answer lies in the reason behind the kink. If the firm raises its price, other firms won't go along, so it will lose lots of market share. However, when the firm lowers price, other firms will go along and the firm won't gain market share. Thus, the firm has strong reasons not to change its price in either direction.

When the demand curve has a kink, the marginal revenue curve must have a gap.

I should emphasize that the kinked demand curve is not a theory of oligopoly pricing. It does not say why the original price is what it is; the kinked demand curve is simply a theory of sticky prices.

The Contestable Market Model

A second model of oligopoly is the *contestable market model*. The **contestable market model** is *a model of oligopoly in which barriers to entry and barriers to exit, not the structure of the market, determine a firm's price and output decisions.* Thus, it emphasizes entry and exit conditions, and says that the price that an oligopoly will charge will exceed the cost of production only if new firms cannot exit and enter the market. The higher the barriers, the more the price exceeds cost. Without barriers to entry or exit, the price an oligopolist sets will be equal to the competitive price. Thus, an industry that structurally looks like an oligopoly could set competitive prices and output levels.

In the contestable market model of oligopoly, pricing and entry decisions are based only on barriers to entry and exit, not on market structure. Thus, even if the industry contains only one firm, it could still be a competitive market if entry is open.

Comparison of the Contestable Market Model and the Cartel Model

Because of the importance of social pressures in determining strategies of oligopolies, no one "oligopolistic model" exists. Oligopolies with a stronger ability to collude (that is, more social pressures to prevent entry) are able to get closer to a monopolist solution. Equilibrium of oligopolies with weaker social pressures and less ability to prevent new entry is closer to the perfectly competitive solution. That's as explicit as we can be.

An oligopoly model can take two extremes: (1) the cartel model, in which an oligopoly sets a monopoly price, and (2) the contestable market model, in which an oligopoly with no barriers to entry sets a competitive price. Thus, we can say that an oligopoly's price will be somewhere between the competitive price and the monopolistic price. Other models of oligopolies give results in between these two.

Q-4 What are the two extremes an oligopoly model can take?

Much of what happens in oligopoly pricing is highly dependent on the specific legal structure within which firms interact. In Japan, where large firms are specifically allowed to collude, we see Japanese goods selling for a much higher price than those same Japanese goods sell for in the United States. For example, you may well pay twice as much for a Japanese television in Japan as you would in the United States. From the behavior of Japanese firms, we get a sense of what pricing strategy U.S. oligopolists would follow in the absence of the restrictions placed on them by law.

NEW ENTRY AS A LIMIT ON THE CARTELIZATION STRATEGY One of the things that limits oligopolies from acting as a cartel is the threat from outside competition. The threat will tend to be more effective if this outside competitor is much larger than the firms in the oligopoly.

For example, small-town banks have a tendency to collude (implicitly, of course), offering lower interest to savers and charging higher interest to borrowers than big banks charge, even though their average costs aren't significantly higher. When I ask small-town banks why this is, they tell me that my perceptions are faulty and that I should mind my own business. But if a big bank, which couldn't care less about increasing the wealth of a small-town banker, enters the town and establishes a branch office, interest rates to savers seem to go up and interest rates to borrowers seem to go down. The big bank can add significant competition—competition that couldn't come from within the town.

On a national scale, the outside competition often comes from international firms. For example, implicit collusion among U.S. automobile firms led to foreign firms' entry into the U.S. automobile market. There are many such examples of this outside competition breaking down cartels with no barriers to entry. Thus, a cartel with no barriers to entry faces a long-run demand curve that's very elastic. This means that its price will be very close to its marginal cost and average cost. This is the same prediction that came from the contestable market theory.

On a national scale, the outside competition comes from international firms.

PRICE WARS   With oligopolies, there's always the possibility of a price war. The reasons for such wars are varied. Since oligopolistic firms know their competitors, they can personally dislike them; sometimes a firm's goal can be simply to drive a disliked competitor out of business, even if that process hurts the firm itself. Passion and anger play roles in oligopoly pricing because interpersonal and interfirm relations are important.

Alternatively, a firm might follow a predatory pricing strategy—a strategy of pushing the price down temporarily to drive the other firm out of business to increase long-term profits. Some argue that Microsoft followed a predatory pricing strategy by virtually giving away its Office Suite on new computer systems to make its software the industry standard. If the predatory pricing strategy is successful, the firm can charge an even higher price because potential entrants know that the existing firm will drive them out if they try to enter. It's this continual possibility that strategies can change that makes oligopoly prices so hard to predict. (In a later chapter we will discuss game theory in detail, since it is an important tool that economists use to study strategic pricing by oligopolies.)

Since we have come to the end of our presentation of the analytics of market structure, a review is in order. The box "A Comparison of Various Market Structures" on page 321 provides that review. It lists the four central market structures, and the similarities and differences among them. It is worth a careful review.

Classifying Industries and Markets in Practice

www
Web Note 15.2
Porter's Five Forces

An industry seldom fits neatly into one category or another. Inevitably, numerous arbitrary decisions must be made as to what the appropriate market is, and whether the industry comes closest to the characteristics of one or the other market structure. So to classify actual industries, a variety of procedures and measures have been developed, and in this section we review those procedures and measures.

To see the problems that arise in classifying industries, consider the banking industry. There are about 6,000 banks in the United States, and banking is considered reasonably competitive. However, a particular small town may have only one or two banks, so there will be a monopoly or oligopoly with respect to banks in that town. Is the United States or the town the relevant market? The same argument exists when we think of international competition. Many firms sell in international markets and, while a group of firms may compose an oligopoly in the United States, the international market might be more accurately characterized by monopolistic competition.

Another dimension of the classification problem concerns deciding what is to be included in an industry. If you define the industry as "the transportation industry," there are many firms. If you define it as "the urban transit industry," there are fewer firms; if you define it as "the commuter rail industry," there are still fewer firms. Similarly with the geographic dimension of industry. There's more competition in the global market than in the local market. The narrower the definition, the fewer the firms.

One of the ways in which economists classify markets in practice is by cross-price elasticities (the responsiveness of a change in the demand for a good to a change in the price of a related good). Industrial organization economist F. M. Sherer has suggested the following rule of thumb: When two goods have a cross-price elasticity greater than or equal to 3, they can be regarded as belonging to the same market.

The North American Industry Classification System

The **North American Industry Classification System (NAICS)** is *an industry classification that categorizes industries by type of economic activity and groups firms with like production processes.* In the NAICS, all firms are placed into 20 broadly

A Comparison of Various Market Structures

Structure / Characteristics	Monopoly	Oligopoly	Monopolistic Competition	Perfect Competition
Number of Firms	One	Few	Many	Almost infinite
Barriers to Entry	Significant	Significant	Few	None
Pricing Decisions	$MC = MR$	Strategic pricing, between monopoly and perfect competition	$MC = MR$	$MC = MR = P$
Output Decisions	Most output restriction	Output somewhat restricted	Output restricted somewhat by product differentiation	No output restriction
Interdependence	Only firm in market, not concerned about competitors	Interdependent strategic pricing and output decision	Each firm acts independently	Each firm acts independently
Profit	Possibility of long-run economic profit	Some long-run economic profit possible	No long-run economic profit possible	No long-run economic profit possible
P and MC	$P > MC$	$P > MC$	$P > MC$	$P = MC$

defined two-digit sectors. These two-digit sectors are further subdivided into three-digit subsectors, four-digit industry groupings, five-digit industries, and six-digit national industry groupings. Each subgrouping becomes more and more narrowly defined. Table 15-1 lists the 20 sectors and shows some subgroupings for one sector, Information, to give you an idea of what's included in each.

When economists talk about industry structure, they generally talk about industries in the four- to six-digit subsector groupings in the United States. This is a convention. Economists are often called on to give expert testimony in court cases, and if an economist wants to argue that an industry is more competitive than its opponents say it is, he or she challenges this convention of using a four- to six-digit classification of

Q-5 Which would have more output: the two-digit industry 21 or the four-digit industry 2111? Explain your reasoning.

321

TABLE 15-1   Industry Groupings in the North American Industry Classification System

Two-Digit Sectors	Three- to Five-Digit Subsectors
11 Agriculture, forestry, fishing, and hunting	
21 Mining	
22 Utilities	
23 Construction	
31–33 Manufacturing	
42 Wholesale trade	
44–45 Retail trade	
48–49 Transportation and warehousing	51 Information
51 Information_____	511 Publishing Industries (except Internet)
52 Finance and insurance	5111 Newspaper, Periodical, Book, and Directory Publishers
53 Real estate and rental and leasing	51111 Newspaper Publishers
54 Professional, scientific, and technical services	
55 Management of companies and enterprises	
56 Administrative and support, and waste management and remediation services	
61 Educational services	
62 Health care and social assistance	
71 Arts, entertainment, and recreation	
72 Accommodation and food services	
81 Other services (except public administration)	
92 Public administration	

Source: U.S. Census Bureau (www.census.gov/eos/www/naics).

industry, asserting that the classification is arbitrary (which it is) and that the relevant market should be the two- to three-digit classification.

Empirical Measures of Industry Structure

To empirically measure industry structure, economists use one of two methods: the concentration ratio or the Herfindahl index.

A **concentration ratio** is *the value of sales by the top firms of an industry stated as a percentage of total industry sales.* The most commonly used concentration ratio is the four-firm concentration ratio. For example, a four-firm concentration ratio of 60 percent tells you that the top four firms in the industry produce 60 percent of the industry's output. The higher the ratio, the closer the industry is to an oligopolistic or monopolistic type of market structure.

> The Herfindahl index is a method used by economists to classify how competitive an industry is.

The **Herfindahl index** is *an index of market concentration calculated by adding the squared value of the individual market shares of all the firms in the industry.* For example, say that 10 firms in the industry each has 10 percent of the market:

$$\text{Herfindahl index} = 10^2 + 10^2 + 10^2 + 10^2 + 10^2 + 10^2 + 10^2 + 10^2 + 10^2 + 10^2$$
$$= 1{,}000$$

> Because it squares market shares, the Herfindahl index gives more weight to firms with large market shares than does the concentration ratio measure.

The Herfindahl index weights the largest firms in the industry more heavily than the concentration ratio because it squares market shares.

The two measures can differ because of their construction, but generally if the concentration ratio is high, so is the Herfindahl index. Table 15.2 presents the four-firm concentration ratio and the Herfindahl index of selected industries.

TABLE 15.2 **Empirical Measures of Industry Structure**

Industry	Four-Firm Concentration Ratio	Herfindahl Index
Poultry	46	773
Soft drinks	52	896
Breakfast cereal	78	2,999
Women's and misses' dresses	21	186
Book printing	38	492
Stationery	51	976
Soap and detergent	38	664
Men's footwear	44	734
Women's footwear	64	1,556
Pharmaceuticals	34	506
Computer and peripheral equipment	49	1,183
Radio, TV, wireless broadcasting	42	583
Burial caskets	73	2,965

Source: *Census of Manufacturers* (factfinder2.census.gov).

The Herfindahl index plays an important role in government policy; it is used as a rule of thumb by the U.S. Department of Justice in determining whether an industry is sufficiently competitive to allow a merger between two large firms. If the Herfindahl index is less than 1,000, the Department of Justice generally assumes the industry is sufficiently competitive, and it doesn't look more closely at the merger. This policy may change in the future.

Q-6 If the four-firm concentration ratio of an industry is 60 percent, what is the highest Herfindahl index that industry could have? What is the lowest?

Conglomerate Firms and Bigness

Neither the four-firm concentration ratio nor the Herfindahl index gives us a picture of corporations' bigness. That's because many corporations are conglomerates—companies that span a variety of unrelated industries. For example, a conglomerate might produce both shoes and automobiles.

To see that concentration ratios are not an index of bigness, say the entire United States had only 11 firms, each with a 9 percent share of each industry. Both indexes would classify the U.S. economy as unconcentrated, but many people would seriously doubt whether that were the case. Little work has been done on classifying conglomerates or in determining whether they affect an industry's performance.

Oligopoly Models and Empirical Estimates of Market Structure

To see how empirical measures of market structure relate to oligopoly models, let's consider the cartel and contestable market models of oligopoly. The cartel model fits best with these empirical measurements because it assumes that the structure of the market (the number of firms) is directly related to the price a firm charges. It predicts that oligopolies charge higher prices than do monopolistic competitors, who in turn charge higher prices than competitive firms charge.

The contestable market model gives far less weight to the empirical estimates of market structure. According to it, markets that structurally look highly oligopolistic could actually be highly competitive—much more so than markets that structurally look less competitive. This contestable market model view of judging markets by

Q-7 The Herfindahl index is 1,500. Using a contestable market approach, what would you conclude about this industry?

performance, not structure, has had many reincarnations. Close relatives of it have previously been called the *barriers-to-entry* model, the *stay-out pricing* model, and the *limit-pricing* model. These models provide a view of competition that doesn't depend on market structure.

To see the implications of the contestable market approach, let's consider an oligopoly with a four-firm concentration ratio of 60 percent and a Herfindahl index of 1,500. Using the structural approach, we would say that, because of the multiplicity of oligopoly models, we're not quite sure what price firms in this industry would charge, but that it seems reasonable to assume that there would be some implicit collusion and that the price would be closer to a monopolist price than to a competitive price. If that same market had a four-firm concentration ratio of 30 percent and a Herfindahl index of 700, the industry would be more likely to have a competitive price.

A contestable market model advocate would disagree, arguing that barriers to entry and exit are what's important. If no significant barriers to entry exist in the first case but significant barriers to entry exist in the second case, the second case would be more monopolistic than the first. An example is the Miami fish market mentioned earlier, where there were 20 sellers (none with a large percentage of the market) and significant barriers to entry (only fishers from the pier were allowed to sell fish there and the slots at the pier were limited). Because of those entry limitations, the pricing and output decisions would be close to the monopolistic price. If you took that same structure but had free entry, you'd get much closer to competitive decisions.

As I presented the two views, I emphasized the differences in order to make the distinction clear. However, I must also point out that there's a similarity in the two views. Often barriers to entry are the reason there are only a few firms in an industry. And when there are many firms, that suggests that there are few barriers to entry. In such situations, which make up the majority of cases, the two approaches come to the same conclusion.

Q-8 The Herfindahl index is 1,500. Using a structural analysis of markets approach, what would you conclude about this industry?

Antitrust Policy

Now that we've gone over the four major market structures in theory, and the way in which industries are classified in practice, let's consider government's role in affecting market structure. That role goes under the name antitrust policy in the United States and competition policy in some other countries.

Judgment by Performance or Structure?

Antitrust policy is *the government's policy toward the competitive process.* It's the government's rulebook for carrying out its role as referee. In volleyball, for instance, the rulebook would answer such questions as: When should a foul be called? When has a person caught and thrown rather than hit the ball over the net? In business a referee is needed for such questions as: When can two companies merge? What competitive practices are legal? When is a company too big? To what extent is it fair for two companies to coordinate their pricing policies? When is a market sufficiently competitive or too monopolistic?

The United States has seen wide swings in economists' prescriptions concerning such questions, depending on which of the two views of competition has held sway. The two competing views are:

1. **Judgment by performance:** *We should judge the competitiveness of markets by the performance (behavior) of firms in that market.*
2. **Judgment by structure:** *We should judge the competitiveness of markets by the structure of the industry.*

Two examples illustrate the difference.

At different times, U.S. antitrust law has been based on two competing views: judgment by performance and judgment by structure.

Standard Oil: Judging Market Competitiveness by Performance

In the late 1880s, a number of trusts (cartels) in the railroad, steel, tobacco, and oil industries were created by what were sometimes called *robber barons* (organizers of trusts who engaged in the exploitation of natural resources and other unethical behavior). The trusts were seen as making enormous profits, preventing competition, and in general bullying everyone in sight. One such cartel was the Standard Oil Trust, created by John D. Rockefeller, which used its monopoly power to close refineries, raise prices, and limit the production of oil. In response the U.S. Congress passed the *Sherman Antitrust Act of 1890*—a law designed to regulate the competitive process. In 1914 the Sherman Antitrust Act was clarified and strengthened with the *Clayton Antitrust Act,* which identified specific practices as illegal and monopolistic. The government brought a lawsuit against Standard Oil for violating the Sherman Antitrust Act.

In 1911 the U.S. Supreme Court handed down its opinion. It was determined that Standard Oil controlled 90 percent of the market and thus was definitely a monopoly. However, the Court decided that the monopolistic structure alone did not violate the Sherman Antitrust Act. To be guilty of antitrust violations there had to be evidence that the firm used its monopoly power to its benefit. In this case, the difference was academic because the court found that Standard Oil had done so and was guilty because it used "unfair business practices." The resolution was to break up Standard Oil, which made the distinction between performance and structure academic.

The structure/performance distinction was also important in a case involving U.S. Steel. Here the Supreme Court ruled that although U.S. Steel controlled a majority of the market and was therefore structural monopoly, it was not a monopoly in performance. That is, it had not used unfair business practices to become a monopolist or once it was a monopolist, and thus it was not in violation of antitrust law. Unlike Standard Oil, U.S. Steel was not required to break up into small companies.

The ALCOA Case: Judging Market Competitiveness by Structure

Judgment by performance was the primary criterion governing antitrust policy until 1945, when the U.S. courts changed their interpretation of the law with the Aluminum Company of America (ALCOA) case. ALCOA was the only producer of aluminum in the United States, a position it built by using its knowledge of the market to expand its capacity before any competitors had a chance to enter the market. Like Standard Oil, it had not used unfair business practices to become a monopolist. This time, the courts focused on the structure of the market and ruled ALCOA to be in violation of antitrust laws, even though it was not guilty of monopoly behavior.

Q-9 How was market competitiveness judged in the Standard Oil and ALCOA cases?

Judging Markets by Structure and Performance: The Reality

Both judgment by structure and judgment by performance have their problems. Judgment by structure seems unfair on a gut level. After all, in economics the purpose of competition is to motivate firms to produce better goods than their competitors are producing, and to do so at lower cost. If a firm is competing so successfully that all the other firms leave the industry, the successful firm will be a monopolist, and on the basis of judgment by structure will be guilty of antitrust violations. Under the judgment-by-structure criterion, a firm is breaking the law if it does what it's supposed to be doing: producing the best product it can at the lowest possible cost.

Supporters of the judgment-by-structure criterion recognize this problem but none-theless favor the structure criterion. An important reason for this is practicality.

Both judgment by structure and judgment by performance have their problems.

An important reason supporting the structure criterion is practicality.

Walmart, State Laws, and Competition

It isn't only the federal government that has laws regulating competition. States do also. One such state law is Arkansas's Unfair Practices Act, which prohibits selling, or advertising for sale, items below cost "for the purpose of injuring competitors and destroying competition." In the early 1990s, three Arkansas pharmacies sued Walmart for violating this law by selling its goods at "too low" a price.

Walmart initially lost the suit in Arkansas; however, in 1995 the Arkansas Supreme Court overturned the lower court decision and held that Walmart's pricing was not part of a strategy to price below cost over a prolonged period.

We may see more such suits, especially in the pricing of prescription pharmaceuticals, since Walmart introduced a $4 price for a 30-day prescription of a variety of generic drugs (including 14 of the top 20 best-selling prescription drugs) and other discount stores followed suit. However, these suits are likely to fail for two reasons. First, Walmart now takes into account state laws, and the $4 program is not available in states where its lawyers see the state laws as a potential problem. And second, the competition has changed. Back in the 1990s, Walmart was competing with local drug

stores that had high profit margins but low volume. Now it's competing with other chains—Kmart, Target, BJ's, Sam's Club—that have entered the prescription drug market and established their own low-cost generic programs.

All of these chains argue that when they charge a low price, they are not doing it to "destroy competition" or "injure competitors," but rather to maintain low prices for consumers. They claim that their pricing policies promote, not destroy, competition.

In principle, most economists agree with Walmart and other chains; new competition, by its very nature, hurts existing businesses—that's the way the competitive process works. Those who don't sell for the lowest price lose, and those who do gain. But most economists also recognize that Walmart's brand of competition can affect the social fabric of small-town economies. A new Walmart store can undermine the town centers and replace them with commercial sprawl on the outskirts of these towns. Whether these externalities are a reason to limit Walmart's aggressive pricing policies is a debatable question.

Judgment by performance requires that each action of a firm be analyzed on a case-by-case basis. Doing that is enormously time-consuming and expensive. In some interpretations, actions of a firm might be considered appropriate competitive behavior; in other interpretations, the same actions might be considered inappropriate. For example, say that an automobile company requires that in order for its warranty to hold, owners of its warranteed vehicles must use only the company's parts and service centers. Is this requirement of the automobile company intended to create a monopoly position for its parts and service center divisions or to ensure proper maintenance? The answer depends on the context of the action.

The problem is that judging each case contextually is beyond the courts' capabilities. There are so many firms and so many actions that the courts can't judge all industries on their performance. To solve this problem the courts limit the cases it looks at using market share, even though it is firms' performance that will ultimately be judged.

Judging by market structure also has difficulties. As you saw in the discussion of monopolistic competition, it's difficult to determine the relevant geographic market (local, national, or international) and the relevant industry (three-digit or five-digit NAICS code) necessary to identify the structural competitiveness of any industry.

The relevant industry question played a large part in the Department of Justice's opposition to a merger between Gillette and Parker Pens in 1993. The government argued that the combined firm would control about 40 percent of the premium-fountain-pen market. The Court, however, allowed the merger, arguing that the relevant market was much larger—the market for premium writing instruments, which also included mechanical pencils, ballpoint pens, and rollerballs. The premium-writing-instruments market had many more competitors than the premium-fountain-pen market.

Similar ambiguities exist with the decision about the relevant geographic market. In the Pabst Brewing case (1966), the definition of the market played a key role. Pabst wanted to merge with the Blatz Brewing Company. On a national scale, both companies were relatively small, accounting together for about 4.5 percent of beer sales in the United States as a whole. Pabst argued that the United States was the relevant market. The Court, however, decided that Wisconsin, where Pabst had its headquarters, was the relevant market, and since the two firms held a 24 percent share of that market, the merger was not allowed.

What should one make of debates regarding relevant markets? The bottom line is that both structure and performance criteria have ambiguities, and in the real world there are no definitive criteria for judging whether a firm has violated the antitrust statutes. A firm isn't at fault or in the clear until the courts make the call.

Both structure and performance criteria have ambiguities, and in the real world there are no definitive criteria for judging whether a firm has violated the antitrust statutes.

Recent Antitrust Enforcement

In recent years few major antitrust cases have been brought, in part because a century of experience has taught business what the law allows, and in part because the government has been lenient in its interpretation of the antitrust laws. That leniency has three interrelated causes. The first is a change in American ideology. Whereas in the 1950s and 1960s the prevailing ideology saw big business as "bad," by the 1980s big business was seen as a combination of good and bad. In this new ideological framework, the political pressure to push antitrust enforcement waned. Second, as the United States became more integrated into the global economy, big business faced significant international competition and hence competition created by U.S. market structure became less important. Third, as technologies became more complicated, the issues in antitrust enforcement also became more complicated for the courts to handle. By the time the legal system had resolved a case, the technology would have changed so much that the issues in that case were no longer relevant. These issues can be seen in two recent cases—Microsoft and AT&T.

Since the 1980s the United States has been more lenient in antitrust cases because of a change in ideology, the globalization of the U.S. economy, and the increasing complexity of technology.

THE MICROSOFT CASE   One of the most important antitrust cases brought in the 1990s was the Microsoft case which raises difficult questions about competition, the competitive process, and government's role in that competitive process.

Microsoft makes computer software. From the company's small start 40 years ago, sales of Microsoft software have grown to account for about 50 percent of the world's software market. Its PC operating system, Windows, accounts for an even larger share—about 90 percent—of the world's computer operating system software market.

Since all software must be compatible with an operating system, the widespread use of Windows gives Microsoft enormous power—power that competitors claim it has used to gain competitive advantage for its other divisions. Competitors' calls for action, and reports of monopolistically abusive acts by Microsoft, led the U.S. Department of Justice in 1998 to charge Microsoft with violating antitrust laws.

The government suit against Microsoft charged the company with being a monopoly and using that monopoly power in a predatory way. Specifically, it charged Microsoft with:

1. Possessing monopoly power in the market for personal computer operating systems.

Nefarious Business Practices

In a secretly recorded comment during a price-fixing meeting, the former president of Archer Daniels Midland (ADM), a major supplier of food and grain, stated, "Our competitors are our friends and our customers are our enemies."

The U.S. antitrust laws concern far more than mergers and market structure; they also place legal restrictions on certain practices of businesses such as price-fixing. By law, firms are not allowed to *explicitly* collude in order to fix prices above the competitive level. A key aspect of the law is the explicit nature of the collusion that is disallowed. Airlines, gas stations, and firms in many other industries have prices that generally move in tandem—when one firm changes its price, others seem to follow. Such practices would suggest that these firms are implicitly colluding, but they are not violating the law unless there is explicit collusion.

To prove explicit collusion is difficult—there must be a smoking gun, and there is seldom sufficient evidence of explicit collusion to prosecute businesses. There are exceptions, however. In 1996, ADM was caught red-handed when one of

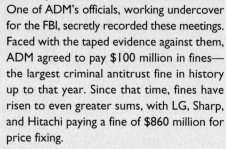

its former officials gave prosecutors tapes of meetings in which price-fixing occurred. Meeting secretly around the world, in countries like Mexico, France, Canada, and Japan, ADM executives tried to fix prices of Lysine, a feed additive, and citric acid.

One of ADM's officials, working undercover for the FBI, secretly recorded these meetings. Faced with the taped evidence against them, ADM agreed to pay $100 million in fines—the largest criminal antitrust fine in history up to that year. Since that time, fines have risen to even greater sums, with LG, Sharp, and Hitachi paying a fine of $860 million for price fixing.

Company	Fine (in millions)
LG, Sharp, and Hitachi (2008–10)	$860
British Airways (2007)	547
Yazahi (2012)	470
Samsung (2005)	300
Cargolux, Nippon, and Asiana (2009)	214
Japan Airlines (2008)	110

2. Tying other Microsoft software products to its Windows operating system.

3. Entering into agreements that keep computer manufacturers that install Windows from offering competing software.

Whether one sees Microsoft as a monopolist depends in part on whether one views it in a static or dynamic framework.

Microsoft had dominated the market for PC operating systems for about a decade. The U.S. Department of Justice argued that this long-standing monopoly position was the result of unfair business practices. Microsoft argued that Windows sold so well because it was a superior product. Microsoft further argued that, because it faced competition from technological change, it was not a monopolist.

Competition came from open-source (free) operating systems such as Linux and Java and more recently "cloud computing" services such as those provided by Internet browser Chrome. Cloud computing provides software services to cell phones, computers, and tablets over the Internet, which eliminates the need for compatibility between hardware and software. Each of these changes has eroded Microsoft's monopoly advantage.

With regard to the antitrust case, in 2000 a judge concluded that Microsoft violated the Sherman Antitrust Act and proposed breaking Microsoft into two companies. Microsoft appealed and eventually the Department of Justice and Microsoft reached an agreement. Microsoft would not be broken up, but its practices would be regulated to prevent predatory behavior that served to raise barriers to entry. This regulation reduced Microsoft's dominance but the development of new technologies has played a larger role in reducing that dominance. As many of the functions of the PC have been

Q-10 What was the resolution of the Microsoft case?

replaced by mobile apps, many of which were not Windows-based. Microsoft's monopoly over operating systems was reduced.

THE AT&T CASE   A second recent case is AT&T. The AT&T you know today isn't the AT&T of the last century. Beginning in 1913 AT&T was what was called a regulated monopoly. It had the exclusive right to provide telephone service in the United States. AT&T controlled 90 percent of the telecommunications market: long-distance and local telephone service and the production of telephones themselves as well as other communications equipment. It was given that right because telephone service required substantial set-up costs—land lines that connect households. To have more than one company stringing competing lines made little sense, making it a natural monopoly. In exchange for exclusive rights to the telephone market, AT&T agreed to be regulated. AT&T was required to provide universal service to all Americans, even those living in rural and remote areas, where service was more costly to provide. Unregulated companies likely would have practiced *cream skimming* (providing service to low-cost areas and avoiding high-cost areas).

In the 1970s technological change fundamentally altered the nature of the long-distance telephone industry. Satellite transmission and fiber optics made physical line connections no longer the only option, so long-distance telephone service was no longer a natural monopoly, and slowly regulators allowed some competition to develop. In 1984, AT&T was broken up by a government antitrust case into seven *Baby Bells,* which continued to supply local telephone service in a regulated industry, and the parent company, AT&T, which could enter any unregulated industry it desired.

The breakup of AT&T was not the end of the changes. The seven Baby Bells merged with one another, and by 2005 only four remained: SBC Communications, Verizon, Bell South, and Qwest. In 1995, AT&T had divided itself into three companies: AT&T, Lucent Technologies, and National Cash Register. Of these, only AT&T remained in the market for communication services, expanding its offerings into wireless communications, digital cable, cable, and long distance. In 2004, however, it withdrew from the residential local and long-distance phone markets. Then in 2005 it was taken over by one of its former parts—SBC Communications, which operated Cingular Wireless—and the combined company chose to use the AT&T name. Then in 2006, the new AT&T was taken over by Bell South, another of the former Baby Bells, and the combined company again called itself at&t (initially in lowercase), making it the new, new at&t. So the name, at&t, still exists, but the company that the name is associated with is quite different from the company that was the subject of the antitrust suit, and it is a company that has twice been taken over by its former parts.

The new AT&T is still facing antitrust issues. In 2011 the Department of Justice sued AT&T and blocked its merger with T-mobile, a smaller cell phone company. The Department of Justice blocked the merger arguing that it would substantially limit competition and allow the combined company to raise prices for consumers.

What we have learned from this experience is that rapid technological change alters the nature of industries and introduces competition in ways that previously had not been possible. The slow moving antitrust laws are usually years behind.

Rapid technological change alters the nature of industries and introduces competition in ways that previously had not been possible.

Assessment of U.S. Antitrust Policy

Economic scholars' overall assessment of antitrust policy is mixed. In certain cases, such as the ALCOA case, most agree that antitrust prosecution went too far. But most believe that other decisions (as in the 1911 Standard Oil case) set a healthy precedent by encouraging a more competitive U.S. business environment. Almost all agree that antitrust enforcement has not reduced the size of firms below the minimally efficient level, the level at which a firm can take full advantage of economies of scale. But they are mixed in their judgments as to whether the enforcement was needed. Performance advocates generally believe that it was not, while structural advocates generally believe that it was. They are also mixed in their judgment about whether any type of antitrust action is feasible in a technologically dynamic industry such as computers or telecommunications.

Conclusion

We've come to the end of our discussion of market structure and government policy toward the competitive process. What conclusion should we reach? That's a tough question because the problem has so many dimensions. What we can say is that market structure is important, and generally more competition is preferred to less competition. We can also say that, based on experience, government-created and protected monopolies have not been the optimal solution, especially when industries are experiencing technological change. But how government should deal with monopolies that develop as part of the competitive process is less clear. Competition has both dynamic elements and market structure elements, and often monopolies that develop as part of the competitive process are temporary—and they will be overwhelmed by other monopolies. Thus, the debate about government entering into the market to protect competition has no single answer, which makes cases like the Microsoft antitrust case difficult to resolve.

Summary

- The two distinguishing characteristics of an oligopolistic market are (1) there are a small number of firms and (2) firms engage in strategic decision-making. *(LO15-1)*

- A contestable market theory of oligopoly judges an industry's competitiveness more by performance and barriers to entry than by structure. Cartel models of oligopoly concentrate on market structure. *(LO15-2)*

- An oligopolist's price will be somewhere between the competitive price and the monopolistic price. *(LO15-2)*

- Industries are classified by economic activity in the North American Industry Classification System (NAICS). Industry structures are measured by concentration ratios and Herfindahl indexes. *(LO15-3)*

- A concentration ratio is the sum of the market shares of individual firms with the largest shares in an industry. *(LO15-3)*

- A Herfindahl index is the sum of the squares of the individual market shares of all firms in an industry. *(LO15-3)*

- Antitrust policy is the government's policy toward the competitive process. *(LO15-4)*

- There is a debate about whether markets should be judged on the basis of structure or on the basis of performance. *(LO15-4)*

- Judgment by performance means judging the competitiveness of markets by the behavior of firms in that market. Judgment by structure means judging the competitiveness of markets by how many firms operate in the industry and their market shares. *(LO15-4)*

- In 2000 the courts found that Microsoft had a monopoly that was protected by barriers to entry and that Microsoft engaged in practices to maintain that monopoly power. Microsoft agreed to stop some practices. *(LO15-4)*

- The antitrust suit against AT&T ended in a settlement that required AT&T to be broken up. AT&T both divided itself and merged with other companies. *(LO15-4)*

Key Terms

antitrust
   policy *(324)*

cartel *(316)*

cartel model of
   oligopoly *(316)*

concentration
   ratio *(322)*

contestable market
   model *(318)*

Herfindahl index *(322)*

implicit collusion *(317)*

judgment by
   performance *(324)*

judgment by
   structure *(324)*

North American Industry
   Classification System
   (NAICS) *(320)*

oligopoly *(315)*

strategic decision
   making *(315)*

Questions and Exercises

1. What distinguishes oligopoly from monopolistic competition? *(LO15-1)*

2. Is an oligopolist more or less likely to engage in strategic decision making compared to a monopolistic competitor? *(LO15-1)*

3. What is the difference between the contestable market model and the cartel model of oligopoly? *(LO15-2)*

4. How are the contestable market model and the cartel model of oligopoly related? *(LO15-2)*

5. In 1982 Robert Crandell, CEO of American Airlines, phoned the Braniff Airways CEO and said, "Raise your fares 20 percent and I'll raise mine the next morning." *(LO15-2)*
   a. Why would he do this?
   b. If you were the Braniff Airways CEO, would you have gone along?
   c. Why should Crandell not have done this?

6. Kellogg's, which controls 32 percent of the breakfast cereal market, cut the prices of some of its best-selling brands of cereal to regain market share lost to Post, which controls 20 percent of the market. General Mills has 24 percent of the market. The price cuts were expected to trigger a price war. Based on this information, what market structure best characterizes the market for breakfast cereal? *(LO15-2)*

7. In 1993 Mattel proposed acquiring Fisher-Price for $1.2 billion. In the toy industry, Mattel is a major player with 11 percent of the market. Fisher-Price has 4 percent. The other two large firms are Tyco, with a 5 percent share, and Hasbro, with a 15 percent share. In the infant/preschool toy market, Mattel has an 8 percent share and Fisher-Price has a 27 percent share, the largest. The other two large firms are Hasbro, with a 25 percent share, and Rubbermaid, with a 12 percent share. *(LO15-3)*
   a. What are the approximate Herfindahl and four-firm concentration ratios for these industries? (Assume all other firms in each industry have 1 percent of the market each.)
   b. If you were Mattel's economist, which industry definition would you suggest using in court if you were challenged by the government?

c. Give an argument why the merger might decrease competition.

d. Give an argument why the merger might increase competition.

8. Which industry is more highly concentrated: one with a Herfindahl index of 1,200 or one with a four-firm concentration ratio of 55 percent? *(LO15-3)*

9. The pizza market is divided as follows: *(LO15-3)*

Pizza Hut	20.7%
Domino's	17.0
Little Caesars	6.7
Pizza Inn/Pantera's	2.2
Round Table	2.0
All others	51.4

   a. How would you describe its market structure?
   b. What is the approximate Herfindahl index?
   c. What is the four-firm concentration ratio?

10. If you were an economist for a firm that wanted to merge, would you argue that the three-digit or five-digit NAICS industry is the relevant market? Why? *(LO15-3)*

11. Suppose you are an economist for Mattel, manufacturer of the doll Barbie, which was making an unsolicited bid to take over Hasbro, manufacturer of the doll G.I. Joe. *(LO15-4)*
   a. Would you argue that the relevant market is dolls, preschool toys, or all toys including video games? Why?
   b. Would your answer change if you were working for Hasbro?

12. What is the difference between judgment by performance and judgment by structure? *(LO15-4)*

13. Is a contestable model or cartel model more likely to judge an industry by performance? Explain your answer. *(LO15-4)*

14. Distinguish the basis of judgment for the Standard Oil and the ALCOA cases. *(LO15-4)*

15. Demonstrate graphically how regulating the price of a monopolist can both increase quantity and decrease price. (Difficult)　(LO15-4)
    a. Why did the regulation have the effect it did?
    b. How relevant to the real world do you believe this result is in the contestable markets view of the competitive process?
    c. How relevant to the real world do you believe this result is in the cartel view of the competitive process?

16. Discuss the effect of antitrust policy in the:　(LO15-4)
    a. monopolistic competition model.
    b. cartel model of oligopoly.
    c. contestable market model of oligopoly.

17. In what market did Microsoft have a monopoly in the late 1990s and early 2000s?　(LO15-4)

18. What technological advances threatened Microsoft's monopoly?　(LO15-4)

19. Why was AT&T given a monopoly in the telephone industry?　(LO15-4)

20. What was the resolution of the AT&T case?　(LO15-4)

Questions from Alternative Perspectives

1. In the past two chapters you have learned much about market power: how it is used, the efficiency implications, and how society has responded. Yet this power remains, albeit minimally checked from time to time. The economist Thorstein Veblen would not be surprised by this. He would argue that firms use market power because they can. How do monopolists use "power" to manipulate outcomes? (Institutionalist)

2. Alexis de Tocqueville once stated that "The Americans have applied to the sexes the great principle of political economy which governs the manufacturers of our age, by carefully dividing the duties of men from those of women, in order that the great work of society may be the better carried on …"
    a. Do you agree with his statement?
    b. What problems might his argument have? (Feminist)

3. In which market structure would women likely be most successful? Why? (Feminist)

4. Does market structure determine firm behavior or does firm behavior determine market structure? (Post-Keynesian)

5. A *BusinessWeek* magazine study of mergers and acquisitions between 1990 and 1995 found that 83 percent of these deals achieved, at best, marginal returns, and 50 percent recorded a loss.
    a. If such mergers are not especially profitable, why do they occur?
    b. U.S. antitrust policy has changed dramatically since the 1960s when the government regularly blocked mergers among companies in the same industry. Today, the federal government is much less active; it allows almost all mergers. Is this new approach justified, or has government just given in to the powers that be?
    c. What antitrust policies would work best in today's U.S. economy? (Radical)

Issues to Ponder

1. A firm is convinced that if it lowers its price, no other firm in the industry will change price; however, it believes that if it raises its price, some other firms will match its increase, making its demand curve more inelastic. The current price is $8 and its marginal cost is constant at $4.
    a. Sketch the general shape of the firm's *MR, MC,* and demand curves and show why there are two possible equilibria.
    b. If there are two equilibria, which of the two do you think the firms will arrive at? Why?
    c. If the marginal cost falls to $3, what would you predict would happen to price?
    d. If the marginal cost rises to $5, what would you predict would happen to price?
    e. Do a survey of five or six firms in your area. Ask them how they believe other firms would respond to their increasing or decreasing price. Based on that survey, discuss the relevance of this kinked demand model compared to the one presented in the book.

2. Private colleges of the same caliber generally charge roughly the same tuition. Would you characterize these colleges as a cartel type of oligopoly?

3. In the 1990s, the infant/preschool toy market four-firm concentration ratio was 72 percent. With 8 percent of the market, Mattel was the fourth largest firm in that market. Mattel proposed to buy Fisher-Price, the market leader with 27 percent.
   a. Why would Mattel want to buy Fisher-Price?
   b. What arguments can you think of in favor of allowing this acquisition?
   c. What arguments can you think of against allowing this acquisition?
   d. How do you think the four-firm concentration ratio for the entire toy industry would compare to this infant/preschool toy market concentration ratio?

4. How would the U.S. economy likely differ today if Standard Oil had not been broken up?

5. In 1992 American Airlines offered a 50-percent-off sale and cut fares. In 1993 Continental Airlines and Northwest Airlines sued American Airlines over this action.
   a. What was the likely basis of the suit?
   b. How does the knowledge that Continental and Northwest were in serious financial trouble play a role in the suit?

6. You're working at the Department of Justice. Ms. Ecofame has just developed a new index, the Ecofame index, which she argues is preferable to the Herfindahl index. The Ecofame index is calculated by cubing the market share of the top 10 firms in the industry.
   a. Calculate an Ecofame guideline that would correspond to the Department of Justice guidelines.
   b. State the advantages and disadvantages of the Ecofame index as compared to the Herfindahl index.

7. What did Adam Smith mean when he wrote, "Seldom do businessmen of the same trade get together but that it results in some detriment to the general public"?

Answers to Margin Questions

1. I would respond that monopolistic competitors, by definition, do not take into account the expected reactions of competitors to their decisions; therefore, they cannot use strategic decision making. I would tell Jean she probably meant, "*Oligopolies* use strategic decision making." (*p. 316; LO15-1*)

2. Maintaining a cartel requires firms to make decisions that are not in their individual best interests. Such decisions are hard to enforce unless there is an explicit enforcement mechanism, which is difficult in a cartel. (*p. 317; LO15-2*)

3. The demand curve perceived by an oligopolist is more elastic above the current price because it believes that others will not follow price increases. If it increased price, its quantity demanded would fall by a lot. The opposite is true below the current price. The demand curve below current price is less elastic. Price declines would be matched by competitors and the oligopolist would see little change in quantity demanded with a price decline. (*p. 318; LO15-2*)

4. The two extremes an oligopoly model can take are (1) a cartel model, which is the equivalent of a monopoly, and (2) a contestable market model, which, if there are no barriers to entry, is the equivalent of a competitive industry. (*p. 319; LO15-2*)

5. The smaller the number of digits, the more inclusive the classification. Therefore, the two-digit industry would have significantly more output. (*p. 321; LO15-3*)

6. The highest Herfindahl index for this industry would occur if one firm had the entire 60 percent, and all other firms had an infinitesimal amount, making the Herfindahl index slightly over 3,600. The lowest Herfindahl index this industry could have would occur if each of the top four firms had 15 percent of the market, yielding a Herfindahl index of 900. (*p. 323; LO15-3*)

7. The contestable market approach looks at barriers to entry, not structure. Therefore, we can conclude nothing about the industry from the Herfindahl index. (*p. 323; LO15-3*)

8. In a market with a Herfindahl index of 1,500, the largest firm would have, at most, slightly under 38 percent of the market. The least concentrated such an industry could be would be if seven firms each had between 14 and 15 percent of the market. In either of these two cases, the industry would probably be an oligopolistic industry and could border on monopoly. (*p. 324; LO15-3*)

9. The Court decided that Standard Oil had engaged in systematic abuse and unfair business practices, and therefore was guilty of antitrust violations and must be broken up. It was judged by performance. In the ALCOA case, the Supreme Court decided the structure of the market, not the company's performance, was the appropriate standard by which to judge cases. (*p. 325; LO15-4*)

10. The resolution of the Microsoft case was that it wouldn't be broken up, but its practices would be regulated. (*p. 328; LO15-4*)

chapter 16

Real-World Competition and Technology

It is ridiculous to call this an industry. This is rat eat rat; dog eat dog. I'll kill 'em, and I'm going to kill 'em before they kill me. You're talking about the American way of survival of the fittest.

—Ray Kroc
(founder of McDonald's)

When Microsoft was designing Zune, the Microsoft workers were sent a link to a video of Steven Jobs (the CEO of Apple) showing Jobs stating, "The only problem with Microsoft is that they have no taste—Absolutely no taste." The goal of Microsoft showing the video to Microsoft workers was to infuriate the Microsoft workers sufficiently so that they would show that not only do they have taste, but that they can bury Apple and its iPod. It was to make the competition with Apple personal. It didn't work, and Apple went public with its "no taste" view of Microsoft in a series of TV ads that portrayed the Apple computer as the tasteful computer compared to a rather stodgy PC.

In earlier chapters we've seen some nice, neat models, but as we discussed in a previous chapter, often these models don't fit reality directly. Real-world markets aren't perfectly monopolistic; they aren't perfectly competitive either. They're somewhere between the two. The monopolistic competition and oligopoly models in previous chapters come closer to reality and provide some important insights into the "in-between" markets, but, like any abstraction, they, too, fail to capture aspects of the actual nature of competition.

In this chapter, I give you a sense of what actual firms, markets, and competition are like. This chapter also discusses an issue that is very much in the news—technology—and relates it to the models we developed earlier and shows how economists' modern models differ from the traditional textbook models.

When reading this chapter, think about the two understandings of competition discussed in the chapter on perfect competition: competition as a process, the end state of which is zero profits, and competition as market structure. In this chapter the focus is on competition as a process—it is a rivalry between firms and between individuals. This competitive process is active in all market forms and is key to understanding real-world competition.

The Goals of Real-World Firms and the Monitoring Problem

Maybe the best place to start is with the assumption that firms are profit maximizers. There's a certain reasonableness to this assumption; firms definitely are concerned about profit, but are they trying to maximize profit? The answer is: It depends.

Short-Run versus Long-Run Profit

The first insight is that if firms are profit maximizers, they aren't just concerned with short-run profit; most are concerned with long-run profit. Thus, even if they can, they may not take full advantage of a potential monopolistic situation now in order to strengthen their long-run position. For example, many stores have liberal return policies: "If you don't like it, you can return it for a full refund." Similarly, many firms spend millions of dollars improving their reputations or building up a brand. Most firms want to be known as good citizens. Such expenditures on reputation and goodwill can increase long-run profit, even if they reduce short-run profit.

The Problem with Profit Maximization

A second insight into how real-world firms differ from the model is that in the real world the decision makers' income is often a cost of the firm. Most real-world production doesn't take place in owner-operated businesses; it takes place in large corporations with eight or nine levels of management, thousands of stockholders whose stock is often held in trust for them, and a board of directors, chosen by management, overseeing the company by meeting eight to ten times a year. Signing a proxy statement is as close as most stockowners get to directing "their company" to maximize profit.

Most real-world production doesn't take place in owner-operated businesses; it takes place in large corporations.

MANAGERS' INCENTIVES Why is the structure of the firm important to the analysis? Because economic theory tells us that, unless someone is seeing to it that they do, self-interested decision makers have little incentive to hold down their pay. But their pay is a cost of the firm. And if their pay isn't held down, the firm's profit will be lower than otherwise. Most firms put some pressure on managers to make at least a predesignated level of profit. (If you ask managers, they'll tell you that they face enormous pressure.) So the profit motive certainly plays a role—but to say that profit plays a role is not to say that firms maximize profit. Having dealt with many companies, I'll go out on a limb and say that there are enormous wastes and inefficiencies in many U.S. businesses.

Q-1 What are two reasons why real-world firms are not pure profit maximizers?

This structure presents a problem in applying the model to the real world. The textbook economic model assumes that individuals are utility maximizers—that they're motivated by self-interest. Then, in the textbook model of the firm, the assumption is made that firms, composed of self-interest-seeking individuals, are profit-seeking firms, without explaining how self-interest-seeking individuals who manage real-world corporations will find it in their interest to maximize profit for the firm. Economists recognize this problem, which was introduced in an earlier chapter. It's an example of the **monitoring problem**—*the need to oversee employees to ensure that their actions are in the best interest of the firm.*

The monitoring problem is that employees' incentives differ from the owner's incentives.

NEED FOR MONITORING Monitoring is required because employees' incentives differ from the owner's incentives, and it's costly to see that the employee does the owner's bidding. The monitoring problem is now a central problem focused on by economists who specialize in industrial organization. They study internal structures of firms and look for a contract that managers can be given: an **incentive-compatible contract** in which *the incentives of each of the two parties to the contract are made to correspond as*

Who Controls Corporations?

When a corporation is formed, it issues stock, which is sold or given to individuals. Ownership of stock entitles you to vote in the election of a corporation's directors, so in theory holders of stock control the company. In practice, however, in most large corporations, ownership is separated from control of the firm. Most stockholders have little input into the decisions a corporation makes. Instead, most corporations are controlled by their managers, who often run them for their own benefit as well as for the owners'. The reason is that the owners' control of management is limited.

A large percentage of most corporations' stock is not even controlled by the owners; instead, it is controlled by financial institutions such as mutual funds (financial institutions that invest individuals' money for them) and by pension funds (financial institutions that hold people's money for them until it is to be paid out to them upon their retirement). Thus, ownership of corporations is another step removed from individuals. Studies have shown that 80 percent of the largest 200 corporations in the United States are essentially controlled by managers and have little effective stockholder control.

Why is the question of who controls a firm important? Because economic theory assumes the goal of business owners is to maximize profits, which would be true of corporations if stockholders made the decisions. Managers don't have the same incentives to maximize profits that owners do. There's pressure on managers to maximize profits, but that pressure can often be weak or ineffective. An example of how firms deal with this problem involves stock options. Many companies give their managers stock options— rights to buy stock at a low price—to encourage them to worry about the price of their company's stock. But these stock options dilute the value of company ownership, decrease profits per share, and can give managers an incentive to overstate profits through accounting gimmicks, as happened at Enron, Xerox, and a number of other firms in the early 2000s.

Self-interested managers are interested in maximizing firm profit only if the structure of the firm requires them to do so.

closely as possible. The specific monitoring problem relevant to firm structure is that often owners find it too costly to monitor the managers to ensure that managers do what's in the owners' interest. And self-interested managers are interested in maximizing the firm's profit only if the structure of the firm requires them to do so.

When appropriate monitoring doesn't take place, high-level managers can pay themselves very well. As can be seen in the table of CEO compensation of selected companies below, many U.S. managers receive multimillion-dollar salaries. But are these salaries too high? That's a difficult question.

www Web Note 16.1
Executive Compensation

Company	CEO Compensation in 2011 (in millions)
McKesson	131.19
Ralph Lauren	66.65
Vornado Realty	64.40
Kinder Morgan	60.94
Honeywell	55.79
Express Scripts	51.52
Priceline.com	50.18
UnitedHealth Group	48.83
Marathon Oil	43.71
Gilead Sciences	43.19

Why Are CEOs Paid So Much?

CEOs are paid more today than they were 25 years ago—a lot more. Today, CEO's pay at top companies is about 250 times that of what an average worker receives, while 25 years ago, CEOs received only 40 times as much. Why the change? Some have suggested that it's just that CEOs are greedy. That's probably true, but it doesn't explain why CEOs are paid so much more today than before, unless they've become a lot greedier, which is unlikely; they've always been greedy. So we have to look elsewhere for an answer.

One thing that's changed in the past 25 years is the bargaining power of workers. Worker's pay is now being held down by competition and outsourcing. (If workers ask for a raise, the company responds "No way" and threatens to shift production to China; the workers are forced to give in to save their jobs.) But CEO's pay is not restrained by outsourcing. (At least not yet.) This means that back in the 1980s, high CEO compensation created labor unrest; today, it does not.

Economists Xavier Gabaix and Augustin Landier of New York University have argued that the rise in CEO's pay is the result of supply and demand forces. They argue that, today, unconstrained supply and demand forces determine pay of CEOs, whereas back in the 1980s, the bargaining considerations of workers partially prevented supply and demand forces from fully operating.

To explain why CEOs are paid so much more today than they were earlier, they argue that the demand for top CEOs has increased significantly in recent years because there are more large firms today than there were 25 years ago, making small differences in CEO performance matter a lot. They further argue that CEO talent is in short supply, which means that the supply curve for top-rate CEOs is highly inelastic, just like the supply curve for top football players, who also get very high pay. Replacing a top CEO by a CEO ranked 250th, they calculate, would reduce a company's market value by 0.016 percent, which for a large firm they calculated to be about $60 million. This means that today large firms are competing for the highly inelastic supply of high-quality CEOs, and the high demand pushes the pay up. So their answer to the question of why CEOs are paid so much more now is that the number of large firms has increased, which has shifted out the demand for CEOs enormously.

This explanation, if correct, offers a policy suggestion for those who feel that the CEOs aren't deserving of their high pay: make the income tax more progressive. A high tax on an inelastic supply will not decrease the quantity supplied significantly, so if one makes the income tax more progressive, it will have little effect on the quantity of CEO effort supplied and thus will have minimal negative effects on efficiency.

One way to get an idea about an answer is to compare U.S. managers' salaries with those in Japan, where the control of firms is different. Banks in Japan have significant control over the operations of firms, and they closely monitor firms' performance. The result is that, in Japan, high-level managers on average earn about one-fifth of what their U.S. counterparts make, while wages of low-level workers are comparable to those of low-level workers in the United States. Given Japanese companies' success in competing with U.S. companies, this suggests that high managerial pay in the United States reflects a monitoring problem inherent in the structure of corporations common to all third-party-payer systems. There are, of course, other perspectives. Considering what some sports, film, and music stars receive places the high salaries of U.S. managers in a different light.

Q-2 Why would most economists be concerned about third-party-payer systems in which the consumer and the payer are different?

What Do Real-World Firms Maximize?

If firms don't maximize profit, what do they maximize? What are their goals? The answer again is: It depends.

Although profit is one goal of a firm, often firms focus on other intermediate goals such as cost and sales.

Real-world firms often have a set of complicated goals that reflect the organizational structure and incentives built into the system. Clearly, profit is one of their goals. Firms spend a lot of time designing incentives to get managers to focus on profit.

But often intermediate goals become the focus of firms. For example, many real-world firms focus on growth in sales; at other times they institute a cost-reduction program to increase long-run profit. At still other times they may simply take it easy and not push hard at all, enjoying the position they find themselves in—being what British economist Joan Robinson called **lazy monopolists**—*firms that do not push for efficiency, but merely enjoy the position they are already in.* This term describes many, but not all, real-world corporations. When Robinson coined the term, firms faced mostly domestic competition. Today, with firms facing more and more global competition, firms are a bit less lazy than they were.

The Lazy Monopolist and X-Inefficiency

Lazy monopolists are not profit maximizers; they see to it that they make enough profit so that the stockholders aren't squealing, but they don't push as hard as they could to hold their costs down. They perform as efficiently as is consistent with keeping their jobs. The result is what economists call **X-inefficiency** *(firms operating far less efficiently than they could technically).* Such firms have monopoly positions, but they don't make large monopoly profits. Instead, their costs rise because of inefficiency; they may simply make a normal level of profit or, if X-inefficiency becomes bad enough, a loss.

The standard model avoids dealing with the monitoring problem by assuming that the owner of the firm makes all the decisions. The owners of firms who receive the profit, and only the profit, would like to see that all the firm's costs are held down. Unfortunately, very few real-world firms operate that way. In reality owners seldom make operating decisions. They hire or appoint managers to make those decisions. The managers they hire don't have that same incentive to hold costs down. Therefore, it isn't surprising to many economists that managers' pay is usually high and that high-level managers see to it that they have "perks" such as chauffeurs, jet planes, ritzy offices, and assistants to do as much of their work as possible.

Q-3 Why doesn't a manager have the same incentive to hold costs down as an owner does?

The equilibrium of a lazy monopolist is presented in Figure 16-1. A monopolist would produce at price P_M and quantity Q_M. Average total cost would be C_M, so the monopolist's profit would be the entire shaded rectangle (areas A and B). The lazy monopolist would allow costs to increase until the firm reached its normal level of profit. In Figure 16-1, costs rise to C_{LM}. The profit of the lazy monopolist is area B. The remainder of the potential profit is eaten up in cost inefficiencies.

The competitive pressures a firm faces limit its laziness.

What places a limit on firms' laziness is the degree of competitive pressures they face. All economic institutions must earn sufficient revenue to cover costs, so all economic institutions have a limit on how lazy and inefficient they can get—a limit imposed by their monopoly position. They can translate the monopoly profit into X-inefficiency, thereby benefiting the managers and workers in the firm, but once they've done so, they can't be more inefficient. They would go out of business.

HOW COMPETITION LIMITS THE LAZY MONOPOLIST   If all individuals in the industry are lazy, then laziness becomes the norm and competitive pressures don't reduce their profits. Laziness is relative, not absolute. But if a new firm comes in all gung-ho and hardworking, or if an industry is opened up to international competition, the lazy monopolists can be squeezed and must undertake massive restructuring to make themselves competitive. Many U.S. firms have been undergoing such restructuring in order to make themselves internationally competitive.

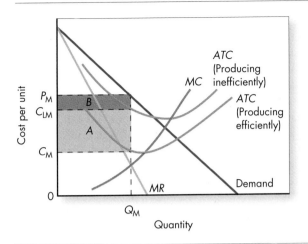

FIGURE 16-1 True Cost Efficiency and the Lazy Monopolist

A monopolist producing efficiently would have costs C_M and would produce at price P_M and quantity Q_M. A lazy monopolist, in contrast, would let costs rise until the minimum level of profit is reached—in this example at C_{LM}. Profit for the monopolist is represented by the entire shaded area, whereas profit for the lazy monopolist is squeezed down to area B.

A second way in which competitive pressure is placed on a lazy monopolist is by a **corporate takeover,** in which *another firm or a group of individuals issues a tender offer (that is, offers to buy up the stock of a company) to gain control and to install its own managers.* In the last few years many of these takeovers were done by private equity firms, which are firms that are not listed on the stock exchange. Most of these private equity firms are primarily investment vehicles, whose expertise is in finance, not in production. They buy up firms that have not been performing well financially and push them to improve their financial payout by becoming more efficient. Usually such tender offers are financed by large amounts of debt, which means that if the takeover is successful, the private equity firm will need to make large profits just to cover the interest payments on the debt.

Managers generally don't like takeovers. A takeover may cost them their jobs and the perks that go along with those jobs, so they'll often restructure the company on their own as a preventive measure. Such restructuring frequently means incurring large amounts of debt to finance a large payment to stockholders. These payments put more pressure on management to operate efficiently. Thus, the threat of a corporate takeover places competitive pressure on firms to maximize profits.

Were profit not a motive at all, one would expect the lazy monopolist syndrome to take precedence. In fact, it's not surprising that nonprofit organizations often display lazy monopolist tendencies. For example, some colleges, schools, libraries, jails, and nonprofit hospitals have a number of rules and ways of doing things that, upon reflection, benefit the employees of the institution rather than the customers. At most colleges, students aren't polled about what time they would prefer classes to meet; instead, the professors and administrators decide when they want to teach. I leave it to you to figure out whether your college exhibits these tendencies and whether you'd prefer that your college, library, or hospital change to a for-profit institution. Studying these incentive-compatible problems is what management courses are all about.

MOTIVATIONS FOR EFFICIENCY OTHER THAN THE PROFIT INCENTIVE

I'm not going to discuss management theory here other than to stimulate your thinking about the problem. However, I'd be remiss in presenting you this broad outline of the monitoring problem without mentioning that the drive for profit isn't the only drive that pushes for efficiency. Some individuals derive pleasure from efficiently run organizations. Such individuals don't need to be monitored. Thus, if administrators are

A corporate takeover, or simply the threat of a takeover, can improve a firm's efficiency.

Q-4 In what way does the threat of a corporate takeover place competitive pressures on a firm?

Web Note 16.2
Creative Destruction

well intentioned, they'll hold down costs even if they aren't profit maximizers. In such cases, monitoring (creating an organization and structure that gives people profit incentives) can actually reduce efficiency! It's amazing to some economists how some nonprofit organizations operate as efficiently as they do—some libraries and colleges fall into that category. Their success is built on their employees' pride in their jobs, not on their profit motive.

Individuals have complicated motives; some simply have a taste for efficiency.

Most economists don't deny that such inherently efficient individuals exist, and that most people derive some pleasure from efficiency, but they believe that it's hard to maintain that push for efficiency year in, year out, when some of your colleagues are lazy monopolists enjoying the fruits of your efficiency. Most people derive some pleasure from efficiency, but, based on their observation of people's actions, economists believe that holding down costs without the profit motive takes stronger willpower than most people have.

The Fight between Competitive and Monopolistic Forces

Even if all the assumptions for perfect competition could hold true, it's unlikely that real-world markets would be perfectly competitive. The reason is that perfect competition assumes that individuals accept a competitive institutional structure—political and social forces that support competition—even though changing that structure could result in significant gains for sellers or buyers. The simple fact is that *self-interest-seeking individuals don't like competition for themselves* (although they do like it for others), and when competitive pressures get strong and the invisible hand's push turns to shove, individuals often shove back, using either social or political means. That's why you can understand real-world competition only if you understand how the invisible hand, social forces, and political pressures push against each other to create real-world economic institutions. Real-world competition should be seen as a process—a fight between the forces of monopolization and the forces of competition.

Competition is a process—a fight between the forces of monopolization and the forces of competition.

How Monopolistic Forces Affect Perfect Competition

Let's consider some examples. During the Depression of the 1930s, competition was pushing down prices and wages. What was the result? Individuals socially condemned firms for unfair competition, and numerous laws were passed to prevent it. Unions were strengthened politically and given monopoly powers so they could resist the pressure to push down wages. The Robinson-Patman Act was passed, making it illegal for large retailers to lower prices to the detriment of local mom-and-pop stores. Individual states passed similar laws, and in the 1990s it was under one of these that Walmart Stores, Inc., lost a court case in which it was accused of charging too-low prices in its pharmacies.

The United States has myriad laws, regulations, and programs that prevent agricultural markets from working competitively.

As another example, consider agricultural markets, which have many of the conditions for almost perfect competition. To my knowledge, not one country in the world allows a competitive agricultural market to exist. The United States has myriad laws, regulations, and programs that prevent agricultural markets from working competitively. U.S. agricultural markets are characterized by price supports, acreage limitations, and quota systems. Thus, where perfectly competitive markets could exist, they aren't allowed to. An almost infinite number of other examples can be found. Our laws and social values and customs simply do not allow perfect competition to work because government emphasizes other social goals besides efficiency. When competition negatively affects these other goals (which may or may not be goals that most people in society hold), government prevents competition from operating.

Economic Insights and Real-World Competition

The extreme rarity of perfectly competitive markets *should not* make you think that economics is irrelevant to the real world. Far from it. In fact, the movement away from perfectly competitive markets could have been predicted by economic theory.

Consider Figure 16-2. Competitive markets will exist only if suppliers or consumers don't collude. If the suppliers producing $0L$ can get together and restrict entry, preventing suppliers who would produce LM from entering the industry, the remaining suppliers can raise their price from P_M to P_L, giving them the shaded area A in additional income. If the cost of their colluding and preventing entry is less than that amount, economic theory predicts that these individuals will collude. The suppliers kept out of the market lose only area C, so they don't have much incentive to fight the restrictions on entry. Consumers lose the areas A plus B, so they have a strong incentive to fight. However, often their cost of organizing a protest is higher than the suppliers' cost of collusion, so consumers accept the restrictions.

Suppliers introducing restrictions on entry seldom claim that the reason for the restrictions is to increase their incomes. Usually they couch the argument for restrictions in terms of the general good, but, while their reasons are debatable, the net effect of restricting entry into a market is to increase suppliers' income to the detriment of consumers.

Q-5 Explain, using supply and demand curves, why most agricultural markets are not perfectly competitive.

How Competitive Forces Affect Monopoly

Don't think that because perfect competition doesn't exist, competition doesn't exist. In the real world, competition is fierce; the invisible hand is no weakling. It holds its own against other forces in the economy.

Competition is so strong that it makes the other extreme (perfect monopolies) as rare as perfect competition. For a monopoly to last, other firms must be prevented from entering the market. In reality it's almost impossible to prevent entry, and therefore it's almost impossible for perfect monopoly to exist. Monopoly profits send out signals to other firms who want to get some of that profit for themselves.

Q-6 Why is it almost impossible for a perfect monopoly to exist?

BREAKING DOWN MONOPOLY   To get some of the profit, firms will break down a monopoly through political or economic means. If the monopoly is a legal monopoly, high profit will lead potential competitors to lobby to change the law underpinning

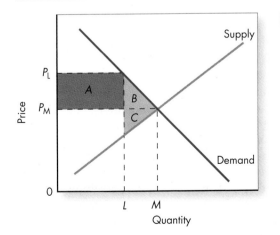

FIGURE 16-2   Movement Away from Competitive Markets

Where suppliers of $0L$ can restrict suppliers of LM from entering the market, they can raise the price of the good from P_M to P_L, giving the suppliers of $0L$ area A in additional income. The suppliers kept out of the market lose area C. The consumers, however, lose both areas A and B. Often the costs of organizing for consumers are higher than the costs for the suppliers, so consumers accept the market restrictions.

that monopoly. If the law can't be changed—say, the monopolist has a patent (which, as I discussed in the chapter on monopoly, is a legal right to be the sole supplier of a good)—potential competitors will generally get around the obstacle by developing a slightly different product or by working on a new technology that avoids the monopoly but satisfies the relevant need.

Say, for example, that you've just discovered the proverbial better mousetrap. You patent it and prepare to enjoy the life of a monopolist. But to patent your mousetrap, you must submit to the patent office the technical drawings of how your better mousetrap works. That gives all potential competitors (some of whom have better financing and already existing distribution systems) a chance to study your idea and see if they can think of a slightly different way (a way sufficiently different to avoid being accused of infringing on your patent) to achieve the same end. They often succeed—so in some cases firms don't apply for patents on new products because the information in the patent application spells out what's unique about the product. That information can help competitors more than the monopoly provided by the patent would hurt them. Instead many firms try to establish an initial presence in the market and rely on inertia to protect what little monopoly profit they can extract.

Establishing an initial presence in a market can be more effective than obtaining a patent when trying to extract monopoly profit.

REVERSE ENGINEERING   Going to the patent office isn't the only way competitors gather information about competing products. One of the other ways routinely used by firms is called **reverse engineering**—*the process of a firm buying other firms' products, disassembling them, figuring out what's special about them, and then copying them within the limits of the law.*

Variations on reverse engineering go on in all industries. Consider the clothing industry. One firm I know of directs its workers to go to top department stores on their lunch hour and buy the latest fashions. The workers bring the clothes back and, that afternoon, the seamstresses and tailors dismantle each garment into its component parts, make a pattern of each part, and sew the original up again. The next day the worker who chose that garment returns it to the department store, saying, "I don't really like it."

Meanwhile the firm has e-mailed the patterns to its Hong Kong office, and two weeks later its shipment of garments comes in—garments that are almost, but not perfectly, identical to the ones the workers bought. The firm sells this shipment to other department stores at one-fourth the cost of the original.

If you ask businesspeople, they'll tell you that competition is fierce and that profit opportunities are fleeting—which is a good sign that competition does indeed exist in the U.S. economy.

Competition and Natural Monopoly

The view one takes of the fight between competitive and monopolistic forces influences one's view of what government policy should be in relation to natural monopolies—industries whose average total cost is falling as output increases. We saw in the chapter on monopolies that natural monopolies can make large profits and that consequently there have been significant calls for government regulation of these monopolies to prevent their "exploitation" of the consumer.

Over the past decade, economists and policy makers have become less supportive of such regulation. They argue that even in these cases of natural monopoly, competition works in other ways. High monopoly profits lead to research on alternative ways of supplying the product, such as sending TV signals through electrical lines or sending phone messages by satellite. New technologies provide competition to existing firms.

New technologies can compete with and undermine natural monopolies.

When this technological competition doesn't work fast enough, people direct their efforts toward government, and political pressure is brought to bear either to control the monopoly through regulation or to break up the monopoly.

REGULATING NATURAL MONOPOLIES   In the past, the pressure to regulate natural monopolies has been stronger than competitive pressure that lowers prices. Regulated natural monopolies have been given the exclusive right to operate in an industry but, in return, they've had to agree to have the price they charge and the services they provide regulated. Regulatory boards control the price that natural monopolies charge so that it will be a "fair price," which they generally define as a price that includes all costs plus a normal return on capital investment (a normal profit, but no economic profit). Most states have a number of regulatory boards.

When firms are allowed to pass on all cost increases to earn a normal profit on those costs, they have little or no incentive to hold down costs. In such cases, X-inefficiency develops with a passion, and such monopolies look for capital-intensive projects that will increase their rate bases. To fight such tendencies, regulatory boards must screen every cost and determine which costs are appropriate and which aren't—an almost impossible job. For example, nuclear power is an extremely capital-intensive method of producing electric power, and regulated electric companies favored nuclear power plants until they were told that some nuclear power plant construction costs could not be passed on.

Once regulation gets so specific that it's scrutinizing every cost, the regulatory process becomes extremely bureaucratic, which itself increases the cost. Moreover, to regulate effectively, the regulators must have independent information and must have a sophisticated understanding of economics, cost accounting, and engineering. Often regulatory boards are made up of volunteer laypeople who start with little expertise; they are exhausted or co-opted by the political infighting they have had to endure by the time they develop some of the expertise they need. As is often the case in economics, there's no easy answer to the problem.

It is because of the problems with regulation that more and more economists argue that even in the case of natural monopoly, no explicit regulation is desirable, and that society would be better off relying on direct competitive forces guided by broader regulatory guidelines emphasizing free entry into the industry. They argue that regulated monopolies inevitably inflate their costs so much and are so inefficient and lazy that a monopoly right should never be granted.

DEREGULATING NATURAL MONOPOLIES   In the 1980s and 1990s, such views led to the deregulation and competitive supply of both electric power and telephone services. Regulators are making these markets competitive by breaking down the layers of the industry into subindustries and deregulating those subindustries that can be competitive. For example, the phone industry can be divided into the phone line industry, the caller service industry, the pay phone industry, and the directory information industry. By dividing up the industry, regulators can carve out the part that has the characteristics of a natural monopoly and open the remaining parts to competition.

Let's take a closer look at the electrical industry. It used to be that electricity was supplied by independent local firms, each providing electricity for its own local customers. Today, however, electricity is supplied through a large grid that connects many regions of the country. With this grid, electricity generated in one area can easily be sent all over the country, and suppliers can compete for customers in a variety of regions. The

Web Note 16.3
Regulating Natural Monopolies

When firms are allowed to pass on all cost increases to earn a normal profit on those costs, they have little or no incentive to hold down costs.

Q-7 What is the problem with regulations that set prices relative to costs?

grid makes competition in power supply feasible, and many states have adopted provisions to open their electricity markets to multiple providers.

The power line industry, however, is not competitive. It would be extremely costly for each company to run a separate power line into your house. That is, the power line industry exhibits *economies of scale.* Because of the economies of scale, the power line industry is the natural monopoly aspect of electrical power supply. The deregulation of electricity involves splitting off the production of electricity from the maintenance of the line—and choosing an appropriate charge for electric line maintenance. While in the newspapers you will likely read that the electrical power industry is being deregulated, that is not quite correct. Only those portions of the market where competition is likely to exist are being deregulated.

How Firms Protect Their Monopolies

The image I've presented of competition being motivated by profits is a useful one. It shows how a market economy adjusts to ever-changing technology and demands in the real world. Competition is a dynamic, not a static, force.

Firms do not sit idly by and accept competition. They fight it. How do monopolies fight real-world competition? By spending money on maintaining their monopoly. By advertising. By lobbying. By producing products that are difficult to copy. By not taking full advantage of their monopoly position, which means charging a low price that discourages entry. Often firms could make higher short-run profits by charging a higher price, but they forgo the short-run profits in order to strengthen their long-run position in the industry.

Cost/Benefit Analysis of Creating and Maintaining Monopolies

Preventing real-world competition costs money. Monopolies are expensive to create and maintain. Economic theory predicts that if firms have to spend money on creating and protecting their monopoly, they're going to "buy" less monopoly power than if it were free. How much will they buy? They will buy monopoly power until the marginal cost of such power equals the marginal benefit. Thus, they'll reason:

- Does it makes sense for us to hire a lobbyist to fight against this law that will reduce our monopoly power? Here is the probability that a lobbyist will be effective, here is the marginal cost, and here is the marginal benefit.

- Does it make sense for us to buy this machine? If we do, we'll be the only one to have it and are likely to get this much business. Here is the marginal cost, and here is the marginal benefit.

- Does it make sense for us to advertise to further our market penetration? Here are the likely various marginal benefits; here are the likely marginal costs.

Examples of firms spending money to protect or create monopolies are in the news all the time. The farm lobby fights to keep quotas and farm support programs. Drug companies spend a lot of resources to discover new drugs they can patent. A vivid example of the length to which firms will go to create a monopoly position is Owens Corning's fight to trademark its hue of pink Fiberglas. Owens Corning spent more than $200 million to advertise and promote its color "pink" and millions more in the court to protect its right to sole use of that hue. Owens Corning has weighed the costs and benefits and believes that its pink provides sufficient brand recognition to warrant spending millions to protect it.

Branding

One of the important ways in which firms try to maintain a monopoly position is called *branding*. U.S. firms spend about $150 billion a year to advertise their products, trying to produce brand names and create a pleasant image in the minds of consumers. Here are a few food-related brand names. I'm sure you know about most, but a couple are still in the process of forming brand recognition.

- *Coffee.* When you think of coffee, you think of Starbucks and inexpensive extravagance. You might not be able to afford a Lexus, but you can afford a Starbucks cup of coffee.

- *Chicken.* Perdue doesn't produce any chicken, but it does do a lot of advertising, and it brands the chickens it sells, so when you think of chicken, you think of Perdue.

- *Bananas.* A banana is a banana is a banana, but only if you haven't been influenced by Miss Chiquita. At its peak, the Chiquita banana jingle was played 376 times a day on radio stations across the United States.

- *Steak.* Most steaks are currently sold generically. Firms such as Omaha Steaks are trying to change that. Don't just buy a steak—buy an Omaha steak.

- *Water.* Firms take water from the tap (or possibly from a spring), run it through some filters, and sell the image of purity by creating a nice-sounding name—Dasani, Vermont Pure …Well, it's better for you than soda.

- *Pork.* Pork tends to be associated with pigs and does not carry a "good-for-you" image. A national association of pork producers is trying to change that image: "Pork—the other white meat."

Establishing Market Position

Some economists, such as Robert Frank at Cornell University, have argued that today's economy is becoming more and more like a monopoly economy. Modern competition, he argues, is a winner-take-all competition. In such a competition, the winner (established because of brand loyalty, patent protection, or simply consumer laziness) achieves a monopoly and can charge significantly higher prices than its costs without facing competition. The initial competition, focusing on establishing market position, is intense.

To see how important establishing a market position is in today's economy, consider the initial public offering (IPO) of new Internet firms that are often highly valued by Wall Street. Many of these firms have no profits and no likelihood of profits for a number of years, but they sell at extraordinarily high stock prices. Why? The reasoning is that these companies are spending money to establish brand names. As their names become better known, they will establish a monopoly position, and eventually their monopoly positions will be so strong that they can't help but make a profit. With the dot-com stock market crash in the early 2000s, this argument was shown to be wrong for most Internet firms. For one or two lucky firms that established their brands, it was true. The problem is that most people have no way of differentiating between the two. When Google made its well-publicized IPO, which attracted much interest, I didn't take part because, on fundamentals, the price seemed high. However, within three months after the IPO, the price of Google stock had doubled from the IPO price and within a year, it was five times as high. (So much for my focus on stock market fundamentals.) I did better with avoiding the Facebook IPO, which also seemed high based on fundamentals. Its price fell soon after its IPO.

In winner-take-all markets, the initial competition is on establishing market position.

Technology, Efficiency, and Market Structure

Technological development has been a driving force in the economy in recent years.

Technological development—*the discovery of new or improved products or methods of production*—has been a driving force in the economy in recent years. As we saw in an earlier chapter on production and cost analysis, technological advance lowers the costs of production and makes economies more efficient—producing more output with the same number of inputs.

Technological advance is a natural outcome of specialization because it requires large investments of time and money in very specialized areas. Specialization allows producers to learn more about the particular aspects of production in which they specialize. As they learn more, they become not only more productive but also more likely to produce technological advances because they gain a deeper understanding of their specialty.

For example, instead of producing an entire line of clothing, companies might specialize in the production of certain types of carbon-based fibers and explore ways of making more useful material. The result of such specialization can be a technological advance such as Gore-Tex—a material that insulates but also "breathes" and thus keeps individuals dry and cool on warm rainy days, and dry and warm on cold rainy or snowy days. Instead of spreading resources to the entire process of making a jacket, a company can concentrate on just one aspect—fibers.

Given the significance of technology, an important question is: What causes technology to grow? Market incentives are an important part of the answer. Before markets existed, economies grew slowly. After markets came into existence in the 1700s, technology advanced more rapidly because individuals gained incentives, in the form of profits, to discover new and cheaper ways of doing things. Globalization of our economy provides an even greater incentive to develop new technologies because the revenue that can be captured from a global market with over 7 billion people (world population) is much greater than the revenue that can be generated from about 320 million people (U.S. population).

Are some market structures more conducive to growth than others? The answer economists have come to is a tentative yes, and it is an answer that makes certain market structures look better than the way they were presented earlier. Let's review what we've learned about market structure. In the basic supply/demand framework, perfect competition is seen as the benchmark—it leads to efficient outcomes. All other market structures lead to some deadweight loss. But the supply/demand framework does not consider technological issues. It implicitly assumes that technology is unchanging or is unaffected by market structure. If market structure does affect technological advance, another type of efficiency must be considered. This efficiency might be called dynamic efficiency. **Dynamic efficiency** refers to *a market's ability to promote cost-reducing or product-enhancing technological change.* Market structures that best promote technological change are dynamically efficient. Oligopoly provides the best market structure for technological advance. To see why, let's look at the four market structures: perfect competition, monopolistic competition, monopoly, and oligopoly. Let's see which have the profit and incentive to innovate.

In considering market structures, dynamic efficiency must be considered as well as static efficiency.

Perfect Competition and Technology

Q-9 Why isn't perfect competition a good market structure for technological advance?

Perfectly competitive firms have no incentive to develop new technologies. Moreover, perfect competitors earn no profits and consequently may not be able to acquire the funds to devote to research and development that leads to technological change. Even if they did, they would gain little from it. A perfectly competitive market would quickly transfer the gains of the innovation to other firms, making it difficult for the innovating firm to recoup the costs of developing the new technology.

Monopolistic Competition and Technology

Monopolistic competition is somewhat more conducive to technological change because firms have some market power. The promise of gaining additional market power provides the incentive to fund research in new technologies. But, as we learned earlier, monopolistic competitors also lack long-run profits. Easy entry limits their ability to recoup their investment in technological innovation. Eventually, their increased market share will deteriorate and they will return to earning normal profits.

Through its support of patents, the United States does provide incentives to innovate. Patents allow the development of new products through the promise of monopoly profits for a specified period of time. Of course, a firm with a patent will change the market structure into a monopoly.

Monopoly and Technology

On the other end of the spectrum is pure monopoly. Monopolies may earn the profits needed for research and development, but they seldom have the incentive to innovate. Since a monopolist's market is protected from entry, the easiest path is the lazy monopolist path. Since many monopolies are created by government (the government gives a monopoly to a specific company), pure monopolists don't face the threat of new competitors. Until recently, European telephone companies and European domestic airlines were monopolies. These industries developed far fewer innovations than did the equivalent U.S. firms that faced more competition, and European industry prices were much higher than those in the United States.

In response to these observations, European governments have moved toward privatization and more competition. Both telecommunications and domestic airlines have been privatized, and their monopolies are being removed. The result has been a fall in prices of their products and expanding new technologies in the telecommunications industries. For example, you can now fly between major European cities on airlines such as easyJet or Ryanair for as low as $25.

Oligopoly and Technology

That leaves oligopoly. Oligopoly is the market structure that is most conducive to technological change. Since the typical oligopolist realizes ongoing economic profit, it has the funds to carry out research and development. Moreover, the belief that its competitors are innovating also forces it to do so. Oligopolists are constantly searching for ways to get an edge on competitors, so significant technological advance takes place in oligopolistic industries.

Oligopoly tends to be most conducive to technological change because it has both the profits and incentives to do so.

Q-10 Why is oligopoly the best market structure for technological advance?

The computer industry is an example of an oligopolistic market that has demonstrated tremendous innovation. Technological progress has been rapid, following *Moore's law*—every 18 months the cost of computing power is cut by half. Another example is the telecommunications industry, which has been experiencing enormous technological change, and will continue to do so in the coming decade.

Some economists, especially those who favor a model in which the threat of competition is enough to keep a firm behaving competitively (a contestable market approach), argue that market structure does not matter for technological progress. It is the conditions of entry that matter. They argue that it is primarily developments in pure science that lead to technological advance. Businesses sample technological advances and develop those that have market potential. They argue that technological advances lead to the formation of oligopolies; oligopolies don't necessarily lead to technological advances. The cigarette industry and the aluminum industry are highly oligopolistic but have had little technological advance. In the steel industry, companies outside the group of existing producers started minimills that led to technological advance. The process did not originate with the oligopolistic steel companies.

Network Externalities, Standards, and Technological Lock-In

Web Note 16.4
Network Economies

In support of the view that technology determines market structure, economists have focused on those aspects of production that involve *network* externalities. An externality, as discussed in earlier chapters, is an effect of a decision on a third party that is not taken into account by the decision maker. A **network externality** occurs *when greater use of a product increases the benefit of that product to everyone.* Social networks such as Facebook exhibit network externalities. If you were the only person in the world on Facebook, it would be pretty useless. As the number of people on Facebook increases, Facebook's value to communication grows enormously. Another example of a product with network externalities is the Windows operating system. It is of much more use to you if many other people use it too, because you can then easily communicate with other Windows users and purchase software based on that platform.

Network externalities are important to market structure because they lead to the development of industry standards. Standards become important because network externalities involve the interaction among individuals and processes. Many examples of the development of industry standards exist. Some are television broadcast standards (they differ in the United States and Europe, which is why U.S. TVs cannot be used in Europe), building standards (there is a standard size of doors), and electrical current standards (220 or 110; AC or DC). One debate over standards is involved with communication devices and what the 5-G network will look like.

> Network externalities lead to market standards and affect market structure.

STANDARDS AND WINNER-TAKE-ALL INDUSTRIES   Network externalities have two implications for the economic process. First, they increase the likelihood that an industry becomes a winner-take-all industry. Early in the development of new products, there may be two or three competing standards, any one of which could be a significant improvement over what existed before. As network externalities broaden the use of a product, the need for a single standard becomes more important and eventually one standard wins out. The firm that gets its standard accepted as the industry standard gains an enormous advantage over the other firms. This firm will dominate the market. Google and the Google search engine is an example of how getting your product accepted as the standard can do wonders for the firm. Facebook is another example. By getting people to accept Facebook as their social network, it undermines the development of alternative social networks.

Once a standard develops, even if other firms try to enter with a better technological standard, they will have a hard time competing because everyone is already committed to the existing industry standard. Deviating from that standard will reduce the benefits of the network externality.

> The first-mover advantage helps explain the high stock prices of start-up technology companies.

Firms in an industry developing a standard will have a strong incentive to be the first to market with the product; they will be willing to incur large losses initially in their attempt to set the industry standard. The "first-mover advantage" helps explain why the stock of small technology companies sold for extremely high prices even though they were having large losses. The large losses were created because the firms were spending money to gain market share so that their products would become the industry standard. If the firm is successful in getting its product accepted as the standard, the demand for the product will rise and it will have enormous profits in the future.

TECHNOLOGICAL LOCK-IN   The second implication of network externalities is that the market might not gravitate toward the most efficient standard. Economists debate how standards can be inefficient and yet be maintained by the first-mover advantage. Some economists argue that the inefficiency can be quite large; others argue that it is small. One aspect of the debate has centered around the QWERTY keyboard on computers. Research by Stanford economist Paul David showed that the arrangement of the keys in the QWERTY keyboard was designed to slow people's typing down so that the keys would not stick on the early mechanical typewriters. As the technology of typewriters improved, the need to slow down typing soon ended, but because the QWERTY keyboard was introduced first, it had become the standard. Other, more efficient keyboards have been proposed but not adopted. The QWERTY keyboard has remained, even with its built-in inefficiencies. David suggested that QWERTY is a metaphor for **technological lock-in**—*when prior use of a technology makes the adoption of subsequent technologies difficult.*

QWERTY is a metaphor for technological lock-in.

David's technological lock-in argument suggests that many of our institutions and technologies may be inefficient. Other economists argue that the QWERTY keyboard was not that inefficient and if it had been, other keyboards would have been adopted. I am not sure who is right in this debate, but it may soon be made obsolete by another technological development: voice recognition software, which will make keyboarding a relic of the past.

The QWERTY debate is a part of a larger debate about the competitive process and government involvement in that process. The issues are somewhat the same as they were in the earlier discussion of government regulation of natural monopolies. Many economists see government involvement as necessary to protect the economy and the consumer. They advocate what economist Brian Arthur calls "a nudging hand" approach, in which the government keeps the competition fair.

Other economists see monopoly as part of the competitive process—something that will be eliminated as competitive forces act against it. Standards will develop, but they will be temporary. If the standards are sufficiently inefficient, they will be replaced, or an entirely new product will come along that makes the old standard irrelevant. For such economists, neither natural monopoly nor technological lock-in is a reason for government interference. Government interference, even the nudging hand, would slow or stop the competitive process and make society worse off.

Modern debates about policy regarding competition take dynamic issues into account, but still leave open a debate about what the role of government should be.

Who is right? My own view leans toward the competitive process view with a nudge here or there, but one cannot be dogmatic about it; each case must be decided on its own merits. Moreover, even in those cases where explicit regulation is not called for, the government must set up appropriate rules and property rights to see that the competitive playing field is reasonably level.

Conclusion

The stories of competition and monopoly have no end. Both are continuous processes. Monopolies create competition. Out of the competitive struggle, other monopolies emerge, only to be beaten down by competition. Technology is a big part of that struggle. Individuals and firms, motivated by self-interest, try to use the changes brought by technology to their benefit. By doing so, they change both the nature of the economy and the direction of technological change itself.

Summary

- The goals of real-world firms are many. Profit plays a role, but the actual goals depend on the incentive structure embodied in the structure of the firm.   *(LO16-1)*

- The monitoring problem arises because the incentives faced by managers are not always to maximize the profit of the firm. Economists have helped design incentive-compatible contracts to help alleviate the monitoring problem.   *(LO16-1)*

- Monopolists facing no competition can become lazy and not hold down costs as much as they are able. X-inefficiency refers to firms operating less efficiently than they could technically.   *(LO16-1)*

- X-inefficiency can be limited by the threat of competition or takeovers. Corporate takeovers often mean change in management.   *(LO16-1)*

- The competitive process involves a continual fight between monopolization and competition. Suppliers are willing to pay an amount equal to the additional profit gained from the restriction. Consumers are willing to pay an amount equal to the additional cost of products to avoid a restriction. Consumers, however, face a higher cost of organizing their efforts.   *(LO16-2)*

- Firms compete against patents that create monopolies by making slight modifications to existing patents and engaging in reverse engineering to copy other firms' products within the limits of the law.   *(LO16-2)*

- The U.S. government is deregulating natural monopolies by dividing the firms into various subindustries, carving out those parts that exhibit the characteristics of a natural monopoly, and opening the remaining parts to competition.   *(LO16-2)*

- Firms will spend money on monopolization until the marginal cost equals the marginal benefit. They protect their monopolies by such means as advertising, lobbying, and producing products that are difficult for other firms to copy.   *(LO16-3)*

- Oligopoly provides the best market structure for technological advance because oligopolists have an incentive to innovate in the form of additional profits and because they have the profits to devote to investing in the research and development of new technologies.   *(LO16-4)*

Key Terms

corporate takeover *(339)*
dynamic efficiency *(346)*
incentive-compatible
 contract *(335)*

lazy monopolist *(338)*
monitoring
 problem *(335)*
network externality *(348)*

reverse engineering *(342)*
technological
 development *(346)*

technological
 lock-in *(349)*
X-inefficiency *(338)*

Questions and Exercises

1. True or false? It is obvious that all for-profit businesses in the United States will maximize profit. Why?   *(LO16-1)*

2. Describe the monitoring problem. How does an incentive-compatible contract address the monitoring problem?   *(LO16-1)*

3. Define *X-inefficiency*. Can a perfect competitor be X-inefficient? Explain why or why not.   *(LO16-1)*

4. Some analysts have argued that competition will eliminate X-inefficiency from firms. Will it? Why?   *(LO16-1)*

5. True or false? If it were easier for consumers to collude than for suppliers to collude, there would often be shortages of goods. Why?   *(LO16-2)*

6. Demonstrate graphically the net gain to producers and the net loss to consumers if suppliers are able to restrict their output to Q_r in the accompanying graph.

Demonstrate the net deadweight loss to society. (*LO16-2*)

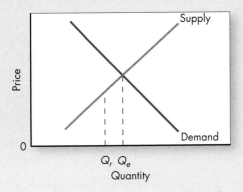

7. Up to how much is the monopolist depicted in the accompanying graph willing to spend to protect its market position? Demonstrate your answer graphically (*LO16-3*)

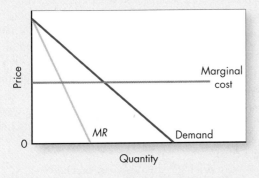

8. True or false? Natural monopolies should be broken up to improve competition. Why? (*LO16-3*)

9. True or false? Monopolies are bad; patents give firms monopoly; therefore, patents are bad. Why? (*LO16-3*)

10. Discuss each of the following market structures in terms of static and dynamic efficiency: (*LO16-4*)
    a. Perfect competition.
    b. Monopolistic competition.
    c. Oligopoly.
    d. Monopoly.

11. What two characteristics does a market structure need to have for firms in that industry to engage in technological advance? What market structure best meets these criteria? (*LO16-4*)

12. Taking into consideration changing technologies, why might the basic supply/demand framework not lead to the most efficient outcome? (*LO16-4*)

13. How do network externalities increase the winner-take-all nature of a market? (*LO16-4*)

14. True or false? Technically competent firms will succeed. Why? (*LO16-3*)

Questions from Alternative Perspectives

1. Some economists have compared managers to politicians.
   a. How do the incentives facing managers resemble those of politicians?
   b. How do they differ?
   c. What does your answer say about the relative value of each to society? (Austrian)

2. Think of the pay of various groups in society.
   a. How does the compensation awarded to heads of religious organizations compare to the salary of CEOs in profit-making organizations?
   b. What is the explanation for this difference?
   c. Should there be a difference? (Religious)

3. In the list of CEOs in the chapter, how many of the CEOs were women? (To find out, you can go to the *paywatch* source, www.paywatch.org, on the web.) What is the likely reason for your finding? (Feminist)

4. While some assets, such as forests, can provide benefits to society in perpetuity, some firms see forests as consumable assets. One example was when corporate raider James

Goldsmith forcibly acquired Crown Zellerbach in Washington State. After doing so, he cut all of Crown Zellerbach's trees, including one 12,000-acre clear-cut, and then sold off all the company's remaining assets piecemeal, a practice called "junk bond forestry." What does this suggest about the long-term environmental sustainability of free market decisions? (Institutionalist)

5. Because the future is inherently uncertain, firms often follow "rules of thumb" to make decisions such as how much capital (factories and machinery for production) to buy and how to price their products. Examples are financial ratios and mark-up pricing.
   a. Does this behavior make sense?
   b. How does uncertainty that firms face encourage firms to use "rules of thumb"?
   c. What implications for economic analysis do firms' use of rules of thumb have? (Post-Keynesian)

6. Large corporations spend tremendous sums in an effort to influence public policy. Some corporations fund

"citizens'" groups to push policies that the corporations want. Giant drug companies fund scientists to prove that the companies' drugs work. Large businesses even hire economists to come up with theories that show why huge businesses and mega-mergers could be beneficial (or at least not harmful).

a. What are some likely results if corporations control "the marketplace of ideas"?
b. What, if anything, should be done about this control? (Radical)

Issues to Ponder

1. Airlines and hotels have many frequent-flier and frequent-visitor programs in which individuals who fly the airline or stay at the hotel receive bonuses that are the equivalent of discounts.
   a. Give two reasons why these companies have such programs rather than simply offering lower prices.
   b. Can you give other examples of such programs?
   c. What is a likely reason why firms don't monitor these programs?
   d. Should the benefits of these programs be taxable?

2. Are managers and high-level company officials paid high salaries because they're worth it to the firm, or because they're simply extracting profit from the company to give to themselves? How would you tell whether you're correct?

3. True or false? Nonprofit colleges must be operating relatively efficiently. Otherwise for-profit colleges would develop and force existing colleges out of business. Why?

4. Author Charles Murray has argued that museums actually inhibit rather than foster the appreciation of art. He points out that the technology exists to make essentially "perfect" copies of any major art work that even the best-trained artistic eye could not differentiate from the original.
   a. What would the introduction of this technology do to art museums?
   b. If that is true, why do you believe that the technology is not used?
   c. How are reproductions of music symphonies handled legally?
   d. What would the prohibition of making recordings of music performances do to the demand for musicians and for symphony halls?
   e. Why are music symphonies handled differently from art?

5. Find a prescription drug that you, someone in your family, or a friend normally takes.
   a. What is the price you (they) pay for it?
   b. What is the lowest online U.S. price for that drug? (Costco is a good place to look.)
   c. If the online price (with shipping) is cheaper, why don't you (they) buy it online?
   d. Now that you have that price information, will you buy the drug online in the future?
   e. What does this process tell you about the competitiveness of the drug market?

6. According to *The Wall Street Journal,* the wholesale price of the generic drug fluoxetine (the generic for Prozac) is $3.60 per 100.
   a. Given that the cost of dispensing them is about $5 to $10 per prescription, how much would you expect the drug to sell for?
   b. In 2008 a prescription for 100 tablets of fluoxetine was selling for $54 at DrugStore.com. It sold for similar prices at other pharmacies. What would you conclude about the market structure, given that information?
   c. At pharmnet.com one could buy 100 fluoxetine tablets for $26. If this is true, what can we say about drug market imperfections?

7. Why would a company want to sacrifice short-run profits to establish market position?

8. The title of an article in *The Wall Street Journal* was "Pricing of Products Is Still an Art, Often Having Little Link to Costs." In the article, the following cases were cited:
   • Vodka pricing: All vodkas are essentially indistinguishable—colorless, tasteless, and odorless—and the cost of producing vodka is independent of brand name, yet prices differ substantially.
   • Perfume: A $100 bottle of perfume may contain $4 to $6 worth of ingredients.
   • Jeans and "alligator/animal" shirts: The "plain pocket" jeans and the Lacoste knockoffs often cost 40 percent less than the brand-name items, yet the knockoffs are essentially identical to the brand-name items.
   a. Do these differences undermine economists' analysis of pricing? Why or why not?
   b. What does each of these examples likely imply about fixed costs and variable costs?
   c. What do they likely imply about costs of production versus costs of selling?
   d. As what type of market would you characterize each of the above examples?

9. Soft-drink companies pay universities for the exclusive "pouring rights" to sell their products on campus. In a recent deal, the University at Buffalo signed a contract with Pepsi for $220,000 per year limiting on-campus soft-drink sales to only Pepsi.
   a. Why would Pepsi agree to pay such a fee?
   b. What would likely happen if there were no pouring rights on campus?

c. Is the sale of pouring rights beneficial to students or harmful to them?

10. Monsanto Corporation lost its U.S. patent protection for its highly successful herbicide Roundup in the year 2000. What do you suppose was Monsanto's strategy for Roundup in the short run? In the long run?

11. One of the things that is slowing the development of nanotechnology is the legal morass of patents that anyone

working with new ideas must deal with. Some have argued that the government should give prizes for new discoveries, such as was offered for the first private flight in space, or as was offered by Napoleon for the discovery of how to store vegetables for long periods, rather than award patents, such as are awarded to drugs.   (*LO16-4*)
a. What is the advantage of prizes over patents?
b. What is the cost?

Answers to Margin Questions

1. Firms are not interested in just short-run profits. They are also interested in long-run profits. So a firm might sacrifice short-run profits for higher long-run profits. Also, those making the decisions for the firm are not always those who own the firm. (*p. 335; LO16-1*)

2. Most economists are concerned about third-party-payer systems because of the problems of monitoring. It is the consumers who have the strongest incentive to make sure that they are getting value for their money. Any third-party-payer system reduces the consumers' vigilance and therefore puts less pressure on holding costs down. (*p. 337; LO16-1*)

3. A manager does not have the same incentive to hold costs down as an owner does because when an owner holds costs down, the owner's profits are increased, but when a manager holds costs down, the increased profits accrue to the owner, not the manager. Thus, the manager has less direct motivation to hold costs down than an owner does. This is especially true if the costs being held down are the manager's perks and pay. (*p. 338; LO16-1*)

4. The threat of a corporate takeover places competitive pressures on firms because it creates the possibility that the managers will be replaced and lose all their perks and above-market-equilibrium pay. (*p. 339; LO16-1*)

5. Most agricultural markets are not perfectly competitive because the gains to producers from moving away from competitive markets are fairly large and, for small deviations from competitive markets, the costs are fairly small to those suppliers and consumers who are kept out. This can be seen in the accompanying graph.

If suppliers producing $0L$ got together and limited supply to L, they could push the price up to P_L and could gain the rectangle A for themselves. Consumers and suppliers who are kept out of the market lose triangles B and C respectively, which, in the diagram, are not only each smaller than A, but also B and C combined are smaller than A. Of course, the area A is lost to the consumers, but the costs of organizing those consumers to fight and protect competition are often prohibitively large. (*p. 341; LO16-2*)

6. It is almost impossible for perfect monopoly to exist because preventing entry is nearly impossible. Monopoly profits are a signal to potential entrants to get the barriers to entry removed. (*p. 341; LO16-2*)

7. The problem with regulation that sets prices relative to costs is that this removes the incentive for firms to hold down costs and can lead to X-inefficiency. While, in theory, regulators could scrutinize every cost, in practice that is impossible—there would have to be a regulatory board duplicating the work that a firm facing direct market pressure undertakes in its normal activities. (*p. 343; LO16-2*)

8. If the additional benefits of creating or maintaining a monopoly exceed the cost of doing so, do it. If they don't, don't. (*p. 344; LO16-3*)

9. Perfect competition is not conducive to technological advance because firms don't earn the profits needed to invest in research and development. It also doesn't have the promise of future above-normal profits needed to motivate researchers to innovate. (*p. 346; LO16-4*)

10. Oligopoly is the best market structure for technological advance because oligopolists have the profits to devote to research and development and have the incentive to innovate. Innovation may provide the oligopolist with a way to increase market share. (*p. 347; LO16-4*)

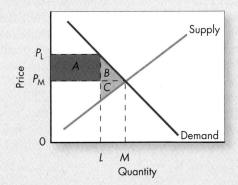

Work and the Labor Market

Work banishes those three great evils: boredom, vice, and poverty.

—Voltaire

Most of us earn our living by working. We supply labor (get a job) and get paid for doing things that other people tell us they want done. Even before we get a job, work is very much a part of our lives. We spend a large portion of our school years preparing for work. Probably many of you are taking this economics course because you've been told that it will help prepare you for a job—or that it will get you more pay than you're getting in your present job. For you, this course is investment in human capital (skills embodied in workers through experience, education, and on-the-job training). If work in the marketplace isn't already familiar to you, once you get out of school it will become so (unless you're sitting on a hefty trust fund or marry somebody who is).

Your job will likely occupy at least a third of your waking hours. To a great extent, it will define you. When someone asks, "What do you do?" you won't answer, "I clip coupons, go out on dates, visit my children . . ." Instead you'll answer, "I work for the Blank Company" or "I'm an economist" or "I'm a teacher." Defining ourselves by our work means that work is more than the way we get income. It's a part of our social and cultural makeup. If we lose our jobs, we lose part of our identity.

There's no way I can discuss all the social, political, cultural, and economic dimensions of work and labor in one chapter, but it's important to begin by at least pointing them out in order to put my discussion of labor markets in perspective. A **labor market** is *a factor market in which individuals supply labor services for wages to other individuals and to firms that need (demand) labor services.* Because social and political pressures are particularly strong in labor markets, we can understand the nature of such markets only by considering how social and political forces interact with economic forces to determine our economic situation.

If the invisible hand were the only force operating, wages would be determined entirely by supply and demand. There's more to it than that, as you'll see, but it shouldn't surprise you that my discussion of the invisible hand and the labor market is organized around the concepts of supply and demand.

Other Factors of Production

The factors of production are sometimes classified as land, labor, and capital, and income from these factors are rent, wages, and interest and profits, respectively. We focus on labor because it is the most important source of income for most of you, and given the limited time in a principles course, choices have to be made. (Opportunity cost rears its head. You can find a discussion of these other factors in the online Chapter 17W, "Nonwage and Asset Income: Rents, Profits, and Interest" at www.mhhe.com/colander9e.) I should, however, note a couple of issues about these other factors of production. First, land as a factor of production depends on property rights. How property rights are determined and structured plays an important role in the amount of rent and the distribution of that rent. Whereas most people would agree that people deserve the fruits of their labor, there is less agreement about rent.

Second, capital is much more difficult to analyze than labor or land. In fact, capital is one of the most difficult aspects of economics, and we do not have a good theory of the rate of interest or profit income that is the result of capital. The modern theory of capital focuses on human capital, intellectual capital, and social capital as well as financial and physical capital. A full analysis of these various elements and the income that derives from their use is far beyond an introductory course.

The Supply of Labor

The labor supply choice facing an individual (that is, the decisions of whether, how, and how much to work) can be seen as a choice between nonmarket activities and legal market activities. Nonmarket activities include sleeping, dating, studying, playing, cooking, cleaning, gardening, and black market trading. Legal market activities include taking some type of paid job or working for oneself, directly supplying products or services to consumers.

Many considerations are involved in individuals' choices of whether and how much to work and at what kind of job to work. Social background and conditioning are especially important, but the factor economists focus on is the **incentive effect** (*how much a person will change his or her hours worked in response to a change in the wage rate*). The incentive effect is determined by the value of supplying one's time to legal market activities relative to the value of supplying one's time to nonmarket activities. The normal relationship is:

> The higher the wage, the higher the quantity of labor supplied.

This relationship between the wage rate and the quantity of labor supplied is shown in the figure in the margin. The wage rate is measured on the vertical axis; the quantity of labor supplied is measured on the horizontal axis. As you can see, the supply curve's upward slope indicates that as the wage rate increases, the quantity of labor supplied increases. Why is that the normal relationship? Because work involves opportunity cost. By working one hour more, you have one hour less to devote to nonmarket activities, which often are simply called *leisure*. Alternatively, if you devote the hour to nonmarket activities, you lose one hour's worth of income from working.

Say, for example, that by working you would have made $10 per hour. If you decide to work two hours less, you'll have $20 less to spend but two hours more available for other activities (including spending the smaller amount of money). When the wage rises, say to $12 per hour, an hour of leisure has a higher opportunity cost. As the cost of leisure goes up, you buy less of it, meaning that you work more.

As I noted in my general discussions of supply and demand, the incentive effects represented by the market supply curve come from individuals' either/or decisions to

Economists focus on the incentive effect when considering an individual's choice of whether and how much to work.

The supply curve for labor is upward sloping; the higher the wage, the higher the quantity of labor supplied.

355

enter, or leave, the labor market and from individuals' decisions to work more, or fewer, hours. Given the institutional constraints in the labor market, which require many people to work a fixed number of hours if they work at all, much of the incentive effect of higher wages influences the either/or decisions of individuals. This affects the labor force participation rate (the number of people employed or looking for work as a percentage of people able to work) rather than adjusting the number of hours worked. For example, when wages rise, retired workers may find it worthwhile to go back to work, and many teenagers may choose to find part-time jobs.

Real Wages and the Opportunity Cost of Work

Q-1 Under the usual conditions of supply, what would you expect would happen to the amount of time you study if the wage of your part-time job rises?

The upward-sloping supply curve of labor tells you that, other things equal, as wages go up, the quantity of labor supplied goes up. But if you look at the historical record, you will see that over the last century, real wages in the United States increased substantially, but the average number of hours worked per person fell. This difference is partly explained by the income effect. Higher incomes make people richer, and richer people can afford to choose more leisure. (See the box "Income and Substitution Effects.")

Given that people are far richer today than they were 50 or 100 years ago, it isn't surprising that they work less. What's surprising is that they work as much as they do—eight hours a day rather than the two or so hours a day that would be enough to give people the same income they had a century ago.

The explanation for why people haven't reduced their hours of work more substantially can be found in how leisure has changed. A century ago, conversation was an art. People could use their time for long, leisurely conversations. Letter writing was a skill all educated people had, and cooking dinner was a three-hour event. If today people were satisfied with leisure consisting of long conversations, whittling, and spending quality time with their families rather than skiing, golfing, or traveling, they could get by with working perhaps only four or five hours per day instead of eight hours. But that isn't the case.

Modern gadgets increase the efficiency of leisure but cost money, which means people must work more to enjoy their leisure.

Today leisurely dinners, conversations about good books, and witty letters have been replaced by "efficient" leisure: a fast-food supper, a home video, and the instant analysis of current events. Microwave ovens, frozen dinners, Pop-Tarts, cellular telephones, the Internet—the list of gadgets and products designed to save time is endless. All these gadgets that increase the "efficiency" of leisure (increase the marginal utility per hour of leisure spent) cost money, which means people today must work more to enjoy their leisure! In the United States, one reason people work hard is so that they can play hard (and expensively).

Economists do not try to answer the normative question of whether people are better off today, working hard to play hard, or simply are more harried.

The fast pace of modern society has led a number of people to question whether we, as a society, are better off working hard to play hard. Are we better off or simply more harried? Most economists don't try to answer this normative question; but they do point out that people are choosing their harried lifestyle, so to argue that people are worse off, one must argue that people are choosing something they don't really want. That may be true, but it's a tough argument to prove.

The Supply of Labor and Nonmarket Activities

In addition to leisure, labor supply issues and market incentives play an important role in other nonmarket activities. For example, a whole set of illegal activities, such as selling illegal drugs, are alternatives to taking a legal job.

Let's say that an 18-year-old street kid figures he has only two options: He can either work at a minimum wage job or deal drugs illegally. Let's say that dealing drugs risks getting arrested or shot, but it also means earning $50 or $75 an hour. Given that

Income and Substitution Effects

Because labor income is such an important component of most people's total income, when wages change other things often do not stay equal, and at times the effect can seem strange. For example, say that you earn $10 an hour and you decide to work eight hours per day. Suddenly demand for your services goes up and you find that you can receive $40 an hour. Will you decide to work more hours? According to the economic decision rule, you will, but you also might decide that at $40 an hour you'll work only six hours a day—$240 a day is enough; the rest of the day you want leisure time to spend your money. In such a case, a higher wage means working less, and the measured supply curve of labor would be backward bending.

Does this violate the economic decision rule? The answer is no, because other things—specifically your income—do not remain equal. The higher wage makes you decide to work more—as the economic decision rule says; but the effect of the higher wage is overwhelmed by the effect of the higher income that allows you to decide to work less.

To distinguish between these two effects, economists have given them names. The decision by a worker to work more hours when his or her pay goes up is called the *substitution effect*. A worker substitutes work for leisure because the price of leisure has risen. The decision to work fewer hours when your pay goes up, based on the fact that you're richer and therefore can live a better life, is called the *income effect*.

It's possible that the income effect can exceed the substitution effect, and a wage increase can cause a person to work less, but that possibility does not violate the economic decision rule, which refers to the substitution effect only.

---

choice, many risk takers opt to sell drugs. When an emergency room doctor asked a shooting victim in New York City why he got involved in selling drugs, he responded, "I'm not going to work for chump change. I make $3,000 a week, tax-free. What do they pay you, sucker?" The doctor had to admit that even he wasn't making that kind of money.

As we discussed in Chapter 1, most low-level drug dealers don't earn anywhere near that pay, but dealing drugs offers a few the chance to advance and earn that and more. For middle-class individuals who have prospects for good jobs, the cost of being arrested can be high—an arrest can destroy their future prospects. For poor street kids with little chance of getting a good job, an arrest makes little difference to their future. For them the choice is heavily weighted toward selling drugs. This is especially true for the entrepreneurial types—the risk takers—the movers and shakers who might have become the business leaders of the future. I've asked myself what decision I would have made had I been in their position. And I suspect I know the answer.

Prohibiting certain drugs leads to potentially high income from selling those drugs and has significant labor market effects. The incentive effects that prohibition has on the choices of jobs facing poor teenagers is a central reason why some economists support the legalization of currently illegal drugs.

Web Note 17.1
Who Works?

Income Taxation, Work, and Leisure

It is after-tax income, not before-tax income, that determines how much you work. Why? Because after-tax income is what you give up by not working. The government, not you, forgoes what you would have paid in taxes if you had worked. This means that when the government raises your marginal tax rate (the tax you pay on an additional dollar of income), your incentive to work falls. Really high marginal tax rates—say 60 or 70 percent—can significantly reduce individuals' incentive to work and earn income.

One main reason why the U.S. government reduced marginal income tax rates in the 1980s was to reduce the negative incentive effects of high taxes. Whereas in the 1950s and 1960s the highest federal U.S. marginal income tax rate was 70 percent,

Q-2 Why do income taxes reduce your incentive to work?

European countries, which have relatively high marginal tax rates, are struggling with the problem of providing incentives for people to work.

today the highest marginal income tax rate is 35 percent. European countries, which have significantly higher marginal tax rates than the United States, are currently struggling with the problem of providing incentives for people to work.

Reducing the marginal tax rate in the United States hasn't completely eliminated the problem of negative incentive effects on individuals' work effort. The reason is that the amount people receive from many government redistribution programs is tied to earned income. When your earned income goes up, your benefits from these programs go down.

Say, for example, that you're getting welfare and you're deciding whether to take an $8-an-hour job. Income taxes and Social Security taxes reduce the amount you take home from the job by 20 percent, to $6.40 an hour. But you also know that the Welfare Department will reduce your welfare benefits by 50 cents for every dollar you take home. This means that you lose another $3.20 per hour, so the marginal tax rate on your $8-an-hour job isn't 20 percent; it's 60 percent. By working an hour, you've increased your net income by only $3.20. When you consider the transportation cost of getting to and from work, the expense of getting new clothes to wear to work, the cost of child care, and other job-associated expenses, the net gain in income is often minimal. Your implicit marginal tax rate is almost 100 percent! At such rates, there's an enormous incentive either not to work or to work off the books (get paid in cash so you have no recorded income that the government can easily trace).

The negative incentive effect can sometimes be even more indirect. For example, college scholarships are generally given on the basis of need. A family that earns more gets less in scholarship aid; the amount by which the scholarship is reduced as a family's income increases acts as a marginal tax on individuals' income. Why work hard to provide for yourself if a program will take care of you if you don't work hard? Hence, the irony in any need-based assistance program is that it reduces the people's incentive to prevent themselves from being needy. These negative incentive effects on labor supply that accompany any need-based program present a public policy dilemma for which there is no easy answer.

Q-3 What is the irony of any need-based program?

The Elasticity of the Supply of Labor

Exactly how these various incentives affect the amount of labor an individual supplies is determined by the elasticity of the individual's labor supply curve.

The elasticity of the market supply curve is determined by the elasticity of individuals' supply curves and by individuals entering and leaving the labor force. Both of these, in turn, are determined by individuals' opportunity cost of working. If a large number of people are willing to enter the labor market when wages rise, then the market labor supply will be highly elastic even if individuals' supply curves are inelastic.

Elasticity of market supply depends on:

1. Individuals' opportunity cost of working.
2. The type of market being discussed.
3. The elasticity of individuals' supply curves.
4. Individuals entering and leaving the labor market.

The elasticity of supply also depends on the type of market being discussed. For example, the elasticity of the labor supply facing one firm of many in a small town will likely be far greater than the elasticity of the labor supply facing all firms combined in that town. If only one firm raises its wage, it will attract workers away from other firms; if all the firms in town raise their wages, any increase in labor must come from increases in labor force participation, increases in hours worked per person, or in-migration (the movement of new workers into the town's labor market).

Existing workers prefer inelastic labor supplies because that means an increase in demand for labor will raise their wage by more. Employers prefer elastic supplies because that means an increase in demand for labor doesn't require large wage increases. These preferences can be seen in news reports about U.S. immigration laws, their effects, and their enforcement. Businesses such as hotels and restaurants often oppose strict immigration laws. Their reason is that jobs such as janitor, chambermaid, and busperson are frequently filled by new immigrants or undocumented workers who have comparatively low wage expectations.

Because of the importance of the elasticity of labor supply, economists have spent a great deal of time and effort estimating it. Their best estimates of labor supply elasticities to market activities are about 0.1 for heads of households and 1.1 for secondary workers in households. These elasticity figures mean that a wage increase of 10 percent will increase the quantity of labor supplied by 1 percent for heads of households (an inelastic supply) and 11 percent for secondary workers in households (an elastic supply). Why the difference? Institutional factors. Hours of work are only slightly flexible. Since most heads of households are employed, they cannot significantly change their hours worked. Many secondary workers in households are not employed, and the higher elasticity reflects new secondary workers entering the labor market.

Immigration and the International Supply of Labor

International limitations on the flow of people, and hence on the flow of labor, play an important role in elasticities of labor supply. In many industries, wages in developing countries are 1/10 or 1/20 the wages in the United States. This large wage differential means that many people from those low-wage countries would like to move to the United States to earn the higher wages. Because they cannot always meet the legal immigration restrictions that limit the flow, many people come into the United States illegally. In addition to about one million legal immigrants per year, up until the recession of 2008, about one million people per year came illegally. Since then, because of stricter enforcement and the economic down turn, there has been a net outflow of illegal immigrants from the United States. Illegal immigrants take a variety of jobs at lower wages and worse conditions than U.S. citizens and legal immigrants are willing to take. The result is that the actual supply of labor is more elastic than the measured supply, especially in those jobs that cannot be easily policed.

In the early 1990s, the European Union introduced open borders among member countries. That institutional change has brought about a more open flow of individuals into higher-wage EU countries from lower-wage EU countries, although other institutionalized restrictions on flows of people, such as language and culture barriers, prevents the EU from being a unified labor market.

www Web Note 17.2
Leaving Home

The Derived Demand for Labor

The demand for labor follows the basic law of demand:

> The higher the wage, the lower the quantity of labor demanded.

This relationship between the wage rate and the quantity of labor demanded is shown in the graph in the margin. Its downward slope states that as the wage rate falls, the quantity of labor demanded rises. The reason for this relationship differs between the demand for labor by self-employed individuals and by firms.

When individuals are self-employed (work for themselves), the demand for their labor is the demand for the product or service they supply—be it cutting hair, shampooing rugs, or filling teeth. You have an ability to do something, you offer to do it at a certain price, and you see who calls. You determine how many hours you work, what price you charge, and what jobs you take. The income you receive depends on the demand for the good or service you supply and your decision about how much labor you want to supply. In analyzing self-employed individuals, we can move directly from demand for the product to demand for labor.

The higher the wage, the lower the quantity of labor demanded.

Derived demand is the demand for factors of production by firms, which depends on consumers' demands.

When a person is not self-employed, determining the demand for labor isn't as direct. It's a two-step process: Consumers demand products from firms; firms, in turn, demand labor and other factors of production. The demand for labor by firms is a **derived demand**—*the demand for factors of production by firms, which depends on consumers' demands.* In other words, it's derived from consumers' demand for the goods that the firm sells. Thus, you can't think of demand for a factor of production such as labor separately from demand for goods. Firms translate consumers' demands into a demand for factors of production.

Factors Influencing the Elasticity of Demand for Labor

Four factors that influence the elasticity of demand for labor are:

1. The elasticity of demand for the firm's good.
2. The relative importance of labor in the production process.
3. The possibility, and cost, of substitution in production.
4. The degree to which marginal productivity falls with an increase in labor.

The elasticity of the derived demand for labor, or for any other input, depends on a number of factors. One of the most important is (1) *the elasticity of demand for the firm's good.* The more elastic the demand for a firm's goods, the more elastic the derived demand. Other factors influencing the elasticity of derived demand include (2) *the relative importance of labor in the production process* (the more important the factor, the less elastic is the derived demand); (3) *the possibility, and cost, of substitution in production* (the easier substitution is, the more elastic is the derived demand); and (4) *the degree to which marginal productivity falls with an increase in labor* (the faster productivity falls, the less elastic is the derived demand).

Each of these relationships follows from the definition of *elasticity* (the percentage change in quantity divided by the percentage change in price) and a knowledge of production. To be sure you understand, ask yourself the following question: If all I knew about two firms was that one was a perfect competitor and the other was a monopolist, which firm would I say is likely to have the more elastic derived demand for labor? If your answer wasn't automatically "the competitive firm" (because its demand curve is perfectly elastic and hence more elastic than a monopolist's), I would suggest that at this point you review the discussion of factors influencing demand elasticity in the chapter on elasticities and relate that to this discussion. The two discussions are similar and serve as good reviews for each other.

Q-4 Name at least two factors that influence the elasticity of a firm's derived demand for labor.

Labor as a Factor of Production

The traditional factors of production are land, labor, capital, and entrepreneurship. When economists talk of the labor market, they're talking about two of these factors: labor and entrepreneurship. **Entrepreneurship** is *labor that involves high degrees of organizational skills, concern, oversight responsibility, and creativity.* It is a type of creative labor.

Entrepreneurship is labor that involves high degrees of organizational skills, concern, oversight responsibility, and creativity.

The reason for distinguishing between labor and entrepreneurship is that an hour of work is not simply an hour of work. If high degrees of organizational skill, concern, oversight responsibility, and creativity are exerted (which is what economists mean by *entrepreneurship*), one hour of such work can be the equivalent of days, weeks, or even years of nonentrepreneurial labor. That's one reason why pay often differs between workers doing what seems to be the same job. It's also why one of the important decisions a firm makes is what type of labor to hire. Should the firm try to hire high-wage entrepreneurial labor or low-wage nonentrepreneurial labor?

In the appendix to this chapter, I formally develop the firm's derived demand. Here in the chapter itself I will simply point out that the demand for labor follows the basic law of demand—the lower the price, the higher the quantity demanded. Figure 17-1 shows a demand-for-labor curve combined with a supply-of-labor curve. As you would expect, equilibrium is at wage W_e and quantity supplied Q_e.

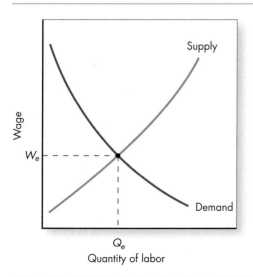

FIGURE 17-1 **Equilibrium in the Labor Market**

When the supply and demand curves for labor are placed on the same graph, the equilibrium wage, W_e, is where the quantity supplied equals quantity demanded. At this wage, Q_e laborers are supplied.

Shift Factors of Demand

Factors that shift the demand curve for labor will put pressure on the equilibrium wage to change. Let's consider some examples. Say the cost of a competing factor of production, such as a machine that also could do the job, rises. That would shift the demand for this factor out to the right, and in doing so put pressure on the wage to rise.

Alternatively, say a new technology develops that requires skills different from those currently being used—for instance, requiring knowing how to use a computer rather than knowing how to use a slide rule. The demand for individuals knowing how to use slide rules will decrease, and their wage will tend to fall.

Another example: Say an industry becomes more monopolistic. What will that do to the demand for labor in that industry? Since monopolies produce less output, the answer is that it would decrease the demand for workers, since the industry would hire fewer of them. The demand for workers would shift in and wages would tend to fall.

Finally, say the demand for the firm's good increases. It's clear that the firm's demand for labor will also increase. The way in which these shift factors work is developed in more detail in the appendix to this chapter.

Q-5 What would happen to a firm's demand for labor if its product became more popular?

TECHNOLOGY AND THE DEMAND FOR LABOR   How will a change in technology affect the demand for labor? This question has often been debated, and it has no unambiguous answer. What economists do know is that the simple reasoning often used by laypeople when they argue that the development of new technology will decrease the demand for labor is wrong. That simplistic reasoning is as follows: "Technology makes it possible to replace workers with machines, so it will decrease the demand for labor." This is sometimes called *Luddite reasoning* because it's what drove the Luddites to go around smashing machines in early-19th-century England.

What's wrong with Luddite reasoning? First, look at history. Technology has increased enormously, yet the demand for labor has not decreased; instead it has increased as output has increased. In other words, Luddite reasoning doesn't take into account the fact that total output can change. A second problem with Luddite reasoning is that labor is necessary for building and maintaining the machines, so increased demand for machines increases the demand for labor.

www   Web Note 17.3
Crowdsourcing

Luddite reasoning isn't *all* wrong. Technology can decrease the demand for certain skills. The computer has decreased demand for calligraphers; the automobile reduced demand for carriage makers. New technology changes the types of labor demanded. If you have the type of labor that will be made technologically obsolete, you can be hurt by technological change. However, technological change hasn't reduced the overall demand for labor; it has instead led to an increase in total output and a need for even more laborers to produce that output.

In the 21st century we're likely to see a continued increase in the use of robots to do many repetitive tasks that blue-collar workers formerly did. Thus, demand for low-skilled manufacturing labor will likely continue to decline, but it will be accompanied by an increase in demand for service industry labor—designing and repairing robots and designing activities that will fill up people's free time.

INTERNATIONAL COMPETITIVENESS AND A COUNTRY'S DEMAND FOR LABOR

Many of the issues in the demand for labor concern one firm's or industry's demand for labor relative to another firm's or industry's demand. When we're talking about the demand for labor by the country as a whole—an issue fundamentally important to many of the policy issues being discussed today—we have to consider the country's overall international competitiveness. A central determinant of a country's competitiveness is the relative wage of labor in that country compared to the relative wage of labor in other countries.

Wages vary considerably among countries. For example, in 2010 workers in the manufacturing industry earned an average of $34.74 an hour in the United States, $43.70 an hour in Germany, and $6.23 an hour in Mexico. Multinational corporations are continually making decisions about where to place production facilities, and labor costs—wage rates—play an important role in these decisions.

> Other factors besides wages play an important role in a firm's decision where to locate.

But why produce in the United States when the hourly rate in Taiwan, for example, is only 1/3 that in the United States? Or in Mexico, where the hourly rate is only about 1/5 that in the United States? The reasons are complicated, but include (1) differences in workers—U.S. workers may be more productive; (2) transportation costs—producing in the country to which you're selling keeps transportation costs down; (3) potential trade restrictions and (4) compatibility of production techniques with social institutions—production techniques must fit with a society's social institutions. If they don't, production will fall significantly.

Number (5) is the *focal point phenomenon*—a situation where a company chooses to move, or expand, production to another country because other companies have already moved or expanded there. A company can't consider all places, and it costs a lot of money to explore a country's potential as a possible host country. For example, Japanese businesses know what to expect when they open a plant in the United States; they don't know in many other countries. So the United States and other countries that Japanese businesses have knowledge about become focal points. They are considered as potential sites for business, while other, possibly equally good, countries are not. Combined, these reasons lead to a "follow-the-leader" system in which countries fall in and out of global companies' production plans. The focal-point countries expand and develop; the others don't.

> Q-6 Name two factors besides relative wages that determine the demand for labor in one country compared to another.

As I have discussed in a number of chapters, the outsourcing that is currently occurring is a reflection of the relative cost differential that firms calculate as they are deciding where to place production units. Initially, that cost differential included large setup costs, making U.S. production cost-effective in many industries despite lower wages elsewhere. As firms have spent the setup costs to establish production facilities abroad, that cost differential relevant to their decisions is increasing, which will mean that U.S.-based production will continue to experience strong pressure to move offshore in the coming decade. Unless offset by new jobs in other industries, the resulting increase in demand for foreign-based workers and decrease in demand for U.S.-based workers will likely put upward pressure on foreign wages and keep strong downward pressure on U.S. wages, limiting wage increases.

Determination of Wages

Supply and demand forces strongly influence wages, but they do not fully determine wages. Real-world labor markets are filled with examples of individuals or firms that resist these supply and demand pressures through organizations such as labor unions, professional associations, and agreements among employers. But, as I've emphasized throughout the book, supply/demand analysis is a useful framework for considering such resistance.

For example, say that you're advising a firm's workers on how to raise their wages. You point out that if workers want to increase their wages, they must figure out some way either to increase the demand for their services or to limit the labor supplied to the firm. One way to limit the number of workers the firm will hire (and thus keep existing workers' wages high) is to force the firm to pay an above-equilibrium wage, as in Figure 17-2(a). Say that in their contract negotiations the workers get the firm to agree to pay a wage of W_1. At wage W_1, the quantity of labor supplied is Q_S and the quantity of labor demanded is Q_D. The difference, $Q_S - Q_D$, represents the number of people who want jobs at wage W_1 but will not be employed. In such a case, jobs must be rationed. Whom you know, where you come from, or the color of your skin may play a role in whether you get a job with that firm.

As a second example, consider what would happen if U.S. immigration laws were liberalized. If you say the supply curve of labor would shift out to the right and the wage level would drop, you're right, as shown in Figure 17-2(b). In it the supply of labor increases from S_0 to S_1. In response, the wage falls from W_0 to W_1 and the quantity of labor demanded increases from Q_0 to Q_1.

In analyzing the effect of such a major change in the labor supply, however, remember that the supply and demand framework is relevant only if the change in the

> Supply and demand forces strongly influence wages, but they do not fully determine wages.

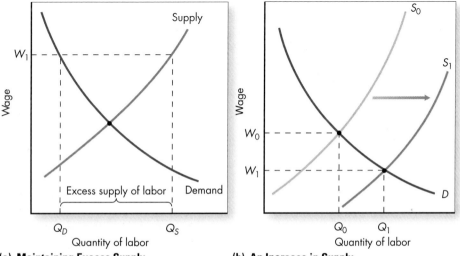

(a) Maintaining Excess Supply

(b) An Increase in Supply

FIGURE 17-2 (A AND B)

The Labor Market in Action

In (a) you can see the effect of an above-equilibrium wage: If workers force the firm to pay them a wage of W_1, more workers will be supplied (Q_S) than demanded (Q_D). With an excess supply of labor, jobs must be rationed. In (b) you can see the effect of an increase in the supply of labor. Assuming the demand for labor remains the same, the increase in the supply of labor will cause the wage level to drop from W_0 to W_1.

Q-7 How could an increase in the supply of labor lead to an increase in the demand for labor?

A monopsony is a market in which a single firm is the only buyer.

A monopsonist takes into account the fact that hiring another worker will increase the wage rate it must pay all workers.

Monopsony

supply of labor doesn't also affect the demand for labor. In reality, a liberalization of U.S. immigration laws might increase the demand for products, thereby increasing the demand for labor and raising wages. When you look at the overall effect of a change, you will often find that the final result is less clear-cut. That's why it's important always to remember the assumptions behind the model you're using. Those assumptions often add qualifications to the simple "right" answer.

Imperfect Competition and the Labor Market

Just as product markets can be imperfectly competitive, so too can labor markets. For example, there might be a **monopsony** (*a market in which a single firm is the only buyer*). An example of a monopsony is a "company town" in which a single firm is the only employer. Whereas a monopolist takes into account the fact that if it sells more it will lower the market price, a monopsonist takes into account the fact that it will raise the market prices if it buys more. Thus, it buys less and pays less than would a market with an equivalent number of competitive buyers.

Alternatively, laborers might have organized together in a union that allows workers to operate as if there were only a single seller. In effect, the union could operate as a monopoly. Alternatively again, there might be a **bilateral monopoly** (*a market with only a single seller and a single buyer*). Let's briefly consider these three types of market imperfections.

MONOPSONY   When there's only one buyer of labor services, it makes sense for that buyer to take into account the fact that if it hires another worker, the equilibrium wage will rise and it will have to pay more to all workers. The choice facing a monopsonist can be seen in Figure 17-3, in which the supply curve of labor is upward-sloping so that the **marginal factor cost** (*the additional cost to a firm of hiring another worker*) is above the supply curve since the monopsonist takes into account the fact that hiring another worker will increase the wage rate it must pay to all workers.

Instead of hiring Q_c workers at a wage of W_c, as would happen in a competitive labor market, the monopsonist hires Q_m workers and pays them a wage of W_m. (A good exercise to see that you understand the argument is to show that where there's a monopsonist, a minimum wage simultaneously can increase employment and raise the wage.)

FIGURE 17-3   **Monopsony, Union Power, and the Labor Market**

A monopsonist hires fewer workers and pays them less than would a set of competitive firms. The monopsonist determines the quantity of labor, Q_m, to hire at the point where the marginal factor cost curve intersects the demand curve. The monopsonist pays a wage of W_m. A union has a tendency to push for a higher wage, W_u, and a lower quantity of workers, Q_u.

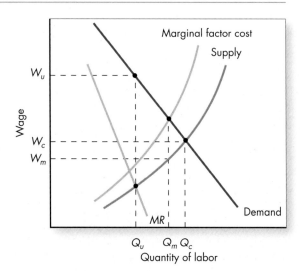

UNION MONOPOLY POWER   When a union exists, it will have an incentive to act as a monopolist, restricting labor supply to increase its members' wages. To do so it must have the power to restrict both supply and union membership. A union would have a strong tendency to act like a monopolist and to move to an equilibrium somewhat similar to the monopsonist case, except for one important difference. The wage the union would set wouldn't be below the competitive wage; instead, the wage would be above the competitive wage at W_u, as in Figure 17-3. Faced with a wage of W_u, competitive firms will hire Q_u workers. Thus, with union monopoly power, the benefits of restricting supply accrue to the union members, not to the firm as in the monopsonist case.

BILATERAL MONOPOLY   As our final case, let's consider a bilateral monopoly in which a monopsonist faces a union with monopoly power. In this case, we can say that the equilibrium wage will be somewhere between the monopsonist wage W_m and the union monopoly power wage W_u. The equilibrium quantity will be somewhere between Q_u and Q_m in Figure 17-3. Where in that range the wage and equilibrium quantity will be depends on the two sides' negotiating skills and other noneconomic forces.

A bilateral monopoly is a market in which a single seller faces a single buyer.

Political and Social Forces and the Labor Market

Let's now consider some real-world characteristics of U.S. labor markets. For example:

1. English teachers are paid close to what economics teachers are paid even though the quantity of English teachers supplied significantly exceeds the quantity of English teachers demanded, while the quantity of economics teachers supplied is approximately equal to the quantity demanded.

2. On average, women earn about 85 cents for every $1 earned by men.

3. Certain types of jobs are undertaken primarily by members of a single ethnic group. For example, a large percentage of construction workers on high-rise buildings are Mohawk Indians. They have an uncanny knack for keeping their balance on high, open building frames.

4. Firms often pay higher than "market" wages.

5. Firms often don't lay off workers even when demand for their products decreases.

6. It often seems that there are two categories of jobs: dead-end jobs and jobs with potential for career advancement. Once in a dead-end job, a person finds it almost impossible to switch to a job with potential.

7. The rate of unemployment among blacks is more than twice as high as the rate among whites.

Supply/demand analysis alone doesn't explain these phenomena. Each of them can, however, be explained as the result of market, political, and social forces. Thus, to understand real-world labor markets, it is necessary to broaden the analysis of labor markets to include other forces that limit the use of the market. These include legal and social limitations on the self-interest-seeking activities of firms and individuals. Let's consider a couple of the central issues of interaction among these forces and see how they affect the labor market.

To understand real-world labor markets, one must broaden the analysis.

Fairness and the Labor Market

People generally have an underlying view of what's fair. That view isn't always consistent among individuals, but it's often strongly held. The first lesson taught in a personnel or human resources course is that people aren't machines. They're human beings with feelings and emotions. If they feel good about a job, if they feel they're part of a team, they will work hard; if they feel they're being taken advantage of, they can be highly disruptive.

Nonwage Income and Property Rights

The four traditional categories of income are wages, rent, profits, and interest. Wages, discussed in the text, are determined by economic factors (the forces of supply and demand), with strong influences by political and social forces, which often restrict entry or hold wages higher than what they would be in a truly competitive market.

The same holds true for nonwage income: payments for use of land (rent), capital (profit), and financial assets (interest). The forces of supply and demand also determine these forms of income. But, as we have emphasized, supply and demand are not necessarily the end of the story. Supply and demand determine price and income, given an institutional structure that includes property rights (the rights given to people to use specified property) and the contractual legal system (the set of laws that govern economic behavior of the society). If you change property rights, you change the distribution of income. Thus, in a larger sense, supply and demand don't determine the distribution of income; the distribution of property rights does.

The system of property rights and the contractual legal system that underlie the U.S. economy evolved over many years. Many people believe that property rights were unfairly distributed to begin with; if you believe that, you'll also believe that the distribution of income and the returns to those property rights are unfair. In other words, you can favor markets but object to the underlying property rights. Many political fights about income distribution concern fights over property rights, not fights over the use of markets.

Such distributional fights have been going on for a long time. In feudal times, much of the land was held communally; it belonged to everyone, or at least everyone used it. It was common land—a communally held resource. As the economy evolved into a market economy, that land was appropriated by individuals, and these individuals became landholders who could determine the use of the land and could receive rent for allowing other individuals to use that land. Supply and demand can explain how much rent will accrue to a landholder; it cannot explain the initial set of property rights.

The type of issues raised by looking at the underlying property rights are in large part academic for Western societies. The property rights that exist, and the contractual legal system under which markets operate, are given. You're not going to see somebody going out and introducing a new alternative set of property rights in which the ownership of property is transferred to someone else. The government may impose shifts at the margin; for example, new zoning laws—laws that set limits on the use of one's property—will modify property rights and create fights about whether society has the right to impose such laws. But there will be no wholesale change in property rights. That's why most economic thinking simply takes property rights as given.

But taking property rights as given isn't a reasonable assumption for the developing countries or the formerly socialist countries still in the process of establishing markets and framing up their structure of property rights. In recent years, institutional economists have redirected their analysis to look more closely at the underlying legal and philosophical basis of supply and demand. As they do so, they are extending and modifying the economic theory of income distribution.

On some assembly-line jobs, it is relatively easy to monitor effort, so individuals can be—and in the past often were—treated like machines. Their feelings and emotions were ignored. Productivity was determined by the speed of the assembly line; if workers couldn't or wouldn't keep up the pace, they were fired.

EFFICIENCY WAGES Most modern jobs, however, require workers to make decisions and to determine how best to do a task. Today's managers are aware that workers' emotional state is important to whether they make sound decisions and do a good job. So most firms, even if they don't really care about anything but profit, will try to keep their workers happy. It's in their own interest to do so. That might mean paying workers more than the going market wage, not laying them off even if layoffs would make sense economically, providing day care so the workers aren't worried about their children, or keeping wage differentials among workers small to limit internal rivalry. Such actions can often make long-run economic sense, even though they might cost the firm in the short run. They are common enough that they have acquired a name—**efficiency wages** (*wages paid above the going market wage to keep workers happy and productive*).

Q-8 Why might efficiency wages make sense in the long run?

366

Views of fairness also enter into wage determination through political channels. Social views of fairness influence government, which passes laws to implement those views. Minimum wage laws, comparable worth laws, and antidiscrimination laws are examples.

COMPARABLE WORTH LAWS   Let's consider one of those, **comparable worth laws,** which are *laws mandating comparable pay for comparable work*—that is, mandatory "fairness." The problem in implementing these laws is in defining what is comparable. Do you define comparable work by the education it requires, by the effort the worker puts out, or by other characteristics? Similarly with pay: Compensation has many dimensions and it is not at all clear which are the relevant ones, or whether the political system will focus on the relevant ones.

Economists who favor comparable worth laws point out that social and intrafirm political issues are often the determining factors in setting pay. In fact, firms often have their own implicit or explicit comparable worth systems built into their structure. For example, seniority, not productivity, often determines pay. Bias against women and minorities and in favor of high-level management is sometimes built into firms' pay-setting institutions. In short, within firms, pay structure is influenced by, but is not determined by, supply and demand forces. Comparable worth laws are designed to affect those institutional biases and thus are not necessarily any less compatible with supply and demand forces than are current pay-setting institutions.

The federal government is not the only government agency that establishes labor laws. State and local governments also do. For example, recently a number of local governments have established "living wage" laws, which are a type of minimum wage law that requires specified employers to pay a "living wage." "Living wage" is most often defined as that wage that would allow one worker, working 40 hours a week, to support a family of four at the poverty level. The analysis of these laws is similar to that of the minimum wage.

Discrimination and the Labor Market

Web Note 17.4
Faculty Hiring Bias

Discrimination exists in all walks of life: On average, women are paid less than men, and blacks are often directed into lower-paying jobs. Economists have done a lot of research to understand the facts regarding discrimination and what can be done about it. The first problem is to measure the amount of discrimination and get an idea of how much discrimination is caused by what. Let's consider discrimination against women.

On average, women receive somewhere around 85 percent of the pay that men receive. That has increased from about 60 percent in the 1970s. This pay gap suggests that discrimination is occurring. The economist's job is to figure out how much of this is statistically significant and, of the portion that is caused by discrimination, what the nature of that discrimination is.

Q-9 True or false? Economic theory argues that discrimination should be eliminated. Why?

Analyzing the data, economists have found that somewhat more than half of the pay difference can be explained by causes other than discrimination, such as length of time on the job. But that still leaves a relatively large difference that can be attributed to discrimination.

Three Types of Direct Demand-Side Discrimination

In analyzing discrimination, it's important to distinguish various types. The first is demand-side discrimination based on relevant individual characteristics. Firms commonly make decisions about employees based on individual characteristics that will affect job performance. For example, restaurants might discriminate against (avoid hiring) applicants with sourpuss personalities. Another example might be a firm hiring more young salespeople because its clients like to buy from younger rather than older

Democracy in the Workplace

In the United States, slavery is illegal. You cannot sell yourself to someone else, even if you want to. It's an unenforceable contract. But work, which might be considered a form of partial slavery, is legal. You can sell your labor services for a specific, limited period of time.

Is there any inherent reason that such partial slavery should be seen as acceptable? The answer to that question is complicated. It deals with the rights of workers and is based on value judgments. You must answer it for yourself. I raise it because it's a good introduction to Karl Marx's analysis of the labor market (which deals with alienation) and to some recent arguments about democracy in the workplace.

Marx saw selling labor as immoral, just as slavery was immoral. He believed that capitalists exploited workers by alienating them from their labor. The best equivalent I can think of is the way most people today view the selling of sex. Most people see selling sex as wrong because it alienates a person from his or her own body. Marx saw all selling of labor that same way. A labor market makes workers see themselves as objects, not as human beings.

The underlying philosophical issues of Marx's concern are outside of economics. Most people in the United States don't agree with Marx's philosophical underpinnings. But it's nonetheless a useful exercise to think about this issue and ask yourself whether it helps explain why we treat the labor market as different from other markets and limit by law the right of employers to discriminate in the labor market.

Some of Marx's philosophical tenets are shared by the modern democracy-in-the-workplace movement. In this view, a business isn't owned by a certain group; it is an association of individuals who have come together to produce a certain product. For one group—the owners of stock—to have all the say as to how the business is run, and for another group—the

regular workers—to have no say, is immoral in the same way that not having a democratic government is immoral. According to this view, work is as large a part of people's lives as is national or local politics, and a country can call itself a democracy only if it has democracy in the workplace.

As with most grandiose ideas, this one is complicated, but it's worth considering because it's reflected in certain laws. Consider, for example, a federal law that limits firms' freedom to close plants without giving advance notice to their workers. The view that workers have certain inalienable rights played a role in passing that law.

For those of you who say "Right on!" to the idea of increasing workers' rights, let me add a word of caution. Increasing workers' rights has a cost. It makes it less likely that firms and individuals who can think up things that need doing will do so, and thus will decrease the number of jobs available. It also will increase firms' desire to discriminate. If you know you must let a person play a role in decisions once you hire that person, you're going to be much more careful about whom you hire.

None of these considerations means that democracy in the workplace can't work. The Brazilian firm Semco is an example. There are various examples of somewhat democratic "firms." Universities are run as partial democracies, with the faculty deciding what policies should be set. (There is, however, serious debate about how well universities are run.) But as soon as you add worker democracy to production, more questions come up: What about consumers? Shouldn't they, too, have a voice in decisions? What about the community within which the firm is located?

Economics can't answer such questions. Economics can, however, be used to predict and analyze some of the difficulties such changes might bring about.

---

employees. If that characteristic can be an identifying factor for a group of individuals, the discrimination becomes more visible.

A second type of demand-side discrimination is discrimination based on group characteristics. This occurs when firms make employment decisions about individuals because they are members of a group who on average have particular characteristics that affect job performance. A firm may correctly perceive that young people in general have a lower probability of staying on a job than do older people and therefore may discriminate against younger people.

A third type of demand-side discrimination is discrimination based on irrelevant individual characteristics. This discrimination is based either on individual characteristics that do not affect job performance or on incorrectly perceived statistical characteristics of groups. A firm might not hire people over 50 because the supervisor doesn't like working with older people, even though older people may be just as productive as, or even more productive than, younger people.

Of the three types, the third will be easiest to eliminate; it doesn't have an economic motivation. In fact, discrimination based on individual characteristics that don't affect job performance is costly to a firm. Competing firms will hire these people and be in a better competitive position because they did so. Market forces will work toward eliminating this type of discrimination.

An example of the success of a firm's policy to reduce discrimination is the decision by McDonald's to create a special program to hire workers with learning disabilities. Individuals who have learning disabilities often make good employees. They tend to have lower turnover rates and follow procedures better than do many of the more transient employees McDonald's hires. Moreover, through their advertising, McDonald's helped change some negative stereotypes about people with disabilities. So in this case market forces and political forces are working together.

If the discrimination is of either of the first two types (that is, based on characteristics that do affect job performance, either directly or statistically), the discrimination will be harder to eliminate. In these cases, not discriminating can be costly to the firm, so political forces to eliminate discrimination will be working against market forces to keep discrimination.

Whenever discrimination saves the firm money, the firm will have an economic incentive to use subterfuges to get around an antidiscrimination law. These subterfuges will make the firm appear to be complying with the law, even when it isn't. An example would be a firm that finds some other reason besides age to explain why it isn't hiring an older person.

Institutional Discrimination

Institutional discrimination is discrimination in which the structure of the job makes it difficult or impossible for certain groups of individuals to succeed. Institutional discrimination does not come from the demand side, but is built into the institutional structure. Consider colleges and universities. To succeed in the academic market, one must devote an enormous amount of effort during one's 20s and 30s. But these are precisely the years when, given biology and culture, many women have major family responsibilities, making it difficult for women to succeed. Were academic institutions different—say, a number of positions at universities were designed for high-level, part-time work during this period—it would be easier for women to advance their careers.

Requiring peak time commitment when women are also facing peak family responsibilities is the norm for many companies, too. Thus, women face significant institutional discrimination.

Whether this institutional discrimination is embodied in the firm's structure or in the family is an open question. For example, sociologists have found that in personal relationships women tend to move to be with their partners more than men move to be with their partners. In addition, women in two-parent relationships generally do much more work around the house and take a greater responsibility for child rearing than men do even when both are employed.

How important are these sociological observations? In discussing discrimination I ask the members of my class if they expect their personal relationships with their partners to be fully equal. The usual result is the following: 80 percent of the women expect a fully equal relationship; 20 percent expect their partner's career to come first. Eighty percent of the men expect their own careers to come first; 20 percent expect an equal relationship. I then point out that somebody's expectations aren't going to be fulfilled. Put simply, most observers believe that the institutional discrimination that occurs in interpersonal relationships is significant.

Three types of demand-side discrimination are:

1. Discrimination based on individual characteristics that will affect job performance.

2. Discrimination based on correctly perceived statistical characteristics of the group.

3. Discrimination based on individual characteristics that don't affect job performance or are incorrectly perceived.

Q-10 Why is discrimination based on characteristics that affect job performance difficult to eliminate?

Institutions can have built-in discrimination.

Economists have made adjustments for these sociological factors, and have found that institutional factors explain a portion of the lower pay that women receive but that other forms of workplace discrimination also explain a portion.

Whether prejudice should be allowed to affect the hiring decision is a normative question for society to settle. In answering these normative questions, our society has passed laws making it illegal for employers to discriminate on the basis of race, religion, sex, age, disability, or national origin. The reason society has made it illegal is its ethical belief in equal opportunity for all, or at least most, individuals. (Gays and lesbians still aren't protected by federal legislation assuring them equal opportunities.)

The Evolution of Labor Markets

Now that we've briefly considered how noneconomic forces can influence labor markets, let's turn our attention to how labor markets developed.

Labor markets as we now know them developed in the 1700s and 1800s. Given the political and social rules that operated at that time, the invisible hand was free to push wage rates down to subsistence level. Workweeks were long and working conditions were poor. Laborers began to turn to other ways—besides the market—of influencing their wage. One way was to use political power to place legal restrictions on employers in their relationship with workers. A second way was to organize together—to unionize. Let's consider each in turn.

Evolving Labor Laws

Laws play an important role in the structure of labor markets.

Over the years, government has responded to workers' political pressure with numerous laws that limit what can and what cannot be done in the various labor markets. For example, in many areas of production, laws limit the number of normal hours a person

In the late 1800s, many workers worked in sweatshops; they often had quotas that required them to work 60 or more hours a week. Fines were imposed for such indiscretions as talking or smiling.

can work in a day to eight. The laws also prescribe the amount of extra pay an employee must receive when working more than the normal number of hours. (Generally it's time-and-a-half.) Similarly, the number and length of workers' breaks are defined by law (one break every four hours).

Child labor laws mandate that a person must be at least 16 years old to be hired. The safety and health conditions under which a person can work are regulated by laws. (For example, on a construction site, all workers are required to wear hard hats.) Workers can be fired only for cause, and employers must show that they had cause to fire a worker. (For example, a 55-year-old employee cannot be fired simply because he or she is getting old.) Employers must not allow sexual harassment in the workplace. (Bosses can't make sexual advances to employees and firms must make a good-faith attempt to see that employees don't sexually harass their co-workers.)

Combined, these laws play an enormously important role in the functioning of the labor market.

Unions and Collective Bargaining

Some of the most important labor laws concern workers' right to organize together in order to bargain collectively with employers. These laws also specify the tactics workers can use to achieve their ends. In the latter part of the 1800s, workers had few rights to organize themselves. The Knights of Labor was formed in 1869, and by 1886 it had approximately 800,000 members. But a labor riot in 1886 turned public opinion against these workers and led to the organization's breakup. In its place, the American Federation of Labor developed and began to organize strikes to achieve higher wages.

Business opposed unions' right to strike, and initially the government supported business. Police and sometimes the army were sent in to break up strikes. Under the then-existing legal structure of the economy, unions were seen as monopolistic restraints on trade and an intrusion into management rights.

In the 1930s, society's view of unions changed (in part as a backlash to the strong-arm tactics used by firms to break up unions), and laws such as the National Labor Relations Act (also called the Wagner Act) were passed guaranteeing workers the right to form unions, to strike, and to engage in collective bargaining. As Figure 17-4 shows, from 1935 to the mid-1950s unions grew significantly in size and importance and remained strong until the late 1970s.

Web Note 17.5
Laws or Contracts?

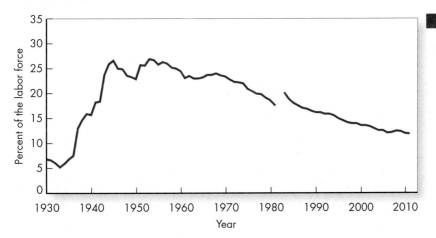

FIGURE 17-4 **Change in Union Membership**

The graph shows union membership from 1930. As can be seen, after the Depression in the 1930s, unions grew in importance. Since the mid-1970s the membership of unions has declined. (Note: The series from 1930 to 1981 excludes members of professional and public employee associations. The series from 1983 and beyond is from *Current Population Statistics*.)

Source: Bureau of Labor Statistics (www.bls.gov).

A closed shop is a firm in which the union controls hiring.

A union shop is a firm in which all workers must join the union.

Businesses weren't happy with unions' increasing strength, and in 1947 they managed to get the Taft-Hartley Act passed. That act placed limitations on union activities. It allowed states to pass "right-to-work" laws forbidding union membership to be made a requirement for continued employment. Moreover, it made **closed shops,** *firms where the union controls hiring,* illegal. Before anyone can be hired in a closed shop, he or she must be a member of the particular union. Federal law does permit **union shops**—*firms in which all workers must join the union.* Individuals are required to join a union after working for the firm for a period of time. The Taft-Hartley Act also outlawed *secondary boycotts.* In a secondary boycott, in order to strengthen its bargaining position, a union gets unions at other firms to force their firms to refuse to buy a firm's products, under threat of a strike.

Union power weakened considerably in 1981, when, in response to a strike by air traffic controllers, President Ronald Reagan fired all the controllers and refused to hire them back. Private firms similarly won the right to hire permanent replacements for striking workers. That stance significantly changed the atmosphere within which unions operate. In 2010, new federal rules strengthened unions by limiting an employer's ability to slow worker elections to establish a union.

Part of the reason labor union membership has declined in recent years is the unions' successes.

As Figure 17-4 shows, the percentage of workers who belong to unions has declined since the 1970s, as unions have lost their bargaining power. Because of that decline, unions don't have the political or economic clout they once had. Part of the reason, ironically, is their success. By pressuring the government to pass laws that protected workers, unions made themselves less necessary. Another part of the reason is the changing nature of production in the United States. Labor unions were especially strong in manufacturing industries. As the relative number of manufacturing jobs has declined in the United States and the number of service jobs has increased, the base of union membership has been reduced. Unions have somewhat compensated for this change by pushing unionization drives among government employees. Today, more than 50 percent of union members work for the government. These unions are becoming stronger and will likely be exerting their influence.

The Labor Market and You

This chapter is meant to give you a sense of how the labor market works. But what does it all mean for those of you who'll soon be getting a job or are in the process of changing jobs? I'll try to answer that question in this last section.

Table 17-1 shows a variety of useful statistics about the labor market. Let's consider how some of them might affect you. For example, consider relative pay of jobs requiring a college degree compared to jobs requiring only a high school diploma. Jobs requiring a college degree pay significantly more, on average, than do jobs requiring only a high school diploma. In recent years the income gap between the two groups has noticeably increased. So the answer to the question of whether it's worthwhile to stick college out for another couple of years and get a degree is probably yes.

Next, consider the salaries of Ph.D.s compared to the salaries of MBAs. A Ph.D. is a person who has gone to graduate school after college, usually for a number of years, and earned an advanced degree called a Doctorate of Philosophy—even though one can earn a Ph.D. in many subjects besides philosophy (such as economics). As you can see, Ph.D.s' starting salaries are lower than salaries of MBAs (masters of business administration) and professionals with other kinds of advanced degrees. Does this mean that Ph.D.s are discriminated against? Not necessarily. It's possible that Ph.D.s'

TABLE 17-1 (A AND B)   Some Typical Starting Salaries

Occupation	Private or Public
Physician assistant	$57,000
Management analyst	44,000
Budget analyst	45,000
Economist	45,000
Secondary school teacher	35,000
Flight attendant	25,000
Insurance underwriter	37,000
Secretary	22,000
Maintenance and Grounds	10,000
Retail sales (salary and commission)	16,000

Degree	Annual Salary[*]
Law (3 years)	
Large firms	$125,000
Small firms	68,000
Engineering	
Bachelor's degree	70,000
Master's degree	85,000
Business	
Bachelor's degree	41,000
Master's (MBA) degree (2 years)	75,000
M.D. (4 years and 3-year internship)	130,000
Ph.D. (5 years)	
In economics	70,000
In humanities	55,000

Sources: Author's estimates based on *Occupational Outlook Handbook, 2011–12* and U.S. Dept. of Labor Statistics (pay varies significantly by region) (www.bls.gov).

(a) Some Typical Starting Salaries of BAs

[*]These figures are rough estimates based on data from the Department of Labor and informal surveys of author.

(b) Starting Salaries for Selected Professional Degrees

lower pay suggests that Ph.D.s derive a "psychic income" from their work in addition to the amount of money they earn.

Since Ph.D.s are often quite smart, their willingness to accept psychic income as a substitute for higher pay suggests that there's much more to consider in a job than the salary. What's most important about a job isn't the wage, but whether you like what you're doing and the life that job provides. (Of course, their lower salaries also could imply that Ph.D.s really aren't so smart.)

So my suggestion to you is definitely to finish college, especially if you enjoy it. (And with books like this, how could you help but enjoy it?) But go to graduate school only if you really enjoy learning. In picking your job, first and foremost pick a job that you enjoy (as long as it pays you enough to live on). Among jobs you like, choose a job in a field in which the supply of labor is limited, or the demand for labor is significantly increasing. Either of those trends is likely to lead to higher wages. After all, if you're doing something you like, you might as well get paid as much as possible for it.

Jobs in which the supply will likely be limited are those in which social or political forces have placed restrictions on entry or those requiring special abilities. If you have some special ability, try to find a job you enjoy in which you can use that ability. You might also look for a job in which entry is restricted, but beware: Jobs that are restricted in supply must be rationed, so while such jobs pay higher wages, you may need personal connections to obtain one of them.

I'm sure most of you are aware that your choice of jobs is one of the most important choices you'll be making in your life. So I'm sure you feel the pressure. But you should also know that a job, unlike marriage, isn't necessarily supposed to be for life. There's enormous flexibility in the U.S. labor market. Many people change jobs six or seven times in their lifetimes. So while the choice is important, a poor choice can be remedied; don't despair if the first job you take isn't perfect. Good luck.

Conclusion

We've come to the end of our discussion about the labor market. As I said at the beginning, most people are defined by their job. Thus the labor market is important, and economic forces play a central role in its operation. But it is also important to remember, precisely because work is so significant to us all, that the labor market is not governed by economic forces alone. Cultural, political, and social forces are central issues in labor markets and in how economic forces play out. So whenever you consider issues involving labor markets, think supply and demand, but also think of people fighting against those forces with political and social pressures to see that economic forces work for, not against, them.

Summary

- Incentive effects are important in labor supply decisions. The higher the wage, the higher the quantity supplied. (*LO17-1*)

- Elasticity of market supply of labor depends on (1) individuals' opportunity cost of working, (2) the type of market being discussed, (3) the elasticity of individuals' supply curves, and (4) individuals entering and leaving the labor market. (*LO17-1*)

- The demand for labor by firms is derived from the demand by consumers for goods and services. It follows the basic law of demand—the higher the wage, the lower the quantity demanded. (*LO17-2*)

- Elasticity of market demand for labor depends on (1) the elasticity of demand for the firm's good, (2) the relative importance of labor in production, (3) the possibility and cost of substitution in production, and (4) the degree to which marginal productivity falls with an increase in labor. (*LO17-2*)

- Technological advances and changes in international competitiveness shift the demand for labor. Both have reduced demand for some types of labor and increased demand for other types. The net effect has been an increase in the demand for labor. (*LO17-2*)

- A monopsony is a market in which a single firm is the only buyer. A monopsonist hires fewer workers at a lower wage compared to a competitive firm. (*LO17-3*)

- A bilateral monopoly is a market in which there is a single seller and a single buyer. The wage and number of workers hired in a bilateral monopoly depend on the relative strength of the union and the monopsonist. (*LO17-3*)

- Firms are aware of workers' well-being and will sometimes pay efficiency wages to keep workers happy and productive. (*LO17-3*)

- Views of fairness in the labor market have led to laws that mandate comparable pay for comparable work. (*LO17-4*)

- Discrimination may be based on (1) relevant individual characteristics, (2) group characteristics, or (3) irrelevant individual characteristics. The easiest to eliminate is discrimination based on irrelevant individual characteristics. The other two are motivated by market incentives. (*LO17-4*)

- Labor laws have evolved and will continue to evolve. Since the 1980s, labor unions have been declining in importance. (*LO17-5*)

Key Terms

bilateral monopoly *(364)*
closed shops *(372)*
comparable worth
  laws *(367)*

derived demand *(360)*
efficiency wages *(366)*
entrepreneurship *(360)*

incentive effect *(355)*
labor market *(354)*
marginal factor cost *(364)*

monopsony *(364)*
union shops *(372)*

Questions and Exercises

1. Why are social and political forces more active in the labor market than in most other markets? *(LO17-1)*

2. Economist Edward Prescott observed that while Americans worked 5 percent fewer hours per week than the French in the 1970s, they worked 50 percent more hours per week in the early 2000s. He found that taxes accounted for nearly all of the difference. What was his likely argument? *(LO17-1)*

3. How is opportunity cost related to the supply of labor? *(LO17-1)*

4. Using the economic decision rule and opportunity cost, explain why an increase in the wage rate increases quantity of labor supplied? *(LO17-1)*

5. Is an increase in the marginal income tax rate reflected by a shift in the after-tax supply of labor or a movement along the supply curve when the pretax wage rate is on the vertical axis? Explain your answer. *(LO17-1)*

6. Using the concept of opportunity cost, explain why welfare programs might increase the number of poor. *(LO17-1)*

7. If the wage goes up 20 percent and the quantity of labor supplied increases by 5 percent, what's the elasticity of labor supply? *(LO17-1)*

8. List four factors that contribute to the elasticity of labor demand. *(LO17-2)*

9. List four shift factors of demand and their effect on demand. *(LO17-2)*

10. The president of the United States receives an annual salary of $400,000. Derek Jeter, shortstop for the New York Yankees, receives $20.6 million annually. *(LO17-2)*
    a. Based on marginal productivity theory, what does this say about their contributions to society?
    b. What qualifications to your answer might you suggest about their relative contributions, and what do your adjustments have to say about marginal productivity theory?

11. Economists Mark Blaug and Ruth Towse studied the market for economists in Britain and found that the quantity demanded was about 150–200 a year, and that the quantity supplied was about 300 a year. *(LO17-3)*
    a. What did they predict would happen to economists' salaries?
    b. What likely happens to the excess economists?
    c. Why doesn't the price change immediately to bring the quantity supplied and the quantity demanded into equilibrium?

12. Demonstrate graphically the effect of a minimum wage law. Does economic theory tell us such a law would be a bad idea? *(LO17-3)*

13. As telecommunications improve, performers can reach larger and larger audiences. In the past, one could only perform in a concert hall; today one can perform for the entire world. How might that change in technology affect the relative pay of performers? *(LO17-3)*

14. New websites such as ifreelance.com have developed a place for companies to post projects for which freelancers can bid. What is the likely effect of this new market on market demand for freelancers? Wages? *(LO17-3)*

15. The town of Oberlin, Ohio, has one hospital. How would you classify this market structure, and what effect will this market structure likely have on wages of nurses in Oberlin compared to a perfectly competitive market structure? Demonstrate your answer graphically. *(LO17-3)*

16. The following statement appeared in a recent article: 7½ cents of every dollar spent at retail stores in America is spent at Walmart. With such market power, Walmart is able to name the price at which it is willing to buy goods from suppliers. *(LO17-3)*
    a. Could this be a correct statement if Walmart's suppliers were operating in a perfectly competitive market?
    b. What if it were operating in an imperfectly competitive market, specifically a monopsonistic market?
    c. What would be the lower limit of the price Walmart could name?

17. Show graphically how a minimum wage can simultaneously increase employment and raise the wage rate. *(LO17-3)*

18. Explain each of the following phenomena using the invisible hand or social or political forces: *(LO17-3)*
    a. Firms often pay higher than market wages.
    b. Wages don't fluctuate much as unemployment rises.
    c. Pay among faculty in various disciplines at colleges does not vary much although market conditions among disciplines vary significantly.

19. A recent study by the International Labor Organization estimates that 250 million children in developing countries between the ages of 5 and 14 are working either full or part time. The estimates of the percentage of children working within particular countries is as high as 42 percent in Kenya. Among the reasons cited for the rise in child labor are population increases and poverty. *(LO17-3)*
    a. Why do firms hire children as workers?
    b. Why do children work?
    c. What considerations should be taken into account by countries when deciding whether to implement an international ban on trade for products made with child labor?

20. a. List three types of demand discrimination.
    b. Which is the most difficult to eliminate? Why?
    c. Which is the easiest to eliminate? Why? *(LO17-4)*

21. Which type of discrimination is easier to address legally—demand side or institutional? Explain your answer. *(LO17-4)*

22. A study in 2005 reported that the average male CEO of Fortune 500 firms is 6 feet, about 2.5 inches more than the average male. Why might this be difficult to eliminate through laws that restrict companies from hiring based on height? *(LO17-4)*

23. According to a study by economists Muriel Niederle and Lise Vesterlund, women are less willing to participate in competitive environments. *(LO17-4)*
    a. What is the potential impact on the number of women in high-level management positions?
    b. If this were the cause of fewer women working in high-level management, would you characterize it as discrimination? If so, what type? If not, why not?

24. Comparable worth laws require employers to pay the same wage scale to workers who do comparable work or have comparable training. What likely effect would these laws have on the labor market? *(LO17-5)*

25. In the early 1990s a teen subminimum training wage law was passed by which employers were allowed to pay teenagers less than the minimum wage. *(LO17-5)*
    a. What effect would you predict this law would have, based on standard economic theory?
    b. In analyzing the effects of the law, Professors Card and Kreuger of Princeton University found that few businesses used it and that it had little effect. Why might that have been the case?

26. In 1993 Congress passed the Family and Medical Leave Act (FMLA), which requires firms with more than 50 employees grant a 12-week unpaid leave of absence for family and medical reasons. What is the likely effect on the demand for female employees? *(LO17-5)*

27. What has happened to union membership in the United States since the 1960s? *(LO17-5)*

28. What is the difference between a union shop and a closed shop? Which did the Taft-Hartley Act make illegal? How have more recent laws changed the role of unions? *(LO17-5)*

Questions from Alternative Perspectives

1. How might the minimum wage lead to greater racial and gender discrimination in the labor market? (Austrian)

2. In his book *Forbidden Grounds,* University of Chicago Professor Richard Epstein argues that federal employment antidiscrimination laws ought to be abolished. [Hint. Reading Westmont College economist Edd Noell's paper "Racial Discrimination, Police Power and the 1964 Civil Rights Act" in Richard Epstein's *Forbidden Grounds: An Evaluation of The Case Against Discrimination Laws* (available on the web at ACE, www.gordon.edu/ace) will be helpful in answering this question.]
   a. How might a Christian economist evaluate the need for federal laws prohibiting racial discrimination?
   b. Why should a Christian economist think more carefully than another economist about the relation between economic liberty and tolerance of the taste for discrimination? (Religious)

3. Gloria Steinem pointed out the following: "I've yet to be on any campus where women weren't worried about some aspect of combining marriage, children, and a career. I've yet to find one where many men were worrying about the same thing."
   a. What does this insight suggest about the working of the labor market in the United States?
   b. Does this male bias in the labor market affect the efficiency of the economy? (Feminist)

4. Table 17-1 provides data about starting salaries for selected professional degrees; in it you can see that Ph.D. economists are paid less than MBAs. If economists are rational, why are they economists? (Institutionalist)

5. Radical economists argue that labor markets are governed by nonmarket forces such as discrimination as well as by the supply and demand for labor. As they see it, poverty and inequality are not aberrations but systematic labor market outcomes. They also believe that unions are much-needed equalizers that help low-wage workers.
   a. How does the radical view of the workings of labor markets and role of unions differ from that presented in your textbook?
   b. In your opinion, how fairly do labor markets operate?
   c. Do labor market outcomes need redress through collective action? (Radical)

6. In firms, the manager is assumed to hold down worker's wages in order to maximize his profits. Who holds down the pay of managers? (Institutionalist)

Issues to Ponder

1. "Welfare laws are bad, not for society, but for the people they are meant to help." Discuss.

2. Which would you choose: selling illegal drugs at $75 an hour (20 percent chance per year of being arrested) or a $6-an-hour factory job? Why?

3. Some economists have argued against need-based scholarships because they work as an implicit tax on parents' salaries and hence discourage saving for college.
   a. If the marginal tax rate parents face is 20 percent, and 5 percent of parents' assets will be deducted from a student's financial aid each year for the four years a child is in school, what is the implicit marginal tax on that portion of income that is saved? (For simplicity assume the interest rate is zero and that the parents' contribution is paid at the time the child enters college.)
   b. How would your answer differ if parents had two children with the second entering college right after the first one graduated? (How about three?) (Remember that the assets will likely decrease with each child graduating.)
   c. When parents are divorced, how should the contribution of each parent be determined? If your school has need-based scholarships, how does it determine the expected contributions of divorced parents?
   d. Given the above, would you suggest moving to an ability-based scholarship program? Why or why not?

4. According to economist Colin Camerer of the California Institute of Technology, many New York taxi drivers decide when to finish work for the day by setting an income goal for themselves. Once they reach it, they stop working.
   a. Is that what you would expect if the drivers are rational?
   b. Prospect theory suggests that people gain less utility from winning a certain sum of money than the utility they would lose if they lost that same sum. How can prospect theory explain the behavior of taxi drivers?

5. In 1997, a Dutch charity sponsored an incentive program in which teachers received prizes equal to about 30 percent of their salary if their students improved their scores on a standardized test.
   a. What effect would you expect the program to have on test scores?
   b. If not all the teachers' students were required to take the test, how would the program have to treat students who did not take the exam?
   c. What would be the most likely way in which the program would change what teachers did?

6. Why might it be inappropriate to discuss the effect of immigration policy using supply and demand analysis?

7. Why is unemployment nearly twice as high among blacks as among whites? What should be done about the situation?

8. Give four reasons why women earn less than men. Which reasons do you believe are most responsible for the wage gap?

9. Interview three married female and three married male professors at your college, asking them what percentage of work in the professor's household each adult household member does.
   a. Assuming your results can be extended to the population at large, what can you say about the existence of institutional discrimination?
   b. If gender-related salary data for individuals at your college are available, determine whether women or men of equal rank and experience receive higher average pay.
   c. Relate your findings in *a* and *b*.

10. In an article in the *Journal of Human Resources* titled "The Economic Reality of the Beauty Myth," economists Susan Averett and Sanders Korenman found that family income of obese women is about 17 percent lower than that of women who are of recommended weight. The differential was less for men than for women.
   a. What conclusions can you draw from these findings?
   b. Do the findings necessarily mean that there is a "beauty" discrimination?
   c. What might explain the larger income penalty for women?

11. More than half of agricultural workers in the United States are undocumented immigrants. Some Americans support strong enforcement of immigration laws that limit the number of workers from Central and South America coming to the United States so that U.S. citizens can get those jobs, while others argue that without them, the jobs that they take will be left unfilled. Who is right?

Answers to Margin Questions

1. Under usual conditions of supply, one would expect that if the wage of my part-time job rises, the quantity of labor I supply in that part-time job also rises. Institutional constraints such as tax considerations or company rules might mean that the quantity of labor I supply doesn't change. However, under the usual conditions of supply, I will study less if the wage of my part-time job rises. (*p. 356; LO17-1*)

2. Taxes reduce the opportunity cost, or relative price, of nonwork activities. So you will substitute leisure for labor as marginal tax rates increase. (*p. 357; LO17-1*)

3. The irony of any need-based program is that such a program reduces people's incentive to prevent themselves from becoming needy. (*p. 358; LO17-1*)

4. Some factors that influence the elasticity of a firm's derived demand for labor include (1) the elasticity of demand for the firm's good; (2) the relative importance of labor in the production process; (3) the possibility, and cost, of substitution in production; and (4) the degree to which marginal productivity falls with an increase in labor. (*p. 360; LO17-2*)

5. The demand for laborers at that firm would shift out to the right. (*p. 361; LO17-2*)

6. Differences among countries in productivity, transportation costs, trade restrictions, and social institutions all determine the relative demand for labor in one country compared to another country. (*p. 362; LO17-2*)

7. If the increase in labor supply leads to an increase in the demand for products in general, the increase in labor supply also will lead to an increase in labor demand. (*p. 364; LO17-3*)

8. Firms might pay workers higher-than-competitive-wages in the long run to cultivate worker loyalty and get workers to work harder. (*p. 366; LO17-3*)

9. False. Economic theory does not argue that discrimination should be eliminated. Economic theory tries to stay positive. Discrimination is a normative issue. If one's normative views say that discrimination should be eliminated, economic theory might be useful to help do that most efficiently. (*p. 367; LO17-4*)

10. Whenever discrimination saves the firm money, the firm will be pressured to discriminate to lower costs to remain competitive. (*p. 369; LO17-4*)

APPENDIX A

Derived Demand

This appendix considers the issues of derived demand in more detail. Although it focuses on the derived demand for labor, you should note that the formal analysis of the firm's derived demand for labor presented in the chapter is quite general and carries over to the derived demand for capital and for land. Firms translate consumers' demands for goods into derived demands for any and all of the factors of production. Let's start our consideration by looking at the firm's decision to hire.

The Firm's Decision to Hire

What determines a firm's decision to hire someone? The answer is simple. A profit-maximizing firm hires someone if it thinks there's money to be made by doing so. Unless there is, the firm won't hire the person. So for a firm to decide whether to hire someone, it must compare the worker's **marginal revenue product** (**MRP**) *(the*

marginal revenue it expects to earn from selling the additional worker's output) with the wage that it expects to pay the additional worker. For a competitive firm (for which $P = MR$), that marginal revenue product equals the worker's **value of marginal product** (**VMP**)—the worker's **marginal physical product** (**MPP**) *(the additional units of output that hiring an additional worker will bring about)* times the price (P) at which the firm can sell the additional product.

Marginal revenue product $= MPP \times P$

Say, for example, that by hiring another worker a firm can produce an additional 6 widgets an hour, which it can sell at $2 each. That means the firm can pay up to $12 per hour and still expect to make a profit. Notice that a key question for the firm is: How much additional product will we get from hiring another worker? A competitive firm can increase its profit by hiring another worker as long as the value of the worker's marginal product (which also equals her marginal revenue product) (*MPP* × *P*) is higher than her wage.

To see whether you understand the principle, consider the example in Figure A17-1(a). Column 1 shows the number of workers, all of whom are assumed to be identical. Column 2 shows the total output of those workers. Column 3 shows the marginal physical product of an additional worker. This number is determined by looking at the change in the total product due to this person's work. For example, if the firm is currently employing 30 workers and it hires one more, the firm's total product or output will rise from 294 to 300, so the marginal product of moving from 30 to 31 workers is 6.

Notice that workers' marginal product decreases as more workers are hired. Why is this? Remember the assumption of fixed capital: More and more workers are working with the same amount of capital and there is diminishing marginal productivity.

Column 4 shows **labor productivity**—*the average output per worker,* which is a statistic commonly referred to in economic reports. It's determined by dividing the total output by the number of workers. Column 5 shows the additional worker's marginal revenue product, which, since the firm is assumed to be competitive, is determined by multiplying the price the firm receives for the product it sells ($2) by the worker's marginal physical product.

Column 5, the marginal revenue product, is of central importance to the firm. It tells the firm how much additional money it will make from hiring an additional worker. That marginal revenue product represents a competitive firm's demand for labor.

Figure A17-1(b) graphs the firm's derived demand for labor, based on the data in column 5 of Figure A17-1(a).

FIGURE A17-1 (A AND B)   **Determining How Many Workers to Hire and the Firm's Derived Demand for Labor**

The marginal revenue product is any firm's demand curve for labor. Since for a competitive firm *P* = *MR,* a competitive firm's derived demand curve is its value of the marginal product curve (*P* × *MPP*). This curve tells us the additional revenue the firm gets from having an additional worker. From the chart in (**a**) we can see that when the firm increases from 27 to 28 workers, the marginal product per hour for each worker is 9. If the product sells for $2, then marginal revenue product is $18, which is one point on the demand curve for labor (point *A* in (**b**)). When the firm increases from 34 to 35 workers, the value of the marginal product decreases to $4. This is another point on the firm's derived demand curve (point *B* in (**b**)). By connecting the two points, as I have done in (**b**), you can see that the firm's derived demand curve for labor is downward-sloping.

1 Number of Workers	2 Total Product per Hour	3 Marginal Physical Product per Hour	4 Average Product per Hour	5 Marginal Revenue Product (*MRP*)
27	270	9.00	10.00	$18
28	279	8.00	9.96	16
29	287	7.00	9.90	14
30	294	6.00	9.80	12
31	300	5.00	9.68	10
32	305	4.00	9.53	8
33	309	3.00	9.36	6
34	312	2.00	9.18	4
35	314		8.97	

(a)

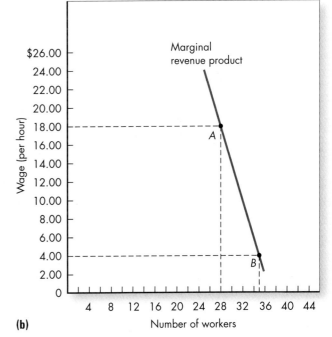

(b)

The resulting curve is the firm's **derived demand curve for labor,** which *shows the maximum amount of labor, measured in labor hours, that a firm will hire.* To see this, let's assume that the wage is $9 and that the firm is hiring 30 workers. If it hires another worker so it has 31 workers, workers' marginal revenue product of $12 exceeds their wage of $9, so the firm can increase profits by doing so. It increases output and profits since the additional revenue the firm gets from increasing workers from 30 to 31 is $12 and the additional cost the firm incurs is the wage of $9.

Now say the firm has hired 4 additional workers so it has 34 workers. As the firm hires more workers, the marginal product of workers declines. As you can see from the graph in Figure A17-1(b), the marginal revenue product of decreasing from 34 to 33 workers is $6. Since the workers' marginal revenue product of $6 is less than their wage of $9, now the firm can increase profits by laying off some workers. Doing so decreases output but increases profit because it significantly increases the average product of the remaining workers.

Only when a worker's wage of $9 equals the marginal revenue product does the firm have no incentive to change the number of employees. In this example, the wage ($9) equals workers' marginal revenue product at 32 workers. When the firm is hiring 32 workers, either hiring another worker or laying off one worker will decrease profits. Decreasing from 32 to 31 workers loses $10 in revenue, but increasing from 32 to 33 workers gains $8 in revenue, but costs $9 in wages. Since the marginal revenue product curve tells the firm, given a wage, how many workers it should hire, *the marginal revenue product curve is the firm's demand curve for labor.*

The fact that the demand curve for labor is downward-sloping means that as more workers are hired, workers' marginal product falls. This might tempt you to think that the last worker hired is inherently less productive than the first worker hired. But that simply can't be because, by assumption, the workers are identical. Thus, the marginal product of any worker must be identical to the marginal product of any other worker, given that a specified number of workers are working. What the falling marginal product means is that *when 30 rather than 25 workers are working,* the marginal product of any one of those 30 workers is less than the marginal product of any one of 25 of those workers when only 25 are working. When the other inputs are constant, hiring an additional worker lowers the marginal product not only of the last worker but also of any of the other workers.

To understand what's going on here, you must remember that when marginal product is calculated, all other inputs are held constant—so if a firm hires another worker, that worker will have to share machines or tools with other workers. When you share tools, you start running into significant bottlenecks, which cause production to fall. That's why the marginal product of workers goes down when a new worker is hired. This assumption that all other factors of production are held constant is an important one. If all other factors of production are increased, it is not at all clear that workers' productivity will fall as output increases.

Why does a firm hire another worker if doing so will lead to a fall in other workers' productivity and, possibly, a fall in the average productivity of all workers? Because the firm is interested in total profit, not productivity. As long as hiring an extra worker increases revenue by more than the worker costs, the firm's total profit increases. A profit-maximizing firm would be crazy not to hire another worker, even if by doing so it lowers the marginal product of the workers.

The economic model of labor markets assumes that marginal productivities can be determined relatively easily. In reality they can't. They require guesses and estimates that are often influenced by a worker's interaction with the person doing the guessing and estimating. Thus, social interaction plays a role in determining wages. If you get along with the manager, his estimate of your marginal productivity is likely to be higher than if you don't. And for some reason, managers' estimates of their own marginal productivity tend to be high. In part because of difficulties in estimating marginal productivities, actual pay can often differ substantially from marginal productivities.

Factors Affecting the Demand for Labor

There are many technical issues that determine how the demand for products is translated through firms into a demand for labor (and other factors of production), but we need not go into them in detail. I will, however, state three general principles:

1. Changes in the demand for a firm's product will be reflected in changes in its demand for labor.
2. The structure of a firm plays an important role in determining its demand for labor.
3. A change in the other factors of production that a firm uses will change its demand for labor.

Let's consider each of these principles in turn.

Changes in the Firm's Demand

The first principle is almost self-evident. An increase in the demand for a product leads to an increase in demand for the laborers who produce that product. The increase in demand pushes the price up, raising the marginal revenue product of labor (which, you'll remember, for a competitive firm is the price of the firm's product times the marginal physical product of labor).

The implications of this first principle, however, are not so self-evident. Often people think of firms' interests and workers' interests as being counter to one another, but this principle tells us that in many ways they are not. What benefits the firm also benefits its workers. Their interests are in conflict only when it comes to deciding how to divide up the total revenues among the owners of the firm, the workers, and the other inputs. Thus, it's not uncommon to see a firm and its workers fighting each other at the bargaining table, but also working together to prevent imports that might compete with the firm's product or to support laws that may benefit the firm.

An example of such cooperation occurred when union workers at a solar energy firm helped fight for an extension of government subsidies for solar energy. Why? Because their contract included a clause that if the solar energy subsidy bill passed, the union workers' wages would be significantly higher than if it didn't. This cooperation between workers and firms has led some economists to treat firms and workers as a single entity, out to get as much as they can as a group. These economists argue that it isn't helpful to separate out factor markets and goods markets. They argue that bargaining power models, which combine factor and goods markets, are the best way to analyze at what level wages will be set. In other words, the cost of labor to a firm should be modeled as if it is determined at the same time that its price and profitability are determined, not separately.

The Structure of the Firm and Its Demand for Labor

The way in which the demand for products is translated into a demand for labor is determined by the structure of the firm. For example, let's consider the difference between a monopolistic industry and a competitive industry. For both, the decision about whether to hire is based on whether the wage is below or above the marginal revenue product. But the firms that make up the two industries calculate their marginal revenue products differently.

The price of a competitive firm's output remains constant regardless of how many units it sells. Thus, its marginal revenue product equals the value of the marginal product. To calculate its marginal revenue product we simply multiply the price of the firm's product by the worker's marginal physical product. For a competitive firm:

Marginal revenue product of a worker =

Value of the worker's marginal product =

MPP × Price of product

The price of a monopolist's product decreases as more units are sold since the monopolist faces a downward-sloping demand curve. The monopolist takes that into account. That's why it focuses on marginal revenue rather than price. As it hires more labor and produces more output, the price it charges for its product will fall. Thus, for a monopolist:

Marginal revenue product of a worker =

MPP × Marginal revenue

Since a monopolist's marginal revenue is always less than price, a monopolist industry will always hire fewer workers than a comparable competitive industry, which is consistent with the result we discussed in the chapter on monopoly: that a monopolistic industry will always produce less than a competitive industry, other things equal.

To ensure that you understand the principle, let's consider the example in Table A17-1, a table of prices, wages,

TABLE A17-1 The Effect of Monopoly and Firm Structure on the Demand for Labor

1 Number of Workers	2 Wage	3 Price P	4 Marginal Revenue (Monopolist) MR	5 Marginal Physical Product MPP	6 Marginal Revenue Product Competitive (MPP × P)	7 Marginal Revenue Product Monopolist (MPP × MR)
5	$2.85	$1.00	$.75	5	$5.00	$3.75
6	2.85	.95	.65	3	2.85	1.95
7	2.85	.90	.55	1	.90	.55

marginal revenues, marginal physical products, and marginal revenue products for a firm in a competitive industry and a monopolistic industry.

A firm in a competitive industry will hire up to the point where the wage equals $MPP \times P$ (columns 5 × 3). This occurs at 6 workers. Hiring either fewer or more workers would mean a loss in profits for a firm in a competitive industry.

Now let's compare the competitive industry with an equivalent monopolistic industry. Whereas the firm in the competitive industry did not take into account the effect an increase in output would have on prices, the monopolist will. It takes into account the fact that to sell the additional output of an additional worker, it must lower the price of the good. The relevant marginal revenue product for the monopolist appears in column 7. At 6 workers, the worker's wage rate of $2.85 exceeds the worker's marginal revenue product of $1.95, which means that the monopolist would hire fewer than 6 workers—5 full-time workers and 1 part-time worker.

As a second example of how the nature of firms affects the translation of demand for products into demand for labor, consider what would happen if workers rather than independent profit-maximizing owners controlled the firms. You saw before that whenever another worker is hired, other inputs constant, the marginal physical product of all similar workers falls. That can contribute to a reduction in existing workers' wages. The profit-maximizing firm doesn't take into account that effect on existing workers' wages. It wants to hold its costs down. If existing workers are making the decisions about hiring, they'll take that wage decline into account. If they believe that hiring more workers will lower their own wage, they have an incentive to see that new workers aren't hired. Thus, like the monopolist, a worker-controlled firm will hire fewer workers than a competitive profit-maximizing firm.

There aren't many worker-controlled firms in the United States, but a number of firms include existing workers' welfare in their decision processes. Moreover, with the growth of the team concept, in which workers are seen as part of a team with managers, existing workers' input into managerial decision making is increasing. In many U.S. firms, workers have some say in whether additional workers will be hired and at what wage they will be hired. Other firms have an implicit understanding or a written contract with existing workers that restricts hiring and firing decisions.

The top five companies to work for based on salary, perks, and fun in 2012 were:

1. Google.
2. Boston Consulting Group.
3. SAS Institute.
4. Wegmans Food Markets.
5. Edward Jones.

Among the reasons Google is on the list is its climbing wall and free laundry. (And its large number of options with a rising stock price.)

Why do firms consider workers' welfare? They do so to be seen as "good employers," which makes it easier for them to hire in the future. Given the strong social and legal limitations on firms' hiring and firing decisions, one cannot simply apply marginal productivity theory to the real world. One must first understand the institutional and legal structures of the labor market. However, the existence of these other forces doesn't mean that the economic forces represented by marginal productivity don't exist. Rather, it means that firms struggle to find a wage policy that accommodates both economic and social forces in their wage-setting process. For example, in 2011 the United Autoworkers Union negotiated multitier wage contracts with auto companies. The companies continued to pay their existing workers a higher wage, but paid new workers a lower wage, even though old and new workers were doing identical jobs. These multitier wage contracts were the result of the interactions of the social and market forces.

Changes in Other Factors of Production

A third principle determining the derived demand for labor is the amount of other factors of production that the firm has. Given a technology, an increase in other factors of production will increase the marginal physical product of existing workers. For example, let's say that a firm buys more machines so that each worker has more machines with which to work. The workers' marginal physical product increases, and the cost per unit of output for the firm decreases. The net effect on the demand for labor is unclear; it depends on how much the firm increases output, how much the firm's price is affected, and how easily one type of input can be substituted for another—or whether it must be used in conjunction with others.

While we can't say what the final effect on demand will be, we can determine the firm's **cost minimization condition**—*where the ratio of marginal product to the price of an input is equal for all inputs.*[1] When a firm is

---

[1]This condition was explicitly discussed in terms of isocost/isoquant analysis in the appendix to Chapter 12.

using resources as efficiently as possible, and hence is minimizing costs, the marginal product of each factor of production divided by the price of that factor must equal that of all the other factors. Specifically, the *cost minimization condition* is

$$\frac{MP_l}{w} = \frac{MP_m}{P_m} = \frac{MP_x}{P_x}$$

where

> w = Wage rate
>
> l = Labor
>
> m = Machines
>
> x = Any other input

If this cost minimization condition is not met, the firm could hire more of the input with the higher marginal product relative to price, and less of other inputs, and produce the same amount of output at a lower cost.

Let's consider a numerical example. Say the marginal product of labor is 20 and the wage is $4, while the marginal product of machines is 30 and the rental price of machines is $4. You're called in to advise the firm. You say, "Fire one worker, which will decrease output by 20 and save $4; spend that $4 on machines, which will increase output by 30." Output has increased by 10 while costs have remained constant. As long as the marginal products divided by the prices of the various inputs are unequal, you can make such recommendations to lower cost.

Conclusion

Changes in these factors make demand for labor shift around a lot. This shifting introduces uncertainty into people's lives and into the economic system. Often people attempt to build up institutional barriers to reduce uncertainty—through either social or political forces. Thus, labor markets function under an enormous volume of regulations and rules. We need to remember that while economic factors often lurk behind the scenes to determine pay and hiring decisions, these are often only part of the picture.

Key Terms

cost minimization
    condition *(382)*
derived demand curve
    for labor *(380)*

labor productivity *(379)*
marginal physical
    product *(MPP) (378)*

marginal revenue product
    (MRP) (378)

value of marginal
    product *(VMP) (378)*

Questions and Exercises

1. Using the information in Figure A17-1, answer the following questions:
   a. If the market wage were $7 an hour, how many workers would the firm hire?
   b. If the price of the firm's product fell to $1, how would your answer to *a* change?

2. If firms were controlled by workers, would they likely hire more or fewer workers? Why?

3. In the 1980s and the 1990s farmers switched from small square bales, which they hired students on summer break to stack for them, to large round bales, which can be handled almost entirely by machines. What is the likely reason for the switch?

4. Should teachers be worried about the introduction of computer- and video-based teaching systems? Why or why not?

5. A competitive firm gets $3 per widget. A worker's average product is 4 and marginal product is 3. What is the maximum the firm should pay the worker?

6. How would your answer to Question 5 change if the firm were a monopolist?

7. Fill in the following table for a competitive firm that has a $2 price for its goods.

Number of Workers	TP	MPP	AP	MRP
1	10		___	
2	19	___		___
3	___	8	___	___
4	___		8.5	___
5	___	___	___	$12

8. Your manager comes in with three sets of proposals for a new production process. Each process uses three inputs: land, labor, and capital. Under proposal *A*, the firm would be producing an output where the *MPP* of land is 30, labor is 42, and capital is 36. Under proposal *B*, at the output produced the *MPP* would be 20 for land, 35 for labor, and 96 for capital. Under proposal *C*, the *MPP* would be 40 for land, 56 for labor, and 36 for capital. Inputs' cost per hour is $5 for land, $7 for labor, and $6 for capital.
   a. Which proposal would you adopt?
   b. If the price of labor rises to $14, how will your answer change?

Nonwage and Asset Income: Rents, Profits, and Interest

> *The first man to fence in a piece of land, saying "This is mine," and who found people simple enough to believe him, was the real founder of civil society.*
>
> —Jean-Jacques Rousseau

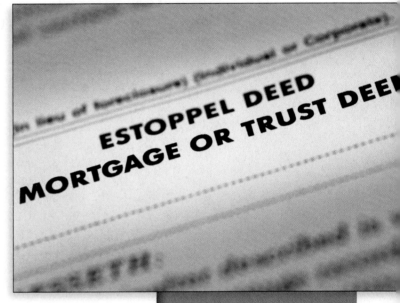

This web chapter can be found at:
www.mhhe.com/colander9e

After reading this chapter, you should be able to:

LO17W-1 Distinguish rent from other types of income and explain the relationship between rent seeking and property rights.

LO17W-2 Define profit and explain its relationship to entrepreneurship.

LO17W-3 Define *interest* and demonstrate how it is used in determining present value.

LO17W-4 Explain the marginal productivity theory of income distribution.

...o Gets What? The Distribution of Income

> *"God must love the poor," said Lincoln, "or he wouldn't have made so many of them." He must love the rich, or he wouldn't divide so much mazuma among so few of them.*
>
> —H. L. Mencken

After reading this chapter, you should be able to:

LO18-1 Explain how income, wealth, and poverty are measured, and how their real-world measures changed over time.

LO18-2 Summarize the socio-economic tensions that high income and wealth inequalities can cause.

LO18-3 Explain why there are so many philosophical debates about equality and fairness, and summarize some of them.

LO18-4 Discuss the practical and theoretical problems of redistributing income.

In 2011, John Hammergren, CEO of McKesson, earned $131 million (base pay plus stock options); that's about $2.5 million per week. Assuming he worked 70 hours per week (you have to work hard to earn that kind of money), that's more than $36,000 per hour.

Today, the average family doctor earns $190,000 per year; that's $3,654 per week. Assuming she works 70 hours per week (she's conscientious, makes house calls, and spends time with her hospitalized patients), that's $52 per hour.

Joe Smith, a cashier in a fast-food restaurant, earns $8 per hour. But to earn enough for his family to be able to eat, he works a lot of overtime, for which he is paid time-and-a-half, or $12 per hour. So he makes about $35,000 per year, or $680 per week, by working 70 hours per week.

Minh Nguyen, a peasant in Vietnam, earns $250 a year; that's $4.80 per week. Assuming he works 70 hours per week (you have to work hard when you are truly poor just to keep from starving), that's 7 cents per hour.

Are such major differences typical of how income is distributed among people in general? Are such differences fair? And if they're unfair, what can be done about them? This chapter addresses such issues. (I should warn you, however: If you're looking for answers, this chapter won't provide them; it will simply make the assumptions on both sides clear.)

The issues addressed in these questions play a fundamentally important role in policy debates today. The reason why is that in the last 20 years the income distribution in the United States has changed considerably. Many formerly middle-income people have moved into the upper-income levels; their wealth and their control of real assets have grown considerably. But simultaneously, lower-income people's income has stagnated or fallen. This change is bringing income distribution issues to center stage in modern policy debates.

In 2006, the housing market, in which many middle-class people had invested a large portion of their wealth, crashed, with prices falling almost 30 percent nationwide and more than 50 percent in some regions. Since most middle-class people had borrowed significant amounts to buy their house, they were highly leveraged—which meant that for many of them the value of their house was less than what they owed on it. Their wealth was wiped out. Combined with a serious recession in which many people lost jobs and could not afford their mortgage payments, this meant that the wealth distribution became even more unequal. The suffering of those who lost their jobs, and lost their wealth, contrasted with the high incomes of Wall Street executives and bankers—many working for the same firms that had been bailed out earlier by the government in the belief that if they went under, the entire economy would collapse—led to what were called "Occupy Wall Street" demonstrations that spread throughout the United States.

Measuring the Distribution of Income, Wealth, and Poverty

There are several different ways to look at income distribution. In the 1800s, economists were concerned with how income was divided among the owners of businesses (for whom profits were the source of income), the owners of land (who received rent), and workers (who earned wages). That concern reflected the relatively sharp distinctions among social classes that existed in capitalist societies at that time. Landowners, workers, and owners of businesses were separate groups, and few individuals moved from one group to another.

Time has changed that. Today workers, through their pension plans and investments in financial institutions, are owners of over 50 percent of all the shares issued on the New York Stock Exchange. Landowners as a group receive a relatively small portion of total income. Companies are run not by capitalists, but by managers who are, in a sense, workers. In short, the social lines have blurred.

This blurring of the lines between social classes doesn't mean that we can forget the question "Who gets what?" It simply means that our interest in who gets what has a different focus. We no longer focus on classification of income by source. Instead we look at how total income is distributed among income groups. How much income do the top 5 percent get? How much do the top 15 percent get? How much do the bottom 10 percent get? Share distribution of income is *the relative division of total income among income groups.*

The share distribution of income is the relative division of total income among income groups.

A second distributional issue economists are concerned with is the socioeconomic distribution of income (*the allocation of income among relevant socioeconomic groupings*). How much do blacks get relative to whites? How much do the old get compared to the young? How much do women get compared to men?

The socioeconomic distribution of income is the relative division or allocation of total income among relevant socioeconomic groups.

The Lorenz Curve

To get a sense of the distribution of income in the United States consider Figure 18-1. It ranks people by their income and tells how much the richest 20 percent (a quintile) and the poorest 20 percent receive. For example, the poorest 20 percent might get 5 percent of the income and the richest 20 percent might get 40 percent. In it you can see that the 20 percent of Americans receiving the lowest level of income got 3.2 percent of the total income. The top 20 percent of Americans received 51.1 percent of the total income. The ratio of the income of the top 20 percent compared to the income of the bottom 20 percent was about 15:1.

The same information can be seen graphically in what is called a **Lorenz curve**—*a geometric representation of the share distribution of income among families in a given*

A Lorenz curve is a geometric representation of the share distribution of income among families in a given country at a given time.

FIGURE 18-1 (A AND B) **A Lorenz Curve of U.S. Income**

If income were perfectly equally distributed, the Lorenz curve would be a diagonal line. In (**b**) we see the U.S. Lorenz curve based on the numbers in (**a**) compared to a Lorenz curve reflecting a perfectly equal distribution of income.

Source: *Current Population Reports*, U.S. Bureau of the Census, 2012 (www.census.gov).

Income Quintile	Percentage of Total Family Income	Cumulative Percentage of Total Family Income
Lowest fifth	3.2%	3.2%
Second fifth	8.4	11.6
Third fifth	14.3	25.9
Fourth fifth	23.0	48.9
Highest fifth	51.1	100.0

(a)

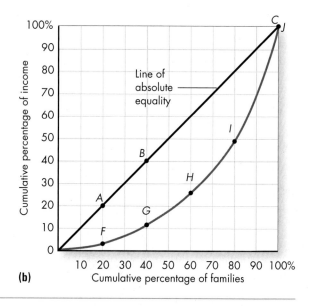

(b)

Q-1 When drawing a Lorenz curve, what do you put on the two axes?

country at a given time. The Lorenz curve measures the cumulative percentage of *families* on the horizontal axis, arranged from poorest to richest, and the cumulative percentage of *family income* on the vertical axis. Since the figure presents cumulative percentages (all of the families with income below a certain level), both axes start at zero and end at 100 percent.

A perfectly equal distribution of income would be represented by a diagonal line like the one in Figure 18-1(b). That is, the poorest 20 percent of the families would have 20 percent of the total income (point *A*); the poorest 40 percent of the families would have 40 percent of the income (point *B*); and 100 percent of the families would have 100 percent of the income (point *C*). An unequal distribution of income is represented by a Lorenz curve that's below the diagonal line. All real-world Lorenz curves are below the diagonal because in the real world income is always distributed unequally.

The blue line in Figure 18-1(b) represents a Lorenz curve of the U.S. income distribution presented in Figure 18-1(a)'s table. From Figure 18-1(a) you know that, in 2011, the bottom 20 percent of the families in the United States received 3.2 percent of the income. Point *F* in Figure 18-1(b) represents that combination of percentages (20 percent and 3.2 percent). To find what the bottom 40 percent received, we must add the income percentage of the bottom 20 percent and the income percentage of the next 20 percent. Doing so gives us 11.6 percent (3.2 plus 8.4 percent from column 2 of Figure 18-1(a)). Point *G* in Figure 18-1(b) represents the combination of percentages (40 percent and 11.6 percent). Continuing this process for points *H, I,* and *C,* you get a Lorenz curve that shows the share distribution of income in the United States in 2011.

U.S. Income Distribution over Time

Lorenz curves are most useful in visual comparisons of income distribution over time and between countries. Figure 18-2 presents Lorenz curves for the United States in 1929, 1970, and 2011. They show that from 1929 to 1970 the share distribution of

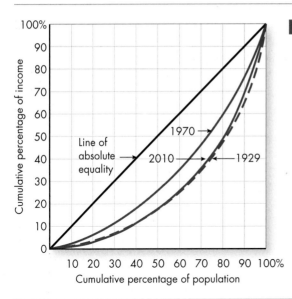

FIGURE 18-2 **Lorenz Curves for the United States: 1929, 1970, and 2011**

The amount of inequality of income distribution has fluctuated in the United States. Until about 1970, it decreased; since then it has increased.

Source: *Current Population Reports*, U.S. Bureau of the Census, 2012 (www.census.gov).

income became more equal. (The curve for 1970 is closer to being a diagonal line than the curve for 1929.) Income of the bottom fifth of families rose by a much higher proportion than did income of the top fifth. That was a continuation of a trend that had begun in the 1920s. In the 1970s that trend stopped and began to reverse. As you can see, from 1970 to 2011 income distribution became less equal. (The curve for 2011 is further from being diagonal than is the curve for 1970.) The income of the bottom fifth of families fell by over 10 percent, while the income of the top fifth rose significantly.

Important reasons for the initial increase in equality are the redistribution measures instituted by the U.S. government between the 1930s and the 1970s, including welfare programs, unemployment insurance, Social Security, progressive taxation (taxation of higher income at higher rates, lower income at lower rates), and improved macroeconomic performance of the economy.

The trend back toward greater inequality starting in the 1970s was caused by a fall in the real income of the poor, when their wage increases didn't keep up with price increases. Part of the reason was globalization; another part is that taxes have become less progressive, government funding for social programs has fallen, and the wages of unskilled and medium-skilled workers have been squeezed by an influx of immigrants into the United States who are willing to work for low wages.

While wages have fluctuated with the business cycle since then, the trend toward greater inequality has continued until about 2011 when the economic downturn reduced income for the rich more than it did for the poor.

The distribution of income over time is not only affected by business cycles, government policy, and competitive pressures; it is also affected by demographic and technological factors. Many families have relatively low income in their early years, relatively higher income in their middle years, and then relatively low income again in their retirement years. The Lorenz curve reflects these differences, so even if lifetime income were equally distributed, income in any one year would not be. Moreover, when the percentages of these groups change, the Lorenz curve will change. For example, as the baby-boom generation retires and no longer works, collective income will fall. That decline in overall income relative to the income of the smaller number of working families will affect the Lorenz curve.

From 1929 to 1970, income inequality in the United States decreased. From 1970 to 2011, it increased.

The effect of technology is a bit different; that effect is easiest to convey with an example. Before the development of radio, TV, records, tapes, CDs, and MP3 players, the number of people who could listen to a performer was limited by how many people could fit in a concert hall. Without recordings or broadcasting to satisfy the demand for entertainment, that meant lots of local singers could earn a decent, but not phenomenal, wage. As recording, broadcasting, and transportation technology progressed, the number of people who could listen to a performance was nearly unlimited and "superstars" were born. The "almost superstars" lost out and were destined to sing for low wages at weddings, bar mitzvah parties, and church recitals, while the superstars became multi-millionaires. Similar changes occurred in sports and other performance activities. The point of the example is that technology can significantly influence income distribution. University of Chicago economist Kevin Murphy argues that as global competition continues to grow, and as telecommunications networks expand, the pressure for income inequality to increase will continue.

> *Technology has played a role in increasing income inequality.*

Defining Poverty

Much of the government's concern with income distribution has centered on the poorest group—those in poverty. Defining poverty is not easy. Do we want to define it as an absolute amount of real income that does not change over time? If poverty were defined as an *absolute* amount of real income, few in the United States would be in poverty today; most of today's poor have higher real incomes than did the middle class 50 or 60 years ago. Or do we want to define it as a *relative* concept that rises as the average income in the society rises? For example, anyone with an income of less than one-fifth of the average income could be defined as being in poverty. If that relative concept of poverty were chosen, then the proportion of people classified as poor would always be the same.

> *Poverty can be defined as a relative or absolute concept.*

> **Q-2** Is the U.S. definition of poverty an absolute or a relative definition?

THE OFFICIAL DEFINITION OF POVERTY   The United States uses a definition of poverty that is a combination of a relative and an absolute measure. Thus, it satisfies neither those who favor an absolute measure nor those who favor a relative measure, and there are calls to increase and calls to decrease the **poverty threshold**—*the income below which a family is considered to live in poverty*. The official definition of poverty is the following:

> A family is in poverty if its income is equal to or less than three times an average family's minimum food expenditures as calculated by the U.S. Department of Agriculture.

> *Poverty is defined by the U.S. government as having an income equal to or less than three times an average family's minimum food expenditures as calculated by the U.S. Department of Agriculture.*

The minimum weekly food budget includes 4 eggs, 1½ pounds of meat, 3 pounds of potatoes, about 4 pounds of vegetables, and other foods; the cost is about $37 per person per week. By the latest calculations, that means that for a family of four, the poverty line is $23,021.

As Table 18-1 shows, using the official poverty measure, the number of people in poverty decreased in the 1960s and then began increasing in the 1970s. In 2011, 46.2 million Americans lived below the poverty threshold.

DEBATES ABOUT THE DEFINITION OF POVERTY   The minimum food budget used to determine the poverty line was determined in the 1960s and has not been recalculated to account for rising standards of living. Thus, it is in principle an absolute measure. Starting in 1969, however, the amount needed to buy that food is adjusted by the rate of inflation rather than by the rise in the price of the originally selected foods. Since food prices have risen by less than the rise in the general price level, the poverty

TABLE 18-1	Number and Percentage of Persons in Poverty

	Number of People (in millions)	Percentage of Population	Poverty Income of Family of 4* (in current dollars)
1960	39.9	22.2%	$ 3,022
1970	24.4	12.6	3,986
1980	29.3	13.0	8,414
1990	33.6	13.5	13,359
2000	31.6	11.3	17,603
2005	37.0	12.6	19,971
2006	36.5	12.3	20,614
2007	37.3	12.5	21,203
2008	39.8	13.2	22,025
2009	43.6	14.3	21,954
2010	46.2	15.1	22,314
2011	46.2	15.0	23,021

*Family of 4 with 2 related children.

Source: *Current Population Reports,* U.S. Bureau of the Census, 2012 (www.census.gov).

threshold has gone up by more than it would have had food prices been used. That means the definition includes significant aspects of relativity; had a purely absolute measure been used, the poverty rate would be considerably lower.

Those who favor a relative measure of poverty argue that our current poverty measure is too low. They point out that food is now closer to one-seventh of a family's total budget, so that food is no longer a good basis for determining the poverty level. Households spend much more now on housing, utilities, health care, and expenses related to work. A poverty threshold that takes different expenses into account raises the poverty threshold and raises the poverty rate from about 15 percent to 23 percent, with millions more people on the poverty roll.

There are arguments that the poverty line is both too high and too low.

Those who favor an absolute measure of poverty argue that the current measure is too high. They point out that U.S. poverty figures do not include in-kind (noncash) transfers such as food stamps and housing assistance. Nor does the current poverty measure take into account underreporting of income, or the savings people have. (Many elderly people may have low incomes but significant wealth, which they could choose to spend.) If we make adjustments for in-kind transfers and underreporting of income, the official number of people in poverty decreases to about 60 percent of the official number. University of Texas economist Daniel Slesnick takes it further and points out that, since the price of food has increased at less than the rate of inflation, a much lower level of expenditures than the amount used to calculate the poverty threshold will provide a "nutritionally adequate diet." Slesnick calculated that when one takes the decrease in the relative price of food into account, the number of people in poverty would have fallen to one-seventh the official count.

Like most economic statistics, poverty statistics should be used with care.

The moral of this debate: Like most economic statistics, poverty statistics should be used with care.

THE COSTS OF POVERTY AND SOCIAL MOBILITY

People who favor policies aimed at achieving equality of income argue that poverty brings significant costs to society. One is that society suffers when some of its people are in poverty, just as the

Web Note 18.1
Poverty and Achievement

entire family suffers when one member doesn't have enough to eat. Most people derive pleasure from knowing that others are not in poverty.

Another cost of poverty is that it increases incentives for crime. People with little income have little to lose. As people's incomes increase they have more to lose by committing crimes, and therefore fewer crimes are committed. Consistent with this argument, the crime rate has largely declined in the 1990s and early 2000s, as the economy grew. When the economy entered a severe recession in 2008, crime rates were expected to rise. They didn't. Instead they fell, bringing into question the importance of poverty for crime.

While crime rates didn't rise, general dissatisfaction with the income distribution did. The sense of fairness that previously existed is giving way to increasing concern about the lack of fairness. Some observers argued that an economic system that led to such large inequalities in income, and left millions without a job or source of income, was unfair. Their complaints often concerned a lack of opportunity for many, and a sense of entitlement of a few. Our society was founded on the belief that if one worked hard one would be rewarded with increasing income and better job prospects for one's children than one's parents had. That belief is being tested, with continued high unemployment and the pressure of globalization holding down wages of jobs in the tradable sectors.

Whereas before, most people accepted that individuals who worked hard could escape poverty, and individuals who didn't work hard would end up, or remain, in poverty. While everyone knew that the poor had it harder, and the rich easier, the United States was seen as a meritocracy, where hard work and ability were key to advancing both economically and socially. In the 1960s and 1970s, studies found that the United States had significant upward and downward mobility, confirming this belief. Recent studies, however, have questioned this view.

Specifically, a recent study by economist Bernt Bratsberg and his colleagues discovered that income mobility has significantly declined in the United States, and that now, the United States has less mobility than Europe. They determined this by ranking countries on a scale of zero to one, with zero meaning perfect mobility (a child's income bears no relation to its parent's income) and one meaning no mobility (a child's income is identical to its parent's income). They found that, for sons, Sweden scored a .2, Britain scored a .36, and the United States scored a .54, suggesting that the United States had only about half as much social mobility as did Sweden and Britain. The situation was worse at the bottom; children born to a family in the bottom fifth of the U.S. income distribution were the least likely to move up. Other studies have confirmed this finding; it is harder for people today to surpass their parents on the income scale than it was a generation ago, and it is much harder for someone in the United States compared to someone in Europe to move up the income scale.

International Dimensions of Income Inequality

Web Note 18.2
International Income
Distribution Data

When considering income distribution, we usually are looking at conditions within a single country. For example, an American among the richest 5 percent of the U.S. population earns approximately 30 times what an American who is among the poorest 20 percent of the American people gets.

There are other ways to look at income. We might judge income inequality in the United States relative to income inequality in other countries. Is the U.S. distribution of income more or less equal than another country's? We could also look at how income is distributed among countries. Even if income is relatively equally distributed within countries, it may be unequally distributed among countries.

The Gini Coefficient

A second measure economists use to talk about the degree of income inequality is the Gini coefficient of inequality. The Gini coefficient is derived from the Lorenz curve by comparing the area between (1) the Lorenz curve and the diagonal (area A) and (2) the total area of the triangle below the diagonal (areas A and B). That is:

Gini coefficient = Area A/(Areas A + B)

A Gini coefficient of zero would be perfect equality, since area A is 0 if income is perfectly equally distributed. The highest the Gini coefficient can go is 1. So all Gini coefficients must be between 0 and 1. The lower the Gini coefficient, the closer the income distribution is to being equal. The Gini coefficient for the United States was 0.48 in 2011.

The following table gives Gini coefficients for a number of other countries. The Gini coefficients for transitional economies such as the Slovak Republic have risen over the last few years because they are now market economies and their incomes are less equally distributed.

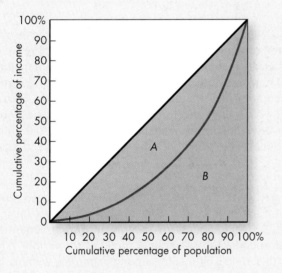

Gini Coefficients for Selected Countries	
Algeria	.353
Bangladesh	.332
Brazil	.519
Canada	.321
Czech Republic	.310
Denmark	.248
Germany	.270
Guatemala	.551
Hungary	.247
Indonesia	.368
Japan	.376
Latvia	.352
Netherlands	.309
Panama	.519
Philippines	.458
Romania	.333
Slovak Republic	.260
South Africa	.650
Thailand	.536
United Kingdom	.340
United States	.477

Source: CIA World Factbook, 2012.

COMPARING INCOME DISTRIBUTION ACROSS COUNTRIES Figure 18-3 gives us a sense of how the distribution of income in the United States compares to that in other countries. We see that the United States has significantly more income inequality than Sweden, but somewhat less than Brazil (and many other developing and newly industrialized countries).

The United States has less income inequality than most developing countries but more income inequality than many developed countries.

An important reason why the United States has more income inequality than Sweden is that Sweden's tax system is more progressive. Until recently (when Sweden's socialist party lost power), the top marginal tax rate on the highest incomes in Sweden was 80 percent, compared to about 35 percent in the United States. Given this difference, it isn't surprising that Sweden has less income inequality.

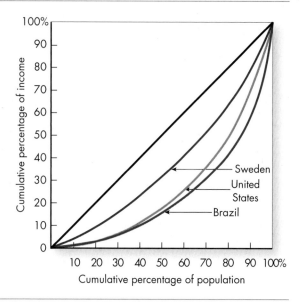

FIGURE 18-3 **U.S. Income Distribution Compared to That of Other Countries**

Among countries of the world, the United States has neither the most equal nor the most unequal distribution of income.

Source: *World Development Report,* The World Bank (www.worldbank.org).

Q-3 How does the income distribution in the United States compare with that in other countries?

INCOME DISTRIBUTION AMONG COUNTRIES   When we consider the distribution of world income, the picture becomes even more unequal than the picture we see within countries. The reason is clear: Income is highly unequally distributed among countries. The average per capita income of the richest countries in the world is more than 100 times the average income of the poorest countries of the world. Thus, a Lorenz curve of world income would show much more inequality than the Lorenz curve for a particular country. Worldwide, income inequality is enormous. A minimum level of income in the United States would be a wealthy person's income in a poor country like Bangladesh.

THE TOTAL AMOUNT OF INCOME IN VARIOUS COUNTRIES   To gain a better picture of income distribution problems, you need to consider not only the division of income but also the total amounts of income in various countries. Figure 18-4 presents per capita income (gross national income) for various countries. Looking at the enormous differences of income among countries, we must ask which is more important: the distribution of income or the absolute level of income. Which would you rather be: one of four members in a family that has an income of $3,000 a year, which places you in the top 10 percent of Bangladesh's income distribution, or one of four members of a family with an income of $12,000 (four times as much), which places you in the bottom 10 percent of the income earners in the United States?

The Distribution of Wealth

In considering equality, two measures are often used: *equality of wealth* and *equality of income.* Because of space limitations, my focus will be on income, but I want to mention wealth. **Wealth** is *the value of the things individuals own less the value of what they owe.* It is a *stock* concept representing the value of assets such as houses, buildings, and machines. For example, a farmer who owns a farm with a net worth of $1 million is wealthy compared to an investment banker with a net worth of $225,000.

Wealth is the value of assets individuals own less the value of what they owe.

FIGURE 18-4   Per Capita Income (Gross National Income) in Various Countries

Income is unequally distributed among the countries of the world. These relative comparisons change considerably over time as exchange rates fluctuate. These estimates are done using the Atlas method, which averages exchange rates over adjacent years. The purchasing power parity estimates would show less inequality.

Source: *World Development Indicators*, 2012 (www.worldbank.org).

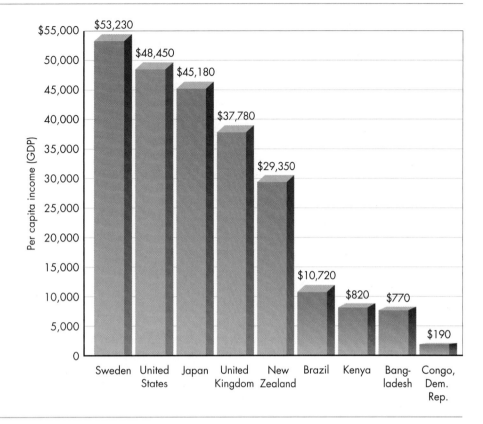

Income is *payments received plus or minus changes in value in a person's assets in a specified time period.* In contrast to wealth, income is a *flow* concept. It's a stream through time. That farmer might have an income of $20,000 a year while the investment banker might have an income of $80,000 a year. The farmer, with $1 million worth of assets, is wealthier than the investment banker, but the investment banker has a higher income.

Income is payments received plus or minus changes in value of a person's assets in a specified time period.

A LORENZ CURVE OF THE DISTRIBUTION OF WEALTH
Figure 18-5 compares the Lorenz curve for wealth in the United States with the Lorenz curve for income in the United States. You can see that wealth in the United States is more unequally distributed than income and that the bottom 40 percent of the U.S. population has close to zero wealth.

In the United States, wealth is significantly more unequally distributed than is income.

HOW MUCH WEALTH DO THE WEALTHY HAVE?
Relative comparisons such as those depicted by Lorenz curves don't give you a sense of how much wealth it takes to be "wealthy." The following numbers provide you with a better sense. Bill Gates, who founded Microsoft and became the richest person in the United States, had a net worth of about $60 billion in 2012. Four of the 15 wealthiest people in the United States were from the Walton family (whose father founded Walmart), each with over $20 billion. Most of us have little chance of joining that group; in fact, most of us have little possibility of becoming one of the top 5 percent of the wealthholders in the United States, which would require total wealth of at least $4 million. Once there was a time when people's ultimate financial goal was to be a millionaire. In the 2000s, the ultimate financial goal for the wealthiest people is to be a billionaire. The millionaire's club is no longer highly exclusive.

Billionaires often lose a billion here, gain a billion there; sometimes they even become multibillionaires. Seldom do they become poor.

The millionaire's club is no longer highly exclusive.

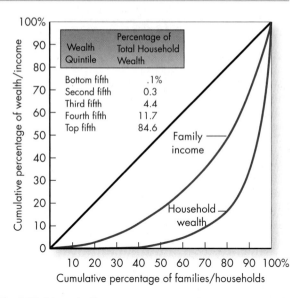

FIGURE 18-5   **Wealth Distribution in the United States and Wealth Compared to Income**

Wealth is much more unequally distributed than income in the United States. In fact, the lowest 40 percent of the population has only .4 percent of the wealth; these people have borrowed nearly as much as they own.

Source: U.S. Bureau of the Census and Edward N. Wolf, New York University (with permission).

Wealth Quintile	Percentage of Total Household Wealth
Bottom fifth	.1%
Second fifth	0.3
Third fifth	4.4
Fourth fifth	11.7
Top fifth	84.6

Of course, people in the club don't always stay there; the club is constantly changing. For example, a number of families who were in the club earlier are no longer in it. Many billionaires lost billions when the world stock market collapsed in 2008 and fell off the list of the world's wealthiest people. Today, some of these people and families might only be multimillionaires.

Socioeconomic Dimensions of Income and Wealth Inequality

The share distribution of inequality is only one of the dimensions that inequality of income and wealth can take. As I mentioned before, the distribution of income according to source of income (wages, rents, and profits) was once considered important. Today's focus is on the distribution of income based on race, ethnic background, geographic region, and other socioeconomic factors such as gender and type of job.

Income Distribution According to Socioeconomic Characteristics

Table 18-2 gives an idea of the distribution of income according to socioeconomic characteristics.

You can see that income differs substantially by type of job, leading some economists to argue that a new professional/nonprofessional class distinction is arising in the United States. Substantial differences also exist between the incomes of women and men, and between whites and blacks.

Income Distribution According to Class

Early economists focused on the distribution of income by wages, profits, and rent because that division corresponded to their class analysis of society. Landowners received rent, capitalists received profit, and workers received wages. Tensions among these classes played an important part in economists' analyses of the economy and policy.

TABLE 18-2 Various Socioeconomic Income Distribution Designations

Median Income, 2011 By Occupational Category	Male	Female
Management	$71,240	$50,804
Business and Financial	63,760	48,724
Health care practitioners	58,708	50,180
Protective service	41,444	31,304
Food preparation	22,308	20,290
Building and grounds cleaning and maintenance	26,104	20,280
Personal care	29,224	21,944
Sales	38,376	31,304
Office and administrative support	34,736	31,908
Farming, fishing, and forestry	23,140	19,292
Construction and extraction	37,336	31,908
Installation, maintenance, and repair	41,964	39,052
Production	33,852	25,220
Transportation and material moving	32,968	25,480

By Age, 2010	Median Individual Income
15–24	$ 9,335
25–34	29,234
35–44	35,918
45–54	35,798
55–64	32,193
Over 65	18,819

By Race, 2010	Median Individual Income
Asian	$65,129
White	55,412
Hispanic origin	38,624
Black	32,229

By Sex	Median Income 1980	1990	2000	2010
Male	$12,530	$20,293	$28,343	$32,137
Female	4,920	10,070	16,063	20,831

Source: *Current Population Reports, Consumer Income,* U.S. Bureau of the Census (www.census.gov).

Even though class divisions by income source have become blurred, other types of socioeconomic classes have taken their place. The United States has a kind of upper class. In fact, a company in the United States publishes the *Social Register,* containing the names and pedigrees of about 25,000 socially prominent people who might be categorized "upper class." Similarly, it is possible to further divide the U.S. population into a middle class and a lower class.

> The United States has socioeconomic classes with some mobility among classes. This is not to say such classes should exist; it is only to say that they do exist.

Class divisions are no longer determined solely by income source. For example, upper-class people do not necessarily receive their income from rent and profits. CEOs of major companies are generally considered upper class, and they receive much of their income as payment for their services. Today we have "upper-class" people who derive their income from wages and "lower-class" people who derive their meager income from profits (usually in the form of pensions, which depend on profits from the investment of pension funds in stocks and bonds). Of course, once people become rich, they earn interest and profits on their wealth as well as income from wages.

THE IMPORTANCE OF THE MIDDLE CLASS What has made the most difference in today's class structure in the United States compared to its class structure in earlier periods and to the structure in today's developing countries is the tremendous growth in the relative size of the middle class. Economists used to see the class structure as a pyramid. From a base composed of a large lower class, the pyramid tapered upward through a medium-sized middle class to a peak occupied by the upper

The class structure in developing countries is a pyramid; in the United States the class structure is more like a pentagon.

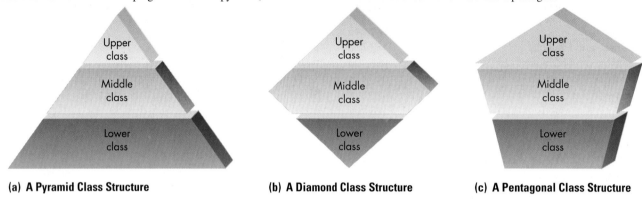

(a) A Pyramid Class Structure   **(b) A Diamond Class Structure**   **(c) A Pentagonal Class Structure**

In the United States, the middle class is the largest class.

class (Figure 18-6(a)). The class structure is still pyramidal in most developing countries. However, in the United States in the 1960s and 1970s, the middle class grew, and the geometric portrayal of the U.S. class structure changed from a pyramid in Figure 18-6(a) to the diamond shape in Figure 18-6(b) with a small upper class, a large middle class, and a small lower class. In the last 20 years, that diamond geometric portrayal has become less appropriate; the middle class itself became split. Some in the middle class have done well and moved into the upper middle class, while others have done poorly, expanding the number at the bottom.

If your job was in a tradable sector such as manufacturing, or was a service that could be outsourced, globalization pushed your wage down or left you unemployed. Those in nontradable sectors such as government workers or semi-skilled service workers such as teachers, whose jobs could not be outsourced or easily replaced with immigrant workers, remained in the middle class. This process, which is continuing, is expanding the lower class to include many formerly in the middle class. Exacerbating the division between the rich and the poor is that those in the lower class are less likely to move up the ladder into the middle class and those in the upper class are also less likely to move down the ladder into the middle class, splitting the upper from the lower class.

Class structure today in the United States has a pentagonal shape.

Today, the pentagonal shape shown in Figure 18-6(c) seems a more appropriate description of the class structure in the United States. The middle class is still relatively large, but the bottom, what some have described as an underclass—a group of people at the bottom who are just getting along and, while they may temporarily escape poverty, are always on the edge of the poverty line—has gotten larger too. This bottom group includes a disproportionate percentage of blacks, and has been expanded by a significant number of undocumented immigrants. These, combined with those formerly in the middle class who lost their "middle-class" jobs, have expanded the bottom group. And the difference is significant. Median wealth of white households, for example, is about 20 times that of black and Hispanic households. The typical Hispanic and black household has about $6,000 in wealth, whereas the typical white family has over $100,000. With the decline of social mobility in the United States, this group of people and their children has only a slight chance of entering into the middle class.

Whatever the best geometric portrayal of the class system, the increase in the relative size of the middle class in developed countries has significantly blurred the distinction between capitalists and workers. In early capitalist society, the distributional fight (the fight over relative income shares) was largely between workers and capitalists. In modern market-based societies, the distributional fight is among various types of individuals. Union workers are pitted against nonunion workers; salaried workers are pitted against workers paid by the hour; government workers are pitted against manufacturing workers. The old are pitted against the young; women are pitted against men; blacks are pitted against Hispanics and Asians, and all three groups are pitted against whites. Such a system exacerbates what is sometimes called class warfare. In the past few years blacks and Hispanics have faced more job losses and housing foreclosures than whites. Nevertheless, according to Pew Research, blacks and Hispanics were more optimistic about their future prospects than whites.

DISTRIBUTIONAL QUESTIONS AND TENSIONS IN SOCIETY   While mainstream economists tend to focus on the share distribution of income, nonmainstream economists tend to emphasize class and group structures in their analysis. Radical economists emphasize the control that the upper class has over the decision process and the political process. Libertarian economists emphasize the role of special interests of all types in shaping government policy. Both radical and libertarian analyses bring out the tensions among classes in society much better than does the mainstream, classless analysis.

When people identify with a particular class or group, they will often work to further the interests of that class or group. They also generally have stronger feelings about inequalities among classes or groups than when they lack that sense of class or group identity. Using a classless analysis means overlooking the implications of class and group solidarity in affecting the tensions in society.

Until recently those tensions showed up every day in political disputes over the tax system, in the quiet fuming of individuals seeing someone else earning more for doing the same job, and in strikes and even riots. Such tensions exist in all countries. In some transitional and developing countries, they break out into the open as armed insurrections or riots over food shortages.

Those tensions have been kept to a minimum in American society. A majority of Americans believe that income distribution is sufficiently fair for them to accept their share more or less contentedly. To remedy the unfairness that does exist, they don't demand that the entire system be replaced. Instead they work for change within the present system. They look to affirmative action laws, comparable worth laws, minimum wage laws, and social welfare programs for any improvement they perceive to be necessary or desirable. There's much debate about whether these government actions have achieved the desired ends, but the process itself reduces tensions and has worked toward maintaining the entire system.

In the past several years individuals on both sides of the political spectrum have become less compromising in their approach. On the right the Tea Party conservatives have called for large cuts in government redistribution programs as part of overall cuts in government. Similarly, on the left, the progressive Occupy movement reflects a discontent about how income distribution is highly skewed toward the top 1 percent and 5 percent of the population.

Income Distribution and Fairness

People's acceptance of the U.S. economic system is based not only on what the distribution of income is but also on what people think it should be and what they consider fair. It is to that question that we now turn. Judgments about whether the distribution of income is fair, or should be changed, are normative ones, based on the values the analyst applies to the situation. Value judgments necessarily underlie all policy prescriptions.

Q-4 How have distributional fights about income changed over time?

Both radical and libertarian analyses bring out the tensions among classes in society much better than does mainstream classless analysis.

Web Note 18.3
Contrasting Analyses

Value judgments necessarily underlie all policy prescriptions.

Philosophical Debates about Equality and Fairness

Depending on one's values, any income distribution can be justified. For example, Friedrich Nietzsche, the 19th-century German philosopher, argued that society's goal should be to support its supermen—its best and brightest. Lesser individuals' duty should be to work for the well-being of these supermen. Bertrand de Juvenal, a 20th-century philosopher, has argued that a high level of income inequality is necessary to sustain the arts, beauty, education, and civilization. He and others say that a world of equally distributed income would be a world without beauty. Even if we don't personally own beautiful, expensive homes, or aren't devoted opera fans, these philosophers argue that our lives are improved because some people do own such homes and because opera performances exist. Inequality creates diversity that enriches the lives of everyone.

Other philosophers disagree strongly. They argue that equality itself is the overriding goal. That view is embodied in the Declaration of Independence: "We hold these truths to be self-evident, that all men are created equal." And for many people the inherent value of equality is not open to question—it is simply self-evident.

Q-5　Is it self-evident that greater equality of income would make the society a better place to live? Why?

Believing that equality is an overriding goal does not necessarily imply that income should be equally distributed. For example, John Rawls (a Harvard University professor who believed that equality is highly desirable and that society's goal should be to maximize the welfare of the least well-off) agreed that to meet that goal some inequality is necessary. Rawls argued that if, in pursuing equality, you actually make the least well-off worse off than they otherwise would have been, then you should not pursue equality any further. For example, say under one policy there would be perfect equality and everyone would receive $10,000 per year. Under another policy, the least well-off person receives $12,000 per year and all others receive $40,000. Rawls argued that the second policy is preferable to the first even though it involves more inequality.

Economists, unlike philosophers, are not concerned about justifying any particular distribution of income. In their objective role, economists limit themselves to explaining the effects that various policies will have on the distribution of income; they let the policy makers judge whether those effects are desirable.

However, in order to judge economic policies, you, in your role as a citizen who elects policy makers, must make certain judgments about income distribution because all real-world economic policies have distribution effects. Accordingly, a brief discussion of income distribution and fairness is in order.

Fairness and Equality

The U.S. population has a strong general tendency to favor equality—equality is generally seen as fair. Most people, including me, share that view. However, in some instances equality of income is not directly related to people's view of fairness. For example, consider this distribution of income between John and Fred:

Q-6　You are dividing a pie among five individuals. What would be a fair distribution of that pie?

John gets $50,000 a year.

Fred gets $12,000 a year.

Think a minute. Is that fair?

The answer I'm hoping for is that you don't yet have enough information to make the decision.

Fairness has many dimensions and it is often difficult to say what is fair and what isn't.

Here's some more information. Say that John gets that $50,000 for holding down three jobs, while Fred gets his $12,000 for sitting around doing nothing. At this point, many of us would argue that it's possible John should be getting even more than $50,000 and Fred should be getting less than $12,000.

What Should Be the Goal of Economic Policy?

Today, most discussions of economic policy focus on a goal of increasing income: Policies that achieve higher income are good; policies that do not are bad. Historically, that has not always been the goal. In the 1800s the economic policy focused on basic goods—distinguishing necessities from luxuries. Only policies that increased basic goods were good; the welfare implications of policies that increased luxuries were much more problematic.

The 1930s marked a major change in how economic policy was conceived. Economics began focusing much more on the utility of all goods, downplaying the distinction between luxuries and basic goods. With this change, the goal of economic policy focused much more on total income, regardless of how that income was divided. The division of goods into necessities and luxuries was seen as adding a normative element to policy that was outside the purview of positive economics.

Recently, Nobel Prize–winning economist Amartya Sen has argued against that utilitarian approach, pointing out that normative elements are unavoidable in policy analysis. He argues that using income as a measure of welfare is not the best approach and has suggested replacing it with a "capabilities" measure. For Sen, the goal of economic policy should be to increase a society's capabilities, which he defines as an individual's freedom within that society to achieve a particular life. For Sen, capabilities are best measured by basic indicators such as life expectancy, literacy, and infant mortality rates—not by income. Poor ratings on such indicators impede people from leading good and happy lives. Sen's work is controversial, but it is important in reminding us that the goals of economic policy should always be kept in mind and that we should not simply accept the goal as being an increase in total income.

But wait! What if we discover that Fred is an invalid and unless his income increases to $15,000 a year he will die? Most of us would change our minds again and argue that Fred deserves more, regardless of how much John works.

But wait! How about if, after further digging, we discover that Fred is an invalid because he squandered his health on alcohol, drugs, and fried foods? In that case some people would likely change their minds again as to whether Fred deserves more.

By now you should have gotten my point. Looking only at a person's income masks many dimensions that most people consider important in making value judgments about fairness.

Three problems in determining whether an equal income distribution is fair are:

1. People don't start from equivalent positions.
2. People's needs differ.
3. People's efforts differ.

Fairness as Equality of Opportunity

When most people talk about believing in equality of income, they often mean they believe in equality of opportunity for comparably endowed individuals to earn income. If equal opportunity of equals leads to inequality of income, then the inequality of income is fair. Unfortunately, there's enormous latitude for debate on what constitutes equal opportunity of equals.

In the real world, needs differ, desires differ, and abilities differ. Should these differences be considered relevant differences in equality? You must answer that question before you can judge any economic policy because to make a judgment on whether an economic policy should or should not be adopted, you must make a judgment about whether a policy's effect on income is fair. In making those judgments, most people rely on their immediate gut reaction. I hope what you have gotten out of the discussion about John and Fred and equality of opportunity is the resolve to be cautious about trusting your gut reactions. The concept of fairness is crucial and complicated, and it deserves deeper consideration than just a gut reaction.

The concept of fairness is crucial and complicated, and it deserves deeper consideration than just a gut reaction.

401

The Problems of Redistributing Income

Let's now say that we have considered all the issues discussed so far in this chapter and have concluded that some redistribution of income from the rich to the poor is necessary if society is to meet our ideal of fairness. How do we go about redistributing income?

First, we must consider what programs exist and what their negative side effects might be. The side effects can be substantial and can subvert the intention of the program so that far less money is available overall for redistribution and inequality is reduced less than we might expect.

Three Important Side Effects of Redistributive Programs

Three side effects of redistribution of income are:

1. The labor/leisure incentive effect.
2. The avoidance and evasion incentive effect.
3. The incentive effect to look more needy than you are.

Three important side effects that economists have found in programs to redistribute income are:

1. A tax may result in people working less (a switch from labor to leisure).
2. People may attempt to avoid or evade taxes, leading to a decrease in measured income.
3. Redistributing money may cause people to make themselves look as if they're more needy than they really are.

All economists believe that people will change their behavior in response to changes in taxation and income redistribution programs. These responses, called *incentive effects of taxation,* are important and must be taken into account in policy making. But economists differ significantly in the size of incentive effects, and empirical evidence doesn't resolve the question. Some economists believe that incentive effects are so high that little taxation for redistribution should take place. They argue that when the rich do well, the total pie is increased so much that the spillover benefits to the poor are greater than the proceeds the poor would get from redistribution. For example, supporters of this view argue that the growth in capitalist economies was made possible by entrepreneurs. Because those entrepreneurs invested in new technology, income in society grew. Moreover, those entrepreneurs paid taxes. The benefits resulting from entrepreneurial action spilled over to the poor, making the poor far better off than any redistribution would. The fact that some of those entrepreneurs became rich is irrelevant because their actions made all society better off.

Q-7 When determining the effects of programs that redistribute income, can one reasonably assume that other things will remain equal?

Other economists believe that there should be significant taxation for redistribution. While they agree that sometimes the incentive effects are substantial, they see the goal of equality overriding these effects.

Politics, Income Redistribution, and Fairness

We began this discussion of income distribution and fairness by assuming that our value judgments should determine the way in which taxes are structured—that if our values lead us to the conclusion that the poor deserved more income, we could institute policies that would get more to the poor. Reality doesn't necessarily work that way. Often politics, not value judgments, plays a central role in determining what taxes individuals will pay. The group that can deliver the most votes will elect lawmakers who will enact tax policies that benefit that group at the expense of groups with fewer votes.

Often politics, not value judgments, plays a central role in determining what taxes an individual will pay.

On the surface, the democratic system of one person/one vote would seem to suggest that the politics of redistribution would favor the poor, but it doesn't. One would expect that the poor would use their votes to make sure income was redistributed to them from the rich. Why don't they? The answer is complicated.

One reason is that many of the poor don't vote because they assume that one vote won't make much difference. As a result, poor people's total voting strength is reduced.

A second reason is that the poor aren't seen by most politicians as a solid voting bloc. There's no organization of the poor that can deliver votes to politicians. A third reason is that those poor people who do vote often cast their votes with other issues in mind. An anti-income-redistribution candidate might have a strong view on abortion as well, and for many the abortion view is the one that decides their vote.

A fourth reason is that elections require financing. Much of that financing comes from the rich. The money is used for advertising and publicity aimed at convincing the poor that it's actually in their best interests to vote for a person who supports the rich. People are often influenced by that kind of biased publicity.

Reasonable-sounding arguments can be made to support just about any position, and the rich have the means to see that the arguments supporting their positions get the publicity. Of course, some of their arguments are also correct. The issues are usually sufficiently complicated that a trained economist must study them for a long time to determine which arguments make sense.

Income Redistribution Policies

The preceding discussion should have provided you with a general sense of the difficulty of redistributing income. Let's now consider briefly how income redistribution policies and programs have worked in the real world. In considering this, it is helpful to keep in mind that government has two direct methods and one indirect method to redistribute income. The direct methods are (1) *taxation* (policies that tax the rich more than the poor) and (2) *expenditures* (programs that help the poor more than the rich). The indirect method involves establishing and protecting property rights. Let's first consider direct methods.

Direct methods of redistribution are taxation and expenditures programs.

TAXATION TO REDISTRIBUTE INCOME   The U.S. federal government gets its revenue from a variety of taxes. The three largest sources of revenue are the personal income tax, the corporate income tax, and the Social Security tax.

State and local governments get their revenue from income taxes, sales taxes, and property taxes. The rates vary among states.

Tax systems can be progressive, proportional (sometimes called *flat rate*), or regressive. A **progressive tax** is one in which *the average tax rate increases with income*. (A progressive income tax schedule might tax individuals at a rate of 15 percent for income up to $20,000; at 25 percent for income between $20,000 and $40,000; and at 35 percent for every dollar earned over $40,000.) It redistributes income from the rich to the poor. A **proportional tax** is one in which *the average rate of tax is constant regardless of income level*. Such a tax might be 25 percent of every dollar earned. It is neutral in regard to income distribution. A **regressive tax** is one in which *the average tax rate decreases as income increases*. It redistributes income from poor to rich. The United States has chosen a somewhat progressive income tax, while the Social Security tax is a proportional tax up to a specified earned income.

Q-8 True or false? A progressive tax is preferable to a proportional tax. Why?

Federal Income Taxes   In the early 1940s, the federal personal income tax was made highly progressive, with a top tax rate of 90 percent on the highest incomes. The degree of progressivity went down significantly through various pieces of legislation after World War II until 1986, when the income tax system was amended to provide for an initial rate of 15 percent and a top rate of 28 percent. (The U.S. income tax also has an earned income tax credit where heads of households earning below a certain amount get a tax credit from government, reducing their taxes, and sometimes providing them with an income subsidy.)

The changes did not reduce the actual progressivity of the personal income tax as much as they seemed to because the 1986 reforms eliminated many of the loopholes in the U.S. Tax Code. Some loopholes had allowed rich people to legally reduce their reported incomes and to pay taxes on those lower incomes at lower rates. The top personal income tax rate on high-income individuals today is 35 percent.

Whereas the personal income tax is progressive, the Social Security tax is initially proportional. All individuals pay the same tax rate on wage income (7.65 percent for employer and 7.65 percent for employee; 15.3 percent for self-employed) up to a cap of about $110,000. Above that income cap, no Social Security tax is due (except for the Medicare portion, which has no cap on the amount to which it is applied). At this income cap, the Social Security tax becomes regressive: Higher-income individuals pay a lower percentage of their total income in Social Security taxes than do lower-income individuals. (They also receive relatively less in Social Security benefits, compared to what they put in. So, while the Social Security tax is regressive, taken as a whole the Social Security system is progressive.)

State and Local Taxes   State and local governments get most of their income from the following sources:

Web Note 18.4
State Lotteries

1. Income taxes, which are generally somewhat progressive.
2. Sales taxes, which tend to be proportional (all people pay the same tax rate on what they spend) or slightly regressive. (Since poor people often spend a higher percentage of their incomes than rich people, poor people pay higher average sales taxes as a percentage of their incomes than rich people.)
3. Property taxes, which are taxes paid on the value of people's property (usually real estate, but sometimes also personal property like cars). Since the value of people's property is related (although imperfectly related) to income, the property tax is considered to be roughly proportional.

When all the taxes paid by individuals to all levels of governments are combined, the conclusion that most researchers come to is that little income redistribution takes place on the tax side. The progressive taxes are offset by the regressive taxes, so the overall tax system is roughly proportional. That is, on average the tax rates individuals pay are roughly equal.

Expenditure programs have been more successful than taxation for redistributing income.

EXPENDITURE PROGRAMS TO REDISTRIBUTE INCOME   Taxation has not proved to be an effective means of redistributing income. However, the government expenditure system has been quite effective. The federal government's expenditures that contribute to redistribution include the following.

Social Security   The program that redistributes the most money is the **Social Security system,** *a social insurance program that provides financial benefits to the elderly and disabled and to their eligible dependents and/or survivors.* Social Security also has a component called **Medicare,** which is a *multibillion-dollar medical insurance system.*

Q-9 True or false? The U.S. Social Security system is only a retirement system.

The amount of an individual's Social Security retirement, disability, or survivors' monthly cash benefits depends on a very complex formula, which is skewed in favor of lower-income workers. The program is not a pension program that pays benefits in proportion to the amount paid in. Many people will get much more than they paid in; some who never paid anything in will get a great deal; and others who paid in for years will get nothing. (No benefits are payable if you die before you retire and leave no survivors eligible for benefits due to your work.) On the whole, the program has been successful in keeping the elderly out of poverty. In addition, Social Security benefits have helped workers' survivors and the disabled.

Today, more than 55 million people receive cash Social Security benefits, many of whom also receive Medicare payments. Total benefits paid, including Medicare, come to over $1 trillion each year.

Public Assistance **Public assistance** programs are *means-tested social programs targeted to the poor, providing financial, nutritional, medical, and housing assistance.* (These programs are more familiarly known as *welfare payments.*) Public assistance programs exist in every state of the union, although the amount paid varies greatly from state to state. The main kinds of public assistance are:

Temporary Assistance for Needy Families (TANF). Provides temporary financial assistance to needy families with children under age 19.

Supplemental Nutritional Assistance Program (SNAP). Provides nutritional assistance in the form of coupons redeemable at most food stores.

Medicaid. Medical assistance for the poor, paid for by the individual states. It's different from, and usually more generous than, Medicare.

General assistance. State assistance to poor people when emergencies arise that aren't taken care of by any of the other programs.

By far the largest proportion of payments goes to needy families with dependent children, especially since these families are usually so poor that, in addition to qualifying for TANF, they meet the eligibility requirements for SNAP and Medicaid.

TANF was instituted by the Personal Responsibility and Work Opportunity Reconciliation Act of 1996 to replace Aid to Families with Dependent Children (AFDC). It has a number of provisions that distinguish it from earlier programs. One important provision is that it establishes a lifetime limit of 60 months (not necessarily consecutive) of benefits. The purpose of the law is to direct welfare recipients to work, and another provision in the law requires welfare recipients to take a job within two years. The law also gives states significant latitude in determining benefits and eligibility criteria. These changes are major ones; they raise many questions about job training and child care. The effects of this law are discussed in the box "From Welfare to Work."

Supplemental Security Income Hundreds of thousands more people would be receiving public assistance if it weren't for **Supplemental Security Income (SSI),** *a federal program that pays benefits, based on need, to the elderly, blind, and disabled.* Although SSI is administered through the Social Security offices, it is unlike Social Security benefits because eligibility for SSI payments is based solely on need. Again unlike Social Security, the recipients pay nothing toward the cost of the program. To be eligible, though, people must have very low incomes and almost no resources except a home, if they are fortunate enough to own one, a wedding ring and engagement ring, and an automobile. Today, over $50 billion is paid in SSI benefits each year.

Unemployment Compensation **Unemployment compensation** is *short-term financial assistance, regardless of need, to eligible individuals who are temporarily out of work.* It is limited financial assistance to people who are out of work through no fault of their own and have worked in a covered occupation for a substantial number of weeks in the period just before they became unemployed.

Normally a person can receive unemployment benefits for only about six months in any given year, and the amount of the benefit is always considerably less than the amount the person earned when working.

A person can't just quit a job and live on unemployment benefits. While receiving unemployment benefits, people are expected to actively search for work. Lower-income workers receive unemployment payments that are more nearly equal to their working wage than do higher-income workers, but there is no income eligibility test. Today, about $150 billion is paid in unemployment benefits each year, although this amount fluctuates with the state of the economy.

From Welfare to Work

In an effort to reduce the negative incentive effects of welfare, in 1996 Congress passed the Personal Responsibility and Work Opportunity Reconciliation Act. The act required recipients of welfare assistance to work after two years on assistance and limited welfare assistance to a total of five years over a lifetime. Part of the act was also designed to offset the taxation implicit in moving from welfare to work, which could be as high as 90 percent or more, since under the old law welfare recipients who earned income above a certain level often lost almost all their welfare benefits.

The act extended funding to the working poor; for example, it provided funding for child care to help mothers move into the workforce and extended Medicaid to include the first year of work. With the changes, the implicit tax on income was reduced to about 40 percent: For every dollar of additional income, people lost 40 cents of benefits. Congress also promised monetary rewards to states that were successful in moving people off the welfare rolls.

This act played an important role in reducing the number of people on welfare from its peak of 14 million in 1994 to about 4 million in 2008, in reducing the average stay on welfare from over eight to under four years, and in reducing the unemployment rate among single mothers.

The largest reduction occurred in the late 1990s and early 2000, when the economy was booming and one could expect the number of welfare recipients to fall anyway. But the reductions continued into the recessions.

The major slowdown that began in 2008, accompanied by the fall in home values, pushed more people into poverty, including many who previously were considered middle class. But that increase in poverty was primarily due to the downturn, and the general feeling in government was that the law has significantly increased the incentives to get off, and stay off, welfare.

Housing Programs   Federal and state governments have many different programs to improve housing or to provide affordable housing. While many of these programs are designed to benefit low-income persons, there are also programs for moderate-income persons and lower-income persons (people whose incomes are lower than moderate but higher than low).

The federal agency overseeing most of these programs, the Department of Housing and Urban Development (HUD), has been criticized for abuse and mismanagement. Hundreds of millions of dollars that could have benefited the poor went instead to developers of housing and other projects, to consultants, and to others who skimmed off money before—or instead of—building or rehabilitating housing. In part because of these problems, federal funding for housing was steadily reduced during the 1980s. Today, about $60 billion is allocated to housing programs each year.

How Successful Have Income Redistribution Programs Been?

Most government redistribution works through its expenditure programs, not through taxes.

After including the effect of both taxes and government programs on the redistribution of income, the after-transfer income is somewhat closer to being equally distributed. Thus government programs have a slight effect on income equality, but it is very small. But because of the incentive effects of collecting and distributing the money, that redistribution has come at the cost of a reduction in the total amount of income earned by the society. The debate about whether the gain in equality of income is worth the cost in reduction of total income is likely to continue indefinitely.

While the direct methods of redistributing income get the most press and discussion, perhaps the most important redistribution decisions that the government makes involve an indirect method, the establishment and protection of property rights. Let's take an example: intellectual property rights. Intellectual property consists of things like a book you've written, a song you've composed, or a picture you've drawn. How these property rights are structured plays a fundamental role in determining the distribution of income.

For example, if strict private property rights are given for, say, a design for a computer screen (e.g., a neat little trash can in the corners and icons of various files), any user other than the designer herself will have to pay for the right to use it. The designer (or the person who gets the legal right to the design) becomes very rich. If no property rights are given for the design, then no payment is made and income is much more equally distributed. Of course, without a promise of high returns to designing a computer screen device, fewer resources will be invested in finding the ideal design. While most people agree that some incentive is appropriate, there is no consensus on whether the incentives embodied in our current property rights structure are too large. I suspect that the trash can (recycling bin) design, while ingenious, would have been arrived at with a much smaller incentive.

The point of the above example is not that property rights in such ideas should not be given out. The point is that decisions on property rights issues have enormous distributional consequences that are often little discussed, even by economists. Ultimately, we can answer the question of whether income redistribution is fair only after we have answered the question of whether the initial property rights distribution is fair.

Q-10 Why are property rights important in the determination of whether any particular income distribution is fair?

The fairness of income depends on the fairness of property rights.

Conclusion

Much more could be said about the issues involved in income redistribution. But limitations of time and space pressure us to move on. I hope this chapter has convinced you that income redistribution is an important but difficult question. Specifically, I hope I have given you the sense that income distribution questions are integrally related to questions about the entire economic system. Supply and demand play a central role in the determination of the distribution of income, but they do so in an institutional and historical context. Thus, the analysis of income distribution must include that context as well as the analyst's ethical judgments about what is fair.

Summary

- The Lorenz curve is a measure of the distribution of income among families in a country. The farther the Lorenz curve is from the diagonal, the more unequally income is distributed. (*LO18-1*)

- The official poverty measure is an absolute measure because it is based on the minimum food budget for a family. It is a relative measure because it is adjusted for average inflation. (*LO18-1*)

- Economic and social mobility in the United States has decreased over the past decades. (*LO18-1*)

- Income is less equally distributed in the United States than in some countries such as Sweden, but more equally distributed than in other countries such as Brazil. There is more income inequality among countries than income inequality within a country. (*LO18-1*)

- Wealth is distributed less equally than income. (*LO18-1*)

- Income differs substantially by class and by other socioeconomic characteristics such as age, race, and gender. (*LO18-2*)

- Fairness is a philosophical question. People must judge a program's fairness for themselves. *(LO18-3)*

- Income is difficult to redistribute because of incentive effects of taxes, avoidance and evasion effects of taxes, and incentive effects of redistribution programs. *(LO18-4)*

- On the whole, the U.S. tax system is roughly proportional, so it is not very effective as a means of redistributing income. *(LO18-4)*

- Government spending programs are more effective than tax policy in reducing income inequality in the United States. *(LO18-4)*

Key Terms

income *(395)*	progressive tax *(403)*	Social Security	unemployment
Lorenz curve *(387)*	proportional tax *(403)*	system *(404)*	compensation *(405)*
Medicare *(404)*	public assistance *(405)*	Supplemental Security	wealth *(394)*
poverty threshold *(390)*	regressive tax *(403)*	Income (SSI) *(405)*	

Questions and Exercises

1. The Lorenz curve for Bangladesh looks like this:

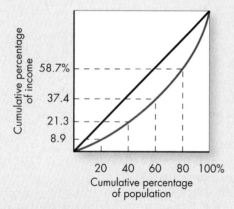

   How much income do individuals in the top income quintile in Bangladesh receive? *(LO18-1)*

2. What would the Lorenz curve for lawyers, represent? *(LO18-1)*

3. Why are we concerned with the distribution of income between whites and blacks, but not between redheads and blondes? *(LO18-1)*

4. The accompanying table shows income distribution data for three countries. *(LO18-1)*

	Percentage of Total Income		
Income Quintile	India	Czech Republic	Mexico
Lowest 20%	8.6%	10.2%	4.4%
Second quintile	12.2	14.3	8.9
Third quintile	15.8	17.5	13.3
Fourth quintile	21.0	21.7	20.4
Highest 20%	42.4	36.3	53.0

   a. Using this information, draw a Lorenz curve for each country.
   b. Which country has the most equal distribution of income?
   c. Which country has the least equal?
   d. By looking at the three Lorenz curves, can you tell which country has the most progressive tax system? Why or why not?

5. Should poverty be defined absolutely or relatively? Why? *(LO18-1)*

6. How does social mobility in the United States compare to that in Britain? Why do you think this is so? *(LO18-1)*

7. Would the Lorenz curve for the world be more or less bowed out compared to the Lorenz curve for the United States? *(LO18-1)*

8. How has the median income of women compared to men changed since 1980? What do you think is the cause? *(LO18-2)*

9. Is the class system in the United States more like a pyramid, diamond, or pentagon? Why is this so? *(LO18-2)*

10. How is the distribution of income related to the emergence of the Tea Party and the Occupy movement? *(LO18-2)*

11. Why did Bertrand de Juvenal argue for a high level of income inequality? *(LO18-3)*

12. In what instance would John Rawls support greater income inequality? *(LO18-3)*

13. In Taxland, the first $10,000 earned per year is exempt from taxation. Between $10,000.01 and $30,000, the tax rate is 25 percent. Between $30,000.01 and $50,000, it's 30 percent. Above $50,000, it's 35 percent. You're earning $75,000 a year. *(LO18-4)*
    a. How much in taxes will you have to pay?
    b. What is your average tax rate?
    c. What is your marginal tax rate?

14. Some economists have proposed making the tax rate progressivity depend on the wage rate rather than the income level. Thus, an individual who works twice as long as another but who receives a lower wage would face a lower marginal tax rate. *(LO18-4)*

    a. What effect would this change have on incentives to work?

    b. Would this system be fairer than our current system? Why or why not?

    c. If, simultaneously, the tax system were made regressive in hours worked so that individuals who work longer hours faced lower marginal tax rates, what effect would this change have on hours worked?

Questions from Alternative Perspectives

1. In a recent study the top 20 percent of Americans had 49.7 percent of the income before taxes and transfers and 48.3 percent after taxes and transfers. The same figures for the bottom 20 percent were 3.4 percent and 4.3 percent respectively.

    a. How much do taxes and transfers "cost" the upper quintile?

    b. How much discretionary income should they be willing to invest to change this situation?

    c. How much discretionary income does the bottom quintile have to prevent such a change? (Institutionalist)

2. In the Old Testament, God promised riches to Israel if Israel kept God's commandments. But in the New Testament, Jesus says that it is easier for a camel to go through the eye of a needle than for a rich man to enter the kingdom of heaven.

    a. Considering the wealth distribution in Figure 18-5, what does this suggest about Americans?

    b. Should government do anything about it?

    c. What do the Old and New Testament teachings suggest about what private individuals ought to do? (Religious)

3. In 2011 the poverty level for a family of four was $23,201.

    a. If one-third of the total income of lower-income households is typically used for food, estimate the amount of money per day per person available for food for a person living at or below the poverty rate.

    b. How much does that leave for this family per month for everything else: rent, utilities, taxes, auto, medical, clothing, and education? (Radical)

4. Say you earn $200, and that the government takes $75 from you in taxes to give to someone else.

    a. How would you feel about that?

    b. What would that transfer likely do to your incentive to work?

    c. What would the government transfer of $75 likely do to the incentive to work of the person who receives the payment?

    d. Would the effect be different if you voluntarily gave $75 to someone else? (Austrian)

5. Antipoverty programs in the United States since the mid-1990s have focused on welfare-to-work programs that compel welfare recipients to take paid jobs. Some economists argue that these programs place women who are not "ready for work" into jobs that are not "ready for mothers" and move them from the ranks of the welfare poor to the working poor.

    a. What policies would be necessary to make U.S. antipoverty programs far more effective?

    b. How could public policy be used to make jobs more "mother-ready" and more likely to lift these women above the poverty line? (Feminist)

Issues to Ponder

1. Some economists argue that a class distinction should be made between managerial decision makers and other workers. Do you agree? Why or why not?

2. If a garbage collector earns more than an English teacher, does that mean something is wrong with the economy? Why or why not?

3. List four conditions you believe should hold before you would argue that two individuals should get the same amount of income.

    a. How would you apply the conditions to your views on welfare?

    b. How would you apply the conditions to your views on how progressive the income tax should be?

    c. If the income tax were made progressive in wage rates (tax rates increase as wage rates increase) rather than progressive in income, would your conditions be better met? Why?

4. Is it ever appropriate for society to:
    Let someone starve?
    Let someone be homeless?
    Forbid someone to eat chocolate?

5. The dissident Russian writer A. Amalrik has written:

    The Russian people . . . have . . . one idea that appears
    positive: the idea of *justice* . . . In practice, "justice"
    involves the desire that "nobody should live better
    than I do" . . . The idea of justice is motivated by ha-
    tred of everything that is outstanding, which we make
    no effort to imitate but, on the contrary, try to bring
    down to our level, by hatred of any sense of initiative,
    of any higher or more dynamic way of life than the
    life we live ourselves.

    What implications would such a worldview have for the
    economy?

6. If you receive a paycheck, what percentage of it is with-
    held for taxes? What incentive effect does that have on
    your decision to work?

7. "There are lies, damned lies, and statistics. Then, there are
    annual poverty figures." Both liberal and conservative
    economists believe U.S. poverty statistics are suspect.
    Here are some reasons:

    (1) They do not take into account in-kind benefits such as
         food stamps and tax credits.
    (2) They do not consider regional cost-of-living
         differences.
    (3) They do not take into account unreported income.

    (4) Food accounts for about one-seventh of a family's
         budget, not one-third.
    (5) Ownership of assets such as homes, cars, and
         appliances is not taken into account.
    a. What would the effect of correcting each of these be
        on measured poverty?
    b. Would making these changes be fair?

8. In "Why Higher Real Wages May Reduce Altruism for
    the Poor," Ball State economist John B. Horowitz considers
    whether redistribution of income is a public good or a
    public bad.
    a. How might income redistribution be considered a
        public good?
    b. How might income redistribution be considered a
        public bad?
    c. What is the likely effect of higher real wages on
        whether income redistribution is perceived to be a
        public good or bad?

9. There are many more poor people in the United States
    than there are rich people. If the poor wanted to, they
    could exercise their power to redistribute as much money
    as they please to themselves. They don't do that, so they
    must see the income distribution system as fair. Discuss.

Answers to Margin Questions

1. When drawing a Lorenz curve, you put the cumulative
    percentage of income on the vertical axis and the
    cumulative percentage of families (or population) on the
    horizontal axis. (*p. 388; LO18-1*)

2. The U.S. definition of poverty is an absolute measure, but
    the way poverty is calculated means that some relativity is
    included in the definition. (*p. 390; LO18-1*)

3. The United States has significantly more income inequal-
    ity than Sweden and Japan, but significantly less than
    Brazil. (*p. 394; LO18-1*)

4. In early capitalist society, the distributional fight was
    between workers and capitalists. In modern capitalist
    society, the distributional fight is more varied. For
    example, in the United States minorities are pitted
    against whites and males against females. (*p. 399; LO18-2*)

5. No, it is not self-evident that greater equality of income
    would make society a better place to live. Unequal
    income distribution has its benefits. Still, most people
    would prefer a somewhat more equal distribution of
    income than what currently exists. (*p. 400; LO18-3*)

6. What is fair is a very difficult concept. It depends on
    people's needs, people's wants, to what degree people are
    deserving, and other factors. Still, in the absence of any

more information than is given in the question, I would
divide the pie equally. (*p. 400; LO18-3*)

7. No, one cannot reasonably assume other things remain
    constant. Redistributive programs have important side
    effects that can change the behavior of individuals and
    subvert the intent of the program. Three important side
    effects are substituting leisure for labor, a decrease in
    measured income, and attempts to appear more
    needy. (*p. 402; LO18-4*)

8. As a general statement, "A progressive tax is preferable to
    a proportional tax" is false. A progressive tax may well be
    preferable, but that is a normative judgment (just as its
    opposite would be). Moreover, taxes have incentive
    effects that must be considered. (*p. 403; LO18-4*)

9. False. The U.S. Social Security system includes many
    other aspects, such as disability benefits and survivors'
    benefits. (*p. 404; LO18-4*)

10. The distribution of initial property rights underlies the
     distribution of income. Those with the property rights
     will reap the returns from those rights. Ultimately, we can
     answer the question whether income distribution is fair
     only after we have answered whether the initial property
     rights distribution is fair. (*p. 407; LO18-4*)

chapter 19

The Logic of Individual Choice: The Foundation of Supply and Demand

> *The theory of economics must begin with a correct theory of consumption.*
>
> —Stanley Jevons

It's Friday night and you've managed to scrimp and save $50 to take a break from classes and buy two tickets, one for yourself and one for a friend, to see the rock concert at the field house. But then you think about it; maybe going to a movie and having a hot fudge sundae after for the two of you would make more sense. Or maybe a big steak dinner just for yourself. Or maybe ordering Chinese. Or maybe studying and giving the money to the homeless shelter. Choices, choices; they are around you all the time.

How individuals make choices is central to microeconomics. It is the foundation of economic reasoning and it gives economics much of its power. The first part of this chapter shows you that foundation and leads you through some exercises to make sure you understand the reasoning. The second part of the chapter relates that analysis to the real world, giving you a sense of when the model is useful and when it's not.

As you go through this chapter, think back to Chapter 1, which set out the goals for this book. One goal was to get you to think like an economist. This chapter, which formally develops the reasoning process behind economists' cost/benefit approach to problems, examines the underpinnings of how to think like an economist.

Rational Choice Theory

Different sciences have various explanations for why people do what they do. For example, Freudian psychology tells us we do what we do because of an internal fight between the id, ego, and superego plus some hangups we have about our bodies. Other psychologists tell us it's a search for approval by our peers; we want to be OK. Economists agree that these are important reasons but argue that if we want an analysis that's simple enough to apply to policy problems, these heavy psychological explanations are likely to get us all mixed up. At least to start with, we need an easier underlying psychological foundation. And economists have one—self-interest. People do what they do because it's in their self-interest.

After reading this chapter, you should be able to:

LO19-1 Discuss the principle of diminishing marginal utility and the principle of rational choice.

LO19-2 Explain the relationship between marginal utility and price when a consumer is maximizing total utility.

LO19-3 Summarize how the principle of rational choice accounts for the laws of demand and supply.

LO19-4 Name three assumptions of the theory of choice and discuss why they may not reflect reality.

Thinking Like a Modern Economist

The Traditional Models as Stepping Stones

A group of economists, called behavioral economists, are beginning to explore consistent deviations from rationality and self-interest, and in doing so they are expanding the building blocks of economics. But doing so has a cost—it complicates the model enormously, and a more complicated model is much more difficult to use. The advantage of using traditional building blocks is that it comes to black-and-white conclusions—and then lets you decide whether the model is or is not applicable.

Behavioral economists recognize the cost and are trying to characterize types of decisions that fit the traditional model and types of decisions that don't. Unfortunately, the work is still in an early stage and they have a long way to go. That's why, at this time, when it comes to teaching economics, almost all economists—including behavioral economists—agree that the best place to start is with models based on the traditional building blocks. That's why this book is structured like it is—it focuses on models with the traditional building blocks, but lets you know that, in their research, modern economists are going beyond the traditional models.

Economists' traditional analysis of individual choice doesn't deny that most of us have our quirks. That's obvious in what we buy. On certain items we're pennypinchers; on others we're big spenders. For example, how many of you or your parents clip coupons to save 40 cents on cereal but then spend $40 on a haircut? How many save 50 cents a pound by buying a low grade of meat but then spend $20 on a bottle of wine, $75 on dinner at a restaurant, or $60 for a concert ticket?

But through it all comes a certain rationality. Much of what people do reflects their rational self-interest. That's why economists start their analysis of individual choice with a relatively simple, but powerful, underlying psychological foundation.

Using that simple theory, two things determine what people do: **utility**—*the pleasure or satisfaction people get from doing or consuming something,* and the price of doing or consuming that something. Price is the tool the market uses to

Web Note 19.1
Utility and Pleasure

Utility is the pleasure or satisfaction that people get from doing or consuming something.

It is important to distinguish between marginal and total utility.

bring the quantity supplied equal to the quantity demanded. Changes in price provide incentives for people to change what they're doing. Through those incentives, the invisible hand guides us all. To understand economics, you must understand how price affects our choices. That's why we focus on the effect of price on the quantity demanded. We want to understand the way in which a change in price will affect what we do.

In summary, economists' theory of rational choice is a simple and powerful theory that shows how these two things—pleasure and price—are related.

Total Utility and Marginal Utility

In thinking about utility, it's important to distinguish between *total utility* and *marginal utility*. **Total utility** refers to *the total satisfaction one gets from consuming a product.* **Marginal utility** refers to *the satisfaction one gets from consuming one additional unit of a product above and beyond what one has consumed up to that point.* For example, eating a whole pound of Beluga caviar might give you 4,700 units of utility.[1] Consuming the first 15 ounces may have given you 4,697 units of utility. Consuming the last ounce of caviar might give you an additional 3 units of utility. The 4,700 is total utility; the 3 is the marginal utility of eating that last ounce of caviar.

An example of the relationship between total utility and marginal utility is given in Figure 19-1. Let's say that the marginal utility of the 1st slice of pizza is 14, and since

---

[1]Throughout the book I choose specific numbers to make the examples more understandable and to make the points I want to make. Economists don't use actual numbers to discuss utility. At the principles level, they use such numbers to make the presentation easier. A useful exercise is for you to choose different numbers and reason your way through the same analysis. In Appendix A, I go through the same analysis without using actual numbers.

FIGURE 19-1 (A, B, AND C) **Marginal and Total Utility**

Marginal utility tends to decrease as consumption of a good increases. Notice how the information in the table (**a**) can be presented graphically in two different ways. The two different ways are, however, related. The downward slope of the marginal utility curve (**c**) is reflected in the total utility curve bowed downward in (**b**). Notice that marginal utility relates to changes in quantity so the marginal utility line is graphed at the halfway point. For example, in (**c**), between 7 and 8, marginal utility becomes zero.

Number of Pizza Slices	Total Utility	Marginal Utility
0	0	
		14
1	14	
		12
2	26	
		10
3	36	
		8
4	44	
		6
5	50	
		4
6	54	
		2
7	56	
		0
8	56	
		−2
9	54	

(a) Utility Table

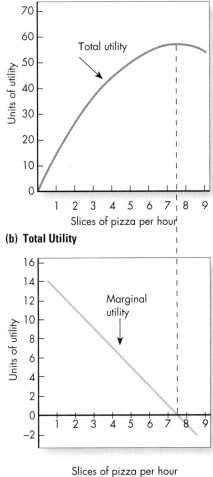

(b) Total Utility

(c) Marginal Utility

you've eaten only 1 slice, the total utility is also 14. Let's also say that the marginal utility of the 2nd slice of pizza is 12, which means that the total utility of 2 slices of pizza is 26 (14 + 12). Similarly for the 3rd, 4th, and 5th slices of pizza, whose marginal utilities are 10, 8, and 6, respectively. The total utility of your eating those 5 pieces of pizza is the sum of the marginal utilities you get from eating each of the 5 slices. The sixth row of column 2 of Figure 19-1(a) shows that sum.

Notice that marginal utility shows up between the lines. That's because it is the utility of *changing* consumption levels. For example, the marginal utility of changing from 1 to 2 slices of pizza is 12. The relationship between total and marginal utility also can be seen graphically. In Figure 19-1(b), we graph total utility (column 2 of the utility table) on the vertical axis and the number of slices of pizza (column 1 of the utility table) on the horizontal axis. As you can see, total utility increases up to 7 slices of pizza; after 8 slices it starts decreasing—after 8 pieces of pizza, you're so stuffed that you can't stand to look at another slice.

In Figure 19-1(c), we graph marginal utility (column 3 of the utility table) on the vertical axis and slices of pizza (column 1) on the horizontal axis. Notice how marginal utility decreases while total utility increases. When total utility stops increasing

Eating contests are proof that, at some point, utility becomes zero.

Q-1 If the total utility curve is a straight line—that is, does not exhibit diminishing marginal utility—what will the marginal utility curve look like?

(between 7 and 8 slices), marginal utility is zero. Beyond this point, total utility decreases and marginal utility is negative. An additional slice of pizza will actually make you worse off.

Diminishing Marginal Utility

Now let's consider the shapes of these curves a bit more carefully: What are they telling us about people's choices? As we've drawn the curves, the marginal utility that a person gets from each additional slice of pizza decreases with each slice of pizza eaten. Economists believe that the shape of these curves is generally a reasonable description of the pattern of people's enjoyment. They call that pattern the **principle of diminishing marginal utility:**

> *As you consume more of a good, after some point, the marginal utility received from each additional unit of a good decreases with each additional unit consumed, other things equal.*

As individuals increase their consumption of a good, at some point, consuming another unit of the product will simply not yield as much additional pleasure as did consuming the preceding unit.

Consider, for example, that late-night craving for a double-cheese-and-pepperoni pizza. You order one and bite into it. Ah, pleasure! But if you've ordered a large pizza and you're eating it all by yourself, eventually you'll enjoy each additional slice less. In other words, the marginal utility you get is going to decrease with each additional slice of pizza you consume. That's the principle of diminishing marginal utility.

Notice that the principle of diminishing marginal utility does not say that you don't enjoy consuming more of a good; it simply states that as you consume more of the good, you enjoy the additional units less than you did the previous units. A fourth slice of pizza still tastes good, but it doesn't match the taste of the third slice. At some point, however, marginal utility can become negative. Say you had two large pizzas and only two hours in which to eat them. Eating the last slice could be pure torture. But in most situations, you have the option *not* to consume any more of a good. When consuming a good becomes torture (meaning its utility is negative), you simply don't consume any more of it. If you eat a slice of pizza (or consume an additional unit of a good), that's a good indication that its marginal utility is still positive.

Rational Choice and Marginal Utility

The analysis of rational choice is the analysis of how individuals choose goods within their budget in order to maximize total utility, and how maximizing total utility can be accomplished by considering marginal utility. That analysis begins with the premise that rational individuals want as much satisfaction as they can get from their available resources. The term *rational* in economics means, specifically, that people prefer more to less and will make choices that give them as much satisfaction as possible. The problem is that people face a budget constraint. They must choose among the alternatives. How do they do that?

SOME CHOICES   Let's start by considering three choices. (Answer each choice as you read it.)[2]

> *Choice 1:*   Between spending another dollar on a slice of pizza that gives you an additional 41 units of utility, or spending another dollar on a hero sandwich that gives you an additional 30 units of utility.

The principle of diminishing marginal utility states that, after some point, the marginal utility received from each additional unit of a good decreases with each additional unit consumed, other things equal.

Diminishing Marginal Utility

Q-2 True or false? Consuming more of a good generally increases its marginal utility. Why?

WWW   Web Note 19.2
Diminishing Marginal Utility

Because people face a budget constraint, they must choose among alternatives.

---

[2]To keep the analysis simple in this example, I consider either/or decisions. Below, I show how to extend the analysis to marginal choices.

Choice 2:   Between reading an additional chapter in this book that gives you an additional 200 units of utility at a cost of one hour of your time, or reading an additional chapter in psychology that gives you an additional 100 units of utility at a cost of 40 minutes of your time.

Choice 3:   Between having your next date with that awesome guy Jerry, which gives you an additional 2,000 units of utility and costs you $70, or taking out plain Jeff on your next date, which gives you an additional 200 units of utility and costs you $10.

The correct choices, in terms of marginal utility, are (1) the pizza, (2) a chapter of this book, and (3) Jerry.

If you answered all three correctly, either you're lucky or you have a good intuitive understanding of the principle of rational choice. Now let's explore the principle of rational choice more thoroughly by considering each of the three examples.

Choice 1   Since the slice of pizza and the hero sandwich both cost $1, and the pizza gives you more units of utility than the hero, the pizza is the rational choice. If you spend $1 on the hero rather than the pizza, you're losing 11 units of utility and not making yourself as happy as you could be. You're being irrational. Any choice (for the same amount of money) that doesn't give you as much utility as possible is an irrational choice.

But now let's say that the price of heroes falls to 50 cents so that you can buy two heroes for the same price you previously had to pay for only one. Let's also say that two heroes would give you 56 units of utility (not $2 \times 30 = 60$—remember the principle of diminishing marginal utility). Which would now be the more rational choice? The two heroes, because their 56 units of utility are 15 more than you would get from that dollar spent on one slice of pizza.

Another way of thinking about your choice is to recognize that essentially what you're doing is buying units of utility. Obviously you want to get the most for your money, so you choose goods that have the highest units of utility per unit of cost. Let's see how this way of thinking about a decision works by considering our second choice.

Choice 2   Here the two alternatives have a cost in time, not money. The analysis, however, is the same. You calculate the marginal utility (additional units of utility) of the choice facing you and divide that by the costs of the activity; that gives you the marginal utility per unit of cost. Then choose the activity that has the higher marginal utility per unit of cost or lower cost per unit of utility. When you do that, you see that this chapter gives you $3^{1}/_{3}$ units of utility per minute ($200/60 = 3^{1}/_{3}$), while the psychology chapter gives you $2^{1}/_{3}$ units of utility per minute. So you choose to read another chapter in this book.[3]

Q-3 Which is the rational choice: watching one hour of CNN that gives you 20 units of utility or watching a two-hour movie that gives you 30 units of utility?

Choice 3   Taking out Jerry gives you $28^{1}/_{2}$ units of utility per dollar ($2,000/\$70$), while taking out Jeff gives you 20 units of utility per dollar ($200/\$10$). So you choose to take out Jerry.[4]

---

[3]As I've pointed out before, I choose the numbers to make the points I want to make. A good exercise for you is to choose different numbers that reflect your estimate of the marginal utility you get from a choice, and see what your rational choices are.

[4]In these examples, I am implicitly assuming that the "goods" are divisible. Technically, this assumption is needed for marginal utilities to be fully specified.

The principle of rational choice tells us to spend our money on those goods that give us the most marginal utility per dollar.

THE PRINCIPLE OF RATIONAL CHOICE   The **principle of rational choice** is as follows: *Spend your money on those goods that give you the most marginal utility (MU) per dollar.* The principle of rational choice is important enough for us to restate.

If $\dfrac{MU_x}{P_x} > \dfrac{MU_y}{P_y}$, choose to consume an additional unit of good *x*.

If $\dfrac{MU_x}{P_x} < \dfrac{MU_y}{P_y}$, choose to consume an additional unit of good *y*.

By substituting the marginal utilities and prices of goods into these formulas, you can always decide which good it makes more sense to consume. Consume the one with the highest marginal utility per dollar.

www
Web Note 19.3
Maximizing Utility

SIMULTANEOUS DECISIONS   So far in discussing our examples, we've considered the choices separately. But in real life, choices aren't so neatly separated. Say you were presented with all three choices simultaneously. If you make all three of the decisions given in the examples, are you being rational? The answer is no. Why? The pizza gives you 41 units of utility per dollar; taking out Jerry gives you 28½ units of utility per dollar. You aren't being rational; you aren't maximizing your utility. It would clearly make sense to eat more pizza, paying for it by cutting the date with Jerry short. (Skip the coffee at the end of the meal.)

But what about the other choice: studying psychology or economics? We can't compare the costs of studying to the costs of the other goods because, as I noted earlier, the costs of both studying alternatives are expressed in terms of time, not money. If we can assign a money value to the time, however, we can make the comparison. Let's say you can earn $6 per hour, so the value of your time is 10 cents per minute. This allows us to think about both alternatives in terms of dollars and cents. Since a chapter in economics takes an hour to read, the cost in money of reading a chapter is 60 minutes × 10 cents = $6. Similarly, the cost of the 40 minutes you'd take to read the psychology chapter is $4.

With these values, we can compare our studying decisions with our other decisions. The value in units of utility per dollar of reading a chapter of this book is:

$$\frac{200}{\$6} = 33\tfrac{1}{3} \text{ units of utility per dollar}$$

So forget about dating Jerry with its 28½ units of utility per dollar. Your rational choice is to study this chapter while stuffing yourself with pizza.

But wait. Remember that, according to the principle of diminishing marginal utility, as you consume more of something, the marginal utility you get from it falls. So as you consume more pizza and spend more time reading this book, the marginal utilities of these activities will fall. Thus, as you vary your consumption, the marginal utilities you get from the goods are changing.

Maximizing Utility and Equilibrium

When do you stop changing your consumption? The principle of rational choice says you should keep adjusting your spending within your budget if the marginal utility per dollar (*MU/P*) of two goods differs. The only time you don't adjust your spending is when there is no clear winner. *When the ratios of the marginal utility to price of the two goods are equal,* you're maximizing utility; this is the **utility-maximizing rule:**

The utility-maximizing rule:

$\dfrac{MU_x}{P_x} = \dfrac{MU_y}{P_y}$

If $\dfrac{MU_x}{P_x} = \dfrac{MU_y}{P_y}$, *you're maximizing utility.*

When you're maximizing utility, you're in equilibrium. To understand how you can achieve equilibrium by adjusting your spending, it's important to remember the principle of diminishing marginal utility. As we consume more of an item, the marginal utility we get from the last unit consumed decreases. Conversely, as we consume *less* of an item, the marginal utility we get from the last unit consumed *increases*. (The principle of diminishing marginal utility operates in reverse.)

Achieving equilibrium by maximizing utility (juggling your choices, adding a bit more of one and choosing a bit less of another) requires more information than I've so far presented. We need to know the marginal utility of alternative amounts of consumption for each choice and how much we have to spend on all those items. With that information, we can choose among alternatives, given our available resources.

An Example of Maximizing Utility

Table 19-1 offers an example in which we have the necessary information to make simultaneous decisions and maximize utility. In this example, we have $7 to spend on ice cream cones and Big Macs. The choice is between ice cream at $1 a cone and Big Macs at $2 apiece. In the table, you can see the principle of diminishing marginal utility in action. The marginal utility (*MU*) we get from either good decreases as we consume more of it. *MU* becomes negative after 5 Big Macs or 6 ice cream cones.

The key columns for your decision are the *MU/P* columns. They tell you the *MU* per dollar spent on each of the items. By following the rule that we choose the good with the higher marginal utility per dollar, we can quickly determine the optimal choice.

Let's start by considering what we'd do with our first $2. Clearly we'd only eat ice cream. Doing so would give us 29 + 17 = 46 units of utility, compared to 20 units of utility if we spent the $2 on a Big Mac. How about our next $2? Again the choice is clear; the 10 units of utility per dollar from the Big Mac are plainly better than the 7 units of utility per dollar we can get from ice cream cones. So we buy 1 Big Mac and 2 ice cream cones with our first $4.

Now let's consider our fifth and sixth dollars. The *MU/P* for a second Big Mac is 7. The *MU/P* for a third ice cream cone is also 7, so we could spend the fifth dollar on either—if McDonald's will sell us half a Big Mac. We ask them if they will, and they

Q-4 True or false? You are maximizing total utility only when the marginal utility of all goods is zero. Explain your answer.

TABLE 19-1 **Maximizing Utility**

This table provides the information needed to make simultaneous decisions. Notice that the marginal utility we get from another good declines as we consume more of it. To maximize utility, adjust your choices until the marginal utility of all goods is equal.

	Big Macs (P = $2)				Ice Cream (P = $1)		
Q	TU	MU	MU/P	Q	TU	MU	MU/P
0	0			0	0		
		20	10			29	29
1	20			1	29		
		14	7			17	17
2	34			2	46		
		10	5			7	7
3	44			3	53		
		3	1.5			2	2
4	47			4	55		
		0	0			1	1
5	47			5	56		
		−5	−2.5			0	0
6	42			6	56		
		−10	−5			−4	−4
7	32			7	52		

tell us no, so we must make a choice between either two additional ice cream cones or another Big Mac for our fifth and sixth dollars. Since the marginal utility per dollar of the fourth ice cream cone is only 2, it makes sense to spend our fifth and sixth dollars on another Big Mac. So now we're up to 2 Big Macs and 2 ice cream cones and we have one more dollar to spend.

Now how about our last dollar? If we spend it on a third ice cream cone, we get 7 additional units of utility. If McDonald's maintains its position and only sells whole Big Macs, this is our sole choice since we only have a dollar and Big Macs sell for $2. But let's say that McDonald's wants the sale and this time offers to sell us half a Big Mac for $1. Would we take it? The answer is no. One-half of the next Big Mac gives us only 5 units of utility per dollar, whereas the third ice cream cone gives us 7 units of utility per dollar. So we spend the seventh dollar on a third ice cream cone.

With these choices and $7 to spend, we've arrived at equilibrium—the marginal utilities per dollar are the same for both goods and we're maximizing total utility. Our total utility is 34 from 2 Big Macs and 53 units of utility from the 3 ice cream cones, making a total utility of 87.

Why do these two choices make sense? Because they give us the most total utility for the $7 we have to spend. We've followed the utility-maximizing rule: Maximize utility by adjusting your choices until the marginal utilities per dollar are the same. These choices make the marginal utility per dollar between the last Big Mac and the last ice cream cone equal. The marginal utility per dollar we get from our last Big Mac is:

$$\frac{MU}{P} = \frac{14}{\$2} = 7$$

The marginal utility per dollar we get from our last ice cream cone is:

$$\frac{MU}{P} = \frac{7}{\$1} = 7$$

The marginal utility per dollar of each choice is equal, so we know we can't do any better. For any other choice, we would get less total utility, so we could increase our total utility by switching to one of these two choices.

Extending the Principle of Rational Choice

Our example involved only two goods, but the reasoning can be extended to the choice among many goods. Our analysis has shown us that the principle of rational choice among many goods is simply an extension of the principle of rational choice applied to two goods. That general principle of rational choice is to consume more of the good that provides a higher marginal utility per dollar.

The Principle of Rational Choice and Utility Maximization

When $\dfrac{MU_x}{P_x} > \dfrac{MU_z}{P_z}$, consume more of good x.

When $\dfrac{MU_y}{P_y} > \dfrac{MU_z}{P_z}$, consume more of good y.

Stop adjusting your consumption when the marginal utilities per dollar are equal.

So the *general utility-maximizing rule* is that you are maximizing utility when the marginal utilities per dollar of the goods consumed are equal.

When $\dfrac{MU_x}{P_x} = \dfrac{MU_y}{P_y} = \dfrac{MU_z}{P_z}$, you are maximizing utility.

When this rule is met, the consumer is in equilibrium; the cost per additional unit of utility is equal for all goods and the consumer is as well off as it is possible to be.

Notice that the rule does not say that the rational consumer should consume a good until its marginal utility reaches zero. The reason is that consumers don't have enough money to buy all they want. They face a budget constraint and do the best they can under that constraint—that is, they maximize utility. To buy more goods, a person has to work more, so she should work until the marginal utility of another dollar earned just equals the marginal utility of goods purchased with another dollar. According to economists' analysis of rational choice, a person's choice of how much to work is made simultaneously with the person's decision of how much to consume. So when you say you want a Porsche but can't afford one, economists ask whether you're working two jobs and saving all your money to buy a Porsche. If you aren't, you're demonstrating that you don't really want a Porsche, given what you would have to do to get it.

Rational Choice and the Laws of Demand and Supply

Now that you know the rule for maximizing utility, let's see how it relates to the laws of demand and supply. We begin with demand. The law of demand says that quantity demanded is inversely related to price. That is, when the price of a good goes up, the quantity we consume of it goes down.

The Law of Demand

Now let's consider the law of demand in relation to our principle of rational choice. When the price of a good goes up, the marginal utility *per dollar* we get from that good goes down. So when the price of a good goes up, if we were initially in equilibrium, we no longer are. Therefore, we choose to consume less of that good. The principle of rational choice shows us formally that following the law of demand is the rational thing to do.

Let's see how. If

$$\frac{MU_x}{P_x} = \frac{MU_y}{P_y}$$

and the price of good *y* goes up, then

$$\frac{MU_x}{P_x} > \frac{MU_y}{P_y}$$

Our utility-maximizing rule is no longer satisfied. Consider the preceding example, in which we were in equilibrium with 87 units of utility (34 from 2 Big Macs and 53 from 3 ice cream cones) with the utility-maximizing rule fulfilled:

$$\underset{\$2}{\underset{\text{Big Mac}}{\frac{14 \text{ units of utility}}{\$2}}} = \underset{\$1}{\underset{\text{Ice cream}}{\frac{7 \text{ units of utility}}{\$1}}} = 7$$

According to the principle of rational choice, if there is diminishing marginal utility and the price of a good goes up, we consume less of that good. Hence, the principle of rational choice leads to the law of demand.

If the price of an ice cream cone rises from $1 to $2, the marginal utility per dollar for Big Macs (whose price hasn't changed) exceeds the marginal utility per dollar of ice cream cones:

Big Mac > Ice cream

$$\frac{14}{\$2} > \frac{7}{\$2}$$

To satisfy our utility-maximizing rule so that our choice will be rational, we must somehow raise the marginal utility we get from the good whose price has risen. Following the principle of diminishing marginal utility, we can increase marginal utility only by *decreasing* our consumption of the good whose price has risen. As we consume fewer ice cream cones and more Big Macs, the marginal utility of ice cream rises and the marginal utility of a Big Mac falls.

This example can be extended to a general rule: If the price of a good rises, you'll increase your total utility by consuming less of it. When the price of a good goes up, consumption of that good will go down. Our principle of rational choice underlies the law of demand:

Quantity demanded rises as price falls, other things constant.

Or alternatively:

Quantity demanded falls as price rises, other things constant.

Q-5 If you are initially in equilibrium and the price of one good rises, how would you adjust your consumption to return to equilibrium?

Income and Substitution Effects

So far I haven't said precisely how much the quantity demanded would decrease with an increase in the price of an ice cream cone from $1 to $2. I didn't because of a certain ambiguity that arises when one talks about changes in nominal prices. To understand the cause of this ambiguity, notice that if the price of an ice cream cone has risen to $2, with $7 we can no longer consume 2 Big Macs and 3 ice cream cones. We've got to cut back for two reasons: First, we're poorer due to the rise in price. *The reduction in quantity demanded because we're poorer* is called the **income effect.** Second, the *relative* prices have changed. The price of ice cream has risen relative to the price of Big Macs. *The reduction in quantity demanded because relative price has risen* is called a **substitution effect.** Technically the law of demand is based only on the substitution effect.

Q-6 What are two effects that generally cause the quantity demanded to fall when the price rises?

To separate the two effects, let's assume that somebody compensates us for the rise in the price of ice cream cones. Since it would cost $10 [(2 × $2 = $4) + (3 × $2 = $6)] to buy what $7 bought previously, we'll assume that someone gives us an extra $3 to compensate us for the rise in price. Since we are not any poorer because of the price change, this eliminates the income effect. We now have $10, so we can buy 2 Big Macs and the 3 ice cream cones as we did before. If we do so, our total utility is once again 87 (34 units of utility from 2 Big Macs and 53 units of utility from 3 ice cream cones.) But will we do so? We can answer that with the table.

	Big Macs (P = $2)				Ice Cream (P = $2)		
Q	TU	MU	MU/P	Q	TU	MU	MU/P
0	0			0	0		
		20	10			29	14.5
1	20			1	29		
		14	7			17	8.5
2	34			2	46		
		10	5			7	3.5
3	44			3	53		

We see that the second Big Mac gives us more *MU* per dollar than the third cone. What happens if we exchange an ice cream cone for an additional Big Mac, so instead of buying 3 ice cream cones and 2 Big Macs, we buy 3 Big Macs and 2 ice cream cones? The *MU* per dollar of Big Macs falls from 7 to 5 and the *MU* per dollar of the ice cream cone (whose price is now $2) rises from 3.5 to 8.5. Our total utility rises to 44 from 3 Big Macs and 46 from 2 ice cream cones, for a total of 90 units of utility rather than the previous 87. We've increased our total utility by shifting our consumption out of ice cream, the good whose price has risen. The price of ice cream went up and, even though we were given more money so we could buy the same amount as before, we did not; we bought fewer ice cream cones. That's the substitution effect in action: It tells us that when the relative price of a good goes up, the quantity purchased of that good decreases, *even if you're given money to compensate you for the rise.*

The Law of Supply

The above discussion focused on demand and goods we consume, but this analysis of choice holds for the law of supply of factors of production, such as labor, that individuals supply to the market, as well as for demand. In supply decisions, you are giving up something—your time, land, or some other factor of production—and getting money in return. To show you how this works, let's consider one final example: how much labor you should supply to the market.

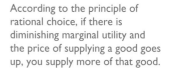

According to the principle of rational choice, if there is diminishing marginal utility and the price of supplying a good goes up, you supply more of that good.

Say that working another hour at your part-time job pays you another $8 and that you currently work 20 hours per week. That additional income from the final hour of work gives you an additional 24 units of utility. Also assume that your best alternative use of that hour—studying economics—gives you another 24 units of utility. (You didn't know economics gave you so much pleasure, did you?) So what should you do when your boss asks you to work an extra hour? Tell her no, you are already satisfying the utility-maximum rule $MU_w/W = MU_s/W$.

$$\frac{\text{Studying}}{24 \text{ units of utility}}{\$8} = \frac{\text{Working}}{24 \text{ units of utility}}{\$8}$$

The price of studying an additional hour is also your wage per hour because that wage is the opportunity cost of studying.

But now say that your boss offers to raise your wage to $8.50 per hour for work you do over 20 hours. That means that both your wage at work and the price of studying have increased. But now you can get more goods for working that additional hour. Let's say that those additional goods raise the marginal utility you get from an additional hour of work to 32 additional units of utility. Now the marginal utility of working an additional hour exceeds the marginal utility of studying an additional hour:

Q-7 Use the principle of rational choice to explain how you would change your quantity of work supplied if your employer raised your wage by $1 per hour.

$$\frac{\text{Studying}}{24 \text{ units of utility}}{\$8.50} < \frac{\text{Working}}{32 \text{ units of utility}}{\$8.50}$$

So you work the extra hour.

Now say your boss comes to you and asks what it would take to get you to work five hours more per week. After running the numbers through your computer-mind, you solve the utility-maximizing rule and tell her, "$10.00 an hour for overtime work and you've got your worker." Combining these hours and wages gives you the supply curve shown in the margin, which demonstrates the law of supply. As you have seen, factor supply curves can be derived from a comparison of marginal utilities for various activities in relation to work.

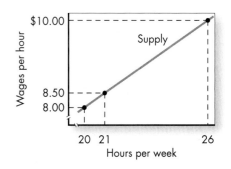

To see that you have the reasoning down, say that an exam is coming and you haven't studied. This will likely raise the marginal utility of studying sufficiently, so you will choose to work less, if you have a choice. What will that change do to your supply curve of labor?

If you answered that it will shift it in to the left, you're in good shape.

Opportunity Cost

Before we leave the principle of rational choice, let's consider how it relates to the opportunity cost concept that I presented in earlier chapters. *Opportunity cost* was the benefit forgone of the next-best alternative. Now that you've been through the principle of rational choice, you have a better sense of what is meant by opportunity cost of a forgone opportunity: It is essentially the marginal utility per dollar you forgo from the consumption of the next-best alternative.

To say $MU_x/P_x > MU_y/P_y$ is to say that the opportunity cost of not consuming good x is greater than the opportunity cost of not consuming good y. So you consume x.

When the marginal utilities per dollar spent are equal, the opportunity cost of the alternatives are equal. In reality, people don't use the utility terminology, and, indeed, a specific measure of utility doesn't exist. But the choice based on the price of goods relative to the benefit they provide is used all the time. Instead of utility terminology, people use the "really need" terminology. They say they will work the extra hour rather than study because they *really need* the money. To say you are working because you "really need" the money is the equivalent of saying the marginal utility of working is higher than the marginal utility of other choices. So the general rule fits decisions about supply, even if most people don't use the word *utility*. The more you "really, really need" something, the higher its marginal utility.

Applying Economists' Theory of Choice to the Real World

Understanding a theory involves more than understanding how a theory works; it also involves understanding the limits the assumptions underlying the theory place on the use of the theory. As I've noted above, economists are questioning some of the assumptions on which traditional economists' analysis of choice is based. Let's consider some of their questions. The first assumption we'll consider is the implicit assumption that decisions can be made costlessly.

The Cost of Decision Making

The principle of rational choice makes reasonably good intuitive sense when we limit our examples to two or three choices, as I did in this chapter. But in reality, we make hundreds of thousands of choices simultaneously. It simply doesn't make intuitive sense that we're going to apply rational choice to all those choices at once. That would exceed our decision-making abilities. This cost of decision making means that it is only rational to be somewhat irrational—to do things without applying the principle of rational choice. Thinking about decisions is one of the things we all economize on.

How real-world people make decisions in real-world situations is an open question that modern economists are spending a lot of time researching. Following the work of Nobel Prize winner Herbert Simon, a number of economists have come to believe that, to make real-world decisions, most people use *bounded rationality*—rationality based on rules of thumb—rather than using the principle of rational choice. They argue that many of our decisions are made with our minds on automatic pilot. This view of rationality has significant implications for interpreting and predicting economic events. For

---

The principle of rational choice states that, to maximize utility, choose goods until the opportunity costs of all alternatives are equal.

Q-8 If the opportunity cost of consuming good x is greater than the opportunity cost of consuming good y, which good has the higher marginal utility per dollar?

Q-9 True or false? Bounded rationality violates the principle of rational choice.

example, one rule of thumb is "You get what you pay for," which means that something with a high price is better than something with a low price. Put technically, we rely on price to convey information about quality. This reliance on price for information changes the inferences one can draw from the analysis, and can lead to upward-sloping demand curves.

A second rule of thumb that people sometimes use is "Follow the leader." If you don't know what to do, do what you think smart people are doing. Consider the clothes you're wearing. I suspect many of your choices of what to wear reflect this and the previous rules of thumb. Suppliers of clothing certainly think so and spend enormous amounts of money to exploit these rules of thumb. They try to steer your automatic pilot toward their goods. The suppliers emphasize these two rules ("You get what you pay for" and "Follow the leader") to convince people their product is the "in" thing to buy. If they succeed, they've got a gold mine; if they fail, they've got a flop. Advertising is designed to mine these rules of thumb.

Advertising is designed to mine rules of thumb.

In technical terms, the "Follow the leader" rule leads to *focal point equilibria,* in which a set of goods is consumed, not because the goods are objectively preferred to all other goods, but simply because, through luck, or advertising, they have become focal points to which people have gravitated. Once some people started consuming a good, others followed.

Given Tastes

A second assumption that behavioral economists are questioning is that our preferences are given and are not shaped by society. In reality, our preferences are determined not only by nature but also by our experiences—by nurture. Let's consider an example: Until it was recently banned, numerous major league baseball players chewed tobacco, but close to zero percent of college professors chewed tobacco. Why? Were major league baseball players somehow born with a tobacco-chewing gene while college professors were not? I doubt it. Tastes often are significantly influenced by society.

CONSPICUOUS CONSUMPTION Another aspect of taste that has been described by economists is **conspicuous consumption**—*the consumption of goods not for one's direct pleasure, but simply to show off to others.* The term was created approximately 100 years ago by the famous institutional economist Thorstein Veblen. Veblen argued that, just as some animals strut around to

Thinking Like a Modern Economist
Mental Accounting

If some of the analysis in this chapter doesn't sit well with you, you're not alone. It assumes that people make decisions on the margin and are able to make mental calculations easily. Behavioral economists, over the past 10 years, have been exploring exactly how people make decisions. The chapter explores a few of them. Here's another.

Consider the following scenario. You buy a $100 ticket to a concert and lose it on the way. If you had another $100, would you buy a replacement ticket and still go to the concert? Most people answer "no." But consider this second scenario. You're on your way to buy a $100 concert ticket and you lose $100 in cash on the way.

You still have enough cash to buy the ticket. Do you? Most people answer "yes."

Why the difference even though the financial situation is equivalent in both situations? Behavioral economists suggest that people make choices within particular mental categories, instead of over all categories. In the first scenario, the ticket was in the "concert" category. Adding another $100 places too much in that mental category. So people decline doing so. In the second scenario, the $100 cash wasn't in the "concert" category, so spending another spare $100 doesn't add to that "concert" category.

Web Note 19.4
Veblen Goods

show their abilities, humans consume to show that they can "afford it." For Veblen, mansions, designer clothing, and $300 appetizers were all examples of conspicuous consumption. He further argued that male industrialists (which were all industrialists at the time) were so busy with business that they didn't have time to show off enough, so they married a trophy spouse whose purpose was to spend their money in a way that showed off their wealth.

TASTES AND INDIVIDUAL CHOICE   One way in which economists integrate the above insights into economics is by emphasizing that the analysis is conducted on the assumption of "given tastes." As discussed above, in reality, economists agree that often forces besides price and marginal utility play a role in determining what people demand. They fully recognize that a whole other analysis is necessary to supplement theirs—an analysis of what determines taste.

Ask yourself what you ate today. Was it health food? Pizza? Candy? Whatever it was, it was probably not the most efficient way to satisfy your nutritional needs. The most efficient way to do that would be to eat only soybean mush and vitamin supplements at a cost of about $300 per year. That's less than one-tenth of what the average individual today spends on food per year. Most of us turn up our noses at soybean mush. Why? Because tastes are important.

I emphasize this point because some economists have been guilty of forgetting their simplifying assumption. Some economists in the 1800s thought that society's economic needs eventually would be fully met and that we would enter a golden age of affluence where all our material wants would be satisfied. They thought there would be surpluses of everything. Clearly that hasn't happened. Somehow it seems that whenever a need is met, it's replaced by a want, which soon becomes another need.

> Somehow, whenever a need is met, it's replaced by a want, which soon becomes another need.

There are, of course, examples of wants being temporarily satisfied, as a U.S. company on a small island in the Caribbean is reported to have discovered. Employees weren't showing up for work. The company sent in a team of efficiency experts who discovered the cause of their problem: The firm had recently raised wages, and workers had decided they could get all they wanted (warm weather, a gorgeous beach, plenty of food, and a little bit of spending money) by showing up for work once, maybe twice, a week. Such a situation was clearly not good for business, but the firm found a solution. It sent in thousands of Sears catalogs (back when Sears sent catalogs), and suddenly the workers were no longer satisfied with what they already had. They wanted more and went back to work to get it. When they were presented with new possibilities, their wants increased. Companies know that tastes aren't constant, and they spend significant amounts of money on advertising to make consumers have a taste for their goods. It works, too.

Web Note 19.5
Tastes and Choices

Tastes are also important in explaining differences in consumption among countries. For example, a Japanese person wouldn't consider having a meal without rice. Rice has a ceremonial, almost mystical value in Japan. In many parts of the United States, supper means meat and potatoes. In Germany, carp (a large goldfish) is a delicacy; in the United States, many people consider carp inedible. In the United States, corn is a desirable vegetable; in parts of Europe, until recently, it was considered pig food.

> **Q-10** Using the principle of rational choice, explain why a change in tastes will shift the demand curve.

To say we don't analyze tastes in the core of economic theory doesn't mean that we don't take them into account. Think back to Chapter 4, when we distinguished shifts in demand (the entire demand schedule shifts) from movements along the demand curve. Those movements along the demand curve were the effect of price. Tastes were one of the shift factors of demand. So economists do include tastes in their analysis; a change in tastes makes the demand curve shift.

> Economists take into account changes in tastes as shift factors of demand.

Making Stupid Decisions

It is hard to make good decisions. You need lots of training—in math, in economics, in logic. Think of kids—do five-year-olds make rational decisions? Some dyed-in-the-wool utilitarians might argue that whatever decision one makes must, by definition, be rational, but such usage makes the concept tautological—true by definition.

When applying the theory of rational choice, most economists agree that some decisions people make can be irrational. For example, they will concede that five-year-olds make a lot of what most parents would call stupid (or irrational) decisions. By a stupid decision, they mean a decision with expected consequences that, if the child had logically thought about them, would have caused the child not to make that particular decision. But five-year-olds often haven't learned how to think logically about expected consequences, so even traditional economists don't assume decisions made by five-year-olds reflect the rational choice model.

DILBERT © reprinted by permission of United Feature Syndicate, Inc.

In the real world, parents and teachers spend enormous effort to teach children what is rational, reasonable, and "appropriate." Children's decision-making process reflects that teaching. But parents and teachers teach more than a decision-making process; they also teach children a moral code that often includes the value of honor and the value of selflessness. These teachings shape their children's decision-making process (although not always in the way that parents or teachers think or hope) and modify their preferences. So our decision-making process and our preferences are, to some degree, taught to us.

Recognizing that preferences and decision-making processes are, to some degree, taught, not inherent, eliminates the fixed point by which to judge people's decisions: Are they making decisions that reflect their true needs, or are they simply reflecting what they have been taught? Eliminating that fixed point makes it difficult to draw unambiguous policy implications from economists' model of rational choice.

Utility Maximization

A third assumption that behavioral economists question is that individuals maximize a utility function that involves getting more for themselves. In experiments, behavioral economists have found that many people don't behave that way—at least in laboratory experiments.

Let's consider one example: the **ultimatum game.** Say that two people are given the opportunity to split $10. One person is allowed to make the decision as to how to divide it. He can keep whatever portion he wants, say $9.90, and give 10 cents to the other, or he could give a 50–50 split. But in the ultimatum game, *the first person only gets the money if the other person accepts the offer. If the second person does not accept, they both get nothing.*

From a purely selfish rationality standpoint, the first individual would keep most of the money, giving only a small amount to the other. Moreover, since the other person comes out better if he accepts even the small amount, he should accept any offer (even one cent) because it makes him better off in terms of his income. So the prediction from the standard economic model is that the first person will keep most of the $10 and the second person will accept whatever amount is offered. But when people play this game, this is not what happens. Instead, generally the first person offers something close to 50–50, which is almost always accepted. However, in instances where the first person offers only a small amount, the offer is generally rejected. It seems that people have a sense of fairness in their decisions, and are willing to pay money (reduce their income) to enforce that sense of fairness.

Behavioral economics is the study of economic choice that is based on realistic psychological foundations.

Three assumptions of the theory of rational choice are:

1. Decisions are costless.
2. Preferences are given.
3. Individuals maximize utility.

425

In other experiments, behavioral economists have found a strong **status quo bias**—*an individual's actions are very much influenced by the current situation, even when that reasonably does not seem to be very important to the decision.* An example of this in the real world occurred when Sweden privatized its social security system. When privatizing retirement, Sweden offered its citizens 456 funds from which to choose to invest. Even though the Swedish government encouraged participants to actively choose their own portfolio, it also offered one of the funds as a default. Even with over 450 other funds from which to choose, 33 percent chose the default fund, a far higher percentage than would be expected if the fund had not been identified as the default.

Given that reality arguing that people are rationally choosing among all alternatives is difficult. As we will discuss in Chapter 22, some behavioral economists have suggested that policy makers can take advantage of this status quo bias when they design policy by structuring programs so that choices are framed in ways that lead people to do what policy makers want them to do. Since individuals are freely choosing, they argue that such policy design does not violate consumer sovereignty.

There are many more such experiments and behavioral economic insights that are changing the face of modern economics. But these insights should be seen as complements to, rather than substitutes for, standard economic reasoning.

Conclusion

This chapter began with a discussion of the simplifying nature of the economists' analysis of rational choice. Now that you've been through it, you may be wondering if it's all that simple. In any case, I'm sure most of you would agree that it's complicated enough. When we're talking about formal analysis, I'm in total agreement.

But if you're talking about informal analysis and applying the analysis to the real world, most economists also would agree that this theory of choice is in no way acceptable. Economists believe that there's more to life than maximizing utility. We believe in love, anger, and doing crazy things just for the sake of doing crazy things. We're real people.

But, we argue, simplicity has its virtue, and often people hide their selfish motivations. Few people like to go around and say, "I did this because I'm a self-interested, calculating person who cares primarily about myself." Instead they usually emphasize other motives: "Society conditioned me to do it"; "I'm doing this to achieve fairness"; "It's my upbringing." And they're probably partially right, but often they hide and obscure their self-interested motives in their psychological explanations. The beauty of the simple traditional economic psychological assumption is that it cuts through many obfuscations (that's an obfuscating word meaning "smokescreens") and, in doing so, often captures a part of reality that others miss. Let's consider a couple of examples.

Why does government restrict who's allowed to practice law? The typical layperson's answer is "to protect the public." The traditional economic answer is that many of the restrictions do little to protect the public. Instead their primary function is to restrict the *number* of lawyers and thereby increase the marginal utility of existing lawyers and the price they can charge.

Why do museum directors almost always want to increase the size of their collections? The layperson's (and museum directors') answer is that they're out to preserve our artistic heritage. The traditional economic answer is that it often has more to do with maximizing the utility of the museum staff. (Economist William Grampp made this argument in a book about the economics of art. He supported his argument by pointing out that more than half of museums' art is in storage and not accessible to the public. Acquiring more art will simply lead to more art going into storage.)

Economists use their simple self-interest theory of choice because it cuts through many obfuscations, and, in doing so, often captures a part of reality that others miss.

Now in no way am I claiming that the traditional economic answer based on pure self-interest is always the correct one. But I am arguing that approaching problems by asking the question "What's in it for the people making the decisions?" is a useful approach that will give you more insight into what's going on than many other approaches. It gets people to ask tough, rather than easy, questions. After you've asked the tough questions, then you can see how to modify the conclusions by looking deeply into the real-world institutions.

All too often, students think of economics and economic reasoning as establishment reasoning. That's not true. Economic reasoning can be extremely subversive to existing establishments. But whatever it is, it is not subversive in order to be subversive, or proestablishment to be proestablishment. It's simply a logical application of a simple idea—individual choice theory—to a variety of problems.

> Approaching problems by asking the question "What's in it for the people making the decision?" is a useful approach that will give you more insight than many other approaches.

Summary

- Total utility is the satisfaction obtained from consuming a product; marginal utility is the satisfaction obtained from consuming one additional unit of a product. *(LO19-1)*

- The principle of diminishing marginal utility states that after some point, the marginal utility of consuming more of the good will fall. *(LO19-1)*

- The principle of rational choice is:

  If $\dfrac{MU_x}{P_x} > \dfrac{MU_y}{P_y}$, choose to consume more of good x.

  If $\dfrac{MU_x}{P_x} < \dfrac{MU_y}{P_y}$, choose to consume more of good y.

  (LO19-1)

- The utility-maximizing rule says:

  If $\dfrac{MU_x}{P_x} = \dfrac{MU_y}{P_y}$, you're maximizing utility; you're indifferent between good x and good y. *(LO19-2)*

- Unless $MU_x/P_x = MU_y/P_y$, an individual can rearrange his or her consumption to increase total utility. *(LO19-2)*

- The law of demand can be derived from the principle of rational choice. *(LO19-3)*

- If you're in equilibrium and the price of a good rises, you'll reduce your consumption of that good to reestablish equilibrium. *(LO19-3)*

- The law of demand is based on the income effect and the substitution effect. The income effect is the reduction in quantity demanded when price rises because the price rise makes one poorer. The substitution effect is the reduction in quantity demanded when price rises because you substitute a good whose price has not risen. *(LO19-3)*

- The law of supply can be derived from the principle of rational choice. *(LO19-3)*

- If your wage rises, the marginal utility of the goods you can buy with that wage will rise and you will work more to satisfy the utility-maximizing rule. *(LO19-3)*

- Opportunity cost is essentially the marginal utility per dollar one forgoes from the consumption of the next-best alternative. *(LO19-3)*

- To apply economists' analysis of choice to the real world, we must carefully consider, and adjust for, the underlying assumptions, such as costlessness of decision making and given tastes. *(LO19-4)*

- The theory of choice assumes decision making is costless, tastes are given, and individuals maximize utility. *(LO19-4)*

- Behavioral economics is the study of economic choice that is based on realistic psychological foundations. *(LO19-4)*

- The ultimatum game suggests that people care about fairness as well as total income. The status quo bias suggests that actions are based on perceived norms. *(LO19-4)*

Key Terms

conspicuous
  consumption *(423)*
income effect *(420)*
marginal utility *(412)*

principle of diminishing
  marginal utility *(414)*
principle of rational
  choice *(416)*

status quo bias *(426)*
substitution effect *(420)*
total utility *(412)*
ultimatum game *(425)*

utility *(412)*
utility-maximizing
  rule *(416)*

Questions and Exercises

1. Explain how marginal utility differs from total utility. *(LO19-1)*

2. According to the principle of diminishing marginal utility, how does marginal utility change as more of a good is consumed? As less of a good is consumed? *(LO19-1)*

3. Complete the following table of Scout's utility from drinking cans of soda and answer the questions below. *(LO19-1)*

Cans of Soda	Total Utility	Marginal Utility
0	—	
1	—	10
2	22	12
3	32	—
4	—	8
5	—	4
6	44	—
7	42	—

a. At what point does marginal utility begin to fall?
b. Will Scout consume the 7th can of soda? Explain your answer.
c. True or false? Scout will be following the utility-maximizing rule by consuming 2 cans of soda. Explain your answer.

4. What key psychological assumptions do economists make in their theory of individual choice? *(LO19-1)*

5. The following table gives the price and total utility of three goods: A, B, and C.

Good	Price	Total Utility							
		1	2	3	4	5	6	7	8
A	$10	200	380	530	630	680	700	630	430
B	2	20	34	46	56	64	72	78	82
C	6	50	60	70	80	90	100	90	80

As closely as possible, determine how much of the three goods you would buy with $20. Explain why you chose what you did. *(LO19-2)*

6. The following table gives the marginal utility of John's consumption of three goods: A, B, and C. *(LO19-2)*

Units of Consumption	MU of A	MU of B	MU of C
1	20	25	45
2	18	20	30
3	16	15	24
4	14	10	18
5	12	8	15
6	10	6	12

a. Good A costs $2 per unit, good B costs $1, and good C costs $3. How many units of each should a consumer with $12 buy to maximize his or her utility?
b. How will the answer change if the price of B rises to $2?
c. How about if the price of C is 50 cents but the other prices are as in *a*?

7. The total utility of your consumption of widgets is 40; it changes by 2 with each change in widgets consumed. The total utility of your consumption of wadgets is also 40 but changes by 3 with each change in wadgets consumed. The price of widgets is $2 and the price of wadgets is $3. How many widgets and wadgets should you consume? *(LO19-2)*

8. Early Classical economists found the following "diamond/water" paradox perplexing: "Why is water, which is so useful and necessary, so cheap, when diamonds, which are so useless and unnecessary, so expensive?" Using the utility concept, explain why it is not really a paradox. (Difficult) *(LO19-2)*

9. State the law of demand and explain how it relates to the principle of rational choice. *(LO19-3)*

10. Suppose a large cheese pizza costs $10 and a calzone costs $5. You have $40 to spend. The marginal utility (*MU*) that you derive from each is as follows: (*LO19-3*)

Number	*MU* of Pizza	*MU* of Calzone
0		
	60	30
1		
	40	28
2		
	30	24
3		
	20	20
4		
	10	10
5		

   a. How many of each would you buy?

   b. Suppose the price of a calzone rises to $10. How many of each would you buy?

   c. Use this to show how the principle of rational choice leads to the law of demand.

11. Your study partner tells you that if you are compensated for the impact on your budget of a rise in the price of a good, your purchase choices won't change. Is he right? Explain. (*LO19-3*)

12. State the law of supply and explain how it relates to opportunity cost. (*LO19-3*)

13. If the supply curve is perfectly inelastic, what is the opportunity cost of the supplier? (*LO19-3*)

14. There is a small but growing movement known as "voluntary simplicity," which is founded on the belief in a simple life of working less and spending less. Do Americans who belong to this movement follow the principle of rational choice? (*LO19-3*)

15. According to Thorstein Veblen, what is the purpose of conspicuous consumption? Does the utility derived from the consumption of these goods come from their price or functionality? Give an example of such a good. (*LO19-4*)

16. Say that the ultimatum game described in the chapter was changed so that the first individual could keep the money regardless of whether the offer was accepted by the second individual or not. (*LO19-4*)

   a. What would you expect would likely happen to the offers?

   b. What would happen to the acceptances?

Questions from Alternative Perspectives

1. The book seems to suggest that all decisions are economic decisions.
   a. Would you agree?
   b. How would tithing fit into the decision-making calculus? (Religious)

2. In his book *Why Perestroika Failed: The Politics and Economics of Socialist Transformation,* Austrian economist Peter Boettke argues that Soviet-style socialist countries had to fail because they could not appropriately reflect individuals' choices. What was his likely argument? (Austrian)

3. The book discusses the issue of decision making in reference to the individual, but generally households, not individuals, make decisions.
   a. How do you think decisions are actually made about issues such as consumption and allocation of time within the household?
   b. Does bargaining take place?
   c. If so, what gives an individual power to bargain effectively for his or her preferences?
   d. Do individuals act cooperatively within the family and competitively everywhere else? (Feminist)

4. Often, people buy a good to impress others and not because they want it.
   a. What implications would such actions have for the application of economic analysis?
   b. How many goods are bought because people want them and how many goods are bought because of advertising and conspicuous consumption? (Post-Keynesian)

5. Most people believe that marginal utility diminishes with each additional dollar of income (or one more dollar is worth more to a poor person than a rich one).
   a. If that is true, how would you design an income tax that imposes an equal burden in lost utility on rich and poor households?
   b. How would your answer differ if the marginal utility of income did not diminish?
   c. How would your answer differ if your goal was to leave households with equal levels of utility from their last dollar of income? (Radical)

Issues to Ponder

1. How would the world be different than it is if the principle of diminishing marginal utility seldom held true?

2. True or false? It is sometimes said that an economist is a person who knows the price of everything but the value of nothing. Why?

3. Assign a measure of utility to your studying for various courses. Do your study habits follow the principle of rational choice?

4. Explain your motivation for four personal decisions you have made in the past year, using economists' model of individual choice.

5. Nobel Prize–winning economist George Stigler explains how the famous British economist Phillip Wicksteed decided where to live. His two loves were fresh farm eggs, which were more easily obtained the farther from London he was, and visits from friends, which decreased the farther he moved away from London. Given these two loves, describe the decision rule that you would have expected Wicksteed to follow.

6. Although the share of Americans who say they are "very happy" hasn't changed much in the last five decades, the number of products produced and consumed per person has risen tremendously. How can this be?

7. Give an example of a recent purchase for which you used a rule of thumb in your decision-making process. Did your decision follow the principle of rational choice? Explain.

8. Economic experiments have found that individuals prefer an outcome where no one is made better off to an outcome where the welfare of only some is improved if that improvement in welfare is unequally distributed. Why do you think this is so?

9. You are buying your spouse, significant other, or close friend a ring. You decide to show your reasonableness and buy a cubic zirconium ring that sells at $\frac{1}{50}$ the cost of a mined diamond and that any normal person could not tell from a mined diamond just by looking at it. In fact, the zirconium will have more brilliance and fewer occlusions (imperfections) than a mined diamond.
   a. How will your spouse (significant other, close friend) likely react?
   b. Why?
   c. Is this reaction justified?

10. Joseph Gallo, the founder of the famous wine company that bears his name, said that when he first started selling wine right after Prohibition (laws outlawing the sale of alcohol), he poured two glasses of wine from the same bottle and put a price of 10 cents a bottle on one and 5 cents a bottle on the other. He let people test both and asked them which they wanted. Most wanted the 10-cent bottle, even though they were the same wine.
   a. What does this tell us about people?
   b. Can you think of other areas where that may be the case?
   c. What does this suggest about pricing?

Answers to Margin Questions

1. If the total utility curve is a straight line, the marginal utility curve will be flat with a slope of zero since marginal utility would not change with additional units. (*p. 413; LO19-1*)

2. False. The principle of diminishing marginal utility is that as one increases consumption of a good, the good's marginal utility decreases. (*p. 414; LO19-1*)

3. Given a choice between the two, the rational choice is to watch CNN for one hour since it provides the higher marginal utility per hour. (*p. 415; LO19-1*)

4. False. You are maximizing total utility when the marginal utilities per dollar are the same for all goods. This does not have to be where marginal utility is zero. (*p. 417; LO19-2*)

5. If I am initially in equilibrium, then $MU_x/P_x = MU_y/P_y = MU_z/P_z$ for all goods I consume. If the price of one good goes up, I will decrease my consumption of that good and increase the consumption of other goods until the equilibrium is met again where $MU_x/P_x = MU_y/P_y = MU_z/P_z$. (*p. 420; LO19-3*)

6. The two effects are the income effect and the substitution effect. (*p. 420; LO19-3*)

7. If offered one more dollar per hour, I would choose to substitute labor for leisure since the price of leisure (pay per hour of work) has increased. Following the principle of rational choice, I would work more to lower the marginal utility of work so that $MU_w/P_w = MU_l/P_l$. (*p. 421; LO19-3*)

8. Good y has the higher marginal utility per dollar since the opportunity cost of consuming good x is the marginal utility per dollar of consuming good y. (*p. 422; LO19-3*)

9. This could be true or false. It depends on how you interpret bounded rationality. If it is interpreted within a costless decision-making environment, it does violate the principle of rational choice since there is no reason to be less than rational. If, however, it is interpreted within a costly decision-making environment, then you can be making decisions within a range because the marginal cost of increasing the range of choices exceeds the marginal benefit of doing so, and in that case bounded rationality is consistent with the principle of rational choice. Information is not costless. (*p. 422; LO19-4*)

10. If a person is in equilibrium and a change in tastes leads to an increase in the marginal utility for one good, he will increase consumption of that good to reestablish equilibrium. A change in tastes will shift a demand curve because it will cause a change in quantity consumed without a change in the good's price. (*p. 424; LO19-4*)

Indifference Curve Analysis

As I stated in the chapter, analyzing individual choice using actual numbers is unnecessary. In the chapter, I asked you to make a deal with me: You'd remember that actual numbers are unnecessary and I'd use them anyway. This appendix is for those who didn't accept my deal (and for those whose professors want them to get some practice in Graphish). It presents an example of a more formal analysis of individual choice.

Sophie's Choice

Sophie is a junk food devotee. She lives on two goods: chocolate bars, which cost $1 each, and cans of soda, which sell for 50 cents apiece. Sophie is trying to get as much pleasure as possible, given her resources. Alternatively expressed, Sophie is trying to maximize her utility, given a budget constraint.

By translating this statement of Sophie's choice into graphs, I can demonstrate the principle of rational choice without ever mentioning any specific amount of utility.

The graph we'll use will have chocolate bars on the vertical axis and cans of soda on the horizontal axis, as in Figure A19-1.

Graphing the Budget Constraint

Let's begin by asking: How can we translate her budget constraint (the $10 maximum she has to spend) into Graphish? The easiest way to do that is to ask what would happen if she spends her $10 all on chocolate bars or all on cans of soda. Since a chocolate bar costs $1, if she spends it all on chocolate bars, she can get 10 bars (point A in Figure A19-1). If she spends it all on cans of soda, she can get 20 cans of soda (point B). This gives us two points.

But what if she wants some combination of soda and chocolate bars? If we draw a line between points A and B, we'll have a graphical picture of her budget constraint and can answer that question because a **budget constraint** is *a curve that shows us the various combinations of goods an individual can buy with a given amount of money*. The line is her budget constraint in Graphish.

To see that it is, say Sophie is spending all her money on chocolate bars. She then decides to buy one fewer chocolate bar. That gives her $1 to spend on soda, which, since those cans cost 50 cents each, allows her to buy 2 cans. Point C (9 chocolate bars and 2 cans of soda) represents that decision. Notice how point C is on the budget constraint. Repeat this exercise from various starting points until you're comfortable with the fact that the line does indeed represent the various combinations of soda and chocolate bars Sophie can buy with the $10. It's a line with a slope of $-\frac{1}{2}$ and intersects the chocolate-bars axis at 10 and the cans-of-soda axis at 20.

To be sure that you've got it, ask yourself what would happen to the budget constraint if Sophie got another $4 to spend on the two goods. Going through the same reasoning should lead you to the conclusion that the budget constraint will shift to the right so that it will intersect the cans-of-soda axis at 28 (point D), but its slope won't change. (I started the new line for you.) Make sure you can explain why.

Now what if the price of a can of soda goes up to $1? What happens to the budget line? (This is a question many people miss.) If you said the budget line becomes steeper, shifting in along the cans-of-soda axis to point E while remaining anchored along the chocolate-bars axis until the slope equals -1, you've got it. If you didn't say that, go through the same reasoning we went through at first (if Sophie buys only cans of soda . . .) and then draw the new line. You'll see it becomes steeper. Put another way, the absolute value of the slope of the curve is the ratio of the price of cans of soda to the price of chocolate bars; the absolute value of the slope becomes greater with a rise in the price of cans of soda.

FIGURE A19-1 **Graphing the Budget Constraint**

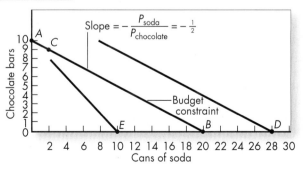

Graphing the Indifference Curve

Now let's consider the second part of Sophie's choice: the pleasure part. Sophie is trying to get as much pleasure as she can from her $10. How do we deal with this in Graphish?

To see, let's go through a thought experiment. Say Sophie had 14 chocolate bars and 4 cans of soda (point *A* in Figure A19-2). Let's ask her, "Say you didn't know the price of either good and we took away 4 of those chocolate bars (so you had 10). How many cans of soda would we have to give you so that you would be just as happy as before we took away the 4 chocolate bars?"

Since she's got lots of chocolate bars and few cans of soda, her answer is probably, "Not too many; say, 1 can of soda." This means that she would be just as happy to have 10 chocolate bars and 5 cans of soda (point *B*) as she would to have 14 chocolate bars and 4 cans of soda (point *A*). Connect those points and you have the beginning of a "just-as-happy" curve. But that doesn't sound impressive enough, so, following economists' terminology, we'll call it an **indifference curve**—*a curve that shows combinations of goods among which an individual is indifferent.* She's indifferent between points *A* and *B*.

If you continue our thought experiment, you'll get a set of combinations of chocolate bars and cans of soda like that shown in the table in Figure A19-2.

If you plot each of these combinations of points on the graph in Figure A19-2 and connect all these points, you have one of Sophie's indifference curves: a curve representing combinations of cans of soda and chocolate bars among which Sophie is indifferent.

Let's consider the shape of this curve. First, it's downward-sloping. That's reasonable; it simply says that if you take something away from Sophie, you've got to give her something in return if you want to keep her indifferent between what she had before and what she has now. The absolute value of the slope of an indifference curve is the **marginal rate of substitution**—*the rate at which one good must be added when the other is taken away in order to keep the individual indifferent between the two combinations.*

Second, it's bowed inward. That's because as Sophie gets more and more of one good, it takes fewer and fewer of another good to compensate for the loss of the good she incurred in order to get more of the other good. The underlying reasoning is similar to that in our discussion of the law of diminishing marginal utility, but notice we haven't even mentioned utility. Technically the reasoning for the indifference curve being bowed inward is called the **law of diminishing marginal rate of substitution**—which tells us that *as you get more and more of a good, if some of that good is taken away, then the marginal addition of another good you need to keep you on your indifference curve gets less and less.*

Even more technically, we can say that the absolute value of the slope of the indifference curve equals the ratio of the marginal utility of cans of soda to the marginal utility of chocolate bars:

$$\left| \text{Slope} \right| = \frac{MU_{soda}}{MU_{chocolate}} = \text{Marginal rate of substitution}$$

That ratio equals the marginal rate of substitution of cans of soda for chocolate bars. Let's consider an example. Say that in Figure A19-2 Sophie is at point *A* and that the marginal utility she gets from an increase from 4 to 5 cans of soda is 10. Since we know that she was willing to give up 4 chocolate bars to get that 1 can of soda (and thereby move from point *A* to point *B*), that 10 must equal the loss of utility she gets from the loss of 4 chocolate bars out of the 14 she originally had. So the marginal rate of substitution of cans of soda for chocolate bars between points *A* and *B* must be 4. That's the absolute value of the slope of that curve. Therefore, her *MU* of a chocolate bar must be about 2.5 (10 for 4 chocolate bars).

FIGURE A19-2   **Sophie's Indifference Curve**

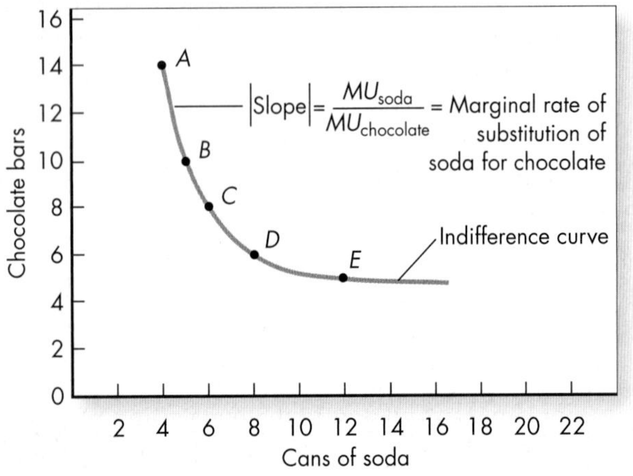

Chocolate Bars	Cans of Soda	
14	4	A
10	5	B
8	6	C
6	8	D
5	12	E

FIGURE A19-3   A Group of Indifference Curves

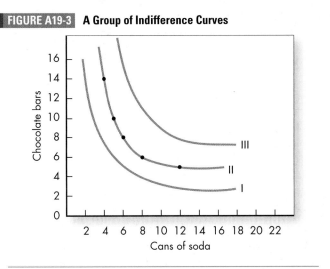

FIGURE A19-3   A Group of Indifference Curves

"prefer-more-to-less" principle would be violated. Say we start at point A: Sophie has 8 chocolate bars and 6 cans of soda. We know that since *A* (8 chocolate bars and 6 sodas) and *B* (6 chocolate bars and 8 cans of soda) are on the same indifference curve, Sophie is indifferent between *A* and *B*. Similarly with points *B* and *C:* Sophie would just as soon have 9 chocolate bars and 7 cans of soda as she would 6 chocolate bars and 8 cans of soda.

It follows by logical deduction that point *A* must be indifferent to *C*. But consider points *A* and *C* carefully. At point *C*, Sophie has 7 cans of soda and 9 chocolate bars. At point *A* she has 6 cans of soda and 8 chocolate bars. At point *C* she has more of both goods than she has at point *A,* so to say she's indifferent between these two points violates the "prefer-more-to-less" criterion. Ergo (that's Latin, meaning "therefore"), two indifference curves cannot intersect. That's why we drew the group of indifference curves in Figure A19-3 so that they do not intersect.

Combining Indifference Curves and Budget Constraints

Now let's put the budget constraint and the indifference curves together and ask how many chocolate bars and cans of soda Sophie will buy if she has $10, given the psychological makeup described by the indifference curves in Figure A19-3.

To answer that question, we must put the budget line of Figure A19-1 and the indifference curves of Figure A19-3 together, as we do in Figure A19-5.

You can continue this same reasoning, starting with various combinations of goods. If you do so, you can get a whole group of indifference curves like that in Figure A19-3. Each curve represents a different level of happiness. Assuming she prefers more to less, Sophie is better off if she's on Curve II than if she's on Curve I, and even better off if she's on Curve III. Her goal in life is to get out to the furthest indifference curve she can.

To see whether you've followed the reasoning, ask yourself the following question: "Assuming Sophie prefers more of a good to less (which seems reasonable), can any two of Sophie's indifference curves cross each other as the ones in Figure A19-4 do?"

The answer is no, no, no! Why? Because they're indifference curves. If the curves were to cross, the

FIGURE A19-4   Why Indifference Curves Cannot Cross

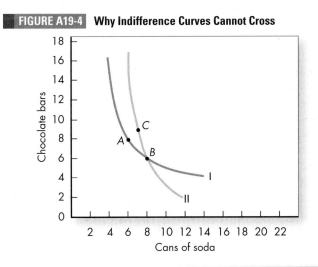

FIGURE A19-5   Combining Indifference Curves and Budget Constraint

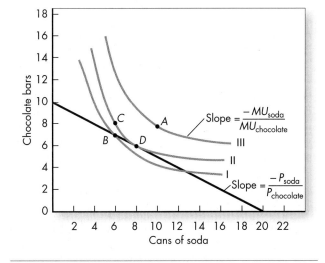

As we discussed, Sophie's problem is to get to as high an indifference curve as possible, given her budget constraint. Let's first ask if she should move to point *A* (8 chocolate bars and 10 cans of soda). That looks like a good point. But you should quickly recognize that she can't get to point *A;* her budget line won't let her. (She doesn't have enough money.) Well then, how about point *B* (7 chocolate bars and 6 cans of soda)? She can afford that combination; it's on her budget constraint. The problem with point *B* is the following: She'd rather be at point *C* since point *C* has more chocolate bars and the same amount of soda (8 chocolate bars and 6 cans of soda). But, you say, she can't reach point *C*. Yes, that's true, but she can reach point *D*. And, by the definition of indifference curve, she's indifferent between point *C* and point *D*, so point *D* (6 chocolate bars and 8 cans of soda), which she can reach given her budget constraint, is preferred to point *B*.

The same reasoning holds for all other points. The reason is that the combination of chocolate bars and cans of soda represented by point *D* is the best she can do. It is the point where the indifference curve and the budget line are tangent—the point at which the slope of the budget line $(-P_s/P_c)$ equals the slope of the indifference curve $(-MU_s/MU_c)$. Equating those slopes gives $(-P_s/P_c) = (MU_s/MU_c)$, or

$$MU_c/P_c = MU_s/P_s$$

This equation, you may remember from the chapter, is the equilibrium condition of our principle of rational choice. So by our Graphish analysis we arrived at the same conclusion we arrived at in the chapter, only this time we did it without using actual numbers. This means that even without a utilometer, economists' principle of rational choice is internally logical.

Deriving a Demand Curve from the Indifference Curve

Not only can we derive the principle of rational choice with indifference curve/budget line analysis, we also can derive a demand curve. To do so, ask yourself what a demand curve is. It's the quantity of a good that a person will buy at various prices. Since the budget line gives us the relative price of a good, and the point of tangency of the indifference curve gives us the quantity that a person would buy at that price, we can derive a demand curve from the indifference curves and budget lines. To derive a demand curve, we go through a set of thought experiments asking how many cans of soda Sophie would buy at various prices. We'll go through one of those experiments.

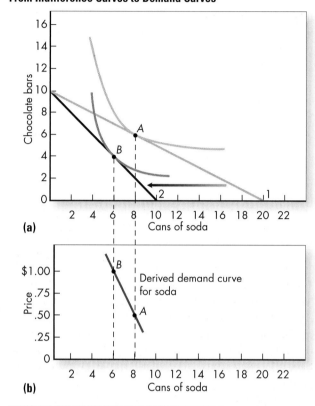

FIGURE A19-6 (A AND B)
From Indifference Curves to Demand Curves

We start with the analysis we used before when Sophie started with $10 and chose to buy 8 cans of soda when the price of a can of soda was 50 cents (point *A* in Figure A19-6(a)). That analysis provides us with one point on the demand curve. I represent that by point *A* in Figure A19-6(b). At a price of 50 cents, Sophie buys 8 cans of soda.

Now say the price of a can of soda rises to $1. That rotates the budget line in, from budget line 1 to budget line 2 as in Figure A19-6(a). She can't buy as much as she could before. But we can determine how much she'll buy by the same reasoning we used previously. She'll choose a point at which her lower indifference curve is tangent to her new budget line. As you can see, she'll choose point *B,* which means that she buys 6 cans of soda when the price of a can of soda is $1. Graphing that point (6 cans of soda at $1 each) on our price/quantity axis in Figure A19-6(b), we have another point on our demand curve, point *B*. Connect these two together and you can see we're getting a downward-sloping demand curve, just as the law of demand said we would. To make sure you understand, continue the analysis for a couple of additional price changes. You'll see that the demand curve you derive will be downward-sloping.

There's much more we can do with indifference curves. We can distinguish income effects and substitution effects. (Remember, when the price of a can of soda rose, Sophie was worse off. So to be as well off as before, as is required by the substitution effect, she'd have to be compensated for that rise in price by an offsetting fall in the price of chocolate bars.) But let's make a deal. You tentatively believe me when I say that all kinds of stuff can be done with indifference curves and budget constraints, and I'll leave the further demonstration and the proofs for you to experience in the intermediate microeconomics courses.

Key Terms

budget constraint *(431)*
indifference curve *(432)*

law of diminishing marginal rate of
    substitution *(432)*

marginal rate of
    substitution *(432)*

Questions and Exercises

1. Zachary has $5 to spend on two goods: video games and hot dogs. Hot dogs cost $1 apiece while video games cost 50 cents apiece.
   a. Draw a graph of Zachary's budget constraint, placing video games on the *y* axis.
   b. Suppose the price of hot dogs falls to 50 cents apiece. Draw the new budget constraint.
   c. Suppose Zachary now has $8 to spend. Draw the new budget constraint using the prices from *b*.

2. Zachary's indifference curves are shown in the following graph. Determine on which indifference curve Zachary will be, given the budget constraints and prices in *a, b,* and *c* from question 1.

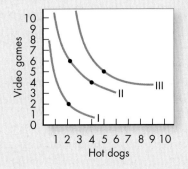

a. Given a choice, which budget constraint would Zachary prefer most? Least?
b. What is the marginal rate of substitution of hot dogs for video games at each of the combinations chosen with budget constraints *a, b,* and *c* in question 1?

3. What would an indifference curve look like if the marginal rate of substitution were zero? If it were constant?

4. What might an indifference curve look like if the law of diminishing marginal utility did not hold?

chapter 20

Game Theory, Strategic Decision Making, and Behavioral Economics

" All men can see the tactics whereby I conquer, but what none can see is the strategy out of which victory is evolved. "

—Sun Tzu

In the movie *A Beautiful Mind,* John Nash and some friends walk into a bar with the idea of meeting some women. They see some women, one of whom is blonde, and discuss their strategy to meet them. Nash tells his friends that if each were to approach the problem on his own, they might all initially go for the blond (whom they consider the most beautiful— OK, so it's a bit clichéish—movies generally are). Nash tells his friends:

> If everyone competes for the blonde, we block each other and no one gets her. So then we all go for her friends. But they give us the cold shoulder, because no one likes to be second choice. Again, no winner. But what if none of us go for the blonde? We don't get in each other's way; we don't insult the other girls. That is the only way we win. That's the only way we all get a girl. (From A *Beautiful Mind:* The Shooting Script, Akiva Goldsman, 2002.)[1]

In the movie this is Nash's eureka moment: Each person, acting in his or her own best interest, will not necessarily arrive at the best of all possible outcomes. Adam Smith is wrong.

Game Theory and the Economic Way of Thinking

The general reasoning process that Nash is portrayed as using captures a central element of the modern economic way of thinking.[2] That central element is *strategic thinking.* Whenever the decisions being analyzed involve interdependent

After reading this chapter, you should be able to:

LO20-1 Explain what game theory is and give an example of a game and a solution to a game.

LO20-2 Discuss how strategic reasoning and backward induction are used in solving games.

LO20-3 Distinguish informal game theory differs from formal game theory.

LO20-4 Describe how the results of game theory experiments challenge some standard economic assumptions.

[1]I am only reporting, not condoning, the portrayal in the movie. I fully agree that Nash's EQ (emotional quotient) and sense of what is socially appropriate can be questioned. If you saw the movie, you probably agree, too.

[2]The reasoning attributed to Nash in the film can also be questioned. (Economists have pointed out that the movie gets the reasoning about the men's best strategy mixed up. Chalk these inaccuracies up to artistic license; it made for a better scene, so the filmmakers didn't care about its being wrong. Their reasoning was probably: Except for economists and mathematicians, no one will notice or care.)

decisions, the decision makers' strategy needs to be considered. Since all types of decisions are interdependent, the study of such interdependent decision-making processes is central to modern economics. In fact, in recent years an entire theory of strategic thinking, called **game theory**—*formal economic reasoning applied to situations in which decisions are interdependent*—has developed.

Game theory is a broad-based approach to understanding human interaction, and is not solely a tool used by economists. All social scientists—political scientists, sociologists, and anthropologists as well as economists—are using game theory more and more as a tool of analysis. Thus, you can see political scientists discussing war strategy and sociologists discussing social relationships in game theoretic terms. In many ways, game theory is the underlying model of the social sciences.

More and more, game theory is becoming the basic tool of modern economics, in many cases replacing supply and demand as economists' core model of choice. Today, when graduate students study microeconomics, they spend more time learning game theory than they spend learning the intricacies of supply and demand models. Game theory has become so important because it is a highly flexible tool that can be applied to many situations without making the restrictive assumptions of the supply/demand model.

> Game theory is formal economic reasoning applied to situations in which decisions are interdependent.

> Q-1 True or false? Game theory is inconsistent with supply/demand analysis. Explain your answer.

Game Theory and Economic Modeling

Before we analyze some specific games, let's step back and reflect on modern economists' modeling method—their way of thinking—and consider where game theory fits within that method. Nobel Prize–winning economist Bob Solow has nicely summarized economists' way of thinking as follows: "You look at a problem; you create a simple model that captures its essence; you empirically test how well that model fits the data, and if it fits, you use that model as a guide to understanding the problem and devising a solution." This method sometimes gets lost as introductory students learn how to apply the models that have already been developed, rather than learning how to develop their own models.

I suspect that oftentimes when you have learned a model, you sensed that it was a stretch to make the model fit real-world situations. Economists share that concern, and are continually tweaking the existing models and developing other models that help us understand real-world problems and issues. That's why game theory developed; it offers a new set of models with which to approach economic issues. Game theory models can be better tailored to fit the actual problem, and thus are more flexible than the standard models. The cost of that flexibility is that individual game theory models are not as broad as the standard models. A different game theory model must be developed for each different situation and for each different set of assumptions. So rather than having a single model with a single equilibrium solution, in game theory there are many models that often have multiple equilibrium solutions. Hence, game theory is really a framework—a method—rather than a finished set of models to mechanistically use in understanding real-world events.

> Game theory models are more flexible than the standard economic models.

The Game Theory Framework

To introduce you to the game theory framework, let's consider a variation of a story told by economists Avinash Dixit and Susan Skeath, in their excellent book on game theory, *Games of Strategy*. In it, four students, who all had A averages, had partied the night before the exam (yes, partying happens) and had slept through the exam. Since they were "A" students, and they felt the professor liked them, they decided to make up a sad sob story and convince her that they should be allowed to take the exam late. So they went to the professor all apologetic, explaining how they had meant to come to the exam, but when they were returning from visiting a sick brother of one of them (who lived 100 miles away), they had had a flat tire. Unfortunately, there was no spare, and it took them five hours to get the flat fixed, making them late for the exam. They knew it wasn't the best story but they figured it was worth a try.

To their surprise the professor agreed with no problem to let them take the exam two days later. So they studied hard, figuring they were a shoo-in for As. The professor put them each in separate rooms and gave them the exam. The first page, worth 10 points, was an easy question, which they all were sure they aced. The second page, however, had just one question, but it was worth 90 points. The question was: "Which tire?"

This is an example of a screening question, which is meant to reveal strategic information about the person who answers. A **screening question** is *a question structured in a way to reveal strategic information about the person who answers.* If they had actually had a flat, the question would be easy to answer, and they would get their As. But if they didn't have a flat (and didn't coordinate their stories beforehand), it is highly unlikely that they would all pick the same answer, and the professor would know that they were lying. Of course, if they had been bright, or had studied game theory, they would have expected that the professor would use such a screening device and would have figured out which tire to say went flat before they went in. But of course, if the professor had taught them game theory, or knew they were even better-than-"A" students, she would have assumed that they would have coordinated their stories about which tire, and she would have worked out an even more elaborate testing strategy to get them to reveal the truth. Game theory studies such issues. Devising such strategies and understanding the strategic interaction of individuals when they take into account the expected reaction of others are the essence of game theory.

You have already seen some of the games that comprise game theory—for example, the ultimatum game in the earlier chapter on individual choice. In the remainder of the chapter, we introduce you to some other games and game theory concepts. The goal of the chapter is not to make you game theorists, but to give you a sense of the way in which economists think and try to understand the many puzzles that are out there.

> A screening question is a question structured in such a way as to reveal strategic information about the person who answers.

The Prisoner's Dilemma

> Web Note 20.1
> The Prisoner's Dilemma

Let's begin with the most famous of all games—the **prisoner's dilemma,** *a well-known two-person game that demonstrates the difficulty of cooperative behavior in certain circumstances.* The standard prisoner's dilemma can be seen in the following example: Two people suspected of committing a crime are brought into the police station and interrogated separately. They know that if neither of them confesses, the police have only enough evidence to charge each with a minor crime for which each will serve 6 months. The police know that too, but they also know that the criminals are guilty of a more serious felony. The police, however, have insufficient evidence to prosecute for the more serious crime. In order to make their case, the police offer each prisoner the following deal if he confesses to the more serious crime:

> "If both you and the other prisoner confess, instead of being sentenced to the maximum 10 years in prison, the two of you will each serve only 5 years in jail. Further, if you confess but the other prisoner doesn't confess, in exchange for your serving as a witness for the prosecution, we will drop the charges for the

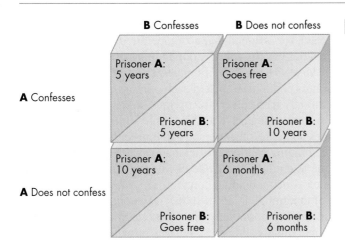

	B Confesses	**B** Does not confess
A Confesses	Prisoner **A**: 5 years / Prisoner **B**: 5 years	Prisoner **A**: Goes free / Prisoner **B**: 10 years
A Does not confess	Prisoner **A**: 10 years / Prisoner **B**: Goes free	Prisoner **A**: 6 months / Prisoner **B**: 6 months

FIGURE 20-1

Prisoner's Dilemma

This payoff matrix illustrates the prisoner's dilemma. If the prisoners could agree not to confess, each would get a light sentence. But each prisoner is offered the chance to go free if he confesses to the crime and agrees to serve as a witness against the other prisoner. With this incentive, both will likely confess and each will be sentenced to 5 years in jail.

lesser felony, and you will be set free. If, however, you don't confess and the other suspect does, you will be sentenced to the maximum 10 years in prison. If neither confesses, both will be charged with the lesser felony and serve 6 months."

The choice each suspect faces is: Do I confess or not confess? The outcome of each choice can be presented in what is called a **payoff matrix**—*a table that shows the outcome of every choice by every player, given the possible choices of all other players*—shown in Figure 20-1. The payoff matrix shows the three elements of any game: the *players* (in this case, two of them, A and B), their possible *strategies* (in this case, to confess or not confess), and the contingent *payoffs* (in this case, their sentences) for each possible outcome.

What strategy will each choose? The combined best option for them, if they could coordinate their actions, is most likely for neither to confess; each gets a short sentence of 6 months. But will they choose that option if they use strategic reasoning? To see whether they do, consider the possibilities each faces. Prisoner A's choices are shown in the rows of Figure 20-1. The blue triangle shows Prisoner A's punishment and the green triangle shows Prisoner B's punishment for each possible outcome. Say that Prisoner A does not confess, putting us in the bottom row of the payoff matrix. He now uses the payoff matrix to consider what options Prisoner B faces. If Prisoner B also does not confess, they both get 6 months in jail (the bottom right corner of the matrix). But if Prisoner B confesses while Prisoner A has not confessed, then Prisoner B will go free. So Prisoner B's best strategy, if Prisoner A does not confess, is to confess; instead of serving a 6-month sentence, he goes free.

Now say that Prisoner A confesses, putting us in the top row of the payoff matrix. In this case, if Prisoner B does not confess, Prisoner B gets 10 years, and if he confesses, 5 years. Again, confessing is Prisoner B's best strategy. Prisoner A concludes that regardless of what he does, Prisoner B's best strategy is to confess, so Prisoner A has to assume that if Prisoner B is following his best options, Prisoner B will confess.

The same reasoning holds for Prisoner B, so each of their optimal strategies (the ones that maximize the expected benefits) is to confess, placing them in the upper left corner of the matrix. Since neither can count on the other *not* to confess, which would lead to the combined best outcome for them, the optimal strategy will be for each to confess because each must assume the other will do the same. Confessing is the rational thing for each prisoner to do. That's why it's called the *prisoner's dilemma*.

A payoff matrix is a table that shows the outcome of every choice by every player, given the possible choices of all other players.

Q-2 In the payoff matrix in Figure 20-1, what is B's best strategy if A confesses?

Q-3 In the payoff matrix in Figure 20-1, what is B's best strategy if A does not confess?

Q-4 If Prisoners A and B are in love and care for each other as they care for themselves, what is the expected outcome of the prisoner's dilemma game?

Q-5 In formal game theory, should cheap talk influence the results?

Web Note 20.2
Cheap Talk

A Nash equilibrium is a set of strategies for each player in the game in which no player can improve his or her payoff by changing strategy unilaterally.

Let's consider the reasoning and assumptions of game theory that led us to the outcome. First, we assumed that the prison sentences capture all the relevant costs and benefits of their decisions. Second, we assumed that no cooperation was possible. The prisoner's dilemma is an example of what is called a **noncooperative game**—*a game in which each player is out for him- or herself and agreements are either not possible or not enforceable.* If the prisoners could have trusted each other to choose the action that helps them both jointly, not only themselves, the optimal strategy is "not to confess," and they both get only a light sentence. Thus, if people's utility functions are interdependent so that each cares about the other person and him- or herself equally, or if the two of them can enter into binding contracts to act that way before they are questioned, then they can escape the dilemma. The "Code of Silence" that is often attributed to the Mafia is an example of such a binding contract; they know that they must do what is in the best interest of the group, or they will be "taken out."

Such binding contracts are seldom possible, which makes the dilemma real for many prisoners, and for many individuals and firms. What is possible is what economists call **cheap talk**—*communication that occurs before the game is played that carries no cost and is backed up only by trust, and not any enforceable agreement.* If standard game theory assumptions hold, cheap talk does not influence the results, since the players cannot trust the other players to follow through on what they say. As producer Samuel Goldwyn said, and baseball star Yogi Berra is famous for repeating, "A verbal contract isn't worth the paper it's written on." But economists have shown that cheap talk might not be so cheap. In many experiments, cheap talk does influence the outcome of a game, especially ones where players have significant difficulty figuring out their optimal strategy. These empirical findings suggest that, to some degree, people do have interdependent utility functions, where each person cares about others as well as him- or herself.

Dominant Strategies and Nash Equilibrium

In analyzing the prisoner's dilemma, notice that the analysis is based on the assumption that the players figure out the other player's best strategy and build into his or her decision the assumption that the other player will choose that best strategy, while taking into account the fact that the first player is doing the same analysis in reverse. In this prisoner's dilemma case, each player has a single best strategy. *A strategy that is preferred by a player regardless of the opponent's move* is called a **dominant strategy.**

A key concept in analyzing games is a concept called a Nash equilibrium, in honor of John Nash, who first proposed it as a solution concept for strategic games. Specifically, a **Nash equilibrium** is *a set of strategies for each player in the game in which no player can improve his or her payoff by changing strategy unilaterally.*[3] A Nash equilibrium is the predicted outcome of a noncooperative game if each player follows his best strategy and assumes that the other players are following their best strategies. The solution to the prisoner's dilemma is a Nash equilibrium.

Notice that the Nash equilibrium doesn't have to be the solution that is jointly best for all players. The solution that is jointly best for both prisoners in the prisoner's dilemma is that neither prisoner confesses. But without the possibility of enforceable cooperation, "not confessing" independently is not the best strategy for either prisoner.

[3]The concept of a Nash equilibrium has a long history and goes back to August Cournot, a French economist in the 1800s, and is sometimes called a Cournot Nash equilibrium. Nash's specific contribution was to prove that all finite games have such equilibria.

The Austan Goolsbee *Check-a-Box* Method for Finding Dominant Strategies and Nash Equilibria

Getting used to thinking in terms of payoff matrices is hard for some students, and economist Austan Goolsbee has pointed out a neat way of finding both *dominant strategies* and *Nash equilibria*. It works by marking the best strategies for each player. Here's how you do it:

1. Put a ✓ for each of B's best strategies.

2. Put an ✗ for each of A's best strategies.

3. Compare ✓'s and ✗'s:

   a. A row with two ✓'s or two ✗'s is a dominant strategy.

   b. A box with a ✓ and an ✗ is a Nash equilibrium.

Let's see how it works with an example. Start by looking at the choices facing individual A—confess or not confess—and ask yourself: What is her best strategy if B confesses? What is her best strategy if B does not confess?

- If B confesses, we are in column 1, and A's best strategy is to confess. Put an ✗ in the upper-left-hand box.

- If B does not confess (column 2), then A's best strategy is to confess, so put an ✗ in the upper-right-hand box.

Continue by asking the same questions for individual B.

- If A confesses, we are in the top row, and B's best strategy is to confess, so put a ✓ in the upper-left-hand box.

- If A does not confess (bottom row), B's best strategy is to confess. So put a ✓ in the lower-left-hand box.

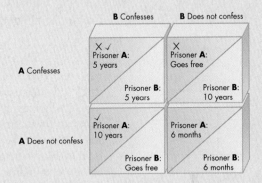

By looking at the pattern of ✓'s and ✗'s, you can make the following conclusions:

- Do any rows have two ✗'s? Yes. *Confessing is a dominant strategy for A.*

- Do any columns have two ✓'s? Yes. *Confessing is a dominant strategy for B.*

- Do any boxes have both a ✓ and an ✗? Yes. *Both A and B confessing is a Nash equilibrium.*

An Overview of Game Theory as a Tool in Studying Strategic Interaction

There are many different assumptions that can be made about the nature of the strategic interaction, and in formal game theory, different assumptions about the nature of those interactions lead to different kinds of games. For example, in the prisoner's dilemma game discussion, we were careful to point out that cooperation was not allowed. In many real-world situations, cooperation is possible, so economists have also developed an analysis of **cooperative games**—*games in which players can form coalitions and can enforce the will of the coalition on its members*. The possibility for cooperation is often greater when a game will be repeated. Because players have the opportunity to communicate, reward, and punish one another in a repeated game, the outcome of a repeated game can often be different from the outcome of a game played just once.

Yet another assumption relates to the order in which players make their decisions. In **sequential games,** *players make decisions one after another, so one player*

www **Web Note 20.3**
Sequential Games

responds to the known decisions of other players. Sequential games stand in contrast to **simultaneous move games,** *where players make their decisions at the same time as other players without knowing what choices the other players have made.* Tic-tac-toe is an example of a sequential game; the prisoner's dilemma and rock-paper-scissors are examples of simultaneous move games.

Often in sequential games, the order makes a big difference. For example, some games have first-mover advantage; tic-tac-toe, for instance. Other games have second-mover advantage. Say Todd and Jenifer both attend the same school. Todd isn't wild about Jenifer, but Jenifer is wild about Todd. They both eat in the same dining hall, which has two tables. If Todd is the first mover, then he ends up sitting with Jenifer since she will always sit at the table with him. If Jenifer is the first mover and chooses a table, Todd will always sit at another table. In this game, the second mover has the advantage.

Some Specific Games

Let's now discuss how game theory can be used as a tool to study strategic interactions by looking at specific games. Let's start with an easy game—tic-tac-toe. Tic-tac-toe is not a very interesting strategic game because it has a clear-cut answer that, I suspect, most of you know. Assuming people want to win and that they behave rationally—that is, they play a strategy that gives them the best chance of winning—tic-tac-toe will always end in a tie.

Formal game theory predicts any tic-tac-toe game (or similar game) will end in a tie because formal game theory assumes all players (1) are fully forward looking, (2) always behave in a manner that gives them the highest payoff, and (3) expect all other players to behave in that same manner. This is what we mean when we say that players are rational.

It is this assumption of rationality that allows us to give precise answers to game theoretic situations. Of course, people aren't always rational, and it is important to remember that formal game theory only provides a prediction about the outcome of a game. Actual behavior may deviate from the formal game theoretic predictions and modern behavioral economists use games in their experiments to discover where people's behavior is predictably irrational.

To compare the theoretical and empirical results, the real-world games that provide the empirical results must correspond to the assumptions of the theoretical model. Unfortunately, real-world games seldom do, which is why economists are turning more and more toward controlled experiments to test the predictions of games. These controlled experiments—either in the field, seeing what actually happens in real life when the games are played under various circumstances, or in the laboratory, where the game is structured to match the assumptions of the theory—are increasing, and the *experimental economics* branch of economics is increasing in importance. (Two economists, Vernon Smith and Danny Kahneman, received the Nobel Prize for their work in experimental economics in 2002.) There is much debate about how much we can rely on such experiments since the controls are never, and often far from, perfect.

Strategies of Players

The analysis of games is often conducted by using a method called **backward induction,** where *you begin with a desired outcome and then determine the decisions that will lead you to that outcome.* With sequential decisions, you continue the backward induction until you arrive at the best strategy for your first move. The tic-tac-toe game is easy to analyze because it is a sequential game with a complete set of choices that can be determined by working backwards from the desired outcome (winning the

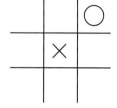

Tic-tac-toe often ends in a tie.

Behavioral economics examines the deviations between formal game theoretical predictions and actual outcomes of games.

In backward induction, you begin with a desired outcome and then determine the decisions that will lead you to that outcome.

Game Theory and Experimental Economics

Game theory has offered significant insight into the structure of economic problems but arrives at the conclusion that a number of alternative solutions are possible. A new branch of economics—experimental economics—has developed that offers insight into which outcome will be forthcoming. Let's consider an example.

When game theorists have done experiments, they have found that people believe that the others in the game will work toward a cooperative solution. Thus, when the gains from cheating are not too great, often people do not choose the individual utility-maximizing position but instead choose a more cooperative strategy, at least initially. Such cooperative solutions tend to break down, however, as the benefits of cheating become larger. Additionally, as the number of participants gets larger, the less likely it is that the cooperative solution will be chosen and the more likely it is that competitive solutions will be chosen.

Experimental economists also have found that the structure of the game plays an important role in deciding the solution. For example, posted-price markets, in which the prices are explicitly announced, are more likely to reach a collusive result than are nonposted- or uncertain-price markets, where actual sale prices are not known. Experiments in game theory are used extensively in designing auctions for allocating such things as telecom licenses or oil leases. Seeing how these auctions were designed gives you a good sense of how game theory, experiments, and real-world experience are combined to design policy.

The policy makers started with the results of the formal game and integrated those into the regulations of the actual bidding process. Then, game theorists pointed out how bidders could exploit loopholes in the regulations. Policy makers then modified the regulations and went through the process again, with game theorists pointing out potential loopholes. Eventually policy makers arrived at the best regulations they could design; then they turned to experimental economists who ran experimental auctions to see if the designs worked—much like airplane designs are tested in wind tunnels before they are actually built. Then the auctions were redesigned, and reconsidered by the game theorists, and, eventually, used as the regulations in auctions.

---

game) to the initial decision of where to place your X or O. Sometimes backward induction leads you to an optimal rollback strategy. *Optimal rollback strategies* are based on assuming your opponent follows her best strategy, which is based on assuming you follow your best strategy, which . . . Optimal rollback strategies are much harder to determine in simultaneous move games because you have to figure out what the person is *likely* to do when you are making your move. (As your hand flies out in a rock-paper-scissors game, you can't base your choice on your opponent's choice in the game.)

DOMINANT STRATEGY   As you saw in the prisoner's dilemma game, in some games, a player will prefer a strategy regardless of the opponent's move. No matter what choice one prisoner makes, assuming the other player is rational, the other prisoner's best strategy is to confess. As I discussed above, such a strategy is called a dominant strategy. So, even though the prisoner's dilemma is a simultaneous game, there is a dominant strategy, with both players "knowing" (given the assumptions of the model) what the other person will do.

A dominant strategy is a strategy that is preferred by a player regardless of the opponent's move.

MIXED STRATEGY   Many simultaneous games don't have a single dominant strategy. Again, consider rock-paper-scissors. Whether you choose rock, paper, or scissors depends on what your opponent chooses. What you don't want to happen is for your opponent to figure out a pattern in your choices. It makes sense to vary your choices randomly so that your opponent has no pattern on which to base his strategy. This strategy is called a **mixed strategy**—*a strategy of choosing randomly among moves.*

Even if a sequential game has an optimal solution, we may not be able to figure out that solution. Sequential move games can involve so many sequential moves that figuring out a rollback strategy is impossible. Chess is an example. Technically chess has a

A mixed strategy is a strategy of choosing randomly among moves.

443

full rollback strategy—once the first move is made, if one had a sufficiently powerful and fast computing ability, that person is the winner. But our computing ability is not sufficient to compute that rollback strategy; chess grand masters have beat computers whose calculations were based on a rollback strategy. But computer chess moves do not have to be based solely on rollback strategies; they can be based on patterns ascertained by studying previous winning strategies. Computers whose strategy was based on a combination of rollback strategies *and* patterns of human play have been able to beat grand masters in chess. Most games that people play in real life are far more complicated than chess, and thus require a combination of intuition, calculation, and common sense.

Strategies in games can change dramatically with just a single change in the rules. Consider the effect of moving from a game played only once to a game played repeatedly. Say you are playing the ultimatum game. In the ultimatum game, two players are offered $10 to split between the two of them, as long as they both agree to accept the money. One player is allowed to decide how to split up the $10, and the other player has the choice of accepting the deal or not accepting the deal.

Q-6 In a single-play ultimatum game, what is the optimal strategy for the first player?

In a single-play ultimatum game, the optimal strategy, assuming people are only concerned with how much money they receive, is clear. The first player's optimal strategy is to give himself almost all the money, say $9.99, offering the second player 1 cent. The second player is clearly better off receiving the 1 cent rather than nothing, so his optimal strategy is to accept. In a repeated-play ultimatum game—a game that will be played a number of times with the same players—the strategy is not so clear-cut. By refusing the 1 cent, the second player can send a signal to the first player that if he wants to keep any of the money, he had better raise his offer. So repeated games offer more possibilities for implicit cooperation than do single-play games. The empirical evidence bears this out.

AN EXAMPLE OF STRATEGY: THE TWO-THIRDS GAME   Let's now consider another game, called the two-thirds game, that demonstrates how backward induction and rollback reasoning work. The two-thirds game is the following: you, and all members of your class, are to choose a number between 0 and 100. You win if the number you have chosen is two-thirds of the average chosen by the class. Before you proceed with reading the chapter, write down your choice.

Now, let's consider your reasoning. First, if you chose a number greater than 67, you were daydreaming rather than thinking. Even if all the other students chose 100, you would still lose, since 2/3 of 100 is 67. Now, let's say you thought a bit and assumed that people would choose randomly, which means that the average would be 50, and 2/3 of it would be 33. That would be a more likely answer, but John Nash wouldn't have thought much of it as an answer. Why? Because don't you think other people are as smart as you—and would use the same reasoning? That's the standard game theory assumption—that people will assume that others will use the best deductive reasoning possible. Making the assumption that people choose the best, we see that it makes sense to assume that people would not initially choose randomly, but instead would reason as you did—and choose 33, 2/3 of which would be 22, so it would make more sense to choose 22. However, even if you chose 22, you are still only partway toward thinking strategically.

Q-7 What is the Nash equilibrium in the two-thirds game?

I say partway to strategic thinking because 22 would not be the solution John Nash would have arrived at. He would have pointed out that if other people were following that same reasoning, they would have arrived at the same conclusion as you did, and would not have put down 22, but would have put down 2/3 of 22, or 14.7, so to choose any number higher than 14.7 is unreasonable. But that is not the end of the rollback

What Game Is Being Played?

In analyzing a game, it is important to know how much players know about the game being played, and whether that knowledge is symmetrical—all players have equal information—or asymmetrical—one player has more information than the others. The implications of asymmetrical knowledge can be seen by considering a game played in the movie *The Princess Bride*. The game is a battle of wits, with the winner getting the heroine, Buttercup. In it, the hero, Westley, offers the villain, the Sicilian, Vizzini, this challenge. Westley places two glasses of wine on the table and states that one contains a deadly poison. The game is for Vizzini to choose a glass, and then for them both to drink. Vizzini accepts the challenge. The scene goes as follows:

> *Westley:* All right: where is the poison? The battle of wits has begun. It ends when you decide and we both drink, and find out who is right and who is dead.

At this point, Vizzini babbles on in order to get Westley to turn around; when Westley does so, Vizzini switches the glasses so that what Westley thinks is his glass is actually the glass that he thinks Vizzini is getting. By this move Vizzini figures he can win the game by changing it to a sequential game—he plans only to drink after Westley has drunk. Since he has switched the glasses, he figures that Westley will only drink if Westley believes that his is not the poisoned glass. Since the glasses are switched, that decision to drink will mean that Vizzini has the nonpoisoned glass, and thus Vizzini can drink safely. (He has switched the game into an asymmetric sequential game where he has the advantage.) The scene continues as follows.

> *Vizzini:* Let's drink—me from my glass, and you from yours. *[Allowing Westley to drink first, he swallows his wine.]*
>
> *Westley:* You guessed wrong.
>
> *Vizzini (roaring with laughter):* You only think I guessed wrong—that's what's so funny! I switched glasses when your back was turned. You fool. You fell victim to one of the classic blunders. The most famous is "Never get involved in a land war in Asia." But only slightly less well known is this: "Never go in against a Sicilian when death is on the line."
>
> *[He laughs and roars and cackles and whoops until he falls over dead.]*
>
> *[At this point the heroine, Buttercup, enters the scene]*
>
> *Buttercup:* To think—all that time it was your cup that was poisoned.
>
> *Westley:* They were both poisoned. I spent the last few years building up an immunity to iocane powder.

The scene makes for some comic relief in the movie, but our interest is in the strategy. Given what Vizzini thought he knew, Vizzini's strategy was sound. But in this case, the game he thought he was playing was not the game he was playing. The game he was actually playing was a game in which he could only lose. This presents another lesson from game theory—often when another individual presents you with a choice, particularly one that seems especially beneficial, the choice you are making will often not be the choice you think you are making, and the game will often be rigged to your disadvantage (you don't have full information). Hence, the general rule of thumb: If it sounds too good to be true, most likely it is.

reasoning. In fact, one can carry the reasoning back further and further, until finally the number you choose approaches zero. In fact, any number other than zero would lose to a smaller number. (This is the rollback strategy in action because the full set of choices is considered in light of the consequences for decisions of all players.) For this game, the Nash equilibrium is zero.

Informal Game Theory and Modern Behavioral Economics

Some games have no Nash equilibrium, and other games have an infinite number of them. Moreover, the probability of all people following their best strategy is highly unlikely, and thus, choosing the Nash equilibrium for the above game would almost always cause you to lose. (Actually, in first-time plays of the two-thirds game, the usual answer comes out with an average of about 30–40.) But then, if we play it again, after we have seen the answer to the first game, the average falls. Figure 20-2 shows the typical outcomes of multiple rounds of play. Initially the average guess is about 35, and it decreases with each additional time played.[4]

Notice that, as the game was played the second time, after the reasoning was explained, the average number chosen by students decreased, and hence moved toward the Nash equilibrium. These results demonstrate another aspect of game theory: players learn, which means that, in practice, repeated games often have different results than one-time games.

Even after the reasoning of the two-thirds game is fully explained to students, the average number they choose never reaches zero, so here we have an example of a game with a Nash equilibrium that, in practice, is not reached. One reason why the Nash equilibrium is not reached is that people's reasoning process is more complicated than assumed by Nash. People do not assume that all other people behave rationally; instead they are making complicated estimates of other people's behavior based on their past behavior and their sense of other people. This means that to apply game theory to real-world problems, game theory must be accompanied by a combination of reasoning, intuition, and empirical study about how people actually behave.

> To apply game theory to real-world problems, game theory must be accompanied by a combination of reasoning, intuition, and empirical study about how people actually behave.

Informal Game Theory

While formal game theory can quickly become very complicated and mathematically intimidating, much of the power of game theory does not lie in its formal application, but rather in its informal application, which simply involves setting up a study of human interactions in a game theoretic or strategic framework. Informal game theory is often called *behavioral game theory* because it relies on empirical observation, not deductive logic alone, to determine the likely choices of individuals. Instead of assuming that people are high-powered calculating machines who can figure out their optimal strategy, no matter how complicated it may be (that's the Nash equilibrium),

---

FIGURE 20-2 **The Two-Thirds Game**

Although when using an optimal roll-back strategy, the solution to the two-thirds game is zero, most people do not choose zero. Instead, as they play the game over and over again, their guesses fall from about 35 in the initial round to the 20s in the third, fourth, and fifth rounds as this graph illustrates.

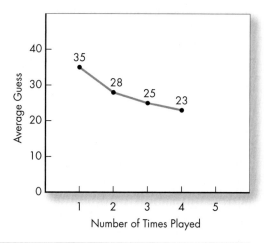

---

[4]For a discussion of evidence about playing the two-thirds game, see Virtudes Alba-Fernández, Pablo Brañas-Garza, Francisca Jiménez-Jiménez, and Javier Rodero-Cosano, "Teaching Nash Equilibrium and Dominance: A Classroom Experiment on the Beauty Contest," *Journal of Economic Education* 37, no. 3 (Summer 2006), pp. 305–22.

The Segregation Game and Agent-Based Modeling

To see the power of Schelling's informal approach to game theory, let us consider one of his thought experiments that uses the game theory framework. In this example, the question he was interested in was why our society is so segregated when much of the population seems to have only slight tendencies toward segregation. As he was thinking of this question, he imagined a society with two types of individuals. Both types had only a slight preference for living next to individuals from their group, but that preference was not strong. His question was: Would that slight preference lead to significant segregation on the aggregate level?

To answer the question, he created a model that consists of a grid. On this grid he assumed people have a slight preference for living next to people with their same characteristics. He then went through a variety of experiments that explored what the result of that slight preference would be. What he discovered was that a slight preference on the individual level could lead to significant aggregate segregation with each group living in segregated areas.

Schelling's "game" has been computerized and can be explored on the web (www.econ.iastate.edu/tesfatsi/demos/schelling/schellhp.htm).

As you play this game, notice that although the game has no single solution, it does give you insight into the process through which segregation comes about. When Schelling first devised his game, powerful computers were still in their infancy. That has now changed. Schelling's approach has led to a whole field of economics, called agent-based modeling, in which agents are "created" in the computer and then allowed to interact. The researchers then look at the resulting patterns that are created and try to use those patterns to understand complex economic phenomena. Ultimately, agent-based computational economics (ACE) modelers hope to create virtual economies, in which one can pretest the effects of policy in the "virtual economy" before one adopts it in practice. We are a long way from that goal, but it has already had some interesting uses. For example, Disneyland has used agent-based modeling to keep its lines as short as possible.

informal game theory looks at how people actually think and behave and is thus empirically based. Informal game theory doesn't provide definite answers; instead, it provides a framework for approaching questions.

This approach to game theory was developed by Nobel Prize winner Thomas Schelling, who argued that much of the power of game theory comes in the framework it provides for thinking about problems, rather than from formal solutions. The power of game theory comes from simply structuring a problem as a strategic interaction problem and writing down a payoff matrix. The box "The Segregation Game and Agent-Based Modeling" explores one of Schelling's informal models.

Real-World Applications of Informal Game Theory

In their book *The Art of Strategy,* economists Avinash Dixit and Barry Nalebuff describe a number of examples of real-world applications of informal game theory. Let's discuss a couple of them. The first involves the TV show *Survivor*—a show that gains much of its interest by creating strategic problems for contestants that are mixed with games of skill. Each week one contestant is eliminated until two are left, at which time all the eliminated contestants get to vote on who wins the grand million-dollar prize. This means that contestants must be ruthless (think about how to get other people thrown off), but also be considered fair and nice in order to get people to vote for them in the final choice. That's the show's hook.

The situation Dixit and Nalebuff describe is probably the most famous episode of the show in which eventually the three players left were Rudy, a former Navy Seal, who was seen as honest and fair and was most people's favorite; Richard, a corporate consultant who was seen as a cold and calculating "pudgy nudist"; and Kelly, a 23-year-old river guide who was also seen as cold and calculating, although maybe a bit less than Richard, and definitely not pudgy. In the final challenge, the three of them had to stand on a pole with one hand on something called the immunity idol for as long as they could. The one who stayed on the longest would win the challenge and would get to decide which two went into the final.

Both Kelly and Richard knew that if Rudy made it to the final, he would win since he was the other players' favorite. So they both wanted Rudy off. The problem for Richard was that he had an alliance with Rudy, and if he won the challenge and kicked Rudy off, he would have to violate the alliance and would likely lose to Kelly in the voting. Thus, the options as seen by Richard:

- Rudy wins—he would pick Richard to continue, but Rudy would beat Richard in the final.

- Kelly wins—she would pick Richard to continue, and it is unclear who would win.

- Richard wins—he would either pick Rudy to continue, but then would lose in the final, or he would pick Kelly to continue, in which case, because he had broken his alliance with Rudy, he would almost certainly lose in the final voting.

Given these options, Dixit and Nalebuff point out that Richard has a dominant strategy—to lose, hoping that Kelly wins. Richard did precisely that—he quit the immunity challenge early; Kelly won the challenge, chose Richard to continue, and, in the final voting, Richard won the million-dollar prize. Rudy cast the deciding vote for Richard, even though Richard's losing on purpose had effectively cost Rudy the game.

A second example they give involves a proposal by Warren Buffett to get a strict campaign finance reform bill passed. In an op-ed piece in the *New York Times,* Buffett proposed banning many types of campaign contributions that most people believe should be banned, doing that would make it more difficult for incumbents to win elections. The problem is that incumbents are the ones who vote on campaign reform bills and they have little incentive to vote for effective campaign finance reform since that would make it hard for them to win elections. Thus, while incumbents want to portray themselves as being in favor of campaign finance reform, they don't really want the bill to pass. To get around the problem, Buffett put forward the following suggestion:

> Well just suppose some eccentric billionaire (not me, not me!) made the following offer: If the bill was defeated, this person—the EB—would donate $1 billion in an allowable manner (soft money makes all possible) to the political party that had delivered the most votes to getting it passed. Given this diabolical application of game theory, the bill would sail through Congress and thus cost our EB nothing (establishing him as not so eccentric after all). (Warren Buffett, "The Billionaire's Buyout Plan," *New York Times,* September 10, 2000.)

The proposal places both Democrats and Republicans in a prisoner's dilemma. Consider their options. If they vote against the bill and the bill is successful, they will deliver $1 billion to the other party, which will give the other party an enormous advantage in the next election, offsetting their advantage in fund-raising. Thus, there is no gain in opposing the bill for a party if the other party supports it. This means that the dominant strategy for both sides would be to support the bill. So the bill would pass.

As a bonus, Buffett noted that the effectiveness of the plan "would highlight the absurdity of claims that money doesn't influence Congressional votes." Unfortunately no eccentric billionaire has come forward with the offer, and with the increase in political party fund-raising, it will likely take an eccentric multibillionaire today to implement it.

There are many more applications of the ideas in informal game theory to the real world, and much of modern economic thinking involves posing problems as strategic games, analyzing the strategic decision-making problem facing both sides, and designing an institutional structure that achieves the goals one wants to achieve.

An Application of Game Theory: Auction Markets

Game theory has highlighted the importance of strategy in individuals' decision making. Looking at problems with this approach has resulted in extraordinarily powerful solutions to economic problems. Let's consider one example that was devised by Nobel Prize–winning economist William Vickrey.

Web Note 20.4
Online Auctions

He analyzed the strategies of people in a standard sealed-bid auction where participants are not aware of other bids. In a standard auction, the person who bids the highest gets the good. Let's say that you are bidding on a computer that you really want, for which you would be willing to pay $500. In this auction, if you were fully rational and Nash-like, would you bid $500? The answer is no; that's not your best strategy; your best strategy is to lower your bid enough so that it is slightly higher than what you expect the next highest bidder to bid. If you believe that to be very low, you can do much better than paying your full price.

Vickrey suggested what is now called the **Vickrey auction**—*a sealed-bid auction where the highest bidder wins but pays the price bid by the next-highest bidder.* He demonstrated that this second-price auction changes the strategy of the bidders, giving them an incentive to bid their true valuation for the good since by bidding his or her true value, a bidder will win the auction without paying the higher amount.

Q-8 How does a Vickrey auction differ from a standard sealed-bid auction?

In a highest bid auction, a bidder's strategy is to not bid the highest, but rather to bid slightly higher than the next-highest bidder. Say you would be willing to pay $500, but you think the next-highest bidder will only bid $220. You might bid $230 since if you bid $500 you would be paying $270 more than you had to pay. In a Vickrey auction, your strategy changes. Since you are not paying your bid, but rather the second-highest bid, you could bid $500, and if the second-highest bidder only bid $220, you would only pay $220.

The advantage of the Vickrey auction bid becomes more apparent when you incorrectly guessed the second-highest bidder's bid. Say that second-highest bid was $300, but you thought it was only going to be $220, so you bid $250. In the standard auction, you would not win—the other bidder would win, even though you were willing to pay more for it. In the Vickrey auction bid, the person who wants it most wins. Vickrey auctions are now often used in auctions for oil lease rights, radio spectrums, and Google's online advertisement program AdWords.

Game Theory and the Challenge to Standard Economic Assumptions

While formal game theory relies upon precise definitions of rationality, informal game theory is used to explore what rationality is and the nature of individuals' utility functions. Modern behavioral economists use an approach that builds on the traditional economics that you've been presented with in earlier chapters—utility maximization, equilibrium, and efficiency—but instead of stopping there, and assuming that the theory has to be right, extends the theory to fit the observations in the real world, modifying the theory where necessary to achieve the fit. This means that instead of exploring the theoretical results of a formal model with a set of assumptions, behavioral economists use *experiments* in which people actually play the formal games to explore the validity of the assumptions in formal game theory and how they might be revised. Work in behavioral economics has led to significant advances in our understanding of the nature of preferences and choice.

For example, one of the basic assumptions of economics is that people are self-interested, and they do what benefits them. In some ways, this assumption is true by definition. One can assume that altruistic people help others because other people's welfare is a component of their utility function. Such a tautological approach to the analysis of choice is not especially helpful, since it is true by definition. Game theory allows us to explore the degree to which, and the nature in which, individuals are concerned with others.

Fairness

Consider a variation of the ultimatum game called the trust game. As with the ultimatum game, the trust game has two players. The first player is given $10 and the choice about how to split it. The difference is that she can either keep it all for herself or "invest" some portion, which is tripled and given to the other player. The second person, called the "trustee," can either keep the now tripled amount or return some portion of it to the first person. At this point the game ends. The Nash equilibrium of this game—what would happen if people are only concerned with themselves, and are fully "rational"—is for the first player to keep the entire $10.

The rollback reasoning (beginning with the last choice) goes like this: The dominant strategy of the "trustee" is to keep any money that is shared since there is no possibility for the first player to reciprocate. Knowing that, the dominant strategy for the first person is to share nothing in the first place. No gains from cooperation are possible.

Experimental evidence shows that, on average, individuals invest about $5 and, on average, trustees return a little less than the investment. It is as if people want to trust and to reward trust. In other experiments, it has been found that people will even spend money of their own to punish others who do not respond "fairly" to offers. So, if people feel someone is being unfair, people will reduce their own income to make that person pay.

Endowment Effects

Another example of empirical work suggesting that people do not behave as the traditional model predicts concerns how people value things. Standard economic theory assumes that value is independent of what you have; that is, preferences are independent of endowment. To test whether this is true, Stanford neuropsychologist Brian Knutson did an experiment where he offered people either an iPod or $100. When given the opportunity to choose between the two, most people chose $100. But when participants were initially given an iPod, but then were offered $100 in exchange for the iPod, most chose to keep the iPod. This is called the *endowment* effect. That ownership increases the value of a good is even confirmed by brain scans that show increased brain activity associated with fear of loss when a good is acquired. Experiments suggest that the traditional assumptions about economic behavior do not always reflect actual behavior.

Web Note 20.5
Opting In or Opting Out?

Framing Effects

Framing effects are the tendency of people to base their choices on how the choice is presented.

Another of the findings of behavioral economics is the importance of **framing effects—** *the tendency of people to base their choices on how the choice is presented.* The classic example of framing effects was presented by Columbia psychologist Amos Tversky and Princeton psychologist Daniel Kahneman. They asked people how they would respond in the following situations regarding 600 people who were threatened by a disease.

Subjects were given the following two undesirable options. In the first experiment, the options were: (A) a guarantee of saving 200 lives for sure but losing the others or (B) a 1/3 chance of saving all 600, but a 2/3 chance of saving no one. Most people chose A over B. Then, they offered the same people the following choices: (A) guaranteed outcome of losing 400 lives for sure but saving the others or (B) a 2/3 chance of 600 dying and a 1/3 chance of no one dying. Most people chose B over A. Now consider the two choices—they are exactly the same, but people responded differently if the choice was presented in the negative rather than the positive frame. This result has been widely duplicated and framing effects are an important part of modern economics.

Q-9 If a firm wants to increase the number of employees who participate in a savings plan, should the enrollment form ask whether the employee wants an automatic withdrawal from a paycheck to retirement or automatic deposit to retirement from a paycheck?

Behavioral Economics and the Traditional Model

There are many more such findings, and behavioral economists are attempting to integrate those findings with traditional economic reasoning. As they do this, the methods of economics are changing. As I stated above, game theory is growing enormously in importance. Why? Because game theory allows a wider range of assumptions than does standard theory—which allows us to state the economic result more precisely. But, as we saw in the example of the two-thirds game, game theory alone does not provide answers. Thus, economists are doing much more in the way of empirical work and incorporating experimental work into their methodology.

Experimental economics is a burgeoning field. It includes laboratory experiments in which assumptions of the economic model are carefully followed, to see how subjects actually respond, and field experiments, in which the precise conditions are not as carefully controlled, but subjects are provided a more realistic setting. Behavioral economists also use computer simulations and even brain scans. One of the branches of behavioral economics is called neuroeconomics, which relies on CAT scans of individuals' brains to study individual choices.

What comes out of behavioral economics is a much more nuanced view of humans. They are purposeful, rather than fully rational; they demonstrate enlightened self-interest rather than greed; and they are boundedly rational rather than fully "Nash-style" rational.

Behavioral economics provides a more nuanced view of human behavior than does standard economics.

The Importance of the Traditional Model: Money Is Not Left on the Table

The fact that people do not act as the traditional economic model predicts does not mean that the traditional assumptions and model are irrelevant—quite the contrary. People acting differently than they would if the standard rationality assumptions hold true creates potential profit opportunities for individuals to take advantage of people's actual behavior. It means that "money is being left on the table." Whenever "money is left on the table," we can expect firms and individuals who understand the economic model to develop businesses and schemes to take that money off the table—to transfer money from those who are acting "irrationally" to those who are acting "rationally." What this means is that the findings of behavioral economics make understanding the logic of the traditional model even more important than it would be if everyone acted according to its assumptions. If you don't understand it, you can expect to lose money to those who do. The point is that the traditional economic model doesn't require everyone, or even a majority of people, to behave in accordance with its assumptions for its predictions to come true. All it takes is a few people to behave rationally because those few can develop businesses and institutions that make people pay for their "irrationality" and lack of self-interest.

Advertising mutual funds is an example. Those advertisements emphasize past performance, and in selling actively managed mutual funds (which have higher

Whenever "money is left on the table," we can expect firms and individuals who understand the economic model to develop businesses and schemes to take that money off the table.

Q-10 If 90 percent of people operate as behavioral economics suggests, does that mean that the standard economic model is no longer applicable?

management fees) firms strongly emphasize past performance, even though past performance of a mutual fund often has little or no predictive power of future earnings of that mutual fund. Often investment companies have many actively managed mutual funds, some of which do well in a specific time period, and some of which do poorly, just because of random variation. With a variety of such funds, they can always have some that have done better than average. When the mutual fund salesman calls his clientele, he will push the actively managed funds that have done well, taking advantage of people's tendency to think that past history is more relevant to future behavior than it often is. Investment salesmen and fund managers make a good living selling such funds—that's the transfer of money from the unwise (in an economic sense) to the wise (in an economic sense). Most economists suggest that the way around this is to buy indexed mutual funds, which are mutual funds that contain a broad set of stocks that reflect the broader market, and are not actively managed. These index funds have much smaller fees and avoid "leaving money on the table" that can be transferred to those who understand the economic model.

Conclusion

Let me now conclude. I hope that this chapter shows you that if you had concerns about whether the traditional models learned in earlier chapters fit reality, they were legitimate concerns. Economic models don't tell you how people should behave, or how they do behave. They aren't meant to do that. Instead, they give insights into how people behave, and how to think strategically. Any economic model must be used with judgment. As Alfred Marshall, an economist whose approach I have followed, said, "The economic model is not a tool that gives answers to questions; it is an apparatus of the mind that helps its possessor come to reasonable conclusions." The overall logic of the economic model provides insight even if most people do not behave as the assumptions predict. Money is not left on the table, and when people act differently than the economic model, we can expect people and firms to figure out ways to take advantage of their behavior.

The economic model is an apparatus of the mind that helps its possessor come to reasonable conclusions.

Those concerns that you had about the relevance of the traditional economic models are also concerns that economists have, and are the basis of current research. In their research economists are pushing the boundaries of the traditional model and are developing new models to include such concerns. Don't think of economic theory as a static, unchanging theory; think of it as a dynamic theory, which is continually taking into account new discoveries and incorporating those discoveries into the model.

Summary

- Game theory is a highly flexible modeling approach that can be used to study a variety of situations in which decisions are interdependent. *(LO20-1)*

- A prisoner's dilemma game is one in which both players have a dominant strategy that leads them to a jointly undesirable outcome. *(LO20-1)*

- A payoff matrix provides a summary of each player's strategies and how the outcomes of their choices depend on the actions of other players. *(LO20-1)*

- A Nash equilibrium is an equilibrium of a game that results from a noncooperative game when each player plays his or her best strategy. With a Nash equilibrium, no player can improve his or her payoff by changing strategy unilaterally. *(LO20-1)*

- A dominant strategy is one that is preferred regardless of one's opponent's move. A mixed strategy is choosing randomly. *(LO20-1)*

- The strategies of players are different in simultaneous and sequential games. *(LO20-2)*

- Sometimes people follow a mixed-strategy of choosing randomly among moves.   (*LO20-2*)

- Behavioral economics examines deviations between formal game theoretical predictions and actual outcomes of games.   (*LO20-3*)

- Insights from behavioral economics can be applied to real-world decision making such as in auctions.   (*LO20-3*)

- Loss aversion and framing effects are examples of findings in behavioral economics that challenge the traditional model's predictions.   (*LO20-4*)

- The traditional model remains relevant because it takes only a few people to realize that money has been left on the table for the results of the standard model to hold.   (*LO20-4*)

Key Terms

backward induction *(442)*
cheap talk *(440)*
cooperative game *(441)*
dominant strategy *(440)*
framing effect *(450)*

game theory *(437)*
mixed strategy *(443)*
Nash equilibrium *(440)*
noncooperative
   game *(440)*

payoff matrix *(439)*
prisoner's
   dilemma *(438)*
screening question *(438)*
sequential game *(441)*

simultaneous move
   game *(442)*
Vickrey auction *(449)*

Questions and Exercises

1. Define the prisoner's dilemma game.   (*LO20-1*)
   a. What assumptions lead to the dilemma?
   b. What creates the possibility of escaping it?
   c. What does the standard model say about your answer to *b*? What does experimental economics say?

2. In the following payoff matrix, Player A announces that she will cooperate.   (*LO20-1*)
   a. How is this likely to change the outcome compared to when neither cooperates?
   b. What does your answer to *a* suggest about the value of cheap talk?
   c. How could Player A make her pronouncement believable?

3. Is the solution to the prisoner's dilemma game a Nash equilibrium? Why?   (*LO20-1*)

4. If a player does not have a dominant strategy, can the game still have a Nash equilibrium?   (*LO20-1*)

5. Two firms have entered an agreement to set prices. The accompanying payoff matrix shows profit for each firm in a market depending upon whether the firm cheats on the agreement by reducing its prices.   (*LO20-1*)
   a. What is the dominant strategy for each firm, if any?
   b. What is the Nash equilibrium, if any?

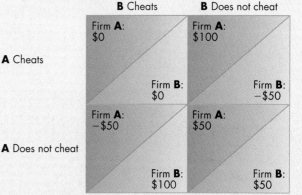

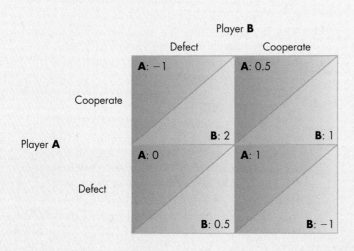

6. Two people are arrested and charged with the same crime. Each is given the opportunity to accuse the other of the crime. The payoff matrix shows how much

time each will serve depending on who rats out whom.   (*LO20-1*)

a. What is the dominant strategy for each, if any?

b. What is the Nash equilibrium, if any?

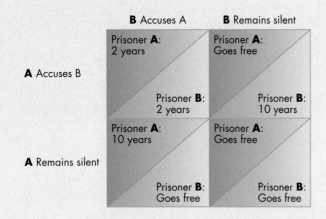

7. For each of the following, state whether Player A and Player B have a dominant strategy and, if so, what each player's dominant strategy is.   (*LO20-1*)

a.

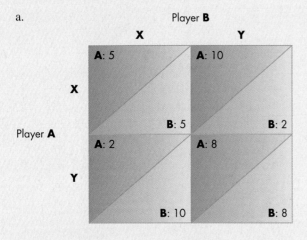

b.

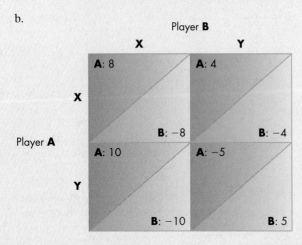

c.

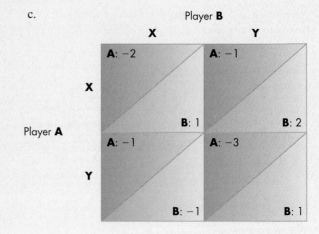

8. Would the results of the prisoner's dilemma game be different if it were a sequential rather than a simultaneous game?   (*LO20-2*)

9. State whether each of the following situations is a simultaneous or sequential game. Explain your answer.   (*LO20-2*)

a. A congressional vote by roll call.

b. The ultimatum game.

c. The Civil War.

d. The segregation game (requires reading the box "The Segregation Game and Agent-Based Modeling" on page 447).

10. Can a player have a rollback strategy in a simultaneous move game?   (*LO20-2*)

11. True or false? If a game has a Nash equilibrium, that equilibrium will be the equilibrium that we expect to observe in the real world.   (*LO20-2*)

12. Why might the multiple-play ultimatum game have a different result than the single-play ultimatum game?   (*LO20-2*)

13. Why do sellers generally prefer a Vickrey auction to a regular sealed bid if sellers don't receive the highest bid in the Vickrey auction?   (*LO20-3*)

14. Say that you are bidding in a sealed-bid auction and that you really want the item being auctioned. Winning it would be worth $250 to you. Say you expect the next-highest bidder to bid $100.   (*LO20-3*)

a. In a standard "highest-bid" auction, what bid would a rational person make?

b. In a Vickrey auction, what bid would he make?

15. When consumers were given the opportunity to select a package of ground beef labeled "75% lean" or a package of ground beef labeled "25% fat," most consumers chose "75% lean." Why? What concept from the chapter does this illustrate?   (*LO20-4*)

16. Why does it take just a few people to act rationally for the standard model to hold?   (*LO20-4*)

Questions from Alternative Perspectives

1. Do you believe people with religious training will arrive at different outcomes than others in a strategic game? Why? Which interaction is preferable? (Religious)

2. Austrian economist Ludwig von Mises defined economics as "the science of human action." Does game theory or standard supply/demand analysis better fit with that definition? Why? (Austrian)

3. Do you believe that women will arrive at different outcomes than men when playing a strategic game? Why? Which is preferable? (Feminist)

4. How does game theory demonstrate the importance of institutions? (Institutionalist)

5. In the opening to this chapter, the author describes a scene in the movie *A Beautiful Mind*. What is disturbing about that scene? Is John Nash representative of economic sensibility? (Feminist)

6. How do the findings of behavioral economics undermine the assumptions of the standard model as to the nature of human beings? (Radical)

Issues to Ponder

1. How is the fact that employers look to see that applicants took difficult courses in college, even though the subject matter has no bearing on the work they will likely do, an example of screening?

2. How is investing in the stock market similar to playing the two-thirds game?

3. In 1950, economists Merrill Flood and Melvin Dresher devised an experiment to challenge the Nash equilibrium. They presented the following payoff matrix to two economists and asked them to play the following game 100 times in succession:

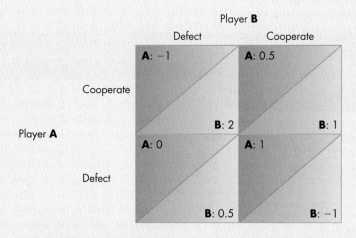

Player **B**

	Defect	Cooperate
Cooperate	A: −1 B: 2	A: 0.5 B: 1
Defect	A: 0 B: 0.5	A: 1 B: −1

Player **A**

a. What is the Nash equilibrium of this payoff matrix?

b. Is the payoff matrix symmetric? If not, who has the advantage? Do you think this affected the strategy of the players? If so, how?

c. In 60 of the 100 games, the players cooperated. Why do you think this was so?

d. What do you suppose the players chose for the 100th play? Why?

4. In 1970 economist Martin Shubik proposed the following game that involved auctioning off a one-dollar bill with the following rules:
   1. The highest bidder wins the dollar bill and pays his bid.
   2. The *second-highest* bidder also has to pay the amount of his last bid—and gets *nothing* in return.
   3. Each new bid has to be higher than the current high bid.
   4. The game ends when there is no new bid within a specified time limit.
   a. When the dollar was auctioned off, do you suppose that the highest bid was less than or greater than a dollar? Why?
   b. Can a rational player ever lose the auction once he has started bidding?
   c. Is it rational to begin bidding?

5. Suppose the two-thirds game described in the chapter were changed to the "average" game, so that the class had to guess a number between 0 and 100, and the person who wins is the person who guesses closest to the average number.
   a. What would the Nash equilibrium likely be?
   b. If your class played this "average" game, would you expect the equilibrium to approach the Nash equilibrium?
   c. If the equilibrium in playing the real-world game is not the Nash equilibrium, what might explain the difference?

6. Say that 90 percent of the people in a market demonstrate loss aversion and 10 percent are "rational." Say that, initially, all people have equal wealth.
   a. How would you expect the wealth distribution to change over time?
   b. Would you expect the traditional model's predictions, which are based on the assumption of rationality, to be correct? Why?

   c. How might you determine the percentage of "rational" people needed for the standard model to give accurate aggregate predictions?

7. In a Vickrey auction how would a person's bid differ if he knew that the seller had someone at the auction submitting a bid for the seller?

Answers to Margin Questions

1. False. The two are not inconsistent. Game theory is a more flexible framework than supply/demand analysis because it can account for less restrictive assumptions compared to supply/demand analysis. (*p. 437; LO20-1*)

2. If A confesses, B's best strategy is also to confess. (*p. 439; LO20-1*)

3. If A does not confess, B's best strategy is to confess. (*p. 439; LO20-1*)

4. Assuming that love means they trust one another, both are more likely to choose to not confess. Each person is willing to do what is necessary to show their love and care for the other. (*p. 440; LO20-1*)

5. Because cheap talk carries no cost and is unenforceable, it is not expected to influence the results of a game. (*p. 440; LO20-1*)

6. The optimal strategy for the first player of a single-play ultimatum game is to offer as little as possible to the

second player because the second player is better off with any amount greater than zero. (*p. 444; LO20-2*)

7. The Nash equilibrium in the two-thirds game is zero. (*p. 444; LO20-2*)

8. In Vickrey auction, the highest bidder wins but pays the second-highest bid, while in a standard sealed bid auction, the highest bidder wins and pays the highest bid. (*p. 449; LO20-3*)

9. Assuming positive framing effects, the question should be framed as a contribution to retirement rather than a withdrawal from a paycheck. (*p. 451; LO20-4*)

10. No, it does not. The remaining 10 percent of rational people will develop businesses to make the remaining 90 percent pay for their irrationality and lead the overall economy to the results of the traditional model. (*p. 451; LO20-4*)

APPENDIX A

Game Theory and Oligopoly

This chapter discussed game theory and its ability to shed light on a broader set of issues than the traditional model. You can see the power of game theory by applying it to oligopoly. As discussed Chapter 15, oligopoly involves *strategic interaction* in which the firms take into account the decisions of the other firms. In all the other basic models—supply/demand, perfect competition, monopolistic competition, and monopoly—firms did not take into

account the decisions of other firms. In those models, firms assumed that their decisions had no effect on other firms' decisions. In perfect competition and monopolistic competition, the argument justifying that assumption was that the firms were so small that their decisions didn't matter to others in the industry; in monopoly, the argument justifying that assumption was that the firm faced no competitors, so there was no other firm to consider. In oligopoly that wasn't the case, which meant that we could not develop a neat formal geometric model of firm behavior.

Game theory allows us to develop more precise models of oligopolistic markets, and of all situations that involve strategic interaction. Thus, game theory can be seen as a complement to, not a replacement for, the supply/demand model. In fact if the game is structured to reflect the assumptions of the supply/demand model, the reasoning in game theory is consistent with supply/demand analysis. Given the same assumptions, game theory comes to the same conclusions as supply/demand analysis.

Prisoner's Dilemma and a Duopoly Example

The easiest application of game theory to oligopoly involves the prisoner's dilemma. To keep the analysis easy, we will assume there are only two firms in the market, which makes the oligopoly what is called a **duopoly**—*an oligopoly with only two firms.* So let us consider the strategic decisions facing a "foam peanut" (packing material) company in a duopoly. Let us assume that the average total cost and marginal cost of producing foam peanuts are the same for both firms. These costs are shown in Figure A20-1(a).

Assume that a production facility with a minimum efficient scale of 4,000 tons is the smallest that can be built. In Figure A20-1(b), the marginal costs are summed and

the industry demand curve is drawn in a way that the competitive price is $500 per ton and the competitive output is 8,000 tons. The relevant industry marginal revenue curve is also drawn.

If the firms can coordinate their actions (fully collude), they will act as a joint monopolist setting total output at 6,000 tons where *MR* = *MC* (3,000 tons each). As you can see in Figure A20-1(a), this gives each a price of $600 with a cost of $575 per ton, for a joint economic profit of $150,000, or $75,000 each. If the firms do not coordinate their actions, they will produce where the *MC* curve intersects the demand curve, setting output at 8,000 tons, producing 4,000 tons each. At this level of output, price is $500 a ton. With average costs of $500, neither earns an economic profit. The firms prefer fully colluding to the situation where they do not coordinate their actions (the competitive equilibrium), where they earn zero economic profit.

If they can ensure that they will both abide by the agreement, the monopolist output will be the joint profit-maximizing output. But the strategic reasoning doesn't end there. What if one firm reasons that it can earn more by cheating on the deal? What if one firm produces 4,000 tons (1,000 tons under the counter)? The additional 1,000 tons in output will cause the price to fall to $550 per ton. The cheating firm's average total costs fall to $500 as its output rises to 4,000, so its profit rises to $200,000. However, the noncheating firm's profit moves in the opposite

---

FIGURE A20-1 (A AND B) Firm and Industry Duopoly Cooperative Equilibrium

In (**a**) I show the marginal and average total cost curves for either firm in the duopoly. To get the average and marginal costs for the industry, you double each. In (**b**) the industry marginal cost curve (the horizontal sum of the individual firms' marginal cost curves) is combined with the industry demand and marginal revenue curves. At the competitive solution for the industry, output is 8,000 and price is $500. As you can see in (**a**), at that price economic profits are zero. At the monopolistic solution, output is 6,000 and price is $600. As you can see in (**a**), *ATC* is $575 at an industry output of 6,000 (firm output of 3,000), so each firm's profit is $25 × 3,000 = $75,000 (the shaded area in (**a**)).

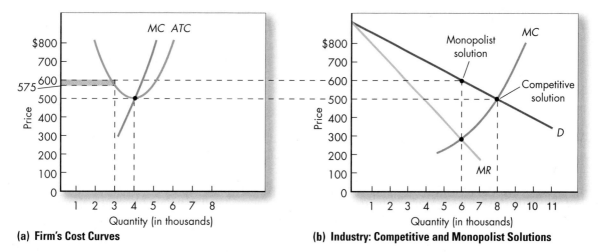

(a) Firm's Cost Curves

(b) Industry: Competitive and Monopolist Solutions

FIGURE A20-2 (A, B, AND C)   **Firm and Industry Duopoly Equilibrium When One Firm Cheats**

Figures (**a**) and (**b**) show the noncheating and the cheating firms' output and profit, respectively, while (**c**) shows the industry output and price. Say they both cheat. The price is $500 and output is 8,000 (4,000 per firm) (point *A* in (**c**)). Both firms make zero profit. If neither cheats, the industry output is 6,000, the price is $600, and their *ATC* is $575. This outcome gives them a profit of $75,000 each and would place them at point *C* in (**c**). If one firm cheats and the other does not, the output is 7,000 and the industry price is $550 (point *B* in (**c**)). The noncheating firm's $75,000 loss is shown by the shaded area in (**a**). The cheating firm's $200,000 profit is shown by the shaded area in (**b**).

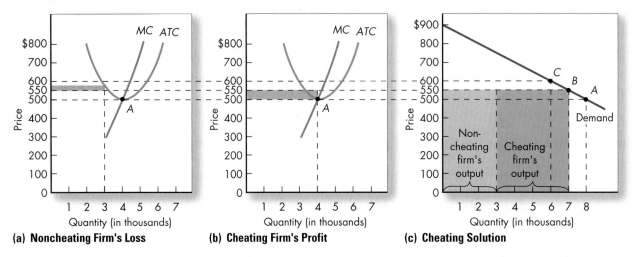

(a) Noncheating Firm's Loss   **(b) Cheating Firm's Profit**   **(c) Cheating Solution**

direction. Its average total costs remain $575, but the price it receives falls to $550, so it loses $75,000 instead of making $75,000. The division of profits and output is shown in Figure A20-2.

In Figure A20-2(a), you can see that the firm that abides by the agreement and produces 3,000 units makes a loss of $75,000; its average total costs are $575 and the price it receives is $550. In Figure A20-2(b), you can see that the cheating firm makes a profit of $200,000; its average costs are $500, so it is doing much better than when it did not cheat. The combined profit of the cheating and the noncheating firms is $125,000 ($200,000 − $75,000 = $125,000), which is lower than if they cooperated. By cheating, the firm has essentially transferred $125,000 of the other firm's profit to itself and has reduced their combined profit by $25,000. Figure A20-2(c) shows how output is split between the two firms.

Once the other firm realizes that the first firm will benefit by cheating and cannot enforce the agreement, it will do better by cheating too. By cheating, it eliminates its loss and the other firm's profit. Output moves to the competitive output, 8,000, and both of the firms make zero profit.

It is precisely to provide insight into this type of strategic situation that game theory was developed. It does so by analyzing the strategies of both firms under all circumstances and placing the combination in a payoff matrix.

Duopoly and a Payoff Matrix

The duopoly presented above is a variation of the prisoner's dilemma game. The results can also be presented in a payoff matrix that captures the essence of the prisoner's dilemma. In Figure A20-3, each square shows the payoff from a pair of decisions listed in the columns and rows.

The blue triangles show A's profit; the green triangles show B's profit. For example, if neither cheats, the result for both is shown in the lower-right square, and if they both cheat, the result is shown in the upper-left square.

Notice the dilemma they are in if cheating cannot be detected. If they can't detect whether the other one cheated and each believes the other is maximizing profit, each must expect the other one to cheat. But if firm A expects firm B to cheat, the relevant payoffs are in the first column. Given this expectation, if firm A doesn't cheat, it loses $75,000. So firm A's optimal strategy is to cheat. Similarly for firm B. If it expects firm A to cheat, its relevant payoffs are in the first row. Firm B's optimal strategy is to cheat. But if they both cheat, they end up in the upper-left square with zero profit.

In reality, of course, cheating is partially detectable, and even though explicit collusion and enforceable contracts are illegal in the United States, implicit collusive contracts are not. Moreover, in markets where similar conditions hold time after time, the cooperative solution

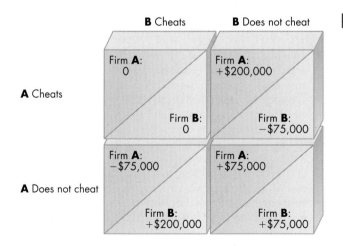

B Cheats   B Does not cheat

A Cheats

Firm **A:**
0

Firm **B:**
0

Firm **A:**
+$200,000

Firm **B:**
−$75,000

A Does not cheat

Firm **A:**
−$75,000

Firm **B:**
+$200,000

Firm **A:**
+$75,000

Firm **B:**
+$75,000

FIGURE A20-3 **The Payoff Matrix of Strategic Pricing Duopoly**

The strategic dilemma facing each firm in a duopoly can be shown in a payoff matrix that captures the four possible outcomes. A's strategies are listed vertically; B's strategies are listed horizontally. The payoffs of the combined strategies for both firms are shown in the four boxes of the matrix, with B's payoff shown in the green shaded triangles and A's payoff shown in the blue shaded triangles. For example, if A cheats but B doesn't, A makes a profit of $200,000, but B loses $75,000.

Their combined optimal strategy is to cartelize and achieve the monopoly payoff, with both firms receiving a profit of $75,000. However, each must expect that if it doesn't cheat and the other does cheat, it will lose $75,000. To avoid losing that $75,000, both firms will cheat, which leads them to the payoff in the upper-left corner—the competitive solution with zero profit for each firm.

is more likely since each firm will acquire a reputation based on its past actions, and firms can retaliate against other firms that cheat. But the basic dilemma remains for firms and tends to push oligopolies toward a zero-profit competitive solution.

The push toward a zero-profit equilibrium can be seen in the price war between Amazon.com and Buy.com. When Amazon.com lowered its threshold for free shipping from $99 to $49, Buy.com responded by offering free shipping on all sales the very next day and then added to that an offer to beat Amazon.com prices by 10 percent. Amazon responded by further reducing its free shipping threshold to $25. Another example is in airline pricing. When a low-fare airline enters a market, the existing airlines generally match, or even go below, the low-fare airline's fare.

Low Price Guarantees:
The Advantage of Rules
or Precommitment

Game theory also sheds light on institutional arrangements of oligopolistic firms. One that has now become standard practice for many oligopolistic firms is the low-price guarantee, in which a store, such as Walmart, states that it will guarantee that the price it charges is lower than the price at any other store in the area. To back up that guarantee, the store offers any customer who finds a lower price a "double the difference back guarantee." One's initial thought likely is that such low-price guarantees are good for consumers—they guarantee consumers low prices. But when considering the low-price guarantee within a game theoretic framework, that conclusion is not so clear.

Notice what the low-price guarantee does for Walmart; it provides information about the pricing of competing firms, and warns the other firms that Walmart will have that information very quickly. Second, consider what this low-price guarantee does to a competitor's, such as Kmart's, strategy. With the low-price guarantee, Kmart knows that if it tries to charge a lower price than Walmart, Walmart will quickly and automatically reduce its price to one even lower. This changes Kmart's strategy since it now makes little sense to try to outcompete Walmart on price. With the guarantee in place, both Walmart's and Kmart's best strategy is not to compete on price. So, paradoxically, the net effect of the "low price guarantee" can be to raise the overall price that consumers pay.

Key Term

duopoly *(457)*

Questions and Exercises

1. Netflix and Blockbuster each expects profit to rise by $100,000 in the coming year. Netflix, thinking that it would like its net profit to rise by more, considers advertising during the Super Bowl. An advertisement on the Super Bowl will cost $80,000. If Netflix advertises, and Blockbuster does not, it expects its profit to rise by $230,000 instead of $100,000, while Blockbuster's profit will rise by only $50,000. Netflix also knows that if it does not advertise, but Blockbuster does, its profit will rise by only $50,000 while Blockbuster's profit will rise by $230,000 instead of just $100,000. If both firms advertise, their profit will rise by the same as if neither had advertised, except each will have spent $80,000 for the ad.
   a. Develop the payoff matrix for the decision facing Netflix and Blockbuster.
   b. Is there a dominant strategy?
   c. If so, what is it?

2. Two firms, TwiddleDee and TwiddleDum, make up the entire market for widgets. They have identical costs. They are currently colluding explicitly and are making $2 million each. TwiddleDee has a new CEO, Mr. Notsonice, who is considering cheating and producing more than he has agreed to produce. He has been informed by his able assistant that if he cheats, he can increase the firm's profit by $1 million at the cost of TwiddleDum losing $1 million of its profits. If both cheat, their profits are $1.5 million each. (TwiddleDum faces the same option.) You have been hired to advise Mr. Notsonice.
   a. Construct a payoff matrix for him that captures the essence of the decision.
   b. If the game is only played once, what strategy would you advise?
   c. How would your answer to b change if the game were to be played many times?

chapter 21

Thinking Like a Modern Economist

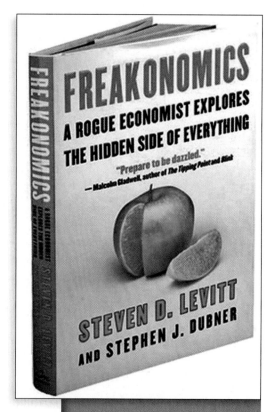

Economics is what economists do.

—Jacob Viner

My son doesn't think much of economists. I know that it's rather common for kids not to have high regard for their parents, but it still hurts. Recently, however, when I was attending a conference and told him that I was on a panel with Steve Levitt, my ranking moved up. In fact my son asked me, "Can you get his autograph for me? He's cool." Steve Levitt's book, *Freakonomics* (written jointly with Stephen Dubner), had hit a chord with my son, and judging from its sales, with lots of other people as well.

I raise this issue here not to sell more copies of Levitt's book (he's sold plenty), but instead to introduce you to what modern economists do, and how what modern economists do relates to the supply and demand model. I include this chapter to disabuse you from thinking that the supply and demand model is the holy grail of economics. Remember Carlyle's comment, "teach a parrot the words 'supply' and 'demand,' and you have an economist." He's wrong; as I stated in an earlier chapter, economists are not parrots, and to understand modern economics you have to know that modern economics uses supply and demand analysis only as a steppingstone. It's an important steppingstone, but still just a steppingstone.

Freakonomics makes the point nicely because if you look in its index, you won't find any entries under supply or demand. The reason isn't because the indexer goofed—it's because Levitt didn't use the formal supply and demand model. Instead, he applied the general ideas behind supply and demand within a variety of other models; most of his conclusions derive from his creative ability to collect data and analyze them with statistical tools. His approach is typical of how modern applied economists approach problems—they collect data, or use data collected by others, and analyze them. The purpose of this chapter is to give you a sense of what modern economists do, and how what you will learn in principles of economics relates to what modern economists do.

A key lesson of this chapter is that *supply and demand is not the glue that holds modern economics together*. Rather, modeling is the glue. When you present a problem or question to an economist, he or she will automatically attempt to reduce that question to a **model**—*a simplified representation of the problem or question that captures the essential issues*—and then work with that model and empirical evidence to understand the problem. The modeling approach is the modern economics approach.

After reading this chapter, you should be able to:

LO21-1 Differentiate traditional economic building blocks from behavioral economic building blocks.

LO21-2 Explain what heuristic models are and how traditional and behavioral heuristic economic models differ.

LO21-3 Distinguish an empirical model from a formal model and list some formal models used by modern economists.

LO21-4 Discuss how modern economics and traditional economics differ in their policy prescriptions.

Q-1 What is the glue that holds modern economics together?

No single model characterizes modern economic models. Modern economists are a highly diverse group of social scientists. What ties them together is their training in modeling and their shared view that incentives are important, and that their models have to capture the importance of incentives.

The Nature of Economists' Models

Economists aren't the only people who use models. Most everyone does. An architect will often create a computer model or a small wooden model of a house he is building. Similarly, an engineer will test a new design with a model. So modeling alone does not distinguish an economist from other scientists and engineers. What does differentiate economists are:

1. The building blocks that economists use in their models and
2. The structure of formal models that economists find acceptable.

Building blocks refer to the assumptions of a model. The structure of a model is the form it takes—verbal, graphical, or algebraic.

By *building blocks* I mean the assumptions that form the basis of economic models. All economists' models hold that incentives are important, but they differ in how they picture people reacting to incentives. For example, you can assume that individuals are selfish, or that individuals care about other people; the models would be different in each instance. By *structure,* I mean the form of the model—for example, a model can be verbal, graphical (for example, the supply/demand model), algebraic with simple equations (for example, $q = 4 - 2P$), or algebraic with highly complex equations[1] (for example,

$$\begin{pmatrix} \delta_t \bar{u}_k(t) \\ \delta_t \bar{v}_k(t) \end{pmatrix} = -k^2 \begin{pmatrix} D_u \bar{u}_k(t) \\ D_u \bar{v}_k(t) \end{pmatrix} + \boldsymbol{R'} \begin{pmatrix} \bar{u}_k(t) \\ \bar{v}_k(t) \end{pmatrix}$$

requiring mind-spinning graduate-level mathematics). The TV show *Numb3rs* is in many ways a description of how modern economists approach problems. In fact, many of the episodes of the show are built around models that modern economists have developed and use in their analysis.

Heuristic models are informal models expressed in words.

Models don't have to be mathematical; economists also use more informal verbal or **heuristic models**—*models that are expressed informally in words*. Models can be physical or they can be virtual models embodied in computer simulations. Computer simulation models also can be interactive where individuals become part of the model. For example, the online virtual world, Second Life, can be thought of as a model of society, and its economy can provide insight for the real-world economy. (Check out how the central authority in Second Life changes the money supply to affect the exchange rate of Second Life currency.) Just like these models, economic models come in many different forms with many different building blocks.

The building blocks and structures of models that economists use have evolved over time. Early economists tended to use a highly restricted set of building blocks and a narrow set of relatively simple (at least compared to their modern alternatives) formal models. **Modern economists** are *economists who are willing to use a wider range of models than did earlier economists.* A major change is that modern economists use a much more *inductive approach* to modeling. An **inductive approach** is *an approach to understanding a problem or question in which understanding*

---

[1]In case you were wondering, this is a reaction diffusion equation expressed in simplifying vector notation. What's a reaction diffusion equation? It's probably better not to ask.

is developed empirically from statistically analyzing what is observed in the data. Models based on an inductive approach are developed by how well they fit the data. Earlier economists were much more likely to use a **deductive approach**—*an approach that begins with certain self-evident principles from which implications are deduced (logically determined).*

Q-2 Are modern economists more likely to use inductive models than earlier economists?

Scientific and Engineering Models

Models can have many purposes. There are models primarily designed to provide understanding of what is happening for the sake of understanding—these are scientific models. Other models can be designed to provide insight into policy issues—these are applied-policy or engineering models. Still other models fall somewhere in between; there is no firm line distinguishing science from engineering. Most of the models you are presented within this book fall more within the applied-policy models. They are designed to provide insight into what is happening in a way that serves as a foundation for a discussion of policy.

Behavioral and Traditional Building Blocks

The traditional building blocks of microeconomics are the assumptions that people are rational and self-interested. What we have called **traditional economists** are *economists who study the logical implications of rationality and self-interest in relatively simple algebraic or graphical models such as the supply and demand model.* (Yes, it is true; by a mathematician's standards, supply and demand models are very simple models. But I agree with you; these simple models are often complicated enough.) Modern economists use supply and demand models, but they also use much more sophisticated models that integrate dynamics and strategic interactions into the analysis.

Traditional economists tend to use simple models based on assumptions of rationality and self-interest.

How much modern economists are willing to deviate from the traditional approach differs among modern economists. For example, some modern economists such as Nobel Prize winner Gary Becker advocate limiting economic models to these traditional building blocks. He writes: "The combined assumptions of maximizing behavior [note: maximizing behavior is how economists interpret rationality], market equilibrium, and stable preferences, used relentlessly and unflinchingly, form the heart of the economic approach." Up until the end of the 1970s, Becker's view predominated among economists. Since the 1980s, however, a group of modern economists has been edging away from these traditional building blocks.

Behavioral Economic Models

The study of models with alternative building blocks has grown so much in recent years that it has acquired a name—**behavioral economics**—*microeconomic analysis that uses a broader set of building blocks than rationality and self-interest used in traditional economics.* Instead of deductively assuming rationality and self-interest, behavioral economists inductively study people's behavior and use those behaviors in their models. Based on these inductive studies, they argue that the assumptions of both rationality and self-interest should be broadened somewhat. Rationality should be broadened to **purposeful behavior**—*behavior reflecting reasoned but not necessarily rational judgment*—and self-interest, to **enlightened self-interest** in which *people care about other people as well as themselves.*

Q-3 If an economist argues that people tend to be purposeful and follow their enlightened self interest, would you most likely characterize that economist as a behavioral or a traditional economist?

Behavioral economics is a leading field of research in economics today. The two important differences between traditional and behavioral building blocks are presented in Table 21-1.

TABLE 21-1	The Different Building Blocks of Traditional and Behavioral Models

Traditional Economics	Behavioral Economics
People are completely rational	People behave purposefully
People are self-interested	People follow their enlightened self-interest

Let's consider another example of behavioral economists' building blocks. Economists Matt Rabin and Ernst Fehr have developed models in which people care about fairness independently of what they themselves get. As discussed in an earlier chapter, they have found that when dividing up a sum of money, people try to divide the sum up fairly rather than giving it all to themselves, even though they could keep it all. In these modern models, the individuals would not be considered solely self-interested but, rather, enlightened self-interested; they care about fairness for its own sake. Economists Herbert Simon and Thomas Schelling have developed models in which people do not behave rationally, at least not in the traditional sense. For example, they have found that people will make choices based on rules of thumb such as "do what you see others doing" without rationally weighing the costs and benefits of each decision. Instead, people follow habit, which is purposeful behavior that reduces the costs of making decisions. Behavioral economists design their models accordingly.

Building blocks are important: They affect how one interprets the results of an analysis; they influence the patterns one sees in a picture. For example, say you observe a firm not taking advantage of its market position. Using traditional building blocks of rationality and self-interest, this would seem very strange. You would look for some hidden reason why the firm isn't taking advantage of that position and keep searching until you find the selfish motive underlying the behavior.

Models based on behavioral building blocks, in which people and firms have goals beyond self-interest, allow researchers to consider the possibility that the firm is not taking advantage of its market position for reasons other than self-interest. Pharmaceutical companies, for example, sell AIDS drugs in African countries at prices far below market price. This could be because of political pressure, but it could also be out of a sense of fairness. A traditional economist would focus on the first; a behavioral economist would consider both possibilities and use empirical data to decide which it is. The point of this example is that an economist who is willing to use a wider set of building blocks sees different information in data than does an economist who uses the traditional building blocks. In modern economics there is a lively debate about what building blocks economists should use.

PREDICTABLE IRRATIONALITY   The key to understanding the difference between behavioral economics and modern traditional economics is to recognize that behavioral economists are not just arguing that people are irrational; they are arguing that people are *predictably irrational* and that actions that traditional economists call irrational might not be irrational when considered in context.[2] For a behavioral economist, rationality comes in many forms, and what's important is that the model captures how people actually behave. Capturing this real-world nature of humans

The assumptions of a model affect the patterns that one sees in the data.

For behavioral economists, universality is less important than the fact that the model captures how people actually behave.

---

[2]An entire book could be written on what is meant by rationality and self-interest, and in some ways, all types of behavior can be considered rational and selfish. So it can be argued that behavioral economists are not arguing that purposeful behavior includes irrational behavior, only that it includes a different type of rationality than is allowed within traditional economics.

requires giving up some of the universality and power of models based on the traditional assumptions. Instead of having one model, one has a collection of models from which to choose for a variety of situations.

Let's consider an example of the difference. Say you are given a choice between two income streams. In the first scenario, you will earn $30,000 the first year, $27,000 the second, and $24,000 the third. In the second scenario, you will earn $24,000 the first year, $27,000 the second, and $30,000 the third. Which would you choose? A model based on traditional rationality predicts you would choose the first, since you will be able to save the additional $6,000 earned the first year, put it in the bank, and end up with more than $30,000 of income in the third year. Since you get more total income with the first stream of income ($24,000 plus the $6,000 from the first year, plus two years of interest on that $6,000), it is "rationally" preferred to the second. But when economists have asked people which stream of income they preferred, economists have found that most people choose the second stream, even when it is explained that they could be better off by choosing the first.

What's going on? Behavioral economists argue that most people recognize that they don't have complete self-control; people believe that they will spend the extra $6,000 earned in the first year rather than save it. Thus, while it may be possible for people to switch the first income stream into an income stream that is preferred to the second, they don't believe that they have the discipline to do so. Thus, they actually prefer the second to the first because it precommits them to saving, and thereby constrains them from doing something they believe they will do, but which they actually don't want to do. They have developed what is called a **precommitment strategy**—*a strategy in which people consciously place limitations on their future actions, thereby limiting their choices.* The behavior is irrational because people tend to choose the stream that results in less total income; it's predictable because in experiments time and time again, people make the same choice. This seemingly irrational choice is not unique to this example but occurs in a variety of contexts.

Q-4 Can adding a constraint on people make them better off?

ARE YOU PREDICTABLY IRRATIONAL?   Economist Dan Ariely, from whose book *Predictably Irrational* many of these examples have been developed, has created a test as a fun way to introduce people to these ideas and to determine whether they exhibit predictably irrational tendencies. (You can take the full test at his book website, www.danariely.com.)

- Does how happy you are with your salary depend on how much you make relative to what your friends, family members, and neighbors make?

- When you are facing a decision to buy something, do you make your decision by considering the pleasure that this item will bring to you and contrast it with all the other possible things that you could buy for the same amount of money, now and in the future?

- How often have you watched your weight, and wanted to skip the dessert at the end of a nice meal out, but once the waiter stopped by with the dessert cart, you ended up ordering the chocolate soufflé?

- Have you ever had a romantic partner in whom you started to lose interest, but when he or she all of a sudden began to grow more distant, your interest rekindled?

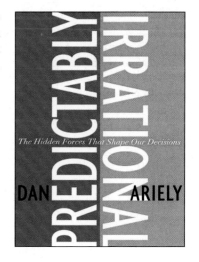

Most people answer these questions yes, no, yes, yes, and yes. These answers are the opposite of what an economist using the traditional building blocks would predict people would answer. Behavioral economics says that we must develop additional economic models that take these predictable behaviors into account.

The Advantages and Disadvantages of Modern Traditional and Behavioral Models

While it may seem that economists would want models that most closely reflect people's behavior, that is not so obvious—models that reflect people's actual behavior don't provide significant insight. For example, a pool player probably does not calculate the angles and spin of a ball to determine how to hit it, but it may make the most sense to assume that she does if one were modeling her behavior. The model may be easier to solve, and may be a better predictor of what will happen, than a model built on her actual behavior. Modern traditional economists emphasize the advantage of simplicity and ease of testing. Having one model means that you can test it and see if it fits reality. With many models, you have to do much more testing. For policy purposes, modern traditional economists argue that a single model that is easy to apply and test is the most useful model.

THE DIFFICULTY WITH BEHAVIORAL BUILDING BLOCKS: TESTING

Modern traditional economists point out that formally moving away from the traditional building blocks is difficult because following one's enlightened self-interest rather than self-interest, and acting purposefully rather than rationally, lead to much less clear-cut models and results. By their nature, behavioral models depend on the specific context of the choices involved; so instead of a single model, there are many. This means that the broader building blocks allow many more patterns to be discerned in the data. That's both an advantage and a disadvantage because it is hard to know which pattern to focus on.

The behavioral economists' answer to this problem is that economists can use laboratory and field experiments, or what is called *experimental economics,* to test alternative building blocks and find those that best describe how people actually behave. Let's consider an example: In an experiment, half the participants are given a mug; the other half are given a pen, each of approximately the same value. The participants were then allowed to exchange one for the other simply by returning the first item. Since who got the pen or the mug was random, the rationality building block would suggest that about half of each group would choose to trade for the other. In fact, only 10 percent of each group chose to trade, suggesting that what one has influences what one wants—in contradiction to the traditional building block of rationality. A behavioral economist would then include **endowment effects** (*people value something more just because they have it*) in their building blocks for models. Endowment effects fit the broader "behaving purposefully" building block; they do not fit the narrower "rationality" building block.

Behavioral economists using *evolutionary models*—models of how an individual's preferences are determined on the basis of natural selection of what is useful for survival—argue that the endowment effect is hardwired into people's brains because it serves a very useful evolutionary function. It makes people happier with what they have, which decreases the social conflict over who gets what. The endowment effect probably makes it possible for parents to put up with their children, and to actually believe that they are close to perfect, even though, to an objective observer, they are far from perfect. In fact, without the endowment effect, we would probably have an online market in children where you could trade yours for someone else's.

TRADITIONAL MODELS PROVIDE SIMPLICITY AND INSIGHT

Modern traditional economists don't agree with the direction that behavioral economics is heading in terms of giving up the old building blocks; they strongly prefer staying with the narrower building blocks of rationality and self-interest. The reason is the simplicity and clarity that come from models with these traditional building blocks; these

Endowment effects—the observation that what one has affects what one wants—is an example of a modern behavioral economics building block.

Neuroeconomics and Microeconomics

Both traditional and behavioral economics generally assume that the most basic building block of economic analysis is the individual. Where the two groups differ is in the assumptions they make about how the individual behaves. Some economists, such as Caltech economist Colin Camerer and University of Zurich economist Ernst Fehr, have questioned whether economists should study building blocks more basic than the individual. They argue that individuals are made up of cells, and that behavior is the result of chemical and electrical processes in the brain. By studying these brain processes, we can better understand an individual's behavior. To do this they perform CT scans of people's brains under a variety of controlled conditions and see what part of the brain is reacting. Their work goes under the name *neuroeconomics*.

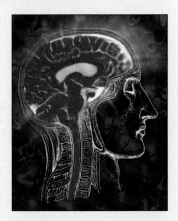

What they have found is that choice is a very complicated electrochemical phenomenon. For example, inconsistent decisions are often not the result of a mistake that would have been corrected if someone had pointed out the inconsistency, but, instead, the result of different electrochemical processes occurring in the brain. People are essentially hard-wired to be inconsistent. In a sense, more than one "you" are making decisions. There is the "emotional you" when your emotions hold sway and the "rational you" when the rational side of your brain holds sway. Depending on which "you" is being affected, the choice that "you" prefer can be quite different. And when both you's are affected, the result is often confusion. (This is a reason why advertisers appeal to both emotion and rationality simultaneously.)

This supports the behavioral economists' argument that we need to use building blocks that are different from the traditional ones. It also opens up a whole new set of possibilities about controlling behavior, such as the precommitment savings strategy discussed in the text. Another example of that precommitment strategy is not keeping dessert in the refrigerator to avoid temptation. Such precommitment strategies allow the "rational you" to win out over the "emotional you."

traditional models give clear-cut results that nicely highlight issues in ways that the modern building blocks do not. It was this view that was expressed by economist Gary Becker when he said that traditional building blocks, used unflinchingly, are the essence of the economic approach. He would argue that behavioral economists have flinched.[3]

Because Becker and other similarly minded economists taught at the University of Chicago, until recently, this unflinching approach was associated with what was called the *Chicago approach* to economics. Recently, however, a number of University of Chicago school economists such as Richard Thaler have begun using a broader set of building blocks, and, as I will discuss below, have been in the forefront of drawing policy implications from models based on modern building blocks.

BEHAVIORAL ECONOMIC MODELS REFLECT OBSERVED BEHAVIOR Behavioral economists' response to Becker and others who advocate sticking with the traditional building blocks is that they agree that the traditional model provides enormous insights, and that *they do not advocate discarding the supply/demand model or*

> Traditional models provide simple and clear results, which can highlight issues that behavioral models cannot.

Web Note 21.1
Predictably Irrational

---

[3]Some economists, called *evolutionary economists,* believe that even this group of building blocks does not go far enough. They advocate thinking of individuals as reflecting their evolutionary tendencies and being shaped by the market into the type of individuals that traditional economists assume are their inherent natures. Others, called *econophysicists* because they are often trained as physicists, argue that for many aggregate issues individual behavior is irrelevant; what happens in the aggregate reflects statistical properties of interactions that are independent of agents and that are independent of the building blocks used within the model.

Q-5 Which are better—models based on traditional building blocks or models based on behavioral building blocks?

the traditional building blocks, especially when teaching economics. Their argument is not that models built on the traditional building blocks—such as supply and demand—are irrelevant; it is simply that the traditional building blocks do not explain everything, and that attempts to use them to explain everything actually undermine our understanding of what models using the traditional building blocks do explain. Behavioral economists argue that empirical work has convincingly shown that people are predictably irrational in some of their behaviors, and modern economics must take that into account.

Eventually, the hope of modern economics is that economists will have a set of models that "explain" the decisions we observe, along with a guide explaining which models fit what situations. Alas, you're not going to get that guide in this book (or in any other textbook). Economists are just not there yet. In fact, we're far from it, and even those who use the new building blocks do not believe that the behavioral models are sufficiently developed to replace the traditional models as the pedagogical core of economics. That's why I focused on the traditional building blocks and the standard supply/demand model throughout the book. But that focus should not lead you to think of the supply/demand model and its assumptions as anything more than a beginning of an introduction to modern economics.

Behavioral and Traditional Informal (Heuristic) Models

As I stated above, economists have many types of models—verbal, empirical, and formal models. Modern economists use all of them. Thus, to understand modern economics, you need to know the various types and their advantages and disadvantages. Let's consider each briefly, starting with heuristic models.

Most of the time when laypeople hear about the results of an economist's analysis, they don't see the underlying formal model. Instead, all they see is a heuristic or verbal discussion that conveys the essence of the model. But if you search deeper into the discussion, you can generally extract the model and see whether the economist is using behavioral or traditional building blocks.

To show you the difference between heuristic models based on traditional building blocks and ones based on broader behavioral building blocks, let's consider some discussions in two popular books that apply economic reasoning to everyday events. That consideration will help clarify the difference between an economist using traditional building blocks and one using behavioral building blocks.

The Armchair Economist: Heuristic Models Using Traditional Building Blocks

Let's begin with a consideration of a model of University of Rochester economist Steven Landsburg. Landsburg calls himself an "armchair economist," by which he means that he provides heuristic models to explain everyday events. For the most part, Landsburg's heuristic models use traditional economic building blocks; he unflinchingly and happily pulls out unexpected implications from models built on those assumptions. Thus, Landsburg is an excellent example of a modern economist who sticks to traditional building blocks.

The particular model of his that I will consider deals with a sometimes taboo topic—sex. His model is designed to make the reader think, and to see how economic reasoning can come to counterintuitive conclusions. Coming to such highly counterintuitive ideas is seen as a strong plus for these models based on traditional building blocks because it gets people to think of questions in a different way than they normally do, and in the process provides important insights.

Steven Landsburg's *An Armchair Economist* is a book based on heuristic models using the self-interest and rationality building blocks.

MORE SEX IS SAFER SEX   In one of his more provocative models (available on *Slate,* www.slate.com/id/2033), Landsburg considers the problem facing Martin, "a charming and generally prudent young man with a limited sexual history, who has been gently flirting with his coworker Joan." Landsburg describes a situation in which Martin and Joan were both thinking that they might go home together after an office party that would be held the next day. However, on the way to the party, Martin notices a Center for Disease Control subway advertisement advocating the virtues of abstinence. Feeling guilty about his thoughts, he decides to stay home rather than to tempt himself. He is being virtuous.

Joan shows up at the party and, in Martin's absence, she hooks up with an "equally charming but considerably less prudent Maxwell." Maxwell is rather careless in practicing safe sex, and the end result of this hookup is that Joan ends up with AIDS—all because Martin was virtuous. (Economic models conveying these parables of the problems with being virtuous have a long history in economics, going back to Bernard Mandeville, who wrote *The Fable of the Bees* back in the 1700s.)

Landsburg then argues that this story demonstrates that Martin's withdrawal from the mating game has made the mating game more dangerous for others. He argues that it follows that the world would be better off (specifically, we could slow the spread of AIDS) if "the Martins of the world would loosen up a little." He then reports some empirical estimates by a Harvard professor that if everyone with fewer than about 2.25 partners per year were to have a few more partners, we could actually slow the spread of AIDS. Landsburg argues the following: "To an economist, it's crystal clear why people with limited sexual pasts choose to supply too little sex in the present: their services are underpriced."

Landsburg's model is meant to shock, which it does. But it is also meant to hone people's reasoning ability, which it also does. It captures the economic insight that when effects of one's decisions on others are not included in a person's decision-making process—that is, where there are externalities—the decision will not lead to the aggregate outcome that most people would prefer. But they are the decisions that Landsburg thinks people will make. Landsburg's model is based on the traditional building block of strong self-interest.

Decisions about sexual activity may have externalities and therefore what is best for the individuals involved may not be best for society.

WHY CAR INSURANCE COSTS MORE SOME PLACES THAN OTHERS

While Landsburg is traditional in his building blocks, he is not always traditional in the formal models he uses, and in some of the issues he studies, he goes far beyond the simple supply/demand model. For example, in another model, he considers the issue of why car insurance costs three times as much in Philadelphia, Pennsylvania, than in Ithaca, New York, even though the theft and accident rates are not significantly different between the two cities. The model he uses is a "path-dependent tipping-point" model with two, rather than one, equilibria. In a tipping-point model, the model can arrive at quite different results depending on people's initial choice. The results are path dependent, and without knowing the path, one cannot predict the equilibrium. Tipping-point models are a type of a broader group of models called **path-dependent models**—*models in which the path to equilibrium affects the equilibrium.* Path-dependent models require a knowledge of the relevant history to reach a conclusion. Were the supply/demand model a path-dependent model, it would not lead to a unique equilibrium price.

The argument Landsburg gives is the following. In the pricing of insurance, there is a feedback effect of the initial choices people make of whether to buy insurance that affects the cost of insurance. If a few people decide not to buy insurance, the costs of insurance to others who do buy insurance will be higher since, if they have an accident with an uninsured driver, their insurance will have to pay. Because insurance costs are

Can You Explain Landsburg's Provocative Insights?

The two arguments that I present in the text are examples of Landsburg's provocative approach, which is characteristic of modern traditional economists. Below are some of his other provocative conclusions based on traditional building blocks. See if you can figure out what the implicit model is that leads to that conclusion. If you can't figure out the model, or want to check your reasoning, his arguments can be found in his book *More Sex Is Safer Sex,* and brief summaries of his reasoning can be found on the text website. (www.mhhe.com/colander9e)

1. Daughters cause divorce.

2. A taste for revenge is healthier than a thirst for gold.

3. A ban on elephant hunting is bad news for elephants.

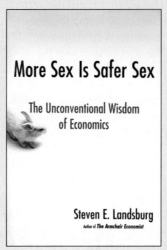

More Sex Is Safer Sex

The Unconventional Wisdom of Economics

Steven E. Landsburg

Author of *The Armchair Economist*

4. Disaster assistance is bad news for the people who receive it.

5. Malicious computer hackers should be executed.

6. The most charitable people support the fewest charities.

7. Writing books is socially irresponsible.

8. Elbowing your way to the front of the water-fountain line is socially responsible.

Many of these are presented a bit in jest (I think)—they are meant to shock and get you to think. But that is precisely how the best advocates of the traditional building blocks use their heuristic models based on traditional building blocks. The models provide you with a different view of an issue, and thereby increase your understanding of what's really going on.

---

higher, even more people drive without insurance, further increasing the rates for those who do buy insurance. Landsburg argues that that is what happened in Philadelphia. In Ithaca, however, the situation went the other way—many initially bought insurance, which meant that insurance costs for everyone were lower, which led others to buy insurance, which led to even lower rates. Both equilibria are self-reinforcing, and, once chosen, are very difficult to change, without a major intervention by government.

Such government interventions go against Landsburg's (and most traditional economists') intuition. Traditional models based on the traditional building blocks without externalities almost inevitably lead to a laissez-faire policy. He states, "For ideological free marketers (like myself), theories (like this one) can be intellectually jarring. We are accustomed to defending free markets as the guarantors of both liberty and prosperity, but here's a case where liberty and prosperity are at odds: By forcing people to act against their own self-interest in the short run, governments can make everybody more prosperous in the long run. . . . Is it worth sacrificing a small amount of freedom for cheaper auto insurance? I am inclined to believe that the answer is yes, but the question makes me squirm a bit."

Here we see a heuristic model based on reasoning that people are rational and self-interested, as in the supply/demand model. But because it is not a supply/demand model with a single equilibrium, it leads to a quite nontraditional result of two possible equilibria. It also leads to a potential policy solution—one requiring all individuals to get insurance. The policy discussion highlighted by this model is highly relevant because it is now part of the debate about health care in the United States. Advocates of government-mandated health insurance argue that an individual's decision to go without health care insurance increases the costs of health care for all, and this has pushed the United States to an undesirable equilibrium. They argue that mandatory insurance would switch the United States to a preferable alternative equilibrium.

The Economic Naturalist: Heuristic Models Using Behavioral Building Blocks

Let's now turn to some models from another popular book, this one by Cornell economist Robert Frank, entitled *The Economic Naturalist*. Frank's approach is very similar to Landsburg's. He observes the events around him and tries to understand them using economic building blocks. The difference between Frank and Landsburg is that Frank is much more willing than Landsburg to go beyond the traditional building blocks. He assumes that people are only *purposeful,* not rational, and that they follow *enlightened self-interest* rather than being only self-interested. This allows for a much wider range of models and set of explanations, as well as a much wider range of policy interventions that follow from the model. We can see the difference by considering two of the models he presents.

WHY ARE PEOPLE MORE LIKELY TO RETURN CASH THAN A LAMPSHADE? The first of his models that we will consider is designed to explain why people are more likely to return cash to a store when given too much change by a cashier than to return the merchandise for which they were not charged. He begins by reporting the results of a survey in which 90 percent of the respondents said they would return $20 to a store if given that amount extra in change, but only 10 percent said they would return a $20 lampshade if the cashier had neglected to charge for it. If people took only their own interests into account, they shouldn't return either.

That people return a $20 lampshade that was mistakenly not scanned less often than they will return an overpayment of $20 in change supports the assumption of purposeful behavior.

He explains this difference in behavior by arguing that people take into account *who* will be hurt by the action. In the case of the cash, the "cashier will have to pay out of her own pocket." Thus, he reasons most people will not want her to be penalized. In the case of the lampshade, it is the store, not the individual, that will suffer the loss, and people are much less worried about hurting stores than they are about hurting people. Notice the difference in Frank's assumption as compared to Landsburg's. In Frank's model, people are somewhat self-interested (they keep the $20 lampshade), but not totally self-interested (they return the $20). Using a model with traditional building blocks, the prediction would be that no one would return the money. Frank's behavioral model allows for the possibility that individuals care about the impact of their actions on others.

WHY DON'T MORE PEOPLE WEAR VELCRO SHOES? A second model found in Frank's book deals with why people continue to wear shoes with shoelaces, even though Velcro shoes are more practical, and, according to Frank, "offer clear advantages over laces" because lace shoes can become untied, causing people to trip and fall. He argues that the reason why shoelaces are still predominant is that the very young (who don't know how to tie shoes) and the very old (who are too feeble to bend down and tie shoes) wear Velcro shoes, and therefore they have become associated with what Frank calls "incompetence and fragility"—characteristics with which most people don't want to be associated.

Where this explanation deviates from the traditional building blocks is the rationality assumption. Using a technology that is less efficient than another (shoelaces over Velcro) is irrational, and thus doesn't make sense. The behavioral assumption in Frank's model is that people care about what other people think about them and thus take social issues, not just economic issues, into account when making their decisions. Behavioral economic models take social dimensions of problems into account; traditional economic models don't.

Behavioral models take social considerations into account; traditional models do not.

Can You Explain Frank's Observations?

The text recounts two heuristic models that are found in Robert Frank's *The Economic Naturalist*. In his review of Frank's book, Vanderbilt economist John Siegfried listed the questions that led to 10 other models in Frank's book. Below is Siegfried's list; I leave it to you to develop the model that would explain the questions.

1. Why does a light come on when you open a refrigerator, but not a freezer?

2. Why do dry cleaners charge more for women's shirts than for men's?

3. Why are brown eggs more expensive than white ones?

4. Why do women endure the discomfort of high heels?

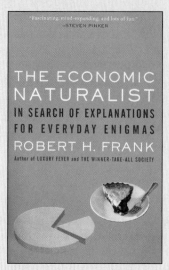

"Fascinating, mind-expanding, and lots of fun."
—STEVEN PINKER

THE ECONOMIC
NATURALIST
IN SEARCH OF EXPLANATIONS
FOR EVERYDAY ENIGMAS
ROBERT H. FRANK
Author of LUXURY FEVER and THE WINNER-TAKE-ALL SOCIETY

5. Why are whales in danger of extinction, but not chickens?

6. If we have Blockbuster video, why don't we have Blockbuster book?

7. Why is there so much mathematical formalism in economics?

8. Why do stores post signs saying that guide dogs are permitted inside?

9. Why do most U.S. department stores put men's fashions on the ground floor?

10. Why is it easier to find a partner when you already have one?

If you want to see the models Frank came up with, see his book *The Economic Naturalist*. Short summaries of the explanations Frank followed can be found on the textbook website. (www.mhhe.com/colander9e).

Q-6 Does the author's tendency to wear Velcro shoes demonstrate that he is beyond social pressures?

I should include an addendum (confession?) to this model; I've worn Velcro shoes for the last 30 years, much to the horror of my children, who asked me not to be seen with them when I wear them. Why do I wear them? I suspect because of my training in traditional economic models. That training has shaped me so that I value efficiency for its own sake. By wearing Velcro shoes I am making a statement to society (I am as much a social creature as others) that I am not driven by social norms about dressing (anyone who has seen my standard attire can attest to the fact that I am not). I consciously do it (at least in the sense of not allowing my wife to put out the clothes she wants me to wear) and, to some degree, I revel in the looks I get because it means that I am free, and efficient, allowing me to consider others slaves of some designer. I tell my kids that some day the world will follow me. They tell me, "Don't hold your breath."

My behavior represents another dimension of behavior that behavioral economists have discovered. Studying a model and using its assumptions can lead you to adopt its assumptions as your own; thus, the models you choose to use to look at the world can influence your behavior. This means that studying economics may not only provide you with insights; it also may change you.

The Limits of Heuristic Models

I could go on with hundreds of these vignettes; they are entertaining, fun, and good practice for the mind. If my sole purpose were to entertain you, I'd include a lot more. But the principles course is meant to do more than entertain; it is meant to teach, and except when they are writing for laypeople, most economists see heuristic models as simply a steppingstone to a more formal model. The reason is that heuristic models are not sufficiently precise, making their validity impossible to test. Think back to the heuristic models we presented and ask yourself how convinced you were by the arguments. Each was relatively easy to modify to come to a different conclusion.

For example, what if Joan had chosen not to hook up with anyone? Or what if she had seen the same abstinence ad as had Martin? Then the argument would have been reversed. Would that mean that the Martins of the world should have less sex? Or what if Velcro shoes suddenly became "in." Would that mean that the more practical solution wins out? So, while the heuristic models embodied in the vignettes are entertaining, it is a fair question to ask whether we really know anything more about the world after learning about the models than we did before. To a scientist the answer is no, we don't, at least in a scientific sense. That's why science is not based on heuristic models.

Empirical and Formal Models

Scientists are very hesitant to base any knowledge on anecdotes or heuristic models, even highly convincing ones. The reason is that they have found that the human mind is extremely good at creating convincing stories that make sense within its own world view or frame, but not necessarily outside of it. They have found that the human mind is what psychologists call a *fast pattern completer*. Heuristic models exploit this tendency in humans that gives people a sense of understanding, but not necessarily a scientific understanding. Scientists argue that to extend a heuristic model to true understanding, you have to quantify and empirically test your arguments.

Q-7 Why are economists very hesitant to base knowledge on heuristic models?

The Importance of Empirical Work in Modern Economics

This leads us to a second important element of modern economics: It is highly empirical. That is, modern economics is based on experiments that can be replicated, or on statistical analysis of real-world observations. While the importance of empirical work has a long history in economics, going back to William Petty in the 1600s, up until the 1940s, economics primarily concentrated on deductive, not inductive, reasoning. That occurred because of the lack of data and the lack of computational power to analyze data.

With the development of **econometrics**—*the statistical analysis of economic data*—in the 1940s, that started to change. But because of limited data and computing power, empirical work in economics did not move to the forefront in economics until the late 1980s when computer power had expanded enough to begin making such an empirical approach useful. At that point, induction started to supplement deduction as the economist's method for understanding the real world. Since the late 1980s this movement toward induction has accelerated, so that today it is fair to say that the development of computing power has fundamentally changed the way economic research is done.

The strong reliance on empirical work is true of all modern economists—both those who use traditional building blocks and those who use behavioral building blocks. Today, much empirical work in economics is not based on formal deductive models, but rather on heuristic models—relatively simple and informal models that capture a possible insight, such as those we discussed above by Frank and Landsburg.

Modern economics—models based on both traditional and behavioral building blocks—relies on experiments and statistical analysis of real-world observations.

The difference between an economic scientist's heuristic model and those of Frank and Landsburg presented above is that the economic scientist doesn't stop with the heuristic model, as did Frank and Landsburg's presentations. He or she builds an empirical model around that heuristic model and supports the argument with empirical evidence. Essentially, what he or she does is to take relationships found in the heuristic model and see if these relationships can be generalized subject to scientifically based statistical studies. Economists call this approach "letting the data speak." To let the data speak, you collect data and analyze them with statistical and econometric tools.

To analyze an issue with an **empirical model**—*a model that statistically discovers a pattern in the data*—researchers empirically study the relationship arrived at in their

A regression finds a line that best fits a combination of points such as the one shown here. It appears from this scatter plot that class size affects the average grade.

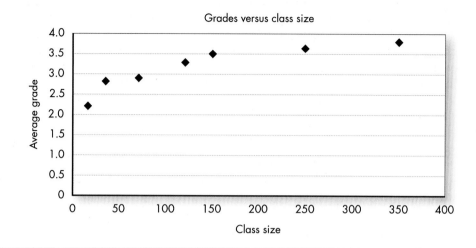

A regression model is a model that statistically relates one set of variables to another.

heuristic models. That's what Steve Levitt did with enormous creativity and success. He looked at a variety of issues: Do sumo wrestlers throw matches? Do basketball teams cheat? And why do drug dealers often live with their mothers? He looks at the data, creates simple informal models and hypotheses, and uses those models to structure his empirical study. For example, he reasoned that if who won sumo wrestling matches did not involve cheating, whether a wrestler was close to winning enough matches to raise his ranking would make no difference as to whether he won a match or not. But he reasoned further that if wrestlers are self-interested and rational, they will have an incentive to agree to quid pro quo arrangements to cheat and throw a match, allowing opponents to win a match in exchange for their throwing a future match. So now he had a testable hypothesis. His hypothesis was: *The closer a wrestler is to raising his rank, the more often his opponent will intentionally lose.* He then collected and statistically analyzed the data. What he discovered was that how close a wrestler was to elimination did make a difference, which allowed him to conclude that sumo wrestlers "cheat."

REGRESSION MODELS   A primary tool of an empirical economist is a **regression model,** *an empirical model in which one statistically relates one set of variables to another,* and the statistical tools that accompany it. For example, say you are wondering if a professor giving higher grades increases the number of students in his class. You would collect data about two variables—the grades he normally gives and enrollment in his classes—giving you a relationship shown in Figure 21-1. Then you would "run a regression," which essentially means that you use a statistical package to find a line that "best fits" the data, where "best fit" means making the distances between that line and the points as small as possible. If the "best fit" line is upward-sloping, as it would be here, then the regression model's answer to the question is a tentative yes, subject to all the things that were held constant and an assumption that causation goes from grades to enrollment.

The "goodness of fit" between the two variables is described by the **coefficient of determination,** which is *a measure of the proportion of the variability in the data that is accounted for by the statistical model.* The larger the coefficient of determination, the better the fit, and if it is a perfect fit, then every point will be on the "best fit" line. This isn't a statistics class so I won't go into further explanation, but that short description should give you a sense of how empirical regression models work. Regression models are the workhorses of much of what applied microeconomists do, and modern economists become almost magicians at pulling information out from data.

Often economists' empirical models explore issues far from the standard domain of economics. One example recounted in Yale professor Ian Ayres' book *Super Crunchers* (a book that nicely explains the importance of data analysis to modern society) is by Princeton professor Orley Ashenfelter. He developed a model that predicted whether a particular year's wine would be a good vintage. He hypothesized that the quality of a wine in a particular year depended on rainfall, weather, and similar elements in that year. He collected all the appropriate data, and then related those data to the price of wine by running a regression. He then developed the following relationship from his regression model:

Wine quality = 12.145 + 0.001 (Winter rainfall) + 0.06 (Average growing-season temperature) − 0.004 (Harvest rainfall)

This relationship tells us that the quality of a Bordeaux wine depends upon rainfall and temperature. He upset "wine connoisseurs" by arguing that his simple regression model does a better job at determining a good year for wine than they do through tasting. Moreover, he argued that his model can determine quality long before wine connoisseurs could even start tasting the wine. So when choosing a wine, forget about sniffing, swirling, and tasting; just get your computer out, collect the data, plug in the numbers, and solve the equation. Is he right? I'm no wine connoisseur, but the people I talk to (admittedly, they tend to be economists) believe that he is.

Another regression model has been used by baseball teams to determine how valuable a prospect is. Econometrically trained specialists collected data on young baseball recruits and ran regressions, finding how different skills are correlated with a team's success. When these specialists did this, they found that bases on balls were almost as important as hits. Thus, they argued that a person's ability to draw a walk should be one of the variables considered in choosing a recruit, something that previously wasn't done. They then used that regression model to predict which young recruit would most likely help a team win. The strategy worked, as discussed by Michael Lewis in *Moneyball;* after using the model, the Oakland Athletics won their division, despite their low payroll. Oakland's success did not go unnoticed; when the Boston Red Sox, a team with a high payroll, started using the model, they won the World Series.

These empirical models are sometimes called *data-mining models,* but I prefer to call them *pattern-finding models*. They play an important role in the modern microeconomist's tool kit and have become more important because of the enormous increase in computing power and statistical software. This increase in computer power allows economic researchers to find stable patterns in data much more easily than before. With sophisticated econometric software, computers can automatically find patterns and turn those patterns into models.

Summarizing: The development of computer power and these empirical models has led to an enormous change in how modern microeconomics is done. For example, when I asked top graduate students as part of an interview what differentiated an economist from another social scientist, they did *not* say that they differed from other social scientists in the building blocks they used. Instead, they said that the difference was the economist's reliance on formal empirical methods.[4]

SIMPLE DATA MODELS: CHARTS, GRAPHS, AND QUANTITATIVE ARGUMENTATION
As a principles student, you will likely not be developing regression models, but you will be building models based on data by developing a chart or a graph that demonstrates how something is changing over time or a pattern

Regression models can reveal all sorts of relationships from the effect of weather on the quality of wine to the contribution of a player's ability to draw a walk toward a team's season record.

---

[4]That may change in the future since other social sciences are becoming much more empirical as well, but for the next decade they will likely still lag behind economics.

that captures the co-movement of two variables. These charts and graphs might not have the full scientific look of a regression model, but they are often more useful. What characterizes the modern economic way of thinking is not the regression model per se, but using quantitative data to make an argument, often by presenting those data with a simple chart or graph.

The Role of Formal Models

Were economic modeling only a matter of data mining, empirical models would replace all other types of modeling, but it is not, and they haven't. Data, by themselves, have no meaning; they have to be interpreted and given meaning, and how one interprets the data depends on the model and the building blocks one has in mind. Either implicitly or explicitly, one's model guides how one organizes the data. That's why theory remains important, and an important part of this principles course is meant to give you practice in understanding the theoretical structure of economic thinking.

You can see the importance of theory by thinking about a magic eye picture—as you change your focus, what you see will change. (You can see a magic eye picture at www.magiceye.com.) A simpler example is the figure of the old woman shown here. Did you see an "old woman"? Most of you will have because that's how I described it. But what if I had said "beautiful young woman" rather than "old woman"? If I had, I suspect you might have seen the picture in a different light. The moral: Which pattern your eye sees in pictures, and even more so in data, depends on the implicit model or frame that you bring to the picture or the data. (If you only see one, keep looking; the eye of the "old woman" is the ear of the beautiful young woman.)

I raise this issue of framing because it highlights the difficulty of pulling information from an empirical model. Two different economists may well see different results even with the same empirical model. Let's consider an example of such a recent debate in economics. The debate concerns the deterrent effect of the death penalty.

In natural science one would determine whether the death penalty has a deterrent effect by doing a controlled experiment that isolates specific variables and changing one variable to see if it causes another to change. But in economics such controlled experiments are generally impossible. An economist can't suggest that we try out the death penalty to see what its deterrent effect would be. So instead of using controlled experiments, economists need to be creative and search for what they call a **natural experiment** (*an event created by nature that can serve as an experiment*) that may help to shed light on an issue.

Doing such a study with existing data, economists Isaac Ehrlich and Joanna Shepherd have found a statistical relationship between the death penalty and the number of murders. In one statistical study, Erlich found that an increase in the number of executions by 1 percent is associated with a decrease in the murder rate by 0.5 percent, while Shepherd found that one execution deterred seven to eight murders. These statistical relationships have been contested by a number of economists. They pointed out that how the variables are specified and the equations mattered. For example, using the same data, economists John Donohue and Justin Wulfers came to quite different conclusions. They stated: "The view that the death penalty deters is still the product of belief, not evidence."

I'm not going to get into the debate here; I don't claim to know who is right. I recount it merely to give you a sense that given the limited ability economists have to conduct controlled experiments, letting the data speak will not necessarily provide the definitive answer. This means that economists, and other social scientists, must rely on their theoretical models to guide them in interpreting data and in drawing out policy implications from their work.

The same pattern can be interpreted in multiple ways. Economists rely on theoretical models to help them interpret the data.

Q-8 True or false? Debates in modern economics will be resolved by letting the data speak.

DIFFERENT TYPES OF FORMAL MODELS THAT ECONOMISTS USE   The above discussion leads us to a third characteristic of modern economics. Earlier economists used models with relatively simple relationships among variables; the supply/demand model is an example of such a simple model. Modern economists—both modern traditional and modern behavioral economists—still use simple models, but they also use models that allow for much more complex relationships among variables than do the simple models. These analytically sophisticated models cannot be expressed in the two-dimensional graphs used by earlier economists.

An example of the difference between earlier economists and modern economists can be seen by considering the "tipping point" model that Landsburg used to analyze differences in car insurance prices. As I stated earlier, that model is a path-dependent model, which technically means that any decision feeds back into the model. In a path-dependent model, you can only know what will happen if you know the path the model takes. Mathematically, specifying path-dependent models is much more complicated than specifying supply/demand models; you have to use an advanced-calculus, differential-equations model rather than a standard algebraic model, or you have to solve it computationally.

Q-9 Is the supply and demand model a path-dependent model?

The reason why formal models have evolved from simple models to more complex and highly technical mathematical models, again, is that technology has changed. In this case, the technology is mathematics. Today's economists are much better trained in mathematics than were earlier economists, which allows economists to go far beyond the interrelationships allowed in supply/demand models. With advances in mathematics, for example, you can have:

- Models with many equilibria, so it is difficult to know what an equilibrium is.
- Models in which not only are the variables related, so too are the changes in variables and the changes in changes in variables.
- Models in which systemic equilibrium involves enormous continual change in the parts so that even though the system is in equilibrium, the individual parts are not.
- Models in which relationships are nonlinear on various levels, and in which an infinitely small change can lead to drastically different results.

The potential interrelationships that can be captured in modern formal models are almost unending, and when one studies the broad range of models with all these potential interrelationships, the number of potential outcomes in the economy is awesome. There is a formal theoretical model that can arrive at just about any possible conclusion.

Which theoretical model is right? Do you choose models with more complex building blocks, as argued by behavioral economists? Or do you choose models with more limiting traditional building blocks? Do you not worry about building blocks? Or do you just worry about which model best fits the empirical evidence? Such questions are the grist of the modern economists' debates. (And you thought we economists were boring people; if my kids only understood how wildly interesting these questions are—would you believe?)

THE TRADE-OFF BETWEEN SIMPLICITY AND COMPLETENESS   You might think that one should use the most complex model with the broadest building blocks because that would give you the broadest approach. But that doesn't necessarily follow. Each new interrelationship involves adding an additional level of technical difficulty, and the more complex the model, the harder it is to arrive at a conclusion. Thus, in their modeling, economists make a continual trade-off between simplicity and completeness. At the principles level, the choice is clear: KISS (Keep It Simple Stupid) rules, which is why the graphical supply/demand model is the workhorse of principles of economics. That's why, even though modern economics goes far beyond supply and demand, the principles course focuses on supply and demand and teaches students the traditional model.[5] Almost all economists agree that for introducing principles students to economic reasoning, used appropriately with sufficient caveats, the supply/demand model is a really neat and useful model. It is the perfect calisthenics of the mind for moving on to models with more complicated behavioral building blocks.

Let me give an example of where the model one uses matters: the state of the aggregate economy in 2008. The question at issue was: Should we be worried about the economy going into a depression or not? The traditional aggregate-supply/aggregate-demand model, which was the standard textbook model, suggested that we should not be concerned. In it, the economy is close to equilibrium, and policies exist to move it to equilibrium if it isn't. That isn't the case for some of the more complex formal models. In these more complex models, the aggregate economy could suddenly change depending on what people believe. You can have what is called a **self-confirming equilibrium**—*an equilibrium in a model in which people's beliefs become self-fulfilling*—so if people think the economy will go into a depression, it will. In some models, what people believe might not even matter; you can have *strange attractor models,* sometimes called **butterfly effect models**—*models in which a small change causes a large effect.* For example, a butterfly flapping its wings in China can cause the output of the U.S. economy to fall significantly. In these models, a small change could tip the economy into a low-growth, high-unemployment equilibrium that would be difficult to escape. In these models, therefore, we had reason to be seriously concerned about the U.S. economy going into a depression. Unfortunately; the continued high unemployment and slow growth since then suggest that the more complicated models were correct.

www   Web Note 21.2
Models in Movies

Game theory models analyze the strategic interaction among individuals.

OTHER FORMAL MODELS   There are many other types of formal models as well. For example, *set theory models* are models based only on formal logical relationships. Yet another is a **game theory model**—*a model in which one analyzes the strategic interaction of individuals when they take into account the likely response of other people to their actions.* Game theory models form the core of much of what is studied in graduate microeconomics today. Thus, the standard graduate microeconomics text has only three supply-and-demand diagrams in an entire 1,000-plus-page book.

More complicated models often yield no analytic solution—that is, you can't solve the set of equations to discover the equilibrium in the model. These complicated analytic models were unusable for a traditional economist because a model that you can't solve analytically didn't provide any insight. That isn't the case for a modern economist. If a modern economist can't solve a model analytically, he or she will estimate the solution by simulating the model with a computer. Computational power replaces

---

[5]I discuss the justification for why the textbooks focus on the supply/demand model and the traditional model, even as the economists in their research have moved from them, in *The Stories Economists Tell* and a *Journal of Economic Education* article, "What Economists Teach and What We Believe." While the supply/demand model captures these ideas, for mathematically inclined students, as Harold Kuhn, a famous mathematical economist, once told his students, the lessons can be generalized into a set of constrained optimization models assuming convex functions, and if principles students were strongly mathematically inclined, many of the models could be presented in calculus format. A brief introduction to the calculus of constrained optimization is available in the *Honors Companion* accompanying this book available on my website, www.mhhe.com/colander9e

analytic elegance. Thus, computer simulation is an important tool of modern economists (both those using behavioral and those using traditional assumptions), and in his or her research a modern economist will often go from struggling with analytically solving a model to simulating it on the computer, and then back to trying to solve it analytically.

Economists use a number of different types of computer simulations. The one described above was a simulation designed to solve a model with a specified set of equations that can't be solved analytically. In those types of simulations, the computer is a computational assistant that can arrive at estimated solutions to complicated analytic sets of equations. This approach is widespread. A more novel approach to computer simulation is designed to deal with problems that are so difficult that you don't even know how to specify the equations. How do economists model when they can't specify the equations that describe the relationships in the model? They use the computer to guide them in specifying the model itself.

This alternative approach to modeling is called the **agent-based computational economic (ACE) model**—*a culture dish approach to the study of economic phenomena in which agents* (encapsulated collections of data and methods representing an entity residing in that environment on the computer) *are allowed to interact in a computationally constructed environment and the researcher observes the results of that interaction.* (For more information about ACE models, see www.econ.iastate.edu/tesfatsi/ace.htm.) ACE modeling is fundamentally different from standard modeling. It is computer based, and it has no equations that have to be solved. Instead, ACE researchers simply try to create virtual computer models that capture the essence of the interdependencies, and then observe the results. So rather than solve a model, you build a computer model with computer agents; you then run the model thousands of times and keep track of the results.

The ACE model is like a petri dish of individual economic actors deployed with specific behaviors. Economists watch and study the relationships and behaviors that develop.

This is a fascinating new approach to modeling complex systems because it allows for all types of interactions. It has the possibility of fundamentally changing the way economists model and how they understand the economy because it allows researchers to consider much more complicated interactions than they could if they had to "solve" the model on their own. For example, ACE models can allow multiple equilibria and the possibility of many levels of path dependency—complications that are beyond traditional models. Recognizing that the models may reflect path dependency, the ACE modeler doesn't run the program once; he or she runs it thousands of times and sees the range of results. So just like engineers are now using virtual computer modeling to design planes and cars, economists are now using virtual computer models to understand how the economy works and to devise policies that might make it work better.

EMPIRICALLY TESTING FORMAL MODELS　With so many different models, one must ask the question: How do you decide which model to use? To decide, economists empirically test alternative models and try to see which one fits best. Essentially this reverses the process used in heuristic empirical modeling, where the data are collected and analyzed before the hypothesis is determined and are then used to determine the hypothesis. With empirically tested formal models, the hypothesis is formulated first—without knowledge of the data—and then the hypothesis is tested to see if the data fit the model. Obviously, formulating hypotheses without knowing the data is difficult, and thus economists try to test hypotheses on "out-of-sample" data—data that were not used in the formulation of the hypothesis. If they don't have such data, they try to develop the data, or something close to them, with experiments and clever observation of events.

Today, fitting the models to the data is much of what modern economists do. "Bringing the model to the data" is a phrase you hear all the time from modern economists.

Modern Traditional and Behavioral Economists

	Earlier Economics	Modern Economics	
		Modern Behavioral Economists	**Modern Traditional Economists**
Assumptions	Rationality Self-interest	Purposeful behavior Enlightened self-interest	Rationality Self-interest
Approach	Deduction	Induction and deduction; emphasis on experimental economics and empirical models	Induction and deduction; emphasis on empirical models
Types of models	Simple supply/demand models	All types including highly complex mathematical models and ACE models	All types including highly complex mathematical models and ACE models

Economists are continually asking questions such as: "How does the model work in out-of-sample data?" "Do we have a natural experiment that we can use to test the model?" "Can we develop a randomized experiment that will test the model?" "Can we design a lab experiment that will test the model?" and "Can we design a field experiment to test the model?"

Such empirical testing requires precision, which means that to truly bring the model to the data, one needs a formal model where all relationships are precisely specified, rather than a heuristic model where relationships are imprecise. Thus, the "empirical models" discussed earlier are quite different from the "empirically tested formal models" that form the foundation of economic science. Empirical models based on heuristic models are fine for policy analysis and for guiding real-world policy decisions that have to be made before one has a full scientific understanding of an issue. These models are absolutely necessary. But before one elevates the insights of the model to the level of full scientific knowledge, one needs much more precise models. As I stated at the beginning of the chapter, most of this book is concerned with engineering models, not scientific models, which is why we will not explore the intricacies of testing formal models.

The difference between the empirical models discussed earlier and the empirically tested formal models described here is a subtle, but important, difference. In a heuristic empirical model, one has only an informal model that lets the data speak first, as heard through your general worldview embodied in your building blocks. After you've heard the data, you can provide an explanation for what you have heard. That explanation will be based on your implicit formal model, *but the empirical model cannot be an explicit test of the model* since the actual model came from the data; there is no formal model to test. To empirically test a formal model or a formalized empirical model developed from a data set, the process is different. Here, one carefully develops the implications of the formal model as they relate to the issue. Then one empirically tests this model's implications against another set of data.

APPLICATION: WHY DID THE PRICE OF CHOCOLATE RISE?   To see how formal models can make a difference in how one thinks about real-world problems, let's consider an example of a puzzle that economists faced. This example gives you a sense of why modern economists have moved to these more complicated models and how the results of the two models differ—even with the same data. The puzzle is the following—the price of chocolate. From 2006 to 2009, the price of chocolate went up to $3,500 a ton from $1,500 a ton. The question is why.

You should be able to give the traditional economic analysis of what likely happened from the analysis of earlier chapters—that explanation would involve supply falling, demand rising, or a combination of the two. (A good exercise is to graph these to see why that would be the explanation.) In a principles course, that would be the right answer. For real-world researchers it is not enough. The problem is that the data don't reveal any apparent shifts in either supply or demand. So why did the price change when supply and demand did not?

Exploring the situation further, economists discovered that there was a structural change in the market. *Hedge funds*—investment funds representing rich investors which had few constraints on what they could buy—that had access to large amounts of credit were moving their investments out of real estate and into commodities over this time period. Chocolate was one of these commodities, but commodities whose prices rose also included oil and grains, both of which also experienced sudden large increases in price during this same time period. These hedge funds did not want the chocolate, and they did not buy chocolate and store it. Instead, they were buying what are called *chocolate futures*—the right to buy chocolate at a specified point in the future at a specified price—in large amounts. Specifically, they increased their demand for chocolate futures from 260 thousand tons to 706 thousand tons over a couple of years, which amounts to an increase from less than 10 percent to more than 20 percent of the total market demand. Prices of chocolate rose to their highest level in more than 30 years.

The question that policy makers posed to economists was whether this hedge fund activity in the futures market was the cause of the rise in the price of chocolate (and other commodities), and if it were the cause, would the rise in price be permanent or temporary? The supply/demand model doesn't directly answer that question. The answer requires an analysis that includes inventories and that captures the relationship between future expected prices—the futures prices of chocolates—and the current price of chocolate. That means that you need a model of intertemporal (across time periods) equilibrium with heterogeneous agents (agents that are not exactly alike).

You also need to figure out how the new behavioral economics building blocks might be playing a role in determining the outcome. For example, one key concept of behavioral economics is anchor points. *Anchor points* are points toward which people gravitate. The existence of anchor points can lead to multiple equilibria for the model. It is possible that the hedge funds increased other participants' anchor point for chocolate prices, which in turn led them to increase their inventory of chocolate. The demand increases and ratifies the increase in price, even though there was no need for price to increase had the anchor point not changed. (I should also point out that hedge funds pay economists large amounts of money to model the economy and to decide where they should invest their funds. So if hedge funds were doing this, it may be because they hired a modern economist who developed a model that showed them how they might do it.)

The analysis quickly becomes complicated, but what is clear is that one needs a more advanced formal model than the supply/demand model to deal with the question. Essentially, the answer economists arrived at was that the hedge fund purchases could have temporarily pushed up the price of chocolate, but did not do so permanently. Later, chocolate prices fell nearly 40 percent amid bumper crops and a continued decline in consumer demand due to a weak global economy.

However, that result isn't much comfort to chocoholics since the models also suggested that the system might take three or four years to adjust, and in the meantime, significant disruption could continue in the chocolate market. Moreover, by then it is possible that the hedge funds could have sold their positions in chocolate futures to others, pocketing their gains. As they do so, one would expect a sudden fall in the price of chocolate significantly below its long-run average. Related puzzles exist in various markets, and economists are hard at work on them. The lesson of this example: Supply and demand are just the beginning for a modern economist.

What Difference Does All This Make to Policy?

Let me now turn to a consideration of what difference these modeling considerations have for policy. The answer is: a lot. Let me briefly distinguish the differences. An economist who concentrates on a single frame tends to be more consistent in his or her policy recommendation. In the past, the framework was that the market is likely the best way to deal with a problem, and that, left alone, the market will guide people toward doing the best they, and society, can, given the constraints. Steven Landsburg nicely summed up what a traditional economist expects in his discussion of the insurance markets.

Modern economists, with their multiple frames, are less sure of the conclusion that the market will solve every problem. They accept that the market has nice properties, but they also find that it has limitations. They know that there are many models where there exists a potential role for public policy in dealing with those limitations. That's why *for a modern economist who uses multiple frames, policy does not follow directly from a model.* As I discussed in the introductory chapter, models provide *theorems*—results that follow logically from a model—not *precepts*—general rules for public policy. Precepts are developed from theorems that follow from various models, along with knowledge of history and of limitations of the models.

Let's consider three examples where a modern economist's precepts might differ from a traditional economist's precepts.

Q-10 If a model tells you that price controls will reduce people's welfare, does it follow that economists will advise governments not to impose price controls?

How much emphasis should be given to benefits of economic growth?

The traditional economist's precept is that more is preferred to less, and that more output is generally good; thus, policies directed at achieving more growth make society better off. The behavioral economic precept is that growth should be questioned. They point out that people's happiness depends on their relative, not their absolute, income after an annual per capita income of about $75,000 is reached. That means that more growth will not necessarily benefit society, and suggests that more focus should be given to how the existing income is distributed, rather than just focusing on total income.

Should the government have done something about the rise in housing prices in the early 2000s?

The earlier precept is that no, government probably shouldn't have. The rise in housing prices that occurred represented people's valuation of the worth of the house. They may have made a mistake in this instance, but there is no reason to believe that the government would have gotten it right, and you can only tell whether houses are overvalued after the fact, not before.

The modern precept (based on dynamic models of interacting agents) for both modern traditional and behavioral economists is that bubbles are possible, and that the housing market in the early 2000s had all the signs of a bubble, which means that the government might have usefully intervened. The bursting of the housing bubble was something that was predictable, and something that policy could have eliminated the need for.

Are people saving enough?

The earlier precept is that people make rational decisions and if they are choosing to save little, that reflects their desires and best estimates of their need. The behavioral economics precept is that how much people save depends on the institutional structure, and with so much of the institutional structure designed to get people to spend, people likely save far too little. But this does not mean that government has to tell people to save more. Instead, government can change the institutional structure and people will save more. For example, as opposed to having to check a box to have some income devoted to savings, saving would become the default option, and people would have to check a box if they don't want to save. By changing the default option on retirement savings plans, one can significantly change the amount people choose to save, leaving people free to make their own decision in both cases.

I could give many more such examples.

Conclusion

This has been a wide-ranging survey of what economists do, and what it means to think like a modern economist. Summarizing, briefly, modern economics goes far beyond supply and demand. Modern microeconomics is open to a wider range of building blocks and models, and is highly empirical. Thinking like a modern economist means approaching problems through modeling, and then relating the results of the model to the empirical evidence. Ultimately, the choice of models is made by empirically testing those models and choosing the one that does the best job of predicting.

The distinction between modern and traditional economists can be overdone. In many ways, the difference is just in when to put real-world complications into the model. Traditional economists use the traditional building blocks, and then adjust the model to fit the more complicated real world. That has the advantage of keeping the basic model clean and as simple as possible, but has the cost of not fitting many real-world situations. Modern economists use more complicated models so that fewer adjustments need to be made. The advantage is that the models better fit more real-world situations, but the disadvantage is that the models are not as clean and clear-cut as the traditional approach.

For teaching purposes, KISS reigns, and most economists, including me, continue to emphasize the traditional micro- and macroeconomic models. Modern insights are added as addenda and modifications.

KISS reigns.

Summary

- Models are the glue that holds economics together. But economists differ in the models that they use. (*LO21-1*)

- A deductive approach is to begin with principles and logically deduce the implications of those

principles. An inductive approach is to develop a model based on patterns in observed data. Modern economists tend to approach models inductively, while traditional economists approach models deductively. (*LO21-1*)

- Behavioral economists replace the traditional assumption of rationality with purposeful behavior and replace self-interest with enlightened self-interested behavior.   *(LO21-1)*

- While models based on modern building blocks often better fit observed behavior, they often do not generalize to contexts outside the one being studied.   *(LO21-1)*

- Heuristic models are models expressed informally in words. They can be based on either traditional building blocks like the models of Landsburg or modern building blocks like the models of Frank.   *(LO21-2)*

- The validity of models often is determined based on their ability to explain real-world data. Thus, models must be tested against the data. This is part of the scientific method.   *(LO21-2)*

- An empirical model is a model that statistically discovers a pattern in the data. For such a model to be scientifically tested, it must be tested against another set of data. A regression model is an example of an empirical model.   *(LO21-3)*

- Two types of models used by modern economists are game-theory models and agent-based computational models.   *(LO21-3)*

- Traditional economists tend to concentrate on a single frame and offer more policy recommendations based on the assumption of a well-functioning market.   *(LO21-4)*

- Modern economists use multiple frames and carefully distinguish theorems that follow from models from precepts that rely on theorems, but also rely on judgments about history and institutions.   *(LO21-4)*

Key Terms

agent-based
  computational
  economic (ACE)
  model *(479)*
behavioral
  economics *(463)*
butterfly effect
  model *(478)*
coefficient of
  determination *(474)*

deductive approach *(463)*
econometrics *(473)*
empirical model *(473)*
endowment effects *(466)*
enlightened
  self-interest *(463)*
game theory
  model *(478)*
heuristic
  model *(462)*

inductive approach *(462)*
model *(461)*
modern
  economist *(462)*
natural
  experiment *(476)*
path-dependent
  model *(469)*
precommitment
  strategy *(465)*

purposeful
  behavior *(463)*
regression
  model *(474)*
self-confirming
  equilibrium *(478)*
traditional
  economist *(463)*

Questions and Exercises

1. How is a model different from the reality that it represents? Give an example.   *(LO21-1)*

2. How does an inductive approach to economics differ from a deductive approach?   *(LO21-1)*

3. What are the two main building blocks for traditional economists? How do they differ from the building blocks of behavioral economists?   *(LO21-1)*

4. How does enlightened self-interest differ from self-interest?   *(LO21-1)*

5. One rule of thumb many people follow is "eat until your plate is clean." How does this rule of thumb violate the rationality assumption?   *(LO21-1)*

6. Name two advantages and two disadvantages of the traditional model.   *(LO21-1)*

7. Name two advantages and two disadvantages of the behavioral model.   *(LO21-1)*

8. In a recent study, when asked to choose between an iPod and $100, people were more likely to choose the money. But when they were given an iPod and then asked if they would trade it for $100, they were more likely to choose the iPod.   *(LO21-2)*
   a. What effect does this reflect?
   b. Is this behavior rational?

9. What is a *heuristic model?* Can a heuristic model be traditional? Why or why not?   *(LO21-2)*

10. Even though the Betamax format for videos is believed to have been better than the VHS format, early market leadership by VHS established VHS as the dominant

choice for videocassette recorders. Some argue that if Betamax had an early lead, it would have been the dominant technology. What kind of equilibrium model best fits this description and why? *(LO21-2)*

11. Why might government intervention make sense in a model of path-dependency but not a supply/demand model? *(LO21-2)*

12. According to economist Robert Frank, why are people more likely to return $20 they'd been given in error in change than a lampshade that had not been scanned at checkout? What does this say about traditional building blocks? *(LO21-2)*

13. Why do economists rely more on empirical evidence today than they did 100 years ago? *(LO21-3)*

14. What does it mean to "let the data speak"? *(LO21-3)*

15. What is a regression? *(LO21-3)*

16. What characteristics would you look for in data to use as a natural experiment? *(LO21-3)*

17. What is an agent-based computational model? *(LO21-3)*

18. Why is "out-of-sample" data important for testing inductive models? *(LO21-3)*

19. True or false? Models provide both theorems and precepts. Explain your answer. *(LO21-4)*

20. State whether each of the policy recommendations is an example of a modern economist's precepts or a traditional economist's precepts. *(LO21-4)*
    a. More goods are preferred to fewer goods.
    b. Banks ought to be required to get approval for new financial instruments.
    c. Firms can decide what information to put on food labels because consumers will demand that relevant information be listed.
    d. Utility companies ought to provide consumers a chart comparing their electricity usage with the average in their neighborhood.

Questions from Alternative Perspectives

1. How might modeling itself frame an economist's analysis, making the economist unable to see basic truths about the way in which society subjugates women? (Feminist)

2. Was Mother Teresa rational? (Religious)

3. It is sometimes said that modern economists pose little questions that can be answered while sociologists pose large questions that cannot be answered. How might that description be related to the economist's modeling approach? (Radical)

4. The book talks as if modern economists have made a large break from traditional assumptions; many heterodox economists see the two as simply minor modifications of the same approach. In what way is that true? (Austrian)

5. If modern economics focuses on empirical models, does that mean that those aspects of life that cannot be quantified are shortchanged? (Institutionalist)

Issues to Ponder

1. What does it mean to assume that people are purposeful in their behavior instead of rational?

2. In one study, a group of Asian-American women were asked to take a math exam. First they were divided into two groups. Before taking the test, individuals in the first group were asked their opinions about coed dorms while the second were asked their family history. Those who had been reminded by the questions that they were women performed worse than those who were reminded that they were Asian. How is this an example of predictably irrational behavior?

3. Is the supply/demand model a path-dependent model? Why or why not?

4. Can an economist who bases her models on traditional building blocks be a modern economist? Why or why not?

5. What might an economist do if he cannot solve a model analytically? (Give up is not an option.)

6. A student is given the option of selecting two homework schedules—one in which three five-page papers and one one-page paper are due at the end of the semester and another in which the first three papers are due the third, sixth, and ninth weeks of the semester and the last paper is due at the end.
    a. Why might a student choose the first option?
    b. Why might a student choose the second option?
    c. Which is the rational choice?

Answers to Margin Questions

1. Modeling, not supply and demand, is the glue that holds modern economics together. (*p. 462; LO21-1*)

2. Because of technological changes in computing, modern economists are more likely to use inductive models compared to earlier economists, who gave more weight to deductive models. (*p. 463; LO21-1*)

3. These are both assumptions associated with behavioral economists. (*p. 463; LO21-1*)

4. It depends on what model you use. In a traditional model it cannot because people choose what is best for them. Thus a constraint upon choice must make them worse off. In a behavioral model, it may make them better off because people are not assumed to have complete self-control. (*p. 465; LO21-1*)

5. It depends. Both have their advantages and disadvantages, and a choice can be made only when one knows the purpose of the model. (*p. 468; LO21-1*)

6. No, it simply demonstrates that he is affected by them in different ways than are other people. (*p. 472; LO21-2*)

7. Economists are hesitant to base knowledge on heuristic models because they are only suggestive, and are subject to people's tendency to be fast pattern completers. Science involves slow, and precise, pattern completion. The rules of scientific models are in many ways rules designed to slow people down and make sure the patterns they complete really do fit together. (*p. 473; LO21-3*)

8. False. While it would be nice if that were the case, the data speak very softly and what one hears depends upon one's frame. Thus, in economics the data seldom provide definitive answers, and economists must rely on their theoretical models to guide them. (*p. 476; LO21-3*)

9. No. In a path-dependent model the path to equilibrium affects the equilibrium. The supply/demand model assumes that is not the case. (*p. 477; LO21-4*)

10. No. One derives theorems (logical implications) from models; policy is based on precepts. Thus, the fact that most economists oppose price controls is based on both a model and judgments about the appropriateness of that model. (*p. 482; LO21-5*)

chapter 22

Behavioral Economics and Modern Economic Policy

> *Nobody's ever gone broke underestimating the intelligence of the general public.*
>
> —H. L. Mencken

When Dutch economist Aad Kieboom was put in charge of the men's restroom at the Amsterdam Airport, he instructed the builders to etch an image of a black housefly on each urinal. As we will see later in the chapter, that directive was an application of modern behavioral economic theory to policy. In this chapter, you will learn why it is, and many other ways in which behavioral economics changes the way economists approach policy.

I begin the chapter by putting the developments in behavioral economic policy in historical perspective, explaining why they developed. I then briefly review the policy implications of the traditional supply/demand models that have been the core of this book's presentation. Finally, I turn to the core of this chapter—behavioral economic policy and how it differs from more traditional economic policy.

Behavioral Economic Policy in Perspective

As discussed in the last chapter behavioral economics is that branch of modern economics that broadens the assumptions about behavior from rationality and self-interest to purposeful behavior and enlightened self-interest. As behavioral economists have broadened the building blocks of their models, they have also started to explore the implications of those broader building blocks for policy. Thus, today a **behavioral economic policy**—*economic policy based upon models using behavioral economic building blocks that take into account people's predictable irrational behavior*—is emerging that complements traditional economic policy.

Behavioral Economics and Economic Engineering

Behavioral economic policy has developed as part of a broader change in the way that economists see their role in policy making. As their understanding of markets has increased, modern economists have moved more heavily into what might be called **economic engineering**—*economics devoted not only to studying markets, but also to designing markets and other coordinating mechanisms.* Economic engineers don't just try to understand the way the economy works as economic scientists do. Economic engineers ask: Can they design mechanisms to better coordinate people's actions?

Q-1 How does economic engineering differ from economic science?

There is not a single market solution; there are hundreds of them.

Q-2 How does a shadow price differ from a normal price?

Shadow price analysis allows you to take morals and social pressures into account in your models.

As modern economists have moved more toward engineering, they have begun to explore a broad range of mechanisms and institutions that solve coordination problems. These mechanisms and institutions are called **coordination mechanisms**—*methods of coordinating people's wants with other people's desires.* All markets are a type of coordination mechanism. There are auction markets, posted price markets, and markets where firms set prices. Each of these mechanisms coordinates wants in a slightly different way. What this means is that there is not a single market solution, but hundreds of them. The economic policy debate is not about whether to have a market solution; the policy debate is what coordinating mechanism will best solve the problem at hand.

Economists began studying coordinating mechanisms by studying markets with money prices. They soon discovered that coordinating mechanisms that don't involve money prices can be modeled as if they do involve prices. To study these coordinating mechanisms, they developed formal models based on **shadow prices**—*prices that aren't paid directly, but instead are paid in terms of opportunity cost borne by the demander, and thus determine his or her choices indirectly.* In these shadow price models, every choice has an associated implicit shadow price, regardless of whether money is exchanged or not. Shadow price models convert opportunity costs to shadow prices.

Shadow price analysis is extremely powerful. For example, it allows you to take morals and social pressure into account in your model. Take stealing, for example. A shadow price of stealing is violating your moral code. If this shadow price is too high, you will choose not to steal. Shadow price models allow you to indirectly measure the price of violating your morals.

Let me give an example of the power of shadow price analysis. In his book *Freedomnomics: Why the Free Market Works,* economist John Lott gives an example of the number of batters hit by a ball when up at bat in the American and National Leagues. Starting in 1973, more batters were being hit in the American League than in the National League. The question was why. Lott developed a shadow price model that determined the cost to a pitcher of throwing a beanball (a pitch aimed at the batter's head). He pointed out that in 1973, the American League instituted the designated hitter (pitchers were exempt from batting). The new rule meant that the pitcher no longer could be hit by a ball thrown by the opposing team's pitcher in retaliation. In his model for American League pitchers that rule change lowered the shadow price of throwing a beanball. The model gave him an explanation: The increase in beanballs in 1973 occurred because the cost of throwing a beanball fell for an American League pitcher. (Applying this insight to policy suggests that to reduce the number of beanballs, the league might raise the money price of pitching a beanball, perhaps by instituting a $10,000 fine for every hit batsman.) Shadow price analysis is central to the way in which economists think about the effect of incentives on an individual's actions and how institutions interact with incentives.

Shadow price analysis has allowed economists to expand the scope of economics.

The introduction of models incorporating shadow price analysis has allowed economists to expand the scope of economics and study a wider range of social coordinating mechanisms, including a number of social problems far removed from traditional economic concerns. For example, a computer program that matches the classes you want to take with the classes that are available would be a coordination mechanism based on shadow prices. Such a program would develop a shadow price for each course and then allocate the classes on the basis of a student's willingness to pay, as determined by the priorities he or she listed in his or her requested courses.

Economists as Mechanism Design Engineers

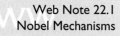

Web Note 22.1 Nobel Mechanisms

The focus on shadow prices has led to the development of a new branch of economics, called *mechanism design,* which is explicitly interested in designing mechanisms to achieve specific ends. **Mechanism design** involves *identifying a goal and then designing a mechanism such as a market, social system, or contract to achieve that end.*

Economists who use mechanism design engineering to develop policy use economic theory as a type of backward induction or reverse engineering process. Instead of building from scratch, taking an existing mechanism apart with the intention of improving it, they begin with the desired outcome and consider what coordinating mechanism will best achieve that outcome. Mechanism design economic engineers use laboratory experiments, field experiments, game theory models, computer simulations, and a variety of other tools to come up with coordinating mechanisms that achieve the desired ends. This branch of modern economics has been extraordinarily influential, and in 2007 the Nobel Prize for Economics went to three economists— Leonid Hurwicz, Eric Maskin, and Roger Myerson—who have done important work in the abstract theory of mechanism design.

Taking this engineering approach to economics also led to a change in the type of models modern economists needed to study markets. Because they were designing mechanisms that had to work, they needed models with assumptions that more precisely matched the institutions they were modeling. As opposed to studying just the simple supply/demand model, modern economists study whether the assumptions of their models match real-world market incentives. Often, they do not.

> Modern economists study whether the assumptions of their models match real-world market incentives.

For example, the supply/demand model assumes that firms maximize profits. But real-world firms' decisions are made by individuals whose incentives may differ from the firm's incentives. When a decision maker's income is not the same as the firm's profit, as is generally the case, the firm's and the decision maker's incentives may be incompatible, and the individual is more likely to make decisions that don't maximize profits. For example, an employee may choose to fly first class with an airline that gives him more frequent flyer miles rather than fly on a low-cost airline, which would have saved the firm money. This behavior shows up as "irrationality" in the traditional supply/demand model because the assumptions don't match the institutional realities. Economists found these "irrationalities" caused by institutional factors throughout the economy.

All types of institutional realities impede the effectiveness of the incentives assumed in economists' models, which changes the way a system works most efficiently. Modern economists call these impediments *incentive compatibility problems.* An **incentive compatibility problem** is *a problem in which the incentive facing the decision maker does not match the incentive needed for the mechanisms to achieve its desired end.* Modern economists have used their insights about incentive incompatibility problems to design mechanisms to align incentives with desired ends.

> **Q-3** Does grading in courses involve an incentive compatibility problem?

The adoption of this mechanism design approach has transformed economic models into an enormously powerful tool for firms and governments. For example, when policy makers needed to figure out how to reduce CO_2 emissions, they turned to economists who designed cap-and-trade for CO_2 emissions. Similarly, when the British government wanted to allocate rights to the radio spectrum, they turned to economists who designed an auction mechanism.

> The adoption of this mechanism design approach has transformed economic models into an enormously powerful tool for firms and governments.

Coordinating mechanisms don't have to be based on money prices. As mentioned above, economists have developed shadow prices that reflect value and costs of constraints in a market. For example, Harvard economist Al Roth used a shadow price model to design the National Residency Matching Program that matches medical students to residency programs. Mechanism design economists also have played an important role in modifying some of the online dating services, and in creating the search algorithms used by Google and Yahoo. All are "coordinating mechanisms" that try to anticipate what the person wants and to match it with what is being offered. These

Markets as Information-Gathering Mechanisms

As economists have begun designing markets, they have discovered that they can take advantage of another useful function of markets—markets' ability to reveal people's collective wisdom. A price in a market represents the collective judgment of what people in the market are willing to pay for a good. Using that insight, economists reasoned: Why not create markets as a way of extracting information from people, that is, to design markets as an information-gathering mechanism? For example, say you are wondering who will win the general election. To make a prediction, economists at the University of Iowa designed an "election futures" market that allows people to "bet" on who is going to win. (A future is the promise to buy an item in the future at a specified price.) For example, you might have bought a *$100 John McCain future* for $45—the price of a $100 John McCain future on October 18th, 2006. So

on that day, people thought that John McCain was going to win the election sufficiently to pay $45 for the possibility of being paid $100. If John McCain had won the election, those who bought the future would have received $100. Because he lost they got nothing. Below is the price history in the market.

The goal of this market is not to provide an opportunity for people to bet. The goal is to predict what candidate is going to win the election. The prices of the futures reflect the collective wisdom of market participants—their predictions of the likelihood of a candidate winning. Thus, if a candidate's $100 future is selling for $20, most people think he is going to lose. You can check out the Iowa Election Futures market at Tipple.410WA. edu/IEM. Do these information markets work? Election futures markets such as this one have done much better at predicting the winners of elections than have the many public opinion polls.

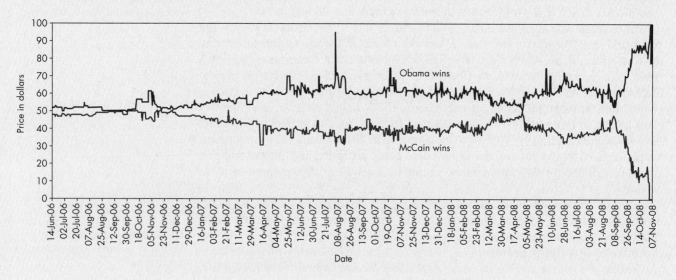

Behavioral Economics and Mechanism Design

Web Note 22.2
The Prediction Market

programs make the systems work better. For example, the New York City Public School Match program that matches students to schools (www.educationsector.org/ usr_doc/ChoiceMatching.pdf) helped increase graduation rates by 13 percentage points. Through shadow price models, all types of allocating and coordinating mechanisms come under the purview of modern economics.

Behavioral Economics and Mechanism Design

Q-4 Why did economists' work in mechanism design lead to a greater interest in behavioral economics?

Mechanism design is important to this chapter because economists' interest in behavioral economics grew out of this engineering approach to economics. As economists started working on real-world problems, they saw that coordination mechanisms did not always work as predicted even when they adjusted for institutional realities. The reason was that their traditional assumptions about human behavior did not always fit reality. So mechanism design economists began to take into account people's predictable irrationalities when designing coordination mechanisms. In order to do that, they had to better understand how people's behavior deviated from the model's predicted behavior, which led to the emergence of behavioral economics. Behavioral economic policies developed as a way of tweaking existing coordinating mechanisms to make them work better, given people's actual behavior.

Let's consider an example of a policy that didn't work as expected and see what behavioral economists say it means for mechanism design. The example involves finding a solution for late pick-ups at a day care center. It seems that a number of day care centers were having a problem getting parents to pick up their kids on time. To solve the problem, the centers followed the traditional economic solution: They imposed a fine for parents who picked up the kids late. The fine established a monetary price for picking up the kids late and was expected to decrease the number late pick-ups. However, that wasn't the result. Instead, the problem worsened; late pick-ups *rose*.

Why did that happen? Behavioral economists argued that the fine "commoditized" the choice. Once a social infraction, late pick-ups became a service parents could buy. Without a fine, the parents felt a moral obligation to pick up the kids on time. There was a high moral shadow price on picking up kids late. The introduction of a fine replaced the moral obligation (shadow price) with a market payment, so the relevant price went down, not up.

Behavioral economists argue that because people are social creatures, the coordinating mechanism that economists design must take into account much more than simple price incentives. It must also include social and moral incentives and the economist's models must include these additional elements as shadow prices. Failure to do so can worsen, rather than improve, the situation. Santa Fe Institute behavioral economist Sam Bowles summarizes the implications behavioral economists drew from this and similar experiments when he argued that traditional economics incorrectly assumes that "policies that appeal to economic self-interest do not affect the salience [importance] of ethical, altruistic, and other social preferences."

The interaction between markets and social and moral incentives is complicated. For example, Bowles also finds that individuals from more market-oriented societies tend to be more moral, which he explains by arguing that "fair-mindedness is essential to the exchange process and that in market-oriented societies individuals engaging in mutually beneficial exchanges with strangers represent models of successful behavior who are then copied by others." The problem for behavioral mechanism design economists is to find the right combination of market, social, and moral incentives that work to solve the particular problem at hand. Knowing what combination requires taking the existing practices and mores in each society and situation into account.

Policy Implications of Traditional Economics

Now that I've given you the context for the development of behavioral economic policy, let's review the policy implications that follow from traditional assumptions to give us a starting point for our consideration of behavioral economic policy. In traditional economics, voluntary trade (without externalities) makes people involved in the trade better off. When people have made all the trades they can, they will be as well off as they can possibly be. If that weren't the case, they would make another trade. The policy implication of the traditional model is that government should stay out of people's way and let them trade. It should step in only to adjust trades that affect people not involved in the exchange—discouraging trades with negative externalities and encouraging trades with positive externalities. The model directs economists toward *laissez-faire*—keep government out of the market, and let people do their own thing.

Of course, economists know that reality is more complicated and that the *theorems* (logical implications of a model, given all assumptions) about the benefits of trade that

Behavioral economic policies developed as a way of tweaking existing coordinating mechanisms to make them work better, given people's actual behavior.

The problem for behavioral mechanism design economists is to find the right combination of market, social, and moral incentives.

The policy implication of the traditional model is that government should stay out of people's way and let them trade.

Q-5 True or false? A traditional economist believes people are always rational.

Web Note 22.3
Irrationality and Cheating

Behavioral economics focuses economists' thinking on people's *predictable irrationality* and designs policies that take people's predictable irrationality into account.

One of the findings of behavioral economics is that choice architecture impacts people's decisions.

Q-6 If an economist believes that choice architecture is important, is he or she more likely to be a traditional economist or a behavioral economist?

follow from the model do not immediately transfer to a *precept* (policy implication of the model as it relates to the real world) of laissez-faire. The precept of laissez-faire is based on more than the model; it is based on value judgments and judgments about how well the model fits reality. For most economists, that laissez-faire precept has lots of exceptions and includes a wide variety of ideas about policy.

These exceptions are, however, exceptions, and, for a traditional economist, the thrust of thinking like an economist means *first* to expect that the market will solve the problem, and *then,* if that doesn't seem be happening, to check why. If the reason why the market isn't working as the model predicted is important, then one modifies the policy precept. Thus, in his *Wealth of Nations,* Adam Smith listed a large number of areas where he believed government should regulate the economy even though his overall model led to laissez-faire.

Behavioral economics complicates the traditional story based on the supply/demand model because it gives up the underlying assumption that people are fully rational and self-interested. Without this assumption, voluntary trade doesn't necessarily make people better off. Instead of focusing economists' thinking on people's rational selves, behavioral economics focuses economists' thinking on people's *predictable irrationality* and designs policies that take people's predictable irrationality into account.

Choice Architecture and Behavioral Economic Policy

One of the findings of behavioral economics is that **choice architecture**—*how choices are presented*—impacts people's decisions. Traditional economic models assume that choice architecture doesn't matter; thus, for example, the models assume that the order in which choices are presented does not matter to a person's choice. If order does matter, then, in the traditional model, the person is being irrational, and if the effect shows up sufficiently so that it is predictable, he is being predictably irrational. If a traditional economist finds that people are predictably irrational, he or she will have to modify the policy implications of his or her theorems as he or she moves to policy precepts.

Behavioral economists argue that modifying precepts after the fact to take predictable irrationality into account isn't enough. They argue that people are predictably irrational in so many areas that economists' models and policy recommendations have to include those predictable irrationalities in both models and policies. Behavioral economic policy—a policy designed to influence people's choice architecture in a way that directs people to make decisions that make them better off under the assumption that they are predictably irrational—does just that.

Two economists leading the charge in creating a separate behavioral economic policy are Chicago professors Richard Thaler and Cass Sunstein.[1] Their book *Nudge* gives a variety of examples of how choice architecture influences decisions and how to design choice architecture to influence behavior. Let's consider a simplification of one of their examples: Carolyn, the director of food services for a large city school system, must choose how to present the food to the students; she has two options:

1. Arrange the food so that the student chooses a healthy lunch, all things considered.

2. Arrange the food so that the students pick the same foods they would choose on their own.

---

[1] Much of the discussion in this chapter is based on Thaler and Sunstein's presentation, including the urinal description that opened the chapter.

Thaler and Sunstein say that a traditional economist would likely choose option two, following the premise that free choice is best. But they argue that traditional economists cannot claim that option two reflects free choice because "what they would choose on their own" depends on how choices are presented. Thaler and Sunstein argue that a behavioral economist would choose option one. Option one gives the students free choice but nudges them to use that free choice to make a "better" selection. Students are still free not to choose healthy food but will be faced with an arrangement of food that will lead more of them to choose healthy food. Thaler and Sunstein call this a **nudge**—*a deliberate design of the choice architecture that alters people's behavior in predictably positive ways.*

Now that I've explained what a nudge is, let's return to the urinal at Amsterdam Airport. What was going on? It turns out that men are not very careful when they relieve themselves and can make quite a mess. They tend to splash a lot. But what Aad Kieboom noticed was that by changing the urinal slightly, the splashing can be reduced. It seems that if men see a fly when they are relieving themselves, they aim for it. If the image of the fly is placed slightly off center in the urinal, the choice architecture is right, and the mess is reduced considerably. His staff found that the "fly-in-the-urinal" reduced spillage by 80 percent.[2]

Nudges are not a new discovery. Private firms use nudges all the time to guide their customers to make choices that benefit the firm. Grocery stores position their highly profitable goods that you are likely to buy on impulse at just the right height and place to get you to buy them—think of the candy at the checkout counter. They also place higher-priced organic foods in a separate section (it reduces price comparison) and place milk at the back of the store (it requires people to walk past, and likely buy, other products along the way). Advertising is another way in which firms nudge their customers. Advertising frames a firm's product in a positive way that the firm's psychologists have found will lead people to develop a desire and need for that product. Advertising nudges seem to be successful since firms spend billions on advertising.

Nudge Policy and Libertarian Paternalism

While the existence of nudges has been well known, what's new in behavioral economic policy suggested by Thaler and Sunstein is the argument that government should use nudges as a policy tool. (We will call the government use of nudges *nudge policy*.) In **nudge policy,** *government structures choices so that people are free to choose what they want, but also more likely to choose what is best for them.*[3]

Nudge policy advocates claim that nudge policy meets what they call a criterion of *libertarian paternalism.* By libertarian, they mean people are still free to choose. They argue that a nudge policy does not go against traditional economics since government is not interfering with people's freedom of choice. By paternalism, they mean people are likely to make better decisions (as judged by an outside beneficent decision maker). Thus, a **libertarian paternalistic policy** is *a policy that leaves people free to choose, but nonetheless guides them toward a choice that a paternalistic observer would see as good for them.* Thaler and Sunstein see their nudge policies as libertarian paternalistic policies. For example, in the spirit of libertarianism, a nudge policy would leave people free to smoke cigarettes, eat lots of candy, or not save for the future (all of which Thaler and Sunstein consider bad) if that's what people really want. But, in the spirit of paternalism, a nudge policy would frame people's choices to engage less often in these activities.

Q-7 A policy designed to structure choices so that people make a certain choice is called what type of policy?

Libertarian paternalistic policy is a policy that leaves people free to choose, but nonetheless guides them toward a choice that a paternalistic observer would see as good for them.

---

[2]There is now a fly-in-the-urinal decal company. You can see it on the web at www.urinalfly.com.

[3]I will discuss the problem of deciding what is "best for them" below.

To give you a sense of how nudge policy would work, let's consider an example. Say you are presented with a retirement savings plan that allows you to save 10 percent of your income. If you choose to save 10 percent, your company will supplement your savings by another 10 percent. To get the company's 10 percent contribution, you have to check a box on the employee savings plan form. Given that choice, economists have found that, even though it seems like a very good deal, often 50 percent of the employees will choose to participate in the savings plan. For traditional economists, that would be the end of the story; they would conclude that 50 percent of the people decided that participating in the savings plan does not make them better off.

For behavioral economists, that is not the end of the story. They point out that people's choices depend on how the choices are framed and, in this case, it depends on what is the default option. What if, instead of having to check a box to *opt into* the savings plan, people had to check a box in order to *opt out* of the savings plan? When framed in this way, a larger percentage of people will choose to participate and a smaller percentage will decline. Behavioral economists ask: Which group is rational: the 50 percent that choose not to participate when they have to opt into the savings plan, or the larger percentage that choose to participate when they have to opt out?

> Behavioral economists point out that people's choices depend on how the choices are framed.

When Are Nudges Needed?

Thaler and Sunstein list various types of choices where they believe that nudges can be useful. Below we consider three.

CHOICES IN WHICH BENEFITS AND COSTS ARE SEPARATED BY TIME

Behavioral economists have found that people tend to make what behavioral economists consider less-than-optimal choices when the benefits and costs of those choices are separated by time. People tend to weight the immediate costs and benefits more, and future costs and benefits less, than if they were given time to reflect on the decision. Such choices present a possibility for policy nudges. Consider weight loss. Many people have a hard time losing weight. Losing weight requires facing an upfront cost (less food and more exercise) and delayed gain (slimmer physique). Many Americans agree that they are overweight and claim to want to lose weight, so designing their choices to make it easier to say no to eating excess food may be warranted.

Similarly, saving requires consuming less now for a delayed benefit of consuming more later. Most people believe that they save too little, and when they look back, they wish that they had saved more. But, of course, by the time they decide they'd made a mistake, it's too late to fix it. So again, here is an opportunity for a useful nudge.

Other examples are exercise and studying. Reflecting back, most of us would have chosen to exercise or study more than we actually did. But when we were making the decision to exercise or study, somehow we just couldn't do it. The treadmill looked like so much work; the textbook (not this one, obviously) was so boring, and the TV show looked so good that we decided to watch it rather than study or exercise. All these are examples of choices in which the benefits and costs are separated by time, and that Thaler and Sunstein see open to nudges.

COMPLICATED CHOICES WITH MANY DIMENSIONS   Complicated choices are another type of choice that people are not good at making, and are therefore good candidates for a nudge. Say you are trying to decide about what type of loan to get for school. You look on the Internet and you find six or seven different options, some of which involve origination fees, some of which don't, some of which involve having your parents cosign the loan, others not, some of which have flexible rates (LIBOR + 2) and some of which have fixed interest rates, some of which involve immediate payback, others that involve payback starting six months after graduation. After spending

hours struggling with them all, your mind swirls. Which one makes sense? Many students decide that there's no good way to figure it out; it's just too complicated. They could use a nudge—giving them some guidance about which is the likely best option. The nudge doesn't preclude them from choosing a different option, but if they can't figure it out, this is the option they are advised to choose.

INFREQUENT CHOICES   An infrequent choice is a third type of decision in which nudge policies may be useful. Infrequent decisions provide little opportunity to practice making choices, evaluate feedback, or explore one's preferences. Making a particular decision for the first time is probably difficult, but if you make a similar set of decisions again and again, through trial and error, you will likely get better, and, eventually, you will get pretty good. Take food shopping: the first time you went to choose a melon, you probably had trouble. But after some practice—sometimes choosing a not-yet-ripe melon and other times hitting the mark—you have gotten pretty good at identifying the feel and smell of a good melon. Repetitive decisions such as these tend to be much more rational and capture what people actually want. Infrequent decisions—such as what college to go to, whom to marry, or what house to buy—are much more difficult.

To learn from frequently made decisions, a person needs feedback—information about the consequences of one's choices. Imagine how difficult it would be to learn how to play the piano on a keyboard that makes no sound. Hearing that wrong note provides immediate feedback on one's playing. Feedback means experiencing the consequences of making a decision.

Frequently made choices also give one a chance to learn about one's preferences or what the advantages of alternative decisions might be. How would you know if you like a caramel rumba Frappuccino until you've tasted one? Trying various flavors of Frappuccino and deciding which one we like is possible, but trying out lots of different mortgages is not. You have to choose a mortgage and predict the outcome based on little to no experience or information. Not surprisingly, people don't make especially good decisions about what type of mortgage to take out. Advocates of nudge policy argue that if people had had nudges telling them the risks of taking out a mortgage based on expected large increases in house prices, the recent subprime mortgage fiasco might have been less of a fiasco.

Two Types of Nudges

The nudges that Thaler and Sunstein propose can be classified as either advantageous default option nudges or information and encouragement nudges. Let's consider both briefly.

ADVANTAGEOUS DEFAULT OPTIONS NUDGES   The first is *advantageous default option policy*. We have already seen an example of how default options influence people's behavior in the savings example discussed earlier. When faced with a choice, people are predisposed to select the default option. By taking advantage of that tendency, economic policy makers can direct people to do what they think is better for them, while still leaving people free to make their own choice. Another example involves health insurance. If employees had to *opt out* of purchasing health insurance, they would be much more likely to buy it, which is presumably the more rational choice. A more controversial example of the default option involves organ donation. If, when people apply for driver's licenses, they had to request that their organs *not be donated,* Thaler and Sunstein argue that more organs would be available for transplant.

INFORMATION AND ENCOURAGEMENT NUDGES   Another type of policy that Thaler and Sunstein recommend can be classified as *information and encouragement*

Three types of choices where nudges may be useful are:

1. choices in which benefits and costs are separated by time,
2. complicated choices with many dimensions, and
3. infrequent choices.

policy. With these policies, government encourages people to make certain choices that government has decided are good for them. An example of an encouragement nudge would be for the government to actively inform people how their energy use compares to the average as a way to encourage people to conserve energy. For example, a number of households in San Marcos, California, were sent a letter telling them how their home energy use compared to the norm. In addition, the letters sent to those who used more-than-average energy were stamped with a frowning emoticon ☹ while the letter to those who had below-average energy use were stamped with a smiling emoticon ☺. The letters reduced energy usage by above-average energy users without affecting the below-average energy users. So the government got people to reduce their energy use without *requiring* energy conservation.

Information nudges come in many forms. One such nudge instituted by colleges to reduce alcohol consumption is advertising the actual drinking habits of college students. This sounds counterintuitive. Wouldn't advertising how much alcohol students drink, when it is illegal for most college students to do so, encourage drinking? Not so. Researchers found that the widespread perception is that college students drink excessively, and that that perception was leading college students to drink to fit in. Such behavior is often referred to as *herding*—behavior in which people mimic what they think other people are doing. The perception that college students drink excessively is inaccurate; students actually drink relatively moderate amounts of alcohol. At the University of Arizona (considered by many as a top party school), for example, the average student drinks one alcoholic beverage a week. By publicizing the fact that most college students don't drink excessively, the herding behavior pushing students towards drinking can be offset and colleges can nudge students to drink less.

Another form of information nudge is designed to guide a person through complicated decisions. The argument for such nudges can be seen with an example. If you are like me, you have a very hard time trying to understand your current cell phone bill. In fact, cell phone bills appear to be designed to confuse. When looking at my bill, I often have no idea how the cost relates to decisions I make about phone calls or whether some other pricing structure or alternative provider would be better. My state of confusion makes it all the harder to decide to change my plan.

Thaler and Sunstein argue that if firms send their customers a complete listing of all the ways they use the phone and all the fees that are charged in a way that can be compared to the pricing plans of other cell phone companies on a comparison website, individuals can make better decisions. They call such nudges RECAP (record, evaluate, and compare alternative prices) nudges.

The Problems of Implementing Nudges

Firms, because they aren't inherently paternalistic, don't necessarily have an incentive to implement the nudges that Thaler and Sunstein advocate. A profit-maximizing firm is out to maximize profit, not to make its customers and employees better off. Sometimes nudges both increase a firm's profits and make a firm's customers and employees better off. But the two goals don't always match. If government is going to consider nudge policies, some method must exist to decide: (1) what nudges to implement and (2) how to get the nudge implemented. Should behavioral economists decide what nudges are appropriate? should businesses? or should government? If the decision maker is different from the one implementing the policy, then some method must exist to get the nudge implemented.

The most likely decision maker will be the political process, which means government. The most likely group to implement many of the nudges that Thaler and Sunstein suggest will be private firms. This presents a problem for nudge policy since it isn't clear that, if it will reduce profits, business will want to implement the nudge in a way that will help the consumer. For example, the likely reason the cell phone bill is so complicated is not that firms don't know that customers would like the information to compare prices—it is *because* the complication makes it hard for customers to compare prices. Thaler and Sunstein recognize this, and accept that many of the nudges they seek to be implemented will require what they call "a very mild form of regulation," which for many economists, makes the nudge something more like a push.

Many nudges are mild forms of regulation.

Distinguishing a Nudge from a Push

In thinking about implementing nudge policies, I find it useful to separate the nudges suggested by behavioral economics into two categories: nudge policy and push policy. If government can institute the behavioral economic policy directly, or if a private firm chooses to implement a policy on its own, it's a nudge. However, if government has to develop a regulation and *requires* firms to implement a particular nudge, the nudge no longer meets the criteria of libertarian paternalism; the nudge is not a nudge, but a push. Thus, in my terminology, the RECAP policy discussed above, when imposed upon firms, is not a nudge; it is a push. Push policies restrict free choice by the firm for the greater good. A **push policy** is *a regulatory or tax policy to get firms or individuals to use "appropriate" nudges.* Such policies involve nudges for the person targeted by the policy but a push for the firm that has to implement the nudge. For example, a push policy might involve government requiring firms to present information in a certain way (as in RECAP), or requiring them to avoid certain actions they currently take.

Q-8 If the government tells a company how to structure the bills it issues, is the policy a nudge policy?

A push policy is a regulatory or tax policy to get firms or individuals to use "appropriate" nudges.

Once one accepts the potential desirability of implementing the insights of behavioral economics through push policies, rather than just through nudge policies, the possibilities for behavioral economic policies increase enormously. For example, push policy might involve government intervening in the market to change incentives through taxation. It could also involve preventing firms from using many of the nudges that they currently use for their advantage. By that I mean that while government may not have yet used the insights of behavioral economics, private firms sure have, and many of the practices that they follow are designed to take advantage of these insights for their own profit, not necessarily to the benefit of the consumer. Firms use their knowledge that people gravitate toward the default option all the time.

For example, when ordering something on the web, you will find that firms often ask whether you want to be included on their mailing list. Often, the box is checked already. To be excluded you have to uncheck the box. Firms can argue that you have a choice whether to be on the list or not. But they know that while you have a choice whether to be on the mailing list, far fewer people choose not to be on the list if the box were left unchecked. Government could require firms to frame the choice so that buyers have to check a box to be included in the mailing list.

Mailing options are another example. Amazon offers free mailing for orders over $25, which it advertises heavily. The default option is the "standard" mailing charge rather than the free mailing option. To get the free mailing, you have to override the default. Moreover, Amazon states that free shipping takes five to nine days rather than three to five days for standard mailing, even though the items are likely sent via the same mailing service. Government could require firms to set the default as the least-cost method of shipment and state shipping time based on actual shipping performance.

Another example of a firm taking advantage of the default option is the lure of free goods when subscribing for a service. For example, book clubs offer you seven books free in exchange for joining, leaving you free to drop out any time. It's a great deal if you drop out, but you can be sure that a sufficient number of people take the default option (staying in the plan), even though they may have wanted to drop out, to warrant book clubs making that offer. Here, government could make book clubs drop new subscribers unless they actively choose to continue beyond the free period. Each of these cases is an example of a push policy because government is regulating the behavior of firms.

Behavioral and Traditional Economic Policy Frames

Adopting the behavioral economic framework opens up many ways in which government can usefully intervene in the market.

As you can see, adopting the behavioral economic framework opens up many ways in which government can usefully intervene in the market. Traditional economists say desires are inherent in each person. Behavioral economists say that desires are affected by context. In fact, one could argue that in order to allow people to express their true desires, all those nudges firms take to benefit themselves would have to be prevented, or countered, by government. For example, if advertising leads people to want things that don't make them happy, on behavioral economic policy grounds, it can be argued that government should implement an information nudge, providing "counter-advertising" that warns people about how firms are trying to change their desires. Countering all nudges by firms would involve a large regulatory presence by government.

Traditional economists say that having more makes you happier. Some behavioral economists suggest that having more is not what makes people happy. Often what makes them happy is having more *than other people.* Relative, not absolute, income matters. That proposition has potentially radical implications for economic policy. Specifically, it introduces the possibility that government can improve society's overall welfare by changing the way in which income is distributed.

The proposition that relative, not absolute, income matters has potentially radical implications for policy.

Cornell behavioral economist Robert Frank has pushed this argument the furthest in terms of implications for behavioral economic policy. He argues that after societies pass a certain threshold level of income, a threshold all Western societies have passed, certain types of material goods don't matter a whole lot to our well being, and crowd out those goods that do matter. He argues that the problem in Western economies is that "people don't spend their extra money in ways that yield significant and lasting increases in measured satisfaction." Instead they spend it on what institutionalist economist Thorstein Veblen called *conspicuous consumption goods*—goods that are bought to show off to the neighbors, rather than for their inherent value. Veblen argued that the rich spend their money on goods such as gigantic mansions and elaborate jewelry that they don't really want for themselves, but want to have as a way of showing off their wealth to others. What matters for the rich is not what they have, but that they outdo the others. As we mentioned before, sometimes rich men even married someone (a trophy wife) whose job was to spend their money in a way that would show off their wealth even more.

Q-9 Do more conspicuous consumption goods make society better off?

Let's consider an example of how relative, not absolute, materialism matters. When we get that super duper, all-stainless-steel barbecue grill with Internet connection and built-in iPod speakers, we are better off. But when the neighbors get the same one, we slip back to being no better off. And if the neighbors get one with a built-in TV too, we are worse off (until we get one with a bigger built-in TV). Society ends up in a type of consumption war in which everyone is trying to outdo the other and no one is better off. (According to some, we might actually be worse off if the additional expenditures required additional work effort and less leisure.)

Frank argues that such consumption wars happen in many areas of our society. An example is houses—they get bigger and bigger, eventually turning into McMansions when much smaller houses would satisfy our needs. Cars are another example—they get bigger and bigger and turn into McHummers when a much less powerful car would do. He calls this push for goods to show off *luxury fever*.

At the same time that people are undertaking this conspicuous consumption, Frank argues that other types of goods—social goods that can be considered *inconspicuous consumption* (goods that are not physical but nevertheless experienced)—are being crowded out. For example, as more people drive bigger cars, traffic becomes congested, noise becomes excessive, the air becomes polluted, and social needs become short-changed. His policy solution is to heavily tax those goods whose consumption value depends on showing off—thereby discouraging their consumption—and use the tax revenue to provide

www   Web Note 22.4
Keeping Up with
the Joneses

Karl Marx and Shove Policy

The arguments for push policy have been suggested by economists in the past. Perhaps the strongest advocate of the general ideas was Karl Marx. Marx argued that the market had a tendency to alienate people from their "true" selves. He argued that people are not born with a collection of inherent wants and desires, but instead develop a collection of wants and needs that reflect the institutions of society. For example, if firms need workers, society creates wants in people that will lead them to work. Thus, many of the wants that people have are created (artificial, not inherent (true) needs). For example, Marx argued that capitalist society created strong tendencies toward wanting materialistic goods. He argued that markets made people competitive, not cooperative; they alienated people from their true self. Markets made people, in the words of Marxist philosopher Herbert Marcuse, one-dimensional people—people who only think of life in terms of material goods, and not in terms of spiritual and social goods.

Those arguments lead to strong policy conclusions that go far beyond nudges, or even pushes. Marx favored what might be called "shove" policy. To stop people from being one dimensional, and to help them escape from their material good fetishes, Marxists argued that we needed a revolution to overthrow the bourgeois capitalist government that legitimized capitalist institutions, and to replace it with a communist government committed to fulfilling humans' true desires. He argued that eventually the communist government would wither away; once people's true desires were fulfilled, government would just no longer be necessary. People's true cooperative selves would overcome their competitive selves. These views led to the communist revolution, and are still held by a number of people throughout the world.

By almost all accounts, communism was not a success. Instead of fulfilling people's true desires, it created shortages and unfairness. Communist governments became seen as the oppressor, and people ultimately decided to overthrow the communist economies and replace them with market economies. This experience soured many economists, and other people, on government policies designed to fill people's "true" wants.

the social amenities that make society better off. He argues that we should structure the economy so that people work a lot less—say three days a week on average—and vacation a lot more. In *Luxury Fever* Frank argues that "reallocations of our time and money in these ways would result in healthier, longer, and more satisfying lives."

Concerns about Behavioral Economic Policies

As you can see, once one opens the gate to using behavioral economic insights, one can easily arrive at a number of policies that extend far beyond traditional economic precepts and nudges. Needless to say, traditional economists have expressed serious misgivings about these behavioral economic policies. In this section I present some of those concerns.

Traditional economists have expressed serious misgivings about these behavioral economic policies.

Few Policies Meet Libertarian Paternalism Criterion

The first concern has already been discussed; the possibility for true nudge policy that meets the libertarian paternalism criterion is very small. Many examples of nudges that advocates of libertarian paternalism give involve government regulation. For example, say the government believes that a particular default option, such as the saving option, will benefit people. If government passes a law that requires firms to make saving the default option, the policy does not meet the libertarian criterion, and thus is more than a nudge. Government is telling the firm what to do. Traditional economists argue that true nudge policies are too small a category to warrant a separate analysis.

Designing Helpful Policies Is Complicated

A second concern is that designing nudge policies quickly becomes complicated, requiring more information than government has. To see the difficulties that even a simple informational policy presents, consider requiring firms to label BST-free milk.

(BST is a cow growth hormone.) That could be seen as simply an information policy, and thus not a strong nudge, despite the fact that labeling would be a government regulation. However, many economists oppose such labeling since most scientific tests have found that milk that comes from cows given the growth hormone BST is no different from milk that does not; they argue that people's concern about BST is itself predictably irrational—people cannot deal with complicated issues. Other economists argue that regardless of what science may conclude, if people believe that BST milk is bad for them, they should be given the information needed to avoid milk with BST; the regulation is simply providing feedback.

The problem is that placing the statement on the milk carton will likely raise people's concerns about the issue and lead some to choose higher-priced milk than they otherwise would. Should the government require such labeling or not, and if so, what other information should be included on the labels? Should people be informed of the antibiotic treatment cows receive, along with many other facts about how cow milk is produced? Where does one draw the line?

It Isn't Clear Government Knows Better

Web Note 22.5
Questioning Nudge Policies

A third concern is that behavioral economic policies (whether true nudge policies or push policies) require government to decide, on the advice of behavioral economists, what is best for people, and what people truly want. For example, a "luxury tax," a policy that Frank and others advocate, involves determining what is a luxury and what is a necessity.

For example, Pennsylvania taxes bathing suits because it consider them luxuries. Even though policies to tax luxuries may seem to resonate with the sense of frustration that many of us feel about perceived excesses of modern society, implementing such a policy requires the government to decide which goods make people truly happy and which goods don't. Doing that isn't easy. If people truly cared about relative, not absolute, income, people would be happy to give up some percentage of their income as long as everyone else did so as well. They are not.

Even if economists could agree that people do not always act in their own self-interest, it isn't clear government can determine what's in people's best interest either.

How can we be sure behavioral economists, or whoever is the decision maker about what nudges and pushes to implement, are right about what is best for people? Even if economists could agree that people do not always act in their own self-interest, it isn't clear government can determine what's in people's best interest either.

Government Policy May Make the Situation Worse

Q-10 What are four concerns about behavioral economic policies?

A fourth concern is that nudge policy substantially increases the potential for *government failure*—where government, in dealing with a problem, actually makes the problem worse. Will government have the willpower to limit its nudges to the set that behavioral economists, or some other group, determine are appropriate? Or will they use nudges in other ways—perhaps to win an election, or to benefit one group over another? Just as traditional economists are concerned with government failure in implementing traditional economic policies to correct for externalities, traditional economists are concerned with government failure in implementing nudge policies.

Traditional economists argue that accepting behavioral economic policy will start the government sliding along a slippery slope.

Traditional economists argue that accepting behavioral economic policy will start the government sliding along a slippery slope. Since the government has a monopoly on power, somehow that monopoly has to be kept in check if it is to benefit the people, not members of the government or its friends. For that reason, early classical economists argued that government power had to be kept under control, even when the appropriate use of power could improve the situation, because one cannot assume that government will appropriately use its power. Because of the fear of an oppressive government, earlier economists felt that, for all its problems, the market with minimal government intervention was often the better alternative. Economics' laissez-faire set of policy precepts arose as part of a liberal tradition that was based upon certain in-alienable rights of the individual that government could not violate. These arguments fit in political philosophy and are outside the confines of this text but they are the ones that a consideration of behavioral economic policy raises.

A Changing View of Economists: From Pro-market Advocates to Economic Engineers

In Chapter 1 I defined economic efficiency as achieving a goal as cheaply as possible and said that economists advise government in how to achieve economic efficiency. The traditional economic model made a shorthand adjustment to interpret the goal of society as designing the economy to maximize people's consumption. Markets tend to do that, and hence the traditional economic model tended to support markets.

Traditional economics justified its concentration on maximizing people's consumption by arguing that people knew what they wanted better than anyone else, and their actions revealed their desires. Consumer sovereignty was not to be questioned. Behavioral economics questions consumer sovereignty and thus opens up a Pandora's box of issues that the traditional economic model keeps out of sight.

Behavioral economics is part of a broader movement in modern economics where economists see themselves as mechanism design engineers. They solve problems by building coordination mechanisms that achieve predetermined goals. Traditional econ-omists' models focus on economic incentives and people's tendency to respond to price incentives. Behavioral economists' models modify that by taking into account people's tendency to be predictably irrational. In doing this, behavioral economics opens up the policy discussion of economics from the traditional economic view that prices and incentives matter to a broader view that *everything matters*. For a behavioral economist, modern economic policy making involves complicated issues, and we need to take into account those complications when designing policy.

Who can argue with the truism that everything matters? Who better than a traditional economist using a behavioral economist's argument? Behavioral economics tells us that people are not good at making decisions when issues are complicated. Economic policy involves very complicated decisions, and the general population and policy makers need a nudge to get them to make good decisions. The traditional model gives them that nudge by concentrating on the most important aspects of choice—price incentives—and not distracting the analysis as behavioral economics does by concentrating on the many ir-rationalities that people exhibit. Furthermore, the traditional model protects individual liberty and prevents the state from trying to shape people's wants. By taking the focus away from that most important incentive, models based on behavioral economic in-sights fail to give people that nudge to concentrate on the most important element—price incentives—and, therefore, are likely to do more harm than good.

I leave it to you to decide which argument is right.

> Behavioral economics questions consumer sovereignty and thus opens up a Pandora's box of issues that the traditional economic model keeps out of sight.

Conclusion

I am a big fan of complexity theory, which pictures the economy as a complex evolv-ing system. But not only is economy evolving, so too is the economics profession. This chapter gives you a sense of that evolution, and the implications of those changes for policy. As you can see, behavioral economics opens up a new set of policy ques-tions and new ways of looking at the world through an economic lens. It shows you that economics is not a single lens, but a set of lenses that recognize that incentives are important, but also recognize that the way in which incentives work is far more com-plicated than any simple model can capture.

Summary

- Mechanism design is an engineering approach to economic problems in which one identifies a goal and then designs a mechanism such as a market, social system, or contract to achieve that goal. *(LO22-1)*

- Behavioral economics is an outgrowth of the mechanism design approach to economics. *(LO22-1)*

- Choice architecture is the context in which decisions are presented. A nudge is designed to influence choice architecture in a way that directs people to make choices that make them better off. *(LO22-2)*

- Nudges are libertarian because people remain free to make choices. They are paternalistic because they change the structure of choices with the intention of influencing people's behavior in a way that improves their choices. *(LO22-2)*

- Nudges can be useful for: (1) choices where benefits and costs are separated by time, (2) complicated choices with many dimensions, and (3) infrequent choices. *(LO22-2)*

- Two categories of nudge polices are (1) advantageous default option policies and (2) information and encouragement policies. *(LO22-2)*

- A true nudge policy leaves everyone free to choose and does not have to be imposed through regulation or taxation. Push policies are government policies requiring firms or individuals to use certain types of nudges. They do not meet the libertarian criterion. *(LO22-3)*

- Government regulation may be required if firms do not want to implement a nudge. Such nudges become pushes. *(LO22-3)*

- Behavioral economic policy is controversial. It is not clear that government can decide what is best for people or, even if they knew what was best, they would implement the policy. Government is subject to failure just as is the market. *(LO22-4)*

Key Terms

behavioral economic
   policy *(487)*
choice architecture *(492)*
coordination
   mechanism *(488)*

economic
   engineering *(487)*
incentive compatibility
   problem *(489)*

libertarian paternalistic
   policy *(493)*
mechanism design *(489)*
nudge *(493)*

nudge policy *(493)*
push policy *(497)*
shadow price *(488)*

Questions and Exercises

1. What is a coordination mechanism? Give an example. *(LO22-1)*

2. True or false? For a market to have a coordination mechanism, money must be exchanged. Explain. *(LO22-1)*

3. True or false? Only money prices affect incentives; shadow prices do not. Explain. *(LO22-1)*

4. What is the incentive compatibility problem? Give an example. *(LO22-1)*

5. What is the primary task of a mechanism design economist? *(LO22-1)*

6. How did mechanism design lead to behavioral economics? *(LO22-1)*

7. Can a model that includes just money price miss relevant prices? Why or why not? *(LO22-1)*

8. How is choice architecture related to behavioral economics and mechanism design? *(LO22-2)*

9. Behavioral economics is a new field in economics. Are nudges new too? *(LO22-2)*

10. What is a nudge policy? Give an example. *(LO22-2)*

11. How can a nudge be defined as libertarian? *(LO22-2)*

12. In what way is nudge policy paternalistic?   (*LO22-2*)

13. Two people are given the choice to participate in a retirement program in which the firm matches contributions. Person A is given a form in which she must check a box to opt into the retirement program. Person B is given a form in which she must check a box to opt out of the retirement program. According to studies, which person is more likely to participate? Or are they equally likely to participate? Explain your answer.   (*LO22-2*)

14. What are three types of choices in which nudges are useful?   (*LO22-2*)

15. Why is a nudge useful for choices where benefits and costs are separated by time?   (*LO22-2*)

16. Why, in the traditional model, is a nudge unnecessary but potentially helpful in the behavioral model?   (*LO22-2*)

17. Classify the following nudges as either a "potentially advantageous default nudge," an "information or encouragement nudge," or "not a nudge."   (*LO22-2*)
    a. A firm redesigns its health enrollment form so that employees must explicitly choose to forgo health insurance.
    b. Your local city sends you an annual report of average water usage per resident with your actual usage along with tips for conserving water.
    c. Government raises the taxes on gasoline to reduce pollution.
    d. A consumer-advocacy group sets up a site with side-by-side comparison of auto-insurance cost based on estimated risk of drivers.

18. Government has provided a way for people to file their tax returns on the Internet to make filing easier and raise compliance. Is this an example of a libertarian paternalistic policy? Explain your answer.   (*LO22-2*)

19. What distinguishes a nudge from a push?   (*LO22-3*)

20. Why would push instead of nudge policies be required? (*LO22-3*)

21. Identify the following as either a nudge, a push, or neither.
    a. The cover of your state tax forms reports that 90 percent of residents pay taxes on time.
    b. If your friends gain weight, you are likely to gain weight too.
    c. Amazon is required by government to set the default mail option as the standard mail rate.
    d. Government taxes in part to redistribute income.
    e. A health insurer issues participants credits for exercising and eating healthy foods that they can use to buy products.

22. How is conspicuous consumption an example of the importance of relative materialism to one's happiness?   (*LO22-3*)

23. How might conspicuous consumption lower total happiness?   (*LO22-3*)

24. What are four reasons to be cautious about nudges?   (*LO22-4*)

25. Why aren't there many libertarian nudge policies?   (*LO22-4*)

26. Assume that government proposes that all employees must be presented with the choice of opting out of a retirement saving program. What assumptions are necessary for this to be a true nudge? Are they reasonable assumptions?   (*LO22-4*)

Questions from Alternative Perspectives

1. Behavioral economics seems to suggest that the "long-term self" rather than the "short-term self" is rational. How do we know that? (Austrian)

2. There is an implicit view in the chapter that if a policy meets the libertarian paternalistic goal, it is a good policy. Is that necessarily the case? (Radical)

3. How does behavioral economics undermine the standard supply/demand model? (Institutionalist)

4. Behavioral economics acknowledges that cultural norms impact people's behavior, something that feminist economists have long included in their analysis. What risks does nudge policy pose for using cultural norms to affect behavior of those in society who have comparatively less power? (Feminist)

Issues to Ponder

1. What mechanism might be developed to determine whether it is appropriate for government to give a nudge?

2. Why were more batters being hit in the American League than in the National League starting in 1973? (Be sure your answer uses shadow prices.)

3. To offset the effect of the designated hitter system, what might the American League do to reduce the number of beanballs thrown?

4. In which of the following cases might a nudge be helpful? Explain why or why not.
   a. Deciding what mortgage is affordable.
   b. Deciding whether to exercise or not on a particular day.

c. Deciding whether to fill your gas tank.
d. Deciding whom to marry.

5. Do we as society focus too much on consumption, and, if so, how would one change that focus?

6. Describe five nudges that firms currently use to get you to do what they want you to do.

Answers to Margin Questions

1. Economic science tries to understand how the economy works; economic engineering tries to design mechanisms to better coordinate people's actions. (*p. 488; LO22-1*)

2. A shadow price is an implicit price of an action whose value is measured in opportunity costs. It does not involve a payment to another person but is estimated by analyzing people's actions. (*p. 488; LO22-1*)

3. Yes, it does. The goal of college is generally thought to be learning. Grading gives one an incentive to learn what is likely to be on the test, not what is necessarily the most useful or important knowledge. (*p. 489; LO22-1*)

4. Economists' work in mechanism design led to a greater interest in behavioral economics because they discovered that people were predictable irrational, and that by taking that predictable irrationality into account, they could design more effective coordination mechanisms. (*p. 490; LO22-1*)

5. False. They believe that people are sometimes irrational but are generally not irrational in a predictable way, and that if they are predictably irrational, that irrationality can

be accounted for as an adjustment to the general model. (*p. 492; LO22-1*)

6. He or she is more likely to be a behavioral economist. (*p. 492; LO22-2*)

7. A policy designed to structure choices so that people make a certain choice is called a nudge policy. (*p. 493; LO22-2*)

8. It depends. From the perspective of the firm, it definitely is not a nudge policy since the firm is being told what to do. It is a push policy. From the perspective of the individual, it can be seen as a nudge policy. (*p. 497; LO22-3*)

9. Not necessarily. Increasing conspicuous consumption goods makes the owner feel better off but makes others feel worse off, and thus does not necessarily make society as a whole better off. (*p. 498; LO22-3*)

10. Four concerns are: (1) there are very few true nudge policies; (2) nudge policies quickly become complicated; (3) governments do not necessarily know what is best; and (4) nudge policies increase the potential for government failure. (*p. 500; LO22-4*)

chapter 23

Microeconomic Policy, Economic Reasoning, and Beyond

> *If an economist becomes certain of the solution of any problem, he can be equally certain that his solution is wrong.*
>
> —H. A. Innis

One important job of economists is to give advice to politicians and other policy makers on a variety of questions relating to social policy: How should unemployment be dealt with? How can society distribute income fairly? Should the government redistribute income? Would a program of equal pay for jobs of comparable worth (a pay equity program) make economic sense? Should the minimum wage be increased? These are tough questions.

In previous chapters, I discussed the formal frameworks that modern economists use to think about such issues. In this chapter I consider economic reasoning in a broader context.

The reason for doing so is that economic reasoning and the supply/demand model are tools, not rules. To draw policy implications from it, the supply/demand model has to be placed in context. Used in the proper context, the supply/demand model is enormously strong, something no one should be without. Used out of context, it can lead to conclusions that don't seem right, and that maybe are not right. Consider the assembly-line chicken-production example in Chapter 12. Some of you may have felt that the assembly-line production of chickens was somehow not right—that the efficiency of the production process somehow did not outweigh the chickens' suffering. Yet the economic model, which focuses on efficiency, directs production toward that assembly line. This chapter considers when you might want to use economic reasoning, and when you might not.

The chapter is divided into two parts. The first part of the chapter extends the supply/demand model to a broader cost/benefit framework, tying together the discussion we had about economic reasoning in the introductory chapters with the chapters that developed the foundations of the supply/demand model. It shows you how economic reasoning is used in practice. The second part of the chapter turns economic reasoning back upon itself, considering not only the benefits (which are considerable) but also the costs of using economic reasoning. In doing so, I discuss how markets that are working perfectly may still lead to outcomes that are undesirable.

Economists' Differing Views about Social Policy

Economists' views on social policy differ widely because:

1. They have different underlying values.
2. They interpret empirical evidence differently.
3. They use different underlying models.

Economists have many different views on social policy because:

1. Economists' suggestions for social policy are determined by their subjective value judgments (normative views) as well as by their objective economic analyses.

2. Policy proposals must be based on imprecise empirical evidence, so there's considerable room for differences of interpretation not only about economic issues but also about how political and social institutions work. Economic policy is an art, not a science.

3. Policy proposals are based on various models that focus on different aspects of a problem.

WWWW   Web Note 23.1
The Clash of the Economists

All three reasons directly concern the role of ideology in economics. However, any policy proposal must embody both economic analysis and value judgments because the goals of policy reflect value judgments. When an economist makes a policy proposal, it's of this type: "If A, B, and C are your goals, then you should undertake policies D, E, and F to achieve those goals most efficiently." In making these policy suggestions, the economist's role is much the same as an engineer's: He or she is simply telling someone else how to achieve desired ends most efficiently. Ideally the economist is as objective as possible, telling someone how to achieve his or her goals (which need not be the economist's goals).

How Economists' Value Judgments Creep into Policy Proposals

Even though economists attempt to be as objective as possible, value judgments still creep into their analyses in three ways: interpretation of policy makers' values, interpretation of empirical evidence, and choice of economic models.

INTERPRETATION OF THE POLICY MAKER'S VALUES   In practice, social goals are seldom so neat that they can be specified A, B, and C; they're vaguely understood and vaguely expressed. An economist will be told, for instance, "We want to make the poor better off" or "We want to see that middle-income people get better housing." It isn't clear what *poor, better off,* and *better housing* mean. Nor is it clear how judgments should be made when a policy will benefit some individuals at the expense of others, as real-world policies inevitably do.

Pareto optimal policies are policies that benefit some people and hurt no one.

Faced with this problem, some academic economists have argued that economists should recommend only **Pareto optimal policies**—*policies that benefit some people and hurt no one.* The policies are named in honor of the famous Italian economist Vilfredo Pareto, who first suggested that kind of criterion for judging social change.[1] It's hard to object to the notion of Pareto optimal policies because, by definition, they improve life for some people while hurting no one.

Q-1   If someone suggests that economists should focus only on Pareto optimal policies, how would you respond?

I'd give you an example of a real-world Pareto optimal policy if I could, but unfortunately I don't know of any. Every policy inevitably has some side effect of hurting, or at least seeming to hurt, somebody. In the real world, Pareto optimal policies don't exist. Any economist who has advised governments on real-world problems knows that all real-world policies make some people better off and some people worse off.

---

[1]Pareto, in his famous book *Mind and Society,* suggested this criterion as an analytic approach for theory, not as a criterion for real-world policy. He recognized the importance of the art of economics and that real-world policy has to be judged by much broader criteria than this.

But that doesn't mean that economists have no policy role. In their policy proposals, economists try to spell out the effects of a policy and whether the policy is consistent with the policy maker's value judgments. Doing so isn't easy because the policy maker's value judgments are often vague and must be interpreted by the economist. In that interpretation, the economist's own value judgments often slip in.

INTERPRETATION OF EMPIRICAL EVIDENCE   Value judgments also creep into economic policy proposals through economists' interpretations of empirical evidence, which is almost always imprecise. For example, say an economist is assessing the elasticity of a product's demand in the relevant price range. She can't run an experiment to isolate prices and quantities demanded; instead she must look at events in which hundreds of other things changed, and do her best to identify what caused what. In selecting and interpreting empirical evidence, our values will likely show through, try as we might to be objective. People tend to focus on evidence that supports their position. Economists are trained to be as objective as they can be, but pure objectivity is impossible.

Let's consider the example of a debate in which some economists proposed that a large tax be imposed on sales of disposable diapers, citing studies that suggested disposable diapers made up between 15 and 30 percent of the garbage in landfills. Others objected, citing studies that showed disposable diapers made up only 1 or 2 percent of the refuse going into landfills. Such differences in empirical estimates are the norm, not the exception. Inevitably, if precise estimates are wanted, more studies are necessary. (In this case, the further studies showed that the lower estimates were correct.) But policy debates don't wait for further studies. Economists' value judgments influence which incomplete study policy makers choose to believe is more accurate.

CHOICE OF ECONOMIC MODELS   Similarly with the choice of models. A model, because it focuses on certain aspects of economic reality and not on others, necessarily reflects certain value judgments, so economists' choice of models must also reflect certain value judgments. Albert Einstein once said that theories should be as simple as possible, but not more so. To that we should add a maxim: Scientists should be as objective and as value-free as possible, but not more so.

> Scientists should be as objective as possible, but not more so.

This book presents primarily mainstream economic models. This includes the standard supply/demand model and the new behavioral models. These models direct us to certain conclusions. Two other general models that some economists follow are a **Marxian (radical) model,** which is *a model that focuses on equitable distribution of power, rights, and income among social classes,* and a **public choice model,** which is *a model that focuses on economic incentives as applied to politicians.* These two models, by emphasizing different aspects of economic interrelationships, sometimes direct us to other conclusions.

Let's consider an example. Mainstream economic analysis directs us to look at how the invisible hand achieves harmony and equilibrium through the market. Thus, when mainstream economists look at labor markets, they generally see supply and demand forces leading to equilibrium. When Marxist economists look at labor markets, their model focuses on the tensions among the social classes, and they generally see exploitation of workers by capitalists. When public choice economists look at labor markets, they see individuals using government to protect their monopolies. Their model focuses on political restrictions that provide rents to various groups. Each model captures different aspects of reality. That's why it's important to be as familiar with as many different models as possible.

> **Q-2** How does a radical analysis of labor markets differ from a mainstream analysis?

> Each model captures different aspects of reality. That's why it's important to be as familiar with as many different models as possible.

The Need for a Worldview

John Maynard Keynes, an economist who gained fame in the 1930s, once said that economists should be seen in the same light as dentists—as competent technicians.

He was wrong, and his own experience contradicts that view. In dealing with real-world economic policy, Keynes was no mere technician. He had a definite worldview, which he shared with many of the policy makers he advised. An economist who is to play a role in forming policy must be willing to combine value judgments and technical knowledge. That worldview determines how and when the economic model will be applied.

Agreement among Economists about Social Policy

Despite their widely varying values, both liberal and conservative economists agree more often on policy prescriptions than most laypeople think they do. They're economists, after all, and their models focus on certain issues—specifically on incentives and individual choice. They believe economic incentives are important, and most economists tend to give significant weight to individuals' ability to choose reasonably. This leads economists, both liberal and conservative, to look at problems differently than other people do.

Many people think economists of all persuasions look at the world coldheartedly. In my view, that opinion isn't accurate, but it's understandable how people could reach it. Economists are taught to look at things in an "objective" way that takes into account a policy's long-run incentive effects as well as the short-run effects. Many of their policy proposals are based on these long-run incentive effects, which in the short run make the policy look coldhearted. The press and policy makers usually focus on short-run effects. Economists argue that they aren't being coldhearted at all, that they're simply being reasonable, and that following their advice will lead to less suffering than following others' advice will. This is not to say that all advice economists give will lead to significant benefits and less suffering in the long run. Some of it may be simply misguided.

The problem economists face is similar to the one parents face when they tell their children that they can't eat candy or must do their homework before they can play. Explaining how "being mean" is actually "being nice" to a six-year-old isn't easy.

A former colleague of mine, Abba Lerner, was well known for his strong liberal leanings. The government of Israel asked him what to do about unemployment. He went to Israel, studied the problem, and presented his advice: "Cut union wages." The government official responded, "But that's the same advice the conservative economist gave us." Lerner answered, "It's good advice, too." The Israeli Labor government then went and did the opposite; it raised wages, thus holding on to its union support in the short run.

Another example comes from a World Bank economist. She had to advise a hospital in a developing country to turn down the offer of a free dialysis machine because the marginal cost of the filters it would have to buy to use the machine significantly exceeded the costs of life-saving medicines that would save even more lives. Economic reasoning involves making such hard decisions.

The best way to see the consistency and the differences in economists' policy advice is to consider some examples. Let's start with a general consideration of economic views on government regulation.

Economists' Cost/Benefit Approach to Government Regulation

Say that 200 people die in a plane crash. Newspaper headlines trumpet the disaster while news magazines are filled with stories about how the accident might have been caused, citing speculation about poor maintenance and lack of government regulation.

The publicity spreads the sense that "something must be done" to prevent such trage-dies. Politicians quickly pick up on this, feeling that the public wants action. They in-troduce a bill outlawing faulty maintenance, denounce poor regulatory procedures, and demand an investigation of sleepy air controllers. In short, they strike out against likely causes of the accident and suggest improved regulations to help prevent any more such crashes.

Economists differ in their views on government regulation of airlines and other businesses, but most find themselves opposing some of the supposedly problem-solving regulations proposed by politicians. They generally adopt a **cost/benefit approach** to problems—*assigning costs and benefits, and making decisions on the basis of the rele-vant costs and benefits*—that requires them to determine a quantitative cost and benefit for everything, including life. What's the value of a human life? All of us would like to answer, "Infinite. Each human life is beyond price." But if that's true, then in a cost/benefit framework, everything of value should be spent on preventing death. People should take no chances. They should drive at no more than 30 miles per hour with air-bags, triple-cushioned bumpers, double roll bars—you get the picture.

It might be possible for manufacturers to make a car in which no one would die as the result of an accident. But people don't want such cars. Many people don't buy the auto safety accessories that are already available, and many drivers ignore the present speed limit. Instead, many people want cars with style and speed.

> Many regulations are formulated for political expediency and do not reflect cost/benefit considerations.

> Cost/benefit analysis is analysis in which one assigns a cost and benefit to alternatives, and draws a conclusion on the basis of those costs and benefits.

The Value of Life

Far from regarding human life as priceless, people make decisions every day that re-flect the valuations they place on their own lives. The table below presents a number of estimates that various economists have made of some of those decisions.

Basis for Calculation	Value of Human Life
Automobile safety features	$5,020,000–7,130,000
Bicycle helmets	1,580,000–5,680,000
Smoke detector purchases	1,010,000–3,380,000
Seat belt usage	1,320,000
Car seats	1,100,000

Car crashes are evidence human life is not beyond price.

These values are calculated by looking at people's revealed preferences (the choices people make when they must pay the costs). To find them, economists calculate how much people will pay to reduce the possibility of their death by a certain amount. If that's what people will pay to avoid death, the value of life can be calculated by multi-plying the inverse of the reduction in the probability of death by the amount they pay. (What is relevant for these calculations is not the actual probabilities but the decision makers' estimate of the probabilities.)

For example, say someone will buy a smoke detector for $25 but won't buy one if it costs more than $25. Also say that the buyer believes that a smoke detector will re-duce the chance of dying in a fire by 1/80,000. That means that to increase the likeli-hood of surviving a house fire by 1/80,000, the buyer will pay $25. That also means that the buyer is implicitly valuing his or her life at roughly $2,000,000 (80,000 × $25 = $2,000,000).

Alternatively, say that people will pay an extra $60 for a set of premium tires that reduces the risk of death by 1/100,000. As opposed to having a 3/100,000 chance per year of dying in a skid on the highway, people driving cars with premium tires have a

> Q-4 If the table in the text correctly describes the valuation individuals place on life with regard to smoke detector purchases and premium tire usage, how would you advise them to alter their behavior in order to maximize utility?

Economists in the Courtroom

Valuing life is more than just an academic exercise. These valuations play an important role in court cases on wrongful death in which one individual sues another for having caused a wrongful death. How do you put a value on the person's life? The courts have to do that—determine how much the defendant will have to pay the plaintiff if the court decides it was a "wrongful death." A court can't simply say that a life is priceless; it relies on economic expert witnesses to provide values.

One way to value life is the method presented in the text—deduce how much people value life from their willingness to take risks. This sounds like a reasonable method, but it has problems that have been much discussed in the literature and in the courtroom. Some of these problems include: small risk values are irrelevant to large risk issues; the variance of estimates is too high to give a reasonable estimate; anonymous lives

are irrelevant in specific cases; people's risk preferences differ; and people's decisions are not fully rational but reflect many other issues such as awareness of the problem and shock value. In fact, there is a whole branch of economics—forensic economics—that looks at such issues.

Another method economists use for valuing life is to calculate the lost earnings and pleasure that someone would have had in his or her remaining lifetime. But this method also has problems since it is difficult to specify either precisely. For example, is a depressed person's life worth less than a happy person's life? Is an investment banker's life worth more than a trainee's life? What is the appropriate discount rate to use to value earnings in different years? Courts have to sort through these many problems, and economists' testimony as expert witnesses often plays a key role in these cases.

---

www Web Note 23.2
The Value of Life

2/100,000 chance of dying $(3/100,000 - 2/100,000 = 1/100,000)$. Multiplying 100,000 (the inverse of the reduction in probability) by $60, the extra cost of the set of premium tires, you find that people who buy these tires are implicitly valuing their lives at $6,000,000.[2] Another way of determining the value that society places on life is to look at awards juries give for the loss of life. One study looking at such awards found that juries on average value life at about $3.5 million.

No one can say whether people know what they're doing in making these valuations, although the inconsistencies in the valuations people place on their lives suggest that to some degree they don't, or that other considerations are entering into their decisions. But even given the inconsistencies, it's clear that people are placing a finite value on life. Most people are aware that in order to "live" they must take chances on losing their lives. Economists argue that individuals' revealed preferences are the best estimate that society can have of the value of life, and that in making policy society shouldn't pretend that life is beyond value.

Economists argue that individuals' revealed choices are the best estimate that society can have of the value of life, and that in making policy society shouldn't pretend that life is beyond value.

Placing a value on human life allows economists to evaluate the cost of a crash. Say each life is valued at $2 million. If 200 people die in that plane accident and a $200 million plane is destroyed, the cost of the crash is $600 million.

Right after the accident, or even long after the accident, tell a mother and father you're valuing the life of their dead daughter at $2 million and the plane at $200 million, and you'll see why economists have problems with getting their views across. Even if people can agree rationally that they implicitly place a value on their own lives, it's not something they want to deal with emotionally, especially after an accident. Using a cost/benefit approach, an economist must be willing to say, if that's the way

---

[2]For simplicity of exposition, I'm not considering risk preferences or other benefits of these decisions, such as lowering the chance of injury.

the analysis turns out, "It's reasonable that my son died in this accident because the cost of preventing the accident by imposing stricter government regulations would have been greater than the benefit of preventing it."

Economists take the emotional heat for making such valuations. Their cost/benefit approach requires them to do so.

Comparing Costs and Benefits of Different Dimensions

After the marginal cost and marginal benefit data have been gathered and processed, one is ready to make an informed decision. Will the cost of a new regulation outweigh the benefit, or vice versa? Here again, economists find themselves in a difficult position in evaluating a regulation about airplane safety. Many of the costs of regulation are small but occur in large numbers. Every time you lament some "bureaucratic craziness" (such as a required weekly staff meeting or a form to be signed assuring something has been done), you're experiencing a cost. But when those costs are compared to the benefits of avoiding a major accident, the dimensions of comparison are often wrong.

For example, say it is discovered that a loose bolt was the probable cause of the plane crash. A regulation requiring airline mechanics to check whether that bolt is tightened and, to ensure that they do so, requiring them to fill out a form each time the check is made might cost $1. How can we compare $1 to the $600 million cost of the crash? Such a regulation obviously makes sense from the perspective of gaining a $600 million benefit from $1 of cost.

But wait. Each plane might have 4,000 similar bolts, each of which is equally likely to cause an accident if it isn't tightened. If it makes sense to check that one bolt, it makes sense to check all 4,000. And the bolts must be checked on each of the 4,000 flights per day. All of this increases the cost of tightening bolts to $16 million per day. But the comparison shouldn't be between $16 million and $600 million. The comparison should be between the marginal cost ($16 million) and the marginal benefit, which depends on how much tightening bolts will contribute to preventing an accident.

Let's say that having the bolts checked daily reduces the probability of having an accident by 0.001. This means that the check will prevent one out of a thousand accidents that otherwise would have happened. The marginal benefit of checking a particular bolt isn't $600 million (which it would be if you knew a bolt was going to be loose), but is

$$0.001 \times \$600 \text{ million} = \$600,000$$

That $600,000 is the marginal benefit that must be compared to the marginal cost of $16 million.

Given these numbers, I leave it to you to decide: Does this hypothetical regulation make sense?

Cost/benefit analysis sometimes leads one to uncomfortable results.

Putting Cost/Benefit Analysis in Perspective

The numbers in our plane crash example are hypothetical. The numbers used in real-world decision making are not hypothetical, but they are often ambiguous. Measuring costs, benefits, and probabilities is difficult, and economists often disagree on specific costs and benefits. Costs have many dimensions, some more quantifiable than others. Cost/benefit analysis is often biased toward quantifiable costs and away from nonquantifiable costs, or it involves enormous ambiguity as nonquantifiable costs are quantified.

The subjectivity and ambiguity of costs are one reason why economists differ in their views of regulation. In considering any particular regulation, some economists will favor it and some will oppose it. But their reasoning process—comparing marginal costs and marginal benefits—is the same; they differ only on the estimates they calculate.

Q-5 Why should you be very careful about any cost/benefit analysis?

WWW Web Note 23.3
Applying Cost-Benefit Analysis

Cost/benefit analysis is often biased toward quantifiable costs.

The Problem of Other Things Changing

A major reason why economists come to different conclusions about policies involves the "other things equal" assumption discussed in Chapter 4. Supply/demand analysis assumes that all other things remain equal. But in a large number of issues it is obvious that other things do not remain equal. However, it is complicated to sort out how they change, and the sorting-out process is subject to much debate. The more macro the issue, the more other things change, and hence the more debate.

Q-6 When using marginal cost/marginal benefit analysis, do "other things remain constant"? Explain.

Let's consider the minimum wage example we discussed in earlier chapters. Suppose you can estimate the supply and demand elasticities for labor. Is that enough to enable you to estimate the number of people who will be made unemployed by a minimum wage? To answer that, ask yourself: Are other things likely to remain constant? The answer is: No; numerous things will change. Say the firm decides to replace these workers with machines. So it will buy some machines. But machines are made by other workers, and so the demand for workers in the machine-making industry will rise. So the decrease in employment in the first industry may be offset by an increase in employment elsewhere.

But there are issues on the other side too. For example, if other things change, workers who get the higher wage may not receive a net benefit. Say you had a firm that was paying a wage lower than the minimum wage but was providing lots of training, which was preparing people for much better jobs in the future. Now the minimum wage goes into effect. The firm keeps hiring workers, but it eliminates the training. Its workers actually could be worse off.

How important are such issues? That's a matter of empirical research, which is why empirical research is central to economics. Unfortunately, the data aren't very good, which is why there is so much debate about policy issues in economics.

There are many more examples of "other things changing," but the above should be sufficient to give you an idea of the problem.

The Cost/Benefit Approach in Context

Economics teaches people to be "reasonable."

Economics teaches people to be reasonable—sickeningly reasonable, some people would say. I hope that you have some sense of what I mean by that. The cost/benefit approach to problems (which pictures a world of individuals whose self-interested actions are limited only by competition) makes economists look for the self-interest behind individuals' actions, and for how competition can direct that self-interest into the public interest.

In an economist's framework,

- Well-intentioned policies often are prevented by individuals' self-interest-seeking activities.
- Policies that relieve immediate suffering often have long-run consequences that create more suffering.
- Politicians have more of an incentive to act fast—to look as if they're doing something—than to do something that makes sense from a cost/benefit point of view.

The marginal cost/marginal benefit story is embodied in the supply/demand framework.

The marginal cost/marginal benefit approach is telling a story. That story is embodied in the supply/demand framework. Supply represents the marginal costs of a trade, and demand represents the marginal benefits of a trade. Equilibrium is where quantity supplied equals quantity demanded—where marginal cost equals marginal benefit. That equilibrium maximizes the combination of consumer and producer surplus and leads to an efficient, or Pareto optimal, outcome. The argument for competitive markets within that supply/demand framework is that markets allow the society to achieve

economic efficiency—*achieving a goal, in this case producing a specified amount of output, at the lowest possible cost.* Alternatively expressed, the story is that, given a set of resources, markets produce the greatest possible output. When the economy is efficient, it is on its production possibility curve, producing total output at its lowest opportunity cost.

The supply/demand framework is logical, satisfying, and (given its definitions and assumptions) extraordinarily useful. That's why we teach it. It gives students who understand it the ability to get to the heart of many policy problems. It tells them that every policy has a cost, every policy has a benefit, and if the assumptions are met, competition sees to it that the benefits to society are achieved at the lowest possible cost. Applied to policy issues, the framework gets you to face trade-offs that you would often rather avoid, and that you likely wouldn't see if you didn't use it. It is what "thinking like an economist" is all about.

Failure of Market Outcomes

A good story emphasizes certain elements and deemphasizes others to make its point. When the moral of the story is applied, however, we have to be careful to consider all the relevant elements—especially those that the story didn't emphasize. That's why in the second part of this chapter I will discuss some implicit assumptions that the supply/demand framework pushes to the back of the analysis and that therefore often don't get addressed in principles courses. I classify these as failures of market outcomes. A **failure of market outcome** occurs *when, even though the market is functioning properly (there are no market failures), it is not achieving society's goals.*

Three separate types of failures of market outcomes will be considered:

1. *Failures due to distributional issues:* Whose surplus is the market maximizing?

2. *Failures due to rationality problems of individuals:* What if individuals don't know what is best for themselves?

3. *Failures due to violations of inalienable or at least partially inalienable rights of individuals:* Are there certain rights that should not be for sale?

I'll discuss an example of each of the three failures of market outcomes and contrast them with market failures. Then I will conclude with a brief discussion of why, even though most economists recognize these failures of market outcomes, they still favor the use of markets for the large majority of goods that society produces.

Distribution

Say that the result of market forces is that some people don't earn enough income to be able to survive—the demand for their labor intersects the supply for their labor at a wage of 25 cents an hour. Also assume there are no market failures. (Information is perfect, trades have no negative externalities, and all goods are private goods.)

The market solution to a wage that is so low the worker can't survive is starvation—people who don't earn enough die. Not all low-wage workers must die, however. As some low-wage workers die, the supply of labor shifts back to the left, raising the wage for the survivors. This process takes time, but eventually all remaining workers will receive a subsistence wage. This is the long-run market solution. Implicit within the supply/demand framework is a Darwinian "survival of the fittest" approach to social policy. Most people would regard the market solution—starvation—as an undesirable outcome. Even though the market is doing precisely what it is supposed to be doing—equating quantity supplied and quantity demanded—most people would not find the outcome acceptable.

DISTRIBUTION OF TOTAL SURPLUS   Let me now relate this distributional issue to the supply/demand framework by considering distribution of consumer

Q-7 True or false? The goal of society is efficiency.

Failure of market outcome occurs when, even though it is functioning properly, the market is not achieving society's goals.

Implicit within the supply/demand framework is a "survival of the fittest" approach to social policy.

Economic Efficiency and the Goals of Society

Economic efficiency means achieving a goal at the lowest possible cost. For the definition to be meaningful, the goal must be specified. Efficiency in the pursuit of efficiency is meaningless. Thus, when we talk about economic efficiency, we must have some goal in mind. In the supply/demand framework, we *assume* the goal is to maximize total utility given the income

people have. Each of the three failures of market outcomes that we discuss in this section represents a situation in which the goals of society cannot be captured by a single measure— where society's goal is more complicated than to maximize total utility—and thus the assumed goal of efficiency (maximizing total utility) is not the only goal of society.

and producer surplus. For most discussions of economic policy, an implicit assumption is that the goal of policy is to create as much total surplus as possible. In a world of only one good and one person, that goal would be clear. But with many goods and many people, what is meant by total surplus in terms of social welfare can be unclear. One reason is that society does not value all surplus equally. In the above starvation example, *the reason most people do not like the market outcome is that they care about not only the size of the total surplus but also how total surplus is distributed.* The supply/demand framework does not distinguish among those who get producer and consumer surplus, and thus avoids that distribution issue.

EXAMPLES OF DISTRIBUTIONAL ISSUES   Let's consider two real-world examples where distributional issues are likely to play a significant role in value judgments about the market outcome. Our economy produces $200-an-ounce olive oil, but it does not provide a minimum level of health care for all. This happens because income distribution is highly unequal. The high income of the wealthy means there is demand for $200-an-ounce bottles of olive oil. (It's all the rage in Silicon Valley.) Businesses establish production facilities to produce it (or any one of a million other luxury items), and it is sold on the market. Selling $200-an-ounce bottles of olive oil is efficient if one's goal is to maximize total consumer and producer surplus. However, given the distribution of income, it would be inefficient to produce health care for the poor. The poor just don't have sufficient income to demand it. Since they have little income, the poor are given little weight in the measure of consumer surplus.

A second example of where distribution of income likely makes a big difference in our normative judgments, and where we would likely not apply the consumer and producer surplus reasoning, concerns the demand for the AIDS drug cocktail. The cocktail can stop AIDS from killing people; thus, the desire for the AIDS cocktail among individuals with AIDS is high. The demand for the drug among those without AIDS is minimal.

In some African countries, almost 30 percent of the population has AIDS. Since consumer surplus reflects desire, one might think that in Africa the consumer surplus from the desire for the AIDS drug cocktail would be enormous. But it isn't. Most people in Africa have relatively little income; in fact, most have so little income that they cannot afford the cocktail at all if it were priced at the U.S. price. Since the price of the cocktail is above their total income, they get no consumer surplus from the cocktail at all in the supply/demand framework: It would be "inefficient" to supply it to them. In the supply/demand framework you can only have a demand for a good if you have the desire *and* the income to pay for it. So, despite the fact that it is inefficient to provide AIDS drugs to low-income Africans, the prices of AIDS drugs to African nations were significantly reduced. Distributional issues trumped efficiency issues.

The point of these examples is not to convince you that the consumer surplus concept is useless. Far from it. For the majority of goods, it is a useful shorthand that demonstrates the power of competitive markets. The point of the examples is to show you the type of case where overriding the supply/demand framework in policy considerations may be socially desirable and efficient if society's goals include a particular distribution of consumer surplus. The sole purpose of society is not to maximize consumer and producer surplus. Society also has other goals. Once these other goals are taken into account, the competitive result may not be the one that is desired.

For many goods, maximizing total surplus is a useful shorthand.

Societies integrate other goals into market economics by establishing social safety nets (programs such as welfare, unemployment insurance, and Medicaid). When individuals are below a certain income, what they receive does not depend solely on what they earn in the market. How high to set a given social safety net is a matter of debate, but favoring the market outcome in most cases is not inconsistent with favoring a social safety net in others.

Consumer Sovereignty and Rationality Problems

John Drunk drinks more than is good for him; he just has to have another drink. He buys liquor voluntarily, so that means buying it makes him better off, right? Not necessarily. Even when they have full information, individuals sometimes do not do what is in their own best interest. If they don't do what's best for themselves, then the market solution—let people enter freely into whatever trades they want to—is not necessarily the best solution. Again, the market is working, but the outcome may be a failure.

This problem is sometimes called *rationality failure of individuals.* The supply/demand framework starts with the proposition that individuals are completely **rational**—that *what individuals do is in their own best interest.* Reflecting on this, however, as we did in earlier chapters, we see that that is not always the case. Most of us are irrational at times; we sometimes can "want" something that we really "don't want." Think of smoking, chocolate, or any other of our many vices. We know those potato chips are bad for us, but they taste so good.

Even if we don't have serious addictions, we may have minor ones; often we don't know what we want and we are influenced by what people tell us we want. Businesses spend over $150 billion every year on advertising in the United States to convince us that we want certain things. Individuals can be convinced they want something that, if they thought further about it, they would not want. The fact that individuals don't know what they want can be a second reason for government intervention—getting people to want what is good for them.

Let's look at an example: The U.S. government has taken the position that if people could be induced to stop smoking, they would be better off. **Sin taxes**—*taxes that discourage activities society believes are harmful (sinful)*—are meant to do just this. Based on the consumer surplus argument, a tax on smoking would create deadweight loss; it would reduce the combination of consumer and producer surplus. But in this case, government has decided that consumer surplus does not reflect individuals' welfare.

Notice the difference between the argument for taxes to change behavior (sin taxes) and the argument for taxes to raise revenue discussed in Chapter 7. When government wants to raise revenue, it takes into account how much deadweight loss is created by the tax. With sin taxes, government is trying to discourage the use of the good that is being taxed and does not take into account deadweight loss. When society takes the position that individuals' demands in the marketplace do not reflect their true welfare, it is not at all clear that the market result is efficient. (See the box "Elasticity and Taxation to Change Behavior.")

Q-8 A cocaine addict purchases an ounce of cocaine from a drug dealer. Since this was a trade both individuals freely entered, is society better off?

Elasticity and Taxation to Change Behavior

A good way to see how economists view the difference between the effect of a sin tax and the effect of a tax to raise revenue is to ask: Would a policy maker rather have an elastic or an inelastic demand curve for the good being taxed? If the purpose is to raise revenue while creating only a minimal amount of deadweight loss, an inelastic demand is preferable. If the purpose is to change behavior, as it is in the example of an alcohol-dependent individual, a more elastic demand curve is better because a relatively small tax can cause a relatively large reduction in purchases.

Consider an example of taxation to reduce consumption. If government believes that smoking is bad for people, it can decrease the amount people smoke by placing a tax on cigarettes. If the demand for cigarettes is inelastic, then the tax will not significantly decrease smoking; but if the demand is elastic, then it will. If demand is inelastic, government may choose alternative methods of affecting behavior, such as advertising campaigns.

Now consider the case in which the government wants to raise revenue. In this case an inelastic demand would be better. That's why most states rely on general sales taxes for revenue—such taxes allow them to raise revenue with relatively little effect on the efficiency of the market.

The following table provides a quick review of when a tax will be most effective, given a particular goal of government.

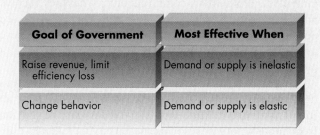

Goal of Government	Most Effective When
Raise revenue, limit efficiency loss	Demand or supply is inelastic
Change behavior	Demand or supply is elastic

Inalienable Rights

Nice Guy wants to save his son, who needs an operation that costs $300,000. He doesn't have that kind of money, but he knows that Slave Incorporated, a newly created company, has been offering $300,000 to the first person who agrees to become a slave for life. He enters into the contract, gets his money, and saves his son. Again, the market is working just as it is supposed to. There's no negative externality, and there's no information problem—Nice Guy knows what he's doing and Slave Inc. knows what it's doing. Both participants in the trade believe that it is making them better off.

Many people's view of the trade will likely be different; they would regard such a market outcome—an outcome that allows slavery—as a market outcome failure. That is why governments have developed laws that make such trades illegal.

As Amartya Sen pointed out (and won a Nobel Prize for doing so), most societies regard certain rights as inalienable. By definition, inalienable rights cannot be sold or given away. There can be no weighing of costs and benefits. For example, the right to freedom is an inalienable right, so slavery is wrong, and any trade creating slavery should not be allowed, regardless of any issues of consumer and producer surplus.

THE NEED TO PRIORITIZE RIGHTS To understand why market outcomes might be undesirable, we have to go back and consider markets in a broader perspective. Markets develop over time as individuals trade to make themselves better off. But markets don't just come into existence—they require the development of property rights for both suppliers and consumers. Each side must know what precisely is being traded. So markets can exist only if there are property rights.

Property rights, in turn, are included in a broader set of rights that are part of society's constitution—the right to vote, the right to free speech, the right to the pursuit of happiness, the right to life. Property rights are subrights to the right to pursue happiness. If property rights conflict with other rights, society must make a judgment

Q-9 True or false? If someone chooses to sell himself into slavery, the individual, and thus society, is better off.

Markets require the development of property rights.

Where to Locate Polluting Industries

Larry Summers, an MIT-trained economist and former president of Harvard University, often carries economic reasoning to its logical conclusion, and talks about it in public, or at least lets it leak out to the public. These traits often get him in hot water. When Larry Summers was chief economist at the World Bank, he signed a memo that argued that the World Bank should encourage more migration of the dirty industries to the LDCs (less-developed countries). Part of the memo stated the following:

> The measurements of the costs of health-impairing pollution depend on the forgone earnings from increased morbidity and mortality. From this point of view a given amount of health-impairing pollution should be done in the country with the lowest cost, which will be the country with the lowest wages. I think the economic logic behind dumping a load of toxic waste in the lowest-wage country is impeccable and we should face up to that.

Based upon cost/benefit analysis and calculations of the "value of life," this reasoning follows, but it is not necessarily the correct reasoning, nor is it reasoning that most people will accept. Here is the response it provoked from Brazil's secretary of the Environment:

> Your reasoning is perfectly logical but totally insane ... Your thoughts [provide] a concrete example of the unbelievable alienation, reductionist thinking, social ruthlessness and the arrogant ignorance of many conventional "economists" concerning the nature of the world we live in ... If the World Bank keeps you as vice president it will lose all credibility. To me it would confirm what I often said ... the best thing that could happen would be for the Bank to disappear.

I leave it to you to sort out which, if any, view is the correct one.

---

about which right has priority. Thus, within the written or unwritten constitution of a society, rights needs to be prioritized.

EXAMPLES OF INALIENABLE RIGHTS   Let's consider a couple of examples. Say I come up to you with a gun and offer you this deal: Your money or your life. This can be viewed as a trade. Because I have the gun, I control whether you live or die. You control the money you have. If we make the "trade," you'll be better off because I don't shoot you and I'll be better off because I'll have more money. But it is not an acceptable trade because the right to your life was inalienable—no one but you owns it; I cannot claim to own it. So, even if the gun gave me the power over your life, it did not give me the right to it. Other moral prohibitions that are related to inalienable rights include those against prostitution, selling body parts, and selling babies.

My point is not that the moral judgments our society has made about these rights are correct; they may or may not be correct. Nor is my point that such trades should not be subjected to the market. My point is that society must make these judgments. Such issues are moral questions and therefore do not have to stand up to the consumer and producer surplus arguments. If something is wrong, it is wrong; whether it is efficient is irrelevant.

Moral judgments must be made about where markets should exist, and someone might decide that the market should be allowed everywhere (that is the libertarian view), but such moral judgments can override consumer surplus arguments about markets achieving efficiency. Consider again the efficient-chicken-farming example discussed in Chapter 12. If you believe that it is immoral to treat chickens the way

Web Note 23.4
A Market for Body Parts

Moral judgments underlie all policy prescriptions.

517

"efficient" farming requires them to be treated, then the fact that the farming is efficient may be irrelevant to you.

Government Failure

Distributional issues, issues of rationality, and the existence of inalienable rights are representative of the types of problems that can arise in the market. For most economists these issues play a role in interpreting the policy results that follow from the economic model presented, even when there is no market failure. But it is important to remember that even these failures of market outcomes do not necessarily call for government action. The reason is government failure.

As I discussed in Chapter 8, if the failure is to be corrected, someone must formulate and enact the policy, and if we believe that government's attempt to correct it will do more harm than good, then we can still support the market as the lesser of two evils. For the government to correct the problem, it must:

1. Recognize the problem.
2. Have *the will* to do something positive about the problem.
3. Have *the ability* to do something positive about the problem.

Government seldom can do all three of these well. Often the result is that government action is directed at the wrong problem at the wrong time.

Probably the most vocal group of economists on the subject of government failure is *public choice economists*. This group, started by James Buchanan and Gordon Tullock, has pointed out that politicians are subject to the laws of supply and demand, like everyone else. Often the result of politics is that the redistribution that takes place does not go from rich to poor, but from one group of the middle class to another group of the middle class. Public choice economists argue that when the government enters the market, the incentives are not to achieve its goal in the least-cost manner; the incentives are to provide a policy that its voting constituency likes. The result is larger and larger government, with little benefit for society, and public choice economists advocate as little government intervention as possible regardless of whether there are market failures or failures of market outcomes.

Economic policy is, and must be, applied within a political context. This means that political elements must be taken into account. Politics enters into the determination of economic policy in two ways, one positive and one negative. Its positive contribution is that politicians take market failures and failures of market outcomes into account when formulating policy. Ultimately the political system decides what externalities should be adjusted for, what is a desirable distribution, what rights are above the market, and when people's revealed demand does not reflect their true demand. To the extent that the government's political decisions reflect the will of society, government is making a positive contribution.

The negative contribution is that political decisions do not always reflect the will of society.[3] The political reality is that, in the short run, people are often governed by emotion, swayed by mass psychology, irrational, and interested in their own rather than the general good. Politicians and other policy makers know that; the laws and regulations they propose reflect such calculations. Politicians don't get elected and reelected by constantly saying that all choices have costs and benefits. What this means is that while policy makers listen to the academic economists from whom they

---

For the government to correct a problem, it must:

1. Recognize the problem.
2. Have the will to deal with it.
3. Have the ability to deal with it.

Economic policy is, and must be, applied in a political context.

Q-10 In what way does government positively contribute to economic policy? In what way does it negatively contribute to economic policy?

---

[3]By even discussing the "will of society" I am avoiding a very difficult problem in political philosophy of what that will is, and how it is to be determined. I leave it to your political science courses to discuss such issues.

The Conventional Policy Wisdom among Economists

Where do economists come out on whether government can correct a failure of market outcomes? The easy answer is that they conclude that to make a policy decision, we must weight the costs of market failure against the costs of government failure. But those costs are often poorly specified and difficult to estimate. Thus, policy considerations require subjective judgments. Let me give you my interpretation of how economists fit these broader considerations into their analysis.

Most economists downplay the distribution issues for the majority of goods, and use distribution in their policy consideration only for the extreme examples, such as those I presented in the text. They believe that it is far better to be open about the distributional goals and to give money directly to individuals, rather than to hide the redistribution by changing the pricing structure through subsidizing goods. Let's take an example: The European Union's agricultural policy currently provides large amounts of price supports for European agricultural production. To keep farmers in business, the prices of agricultural goods are kept high. If the social decision were to keep farmers in business, most economists, however, would prefer to see the EU provide direct subsidies to farmers. Then the policy of redistribution is clear to everyone, and is far less costly in terms of both efficiency and implementation.

The "rights argument" plays a role in all economists' policy arguments. Almost all economists oppose selling citizenship. All oppose slavery. All see economic policy as being conducted

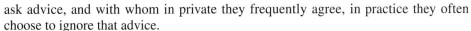

within a constitutional setting, and that means that inalienable rights come before market efficiency.

There are, of course, areas of ambiguity—allowing the regulated sale of body parts from individuals who have died is one such area. Let's consider it. There is currently a shortage of organs for transplants. When someone dies, from a medical perspective his or her organs can usually be "harvested" and used by someone else—but only if the deceased had signed a donor card. If the family of the deceased donor were given $5,000 for burial expenses, some economists argue, the shortage of transplant organs would disappear and everyone would be better off—the family could give the deceased a much nicer funeral and people needing the organs could live. My feeling is that economists are more open to such market solutions than the general public, but there is nothing in economics that requires such solutions.

The argument about problems arising from rationality issues is also accepted by most economists, but they downplay it for most nonaddictive goods. The reason is that while it is true that individuals may not know what they want, it is far less likely that the government will know better. Based on that view, on average, the acceptance of consumer sovereignty, and the market result, is probably warranted. Exceptions include children and some elderly. How to deal with addictive goods is still very much in debate among economists, and there is no conventional wisdom.

ask advice, and with whom in private they frequently agree, in practice they often choose to ignore that advice.

Because government both adjusts for failures of market outcomes and is subject to short-run political pressures, the way in which economic reasoning influences policy can be subtle. Sometimes we see elaborate charades acted out: Politicians put forward bills that from a cost/benefit viewpoint don't make sense but that make the politicians look good. They hope the bills won't pass, but they also hope that presenting them will allow enough time to pass so that emotions can cool and a more reasonable bill can be put forward. Other times, compromise bills are proposed that incorporate as much cost/benefit policy as possible, but also appeal to voters' emotional sense. In short, economic policy made in the real world reflects a balancing of cost/benefit analysis and special interest desires.

Conclusion

Adam Smith, the creator of modern economics, was a philosopher; his economics was part of his philosophy. Before he wrote the *Wealth of Nations*, in which he set out his argument for markets, he wrote a book called *The Theory of Moral Sentiments*, in which he laid out his broader philosophy. That foundation, in turn, was part of the Scottish Enlightenment, which spelled out what was meant by a good society and how individuals' and society's rights should be considered. Any economic policy issue must be interpreted within such a broad philosophical framework. Clearly, an introductory course in economics cannot introduce you to these broader philosophical and political issues. But it can point out to you their importance, and that economic policy arguments must fit within that broader context.

Economics provides the tools, not the rules, for policy.

This chapter was written to give you a sense of that broader context—economics provides the tools, not the rules, for policy. Cost/benefit analysis and the supply/demand framework are powerful tools for analyzing issues and coming up with policy conclusions. But to apply them successfully, they must be applied in context.

Applying economics is much more than muttering "supply and demand." Economics involves the thoughtful use of economic insights and empirical evidence.

Thomas Carlyle, who, as we saw in the introductory quotation to Chapter 4, argued that all you have to do is teach a parrot the words *supply* and *demand* to create an economist, was wrong. Economics involves the thoughtful use of economic insights and empirical evidence. If this chapter gave you a sense of the nature of that thoughtful application along with the core of economic reasoning, then it succeeded in its purpose.

Summary

- Economists differ because of different underlying value judgments, because empirical evidence is subject to different interpretations, and because their underlying models differ. *(LO23-1)*

- Value judgments inevitably work their way into policy advice, but good economists try to be objective. *(LO23-1)*

- Economists tend to agree on certain issues because their training is similar. Economists use models that focus on economic incentives and rationality. *(LO23-1)*

- The economic approach to analyzing issues is a cost/benefit approach. If the marginal benefits exceed the marginal costs, do it. If the marginal costs exceed the marginal benefits, don't do it. *(LO23-2)*

- People make choices every day that reveal the value that they place on their lives. The value of life is calculated by multiplying the inverse of the reduction in the probability of death by the amount individuals pay for that reduction. *(LO23-2)*

- Collecting and interpreting empirical evidence is difficult, which contributes to disagreements among economists. *(LO23-2)*

- The cost/benefit approach and the supply/demand framework deemphasize the possibility that market outcomes may be undesirable to society. *(LO23-2)*

- Three failures of market outcomes are: (1) failures due to distributional issues, (2) failures due to rationality problems of individuals, and (3) failures due to violations of inalienable rights. *(LO23-3)*

- Although an implicit assumption in most policy discussions is that the goal of policy is to maximize consumer and producer surplus, society does care about how that total surplus is distributed. *(LO23-3)*

- The supply/demand framework assumes that individuals are rational. Individuals are not always rational in practice. Their actions are swayed by addictions, advertising, and other pressures. *(LO23-3)*

- Some rights, called inalienable rights, cannot be bought and sold. What rights are inalienable are moral judgments that do not have to stand up to the same cost/benefit framework. *(LO23-3)*

- Economics provides the tools, not the rules, for policy. *(LO23-4)*

- Economics involves the thoughtful use of economic insights and empirical evidence. *(LO23-4)*

Key Terms

cost/benefit
   approach *(509)*
economic
   efficiency *(513)*

failure of market
   outcome *(513)*
Marxian (radical)
   model *(507)*

Pareto optimal
   policy *(506)*
public choice
   model *(507)*

rational *(515)*
sin tax *(515)*

Questions and Exercises

1. Could anyone object to a Pareto optimal policy? Why? *(LO23-1)*

2. Would it be wrong for economists to propose only Pareto optimal policies? *(LO23-1)*

3. Would all economists oppose price controls? Why or why not? *(LO23-1)*

4. In the early 1990s, the 14- to 17-year-old population fell because of low birth rates in the mid-1970s. Simultaneously the combined decisions of aging baby boomers to have kids resulted in an increase in the number of babies and hence in an increase in the number of parents needing baby-sitters. What effect will these two events likely have on: *(LO23-2)*
   a. The number of times parents go out without their children?
   b. The price of baby-sitters?
   c. The average age of baby-sitters?
   d. Should government require a minimum wage and age of baby sitters?

5. Should the buying and selling of body organs be allowed Why or why not? *(LO23-2)*

6. In the 1970s legislators had difficulty getting laws passed requiring people to wear seat belts. Now not only do most people wear seat belts, many cars have air bags too. Do people value their lives more today? *(LO23-2)*

7. Economist Steven D. Levitt estimated that, on average, for each additional criminal locked up in the United States, 15 crimes are eliminated. In addition, although it costs about $30,000 a year to keep a prisoner incarcerated, the average prisoner would have caused $53,900 worth of damage to society per year if free. If this estimate is correct, does it make economic sense to build more prisons? *(LO23-2)*

8. If one uses a willingness-to-pay measure in which life is valued at what people are willing to pay to avoid risks that might lead to death, the value of a U.S. citizen's life is $2.6 million, a Swede's life is worth $1.2 million, and a Portuguese's life is worth $20,000 (according to an article in the *Journal of Transport Economics and Policy*). *(LO23-2)*
   a. What policy implications does this value schedule have?

   b. Say you operate an airline. Should you spend more on safety precautions in the United States than you do in Portugal?

9. In "Valuing Reduced Risks to Children: The Case of Bicycle Safety Helmets," economists Robin R. Jenkins, Nicole Owens, and Lanelle Bembenek Wiggins estimate the value of the lives of children by using parents' willingness to purchase bicycle helmets. Wearing a helmet reduces the probability of death frombicycling by .0000041. The annualized cost of a helmet is $6.51. *(LO23-2)*
   a. What economic concept is their study based on?
   b. Assuming helmets are worn 100 percent of the time, what is the value of life parents place on a child as revealed by their purchase of a bicycle helmet?
   c. What happens to the value-of-life estimate if parents expect their children to wear the helmets less than 100 percent of the time?

10. What are three ways in which a well-functioning market might result in undesirable results? *(LO23-3)*

11. Until recently, China had a strict one-child-per-family policy. For cultural reasons, families favor boys and there are now many more male than female children born in China. How is this likely to affect who pays the cost of dates in China in 15 to 20 years? Explain. *(LO23-3)*

12. As organ transplants become more successful, scientists are working on ways to transplant animal organs to humans. Pigs are the odds-on favorites as "donors" since their organs are about the same size as human organs. *(LO23-3)*
   a. What would the development of such organ farms likely do to the price of pigs?
   b. If you were an economic adviser to the government, would you say that such a development would be Pareto optimal (for humans)?
   c. Currently, there is a black market in human organs. What would this development likely do to that market?

13. Why are economists' views of politicians cynical? *(LO23-4)*

14. Anthony Zielinski, a member of the Milwaukee Board of Supervisors, proposed that the county government sell the organs of dead welfare recipients to help pay off the welfare recipients' welfare costs and burial expenses. What was the likely effect of that proposal? Why? (LO23-4)

15. What is the basis for the opinions of public choice economists about government's ability to correct market failures? (LO23-4)

Questions from Alternative Perspectives

1. Even though a policy's stated goals may be laudable, its actual outcome can often cause serious problems.
   a. How much does it matter to an economist how closely a policy's goals match its outcome?
   b. How much does it matter to a politician? (Austrian)

2. In standard textbook economic analysis, institutions are often portrayed as creating market failures.
   a. Give an example of market failure caused by an institution not discussed in the text.
   b. What would a free market advocate likely say should be done about the failure?
   c. How would an Institutionalist likely respond? (Institutionalist)

3. The text deemphasizes the fact that people are social creatures who feel a need to conform to norms; Post-Keynesians emphasize norms.
   a. Who shapes these social norms?
   b. Does society as a whole benefit from these norms?
   c. How does the existence of these norms affect the analysis presented in the text about the way markets work? (Post-Keynesian)

4. Critics have pointed out a number of flaws in cost/benefit analysis: It assigns a dollar value to things that are not commodities such as human life; it places a price on public goods that we consume collectively (such as air quality); it downgrades the importance of the future through its discount rates; and it ignores distributional issues and issues of fairness.
   a. How reliable do you consider cost/benefit analysis as a policy analysis tool?
   b. Does cost/benefit analysis work better in some situations and worse in others? (Be sure to give some examples and to explain your overall position.) (Radical)

5. In his paper "Why Did the Economist Cross the Road? The Hierarchical Logic of Ethical and Economic Reasoning," economist Andrew Yuengert of Pepperdine University argues that "economists often give truncated justifications for their activities as economists out of fear that 'ethical' considerations will render their conclusions unscientific."
   a. Do you agree with this view?
   b. How might the presentation of economics change if economists did not have that fear? (Religious)

Issues to Ponder

1. In cost/benefit terms, explain your decision to take an economics course.

2. How much do you value your life in dollar terms? Are your decisions consistent with that valuation?

3. If someone offered you $1 million for one of your kidneys, would you sell it? Why or why not?

4. The technology is now developing so that road use can be priced by computer. A computer in the surface of the road picks up a signal from your car and automatically charges you for the use of the road.
   a. How could this technological change contribute to ending bottlenecks and rush-hour congestion? Demonstrate graphically.
   b. How will people likely try to get around the system?
   c. If people know when the prices will change, what will likely happen immediately before? How might this be avoided?

5. According to U.S. government statistics, the cost of averting a premature death differs among various regulations.

Car seat belt standards cost $100,000 per premature death avoided, while hazardous waste landfill disposal bans cost $4.2 trillion per premature death avoided. If these figures are correct, should neither, one, the other, or both of these regulations be implemented?

6. Technology will soon exist such that individuals can choose the sex of their offspring. Assume that technology has now arrived and that 70 percent of the individuals choose male offspring.
   a. What effect will that have on social institutions such as families?
   b. What effect will it have on dowries—payments made by the bride's family to the groom—which are still used in a number of developing countries?
   c. Why might an economist suggest that if 70 percent male is the expectation, families would be wise to have daughters rather than sons?

7. In a study of hospital births, the single most important prediction factor of the percentage of vaginal births as

opposed to Caesarean (C-section) births was ownership status of hospitals—whether they were for-profit or nonprofit.

a. Which had more C-sections, and why?

b. What implications about the health care debate can you draw from the above results?

c. How might the results change if the for-profit hospital received a fixed per-patient payment—as it would in a managed care system?

8. Why might an economist propose a policy that has little chance of adoption?

9. The number of auto accidents per year is the equivalent of a 737-plane crash every day. In the book *Why Not?* Yale professors Barry Nabalof and Ian Ayres suggest that computers that record driver behavior (similar to the black boxes in planes that record crashes) be installed in cars. In trials where such computers were installed in cars, crash rates fell by one-third.

a. If these boxes cost $100 each, and their installation reduces the probability of a crash that costs an average of $30,000 in damage to persons and vehicles, do such boxes make sense?

b. If they do make sense, what is a reason they are not installed?

c. In what cars will they likely be installed first?

d. What will their installation likely do to driving habits?

10. According to economists Henry Saffer of Kean University, Frank J. Chaloupka of the University of Illinois at Chicago, and Dhaval Dave of CUNY Graduate Center, using the criminal justice system to deter one person from using drugs costs $1,733, and using treatment centers costs $1,206.

a. Which of the two programs would you recommend?

b. What additional information do you need to determine whether either is worth pursuing?

c. The authors estimated that the social cost to society of a person using drugs is $897. Based on this information alone, should the government spend the money on drug control?

11. Michael Tanner and Stephen Moore of the Cato Institute recently calculated the hourly wage equivalent of welfare for a single mother with two children for each of the 50 United States. Their estimates ranged from $17.50 an hour for Hawaii to $5.33 in Mississippi. What do you suppose were their policy recommendations? What arguments can be made to oppose those prescriptions?

Answers to Margin Questions

1. I would respond that in the real world, Pareto optimal policies don't exist, and all real-world policies designed to make someone better off will make someone worse off. In making real-world policy judgments, one cannot avoid the difficult distributional and broader questions. It is those more difficult questions, which are value-laden, that make economic policy an art rather than a science. (*p. 506; LO23-1*)

2. A radical analysis of the labor market differs from the mainstream analysis in that it emphasizes the tensions among social classes. Thus, a radical analysis will likely see exploitation built into the institutional structure. Mainstream analysis is much more likely to take the institutional structure as given and not question it. (*p. 507; LO23-1*)

3. Oftentimes being "mean" in the short run can actually involve being "nice" in the long run. The reason is that often policy effects that are beneficial in the long run have short-run costs, and people focusing on those short-run costs see the policy as "mean." (*p. 508; LO23-1*)

4. To maximize utility, one would expect that the marginal value per dollar spent should be equal in all activities. Thus, if the table is correct, it would suggest that you should be far less concerned about premium tire usage and far more concerned about whether your house has smoke detectors or not. (*p. 509; LO23-1*)

5. Costs and benefits are ambiguous. Economists often disagree enormously on specific costs and benefits, or the costs and benefits are difficult or impossible to quantify. Thus, you should be extremely careful about using a cost/benefit analysis as anything more than an aid to your analysis of the situation. (*p. 511; LO23-2*)

6. Other things do not always remain constant. The more macro the issue, the more things are likely to change. These changes must be brought back into the analysis, which complicates things enormously. (*p. 512; LO23-2*)

7. False. Efficiency is achieving a goal as cheaply as possible. Stating efficiency as a goal does not make sense. (*p. 513; LO23-3*)

8. No. The cocaine addict may be responding to the cravings created from the addiction, and not from any rational desire for more cocaine. Society may not be better off. (*p. 515; LO23-3*)

9. False. Society may find that personal freedom is an inalienable right. Selling such a right may make society worse off. (*p. 516; LO23-3*)

10. Government makes a positive contribution by adjusting for market failures and failures of market outcomes. Government may make a negative contribution because government is swayed by short-run political pressures. (*p. 518; LO23-4*)

Glossary

A

Adverse Selection Problem   A problem that occurs when buyers and sellers have different amounts of information about the good for sale.

Agent-Based Computational Economic (ACE) Model   A culture dish approach to the study of economic phenomena in which agents are allowed to interact in a computationally constructed environment and the researcher observes the results of that interaction.

Annuity Rule   The present value of any annuity is the annual income it yields divided by the interest rate.

Antitrust Policy   The government's policy toward the competitive process.

Art of Economics   The application of the knowledge learned in positive economics to the achievement of the goals one has determined in normative economics.

Average Fixed Cost   Fixed cost divided by quantity produced.

Average Product   Output per worker.

Average Total Cost   Total cost divided by the quantity produced.

Average Variable Cost   Variable cost divided by quantity produced.

B

Backward Induction   You begin with a desired outcome and then determine the decisions that will lead you to that outcome.

Balance of Trade   The difference between the value of the goods and services a country imports and the value of the goods and services it exports.

Bar Graph   A graph where the area under each point is filled in to look like a bar.

Barriers to Entry   Social, political, or economic impediments that prevent firms from entering a market.

Behavioral Economic Policy   Economic policy based upon models using behavioral economic building blocks that take into account people's predictable irrational behavior.

Behavioral Economics   Microeconomic analysis that uses a broader set of building blocks than rationality and self-interest used in traditional economics. The study of economic choice that is based on realistic psychological foundations.

Bilateral Monopoly   A market with only a single seller and a single buyer.

Budget Constraint   A curve that shows us the various combinations of goods an individual can buy with a given amount of money.

B

Business   A private producing unit in our society.

Butterfly Effect Model   A model in which a small change causes a large effect.

C

Capitalism   An economic system based on the market in which the ownership of the means of production resides with a small group of individuals called capitalists.

Cartel   A combination of firms that acts as if it were a single firm.

Cartel Model of Oligopoly   A model that assumes that oligopolies act as if they were monopolists that have assigned output quotas to individual member firms of the oligopoly so that total output is consistent with joint profit maximization.

Cheap Talk   Communication that occurs before a game is played that carries no cost and is backed up only by trust, and not any enforceable agreement.

Choice Architecture   The context in which decisions are presented.

Closed Shop   A firm where unions control the hiring.

Coefficient of Determination   A measure of the proportion of the variability in the data that is accounted for by the statistical model.

Comparable Worth Laws   Laws mandating comparable pay for comparable work.

Comparative Advantage   The ability to be better suited to the production of one good than to the production of another good.

Complements   Goods that are used in conjunction with other goods.

Concentration Ratio   The value of sales by the top firms of an industry stated as a percentage of total industry sales.

Conspicuous Consumption   The consumption of goods not for one's direct pleasure, but simply to show off to others.

Constant Returns to Scale   A situation in which long-run average total costs do not change with an increase in output.

Consumer Sovereignty   The principle that the consumer's wishes determine what's produced.

Consumer Surplus   The difference between what consumers would have been willing to pay and what they actually pay. Also, the value the consumer gets from buying a product less its price.

Contestable Market Model   A model of oligopoly in which barriers to entry and barriers to exit, not the structure of the market, determine a firm's price and output decisions.

Contractual Legal System   The set of laws that govern economic behavior.

Cooperative Game   A game in which players can form coalitions and can enforce the will of the coalition on its members.

Coordinate System   A two-dimensional space in which one point represents two numbers.

Coordination Mechanisms   Methods of coordinating people's wants with other people's desires.

Corporate Takeover   An action in which another firm or a group of individuals issues a tender offer (that is, offers to buy up the stock of a company) to gain control and to install its own managers.

Corporation   A business that is treated as a person, legally owned by its stockholders. Its stockholders are not liable for the actions of the corporate "person."

Cost Minimization Condition   A situation where the ratio of marginal product to the price of an input is equal for all inputs.

Cost/Benefit Approach   Assigning costs and benefits, and making decisions on the basis of the relevant costs and benefits.

Cross-Price Elasticity of Demand   The percentage change in demand divided by the percentage change in the price of a related good.

Currency Appreciation   A change in the exchange rate so that one currency buys more units of a foreign currency.

Currency Depreciation   A change in the exchange rate so that one currency buys fewer units of a foreign currency.

D

Deadweight Loss   The loss of consumer and producer surplus from a tax.

Deductive Approach   An approach that begins with certain self-evident principles from which implications are deduced (logically determined).

Demand   A schedule of quantities of a good that will be bought per unit of time at various prices, other things constant.

Demand Curve   The graphic representation of the relationship between price and quantity demanded.

Demerit Good or Activity   A good or activity that government believes is bad for people even though they choose to use the good or engage in the activity.

Depreciation   A measure of the decline in value of an asset that occurs over time through use.

Derived Demand   The demand for factors of production by firms, which depends on consumers' demands.

Derived Demand Curve for Labor   A curve that shows the maximum amount of labor, measured in labor hours, that a firm will hire.

Direct Regulation   A program in which the amount of a good people are allowed to use is directly limited by the government.

Direct Relationship   A relationship in which when one variable goes up, the other goes up too.

Diseconomies of Scale   Situation when the long-run average total costs increase as output increases.

Dominant Strategy   A strategy that is preferred by a player regardless of the opponent's move.

Duopoly   An oligopoly with only two firms.

Dynamic Efficiency   A market's ability to promote cost-reducing or product-enhancing technological change.

E

Econometrics   The statistical analysis of economic data.

Economic Decision Rule   If the marginal benefits of doing something exceed the marginal costs, do it. If the marginal costs of doing something exceed the marginal benefits, don't do it.

Economic Efficiency   Achieving a goal at the lowest possible cost.

Economic Engineering   Economics devoted not only to studying markets, but also to designing markets and other coordinating mechanisms.

Economic Force   The necessary reaction to scarcity.

Economic Model   A framework that places the generalized insights of a theory in a more specific contextual setting.

Economic Policy   An action (or inaction) taken by government to influence economic actions.

Economic Principle   A commonly held economic insight stated as a law or general assumption.

Economic Profit   Explicit and implicit revenue minus explicit and implicit cost. Also, a return on entrepreneurship above and beyond normal profits.

Economically Efficient   A method of production that produces a given level of output at the lowest possible cost.

Economics   The study of how human beings coordinate their wants and desires, given the decision-making mechanisms, social customs, and political realities of the society.

Economies of Scale   Situation when long-run average total costs decrease as output increases.

Economies of Scope   Situation when the costs of producing products are interdependent so that it's less costly for a firm to produce a good when it's already producing another.

Efficiency   Achieving a goal as cheaply as possible. Also: Using as few inputs as possible.

Efficiency Wages   Wages paid above the going-market wage to keep workers happy and productive.

Efficient   Achieving a goal at the lowest cost in total resources without consideration as to who pays those costs.

Effluent Fees   Charges imposed by government on the level of pollution created.

Elastic   The percentage change in quantity is greater than the percentage change in price ($E > 1$).

Embargo   A total restriction on the import or export of a good.

Empirical Model   A model that statistically discovers a pattern in the data.

Endowment Effects   People value something more just because they have it.

Enlightened Self-Interest   People care about other people as well as themselves.

Entrepreneur   An individual who sees an opportunity to sell an item at a price higher than the average cost of producing it.

Entrepreneurship   The ability to organize and get something done. Also: Labor services that involve high degrees of organizational skills, concern, oversight responsibility, and creativity.

Equilibrium   A concept in which opposing dynamic forces cancel each other out.

Equilibrium Price   The price toward which the invisible hand drives the market.

Equilibrium Quantity   The amount bought and sold at the equilibrium price.

Excess Demand   Situation when quantity demanded is greater than quantity supplied.

Excess Supply   Situation when quantity supplied is greater than quantity demanded.

Exchange Rate   The price of one country's currency in terms of another currency.

Excise Tax   A tax that is levied on a specific good.

Experimental Economics   A branch of economics that studies the economy through controlled laboratory experiments.

Externality   An effect of a decision on a third party not taken into account by the decision maker.

F

Failure of Market Outcome   A situation in which, even though the market is functioning properly (there are no market failures), it is not achieving society's goals.

Fallacy of Composition   The false assumption that what is true for a part will also be true for the whole.

Firm   An economic institution that transforms factors of production into goods and services.

Fixed Costs   Costs that are spent and cannot be changed in the period of time under consideration.

Framing Effect   The tendency of people to base their choices on how the choice is presented.

Free Rider Problem   Individuals' unwillingness to share in the cost of a public good.

Free Trade Association   A group of countries that have reduced or eliminated trade barriers among themselves.

G

Game Theory   Formal economic reasoning applied to situations in which decisions are interdependent.

General Agreement on Tariffs and Trade (GATT)   A regular international conference to reduce trade barriers held from 1947 to 1995. It has been replaced by the World Trade Organization (WTO).

General Rule of Political Economy   When small groups are helped by a government action and large groups are hurt by that same action, the small group tends to lobby far more effectively than the large group.

Global Corporation   A corporation with substantial operations on both the production and sales sides in more than one country.

Globalization   The increasing integration of economies, cultures, and institutions across the world.

Good/Bad Paradox   The phenomenon of doing poorly because you're doing well.

Government Failure   A situation in which the government intervention in the market to improve market failure actually makes the situation worse.

Grandfather   To pass a law affecting a specific group but providing that those in the group before the law was passed are exempt from some provisions of the law.

Graph   A picture of points in a coordinate system in which points denote relationships between numbers.

H

Herfindahl Index   An index of market concentration calculated by adding the squared value of the individual market shares of all firms in the industry.

Heuristic Model   A model that is expressed informally in words.

Households   Groups of individuals living together and making joint decisions.

I

Implicit Collusion   A type of collusion in which multiple firms make the same pricing decisions even though they have not explicitly consulted with one another.

Incentive Compatibility Problem   A problem in which the incentive facing the decision maker does not match the incentive needed for the mechanism to achieve its desired ends.

Incentive-Compatible Contract A contract in which the incentives of each of the two parties to the contract are made to correspond as closely as possible.

Incentive Effect How much a person will change his or her hours worked in response to a change in the wage rate.

Income Payments received plus or minus changes in the value of a person's assets in a specified time period.

Income Effect The reduction in quantity demanded because price increases make us poorer.

Income Elasticity of Demand The percentage change in demand divided by the percentage change in income.

Indifference Curve A curve that shows combinations of goods among which an individual is indifferent.

Indivisible Setup Cost The cost of an indivisible input for which a certain minimum amount of production must be undertaken before the input becomes economically feasible to use.

Inductive Approach An approach to understanding a problem or question in which understanding is developed empirically from statistically analyzing what is observed in the data.

Industrial Revolution A time when technology and machines rapidly modernized industrial production and mass-produced goods replaced handmade goods.

Inefficiency Getting less output from inputs that, if devoted to some other activity, would produce more output.

Inefficient Achieving a goal in a more costly manner than necessary.

Inelastic The percentage change in quantity is less than the percentage change in price ($E < 1$).

Infant Industry Argument The argument that with initial protection, an industry will be able to become competitive.

Inferior Good Good whose consumption decreases when income increases.

Inherent Comparative Advantage Comparative advantage that is based on factors that are relatively unchangeable.

Institutions The formal and informal rules that constrain human behavior.

Interest The income paid to savers—individuals who produce now but don't consume now.

Interpolation Assumption The assumption that the relationship between variables is the same between points as it is at the points.

Inverse Relationship A relationship between two variables in which when one goes up, the other goes down.

Invisible Hand The price mechanism; the rise and fall of prices that guide our actions in a market.

Invisible Hand Theorem A market economy, through the price mechanism, will tend to allocate resources efficiently.

Isocost Line A line that represents alternative combinations of factors of production that have the same costs.

Isoquant Curve A curve that represents combinations of factors of production that result in equal amounts of output.

Isoquant Map A set of isoquant curves that show technically efficient combinations of inputs that can produce different levels of output.

J–K

Judgment by Performance To judge the competitiveness of markets by the performance (behavior) of firms in that market.

Judgment by Structure To judge the competitiveness of markets by the structure of the industry.

L

Labor Market The factor market in which individuals supply labor services for wages to other individuals and to firms that need (demand) labor services.

Labor Productivity The average output per worker.

Laissez-Faire An economic policy of leaving the coordination of individuals' actions to the market.

Land Bank Program A program in which government supports prices by giving farmers economic incentives to reduce supply.

Law of Demand Quantity demanded rises as price falls, other things constant. Also can be stated as: Quantity demanded falls as price rises, other things constant.

Law of Diminishing Marginal Productivity As more and more of a variable input is added to an existing fixed input, eventually the additional output one gets from that additional input is going to fall.

Law of Diminishing Marginal Rate of Substitution As you get more and more of a good, if some of that good is taken away, then the marginal addition of another good you need to remain on the same indifference curve gets less and less.

Law of One Price The wages of workers in one country will not differ significantly from the wages of (equal) workers in another institutionally similar country.

Law of Supply Quantity supplied rises as price rises, other things constant. Also can be stated as: Quantity supplied falls as price falls, other things constant.

Lazy Monopolist A monopolist that does not push for efficiency, but merely enjoys the position it is already in.

Learning by Doing As we do something, we learn what works and what doesn't, and over time we become more proficient at it.

Libertarian Paternalistic Policy A policy that leaves people free to choose, but nonetheless guides them toward a choice that a paternalistic observer would see as good for them.

Line Graph   A graph where the data are connected by a continuous line.

Linear Curve   A curve that is drawn as a straight line.

Long-Run Decision   A decision in which a firm chooses among all possible production techniques.

Lorenz Curve   A geometric representation of the share distribution of income among families in a given country at a given time.

Luxury   A good that has an income elasticity greater than 1.

M

Macroeconomic Externality   An externality that affects the levels of unemployment, inflation, or growth in the economy as a whole.

Macroeconomics   The study of the economy as a whole, which includes inflation, unemployment, business cycles, and growth.

Marginal Benefit   Additional benefit above the benefits already derived.

Marginal Cost (*MC*)   Additional cost over and above the costs already incurred. Also: Increase (decrease) in total cost from increasing (or decreasing) the level of output by one unit. Also: The change in total cost associated with a change in quantity.

Marginal Factor Cost   The additional cost to a firm of hiring another worker.

Marginal Physical Product (*MPP*)   The additional units of output that hiring an additional worker will bring about.

Marginal Product   The additional output that will be forthcoming from an additional worker, other inputs constant.

Marginal Productivity Theory   Factors are paid their marginal revenue product (what they contribute at the margin to revenue).

Marginal Rate of Substitution   The rate at which one good must be added when the other is taken away to keep the individual indifferent between the two combinations. Also: The rate at which one factor must be added to compensate for the loss of another factor to keep output constant.

Marginal Revenue (*MR*)   The change in total revenue associated with a change in quantity.

Marginal Revenue Product (*MRP*)   The marginal revenue a firm expects to earn from selling an additional worker's output.

Marginal Social Benefit   The marginal private benefit of consuming a good plus the benefits of the positive externalities resulting from consuming that good.

Marginal Social Cost   The marginal private costs of production plus the cost of the negative externalities associated with that production.

Marginal Utility   The satisfaction one gets from consuming one additional unit of a product above and beyond what one has consumed up to that point.

Market Demand Curve   The horizontal sum of all individual demand curves.

Market Economy   An economic system based on private property and the market in which, in principle, individuals decide how, what, and for whom to produce.

Market Failure   A situation in which the invisible hand pushes in such a way that individual decisions do not lead to socially desirable outcomes.

Market Force   An economic force that is given relatively free rein by society to work through the market.

Market Incentive Plan   A plan requiring market participants to certify that they have reduced total consumption—not necessarily their own individual consumption—by a specified amount.

Market Supply Curve   The horizontal sum of all individual supply curves. Also: Horizontal sum of all the firms' marginal cost curves, taking account of any changes in input prices that might occur.

Marxian (Radical) Model   A model that focuses on equitable distribution of power, rights, and income among social classes.

Mechanism Design   Identifying a goal and then designing a mechanism such as a market, social system, or contract to achieve that end.

Medicare   A multibillion-dollar medical insurance system.

Merit Good or Activity   A good or activity that government believes is good for you, even though you may not choose to consume the good or engage in the activity.

Microeconomics   The study of individual choice, and how that choice is influenced by economic forces.

Minimum Efficient Level of Production   The amount of production that spreads setup costs out sufficiently for a firm to undertake production profitably.

Minimum Wage Law   A law specifying the lowest wage a firm can legally pay an employee.

Mixed Strategy   A strategy of choosing randomly among moves.

Model   A simplified representation of the problem or question that captures the essential issues.

Modern Economists   Economists who are willing to use a wider range of models than did earlier economists.

Monitoring Costs   Costs incurred by the organizer of production in seeing to it that the employees do what they're supposed to do.

Monitoring Problem   The need to oversee employees to ensure that their actions are in the best interest of the firm.

Monopolistic Competition   A market structure in which many firms sell differentiated products; there are few barriers to entry.

Monopoly A market structure in which one firm makes up the entire market.

Monopsony A market in which a single firm is the only buyer.

Most-Favored Nation A country that will be charged as low a tariff on its exports as any other country.

Movement along a Demand Curve The graphical representation of the effect of a change in price on the quantity demanded.

Movement along a Supply Curve The graphical representation of the effect of a change in price on the quantity supplied.

N

Nash Equilibrium A set of strategies for each player in the game in which no player can improve his or her payoff by changing strategy unilaterally.

Natural Experiment A naturally occurring event that approximates a controlled experiment where something has changed in one place but has not changed somewhere else. That is, an event created by nature that can serve as an experiment.

Natural Monopoly An industry in which a single firm can produce at a lower cost than can two or more firms. Also: An industry in which significant economies of scale make the existence of more than one firm inefficient.

Necessity A good that has an income elasticity less than 1.

Negative Externality The adverse effect of a decision on others not taken into account by the decision maker. When the effects of a decision not taken into account by the decision maker are detrimental to others.

Network Externality The phenomenon that the greater use of a product increases the benefit of that product to everyone.

Noncooperative Game A game in which each player is out for him- or herself and agreements are either not possible or not enforceable.

Nonlinear Curve A curve that is drawn as a curved line.

Nonrecourse Loan Program A program in which government "buys" goods in the form of collateral on defaulting loans.

Normal Good A good whose consumption increases with an increase in income.

Normal Profit The amount the owners of business would have received in the next-best alternative. Also: Payments to entrepreneurs as the return on their risk taking.

Normative Economics The study of what the goals of the economy should be.

North American Industry Classification System (NAICS) An industry classification that categorizes industries by type of economic activity and groups firms with like production processes.

Nudge A deliberate design of the choice architecture that alters people's behavior in predictably positive ways.

Nudge Policy Policy in which government structures choices facing people so that they are free to choose what they want, but also more likely to choose what is best for them.

O

Oligopoly A market structure in which there are only a few firms and firms explicitly take other firms' likely response into account; there are often significant barriers to entry.

Opportunity Cost The benefit you might have gained from choosing the next-best alternative.

Optimal Policy A policy in which the marginal cost of undertaking the policy equals the marginal benefit of that policy.

P

Pareto Optimal Policy A policy that benefits some people and hurts no one.

Partnership A business with two or more owners.

Patent The legal protection of a technical innovation that gives the person holding it sole right to use that innovation. (Note: A patent is good for only a limited time.)

Path-Dependent Model A model in which the path to equilibrium affects the equilibrium.

Payoff Matrix A table that shows the outcome of every choice by every player, given the possible choices of all other players.

Perfectly Competitive Market A market in which economic forces operate unimpeded.

Perfectly Elastic Quantity responds enormously to changes in price ($E = \infty$).

Perfectly Inelastic Quantity does not respond at all to changes in price ($E = 0$).

Pie Chart A circle divided into "slices of pie," where the undivided pie represents the total amount and the pie slices reflect the percentage of the whole pie that the various components make up.

Positive Economics The study of what is and how the economy works.

Positive Externality When the effects of a decision not taken into account by the decision maker are beneficial to others.

Poverty Threshold The income below which a family is considered to live in poverty.

Precepts Policy rules that conclude that a particular course of action is preferable.

Precommitment Strategy A strategy in which people consciously place limitations on their future actions, thereby limiting their choices.

Present Value A method of translating a flow of future income or savings into its current worth.

Price Ceiling A government-imposed limit on how high a price can be charged. In other words, a government-set price below the market equilibrium price.

Price-Discriminate To charge different prices to different individuals or groups of individuals.

Price Elasticity of Demand The percentage change in quantity demanded divided by the percentage change in price.

Price Elasticity of Supply The percentage change in quantity supplied divided by the percentage change in price.

Price Floor A government-imposed limit on how low a price can be charged. In other words, a government-set price above equilibrium price.

Price Stabilization Program A program designed to eliminate short-run fluctuations in prices, while allowing prices to follow their long-run trend line.

Price Support Program A program designed to maintain prices at higher levels than the market prices.

Price Taker A firm or individual who takes the price determined by supply and demand as given.

Principle of Diminishing Marginal Utility As you consume more of a good, after some point, the marginal utility received from each additional unit of a good decreases with each additional unit consumed, other things equal.

Principle of Rational Choice Spend your money on those goods that give you the most marginal utility (*MU*) per dollar.

Prisoner's Dilemma A well-known game that demonstrates the difficulty of cooperative behavior in certain circumstances.

Private Good A good that, when consumed by one individual, cannot be consumed by another individual.

Private Property Right Control a private individual or firm has over an asset.

Producer Surplus Price the producer sells a product for less the cost of producing it.

Production The transformation of factors into goods and services.

Production Function The relationship between the inputs (factors of production) and outputs.

Production Possibility Curve (PPC) A curve measuring the maximum combination of outputs that can be obtained from a given number of inputs.

Production Possibility Table A table that lists a choice's opportunity costs by summarizing what alternative outputs can be achieved with given inputs.

Production Table A table showing the output resulting from various combinations of factors of production or inputs.

Productive Efficiency Achieving as much output as possible from a given amount of inputs or resources.

Profit What's left over from total revenues after all the appropriate costs have been subtracted. That is, Total revenue − Total cost. Also: A return on entrepreneurial activity and risk taking.

Profit-Maximizing Condition $MR = MC = P$.

Progressive Tax A tax whose rates increase as a person's income increases.

Property Rights The rights given to people to use specified property as they see fit.

Proportional Tax A tax whose rates are constant at all income levels, no matter what a taxpayer's total annual income is.

Public Assistance Means-tested social programs targeted to the poor and providing financial, nutritional, medical, and housing assistance.

Public Choice Economist An economist who integrates an economic analysis of politics with an analysis of the economy.

Public Choice Model A model that focuses on economic incentives as applied to politicians.

Public Good A good that if supplied to one person must be supplied to all and whose consumption by one individual does not prevent its consumption by another individual. That is, a good that is nonexclusive and nonrival.

Purposeful Behavior Behavior reflecting reasoned but not necessarily rational judgment.

Push Policy A regulatory or tax policy to get firms or individuals to use "appropriate" nudges.

Q

Quantity Demanded A specific amount that will be demanded per unit of time at a specific price, other things constant.

Quantity Supplied A specific amount that will be supplied at a specific price, other things constant.

Quasi Rent Any payment to a resource above the amount that the resource would receive in its next-best use.

Quota A quantity limit placed on imports.

R

Rational An adjective used to describe behavior individuals undertake in their own best interest.

Regression Model An empirical model in which one set of variables is statistically related to another.

Regressive Tax A tax whose rates decrease as income rises.

Regulatory Trade Restrictions Government-imposed procedural rules that limit imports.

Rent The income from a factor of production that is in fixed supply.

Rent Control A price ceiling on rents, set by government.

Rent Seeking The restricting of supply in order to increase the price suppliers receive.

Rent-Seeking Activity Activity designed to transfer surplus from one group to another.

Resource Curse The paradox that countries with an abundance of resources tend to have lower economic growth and more unemployment than countries with fewer natural resources.

Reverse Engineering The process of a firm buying other firms' products, disassembling them, figuring out what's special about them, and then copying them within the limits of the law.

Rule of 72 The number of years needed for a certain amount to double in value is equal to 72 divided by the rate of interest.

S

Scarcity The goods available are too few to satisfy individuals' desires.

Screening An action taken by an uninformed party that induces the informed party to reveal information.

Screening Question A question structured in a way to reveal strategic information about the person who answers.

Self-Confirming Equilibrium An equilibrium in a model in which people's beliefs become self-fulfilling.

Sequential Game A game where players make decisions one after another, so one player responds to the known decisions of other players.

Shadow Price A price that isn't paid directly, but instead is paid in terms of opportunity cost borne by the demander, and thus determines his or her action indirectly.

Share Distribution of Income The relative division of total income among income groups.

Shift in Demand The graphical representation of the effect of anything other than price on demand.

Shift in Supply The graphical representation of the effect of a change in a factor other than price on supply.

Short-Run Decision A decision in which the firm is constrained in regard to what production decisions it can make.

Shutdown Point The point below which the firm will be better off if it temporarily shuts down than it will if it stays in business.

Signaling An action taken by an informed party that reveals information to an uninformed party and thereby partially offsets adverse selection.

Simultaneous Move Game A game where players make their decisions at the same time as other players without knowing what choice the other players have made.

Sin Tax A tax that discourages activities society believes are harmful (sinful).

Slope The change in the value on the vertical axis divided by the change in the value on the horizontal axis.

Social Security System A social insurance program that provides financial benefits to the elderly and disabled and to their eligible dependents and/or survivors.

Socialism An economic system based on individuals' goodwill toward others, not on their own self-interest, and in which, in principle, society decides what, how, and for whom to produce.

Sole Proprietorship A business that has only one owner.

Sovereign Wealth Funds Investment funds held by governments.

Status Quo Bias An individual's actions are very much influenced by what the current situation is, even when that reasonably does not seem to be very important to the decision.

Stock A certificate of ownership in a company.

Strategic Bargaining Demanding a larger share of the gains from trade than you can reasonably expect.

Strategic Decision Making Taking explicit account of a rival's expected response to a decision you are making.

Strategic Trade Policy Threatening to implement tariffs to bring about a reduction in tariffs or some other concession from the other country.

Substitute A good that can be used in place of another good.

Substitution Effect The reduction in quantity demanded because relative price has risen.

Sunk Cost Cost that has already been incurred and cannot be recovered.

Supplemental Security Income (SSI) A federal program that pays benefits, based on need, to the elderly, blind, and disabled.

Supply A schedule of quantities a seller is willing to sell per unit of time at various prices, other things constant.

Supply Curve A graphical representation of the relationship between price and quantity supplied.

T

Tariff An excise tax on an imported (internationally traded) good.

Tax Incentive Program A program using a tax to create incentives for individuals to structure their activities in a way that is consistent with the desired ends.

Team Spirit The feelings of friendship and being part of a team that bring out people's best efforts.

Technical Efficiency   A situation in which as few inputs as possible are used to produce a given output.

Technological Change   An increase in the range of production techniques that leads to more efficient ways of producing goods as well as the production of new and better goods.

Technological Development   The discovery of new or improved products or methods of production.

Technological Lock-In   The prior use of a technology makes the adoption of subsequent technologies difficult.

Theorems   Propositions that are logically true based on the assumptions in a model.

Third-Party-Payer Market   A market in which the person who receives the good differs from the person paying for the good.

Total Cost   The explicit payments to the factors of production plus the opportunity cost of the factors provided by the owners of the firm.

Total Revenue   The amount a firm receives for selling its product or service plus any increase in the value of the assets owned by the firm.

Total Utility   The total satisfaction one gets from consuming a product.

Trade Adjustment Assistance Programs   Programs designed to compensate losers for reductions in trade restrictions.

Trade Deficit   When imports exceed exports.

Trade Surplus   When exports exceed imports.

Traditional Economists   Economists who study the logical implications of rationality and self-interest in relatively simple algebraic or graphical models such as the supply and demand model.

Transferable Comparative Advantage   Comparative advantage based on factors that can change relatively easily.

U

Ultimatum Game   A game in which the person only gets the money if the other person accepts the offer. If the second person does not accept, they both get nothing.

Unemployment Compensation   Short-term financial assistance, regardless of need, to eligible individuals who are temporarily out of work.

Union Shop   A firm in which all workers must join the union.

Unit Elastic   The percentage change in quantity is equal to the percentage change in price ($E = 1$).

Utility   The pleasure or satisfaction that one expects to get from consuming a good or service.

Utility-Maximizing Rule   Utility is maximized when the ratios of the marginal utility to price of two goods are equal.

V

Value of Marginal Product (*VMP*)   An additional worker's marginal physical product multiplied by the price at which the firm could sell that additional product.

Variable Costs   Costs that change as output changes.

Vickrey Auction   A sealed-bid auction where the highest bidder wins but pays the price bid by the next-highest bidder.

W

Wealth   The value of the things individuals own less the value of what they owe.

Welfare Loss Triangle   A geometric representation of the welfare cost in terms of misallocated resources caused by a deviation from a supply/demand equilibrium.

X–Y

X-inefficiency   The underperformance of a firm that has a monopoly position. The firm operates far less efficiently than it could technically.

Z

Zoning Laws   Laws that set limits on the use of one's property.

A

Ads (noun)   Short for "advertisements."

Ain't (verb)   An ungrammatical form of "isn't," sometimes used to emphasize a point although the speaker knows that "isn't" is the correct form.

All the Rage (descriptive phrase)   Extremely popular, but the popularity is likely to be transitory.

American League (name of an organization)   An association of baseball teams. The United States has two baseball associations—the other is the National League.

Andy Warhol (proper name)   American artist who flourished in the period 1960–1980. He was immensely popular and successful with art critics and the intelligentsia, but, above all, he gained worldwide recognition in the same way and of the same quality as movie stars and athletes do. His renown has continued even after his death.

Automatic Pilot (noun)   To be on automatic pilot is to be acting without thinking.

B

Baby Boom (noun)   Any period when more than the statistically predicted number of babies are born. Originally referred to a specific group: those born in the years 1945–1964.

Baby Boomers (descriptive phrase)   Americans born in the years 1945 through 1964. An enormous and influential group of people whose large number is attributed to the "boom" in babies that occurred when military personnel, many of whom had been away from home for four or five years, were discharged from military service after the end of World War II.

Backfire (verb)   To injure a person or entity who intended to inflict injury.

Balloon (verb)   To expand enormously and suddenly.

Barista (noun)   The name given to a worker at a "high-class" coffee shop.

Bases on Balls (descriptive phrase)   A strategy in the game of baseball. If a pitcher throws a long enough succession of defective throws, the batter gets to run—or walk—to first base without having hit any balls.

Bean (noun)   A person's head; also a person's mind or intellectual ability. ("Bean" is American slang for "head.")

Beanball (noun)   A ball thrown with the intention of hitting the opponent on the head.

Beluga Caviar (noun)   The best, most expensive, caviar.

Benchmark (noun)   A point of reference from which measurement of any sort may be made.

Better Mousetrap (noun)   Comes from the proverb "Invent a better mousetrap and the world will beat a path to your door."

Bidding (or Bid) (verb sometimes used as a noun)   Has two different meanings. (1) Making an offer, or a series of offers, to compete with others who are making offers. Also the offer itself. (2) Ordering or asking a person to take a specified action.

Big Bucks (noun)   Really, really large sum of money.

Big Mac (proper noun)   Brand name of a kind of hamburger sold at McDonald's restaurants.

Bind (noun)   To "be in a bind" means to be in a situation where one is forced to make a difficult decision one does not want to make—where any decision seems as if it would be wrong, or at least undesirable.

Blow Off (verb)   To treat as inconsequential; to deal superficially with something.

Blue-Collar (adjective)   Description of manufacturing work, contrasted with white-collar or administrative work.

Blue-Collar America (noun)   That portion of the U.S. population that works in manufacturing and in manual labor jobs.

Booming (adjective)   Being extraordinarily and quickly successful.

Boost (verb and noun)   To give a sudden impetus, or boost, to something or someone.

Boston Red Sox (compound noun)   A U.S. baseball team.

Botched (adjective)   Operated badly; spoiled.

Brick-and-Mortar (adjective)   A company that has a physical presence such as a building. Brick-and-mortar contrasts with companies with a presence only on the Internet.

Bring Home (verb)   To emphasize or convince.

Bronco Bull   A bull ridden in a rodeo. The rider's objective is to stay on the bull until he wrestles it to the ground or is thrown off.

Buffalo (adjective, as used in this book)   "Buffalo chicken wings" are a variety of tempting food developed in, and hence associated with, the city of Buffalo. (Not all chicken wings are Buffalo chicken wings.)

Busch Stadium (name of a stadium)   Anheuser-Busch is a firm that produces widely consumed brands of beer. Its home offices are in St. Louis. It bought naming rights to Busch Stadium in St. Louis, MO.

C

Cachet (noun)   Prestige, distinction, high quality. This word is borrowed from French and is pronounced "ca-SHAY."

Call (verb)   In sports refereeing, one meaning of "to call" is for the referee to announce his or her decision on a specific point.

Calvin Coolidge (proper name)   President of the United States 1923–1929.

Catch (noun)   A proviso; an unexpected complication.

Central Park West (proper noun)   A fashionable and expensive street in New York City.

CEO (noun)   Abbreviation of "chief executive officer."

Charade (noun)   A pretense, usually designed to convince someone that you are doing something that you are definitely not doing.

Chit (noun)   Type of IOU (see IOU) or coupon with a designated value that can be turned in toward the purchase or acquisition of some item.

Chump Change (noun)   Insignificant amount of money earned by or paid to a person who is not alert enough to realize that more money could rather easily be earned.

Clear-cut (adjective)   Precisely defined.

Clip Coupons (verb)   To cut coupons out of newspapers and magazines. The coupons give you a discount on the price of the item when you present the item and the coupon at the cashier's counter in a store. It can also mean collecting interest on bonds. (In earlier times, bonds had coupons attached. The holders clipped them and sent them in to the bond issuer to collect the bond's interest.)

Clout (noun)   Influence or power.

Coined (verb)   Invented or originated.

Coldhearted (adjective)   Without any sympathy; aloof; inhuman.

Cookie Monster (proper noun)   Character in the television show *Sesame Street.* (Also see "Elmo.")

Co-opted (adjective)   Overwhelmed.

Cornrows (noun)   Hair style in which hair is braided in shallow, narrow rows over the entire head.

Corvette (noun)   A type of expensive sports car.

Costco (proper noun)   Name of a chain of big stores selling groceries and other items at a sharp discount. Usually the items are packaged in large quantities—for example, 50-pound bags of flour.

Couch (verb)   To construct and present an argument.

Crack (noun)   A strong form of cocaine.

D

Deadbeat (noun)   Lazy person who has no ambition, no money, and no prospects.

Deadweight (noun)   Literally, the unrelieved weight of any inert mass (think of carrying a sack of bricks); hence, any oppressive burden.

Decent (adjective)   One of its specialized meanings is "of high quality."

Doodle (noun and verb)   Idle scribbles, usually nonrepresentational and usually made while actively thinking about something else, such as during a phone conversation or sitting in a class.

Doritos (proper noun)   Brand name of a type of snack in chip form. The label lists its principal ingredient as corn, but it contains at least 30 other ingredients, many of them chemical.

Dr. Seuss Book (noun)   A book by a favorite U.S. children's author.

Drop in the Bucket (noun)   Insignificant quantity compared to the total amount available.

Dyed-in-the-Wool (adjective)   Irretrievably convinced of the value of a particular course of action or of the truth of an opinion. Literally, wool that is dyed after it is shorn from the sheep but before it is spun into thread.

E

Elmo (proper noun)   Character in the television show *Sesame Street.* (Also see "Cookie Monster.")

'Em (pronoun)   Careless way of pronouncing "them." Written out, it reproduces the sound the speaker is making.

Emotional Quotient (EQ) (noun)   The ability to relate to others. It is a play on the concept IQ or intelligence quotient. There is no EQ measure or test.

Establishment (noun and adjective)   Noun: the prevailing theory or practice. Adjective: something that is used by people whose views prevail over other people's views.

Eureka Moment (noun)   "Eureka" is Greek for "I have found it!" Means having a sudden insight. Aristophanes is said to have cried out "Eureka," jumped out of his bath, and run down the street crying "Eureka!" when it struck him suddenly that the weight of water displaced by a submerged body is the same as the weight of the body being displaced.

F

Fake (verb)   To fake is to pretend or deceive; to try to make people believe that you know what you're doing or talking about when you don't know or aren't sure.

Fiberglas (proper noun)   A brand of insulating material.

Fire (verb)   To discharge an employee permanently. It's different from "laying off" an employee, an action taken when a temporary situation makes the employee superfluous, but the employer expects to take the employee back when the temporary situation is over.

Fix (verb)   To prepare, as in "fixing a meal." This is only one of the multiplicity of meanings of this verb.

Fleeting (adverb)   This word's usage is elegant and correct, but rare. It means transitory or short-lived.

Flipside (noun)   The other side of a two-sided object or of a two-sided argument or situation. Origin: In the days before tape and DVD, music was recorded on large disks, made of vinyl or other material. Both sides of the disk were used, thus—the flipside.

Flop (noun) A dismal failure.

Follow Suit (verb) To do the same thing you see others do. Comes from card games where if a card of a certain suit is played, the other players must play a card of that suit, if they have one.

Follow the Leader (noun) Name of a children's game. Metaphorically, it means to do what others are doing, usually without giving it much thought.

Form Follows Function (description) A phrase borrowed from architecture, where it means that the architect determines what a building is to be used for, and then designs the building to meet the demands of that use, or function.

Fourth Sector (noun) An additional sector in the U.S. economy in addition to the typical three: government, private business, and nonprofit.

Front (noun and verb) Activity undertaken to divert attention from what is.

Funky (adjective) Eccentric in style or manner.

G

Gadget (noun) Generic term for any small, often novel, mechanical or electronic device or contrivance, usually designed for a specific purpose. For instance, the small wheel with serrated rim and an attached handle used to divide a pizza pie into slices is a gadget.

Gas-Guzzling (adjective) Describes motor vehicles that use a noneconomical or excessive amount of gasoline.

Gee (expletive) Emphatic expression signaling surprise or enthusiasm.

Get You Down (descriptive phrase) Make you depressed about something or make you dismiss something altogether. (Do not confuse with "get it down," which means to understand fully.)

G.I. Joe (noun) A toy in the form of a boy (as "Barbie" is a girl). The original meaning was "government issue"—i.e., an item such as a uniform issued by the U.S. government to a member of the U.S. armed forces, and, by extension, the person to whom the item was issued.

Giveaways (noun) Something, usually valuable, that you confer without receiving anything tangible in return. In this book, it refers to Congress enacting tax cuts that are insignificant to all but people who are already rich.

GM (noun) The General Motors automobile company.

Go-Cart (noun) A small engine-powered vehicle that is used for racing and recreation.

Gold Mine (noun) Metaphorically, any activity that results in making you a lot of money.

GOP This acronym stands for "Grand Old Party." The GOP is the Republican political party.

Got It Made (descriptive phrase) Succeeded.

Grind (noun) Slang for necessary intense effort that may be painful but will likely benefit your understanding.

Groucho Marx (proper name) A famous U.S. comedian (1885–1977).

Gung-ho (adjective) Full of energy and eager to take action.

Guns and Butter (descriptive phrase) Metaphor describing the dilemma whether to devote resources to war or to peace.

Guzzle, Guzzler (verb and noun) Verb: to consume something greedily, wastefully, and rapidly. Noun: an object (or a person) that guzzles.

H

Haggling (noun) Bargaining, usually in a petty and confrontational manner.

Hangover (noun) The queasy feeling, usually accompanied by a headache, that can afflict a person who has gotten drunk. The feeling can last for hours after the person is no longer actually drunk.

Hard Hit (adjective) Affected in a negative way, often severely.

Hard Liquor (noun) Alcoholic beverages with a high content of pure alcohol. Beer and wine are not "hard liquor," but most other alcoholic drinks are.

Hassle (noun and verb) Noun: unreasonable obstacle. Verb: to place unreasonable obstacles or arguments in the way of someone.

Hawking (adjective) Selling aggressively and widely.

Hefty (adjective) Large; substantial.

Hero Sandwich (noun) A type of very large sandwich.

Highfalutin (adjective) American slang term meaning pretentious, self-important, supercilious.

Hitting the Mark (expression) Achieving your purpose.

Holds Its Own (descriptive phrase) Refuses to give up, even in the face of adversity or opposition.

Home Free (descriptive phrase) Safe and successful.

Hook (noun) Strategy to engage your attention.

Hot Dog (noun) A type of sausage.

I

"In" (preposition sometimes used as an adjective) Placed within quotation marks to show it is used with a special meaning. Here it is used as an adjective, to indicate "fashionable or popular, usually just for a short period." To be "in" means to be associated with highly desirable people (the "in" people).

Incidentals (noun) Blanket term covering the world of small items a person uses on a daily basis as the need happens to arise—that is, needed per incident occurring. Examples are aspirin, combs, and picture postcards.

IOU (noun) A nickname applied to a formal acknowledgment of a debt, such as a U.S. Treasury bond. Also an informal but written acknowledgment of a debt. Pronounce the letters and you will hear "I owe you."

iPod (proper name) A compact digital music player designed by Apple Inc.

It'll (contraction) "It will."

J

Jarring (adjective) Extremely surprising and unexpected occurrence, usually slightly unpleasant.

JetBlue (proper name) A low-cost U.S. airline, which is actively entering new markets.

Junk Food (noun) Food that tastes good but has little nutritional value and lots of calories. It is sometimes cheap, sometimes expensive, and it's quick and easy to buy and eat.

Just Say No (admonition) Flatly refuse. This phrase became common in the 1980s after Nancy Reagan, the wife of the then-president of the United States, popularized it in a campaign against the use of addictive drugs.

K

Ketchup (noun) Spicy, thick tomato sauce used on, among other foods, hot dogs.

Knockoff (noun) A cheap imitation.

L

Laetrile (noun) Substance derived from peach pits, thought by some people to be a cure for cancer.

Lay Off (verb) To discharge a worker temporarily.

Lemon (noun) Slang term for an object that is irreparably faulty. It's usually something for which you have paid a substantial amount of money and by whose performance you feel cheated.

Levi's (noun) Popular brand of jeans.

Like Greek (descriptive phrase) Incomprehensible (because in the United States, classical Greek is considered to be a language that almost no one learns).

Lion's Share (noun) By far the best part of a bargain.

Lobby (verb and noun) Verb: to attempt by organized effort to influence legislation. Noun: an organized group formed to influence legislation. A lobbyist is a member of a lobby.

Lousy (adjective) Incompetent or distasteful.

M

Mazuma (noun) U.S. slang term for money. It was used in the first half of the 20th century but is now rare, to say the least.

MBA (noun) An academic degree: master of business administration.

Medicaid (proper noun) Health insurance program for low-income people. It is administered jointly by the U.S. government and the individual states.

Medicare (proper noun) U.S. government health insurance program for people who are disabled or age 65 and over. There is no means test.

Messed Up (adjective) Damaged or badly managed.

Mother of Necessity A witty remark that reverses the terms of a famous saying, "Necessity is the mother of invention."

Mousetrap (noun) Producing a better mousetrap is part of the saying, "Make a better mousetrap and the world will beat a path to your door." Metaphorically, producing a better mousetrap stands for doing anything better than it has previously been done.

N

NA (abbreviation) "Not available."

NATO (noun) North American Treaty Organization. Western alliance for joint economic and military cooperation. It includes the United States, Canada, and several European nations.

National League (name of an organization) An association of U.S. baseball teams. The United States has two baseball associations—the other is the American League.

Nature of the Beast (descriptive phrase) Character of whatever you are describing (need not have anything to do with a "beast").

Nerd (noun) An insignificant and uninteresting person or a person so absorbed in a subject that he or she thinks of nothing else and is therefore boring.

Nickel-and-Dimed (adjective) Worried over every expenditure, even tiny sums like nickels and dimes; also having the last tiny sum of money extracted.

Nirvana (noun) This word is adopted from Buddhism. Its religious meaning is complicated, but it is used colloquially to mean salvation, paradise, harmony, perfection.

No Way (exclamation) Emphatic expression denoting refusal, denial, or extreme disapproval.

Nobel Prize (adjective/noun) A prestigious money prize awarded annually from a fund set up in 1901 by the will of Alfred Nobel, the inventor of dynamite. The prizes are in several categories: physics, chemistry, physiology and medicine, literature, and economics. Nobel also established the Nobel Peace Prize, distinguished by the word "peace."

Nudge (noun and verb) Noun: little push. Verb: to give a little push.

O

Oakland Athletics (adjective/noun) A U.S. major league baseball team.

Occupy Movement (proper noun) A protest movement against income inequality that started with an occupation of Zuccotti Park in Wall Street, New York City.

Off-the-Cuff (adjective) A quick, unthinking answer for which the speaker has no valid authority (comes from the alleged practice of writing an abbreviated answer on the cuff of your shirt, to be glanced at during an examination).

Oliver Wendell Holmes Jr. (proper name) A justice of the U.S. Supreme Court, famous for his wit, his wisdom, his literary ability, his advocacy of civil rights, and his long life (1841–1935).

On Their Toes (descriptive phrase) Alert; ready for any eventuality.

P

Pandora's Box (complex noun) An allusion to a Greek myth. To release a cloud of troubles. Pandora, a figure in Greek mythology, was given a box but told not to open it. She could not resist, and the opened it. It was filled with all the problems of the universe, which escaped to plague us forever.

Park Avenue (noun) An expensive and fashionable street in New York City.

Part and Parcel (noun) An integral element of a concept, action, or item.

Peanuts (noun) Slang for a small amount, usually money but sometimes anything with a small value.

Peer Pressure (descriptive phrase) Push to do what everyone else in your particular group is doing.

Perks (noun) Short for "perquisites."

Pie (noun) Metaphor for the total amount of a specific item that exists.

Piecemeal (adverb) To do something bit by bit instead of all at once.

Pitcher (noun) In the game of baseball, the player who throws—or "pitches"—the ball to the player who is waiting to strike it.

Pop-Tart (noun) Brand name of a type of junk food. It's a sweet filling enclosed in pastry that you pop into the toaster and when the pastry is hot, it pops out of the toaster.

Populist (noun and adjective) Noun: a member of a political party that purports to represent the rank and file of the people. Adjective: a political party, a group, or an individual that purports to represent rank and file opinion.

Pound (noun) Unit of British currency.

Powers That Be (expression) People or institutions that have power such that there is nothing one can do to influence those people or institutions—or at least nothing easy.

Practice Makes Perfect (expression) The grammar of this phrase is illogical but the meaning is clear.

Premium Tires All Round (descriptive phrase) Premium tires are tires of superior quality. When all the tires on your vehicle are premium tires, you have them "all round."

Proxy (noun) A stockholder can give a "proxy" to the firm. It is an authorization that permits the firm's officials to vote for the proposition that the stockholder directs them to vote for. By extension, proxy means a substitute.

Ps and Qs See under *Mind.*

Pub (noun) Short for "public house," a commercial establishment where alcoholic drinks are served, usually with refreshments and occasionally with light meals.

Q

Quip (noun and verb) Noun: a jocular remark. Verb: to make a jocular remark.

R

Raise Your Eyebrows (verb) To express surprise, usually by a facial expression rather than vocally.

Red Flag (noun) A red flag warns you to be very alert to a danger or perceived danger. (Ships in port that are loading fuel or ammunition raise a red flag to signal danger.)

Red-Handed (adjective) Indisputably guilty. Comes from being found at a murder or injury scene with the blood of the victim on one's hands.

Relief (noun) This term was an informal one, applied specifically to the financial assistance people in the United States received from the government during the Great Depression (1929 until about 1941). It arose because of a government program administered by the Works Progress Administration (WPA) formed to create jobs, and hence to employ people who otherwise would have been unemployed.

Right On! (exclamation) Expression of vigorous, often revolutionary, approval and encouragement.

Ritzy (adjective) Very expensive, fashionable, and ostentatious. Comes from the entrepreneur Caesar Ritz, a Swiss developer of expensive hotels, active in the first quarter of the 20th century. Upscale, fancy. Has overtones of ostentation.

Rock Bottom (noun) To reach the absolute limit of one's endurance or resources.

Rule of Thumb (complex noun) Judgment based on practical experience rather than on scientific knowledge.

Comes from habit of using the space between the tip to the first joint of your thumb as being about an inch—good enough for the task at hand but not precise.

S

Saks (proper name)   A midsize department store that sells expensive, fashionable items. There are very few stores in the Saks chain, and Saks stores are considered exclusive.

Savvy (adjective)   Slang term meaning very knowledgeable. Adaptation of the French verb *savoir,* meaning "to know."

Scab (noun)   Person who takes a job, or continues in a job, even though workers at that firm are on strike.

Scraps (noun)   Little pieces of leftover food. Also little pieces of anything that is left over: for example, steel that is salvaged from a wrecked car.

Scrooge (proper name)   Character in Charles Dickens' *A Christmas Carol,* an English story written in the mid 1850s. He was unbelievably miserly and disagreeable (but in the story he reformed).

Sears Catalog (noun)   Sears, Roebuck and Co. is a large chain of stores that sells a wide variety of goods. Before shopping malls, interstate highways, and the Internet, Sears used to have a huge mailing list to which it sent enormous catalogs. A person receiving such a catalog would have information about, and access to, thousands of items, many of which the person might not have known existed before the catalog provided the prospect.

Set Up Shop (verb)   To go into business.

Shivering in Their Sandals (descriptive phrase)   Adaptation of standard English idiom *shivering in their shoes,* which means being afraid.

Shoo-in (noun)   Highly probable (as in "you are a shoo-in" to get an A).

Shorthand (noun)   Any of several systems of abbreviated writing or writing that substitutes symbols for words and phrases. Shorthand was widely used in business until the introduction of mechanical and electronic devices for transmitting the human voice gradually made shorthand obsolete. Today it means to summarize very briefly or to substitute a short word or phrase for a long description.

Show-off (verb and noun)   To be blatant and vulgar in displaying a possession or accomplishment. The person who is a show-off is displaying conspicuous consumption.

Significant Other (noun)   A person with a close relationship with an individual, often a romantic interest.

Sixpence (noun)   A British coin that is no longer in use. It represented six British pennies; its U.S. equivalent in the 2000s would be about a nickel.

Skin of One's Teeth (descriptive phrase)   To succeed by the skin of one's teeth means to just barely succeed. A micromeasure less and one would not have succeeded.

Smoke Screen (noun)   Metaphorically, anything used intentionally to hide one's true intentions.

Smoking Gun (noun)   This term has come to stand for any indisputable evidence of guilt or misdeeds.

Soft Drink (noun)   Nonalcoholic beverage.

Sourpuss (noun)   Dour; sulky; humorless. Derives from *sour,* which is self-explanatory, and *puss,* a slang word for "face."

Spoils (noun)   Rewards or advantages gained through illegal or unethical activity.

Squash (verb)   To crush or ruin.

Stay on Their Toes (idiom)   To be alert.

Steady (noun)   A person to whom you are romantically committed and with whom you spend a lot of time, especially in social activities.

Stealth Gains (noun)   Gains that occur unbeknownst to you.

Sticky (adjective)   Resistant to change, as if glued on.

Sucker (noun)   A gullible person.

Super Bowl (noun)   Important football game played annually that attracts millions of viewers (most of them see the game on TV).

Sweetheart Contract (noun)   A contract where one party to the contract is given all, or almost all, the advantage; specifically, a contract between an employer and the workers' union where the employer gains the advantage and the contract on the workers' side has been arranged by a union official who secretly gives up advantages for the workers in return for significant advantage for the official.

T

Tables Were Turned (descriptive phrase)   The advantage of one side over the other reverses so that now the winner is the loser and the loser is the winner.

Tacky (adjective)   In very poor taste.

Taco Technician (noun)   A name given to a worker at a fast-food restaurant specializing in Mexican foods.

Take a Flier (expression)   To take a chance; to undertake a risky action in the hope that you will be lucky.

Take the Heat (verb)   To accept all criticism of one's action or inaction, whether or not one is actually the person that should be blamed.

Time-and-a-Half (noun)   In labor law, 150 percent of the normal hourly wage.

To Be in Hot Water (descriptive phrase)   To be in trouble.

Ton (noun)   A ton weighs 2,000 pounds and an English ton (often spelled "tonne") weighs 2,240 pounds. In this book the term is used most frequently to mean simply "a large quantity."

Tough (adjective)   Very difficult.

Trendy (adjective)   A phenomenon that is slightly ahead of traditional ways and indicates a trend. Something trendy may turn into something traditional, or it may fade away without ever becoming mainstream.

Trophy Spouse (noun)   A spouse (usually the wife) who is young, beautiful, and perhaps famous and/or rich who has been married to an older—sometimes much older—very successful and rich person, usually after divorcing one or more previous spouses. The trophy spouse is just that—a trophy. (See "show-off.")

Truck (verb)   To exchange one thing for another. This was Adam Smith's definition in 1776 and it is still one of the meanings of the verb.

Truth (noun)   When capitalized (other than at the start of a sentence) true beyond any doubt (as opposed to "truth"—the best truth we have at the moment).

Tune In (verb)   To become familiar with.

Turf (noun)   Territory, especially the figurative territory of a firm.

Turn of the Century (expression)   The few years at the end of an expiring century and the beginning of a new century. For example: 1998–2002.

Turn Up One's Nose (verb)   To reject.

Twinkies (noun)   Brand name of an inexpensive small cake.

U

Union Jack (noun)   Nickname for the British flag.

Up at Bat (expression)   From the sport of baseball. A player (the "batter") who is in the position ("home plate") where a player from the opposing team (the "pitcher") will throw the ball to him. The player to whom the ball is thrown is "up at bat." Thus, to be up at bat can mean being ready to meet an impending emergency or other situation.

Up in Arms (adjective)   Furious and loudly protesting. Comes from the use of *arms* to stand for *firearms.*

V

Vanity License Plate (descriptive phrase)   One-of-a-kind motor vehicle license plate issued to your individual specification. It might have your name, your profession, or any individual set of letters and numbers you choose that will fit on the plate.

Vignette (noun)   Short little story that uses a few words to illustrate or reinforce a point.

W–Y

Wadget (noun)   Term used by economists to stand for any manufactured good except goods designated as widgets. (See widget.)

Walmart (proper name)   A very large store that sells thousands of inexpensive items. There are thousands of Walmarts in the United States and the company has expanded into foreign markets.

Wheaties (proper noun)   Name of a brand of dry breakfast cereal.

White Elephant (noun)   Property requiring expensive care but yielding little profit; trinket without value to most people but esteemed by a few. There are real white elephants, which are albinos. They are rare and therefore expensive and high-maintenance.

White Knight (noun)   A company that comes to the rescue of another company. The term comes from the game of chess—some chess sets have white pieces and black pieces—and from the children's book *Alice Through the Looking Glass,* where the story is structured as a game of chess and a chess piece, the white knight, tries to rescue Alice.

Whopper (proper noun)   Brand name of a kind of hamburger sold at Burger King restaurants.

Widget (noun)   The opposite of a wadget. (See wadget.)

Wild About (descriptive phrase)   Extremely enthusiastic about undertaking a particular action or admiring a particular object or person.

Wind Up (descriptive phrase)   To discover that you have reached a particular conclusion or destination.

With It (descriptive phrase)   Highly popular.

With-It (adjective)   Current in one's knowledge.

Workhorse (noun)   Common, everyday method of accomplishing a task—nothing fancy. A "workhorse" in actuality is a strong horse of no particular beauty or attraction but is useful for pulling heavy loads in situations where using a machine is impractical.

World Series (complex noun)   At the end of the baseball season the two opposing teams left after the season's contests have eliminated all the other teams meet each other. The winner in this "World Series" wins the season.

World War I (proper noun)   1914–1918. The United States did not enter until 1917.

World War II (proper noun)   1938–1945. The United States did not enter until 1941.

Wound Up (past tense of verb *wind up*)   To have found oneself in a particular situation after having taken particular actions.

Writ Large (adjective)   Strongly emphasized; defined broadly. ("Writ" is an obsolete form of the word "written.")

Writing on the Wall (descriptive phrase)   To see the writing on the wall is to realize that a situation is inevitably going to end badly. It comes from the Biblical story that Nebuchadnezzar, king of Babylon, saw a fatal prediction written on a wall.

Z

Zune (proper name)   A compact digital music player designed by Microsoft to compete with the iPod.

Photo Credits

CHAPTER 1

Page 4: © Hulton-Deutsch Collection/Corbis; **p. 9:** Bleichroder Print Collection, Baker Library, Harvard Business School; **p. 11:** © Rachel Epstein/PhotoEdit; **p. 14:** © Getty Images; **p. 16:** Larry Lee Photography/Corbis. All Rights Reserved RF; **p. 18:** © AP Photo/Alden Pellett.

CHAPTER 2

Page 24: Glow Images RF; **p. 32:** (Stock Market) © Photodisc/Getty Images RF, (Yard Sale) © Jon Riley/Getty Images RF; **p. 35:** © Camera Press/Redux Pictures; **p. 36:** Image courtesy of the Foresight Institute and the Institute for Molecular Manufacturing (IMM), www.imm.org.

CHAPTER 3

Page 51: © Getty Images; **p. 54:** © AP Photo; **p. 63:** © UIA via Getty Images.

CHAPTER 4

Page 77: © Mike Ditz/2007 Transtock.com; **p. 86:** U.S. Coast Guard Photo by Petty Officer 3rd Class Patrick Kelley; **p. 89:** © The McGraw-Hill Companies, Inc./Gary He, photographer RF.

CHAPTER 5

Page 100: © National Oceanic and Atmospheric Administration/Department of Commerce; **p. 107:** © Rachel Epstein/PhotoEdit.

CHAPTER 6

Page 122: © AP Photo/Rick Maiman; **p. 128:** © Erica S. Leeds RF; **p. 129:** © Tony Freeman/PhotoEdit; **p. 135:** © AP Photo/Neil Redmond.

CHAPTER 7

Page 144: George Cruikshank, Plucking a Goose, c. 1824. Pen and brown ink. Collection Grunwald Center for the Graphic Arts. Richard Volger Cruikshank Collection, Hammer Museum, Los Angeles. Photography by Robert Wedemeyer.; **p. 147:** © Royalty-Free/Corbis RF; **p. 151:** © BananaStock/JupiterImages; **p. 162:** Courtesy of David Colander.

CHAPTER 8

Page 164: © Getty Images; **p. 168:** © Photolink/Getty Images RF; **p. 177:** © Royalty-Free/Corbis RF; **p. 179:** © Carl De Souza/AFP/Getty Images.

CHAPTER 8W

Page 185: Joeseph Sohm-Visions of America/Getty Images RF; 8W.1: Joeseph Sohm-Visions of America/Getty Images RF; 8W.2: © Business Wire, General Mills/AP Images; 8W.3: Courtesy of U.S. Department of Agriculture; 8W.4: © Scenics of America/PhotoLink RF.

CHAPTER 9

Page 186: © Steve Allen/Brand X Pictures/Getty Images RF.

CHAPTER 10

Page 205: © Mike Nelson/AFP/Getty Images; **p. 214:** © C. Sherburne/PhotoLink RF; **p. 217:** © Paul Conklin/PhotoEdit.

CHAPTER 11

Page 226: © The McGraw-Hill Companies, Inc./Jill Braaten, Photographer RF; **p. 229:** (tl) © GeoStock/Getty Images RF, (tr) © Neil Beer/Getty Images RF, (bl) © PRNewsFoto/AK Steel/AP Images RF, (br) © PRNewsFoto/The HON Company/AP Images RF; **p. 239:** "Book Cover" from HORTON HATCHES THE EGG by Dr. Seuss, TM & Copyright © by Dr. Seuss Enterprises, L.P. 1940, renewed 1968. Used by permission of Random House Children's Books, a division of Random House, Inc.

CHAPTER 12

Page 245: D. Hurst/Alamy RF; **p. 247:** © PRNewsFoto/Mazda North American Operations/AP Images RF; **p. 249:** © Kent Knudson/PhotoLink RF; **p. 252:** © Spencer Grant/PhotoEdit; **p. 255:** (l) © Bettmann/Corbis, (r) © Photodisc/Getty Images RF, **p. 256:** (t) © Digital Vision/PunchStock RF, (b) © Image Source/Getty Images RF.

CHAPTER 13

Page 267: © JP Laffont/Sygma/Corbis; **p. 270:** Courtesy of Priceline.com; **p. 280:** © Bob Krist/Corbis; **p. 282:** © RICK WILKING/Reuters/Corbis.

CHAPTER 14

Page 288: © Washington Post/Getty Images; **p. 296:** © Vincent Hobbs/SuperStock; **p. 300:** Used with permission from Ralph Anspach and University Games.

CHAPTER 15

Page 315: © Kraig Scarbinsky/Getty Images; **p. 326:** © David McNew/Getty Images; **p. 327:** Microsoft product shot(s) reprinted with permission from Microsoft Corporation; **p. 328:** © AFP/Getty Images.

CHAPTER 16

Page 334: © AP Photo/John Froschauer; **p. 336:** © Bob Daemmrich/Corbis; **p. 337:** © Roy McMahon/Corbis RF; **p. 345:** © The McGraw-Hill Companies, Inc./Jill Braaten, photographer RF.

P

CHAPTER 17

Page 354: © Bill Lai/Getty Images; **p. 370:** © Bettmann/Corbis.

CHAPTER 17W

Page 385: © Jack Star/PhotoLink/Getty Images RF; p. 17W-1: © Jack Star/PhotoLink/Getty Images; p. 17W-11: Bleichroder Print Collection, Baker Library, Harvard Business School.

CHAPTER 18

Page 386: (t) © Comstock/PunchStock RF; (b) © Design Pics/Con Tanasiuk RF.

CHAPTER 19

Page 411: © Fancy Collection/SuperStock RF; **p. 413:** © Chris Hondros/Getty Images; **p. 423:** (t) © Royalty-Free/Corbis RF; (b) © age fotostock/SuperStock.

CHAPTER 20

Page 436: © Twentieth Century Fox/Photofest; **p. 445:** © Twentieth Century Fox/Photofest; **p. 447:** © Bill Inashita/CBS Archive via Getty Images.

CHAPTER 21

Page 461: Book cover of Freakonomics by Steven D. Levitt and Stephen J. Dubner, William Morrow Publishers. Photo © Roberts Publishing Services; **p. 465:** Book cover of Predictably Irrational by Dan Ariely, HarperCollins Publishers. Photo © Roberts Publishing Services; **p. 466:** Image from Robert Bloomfield's Mentanomics™, Used by permission; **p. 467:** © Brand X Pictures/PunchStock RF; **p. 468:** Book cover of Armchair Economist by Steven E. Landsburg, The Free Press, Division of Simon & Schuster, Inc. Photo © Roberts Publishing Services; **p. 470:** Book cover of More Sex is Safer Sex: The Unconventional Wisdom of Economics by Steven E. Landsburg, The Free Press, Division of Simon & Schuster, Inc. Photo © Roberts Publishing Services; **p. 471:** Prada shoes product, © PRADA 2008; **p. 472:** Book cover of The Economic Naturalist by Robert H. Frank, Basic Books. Photo © Roberts Publishing Services; **p. 474:** © Nice One Productions/Corbis RF; **p. 476:** Original image from an anonymous German postcard, circa 1888, public domain.

CHAPTER 22

Page 487: © Roberts Publishing Services.

CHAPTER 23

Page 505: © AP Photo/Ron Edmonds; **p. 509:** © Royalty-Free/Corbis RF; **p. 510:** © Royalty-Free/Corbis RF; **p. 517:** © Comstock Images/Alamy RF; **p. 519:** Courtesy of UNOS.

Index

Page numbers followed by n refer to notes.

List of Boxes

THINKING LIKE A MODERN ECONOMIST